From Puvis de Chavannes to Matisse and Picasso

Toward Modern Art

From Puvis de Chavannes to Matisse and Picasso
Toward Modern Art

edited by Serge Lemoine

With 623 illustrations, 480 in colour

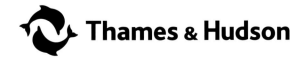
Thames & Hudson

cover
Pierre Puvis de Chavannes,
Summer, detail, 1891
The Cleveland Museum of Art

Pablo Picasso,
Bathers Watching an Airplane, 1920
Paris, Musée Picasso

page 5
Pierre Puvis de Chavannes,
Bathers, detail, 1890 circa
Toronto, Art Gallery of Ontario

page 9
Henri Matisse,
Sketch for "Music," 1907
oil on canvas, 73.4 x 60.8 cm
New York, The Museum of Modern Art.
Gift of A. Conger Goodyear in honor
of Alfred H. Barr, Jr.

page 10
Pablo Picasso,
Large Bather, detail, 1921
Paris, Musée de l'Orangerie

First published in the United Kingdom in 2002 by Thames & Hudson Ltd,
181A High Holborn, London WC1V 7QX

© 2002 by SIAE
© 2002 RCS Libri Spa

British Library Cataloguing-in-Publication Data
A catalogue record for this book is available from the British Library

ISBN 0-500-23796-4

Printed and bound in Italy

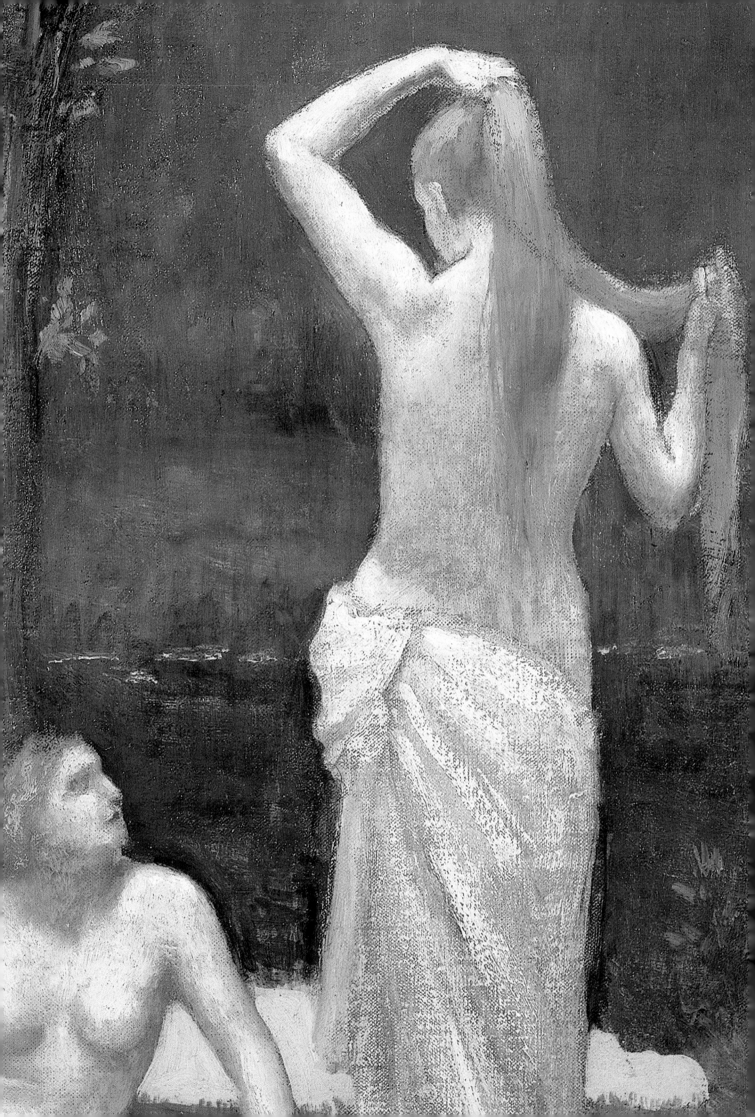

PALAZZO GRASSI

Palazzo Grassi S.p.A.
San Samuele 3231 - Venice

Over the years, Palazzo Grassi has dedicated various exhibitions to individual artists and artistic movements of the twentieth century, aiming to build up a picture of the development of modern art through an exploration of its history, concerns and forms of expression. This exhibition, *From Puvis de Chavannes to Matisse and Picasso*, looks at the crucial period of the emergence of modern art—from the end of the nineteenth to the beginning of the twentieth century—with the curator, Serge Lemoine, offering a detailed and innovative reading that emphasizes the importance of the influence Puvis de Chavannes had on the most significant artists of that period.

The exhibition presents not only the work of Puvis de Chavannes, a great artist who—thanks to this opportunity—will become better known in Italy, but also the work of all those artists such as Gauguin, Seurat, Matisse and Picasso who demonstrably took Puvis de Chavannes as a point of reference in their own artistic endeavours.

The originality of the approach adopted, and the wealth and quality of the works on display make the exhibition noteworthy for various reasons: as a rigorous study in art history, as a compendium of detailed information, as an opportunity to engage with some of the artists and masterpieces that are most representative of modern art.

The success of this ambitious project is due to the work of Serge Lemoine and all those who have made a valuable contribution to the creation of the show, in particular Gae Aulenti for the exhibition design and Pier Luigi Cerri for the graphics. And finally one cannot but mention our deep gratitude to those who have lent works; it is their ready collaboration which has made it possible to meet the challenge of such a demanding exhibition.

Cesare Annibaldi

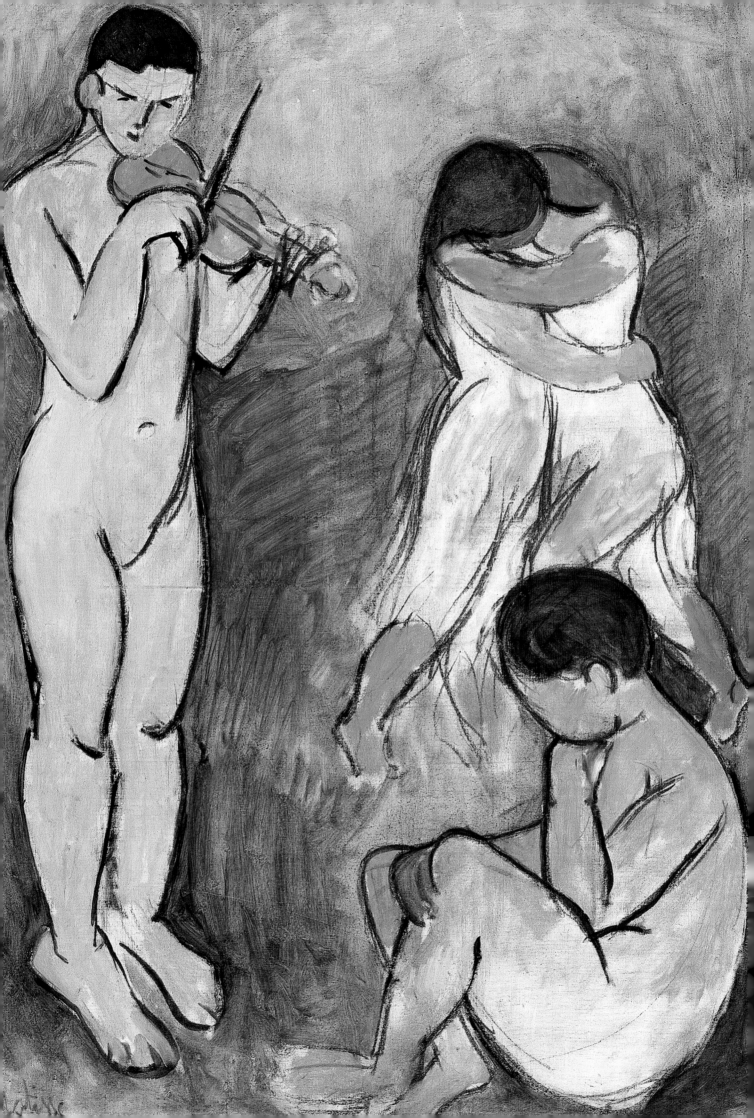

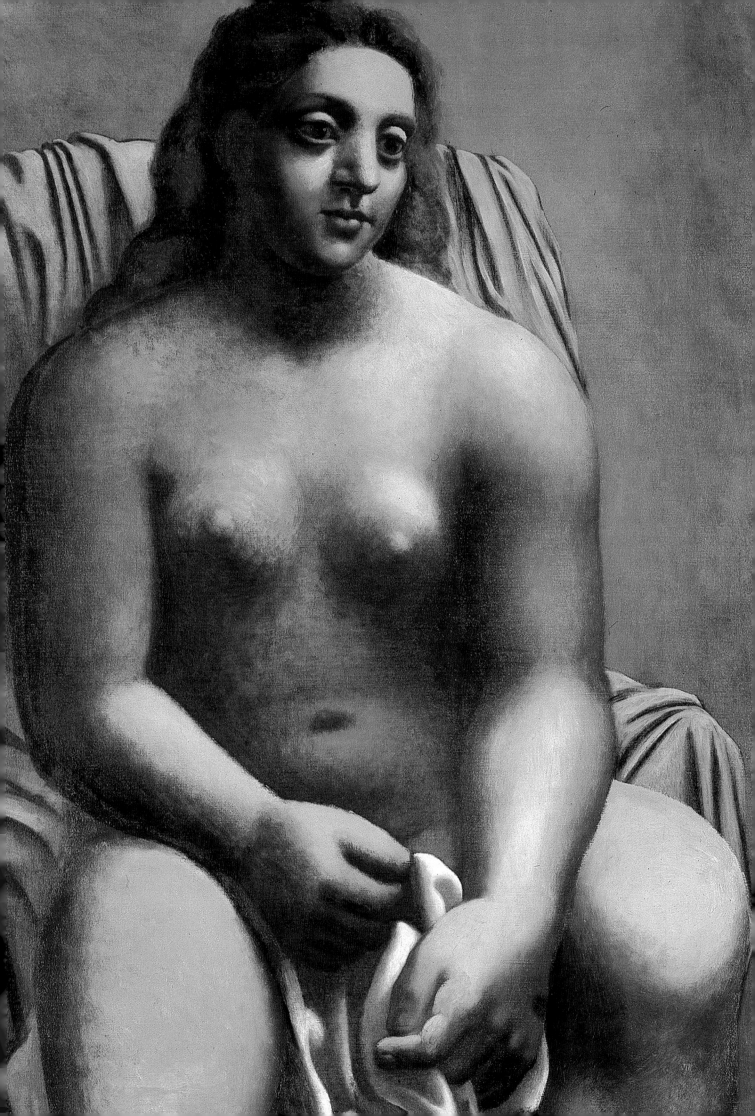

Aberdeen, Art Gallery and Museums
Aix-en-Provence, Musée Granet
Amsterdam, Fridart Stichting
Amsterdam, Van Gogh Museum
Basel, Öffentliche Kunstsammlung
Kunstmuseum
Berlin, Staatliche Museen zu Berlin,
Neue Nationalgalerie
Bielefeld, Kunsthalle
Blessington, Lady Beit
Boston, Museum of Fine Arts
Brooklyn, Museum of Art
Brussels, Musées Royaux des Beaux-Arts
de Belgique
Budapest, Szépúmvészeti Múzeum
Buffalo, Albright Knox Art Gallery
Bulle, Musée Gruérien
Cahors, Musée Henri Martin
Copenhagen, Statens Museum for Kunst
Den Haag, Gemeentemuseum Den Haag
Duisburg, Wilhelm Lehmbruck Museum
Dunkerque, Musée des Beaux-Arts
Düsseldorf, Stiftung Museum Kunst Palast
Edinburgh, National Gallery of Scotland
Frankfurt, Städelsches Kunstinstitut
Geneva, Galleria Jan Krugier, Dietesheim
et Cie
Geneva, Petit Palais, Musée d'Art Moderne
Göteborg, Konstmuseum
Gent, Musée d'Art et d'Histoire de la Ville
Halle, Staatliche Galerie Moritzburg,
Landeskunstmuseum, Sachsen-Anhalt
Hamburg, Hamburger Kunsthalle
Hannover, Niedersächsische
Sparkassestiftung
Helsinki, Ateneum Art Museum, Finnish
National Gallery
Helsinki, Sigrid Jusélius Foundation
Jona, Thomas Schmidheiny
Kiel, Kunsthalle zu Kiel
Leipzig, Museum der bildenden Künste
Lille, Palais des Beaux-Arts
London, Tate Gallery
London, The National Gallery
Lugano, Museo Cantonale d'Arte
Lyon, Musée des Beaux-Arts
Mâcon, Musée des Ursulines
Madrid, Museo Nacional de Arte Reina
Sofía
Mainz, Landesmuseum
Metz, Musées de la Cour d'Or
Tsu-Shi Mie Kan, Mie Prefectural Art
Museum
Milan, Civica Galleria d'Arte Moderna
Milan, Claudia Gian Ferrari
Musée de Brest
Musée de Grenoble
Museo d'Arte Moderna e Contemporanea
di Trento e Rovereto
Neuchâtel, Musée d'Art et d'Histoire
Neuss, Clemens-Sels-Museum
New Haven, Yale University Art Gallery
New York, Solomon R. Guggenheim
Museum

New York, The Metropolitan Museum
of Art
New York, The Museum of Modern Art
Nice, Musée Matisse
Oslo, Munch-Museet
Oslo, Nasjonalgalleriet
Otterlo, Kröller-Müller Museum
Paris, Centre Georges Pompidou, Musée
National d'Art Moderne
Paris, Daniel Malingue
Paris, Fonds national d'art contemporain,
Ministère de la culture
Paris, Jean-François Heim collection
Paris, Musée d'Art Moderne de la Ville
Paris, Musée de l'Orangerie
Paris, Musée d'Orsay
Paris Musée Maillol
Paris, Musée Picasso
Paris, Musée Rodin
Paris, Paul and Adrien Maeght collection
Paris, Petit Palais, Musée des Beaux-Arts
de la Ville de Paris
Paris, Rhodia Dufet-Bourdelle collection
Philadelphia, Philadelphia Museum of Art
Quimper, Musée des Beaux-Arts
Rome, Galleria Nazionale d'Arte Moderna
Rouen, Musée des Beaux-Arts
Saint-Étienne, Musée d'Art Moderne
Saint-Germain-en-Laye, Musée
Départemental Maurice Denis
Saint Louis, The Saint Louis Art Museum
Saint Louis, Washington University
Gallery of Art
Saint-Tropez, Musée de l'Annonciade
San Antonio, Walter F. Brown
Saint Petersburg, Museo di Stato Russo
Stuttgart, Staatsgalerie
Stockholm, Thielska Galleriet
The City College of New York
Toronto, Art Gallery of Ontario
Toulouse, Musée des Augustins
Turin, Galleria Civica d'Arte Moderna
e Contemporanea, Fondazione Guido
ed Ettore de Fornaris
Washington, National Gallery of Art
Williamstown, Sterling and Francine Clark
Art Institute
Winterthur, Villa Flora
Zurich, Katharina Büttiker collection,
Galerie Wühre 9 Art deco
Zurich, De Pury & Luxembourg
Zurich, Stiftung Sammlung E.G. Bührle
Zurich, Kunsthaus

and all those who wish to remain
anonymous.

For their support and their precious advices
the curator would like to thank:

Anne Baldassari, Marie-Laure Bernadac,
Irène Bizot, Ursula Bode, Olivier Bonfait,
Marie-Christine Boucher, Christian Briend,
S.E. François Bujon de l'Estang, Françoise
Cachin, Beverley Calté, Marie-Lothika
Charuau, Catherine Chevillot, Gilles
Chazal, Juliane Casandier, Jean-Michel
Coulais, Corinne Cuellar-Nathan, Claire
Denis, Anne Distel, Marina Distel, Mercè
Doñate i Font, Giselle Eberhard, Serge
Fauchereau, Vitali Fedorenko, Marina
Ferretti, Maria Teresa Fiorio, Francesc
Fontbona de Vallescar, Jean Gautier,
Claudia Gian Ferrari, Paul Josefowitz,
Rudolf Koella, Pierre Korzilius, Rémi
Labrusse, Marit Lange, Marie Lemoine,
Thomas Llorens, Bertrand Lorquin,
Francine Mariani-Ducray, Rainer-Michael
Mason, Emmanuelle de Montgazon, Jean-
Michel Nectoux, Monique Nonne, Anne
Perrot, Anne Pingeot, Vincent Pomarède,
Bertrand Puvis de Chavannes, Pierre
Rosenberg, Elisabeth Salvan, Helmiriitta
Sariola, Jeanine Scaringella, Aurora Scotti,
Jean Serroy, André Siganos, Béatrice Violle,
Richard Wattenmaker, Wolfgang Werner

Invaluable help has been given by Laurence
Zeiliger, of the Musée de Grenoble
Archives, and by her assistants, Gérard
Ponson and Bertrand Pauty.
The Archives of the Musée d'Orsay
have also contributed to the making
of this catalog.
Liason with the press was made possible
by Olivier Tomasini of the Musée
de Grenoble, and Aggy Lerolle
of the Musée d'Orsay.

Exhibition

Curator
Serge Lemoine

with Marianne Le Pommeré,
who has collaborated in the making of the
exhibition from its beginning to its end

Curatorial advisory
Tomas Sharman

Installation
Gae Aulenti
with Francesca Fenaroli

Graphic design
Studio Cerri & Associati
with the collaboration of
Dario Zannier

Lighting consultant
Piero Castiglioni

Press office
Mario Spetia, *Fiat press office coordination*

Lucia Pigozzo

Secretary in Paris
Domitille d'Orgeval

Catalog

Editorial director
Mario Andreose

Chief editor
Elisabetta Sgarbi

Coordinating editor
Marina Rotondo

Editorial collaboration
Giovanna Vitali

Editing
Paula Billingsley

Graphic design
Sabina Brucoli

Iconographic research
Silvia Borghesi

Translations
Line Henriksen
Judith Schub
Jeremy Scott
Ruth Waaler
Susan Wise
John Young

Technical staff
Sergio Daniotti
Valerio Gatti

Contents

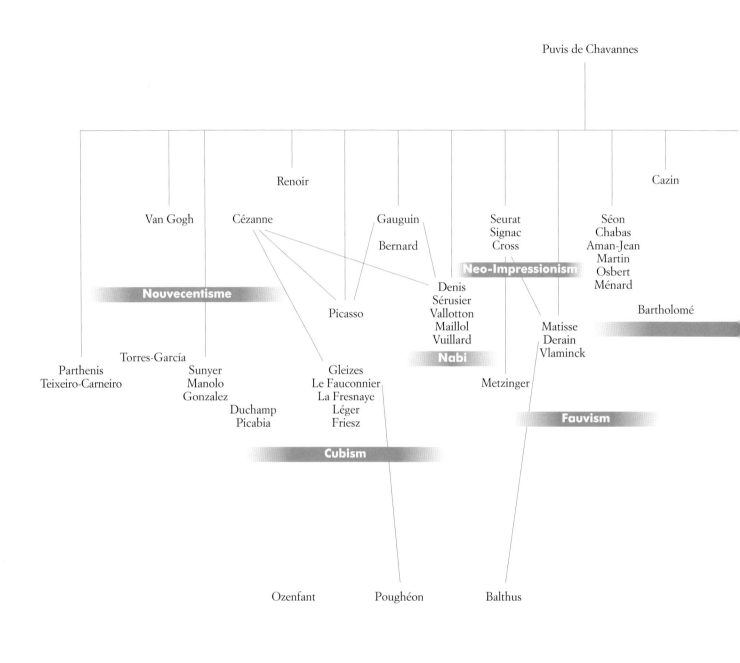

Puvis de Chavannes

Cazin

Renoir

Van Gogh   Cézanne   Gauguin   Seurat   Séon
                                                               Signac   Chabas
                                             Bernard   Cross   Aman-Jean
                                                                               Martin
                                                                               Osbert
Neo-Impressionism   Ménard

                                                      Denis   Bartholomé
Nouvecentisme   Sérusier
                                                      Vallotton   Matisse
                             Picasso   Maillol   Derain
                                                      Vuillard   Vlaminck

Torres-García   **Nabi**

Parthenis   Sunyer   Gleizes
Teixeiro-Carneiro   Manolo   Le Fauconnier   Metzinger
                           Gonzalez   La Fresnaye
              Duchamp   Léger   **Fauvism**
              Picabia   Friesz

                              Cubism

Ozenfant   Poughéon   Balthus

Spain
Portugal   France
Greece

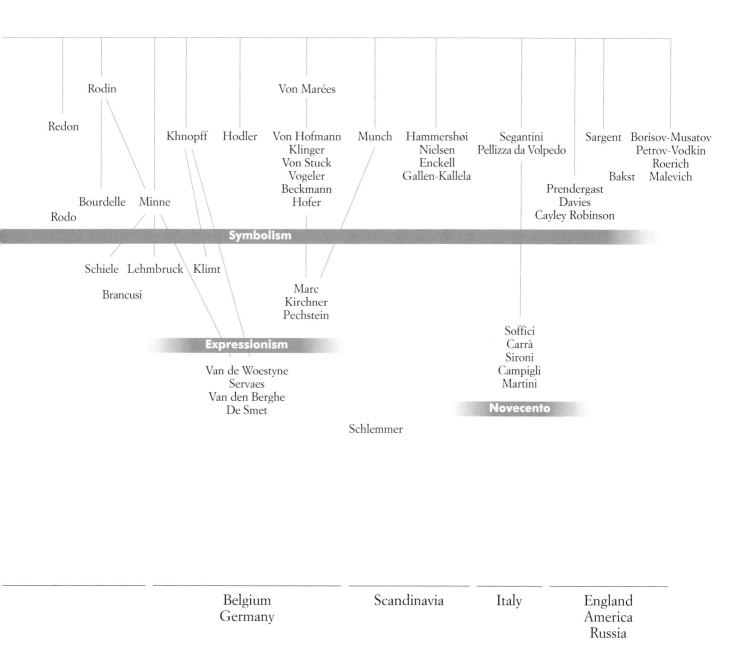

Redon

Rodin

Bourdelle   Minne

Rodo

Khnopff   Hodler

Von Marées

Von Hofmann
Klinger
Von Stuck
Vogeler
Beckmann
Hofer

Munch

Hammershøi
Nielsen
Enckell
Gallen-Kallela

Segantini
Pellizza da Volpedo

Sargent   Borisov-Musatov
Petrov-Vodkin
Roerich
Bakst   Malevich

Prendergast
Davies
Cayley Robinson

Symbolism

Schiele   Lehmbruck   Klimt

Brancusi

Marc
Kirchner
Pechstein

Expressionism

Van de Woestyne
Servaes
Van den Berghe
De Smet

Schlemmer

Soffici
Carrà
Sironi
Campigli
Martini

Novecento

Belgium
Germany

Scandinavia

Italy

England
America
Russia

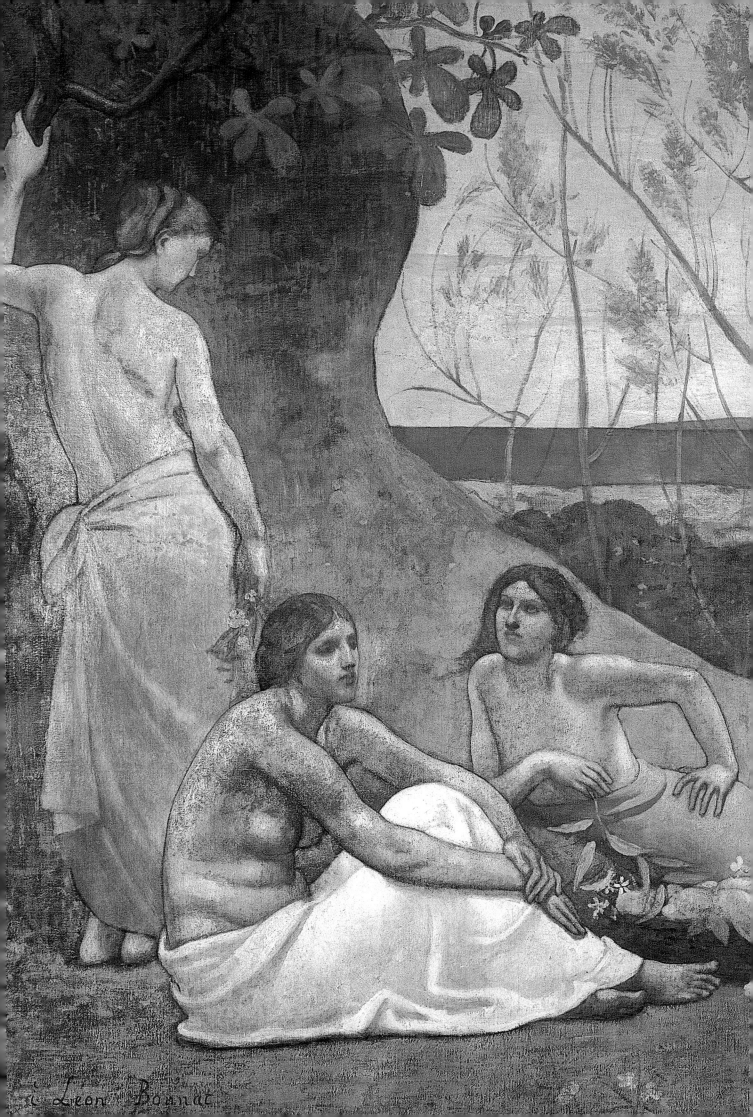

Léon Bonnat

Serge Lemoine

The Creator

There is an artist whose influence on the history of art in the late nineteenth and the early twentieth centuries was of great consequence. Throughout Europe and in America. His name has not fallen into oblivion. Yet in our day it no longer reflects that importance nor that status, since it is neither Monet nor Van Gogh, nor Rodin nor even Cézanne, nor any other name the public is so fond of, shown everywhere, reaching astronomical prices in auctions, appearing in books and on the covers of high-circulation magazines. It is that of the French painter, Pierre Puvis de Chavannes, who lived from 1824 to 1898.

History

Today the history of modern art, to thus define twentieth-century art and looking at it from our contemporary vantage point, is told in elementary, linear terms: we all know it. It starts with Impressionism, where Manet, Monet, Renoir, Degas are indistinctly associated, followed by Post-Impressionism with Seurat, Van Gogh, Gauguin and Cézanne; it continues with Fauvism and Matisse, through Picasso and Cubism, reaching abstraction with Kandinsky. Surrealism, which comes later, is to be added although it is difficult to place it in that sequence. The rest proceeds accordingly. Nowadays this interpretation is accepted—and has been for some time—by the majority of historians, critics, and the public whose tastes and values it conditions, and even by most artists.

Yet such a historical description, in which Impressionism is considered the source of modern art, presents, and has always presented, a great number of issues that remain unexplained and inexplicable, as soon as it is examined without preconceptions, like the transition from Monet to Cubism through Cézanne, or from Cubism to abstraction, when the art of Mondrian and Malevich, not to mention Kandinsky and Kupka, has so many spiritualist implications. To be more explicit, can Picasso's works of the Blue and Pink Periods be explained in terms of Toulouse-Lautrec, Steinlen, or even Gauguin, as is done? What relationship with prior works is to be found in the Matisse of *Luxe, calme et volupté* with its Divisionist technique, *Bonheur de vivre* with its vivid, rapid and undulating touches of color, the two versions of *Luxe* in which line suddenly prevails at the expense of color, and lastly, *Music* and *Dance* with their bright contrasting uniform hues?

Further along in the twentieth century, what is one to think of Picasso's subjects during his so-called "Neoclassical" or "Ingresque" period, and of their treatment? Just where do they come from, those frieze-like compositions with their singular colors, parallel bands of earth, sea and sky, and themes that are so particular, which the artist would continue to use up to his "monstruous" figures of the 1930s? Just why did Matisse remain faithful to the theme of dance when he executed Dr. Barnes's commission, and why did he treat the lunettes of the building with those forms, those flat, uniform colors?

During the last part of the nineteenth century and around 1900, why does one run into so many painters in the world who have nothing in common with Impressionism, and who no longer belong to the category of academic and eclectic art commonly qualified as "*art pompier*"? Every one of these artists, including a fair number of sculptors, display a great unity of style and content in their production that causes them to be grouped today under the denomination of Symbolism, a trend to which even Gauguin, with his philosophical subjects, belongs. A complete opposite, Seurat: but nor do his compositions reveal any reminiscences of Impressionism.

These few questions, raised helter-skelter among innumerable other ones, cannot be answered when they are considered from the point of view of Monet's, or even Cézanne's posterity. They might confirm the theory of the "break," a break between the art of the past and that of the twentieth century, so dear to those spirits that reject the latter as a whole and sigh for "bygone craftsmanship."

Is it feasible today to challenge that univocal history, that has become tradition, some might say vulgate, that appears to be so unsatisfactory with respect to the wealth and complexity of its manifestations? One must leave aside ready-made formulas and prejudices, and go back to history itself to concentrate on the facts and their manifestations, and then examine what has taken place since the beginning of modern art, rather than the reverse, that is, start with what is known and accepted today and go back in time. Such a reappraisal enables us to understand that as early as 1865 there was a painter who was not part of the fashionable trends

1. Pierre Puvis de Chavannes,
Pleasant Land, detail, 1882.
Bayonne, Musée Bonnat

of fossilized tradition, nor an Impressionist, Realist, or academic, and who contributed a new language and powerful, simple concepts as well as an artistic ideal. These concepts were so thoroughly appreciated by his contemporaries, the next generations, and the public less than twenty years later, that they exerted a profound influence all over the world and lasted until late in the following century. That painter, as we already claimed, is Puvis de Chavannes.

Fame
His art—expressed in monumental decorative schemes covering huge surfaces that were integrated into the architecture, and in easel paintings of all sizes, some of large format—has two main components: a subject and a form. The latter consists of simplified pictorial elements, that can go as far as schematization, a concise draftsmanship, an economy of muted shades, a decided flatness at the expense of illusionistic depth. As for his technique, it is unaffected and occasionally crude, even in the small formats. The content is based on allegory, and shows a preference for simple themes that are displayed without narration or psychology, but which emanate a poetry, that may be elegiac, gloomy or even tragic.

The paintings *Hope* (1872), *Young Women by the Sea* (1879)*,* and *Dream* (1883), with their directly approached subject, their silence and their utterly timeless appearance, are true pictorial poems, that are achieved through their rarefied composition, the inter-locking of the forms and the accurate appropriateness of their colors, while the two versions of *The Prodigal Son* (1879), and even more so *The Poor Fisherman* (1881), with its utter bareness, express dereliction and poverty, without literary or picturesque effects. As for the large decorations, those of the Musée de Picardie in Amiens in their two stages (1861–65 and 1880–82), and in particular the one titled *Ludus pro Patria*; the composition *Pleasant Land* painted in 1882 for Léon Bonnat's residence in Paris; the monumental paintings of the Musée des Beaux-Arts in Lyon (1884–86) and especially *The Sacred Wood Dear to the Arts and Muses*; the two cycles dedicated to the story of Saint Genevieve in the Panthéon in Paris (1874–78 and 1893–98), their scope, ambition, science and simplicity reveal a perfect balance between subject and the form in which it is expressed, painting and space, poetic invention and the constraints of the wall.

That art of composing with such ease, illustrating with such clarity, simplifying everything including the brushstroke, getting to the essence without overlooking detail, creating lasting images without being narrative, explains Puvis de Chavannes's singular position in his day. As soon as he found his own way in the 1860s, his style had nothing to do with that of the different figures of the art of the Second Empire and the Third Republic, neither Cabanel nor Baudry, neither Bonnat nor Meissonnier, who triumphed in the Salon where he too exhibited. He had nothing in common with the art of the Impressionists and the Salon des Refusés, neither with Manet, nor Pissarro nor Monet, there was no realistic interpretation of landscape and atmosphere, nor any fondness for still life, nor attraction to the ephemeral and the changing, or any recording of the anecdote nor representation of the everyday commonplace. Only Degas, with his rigor and his daring, shows true affinities with Puvis de Chavannes: at the beginning of their careers, did they not both refer to the same model, Ingres, along with fourteenth-century mural art?

Puvis de Chavannes's monumental decorative schemes, paintings, and drawings, which betoken the most accomplished art, the most unrelated to the times yet the most directly connected to the grand tradition, enable us to grasp the influence he had on his contemporaries and the next generations, whereas the Impressionists's art had no effect, except that of stirring healthy reactions against it; and that of Degas, which was too particular, had no noticeable posterity. Puvis de Chavannes's position was comparable but superior to that of Jean-François Millet several years earlier, who also left his mark for the same reasons—the sense of synthesis, the reduction to types, the expression of timelessness and creation of strong, unforgettable images—on artists like Van Gogh, Seurat, Gauguin, Segantini and countless other painters, who were to emulate, occasionally at the same time, the works of one or the other of these masters.

The authority Puvis de Chavannes wielded finds a good illustration in the banquet offered in his honor in 1889 in Paris. Planned and presided over by Auguste Rodin, it gathered 550 persons, painters, sculptors, poets, writers, critics, composers, politicians, civil servants, art lovers, happy to show him their admiration. In his lifetime, entire generations of artists, in particular from Scandinavia, Germany, Switzerland, America, flocked to the French capital, choosing his art as their model. Puvis de Chavannes at the time played the same role as David around 1800, one that after him would be Mondrian's, and his fame contributed to consolidate Paris as the capital of art. He died in 1898, universally admired.

The Eclipse

His fame did not prevent him from falling into disfavor. After World War I, his name began to be forgotten by public opinion, historians, critics and artists, despite the fact that several books appeared glorifying his art, including the one by Camille Mauclair. And yet at the very same time, the reputations of a few of his most brilliant disciples, Bonnard and Vuillard, Matisse and Picasso, were spreading, and young, more or less marginal painters like Balthus, were in turn discovering him. Neglect and then oblivion soon led to incomprehension and even a complete misinterpretation of his work.

It is possible to see the reasons, yet not easy to explain them without appearing to over-simplify. The first aspect has to do with Puvis de Chavannes's preferred means of expression, monumental painting, that gradually became unfashionable owing to the transformation of architecture combined with the evolution of taste. The decorative scheme of the Palais de Chaillot, built in Paris in 1937, was similar to those of the same period in official buildings in Italy, Germany and the USSR, and is to be considered one of the last expressions of a way of conceiving the integration of the arts, at a time when Rietveld's Schröder house in Utrecht, Gropius's Bauhaus in Dessau, Mies van der Rohe's German pavilion in Barcelona, and Le Corbusier's villa Stein-de Monzie in Garches had already revolutionized the art of building.

There is another reason of a different order that has as much to do with the field of sensibility as with the evolution of mentalities: we can discern it in the growing taste for a kind of painting that is immediately accessible and has nothing to prove, Picasso's *Guernica* and certain Surrealist paintings illustrating exactly the opposite. In other words, the triumph of Impressionism, which appeals to immediate sensation, whereas "old" painting is held to be difficult or even grim. Deeply-thought out composition is cast aside for improvised painting, which is expressed by slapdash craftsmanship or, on the contrary, ploddingly overdone as in Van Gogh. The final result: small and medium-size formats became popular, art in the first half of the twentieth century having entirely, barring exceptions, shifted its ambition: easel painting, faster done, cheaper, easy to move, showable and sellable, lastingly won out over "great painting."

All these features, revealing essential changes in mentalities and habits, ended up by prevailing as the sole criteria of modernism: they would lead to a series of misunderstandings, beginning with the one whereby Puvis de Chavannes's art, despite the evidence, would become identified with "*art pompier*." That misconception reached a climax in Paris in 1968 when his painting at the Sorbonne was ridiculed at the time the University of Paris was occupied by demonstrators, several of whom—true barbarians—even suggested destroying it. That state of mind was also expressed when Surrealism had finally won its ground and explaining it and seeking out its sources had become necessary, just when Symbolism was beginning to surface again. It was then that the figure of Gustave Moreau, whose work was so literary yet of an inferior pictorial quality, was rehabilitated, while Puvis de Chavannes was even more obfuscated and misunderstood.

Thus, during the second half of the twentieth century and in step with Marcel Duchamp's rising importance, whether it be legitimate or based on mistaken beliefs, the art of Puvis de Chavannes was forgotten. Beginning in the 1970s, a series of exhibitions and books would undertake a reappraisal, first of all of Symbolism, a movement that had been entirely neglected because of the exclusive taste for Impressionism. In 1976, the exhibition *Le Symbolisme en Europe* was therefore able to draw up a first inventory of that singular art, in which Puvis de Chavannes was just one name among many others. The following year, the book *Journal du Symbolisme* by Robert L. Delevoy sought to provide explanations and interpret the complexity of trends within that movement: Puvis de Chavannes was not overlooked, however, he was presented therein as less important than Moreau or the Pre-Raphaelite

2. Pierre Puvis de Chavannes,
The Dream, 1883.
Paris, Musée d'Orsay

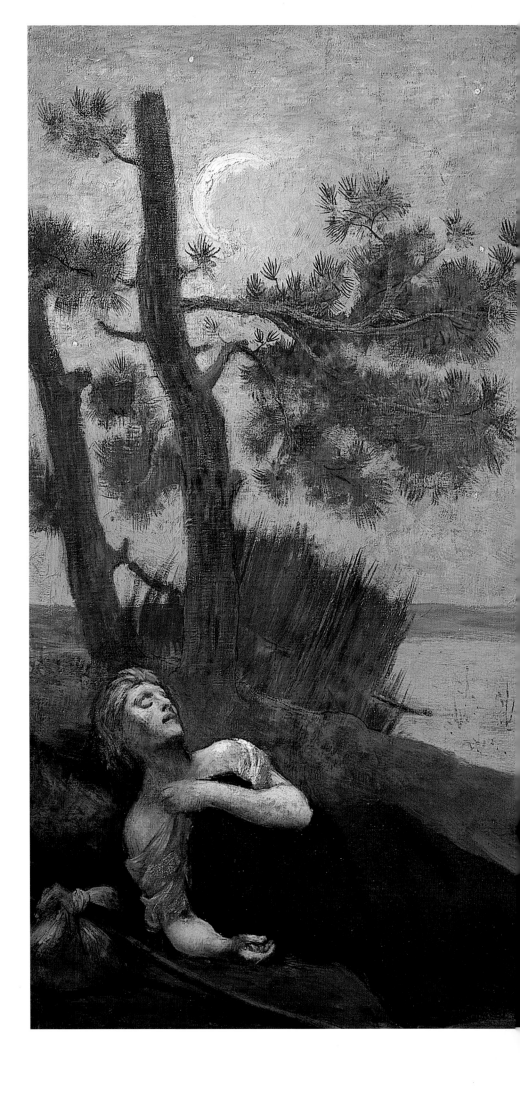

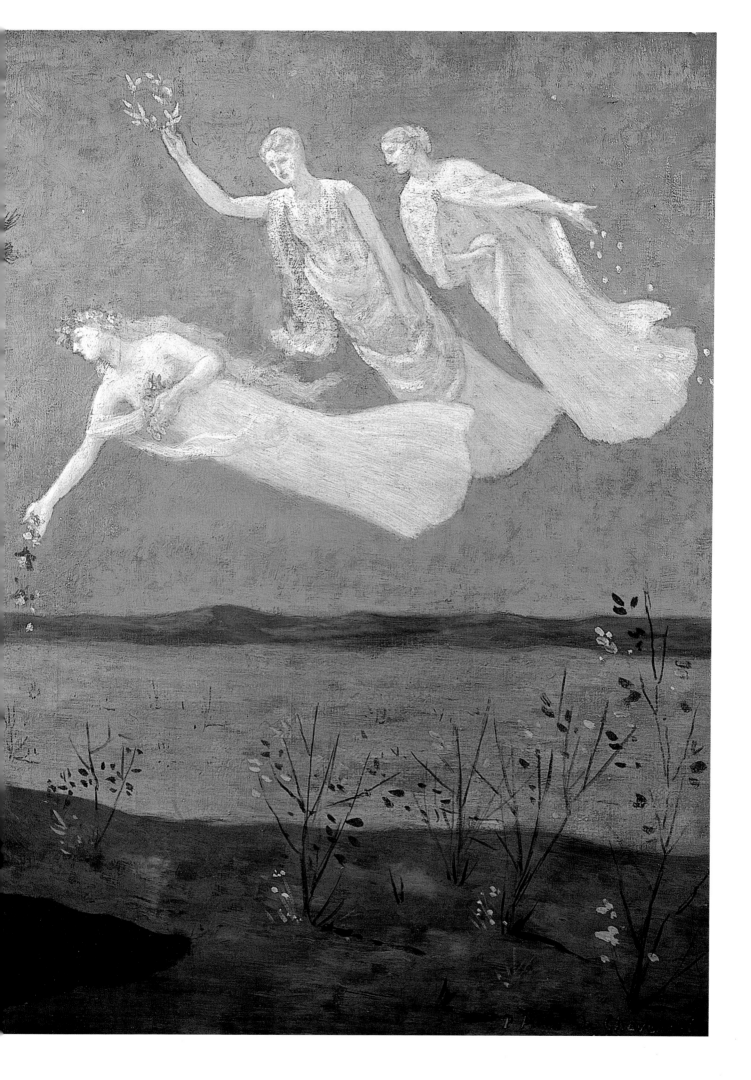

artists. In 1995, the enthralling Montreal exhibition *Paradis perdus: l'Europe symboliste* considered the events of that period from an iconographic point of view, striving to present it in a literary manner and failing to appreciate the role Puvis de Chavannes had played. Again in 1999, the exhibition at the Musée d'Ixelles *Les Peintres de l'âme. Le Symbolisme idéaliste en France* mentioned the existence of Puvis de Chavannes without pointing out his past supremacy. Finally the exhibition at the Royal Academy of London titled *1900 Art at the Crossroads*, organized for the year 2000, simply offered an overview devoid of main lines of direction or hierarchy, and Puvis de Chavannes, who had died in 1898, was missing, whereas he should have been one of the leading references of the period. Last of all and in another register, one will be amused to note, since it is a perfect illustration of that same frame of mind, Georges Banu's work *L'Homme de dos, peinture et théâtre*, which came out in 2000 and was hailed by the critics, where Puvis de Chavannes's name was not even mentioned.

The Contradiction

Rehabilitation of Puvis de Chavannes, as well as emphasis on the role he played in his day and the influence he exerted later on, came from across the Atlantic. By 1945, the American art historian Robert Goldwater, inspired, he claimed, by a suggestion from Alfred H. Barr himself, had already published an article on the subject. Then in 1975, Richard J. Wattenmaker, at the time chief curator of the Art Gallery of Ontario in Toronto, held a first exhibition on Puvis de Chavannes in which he proved, with deep insight and a perfect grasp of the importance of the fact, how great his influence had been. At the time counter to the mainstream, his splendid undertaking remained limited and unique, despite Hilton Kramer's favorable review in the *New York Times* which, to tell the truth, appeared shortly before the show closed.

The first retrospective devoted to Puvis de Chavannes was organized in Paris by Jacques Foucart and Louise d'Argencourt, before traveling to Ottawa. Despite its quality and scope, reception was poor and did not alter the opinion on the artist, nor did the very erudite catalog of Puvis de Chavannes's drawings conserved at the Musée du Petit Palais in Paris, which was published in 1979 by Marie-Christine Boucher, and which did, however, confirm the artist's importance as a draftsman. There followed afterthoughts, various mentions, a few specifications, the ones by Pierre Vaisse for instance, who underlined in 1983 the connection between the art of Ferdinand Hodler and that of Puvis de Chavannes, while Françoise Cachin in turn pointed out Gauguin's ties with Puvis in her book on the Tahiti painter published in 1988. Pierre Schneider, in his 1984 milestone book on Matisse, stressed what the author of *Dance* owed to Puvis. And Paul-Louis Mathieu, who examined the period from an historical point of view in *La Génération symboliste* of 1990, underscored the figure of Puvis de Chavannes. Anne Distel and especially Michael F. Zimmermann, in their respective studies of Seurat's work published in 1991, showed to what degree the art of the Lyon master had nurtured the inventor of Pointillism. Kenneth E. Silver, in his 1991 book titled *Vers le retour à l'ordre* was fully aware that Picasso's sources after World War I were to be sought in Puvis de Chavannes, as Anne Eggum did in 1992 for Edvard Munch in her biography of the artist, appearing in the catalog *Munch et la France*. In 1995, Pierre Daix in his *Dictionnaire Picasso* referred to Puvis as the source of the painter's Blue and Pink Periods. The exhibition *Pierre Puvis de Chavannes* at the Van Gogh Museum of Amsterdam in 1999, curated by Aimée Brown Price, insisted in turn on the importance of Puvis's art, and briefly recalled his influence, by means of several examples. Last of all, in 2000, at the Statens Museum for Kunst in Copenhagen, Peter Nørgaard Larsen demonstrated Puvis's vital role in that part of Europe, in the exhibition titled *Symbolism in Danish and European Painting 1870–1910*. However, those events have still not succeeded in revising the overall perception of Puvis de Chavannes's work. Compared to the prestige of the names of Manet, Monet, Van Gogh, and those of Cézanne and Gauguin, the figure of Puvis de Chavannes has not yet been rehabilitated. One only has to see in order to understand.

In the 1860s, Puvis de Chavannes's style had evolved in the compositions for the Musée de Picardie in Amiens, where he placed his panels *Work* and *Rest, War* and *Peace*, which were completed by the composition *Ave Picardia Nutrix*, and which spanned the years 1861 to 1865, plus the two decorations for the Palais Longchamp in Marseille (1867–69). His art, that was to continue to develop over thirty years, would be known, widespread, viewed and discussed, to the point of provoking veritable rejections as well as fervent enthusiasm. And his fame would continue to grow. Concurrently with public commissions for Poitiers, Lyon, Rouen, the Panthéon, the Sorbonne and lastly the Boston Library, one exhibition at the Salon followed another, with the same works being shown more than once. Before being installed in the buildings, the monumental compositions were also exhibited as soon as they were completed, so that the public and artists could see them, in the same way their cartoons and reduced copies were shown later on. The galleries, in particular Durand-Ruel in Paris and New York, showed his work exhaustively on several occasions, and in 1899 after his death, while a tribute to him was held at the Salon d'Automne in 1904. He exhibited alone or in group shows on different occasions in Paris and abroad, in Brussels, Venice, Scandinavia, Germany, Italy, and America. Puvis de Chavannes was known, understood and admired, and his influence was immediately felt.

His Peers
Early in their careers, Puvis de Chavannes and Degas were quite close, and then they parted ways. But Degas, who collected Puvis's drawings, continued to pay attention to his art and at the end of his life rediscovered some of his friend's solutions in his own works on paper. Odilon Redon was strongly influenced by Puvis, and would retain his chalky, unpolished, hazy backgrounds, his succinct forms, and of course his fondness for the line: his paintings frequently seemed to be enlarged details of Puvis's compositions, like *The Prisoner* (Cologne, Wallraf-Richartz Museum). Eugène Carrière, who was a friend of Puvis and painted his portrait (Lyon, Musée des Beaux-Arts), did not fail to be influenced by him, his work becoming as flowing and evanescent as Puvis's was firm and composed: the painting *The Young Mothers* (1906, Paris, Petit Palais, Musée des Beaux-Arts de la Ville) looks like a copy of the central part of *The Sacred Wood*. When everything was against them, the Impressionist painters, who were nevertheless defended by Puvis, were able to take his example into consideration: In this way, Auguste Renoir's painting *The Bathers* (1887, Philadelphia, Philadelphia Museum of Art), appears more completely Puvisesque in its subject, composition and treatment of forms than Ingresque, as has been said. Even the highly personal Auguste Rodin was deeply indebted to Puvis's art and his treatment of the subject, as we can see in particular in the bearing of the statue *The Age of Bronze* (1875–77, Paris, Musée Rodin), and in its movement and the accuracy of its contour. Rodin was the one to arrange the banquet given in Puvis's honor for his seventieth birthday, and remained one of his most enthusiastic admirers until the end of his life. Along with France, Germany: Hans von Marées came to Paris at an early age in 1873–74, and deeply impressed by Puvis's compositions, remained loyal to him leaving in turn a decisive legacy to German art.

The Echo
After the generation of artists born in the 1840s came that of the painters customarily called Post-Impressionists—a term that should be discarded today—and that of the Symbolist artists, whom cannot be dissociated from one another: was not Seurat a friend of Aman-Jean? And Gauguin is obviously a Symbolist artist, like many Nabis, who emulated him just as they did Puvis.
The Neo-Impressionists were among Puvis's first disciples, the ones who textually borrowed his lesson and even his solutions, transposing them in modern subjects. From the start, Georges Seurat painted a *Tribute to Puvis de Chavannes* (1883–84, Paris, private collection) in a rough sketch showing *The Poor Fisherman* placed on an easel outdoors. The trend was set. *Bathers at Asnières* (1883–84, London, National Gallery), so impressive in its stillness, its pale colors and utter simplification, borrows the tripartite arrangement of *Pleasant Land*, the rear-view and profile placement of the figures, the play of arabesques Puvis had invented, and which the painting *Sunday Afternoon on the Island of La Grande Jatte* (1884–85, Chicago, The Art Institute) would carry to its ultimate consequences with its frieze-like composition, stylized figures incorporated into a décor rhythmized by the layout of the trees, its oblong rectangular format, and monumental dimensions. *The Models* (1886–88, Merion, The Barnes Foundation) flippantly plays with sequences of lines, while the composition of

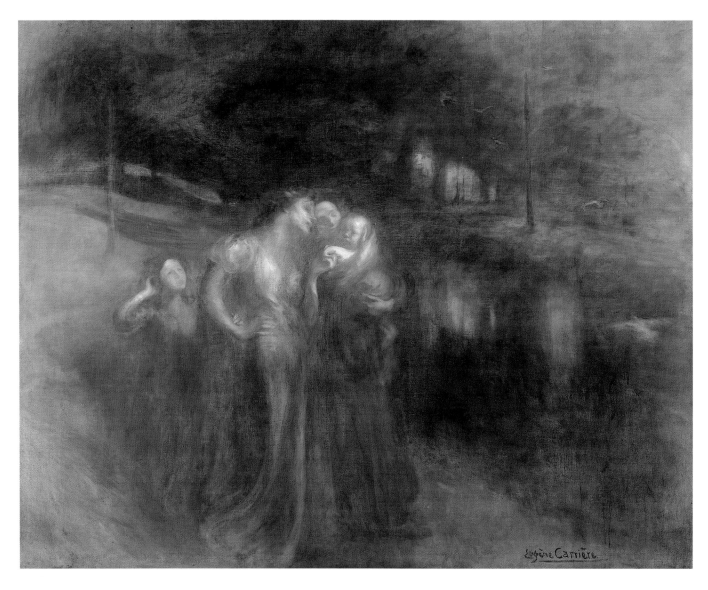

3. Eugène Carrière,
The Young Mothers, 1906.
Paris, Petit Palais, Musée
des Beaux-Arts de la Ville

Circus Sideshow (1887–88, New York, The Metropolitan Museum of Art), radicalizes Puvis's teaching, by emphasizing frontality, lack of depth and the succession of rhythms.
Paul Signac, who was Seurat's friend, was to return at a later date to Puvis's conceptions in *Women at the Well* (1892, Paris, Musée d'Orsay) and several other landscapes (*Saint-Tropez The Door*, 1896, Bucharest, National Fine Arts Museum of Romania), but his most important work, *In the Time of Harmony* (1893–95, Montreuil, Hôtel de Ville), looks like a transposition of *Pleasant Land*. As for Henri Edmond Cross, he seems more literal, but also more stylized as well, *Evening Breeze* (1893–94, Paris, Musée d'Orsay) appearing to be a thoroughly idealized evocation of Eden. The other Pointillists, Théo Van Rysselberghe and Hippolyte Petitjean, illustrated identical themes that Maximilien Luce pursued in a casual vein up to the 1930s.
Along with Seurat, Paul Gauguin is the artist who most closely studied Puvis de Chavannes. When he left for Tahiti in 1891, he took along a reproduction of *Hope* (nude) by Puvis, that he quoted in particular in one of his paintings, *Still Life with "Hope"* (1901, private collection). A late starter who had to feel his way, as soon as he moved to Pont-Aven he became Puvis's main disciple and remained so until the end,. He was even more faithful than Seurat, since he retained and developed figuration, directing it toward symbols and philosophical meditation. Still, he was also freer, since he was successful in combining arabesque and color and went further in abstraction, that is, non-realism. *Youths Bathing* (1888, Hamburg, Kunsthalle) and *Young Boys Wrestling* (1888, London, private collection) might be

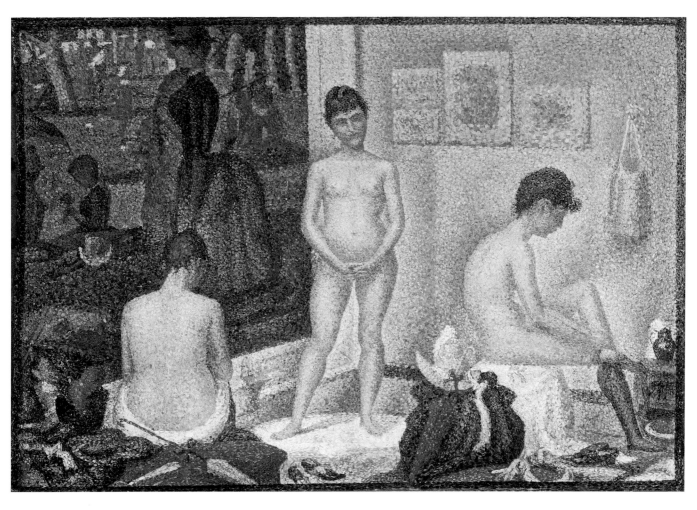

literal quotations from motifs of *Pleasant Land*, whereas the composition of his paintings, the relationship of the figures with the background, the themes illustrated in *Ta Matete* (1892, Basel, Kunstmuseum), a group of figures; *Vairumati* (1897, Paris, Musée d'Orsay), an isolated figure; *Two Tahitian Women on a Beach* (1892, Honolulu, Honolulu Academy of Arts), silhouettes seen in rear view standing out against the horizontal parallels of the landscape; and the humanist and esoterical epitome embodied in *Where Do We Come from? What Are We? Where Are We Going?* (1897, Boston, Museum of Fine Arts), in their rendering and their interpretation of Puvis, constitute the highest tribute he could receive. The rear-view or profile figures, the stylized elements of the setting, vegetation and architecture, the animals, horses, pigs, dogs and cows painted so synthetically, the accessories and all the simplified objects, and, finally, the ambition of the subjects to achieve universality denote the many elements Gauguin had been able to perceive and make his own in Puvis de Chavannes's art. And he would influence Emile Bernard, who would look at Puvis on his own, as can be seen in his painting *Bathers with Red Cow* (1889, Paris, Musée d'Orsay).

Vincent Van Gogh deeply admired Puvis, as his letters prove, but to a lesser degree his painting. As for Paul Cézanne, he would borrow frontality from Puvis, which he would employ in his landscapes and his figures, the tripartite arrangement of space—with earth, sea and sky (*L'Estaque, View of the Gulf of Marseille*, c. 1878–79, Paris, Musée d'Orsay), as has been seen in *Pleasant Land* and, of course, in the cycle of the *Bathers*—the vast compositions, incorporating figures, seen standing from the back or in profile, crouching or coming out of the water in rear view in a landscape rhythmized by trees.

The Diffusion

As we know, Seurat, Van Gogh and Cézanne had a decisive influence on the following generations. First of all, that of the Nabi artists that appeared around 1890 and was also involved

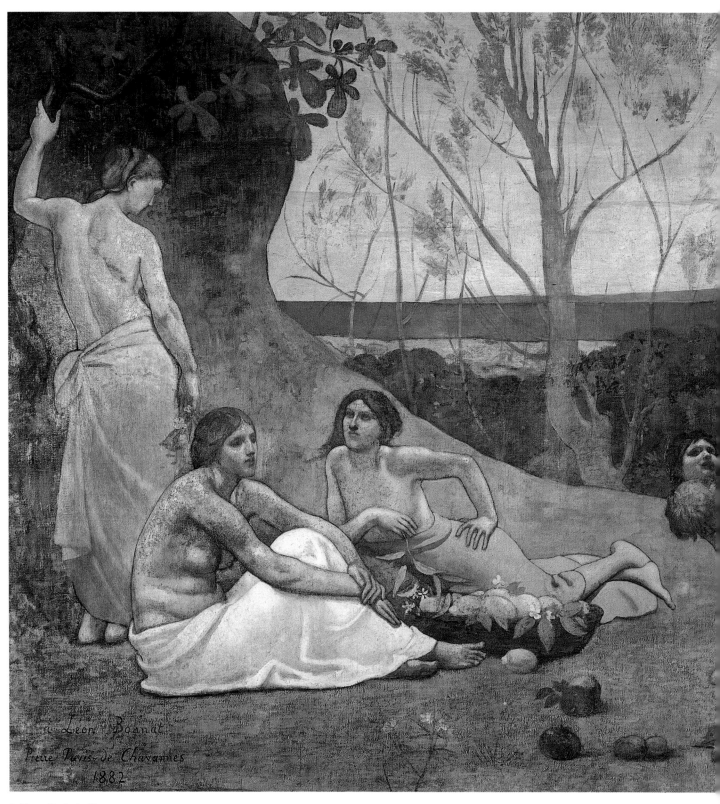

5. Pierre Puvis de Chavannes,
Pleasant Land, 1882.
Bayonne, Musée Bonnat

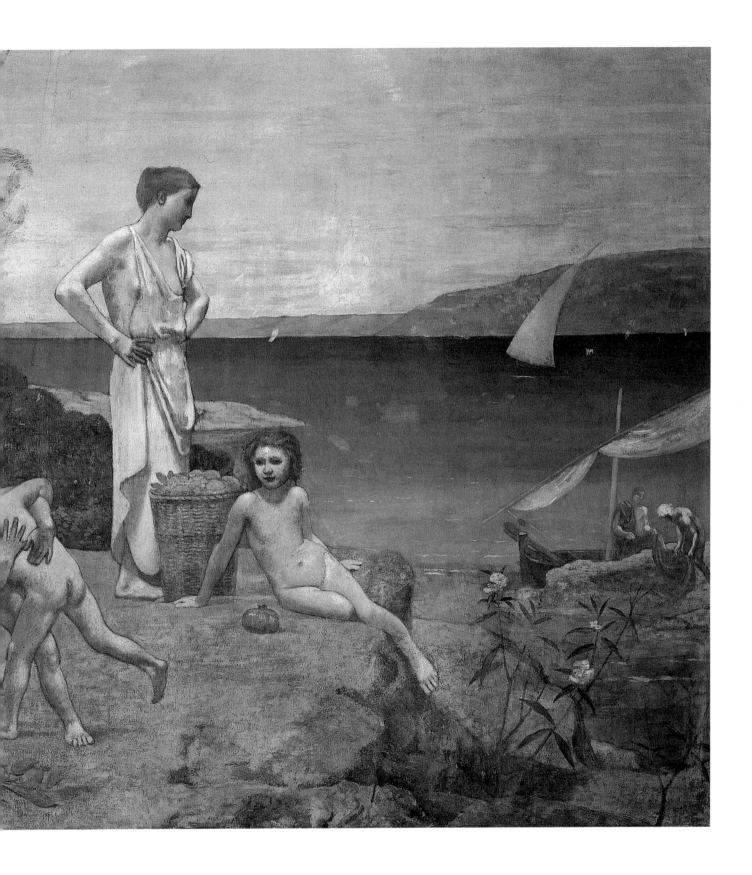

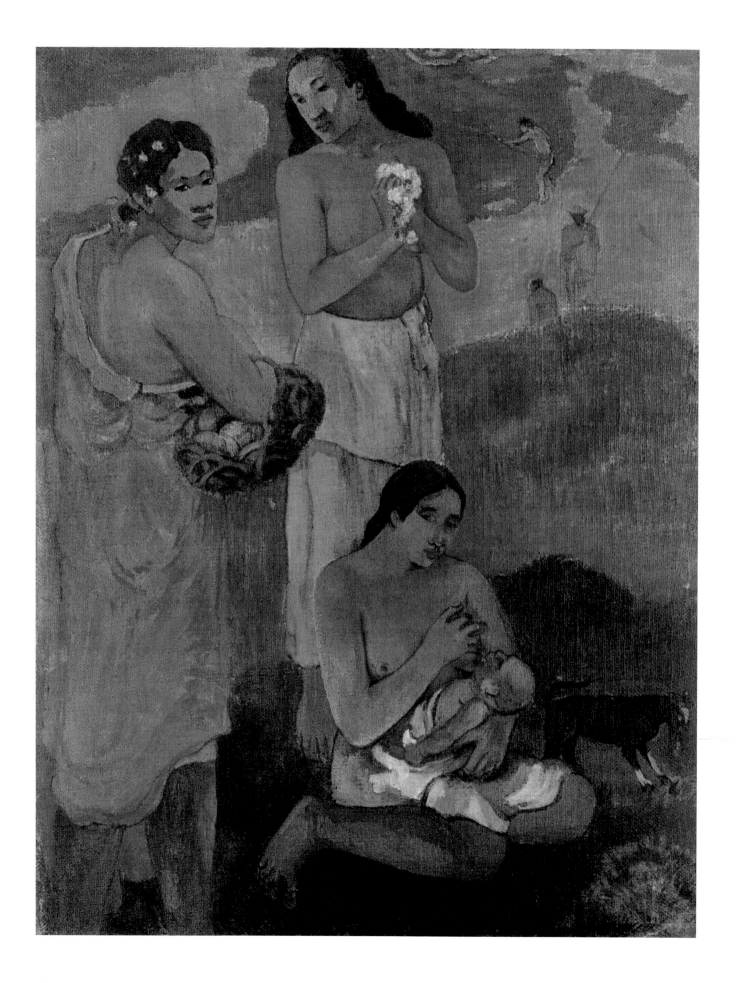

7. Paul Cézanne,
Bathers at Rest, 1875–76.
Merion, The Barnes Foundation

8. Paul Cézanne,
Three Female Bathers, 1879–82.
Paris, Petit Palais, Musée
des Beaux-Arts de la Ville

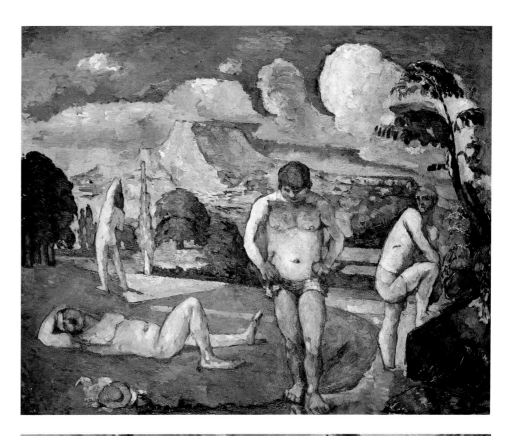

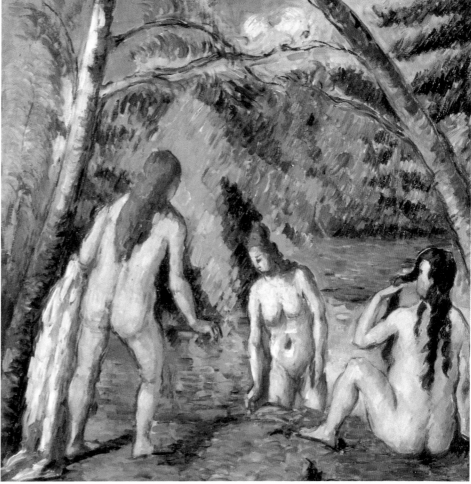

opposite page
6. Paul Gauguin, *Women on the
Seashore (Motherhood)*, 1899.
Saint Petersburg,
The Hermitage Museum

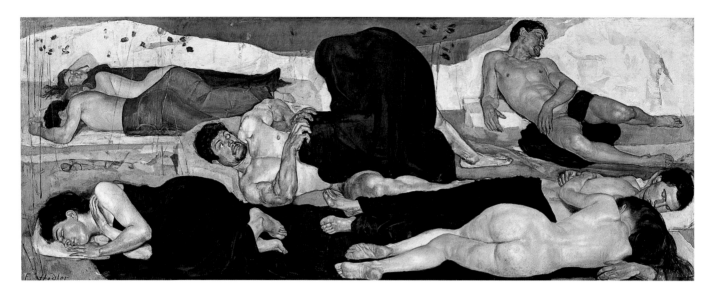

with Symbolism, which was of the same period, and which shall be discussed later: After all, *The Talisman* (1888, Paris, Musée d'Orsay) by Paul Sérusier was painted under Gauguin's guidance, and did not Maurice Denis render a *Tribute to Cézanne* (1900, Paris, Musée d'Orsay)? Yet, on close examination, it is to Puvis de Chavannes that they owe their art. First and foremost, Maurice Denis, whose admiration was boundless as we see in his *Diary*. He mulled over, assimilated and developed the ideas contained in *Young Women by the Sea* and in *Sacred Wood*: the frieze-like composition, the expression of space, the choice of colors in which muted shades prevail, the forms reduced to the decorative arabesque, which would become the leitmotiv of Art Nouveau and whose early stages can be found in Gauguin; last of all, the expression of rhythm, produced by the position of the figures and their relationship with the trees. Maurice Denis is famed for his definition of painting as "a flat surface covered by colors assembled in a certain order." Yet, paradoxically, the subject plays an essential part in his work, as can be seen both in his contemporaneous and timeless representations, titled *Bathers at Perros-Guirec*, or else *The Muses, The Orchard of the Wise Virgins* and *Sacred Wood.*

In his early days, Pierre Bonnard did not fail to emulate inventions from *Inter Artes et Naturam*, as we can see in his painting *The Big Garden* (1898, Paris, Musée d'Orsay), even in its horizontal format. Likewise, Edouard Vuillard had perfectly assimilated Puvis's arrangements, that he found in intimist subjects like *Green Interior* (1891, New York, The Metropolitan Museum of Art) as well as in the large ensemble of decorative panels based on the theme of *Public Gardens* (1894, lost). Ker-Xavier Roussel followed suit with his representations of contemporary scenes which he then abandoned for far more literal evocations of antiquity. The other Nabi painters, Paul Sérusier, Jan Verkade, Charles Filiger, Paul Ranson, Pierre Girieud were undoubtedly followers of the Gauguin of Pont-Aven and of Emile Bernard, but they were above all loyal disciples of Puvis de Chavannes, occasionally converting his themes to esoterism, as in *Nabi Landscape* by Paul Ranson (London, private collection).

Within that group, Aristide Maillol's position was special. As a painter first, he was entirely under the sway of Puvis's art, as can be seen in the copy he made in 1887 of *The Poor Fisherman* (Paris, Musée d'Orsay). He quickly and precociously found his own style within the world of Puvis (*The Crown of Flowers [A Meadow Subject]*, 1889, Copenhagen, Ny-Carlsberg Glyptothek), even drawing his inspiration from *Christian Inspiration*, the most ignored panel of the stairway of the Musée des Beaux-Arts of Lyon (*Portrait of Aunt Lucie*, 1892, private collection). When, after 1895, he began practicing sculpture, he invented a world of smooth, full forms, sensuous and idealized, that owes nothing to Rodin and everything, including the use of allegory to Puvis. Félix Vallotton, with his peculiar style and critical vision, was nonetheless a perfect adept of Puvis, as attested so well by the engraved portraits he made of him, the numerous figures and the layout of the painting *Bathing on* a *Summer Evening* (1892–93, Zurich, Kunsthaus), as well as by his landscapes treated in the classicizing manner, and his contemporary motifs (*On the Beach*, 1899, Switzerland, private collection).

At the same time, about 1895, a second Neo-Impressionist movement was launched, stemming from the art of Paul Signac and then evolving into a simpler Divisionism, as shown in the exhibition at the Landesmuseum of Münster and the Musée de Grenoble in 1996–97. Signac, just like Cross, who was his neighbor on the Mediterranean coast, had an enormous influence everywhere, in France, in Holland, and in Germany thanks especially to Count Kessler around 1900, at a time when Cézanne's name was still practically unknown. His technique blended remarkably with the art of composition that he owed to Puvis and was already visible in *In the Time of Harmony*. That new language would contribute to increase the diffusion of Puvis's art in another direction, which would be confirmed in Matisse and his painting *Luxe, calme et volupté* (1905, Paris, Musée d'Orsay), in Derain and his composition appropriately titled *The Golden Age* (1905, Teheran, Museum of Modern Art), and in Jean Metzinger (*Landscape, Sunset*, 1907, Otterlo, Rijksmuseum Kröller-Müller): Indeed in these works, the subject, forms and composition belonged to Puvis, while the color and treatment were Signac's.

Other Countries

Symbolism is the other great issue. It sprang up during the 1880s, and soon spread all over Europe, eventually becoming an authentic artistic movement that associated all forms of expression, from painting to poetry, sculpture and drama. Contrary to Naturalism and therefore anti-Impressionist, it sought to express philosophical reflections on life, death, the world or dreams, by means of images that assumed the form of symbols that were more or less explicit and played on correspondences. These reflections, often invested with mysticism and esoterism, opened onto highly subjective and sometimes hermetic visions, glorifying the weird, the fantastic or sheer dread. Symbolism cannot be boiled down to a tendency or a style: it blended very different strains, one of which was obviously animated by Paul Gauguin, and others by certain Nabis, who called themselves "initiates." For the most part, Symbolism's matrix was not Gustave Moreau, as has been repeated groundlessly, but above all without looking at the art of Puvis de Chavannes. *Death and the Maidens, Hope, The Poor Fisherman, The Dream, Orpheus, The Sheperd's Song*, like the large decorations such as *Pleasant Land* and *The Sacred Wood*, represent familiar myths or simple, fundamental allegories, which were so elaborated, that is, so totally devoid of naturalism, that they would serve as models for every generation of Symbolist painters, beginning with that of Odilon Redon, as has already been seen, up until 1914 and even later. Puvis de Chavannes's art constitutes the major fulcrum of European Symbolism around which that movement was arrayed.

In France first of all, with the exception of Raphaël Collin who vulgarized his art, his disciples and pupils, Jean-Charles Cazin, Alexandre Séon, Alphonse Osbert and Henri Martin paraphrased it, transposed it or accentuated its features after the fashion of all mannerisms (Alphonse Osbert, *The Mystery of the Night*, 1897, Paris, private collection). Each of them would develop one particular aspect, starting from the landscape, the figure, classical or profane themes, such as Paul Chabas, Henri Le Sidaner, Emile-René Ménard. Edmond Aman-Jean, Seurat's fellow student and friend, whose art also appears to be close to that of Maurice Denis in its ideals, would dwell on compositions in which the decorative aspect prevailed (*Girl with Peacock*, 1895, Paris, Musée des Arts Décoratifs). The sculptors did not stay on the sidelines, for example Albert Bartholomé, but the other sculptors preferred to stick to allegory, as had Puvis: that is the case of Antoine Bourdelle in the heroic genre or of Joseph Bernard in the graceful manner.

Symbolism was even more widely diffused in Germany and Switzerland, since Impressionism had not found a fertile soil in those two countries. It was to develop there from Puvis de Chavannes, as well as from Arnold Böcklin himself. Both can, moreover, be connected in many respects: their art is often comparable and their evolution parallel, although Böcklin did not turn to mural painting.

Hans von Marées, as has been seen, was the first German painter to emulate Puvis de Chavannes. The founder of modern art in his country, together with Böcklin, he himself would exert considerable influence on Max Klinger, who was also under the sway of the Basel painter: but the work *L'Heure bleue*, painted in 1873 and undertaken when the artist was still in Paris, is a sure sign that Klinger had known how to look at Puvis. That is also the case of Franz von Stuck and even more so of Ludwig von Hofmann, whose entire oeuvre stems from Puvis (*Idolino*, c. 1892, Bielefeld, Kunsthalle), up to his mural compositions for Weimar. Hofmann, who would evolve in remarkable fashion toward a greater stylization, is a key figure given the influence he had on Expressionist painters such as Ernest-Ludwig Kirchner and Max Pechstein. In the 1890s, one of the prime movers in the Worpswede school, Heinrich Vogeler, borrowed Puvis's themes, converting them to a rather naïve simplification. This clearly explains why so many elements in Paula Modersohn-Becker evoke Gauguin as much as the author of *The Sacred Wood.* Besides Hans von Marées, Puvis can be found in the early works of Max Beckmann, Franz Marc and Karl Hofer, the latter remaining loyal to the French master throughout his entire career (*Three Bathing Youths,* 1907, Winterthur, Kunstmuseum).

But the great figure of Symbolism in that part of Europe is the Swiss painter Ferdinand Hodler, who became equally famous in Germany. From the start, his ambition was to vie with Puvis, and he immediately became engaged in his field of predilection, that of mural painting (*Architecture, Art of the Engineer*, 1889–90, Zurich, private collection). In Paris, he exhibited works that Puvis saw and admired, like *Night* (1889–90, Bern, Kunstmuseum). By the subjects he tackled, in which he illustrated his vision of man and the universe, in his landscapes as in his simplest portraits, Hodler, like Gauguin, created a style that, while remaining loyal to Puvis, was one of the most original and promising developments of the future.

Expansion

At that time, Belgium was as close to Germany and Central Europe as it was to France. It represented, with the Groupe des XX in particular, an extremely important center for both literary and artistic Symbolism, owing to two personalities, the painter Fernand Khnopff and the sculptor George Minne. Having received his training from Xavier Mellery, who himself was under Puvis de Chavannes's influence, Khnopff is in fact the founder of Belgian Symbolism that would later nurture Surrealism. Khnopff looked directly at Puvis's works, as can be seen from *Memories* (1889, Brussels, Musées Royaux des Beaux-Arts), with its frieze-like composition and the repetition of seven identical figures in front of a flat space formed by horizontal parallels. In turn, Khnopff would leave his mark on the Viennese Gustav Klimt, which would explain why the *Beethoven frieze* created for the Secession building in Vienna is so reminiscent of the French painter.

George Minne had been Rodin's pupil and owed him a great deal, but it was Puvis de Chavannes's art that enabled him to break away from that of Rodin. Just like Khnopff and Hodler, he would make use of a single, identically repeated motif: in *Fountain of Five Kneeling Youths* (c. 1898, Ghent, Musée Royal des Beaux-Arts), the same slender figure of a kneeling boy is repeated five times around a circular base, a layout that simultaneously shows the subject in rear view, profile and front view. The rhythm Puvis had so beautifully developed in his murals achieved here a spatial expression that would become amazingly popular, especially in Germany: George Minne inspired all of Wilhelm Lehmbruck's art, as well as Constantin Brancusi's first steps, and we can even see reminiscences of him in Oskar Schlemmer. His figures, with their odd bearing and full of morbidness, largely generated those of Egon Schiele and Oskar Kokoschka. Another Belgian sculptor is to be mentioned for the development of his career, Constantin Meunier, and a painter, Henri Evenepoel. It is easy to see the contours of a world emerge, with its channels, its correspondences, and what unites all these seemingly so different creations: At a certain point, they all present common features, behind which we can always find the masterful oeuvre of Puvis de Chavannes.

With Giovanni Segantini, Italy was to be represented by one of the most appealing exponents of Symbolism. His figures, and the treatment of forms and subjects drawn from peasant life, are marked by the art of Jean-François Millet, and this is clear in his drawings, but his compositions owe more to the world of Puvis de Chavannes: see *Love at the Fountain of Life*, whose very title is already so revealing (1896, Milan, Galleria Civica d'Arte Moderna). Giuseppe Pellizza da Volpedo, whose subjects and style would mark the Futurist artists befo-

10. Alexandre Séon, *The Star.* Private collection

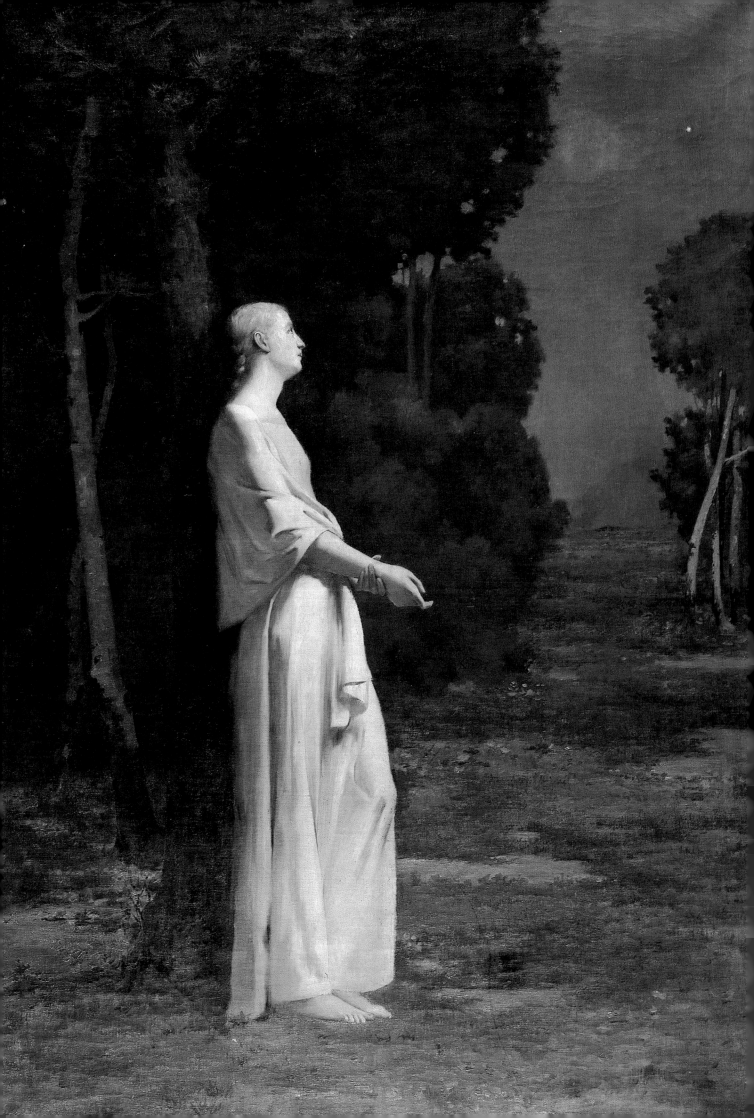

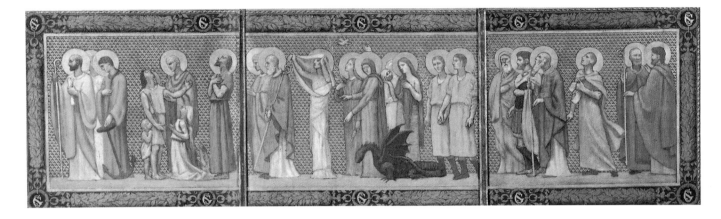

11. Pierre Puvis de Chavannes, *Legendary Saints of France*, 1879. Philadelphia Museum of Art

re they discovered Cubism, retained Puvis's main characteristics, as in *The Round* (1902–03, Milan, Galleria Civica d'Arte Moderna).

After Germany, it was in Scandinavia that Symbolism found its favorite ground, albeit in an exceedingly melancholy, pessimistic version, as can be imagined. Two different currents traverse it, opposed in their aesthetics, yet both under the sway of the art of Puvis, who appears to have so literally enthralled the artists of Norway, Sweden, Finland and Denmark that nearly all of them went to Paris to see the master's works, whose appeal might be compared to that of Raphael in Rome. One of these two strains put a particular emphasis on line, the accuracy of the contour at the expense of color and a careful composition: this is apparent in the paintings by Ejnar Nielsen, Magnus Enckell, Beda Stjernschantz, and Laurits Andersen Ring. Instead, Akseli Gallen-Kallela adopted a simpler draftsmanship, but much brighter colors. As for Vilhelm Hammershøi, it is obvious where his leitmotiv of the rear-view figure came from. His early linear style emulating classicism evolved into a slightly blurred contour, while he obsessively transposed into everyday life Puvis's neutral theatricality.

The other Scandinavian current of Symbolism is entirely embodied in the Norwegian painter Edvard Munch, whose oeuvre is immense and whose posterity is impressive, especially in Central and Northern Europe. If we measure to what degree Munch was able to appropriate Puvis de Chavannes's contribution—and he would prove it all his life, in *Puberty* (1894–95, Oslo, Nasjonalgalleriet), which is the northern version of *Hope; Bathing Men* (1907, Helsinki, Ateneum) belonging to his Warnemünde period, where we again have the motif of the ring behind a sequence of standing figures seen from the front, back or in profile; and in all his friezes bearing the title *Frieze of Life* (1899–1900, Oslo, Nasjonalgalleriet)—we can just imagine the consequences of his legacy: This is the case of Mondrian whose *Woods near Oele* (1906, The Hague, Gemeentemuseum) comes straight from Munch's *The Voice* (1893, Oslo, Munch Museet), and whose approach cannot be understood without referring to Puvis. Munch created an entirely personal vision as did Gauguin and Hodler, in which the perfectly assimilated presence of Puvis continued nonetheless to play a role.

Russia was to be at the same time an important center for Symbolism and for the diffusion of Puvis's aesthetic. A number of painters claimed to be more or less literal followers of the French master, among whom Viktor Borissov-Moussatov, Mikhail Nesterov, Nikolai Roerich and Kuz'ma Petrov-Vodkin. Léon Bakst's sets and costumes for the theater can be clearly observed in this context as well as Kasimir Malevich's first Symbolist works (*Prayer–Study for a Fresco*, 1907, Saint Petersburg, Russian State Museum), and those of Wassily Kandinsky, expressed, on the other hand, through the use of the Divisionist technique (*Sunday. Old Russia*, 1904, Rotterdam, Boijmans-Van Beuningen Museum).

Every other country was influenced by Puvis to a certain extent: England, with William Rothenstein, Frederick Cayley Robinson and Augustus John; America, especially with John S. Sargent, who as a matter of fact would be commissioned to execute a decoration for the Boston Library after Puvis, Mary Cassatt, Maurice Prendergast, Arthur Glackens, Arthur B. Davies and Bryson Burroughs, his most conscientious disciple and a museum curator; while Greece would boast Constantinos Parthenis; and Portugal, Antonio Teixeiro-Carneiro.

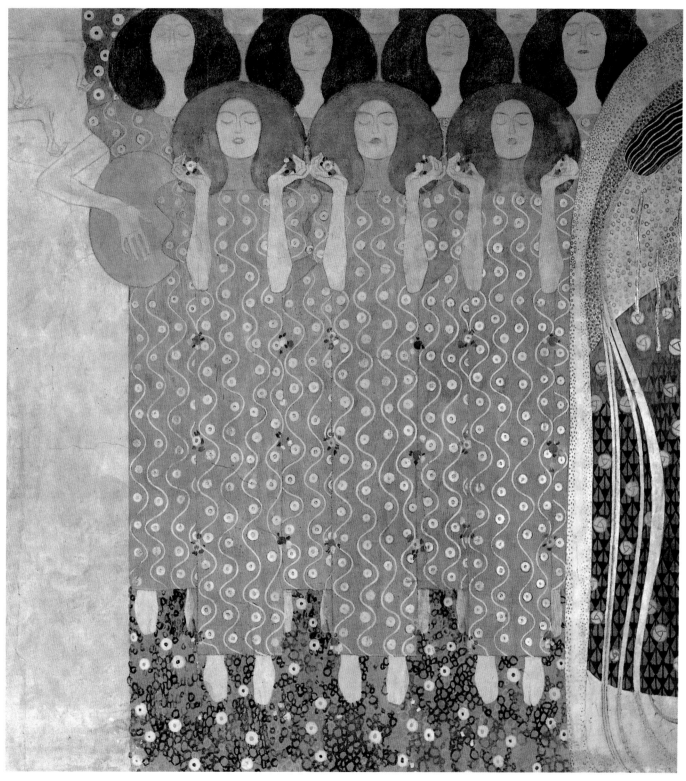

12. Gustav Klimt,
The Choir of the Angels in Paradise,
detail of the
Beethoven Frieze, 1902.
Vienna, Österreichische Galerie

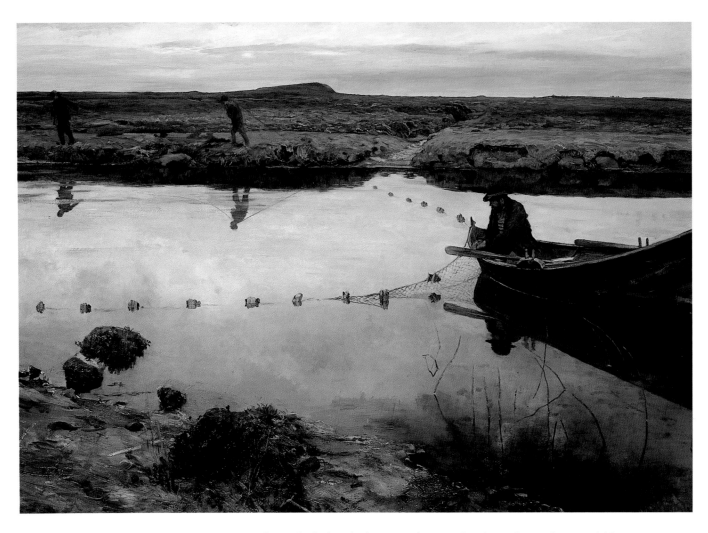

13. Eilif Peterssen,
*Salmon Fishermen on
Figgen River*, 1889.
Lillehammer, Kunstmuseum

Spain was to be included with the special example of Catalonia that would become an authentic Puvis land, giving rise to Picasso. A School of Decoration was formed in Barcelona around Joaquín Torres-García, who in turn discovered Puvis's work in 1907, and made it his ideal. Devoted to monumental art, it included artists such as Josep Obiols, Jaume Querol, Lluis Puig, Manel Cano, Tomas Aymat, and Josep-Maria Marqués-Puig. Torres-Garcia is the most singular example of Puvis's sway on an artist. The paintings and decorations he made before he left Barcelona represent a nearly identical, yet cruder, reappropriation, of Puvis's aesthetic. He would remain loyal to him throughout the 1920s, producing astonishing paintings imitating classical frescoes framed by architectural elements in wood, a key for understanding his later reliefs just before he discovered Mondrian's art in Paris, founded Cercle et Carré with Michel Seuphor, and went abstract. During the 1930s, he would once again show how devoted he was to Puvis, whom in fact he had not given up. After 1945, he still appealed to those fundamentals even in his most transposed allegories. Torres-García and his circle are only one of the elements that Catalonia produced under the name of Noucentisme: but Joaquim Sunyer, the sculptors Manolo and Josep Clarà and Julio González when he was still a painter (*Girls Sleeping on the Beach*, 1914, Barcelona, Museu Nacional d'Art de Catalunya) are proof of Puvis's presence in that country.

Symbolism spread throughout Europe and, in particular, as we have just seen, in a component that was essentially influenced by Puvis de Chavannes's art. Of course there were other factors involved, since the paths of creation are countless and formed by many crossings. This kind of discussion, appraisal and commentary demands endless nuances, or else it appears too elementary. The fact remains that the new trends of modern art that began to develop in the early twentieth century were steeped in this fundamental movement. Such was the context in which Picasso would embark on his career.

14. Pierre Puvis de Chavannes,
The Poor Fisherman, 1881.
Paris, Musée d'Orsay

Picasso and Matisse

In 1900, Pablo Picasso appeared in Paris, a city taken up with the World Fair and steeped in Puvis's aesthetic. He saw Puvis's works exhibited at the Fair, and must have certainly gone to the Panthéon, the Hôtel de Ville, and the Sorbonne, inasmuch as hailing from Barcelona he was already familiar with everything Puvis's art represented: Hence, beginning in 1902, his paintings and drawings of the Blue Period with their cold color, like the blue of *Saint Genevieve Watching over Paris*, their simplified, heightened forms, their lack of depth, their frontality and their very melancholy subjects. That sadness, the same as in *Prodigal Son*, permeates paintings like *The Fisherman's Goodbye* (1902, Japan, private collection)*, La Vie* (Cleveland, The Cleveland Museum of Art), and *The Tragedy* (1903, Washington, National Gallery), whose titles speak for themselves.

We should look at the Pink Period as a confirmation of the preceding one. Here Picasso went further in assimilating and transposing Puvis's contributions, in particular in the interpretation of space and the placing of figures within it. *Acrobat on a Ball* (1905, Moscow, Pushkin Museum) is certainly his masterpiece in this genre, with the succession of planes reduced to verticality and the sequence of figures, from the man seen from the rear with his accurate outline through the arabesque of the young acrobat on his ball to the distant horse. Picasso then proceeded to drastically simplify his images, which became veritable details—entirely revisited—of Puvis's compositions (*The Two Brothers*, 1906, Basel, Kun-

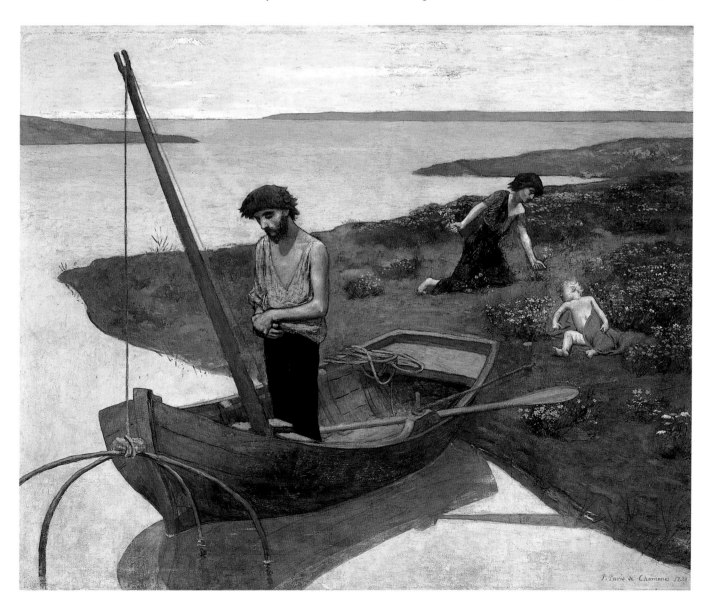

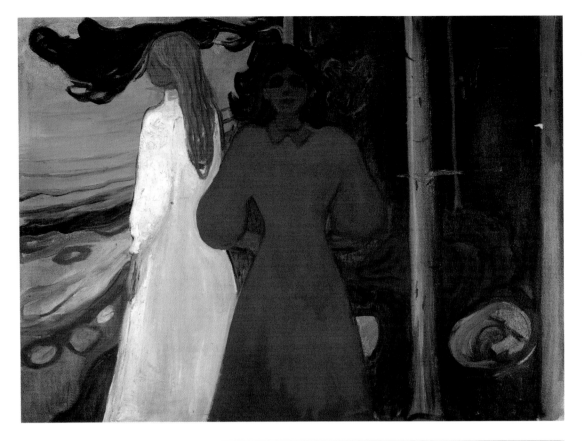

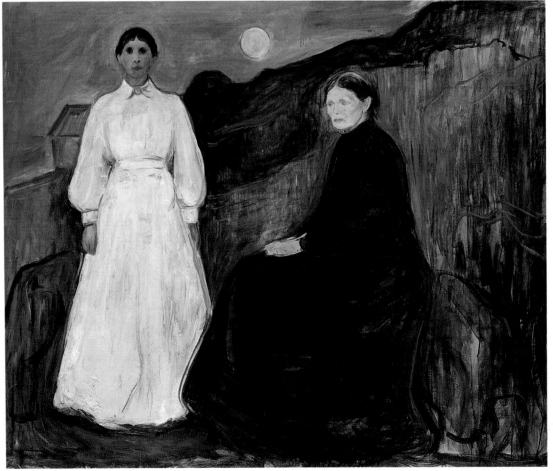

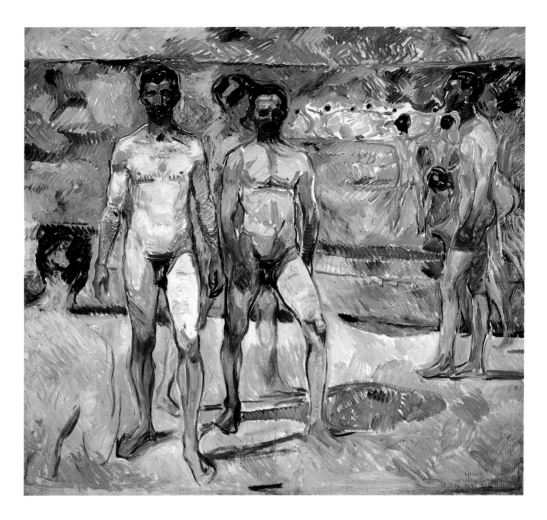

stsmuseum). That evolution, naturally associated with other factors, would lead him to Cubism. But we should point out that the composition of the *Demoiselles d'Avignon* (1907, New York, The Museum of Modern Art), its very format, its frontality, the layout of the vertical figures and even the crouching rear-view one, are right out of Puvis's world. Just prior to the birth of Analytic Cubism, Picasso again composed *Large Nude by the Sea* (1908–09, New York, The Museum of Modern Art), which features merely a standing figure holding a drapery, seen in profile, one arm raised, painted in shades of pink and gray, standing out against a background of three horizontal parallels representing earth, sea and sky: did that bather not come straight out of *Pleasant Land*?

Henri Matisse discovered or rallied the art of Puvis a bit later than Picasso. We have seen all that *Luxe, calme et volupté* (1905, Paris, Musée d'Orsay) owed to Signac, including the subject and the composition inspired by Puvis. Up until 1916, his presence would be felt. The subject of *Le Bonheur de vivre* (1905–06, Merion, The Barnes Foundation) is indeed that of a timeless pastoral scene, where in the center we see the motif of dancers in a ring, a reinterpretation of the group in the painting *Death and the Maidens*. Having parted with Fauvism, Matisse would come back to the expression of the line in his first version of *Le Luxe* (1907, Paris, Centre Georges-Pompidou, Musée National d'Art Moderne) whose layout and subject should be viewed as a transposition of *Young Women by the Sea*, an option the second version of that composition carried further (*Le Luxe II*, 1907, Copenhagen, Statens Museum for Kunst). The following year, the same appropriation of Puvis's themes, the subject and the form, together with a desire for the decorative, returned in *Bathers with a Turtle* (1908, St Louis, St Louis Art Museum) at the expense of radical simplification: a flat background formed by parallel bands of color, neither decoration nor detail, figures that are unrealistic since they are subject to the needs of the composition. In 1909–10, Matisse painted *Music* and *Dance* (Saint Petersburg, The Hermitage Museum), confirming his earlier achievements. *Dance* returns to the central motif of *Le Bonheur de vivre*, that now takes up the entire surface of the painting: the figures, reduced to a series of curves and counter-curves forming a loop, are inscribed in an abstract landscape consisting of just two strictly flat registers, painted in saturated color, green below, the other blue: Puvis's lesson, carried to its ultimate consequences. Later on, in 1916, Matisse was to come back to one of Puvis de Chavannes's favorite themes: the expression of rhythm by the succession of verticals in an oblong rectangular format, with the insertion of figures in a landscape enhanced by trees. At that time, Matisse painted *Bathers by a River* (Chicago, The Art Institute) where, in the monumental format of Puvis, sketchily rendered plant figures and motifs were directly placed side by side, enclosed in vertical registers, the ensemble producing a sense of extraordinary power but of masterful brutality as well.

André Derain, one of the leading personalities of Fauvism, also took advantage of Puvis de Chavannes's oeuvre as well, offering his own interpretation of it in *The Golden Age* (1905, Teheran, Museum of Modern Art) with its self-explanatory title. The following year, *Dance* (1906, Amsterdam, Fridart Foundation) confirmed that direction in a wealth of decorativeness, while *Bathers* (1907, New York, The Museum of Modern Art) simplified radically and somewhat crudely one of the master's themes, presenting three schematic figures in an indistinct landscape, that is, forms giving rhythm to a pictorial surface. Maurice de Vlaminck, although reputedly so unpolished, did not ignore Puvis in his compositions, nor did Georges Rouault, Gustave Moreau's closest pupil, who took over Puvis's principles in *Riders in the Twilight* (1904, Zurich, Bührle Foundation Collection). Picasso and Matisse of course are not the only ones. When one understands that Marcel Duchamp and Francis Picabia belonged to that same world, it is easier to interpret their later work. With its primitivist aspect borrowed from Emile Bernard, the painting *The Bush* by Marcel Duchamp (1911, Philadelphia, The Philadelphia Museum of Art) is a perfect expression of a Symbolist conception, as is Picabia's *Adam and Eve* (1911, Paris, private collection). Concurrently with Picasso, many other artists who were Cubist or who became so would display the influence they received from Puvis: such is the case of Albert Gleizes with *Bathers* (1912, Paris, Musée Municipal d'Art Moderne), Othon Friesz with *Bathers of Andelys* (1908, Geneva, Musée du Petit Palais), Henri Le Fauconnier with *Abundance* (1910, The Hague, Gemeentemuseum), Roger de La Fresnaye with *Nude in a Landscape* (1910, Paris, Centre Georges-Pompidou, Musée National d'Art Moderne), as well as Fernand Léger, whose painting *Nudes in the Forest* (1909–10, Otterlo, Rijksmuseum Kröller-Müller) with its oblong horizontal format and the profusion of off-keel cylinders in a twilight that makes an interpretation difficult, presents a solid orthogonal composition in which the figures and the perfectly integrated landscape express a great energy.

Elsewhere, in Germany, as we have already seen, the Expressionist painters, those of the Brücke and the Blaue Reiter groups, especially Franz Marc, who were inspired by Ludwig von Hofmann and later by Hans von Marées in their creations would also adopt several aspects of Puvis, much like Max Beckmann did in his early days. In Belgium, Symbolism would continue to foment the first group of Laethem-Saint-Martin which before embracing Cubist manners *à la* Zadkine and joining up with Expressionism was to be largely nurtured by references to Puvis, as we can see in the works of Gustave Van de Woestyne, Léon and Gustave De Smet, Frits Van den Berghe, as well as in the very different ones of Albert Servaes.

Later in the Twentieth Century
After World War I the tone was to change, but there is no need to discuss the notion of a return to order here. In 1917, Picasso had already developed his so-called "Ingresque" style in the portraits he drew. In 1920, his paintings begin to reflect a new interest in construction and the assertion of volume which was far less "classicizing" or "Neoclassic" than entirely in the spirit of Puvis: in *Women and Child by the Sea* (1921, Chicago, The Art Institute), the arrangement of the figures inside a triangle, the profile presentation, the silhouette of the group standing out against a background of parallel horizontals, the color range and the absence of shading revisit the notions present in *Antique Vision*. The famous painting *Three Women at the Spring* (1921, New York, The Museum of Modern Art) entirely be-

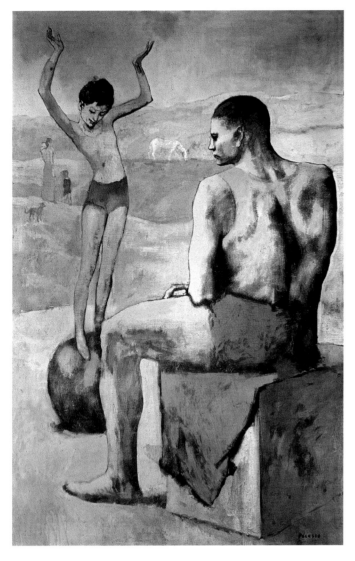

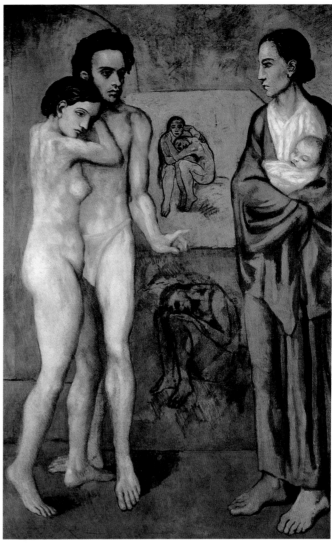

18. Pablo Picasso,
Acrobat on a Ball, 1905.
Moscow, Pushkin Museum

19. Pablo Picasso, *La Vie*, 1903.
The Cleveland Museum of Art

longs to that manner, just like *Seated Bather* (1930, New York, The Museum of Modern Art),
which returns to that same motif, this time monstrously distorted, set in front of the tripartite
décor.

Therefore Picasso was totally faithful to Puvis's ideal. Although with less assertiveness, Fernand Léger was too, illustrating in turn the theme of *Dance* (1929, Grenoble, Musée de
Grenoble) in which he retained only two animated, hieratic figures. After Purism, Amédée
Ozenfant found the humanist figuration again in allegories *à la* Puvis (*The Bather's Grotto*, 1930, Grenoble, Musée de Grenoble). At the time, Italy was not left behind, as the interest of a number of *Novecento Italiano* artists indicates. When they left behind the world
of metaphysical painting, even Carlo Carrà, and Mario Sironi, Massimo Campigli, and Mario
Mafai in turn would follow Puvis's precepts, while the sculptor Arturo Martini would create *The Fisherman's Wife* (1930, Milan, private collection) which conforms in every aspect
to the spirit of its model.

In that context and at the crossroads of multiple influences, we have Balthus, close to Derain and to the Surrealist universe (*The Mountain*, 1937, New York, The Metropolitan Museum of Art), or in another register, Robert Poughéon, whose compositions combine Ménard's solutions with those of André Lhote (*The Dioscuri*, 1939, private collection).

At the time, Puvis de Chavannes could continue to inspire Othon Friesz on the one hand,
who openly referred to the French tradition, and on the other, Henri Matisse who, after his
Nice period, rekindled his daring and returned to the theme of dance, and executed in
1930–31 a commission from Dr. Barnes, who asked him to decorate the premises of his foun-

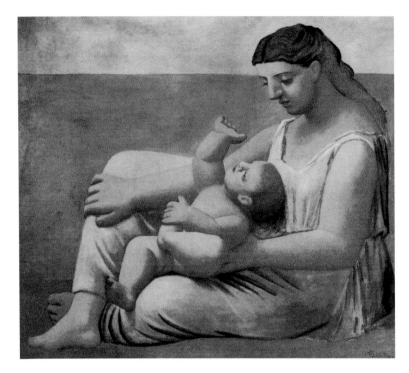

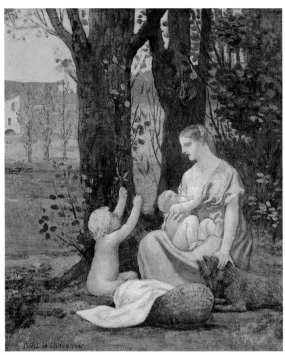

20. Pablo Picasso, *Woman and Child by the Sea*, 1921. Chicago, The Art Institute

21. Pierre Puvis de Chavannes, *Charity*, 1887. Private collection

dation at Merion. Matisse opted for sequences of figures, enlarging the forms of *Dance* he had executed for Shchukin and treating them in large simplified flat tints. Even their placement within the architecture reminds us, with its lunettes, of the arrangement of Puvis's decoration in the Boston Library which he assimilated perfectly. In Matisse's last period, that of the cut-out gouaches, the memory of Puvis would last, especially in the series of *Blue Nudes*, which represent crouching figures that were drawn, after having been stylized, from figures in *Le Bonheur de vivre* (*Blue Nude II*, 1952, Paris, Centre Georges-Pompidou, Musée National d'Art Moderne). How better to express that memory than in the *Back* series? Is not that motif—which he created in 1913, then went back to the same year, again in 1916–17, and finally in 1930—that of the central figure in *Young Women by the Sea*?

Nor did Picasso forget. After the war, during the period at Antibes, he painted *La Joie de vivre or Antipolis* (1949, Antibes, Musée Picasso) in which the format, an oblong rectangle, the frieze-like composition, the stylized forms, the simple, flat planes of color, and the subject itself declare their origin. At the time he decorated the chapel of the château of Vallauris in 1952, he made use of layouts and correspondences as had Puvis, even in the themes, *War, Peace*, similar to the Amiens cycle. Lastly, *Fall of Icarus* (1958), the commission for the UNESCO building in Paris, should also be seen in that perspective. Criticized at the time for its treatment, judged careless, and its subject, difficult to interpret, that mural should be viewed like a composition *à la* Puvis with its background, its color scheme in which ochres and blues dominate, and the layout of the figures, some standing, others lying on the ground. While the title, chosen in fact by Gaéton Picon, adds to the confusion, the one by Picasso was perfectly illuminating: "The triumph of the forces of life and of the spirit over evil."

Style

Puvis's art, after the early years and during the course of its evolution of more than thirty years, can be divided into three major periods: the one illustrated by paintings like *Hope* or the first decorative cycle of the Panthéon; the second, represented by the monumental compositions, for instance *Pleasant Land* and *Sacred Wood*; and the last, that of the Boston Library. All three contribute to Puvis de Chavannes's style, whose components we can now try to define: they have as much to do with the type of subjects represented as with their expression by pictorial means. Puvis uses allegory, choosing the simplest possible: one symbol, one idea per form, even per composition. Neither narration, nor psychology. Instead, gestures, postures, situations. No portrait, no anecdote nor particularity: stylized counte-

22. Henri Matisse, *Le Luxe I*, 1907. Paris, Musée National d'Art Moderne, Centre Georges-Pompidou

23. Pierre Puvis de Chavannes, *Young Women by the Sea*, 1879. Paris, Musée d'Orsay

nances, essential silhouettes that become archetypes, abstract animals, timeless backgrounds. No effects, a sense of measure. Hence the overall impression produced by this painting: it is mute, silent. And essentially visual.

The means to achieve that result call upon structure and rhythm in the composition, and scrupulously comply with the two principal laws ruling the integration of painting in architecture: the law of the wall and of the frame. The wall will be emphasized by verticality, meaning lack of depth, the distribution of its compartments either in parallel bands or three parts, and the rhythm created by the forms marking it. On that surface thus distributed, we then have forms that are simplified, barely modeled or used in flat tints, creating sequences, and united by the play of correspondences. There is an economy of colors and close-set values in order to avoid creating marked contrasts. The overall appearance, opaque and sometimes chalky, is similar to that of frescoes; it is obtained by using a dry material, with scarcely any binder, and a broad, at times thick, brushstroke that may give the impression of having been scraped, even in the small formats.

The law of the frame that essentially concerns monumental painting was respected to the letter by Puvis who, in his compositions, took into consideration the situation of the painting in space and in its location: an oblong strip, a vertical surface, a triptych, a door frame, a tympanum, and solutions adapted to each configuration. Often they were all the more appropriately selected from a repertory that Puvis gradually amassed, as Rodin was to do, and were improved on and used over and over according to his needs: thus the motif formed by the central figure of the seated woman with her child in *Summer* (1873, Paris, Musée d'Orsay). Lastly, the rear-view figures that appear throughout the work like a leitmotiv, the theme of the dance, the flying forms of *The Dream*, *The Sacred Wood* of Lyon, the *Muses* of Boston, the layouts of *Hope* and *The Poor Fisherman*, *The Prodigal Son* and *The Toilette* (1883, Paris,

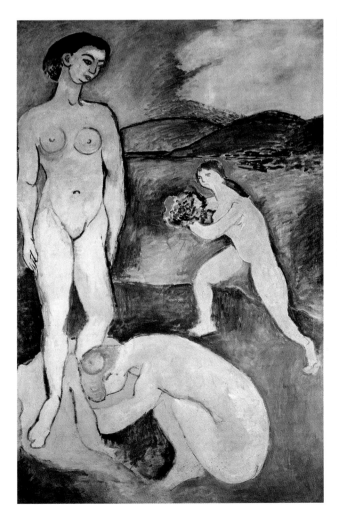

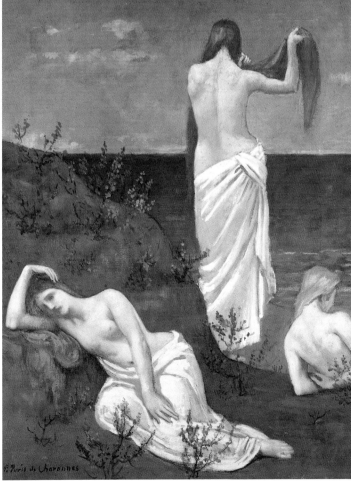

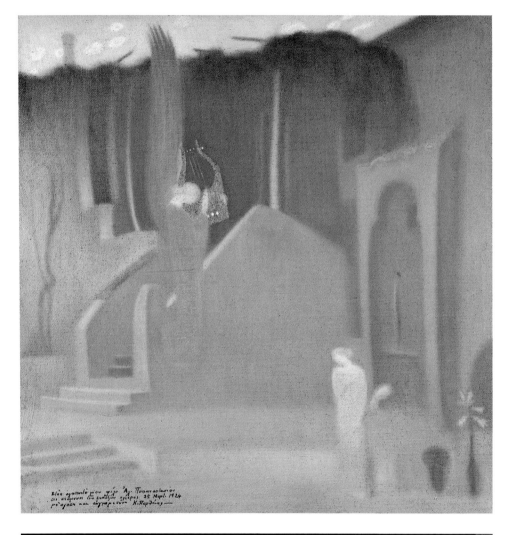

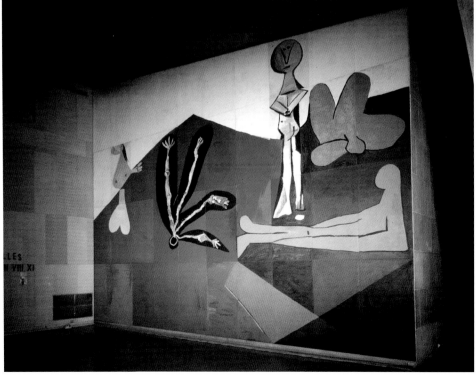

26. Henri Matisse, *Blue Nude II*,
1952. Paris, Musée National d'Art
Moderne, Centre Georges-
Pompidou

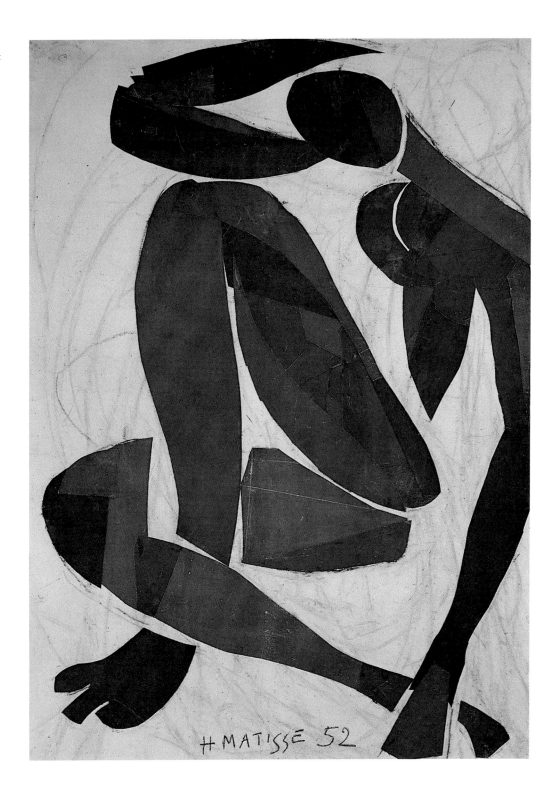

opposite page
24. Constantinos Parthenis,
The Annunciation, 1911
Athens, Museum Alexandros
Soutzos

25. Pablo Picasso,
Fall of Icarus, 1958
Paris, Maison de l'Unesco

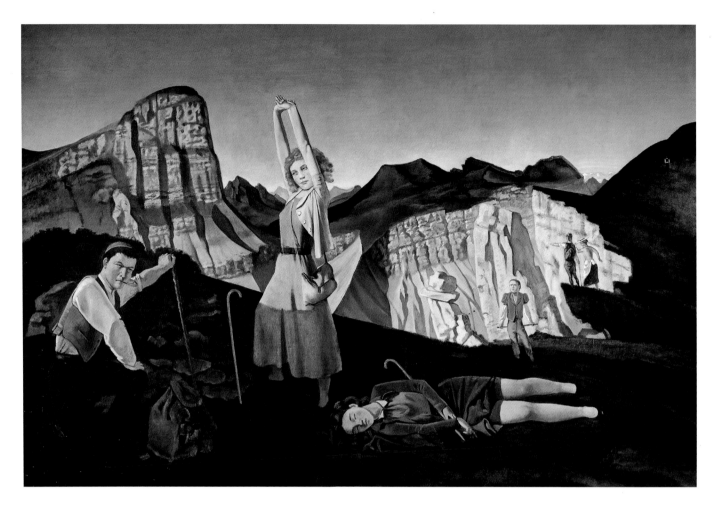

27. Balthus, *The Mountain*, 1937.
New York, The Metropolitan
Museum of Art

Musée d'Orsay) are just so many images or motifs of sheer creation that have been rendered unforgettable and express one of the highest degrees of the art of painting.

From 1880 on, Puvis de Chavannes dominated his age, and his ascendancy produced Raphaël Collin as well as Paul Gauguin, and the utterly different visions of Seurat and Munch, Bourdelle and Maillol. Furthermore, it allows for a profound understanding of the works of Picasso and Matisse and, through their differences, that which unites them. His influence did not just effect the field of painting and sculpture, but touched also on the decorative arts and in particular the art of stained glass, as it was practiced by Art Nouveau glassmakers like Emile Gallé. In the applied arts, especially in posters, he served as a model for the creations of Eugène Grasset and Carlos Schwabe, as well as the illustrations of Henri Rivière. His aesthetic left its mark on countless photographers, particularly in the period of Pictorialism, as we can see in the pictures by Heinrich Kühn, Clarence White and Gertrude Käsebier. In drama, when Symbolism countered Realism, scenography borrowed all its characteristics from Puvis's art; first of all in the Théâtre d'Art directed by Paul Fort, and later by Lugné-Poe, whose childhood friends had been Sérusier, Maurice Denis, Gauguin and Vuillard in particular. His influence can also be detected in the early cinema: the first great French cinema director and theoretic, Louis Feuillade, wrote in *La Série esthétique* in 1910 a manifesto for "film authors" in which he proposed "the art of painting" as an example, citing that of Puvis in particular. Puvis de Chavannes also left his mark on those composers with whom he was associated and whom he inspired, such as Ernest Chausson, Claude Debussy and especially Erik Satie. Many writers admired him, including Emile Zola, Joris-Karl Huysmans, Alfred Jarry and Catulle Mendès, and honoring him along with the hundred poets of the Album des Poètes that Rodin solemnly offered him on the occasion of the banquet, were Emile Verhaeren, Rémy de Gourmont, Georges Rodenbach, Henri de Régnier, Jean Richepin, José-Maria de Hérédia, Paul Verlaine, Paul Fort and Stéphane Mallarmé.

The End of the Misconception

What artist, since the sixteenth century and by the sole means of his art, has received such recognition, especially from other artists, and exerted such a supremacy in his lifetime, one that later influenced so many and so different generations? Puvis de Chavannes created—even if the word may be meaningless for some—a universal art that commanded admiration by its simplicity and harmony. Composition, expressiveness of forms and colors and subject were so thoroughly blended that their effect was immediate and then became eternal.

Puvis's clear and comprehensible work offers models that can be reproduced, assimilated, transposed and combined: one need only keep a structure, a group of forms, a line, a color combination, a part, a detail, an ensemble, an image. Starting from there, each was able to make his own way. Puvis de Chavannes is an artist who embraced a tradition that he was able to keep alive, built his own vision and paved the way for the future. How can we even conceive of a break that can be neither described nor situated, when we can observe, on the other hand, an authentic continuity in the history of art between the nineteenth and the twentieth centuries that Puvis's art and posterity insured. Does not such a natural sequence, such a continuous transition, once again offer an illustration of the life of forms and the proof that history has not come to an end?

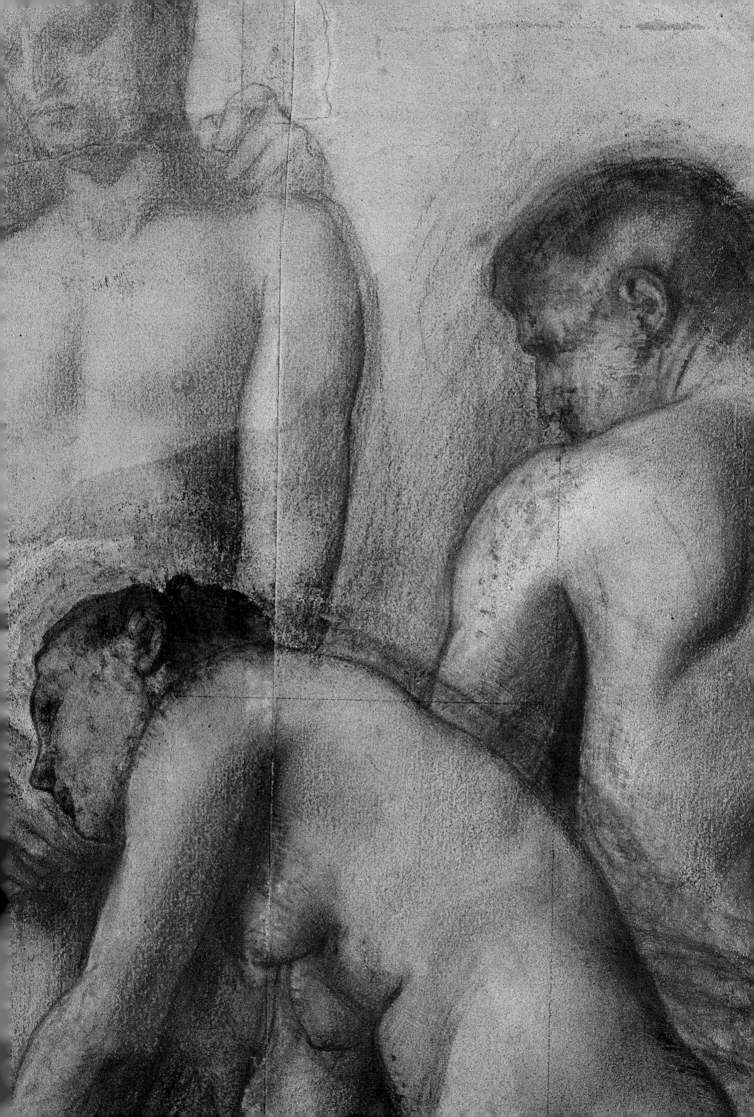

Anomalous—that is how Puvis de Chavannes could appear to his contemporaries, even those among them who were his most ardent admirers. For example, Camille Mauclair, who was often wide of the mark in his appreciation of the moderns of the early twentieth century and yet wrote what remains one of the best books on Puvis de Chavannes, would describe the artist as an "isolated phenomenon."[1] And in 1909, when Léonce Bénédite, curator of the Musée de Luxembourg, drew up his panorama of nineteenth-century painting, he was clearly uncertain as to where Puvis de Chavannes should be placed. In the end, he left him in some sort of "no man's land" half way between the Impressionists and the painters of the "new generation" who were "striving to rejuvenate the traditions of history painting, the nude and the portrait." After the ill-matched bag of Jules Lefebvre, Tony Robert-Fleury, Ferdinand Humbert, Benjamin Constant, Fernand Cormon, Albert Maignan, Luc Olivier-Merson, Raphael Collin and François Flameng—but before Degas and Renoir—came Puvis de Chavannes, "whose monumental work has entirely dominated our age."[2] This uncertain position is indicative of the difficulty still encountered when it comes to defining Puvis de Chavannes's work; for a time, the artist was confused with the arch-conventionalists—even if that category of *les pompiers* has now revealed itself to be obsolete—and yet he was undoubtedly one of the very first "prophets" of modern painting. When, in 1896, Zola was drawing up his pessimistic "assessment of the last thirty years," he was careful not to forget Puvis, recognizing his achievement in this brief statement: while light painting was triumphant and academic painting was foundering, "Puvis de Chavannes continued to grow in his solitary labor as a pure artist."[3] And it was this independence and this solitude that guaranteed the anomalous painter his henceforth central position; the result was that Puvis de Chavannes's art would exercise an influence that was both varied and continual. With such a free artist, other artists could and would enter into a perfectly free exchange.

At first, Puvis seems to have chosen the status of outsider, which later was a position others recognized as his right. He first came to the public's attention in 1859 with his *A Return from the Hunt* and established a name for himself at the 1861 Salon with his diptych of *Peace* and *War*; however, a certain mystery hangs over the beginnings of his career and training. What we do know is that, very briefly, he was the pupil of Scheffer, Delacroix and Couture, and that he would unsuccessfully submit to the Salon a series of paintings of a pathos, violence and confusion which are the very antithesis of the self-mastery and serenity that characterize his post-1860 works. Puvis de Chavannes himself said that he had encountered his "road to Damascus" when decorating the salon of the family house at Brouchy, where the requirements of simplicity and legibility first began to force themselves upon him. However, all "roads to Damascus" involve some terrible upheaval and one must take the artist at his word when he uses that comparison. Nevertheless, there remains the mystery of those years during which Puvis de Chavannes passed from the Courbetesque Realism of *The Village Firemen* (c. 1857), the amazing crimson splurge of *Mademoiselle de Sombreuil Drinking a Glass of Blood to Save Her Father's Life* (1850)—something that not even Delacroix would have dared—and the Decampsesque chiaroscuro and brutality of his *The Martyrdom of Saint Sebastian* to those calm paradisiacal paintings installed in the Musée d'Amiens after 1860. One would have expected some sort of dialogue and engagement with the work of Ingres, but it is covered over by the very savagery of the line. What is not obliterated is the presence of Chassériau, who would remain Puvis's most cherished model, the artist who introduced him to the art of mural painting. However, unlike Chassériau, Puvis de Chavannes has no genius for synthesis. He is too excessive in his approach to ever rise to the status of a master, to ever fit into a direct line of descent. He is like a convert who maintains the selfsame virtues each time he passes from one church to another; and the characteristics of the soft and gentle Puvis will always remain willpower, perseverance, a continuity in draftsmanship and a certain tension, power and even violence in execution. The meditative artist exudes the energy that is always to be found among the great solitaries. Over and over again one sees critics faced with this problem of situating Puvis de Chavannes with regard to his contemporaries and the great artistic movements of his day. And over and over again Puvis is surprising not only because he seems to stand outside the "modernity" of the moment, but also because his painting is intriguing and interesting precisely because of the faults or qualities (depending on your point of view) that seem to be his alone. Using broad categorizations, one might simplify things and say that Puvis de Chavannes was reproached for three things: he failed to meet the canon of great idealist art; he remained too distant from the Naturalists and the independents; he was never really a Symbolist.

1. Pierre Puvis de Chavannes,
Study of Four Figures for "Rest,"
detail, c. 1862.
Paris, Musée d'Orsay

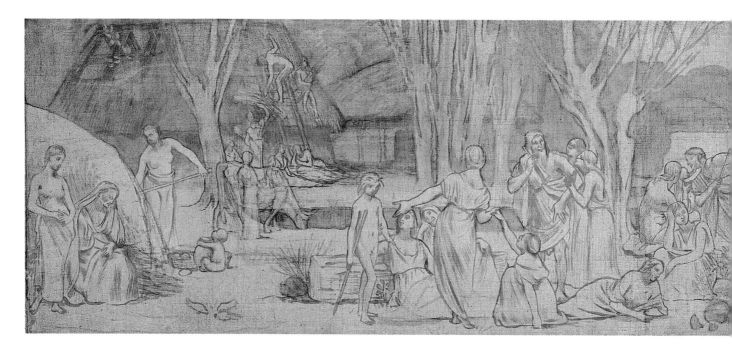

2. Pierre Puvis de Chavannes,
Study for "Ludus pro Patria," c. 1879
Paris, Musée d'Orsay

The most striking and evident feature for his contemporaries was how he distanced himself from that descriptive and analytical fervor that—in the genres of history-painting and landscape—can be traced through Courbet, Manet and Jean-Paul Laurens to the Impressionists. Mauclair commented that Puvis de Chavannes "was never successful among the partisans of an art that was directly and solely figurative; art that—whether academic, Realist or Impressionist—does nothing but stimulate the eye, offering purely sensorial pleasures."[4] Though rather forced in its analysis, this is a valid general comment. The passion for the real—be it filtered by the eye or translated from history—was the rallying-cry of art in the second half of the nineteenth century, and Puvis de Chavannes seems to have been indifferent to it. How else is one to explain the violence in the comments of Castagnary, which are undoubtedly one of the clearest statements we have of the extent to which Puvis de Chavannes could shock the "moderns" of the period 1860–80. In his *Salon* of 1863, Castagnary draws up a clear picture of the "three contemporary schools." According to him, "the Classical School" and the "Romantic School" belong to the distant and recent past respectively. The present and the future belong, however, to the "Naturalist School," which holds that "art is the expression of life in all its forms and degrees; its sole goal is to reproduce nature by bringing it to the maximum of its power and intensity." Thus, for Castagnary, the important figures are Daubigny, the creator of *The Grape Harvest*; Courbet, whose *Return from the Conference* was banned from exhibition; and Millet, the painter of *Peasant Resting on His Hoe*. In the "Classic School," Castagnary includes Flandrin—who, in the absence of Ingres, has become "the king of these pale regions"—Baudry, Cabanel, Hébert, Bouguereau and Puvis de Chavannes, who, it should be emphasized, he considered "one of the two truly important men in this list" (the second, rather unexpectedly, was Duveau, a specialist in paintings of shipwrecks and people lost at sea, who would however fail to live up to his promise). As far as Castagnary was concerned, Puvis de Chavannes's *Work* and *Rest* in no way rendered the reality of their subject matter, because the artist "does not require anything of nature or of his life models; his figures are imaginary, without racial characteristics or individuality; his landscapes have no time, climate or light." Castagnary argues that this representation of work cannot satisfy those who are looking for a contemporary rendition of social reality: "to complete the idea behind the work, you could have—you should have—added grape-gatherers, harvesters, masons, mechanics, engineers, and so on." As for the allegory, that really drove the critic to despair because it left so much room for interpretation: "I cannot grasp the possible relation between the picture before my eyes and the purpose the artist set himself in painting it."[5] He was disappointed both by the subject matter of the painting and the thinking behind it.

In 1869, when commenting on the canvases destined to decorate the main staircase of the Musée des Beaux-Arts in Marseille's Palais Longchamp, Castagnary would go through the annual reit-

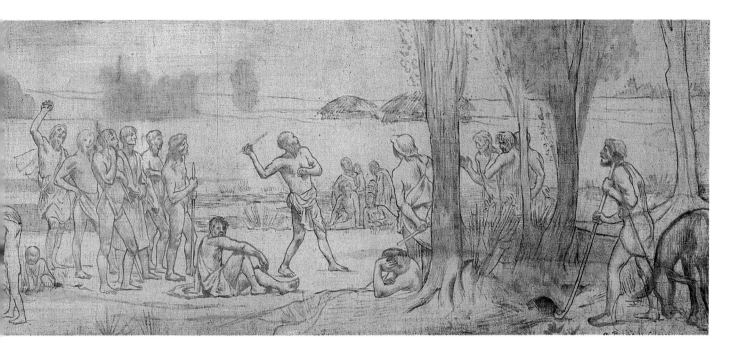

eration of his reservations about the artist. "M. Puvis de Chavannes neither draws nor paints. . . Does he at least compose in the same way as nature does, using living things—be they men, animals or trees? No." He then goes on to suggest another painting altogether that Puvis de Chavannes might have created "with porters moving around, with grain arriving, with the wheat piled up on the flags of the quayside . . . all under a bright sun and set against a blue sea . . . an original, powerful and grandiose spectacle, just asking to be reproduced on canvas."[6] Castagnary, it seems, has not gone any further than Joseph Vernet! The fact that in his *Marseille, Gateway to the Orient*, Puvis de Chavannes had gone further than ever before in the precise evocation of a specific location, did not much impress the critic, who considered the truly important painting in the 1869 Salon to be Courbet's *The Killing of the Stag*. Even if, as in 1872, Castagnary might acknowledge the strength of Puvis's "convictions," he can never accept his aesthetics. And yet after 1870 it seemed that mural commissions were being equally divided between, on the one side, *naturalistes* such as Detaille, Cormon, Laurens and Flameng, and on the other, Puvis de Chavannes alone. Powerless to do anything about it, the partisans of Naturalism, then in the majority, could only stand by and watch this strange turn of events, marveling at what they saw.

The reservations of the partisans of Naturalism—who held that a concern for truth should not lead to a sacrifice of volume and color, of density and texture in the rendition of beings and things—were echoed and compounded by those voiced from within the so-called School of Tradition. They too did not recognize that, with each passing Salon, it was Puvis de Chavannes who seemed to embody a possible present and future for *la grande peinture,* at exactly the moment in which people might well have asked themselves if such painting was actually destined to disappear altogether. This lack of understanding among the last remaining troops of tradition—who should have seen Puvis de Chavannes as their Leonidas—found concrete expression in the discussion of his draftsmanship. Puvis de Chavannes simply did not know how to draw; he had no knowledge of anatomy; he was the bad student who never managed to pass from the real to the ideal. This feeling is well illustrated by the comments made by Theodor de Wyzewa in 1894. He wrote that one had to admit "this truth: that the paintings of M de Chavannes are very badly drawn; that their colors may be pleasant but are very rudimentary. . . . It is a fact that M. de Chavannes's figures are deformed in some part of their body, with limbs that are asymmetrical or badly linked to the body . . . with weak poses and gestures. . . . It is a fact that the colors in this painting are washed-out, deadened, reduced to the slightest role possible. There is neither draftsmanship nor color; or rather there is detestable draftsmanship and almost non-existent color."[7] Fed up with a literature and painting afflicted by excessive reality, by "so-called truths," Wyzewa saw that Puvis de Chavannes might have been the artist best-suited to open the way to a new era in art. However, the artist's style troubled him because it remained almost untouched by academic skill and

3. Jean-François Millet,
Farmer Resting,
The Hague, Mesdag Museum

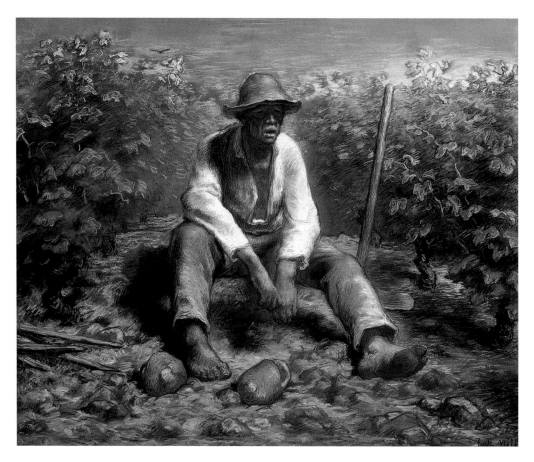

knowledge—that knowledge enjoyed by Baudry and Bouguereau; because the ever more apparent clarity of his art seemed to be bathed in a totally different light than that observed by the Impressionists; because his manner of painting seemed so slight and dry alongside the feeling for the tactile that was shared by such different artists as Manet, Meissonier, Monet and Bonnat. And if Edmond About is so cutting and unjust towards Puvis de Chavannes, it is because he feels he owes a debt of friendship and loyalty to Paul Baudry, whom he argues is the true great mural artist. According to About, in 1881 the real masterpiece recognized by "the election jury, which has done itself honor by giving the finest place in the exhibition to [this] great painting by Paul Baudry," is *The Glorification of the Law* commissioned for the ceiling of the large Audience Room in the Court of Cassation in Paris. It is revealing that About cannot avoid bringing in Puvis de Chavannes, and requires that one appreciate Baudry by measuring him against the artist who is felt to be less a rival than a successor. Like Puvis, Baudry is a reflective painter. "The artist has a bit more literature and philosophy than one usually finds in a painter; before taking up his pencil, he ponders and meditates, working out his allegories at length." But, unlike Puvis de Chavannes, Baudry likes "to paint"; he "throws himself into forms and colors like a young colt." As the foyer to the Opéra shows, it is Baudry who is the new Raphael of modern times; he is the one who has equal mastery of thought and expression. And About offers this piece of advice to the young: "those who lose themselves in their daydreams to the point where they lose sight of draftsmanship and color will soon degenerate into Puvis de Chavannes."[8] What this reveals is astonishing: even his opponents take Puvis de Chavannes as being the person against whom one has to define oneself. The 1881 Salon was a grand-scale premiere for the new Republic, and within it Puvis de Chavannes definitely emerged as the most original painter present. The gold medal awarded to Baudry had something of the air of recognition for services past; it was a leave-taking of the most gifted heir of the great tradition, the virtuoso of eclecticism, the modernizer of allegory, the heir of the Venetians; as Jules Claretie would put it "his was great Art without ennui." However, Detaille's *Distribution of the Flags*, an immense commentary on the July 14 ceremony in 1880, was an unexpected flop. This enormous "colored lithograph"—to use Emile Delarue's description of the work—revealed the vanity of excessive realism applied on a grand scale. Detaille was so vexed

opposite page
4, 5. Pierre Puvis de Chavannes,
Rest and *Work*, 1867.
Washington, D.C.,
National Gallery of Art

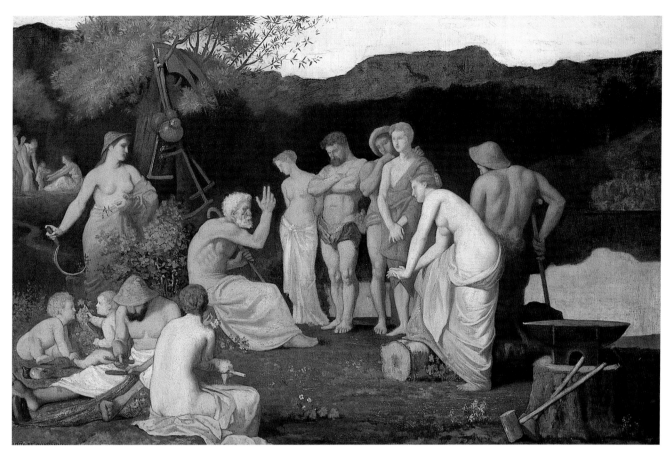

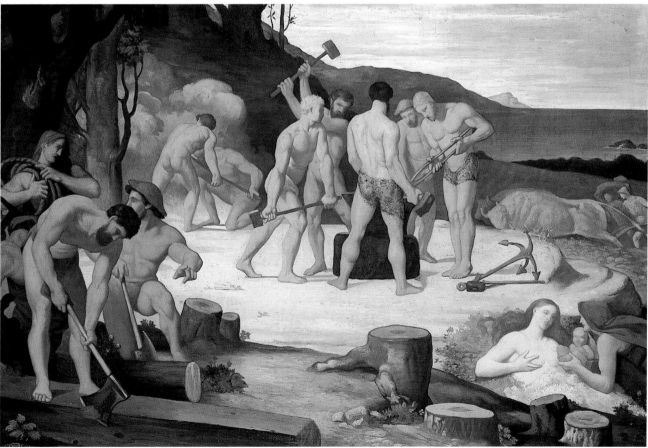

6. Edouard Manet,
*Portrait of M. Pertuiset,
the Lion-hunter*, 1881.
São Paulo, Museu de Arte

by the reception the work received that he actually destroyed it. Manet too would receive no better reception, his new work being considered unrecognizable as his. The *Portrait of M. Pertuiset, the Lion-hunter* seemed too purple, awash in those violet shades that would soon rouse the ire of Zola. Huysmans considered the work a veritable disaster. The paradox was that this portrait would be compensated with the medal that meant Manet could no longer be rejected by the jury. As for Charles Cazin's *Remembrance of a Feast*, it astonished people with its quintessential use of allegory. As a matter of fact, the artist, who was looked upon as a disciple of Puvis de Chavannes, was acting as his master's foil because, seen alongside the overly complex *Holiday*, *The Poor Fisherman* came across as all the more moving and fascinating. The "pallor of the palette" was now overlooked, and there was no criticism of the "reality" of the figures and landscape. In his article in *Le Temps*, Paul Mantz rallied to the Puvis de Chavannes camp: from this "very slight use of draftsmanship, color and light" emerges an "emotion," a poignant image imposes itself on our attention.[9] It was finally being recognized that, with his own very particular means, Puvis de Chavannes was actually saying more than anyone else.

As well as being beleaguered on the Realist and idealist fronts, Puvis de Chavannes was also soon under attack from the Symbolists. Here again, it is worth quoting Camille Mauclair, who generally was so entirely favorable to the artist. According to the writer, Puvis de Chavannes avoided falling "into the errors committed by other modern painters of allegorical decoration"; he did not have "the brutality and poor taste of Böcklin, the dryness of Watts, the distinguished anemia of Burne-Jones, the—at times, amphigoric—hermeticism of Holman Hunt, or the morbid preciosity of Fernand Khnopff." Leaving aside the validity of Mauclair's assessments of those artists, one should here underline the essential point that emerges: in his intellectual ambitions and stylistic choices, Puvis de Chavannes is a foreigner among foreigners. "With regard to all these curious spirits, all these searchers who may vary in talent but are all equally tormented, these Pre-Raphaelites, Neo-Primitives and Academicists. . . . Puvis de Chavannes remains as isolated as he is when seen in relation to Realists or Impressionists, who simply strive for the rendition of sen-

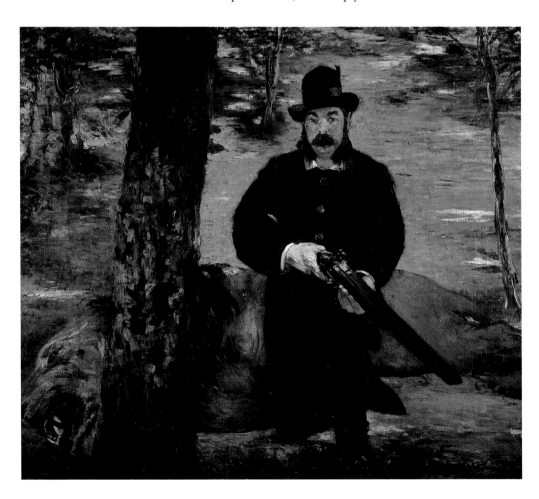

opposite page
7. Pierre Puvis de Chavannes,
Study of Four Figures for "Rest,"
c. 1862.
Paris, Musée d'Orsay

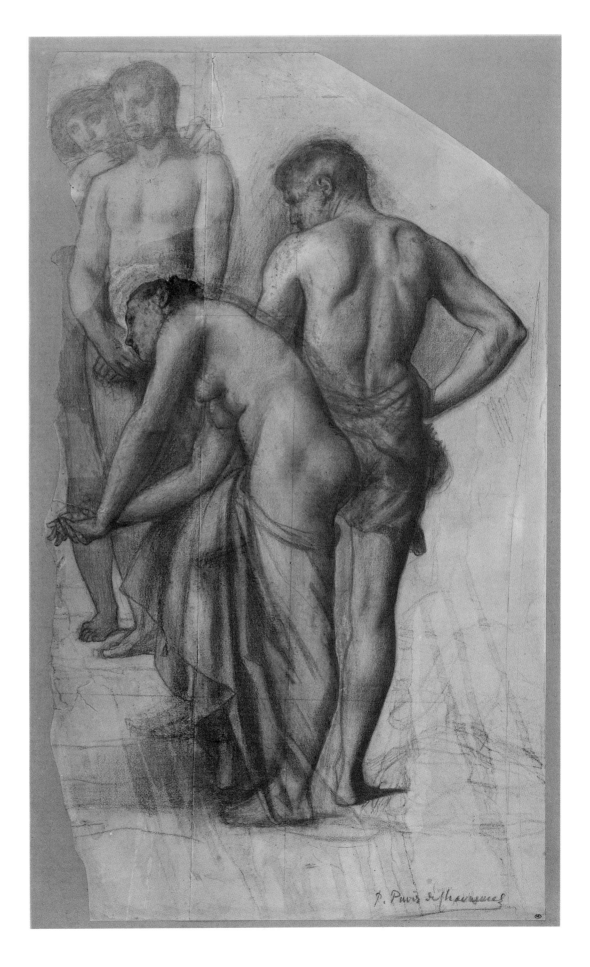

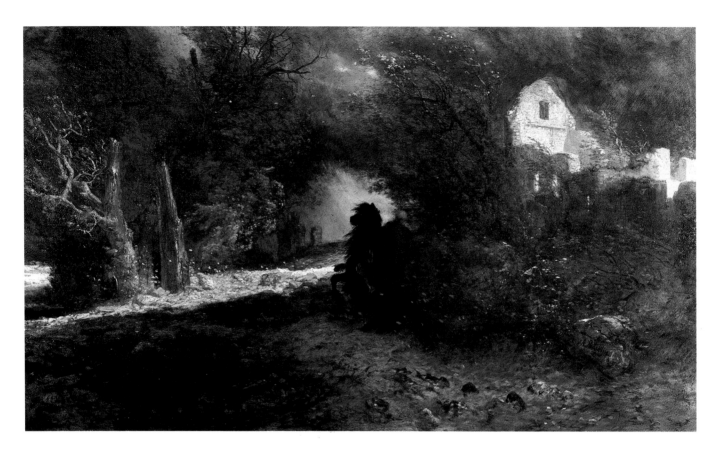

sation, the notation of the moment, without any cerebral life."[10] To his contemporaries, Puvis de Chavannes may at first have seemed to be the father of a Symbolist movement which reacted against realist immediacy and favored an art of ideas, if not of ideals; however, later, his simplicity and his lack of interest in the complexities of allegory turned him into something of an anti-Gustave Moreau. Indeed, in comparison to the complicated art of the *fin du siècle*, Puvis de Chavannes emerged as an irenic classical painter—the incarnation of a Raphael who had survived into the days of Mannerism and Caravaggio!

In his summary of contemporary art in 1896, Zola showed his irritation with all those "modernities" of the period 1860–70 which had become rather commonplace and habitual. "Oh, the horizons where the trees are blue, the waters red and the skies green! It is terrible, terrible, terrible." He detested the "line" of independents in 1874, just as much as the avatars of a movement of "natural protest against triumphant Realism" (which according to him, simply resulted in vaporous and "asexual" "soul painting"). And for all this he identifies an unexpected culprit: "here, I think that the blame belongs to the great and pure artist Puvis de Chavannes. His aftermath has proved disastrous, even more disastrous than that of Manet, Monet and Pissarro."[11] And thus, the isolated Puvis gets placed at the head of a line of followers; he becomes the master of a school that he had never intended to found. The reversal here is astonishing. In the 1900s, the solitary Puvis de Chavannes has become a fixed point of reference, while once he had seemed an unredeemed figure who could not be fitted into the art scene. Here, one can trust Zola's judgment: the anomalous had, indeed, become one of the two central figures around which the painting of the second half of the nineteenth century fell into place. He and Manet formed one of those frequently-cited couples which, just like Poussin and Rubens or Ingres and Delacroix, occur at regular intervals as an embodiment of the antithetical approaches to human life and artistic desire.

And what was it that made Puvis de Chavannes irredeemable? This is the essential question, because it is the criticisms made of him by his contemporaries that enable us to best assess his originality, at the same time as explaining—and justifying—the extent of his influence. What never failed to amaze about this painter of ideas was that he spoke a simple language. In an era when allegory enjoyed great cachet, when the subtlest concepts and all the professions and inventions of the modern world could find new—and often esoteric—expression in figurative works (look, for example, at the walls of the Hôtel de Ville in Paris), Puvis de Chavannes was both surprising and attractive because his meaning was immediately clear. Here again, one might quote Camille Mauclair in his summary of this consensus of opinion regarding the artist's legibility: "Of all allegorical paintings, of all the mural decorations concealing some hidden meaning, none is as clear, simple and humanly direct as the work of Puvis de Chavannes."[12] Clarity, simplicity and humanity—these are the three virtues, the three guardian angels that have guaranteed the continued standing of the artist. The inevitable question that reemerges with regularity is: Was Puvis de Chavannes a Symbolist or not? And in answering no, one always makes reference to the evident clarity in the *signifié* (the reverse side of the *signifiant*).

One does not need an explanatory booklet when looking at a painting by Puvis de Chavannes, no particular knowledge or expertise is required. All that is demanded is that one be part of humankind. And yet, in that century of history and nationalism, could one appeal to that which draws together all humanity and eschew membership of a particular era and a particular nation? That is clearly the great paradox and the remarkable strength of Puvis. The contrast that can be seen on the walls of the Panthéon—between the works of Jean-Paul Laurens, which reveal such attention to historical, ethnographic and sociological exactitude, and the works of Puvis, which at one and the same time are so detached and yet so contemporary—in effect defines the sensibility of an entire era. The comparison between the two is as revealing for the nineteenth century as that between Corneille and Racine is for the seventeenth, or Voltaire and Rousseau for the eighteenth. Even when he is dealing with precise historic events such as the Battle of Poitiers, describing a real location such as the Port of Marseille, or even rendering contemporary clothing (as in Rouen), Puvis always steers clear of too much historical or geographical detail. His sole true subject matter was the continuity of human life. In his work, the possibility of classical inspiration in the heart of the nineteenth century is expressed not by reference to some historical type—for example, the evocation of some model drawn from classical antiquity or the Renaissance—but by the simple restitution of what is essential in the life of humankind, in any age, in any nation.

Puvis de Chavannes had to strive with particular determination to achieve this ambition without falling into the eclectic or the anecdotal. The types of humanity as presented by the artist have, in fact, raised legitimate questions. Whether painted nude or clothed, his figures comply with no specific canons. In the century of Darwin, which was fascinated by the evolution of species, by problems of race and ethnography, of social origins and membership, it was inevitable that questions were raised about the way Puvis de Chavannes interpreted and depicted the human body. In each picture there were no precise references. Was he painting Greeks, Romans, Franks, Picards or the people of Rouen? Did his characters belong to a period of prehistory? Were they still underwritten by that concern for ideal beauty that was so dear to the Academy? The human type as depicted by Puvis de Chavannes never ceased to intrigue. Some suggested it represented the "Gallo-Roman" type—that is, a synthesis of the barbaric and the Hellenistic. For his part, Mauclair saw "a society outside time . . . real [and yet] without a precise date," a "pastoral primitivism that was neither Greek, biblical nor Roman." And thus one comes to that mighty word "primitivism," which would be so rich in consequences and associations. However, man as depicted by Puvis de Chavannes no longer lives in paradise alongside some paleolithic marsh; unlike the heroes painted by Cormon, they would find no place in the Musée de Saint-Germain-en-Laye. "Puvis has traced humanity through that period which comes after the age of caves but precedes the period of defined civilizations and nations."[13] Without endorsing Mauclair's reading of historical periods, one can see that Puvis de Chavannes occupies a place apart—somewhere between the reevocation of golden ages, the search for the islands of the "noble savage" and precise historical and sociological recreations of the past. With Puvis de Chavannes, primitivism became the great obsession. He invents it to recount stories of an eternal humankind, a terrestrial paradise where the fundamental needs, basic feelings and essential requirements which are the lot of humanity can find concrete development and expression in all their inherent simplicity. Undoubtedly, Puvis de Chavannes was the one who showed his contemporaries that the moderns too could claim their place in eternity. And to the task, he brought a style that seemed so strange to an age in which the world of painting was dominated by lyrical expressions, stylistic refinements and chromatic exactitude. Théophile Gautier immediately saw the new possibilities raised by this unknown artist. "Are they cartoons, tapestries or rather frescoes taken from some unknown Fontainebleau?" he asked when looking at *War* and *Peace* in the 1861 Salon. "What process did

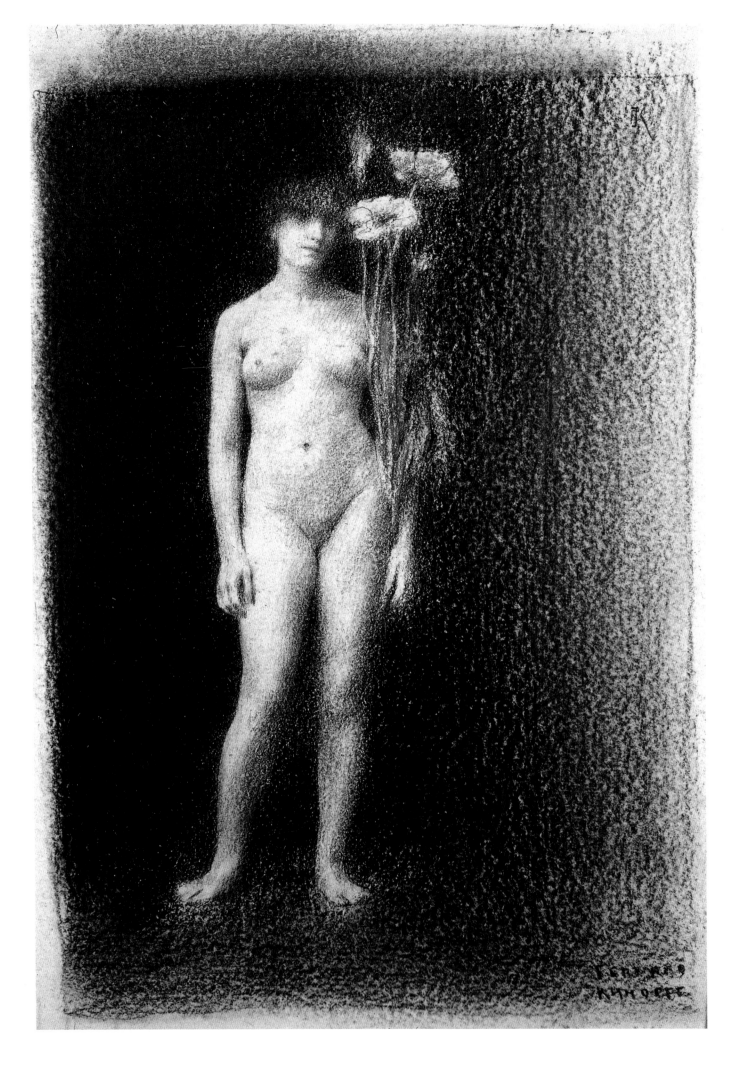

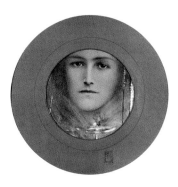

10. Fernand Khnopff,
Woman with Blue Cyclamen,
Ghent, Musée des Beaux-Arts

he use in painting them. . . . One isn't too sure, given that the range used is so strange. . . . In a time of prose and realism, this young artist is naturally epic, heroic and monumental, thanks to a bizarre recurrence of an old genius."[14] The best minds—if not painters—of the day were striving to find a way of reconciling the charm of easel painting and the blandishments of oil with the requirements of mural art and the matte finish of frescoes. The restitution of that venerable and ancient technique appeared as one of the highest ambitions of art; however, so far none of the attempts to revive fresco painting had been convincing (the lamentable example of Mottez's work at Saint-Germain-L'Auxerrois was significant). The compromise solution was a resort to painting on wax—*à la* Hippolyte Flandrin—thus uniting the advantages of fresco and easel painting. However, most artists simply stuck their canvases onto the wall. Here again, Puvis de Chavannes can be seen as sharing—and yet standing apart from—this approach: He did paint on canvas, but with full respect for the requirements of mural art (a famous anecdote concerns one of the artists at the Panthéon who, impatient with mural art as such, declared he had no intention of adapting his style, and then received this reply from Puvis de Chavannes: "Well then, the wall will puke back on you"). Again the artist reversed the situation. Not content with simply painting for walls, when it came to producing easel works, he eschewed the idea of the *morceau* and endowed the work with all the qualities of a fresco. Thus he was the artist who found a "way out," who proposed a solution to the "impasse" that had been created in *la grande peinture* since "the collapse of classical principles." According to Zola, he alone " knows how to be interesting and lively, by simplifying line and painting in uniform tones."[15]

And thus the particular status of Puvis de Chavannes at the end of the century was confirmed. While remaining outside all the movements and passions that dominated the world of art, he nevertheless occupied a central position in that world. The artist who never really had a studio or disciples would be honored by that famous banquet of 1895, a manifestation of affection and admiration held to celebrate the man and his work, the rigor of a life and oeuvre that had remained faithful to a few great intuitions. Puvis de Chavannes would never fit into the Académie des Beaux-Arts; independence was too vital to him. However, Léon Bonnat, whose Realist style was the very opposite of Puvis de Chavannes's, would in 1882 see in *Pleasant Land* the most moving manifestation of "great art," obtained "not through the vain formulae of the schools but through the free interpretation of nature . . . to then translate the ravishment of an inner dream into a language of which Puvis de Chavannes is the inventor and master."[16] And yet while Puvis was a powerfully influential presence, precise accounts of that presence are rare, even if the works being produced show that the artist's oeuvre was being looked at and meditated upon. This was the last of the painter's miracles. This man of freedom, enabled others to enter into a free engagement with him and his work; there was no subjugation to the usual bonds of influence. Puvis de Chavannes already occupied the best possible place—that is, the eyes and hearts of all those who had in contemplating his works become, perhaps not his disciples, but certainly his friends. Indeed, one might say that the footnote to the artist's career was written by Henri Focillon: "All those who attempted [and one would add, will attempt] to restore serenity of form and decor have admired or meditated upon [one would add, will admire or meditate upon] the art of Puvis de Chavannes."[17]

[1] C. Mauclair, *Puvis de Chavannes*, Paris, Plon, 1928, p. 149.
[2] L. Bénédite, *La peinture du XIXème siècle d'après les chefs-d'oeuvre des maîtres. . .* , Paris, Flammarion, n.d. [1909], p. 169.
[3] E. Zola, "Peinture," *Le Figaro,* May 2, 1896. See *Le Bon Combat, de Courbet aux impressionnistes*, critical edition by J.P. Bouillon, Hermann, 1974, p. 263.
[4] Mauclair, *op. cit,* p. 27.
[5] J.A. Castagnary, *Salons (1857–1870)*, Paris, Charpentier, 1892. "Salon de 1863," vol. 1, pp. 105 and 130.
[6] *Ibidem*, "Salon de 1869," pp. 335–36.
[7] T. de Wyzewa, *Peintres de Jadis et d'Aujourd'hui*, Paris, 1903, p. 364.
[8] E. About, *Le Décaméron du Salon de peinture pour l'année 1881*, Paris, Librairie des Bibliophiles, 1881, p. 15.
[9] P. Mantz, in *Le Temps*, May 22, 1881.
[10] Mauclair, *op. cit.,* pp. 153–54.
[11] Zola, *op. cit.*, p. 262.
[12] Mauclair, *op. cit.,* p. 22.
[13] *Ibidem*, p. 122.
[14] T. Gautier, in *Le Moniteur Universel*, May 25, 1861.
[15] Zola, "Salon de 1875," in *Le Bon Combat, op. cit.* p. 164.
[16] A. Michel and J. Laran, *Puvis de Chavannes,* Paris, 1911, p. 78.
[17] H. Focillon, *La peinture au XIXème et au XXème siècle. Du réalisme à nos jours*, Paris, 1928, p. 250.

opposite page
9. Fernand Khnopff,
Nude with Flowers,
Brussels, private collection

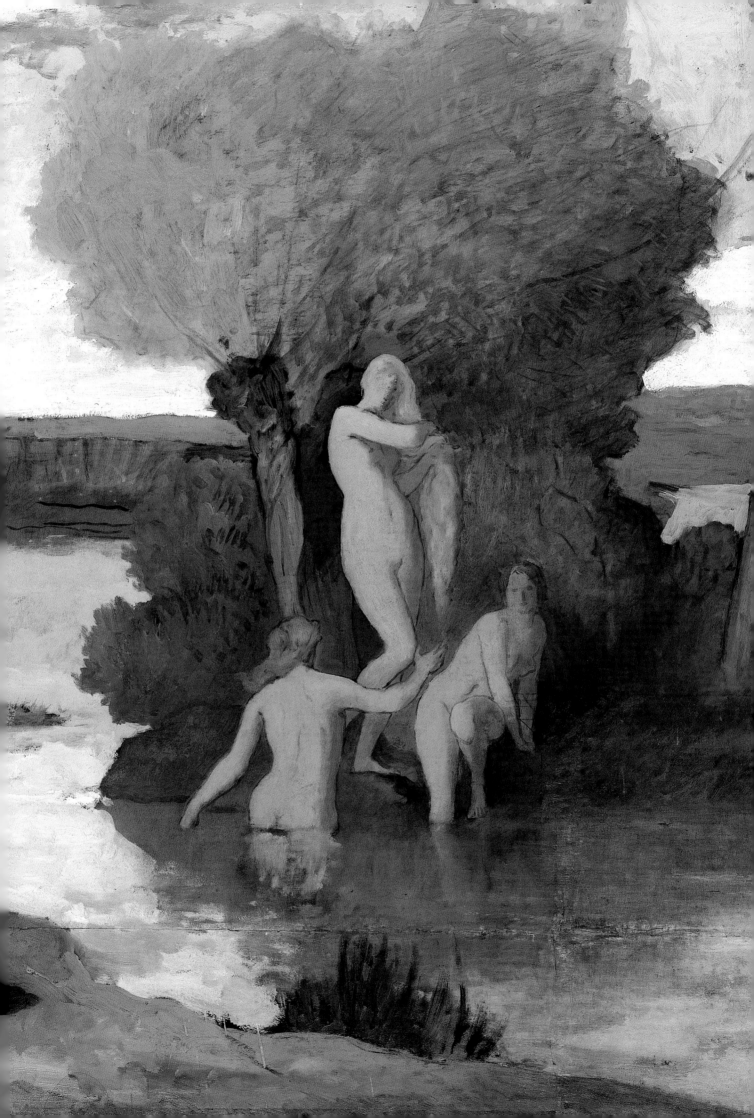

Puvis de Chavannes's Critical Fortune

Puvis de Chavannes had a horror of the 'blahblahblah' of art critics and was ready to make ironic remarks about the inspiration for his paintings in his commentaries to critics.
L. Wehrlé[1]

Over the course of his fifty years as an artist, from 1848 to 1898, Pierre Puvis de Chavannes's work went from not being noted at all in the critical press (the first decade, his style steeped in Romanticism), to reactions that ranged from enthusiastic praise to paroxysms of outrage. Critics who admired his work did so for a variety of disparate and often conflicting reasons. The responses that Puvis's work elicited and their sundry rationales are the subject of Robert Goldwater's classic, seminal analysis "Puvis de Chavannes: Some Reasons for a Reputation."[2] The almost universal esteem that he noted for Puvis when he reached his innovative mature idiom in the 1880s had glaring exceptions.

Decade by decade, the critical response to Puvis's work changed and so too did its focus. In the 1860s, as Puvis found his aesthetic footing, he was favored with a few lengthy, perceptive, and searching discussions of his monumental murals, with which he aimed to make his reputation. The prolific literary figure Théophile Gautier, who prided himself on having been the first to discover Puvis in 1859[3] and remained a staunch supporter, explained that Puvis's murals fulfilled the special requirements of wall decorations, such as planarity and simplicity. He justified the peculiarity of their curiously muted colors by comparing them to frescoes and tapestries, the latter a standard trope in late nineteenth-century criticism for flattened compositions of even tonalities.[4] The critics Paul Mantz and Gustave Planche welcomed these huge paintings for their ambitiousness, in the great French tradition. By 1863 the critic Arthur Stevens wrote that Puvis was "seeking style over everything and walking on the path to great painting, to decorative art."[5]

By the 1870s Philippe Burty recognized that Puvis de Chavannes's exceptional innovation was to have developed a decorative aesthetic for his murals that he brought to all his painting[6]—only to decry it. He found certain paintings effective when considered as *décor*, but unacceptable as autonomous works of art (*tableaux*). As he wrote, "They shock as paintings [*tableaux*] because of their sketchy appearance and indications of scumbling. Seen in place and as *décors*, they have a limpid value and a frankness of effect which are undeniable."[7] Similarly, though a score of years later, in a letter to his son, Camille Pissarro called such a decorative panel by Puvis presented as an independent easel painting an "anomaly."[8]

By the early 1880s Puvis's images changed and so did the context of understanding.[9] Critics changed too; their proclivities and prowess affected their understanding as did their age and generation. Moreover, not all critics were constant.

Edmond About's (1828–86)[10] early praise of Puvis's murals made his later criticism the more painful.[11] About, who commended Puvis's first monumental paintings as special undertakings for which he merited "le titre glorieux de décorateur,"[12] came to address him as "mon cher Pierrot,"[13] but found fault with his 1869 murals for the new art museum at Marseille for their lack of finish: "Nothing forces you to exhibit two paintings henceforth if you have the time to finish only one; you can develop your drawing at leisure and pick up refinement which is the *only* thing that you lack."[14] Puvis tried to be conciliatory,[15] but felt betrayed by About and his "exquisite malice."[16] As Puvis's art became more radical, critics like About grew even less sympathetic. About made what Puvis de Chavannes took to be a particularly perfidious pronouncement concerning his 1881 *The Poor Fisherman* (Paris, Musée d'Orsay), "a laborious mistake" ("un erreur laborieuse") that made the artist "a solemn and committed caricaturist" ("un caricaturiste solennel et convaincu").[17] And in 1883 he published this scathing assessment: "When Hell needs repaving, like the Champs Elysées, it will not fail to commit the enterprise to M. Puvis de Chavannes. This artist is, *par excellence*, the man of good intentions, I will even say, of great intentions and vast ideas. For more than twenty years, he has promised himself and he has promised us a masterpiece which he will never execute, for he does not know how either to paint or draw, and he proudly parades an encyclopedic ignorance of every corner of the domain of art. The lack of a primary education is unhappily, without remedy; neither courage nor perseverance, nor even a certain nobility of soul, will produce an epic in twelve cantos for a dreamer who has not gone to primary school and who lacks not only prosody but the most ordinary spelling."[18] In fact, *The Poor Fisherman* evoked a plethora of unusually livid critical rage.[19]

It was deplored by the critic Albert Wolff (1835–91), though he too had taken kindly to

1. Pierre Puvis de Chavannes, *The River*, detail. New York, The Metropolitan Museum of Art, Catharine Lorillard Wolfe Collection, Wolfe Fund

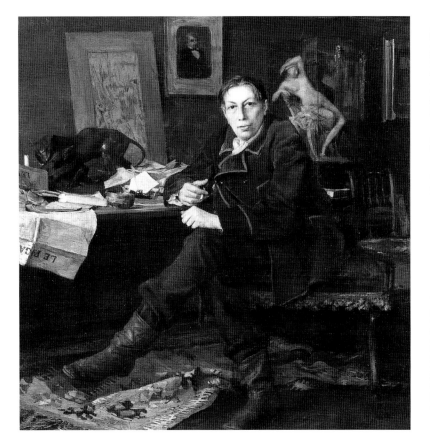

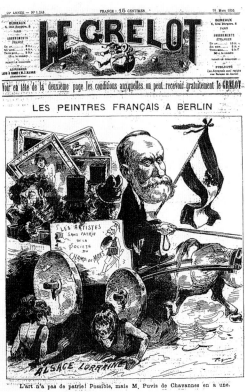

2. Jules Bastien-Lepage,
Portrait of Albert Wolff, 1881.
Shaker Heights, Butkin Collection

3. Jules Bastien-Lepage,
Caricature of Puvis de Chavannes
(cover of *Le Grelot*,
March 10, 1895)

Puvis's murals—Puvis had even dedicated a reduced section of his *Saint Genevieve* mural to him (Otterlo, Rijksmuseum Kröller-Müller), pictured behind him in Jules Bastien-Lepage's 1881 portrait of the influential, long-time critic for the *Figaro* (Shaker Heights, Ohio, Collection Mrs. N.L. Butkin, fig. 2). That the powerful Wolff now turned against his work was difficult for Puvis; but that Puvis's reduced version of *Pleasant Land* (New Haven, Yale University Art Gallery) of 1882 was in his collection would seem to indicate a reconciliation.[20] Wolff was not always respected; in 1892 *The Boston Evening Transcript* published this caustic evaluation:[21] "Anecdotes about the late Albert Wolff of the Paris *Figaro* abound, and all the writers seem to agree that he was witty . . . and entirely unscrupulous. It is odd that anyone should suppose that his criticisms were taken seriously. We all liked to read his nicely turned epigrams, but no one ever regarded that sort of stuff as art criticism. The real art critics of Paris are such men as Paul Mantz, Charles Clément, Paul Leroi, the writers for the *Débats*, the *Temps*, the *Gaulois*, the *Dix-neuvième Siècle*, *L'Art* and the *Gazette des Beaux-Arts*. Those are the solid organs of public opinion in France, and not the frothy *Figaro*, which everybody reads and nobody believes."[22]

Indeed, in the 1890s, Puvis's work was regularly featured in the popular *Figaro-Salon* (headed for a short time by Wolff), that gave it pride of place in its large format reproductions, but usually had little to say about the art that was illustrated. Indeed, by the end of the century much about criticism had changed from an occupation-cum-vocation of those with a literary background to a professionalized and routinized journalistic industry in which criticism proliferated but thoughtful discussion became a rarity, often replaced by reiterated received ideas.[23]

Joris-Karl Huysmans recognized Puvis's originality, in utter contrast to the usual *pasticheurs* (imitators) who filled the Salons, but was not sure what to make of it.[24] He was absolutely conflicted—both attracted and repulsed—and finally abandoned himself to the headlong critical propulsion of his prose, at Puvis's expense: "I shall finish, God forgive me . . . by experiencing an irrational admiration for the work of Puvis de Chavannes! It is certain that in face of these boring imitations [by other artists], *The Prodigal Son* and *Young Girls by the Seaside* are the real marvels. It is always the same pale color, the same appearance of fresco, always angular and hard, that irritates, as customary, with his pretensions of naïveté and his affectation of the simple; and nonetheless, however incomplete he can be, that painter has talent . . . he even achieves . . . a certain grandeur. One admires his efforts, one wants to applaud him; then one revolts. . . ."[25]

He struggled to understand how to frame this new work aesthetically, but was unable to evaluate the images except from a bias born from Realism. While much new French painting in the second half of the nineteenth century met with mixed responses, it was rare that an individual critic would be so unnerved, baffled, and torn as Huysmans at what he called the "strange" *Poor Fisherman*: "a twilight painting . . . dry, hard, feigning as usual a naïve stiffness. . . . In front of this canvas, I shrug my shoulders, irritated by this monkey business of biblical grandeur . . . then, just the same I feel taken with pity and indulgence, for it is the work of someone gone astray, but it is also the work of a committed artist who mistrusts the infatuation of the public and who, contrary to other painters, disdains getting messed up in the cesspool of fashion. In spite of the repulsion that wells up in me when I am in front of this painting, I cannot prevent myself from having a certain attraction to it when I am far from it."[26] There were so many strings to Puvis's bow, so many aspects to his imagery, that one and the same painting could elicit fiercely contrary reactions.

Though Jules Castagnary came eventually to champion Puvis de Chavannes's work (by 1887), like About and Huysmans he earlier complained that Puvis did not have the fundamental technique required of an artist. A consentient opinion was that Puvis was willfully naïve, a poor draftsman, and a coarse painter. Moreover, it was no compliment when Castagnary, a proponent of Realism, wrote that Puvis "does not draw or paint; he composes, that's his specialty."[27] This condemnation utterly contrasts to the evaluation of a group of younger critics much taken with the originality of *The Poor Fisherman*,[28] just what was excoriated by the old guard. Indeed, Maurice Denis, painter, ardent admirer, and penetrating commentator on Puvis's work launched his famous definition of "néo-traditionnisme," manifesto of a new kind of painting in which the composition and color were paramount—immediately after his discussion of Puvis's compelling canvas: "Se rappeler qu'un tableau—avant d'être un cheval de bataille, une femme nue ou une quelconque anecdote—est essentiellement une surface plane recouverte de couleurs en un certain ordre assemblées."[29]

While older critics waxed and then waned in ardor, by the late 1880s younger writers—Félix Fénéon,[30] Albert Aurier, Alphonse Germain,[31] Gustave Geffroy—receptive to a new aesthetic frame of reference and lexicon of terms, such as the decorative, gave Puvis a higher approval rating. Aurier (1865–92), who wrote for the *Mercure de France* from 1888 until his premature death, put great store in originality, simplification, and the role of the decorative in painting. He classified artists as "ouvriers" or "chercheurs" (workers or searchers), and maintained that great art was made by isolated artists,[32] surely he would have put Puvis de Chavannes with the last two groups.[33] Gustave Geffroy (1855–26) often wrote on Puvis,[34] and in a late rejoinder to the kind of criticism About had made in the 1860s, explained that though Puvis's work might seem unfinished, it was not; the absolute simplicity of images delimited by only a few lines was meant to be.[35] Moreover, the singularity of Puvis's work precluded successful imitation; there was only one Puvis as there was only one Manet.[36]

Criticism helps contextualize a work of art by alerting readers to a contemporary understanding of its elements and the values put upon them. Critics help establish whether we are seeing the same thing.[37] Sâr Joséphin Péladan was among the first to insist that ideological biases affect criticism;[38] critics sometimes have an ax to grind.[39] A sizable recent literature, the result of a small stampede in this analytical direction, has both humanized and examined critics in terms of their politics to get at the meaning of their criticism. Thus, Camille Mauclair's admiration for Puvis is that of one who favored the intellectual, nationalistic strains of a great French decorative art.

To Edmond de Goncourt, Puvis de Chavannes was a bad joke. He was infuriated by the flatness of his representations, for one, which he compared to that of Javanese idols. His abuse also centered on Puvis's stiff manner, how "découpées" his figures looked; those of *The Sacred Wood* as if they were "fabricated out of cut-out boards. Oh, idealist painting!"[40]

A typical comment was that of May 6, 1886—gone round again to Puvis's muffled colors, just what Gautier, over a score of years earlier, had tried to validate: "What can charm in a Puvis de Chavannes? Is it this sad color of old, faded *greens*? Is it the spiritless drawing, without accentuation, without feeling . . . the stupidest of all the drawing I have ever seen? . . . I believe the critic has never swallowed as a true painter a man as bereft of all pictorial qualities and as laboriously unsophisticated and as idiotically a plagiarist of the past."[41] With further consternation he wrote on June 28, 1887, "That Puvis de Chavannes! To think that there are so many fine blank spaces on our public monuments which are condemned to be soiled by his sad grisailles which are so badly, or worse so stupidly drawn! Since painting began I know of no painter whose drawing was so banal [pudgy]."[42] Doubtless reflecting wider views, he spared no cleverly devastating remark at Puvis's expense—at least recording his comments in his private journal. Indeed, Puvis's work evoked a considerable critical commentary of this more private nature: fulminations as well as searching, appreciative analyses in the personal journals and correspondence of such articulate artists and connoisseurs as Van Gogh and Maurice Denis.

As Puvis arrived at his characteristic idiom in the 1870s his work garnered the tribute of mischievous caricatural parodists—long used to ridicule the unusual, innovative, and original in art—and his titles were not spared ridicule either. Indeed, he himself frequently enough was so honored as a caricatural portrait on the cover of *Le Grelot* testifies (fig. 3).[43] The caricaturist Cham[44] (1819–79), who routinely and hilariously lampooned paintings at the official Salons, did not spare Puvis's paintings; and others also joined the fray. These shrewd satires graphically point up the new and unexpected by exaggerating them. So the slender figure and stiff pose of Puvis's *Hope* (Salon of 1872, Baltimore, Walters Art Gallery) was made bonier and more derisively angular still. Petit Bob, Gyp, and Grelot also signaled what was "wrong" or untoward in Puvis's work: his rhythmic repetitions of motifs became endlessly and ineluctably rhythmic; trees and foliage appeared at calibrated intervals, the rigid figures in *The Sacred Wood Dear to the Arts and Muses* of 1884 recur in "*The sacred wood* dear to woodworkers for Karlutain. . . ."[45] The fabulously witty proto-dada group of "incohérènts" didn't stop there; among their wickedly irreverent names for Puvis were "Pubis de cheval, Pue Vice de Chats (Vannes), Puvis de Davannes."[46]

Sensitive to and deeply discouraged by the slightest criticism[47] and troubled by its vagaries, Puvis mocked adverse appraisals as misguided and pointed out their tremendous inconsistencies: one critic called his images "le rebut de l'imagerie d'Epinal," (the scum of Epinal imagery) referring to the flat, crude-seeming popular broadsides printed during the nineteenth century, while another compared his drawings to those of Michelangelo[48] (actually both were right).

Puvis's reputation was at its apogee in the 1890s, and many praised his work—often misconstruing it however. They saw his murals (painted on canvas to be installed), at the Salons where they were decontextualized—severed from the surrounds of their destination, and building type—museum, library, or city hall; absent the raison d'être of countless formal determinants, and the program and painting cycle to which they were keyed. More than one critic, basing his ideas on the works seen *seriatim* rather than *in situ* was thus misled to their final appearance and iconographic meaning.[49]

At the end of his life Puvis was almost universally admired, which one critic ascribed to the artist's longevity—all his detractors had died and enthusiasts had been born.[50] In the twentieth century, Puvis's critical fortunes were often governed by the ongoing problem of having his murals so dispersed as to be virtually unavailable for examination. Their most compelling qualities—monumental scale, large expanses of flat, clear color, fantastic chalky colors, dry grainy textures, and containment in wide, ornamental borders—cannot be transmitted in reproduction.[51] Moreover, as Meyer Schapiro pointed out with his usual acumen and prescience, commentators who work from black and white photographs are relegated to discussions of formal attributes and iconography. By the 1920s, as the painter and writer Jacques-Emile Blanche allowed—and regretted—in his correspondence with Maurice Denis, Puvis was no longer in fashion, he "n'est à la mode, ni chez les Fauves, ni chez les Académiques."[52]

4. Puvis de Chavannes in his Place Pigalle studio in Paris, 1884–87.

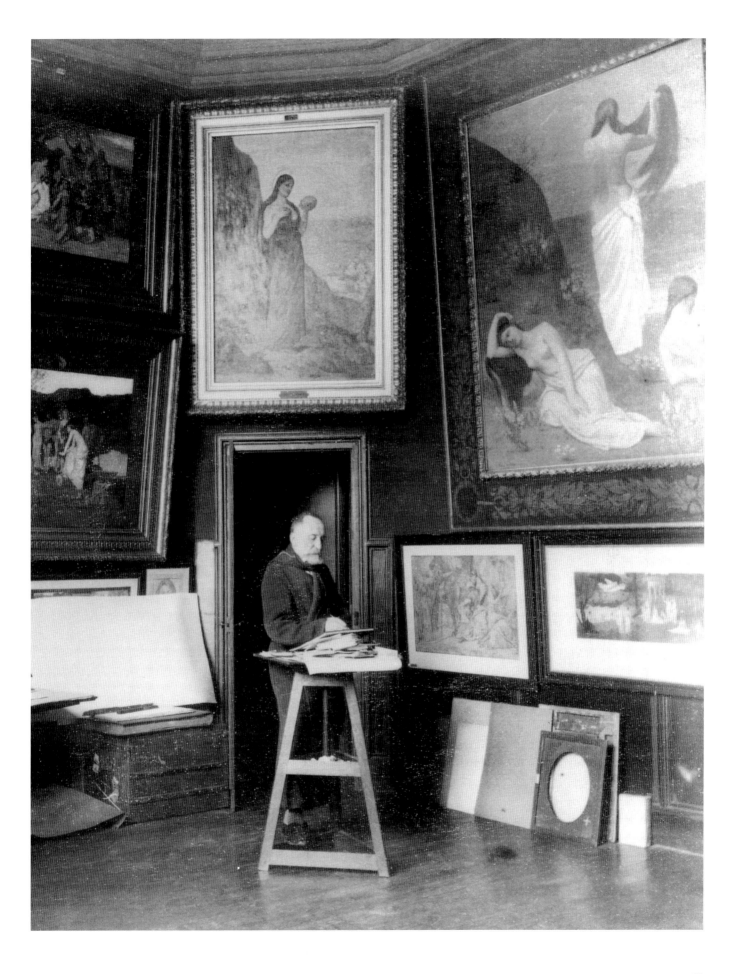

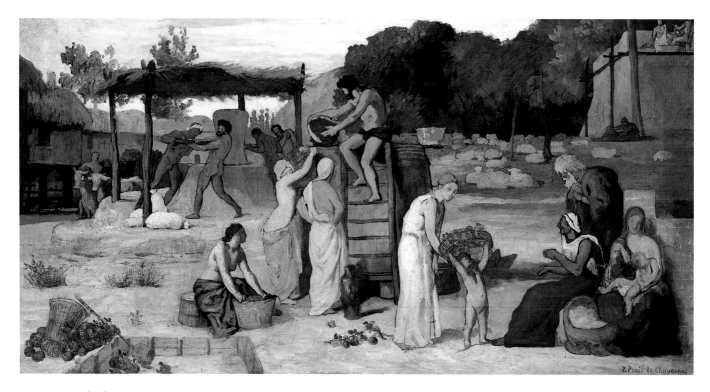

5. Pierre Puvis de Chavannes,
The Cider.
New York, The Metropolitan
Museum of Art, Catharine
Lorillard Wolfe Collection,
Wolfe Fund

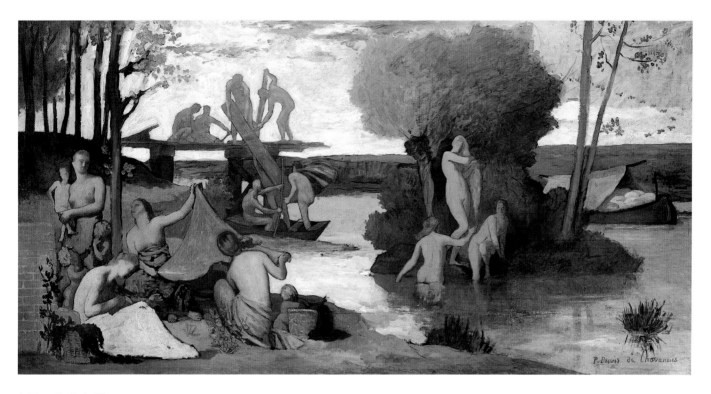

6. Pierre Puvis de Chavannes,
The River.
New York, The Metropolitan
Museum of Art, Catharine Lorillard
Wolfe Collection, Wolfe Fund

Critics have long found Puvis's works difficult to classify, contributing to their discomfiture and his neglect. With new opportunities to see his work and contexts for understanding it—as through the propagation of his ideas to other artists of many lands, what the current exhibition endeavors to show—Puvis's work may be seen and evaluated anew. Thus, the current exhibition is another step in remedying his critical fortune.

[1] Puvis de Chavannes "avait horreur d'un certain blablabla de critique d'art, et il ironisait volontiers dan [sic] les commentaires qui leur inspirait sa peinture. . . ." L. Wehrlé, in an undated letter, Déubergue Collection, Paris. Wehrlé published many of the two hundred letters his mother had collected in *La Revue de Paris*, XI, February 1, 1911, pp. 449–77.

[2] *Art Bulletin*, XXVIII, March 1946, pp. 33–43; Goldwater thanks Alfred H. Barr, Jr., director of the Museum of Modern Art in New York, for having suggested the topic to him—the latter must also have been fascinated by Puvis and his place in modernism.

[3] He wrote on him that year and for a number of years in *Le Moniteur Universel*.

[4] Used, for example, to explain the appearance of paintings by Seurat and Cassatt later (and not so used as an antifeminist attack as alleged by one art historian). See also P. Vaisse, "La Querelle de la Tapisserie au début de la IIIe République," *Revue de l'Art*, no. 22, 1973, pp. 66–86.

[5] "cherchant pardessus tout le style et marchant dans la voie de la grande peinture, de l'art décoratif." A. Stevens, *Le Salon de 1863*, Paris, 1866, p. 132.

[6] For the formulation of this, Puvis's special manner, see A. Brown Price, "The Decorative Aesthetic in the Work of Pierre Puvis de Chavannes," ("L'esthétique décorative de Puvis de Chavannes") in L. D'Argencourt, J. Foucart et al, *Puvis de Chavannes, 1824–1898*, exh. cat., Paris, Grand Palais, and Ottawa, National Gallery of Canada, 1976–77, pp. 21–28. Criticism has a dialogic relationship with the development of Puvis's work, the latter is summarized in my essay, "Pierre Puvis de Chavannes. The Development of a Pictorial Idiom," in A. Brown Price, *Pierre Puvis de Chavannes*, exh. cat., Van Gogh Museum, Amsterdam (February 25–May 29, 1994), Amsterdam, Zwolle, 1994, pp. 11–23. These ideas are further developed in my forthcoming monograph on the artist which also comprises a catalogue raisonné of the painted work.

[7] "Elles heurtent comme tableaux, par leur aspect d'ébauches, par leurs indications de frottis. Elles ont, en place et comme décors, une valeur de clarté, de franchise d'effet qui ne sont pas niables. . . ." P. Burty, "The Exhibition of the 'Intransigeants,'" *The Academy*, IX, April 15, 1876, p. 364, quoted by S.Z. Levine, "Décor/Decorative/Decoration in Claude Monet's Art," *Arts*, LI, February 1977, p. 137; and idem, "Exposition des impressionistes," *La République française*, XXV, April 25, 1877, n.p.; the latter also quoted in M. Ward, "Impressionist Installations and Private Exhibitions," *The Art Bulletin*, LXXIII, December 1991, p. 604.

[8] Letter to Lucien of November 21, 1895, in J. Bailly-Herzberg, *Correspondance de Camille Pissarro*, Paris, 1989, vol. 4, p. 119.

[9] The complex issues in the reception and evaluation of Puvis's drawings and the dynamics itself of change are perceptively addressed by Jon Whiteley in "The Role of Drawing in the Work of Puvis de Chavannes," in Brown Price, *Pierre Puvis de Chavannes, op. cit.*, pp. 28–36.

[10] About was a novelist, essayist, and playwright; he wrote for *Journal des débats* and from May 1872 he was manager of *Le XIXè siècle*.

[11] Puvis reported his distress in a letter of May 13, 1884 to his family, private collection, France.

[12] E. About, "Peinture décorative," in *Dernières lettres d'un bon jeune homme*, Paris, 1863, pp. 217–18, 221–22, 223.

[13] See letters and thanks from 1861, May 11, 1866, May 8, 1867, and July 2, 1869; correspondence in a private collection, France.

[14] "Rien ne te force désormais à exposer deux tableaux si tu n'as pas le temps que d'en finir un; tu peux pousser ton dessin à loisir et accrocher le fin qui *seul* te manques." Private collection, France.

[15] A note of May 17, 1874, private collection, France.

[16] "la malveillance la plus recherché. . . ." Private collection, France.

[17] See their correspondence and "Edmond About, écrivain et critique d'art (1828–1885)," *Le Petit Journal des Grandes Expositions*, no. 14, n.d. [1985], pp. 1, 3.

[18] "Lorsque l'enfer voudra se faire paver à neuf, comme les Champs Elysées, il ne manquera pas de confier l'entreprise à M. Puvis de Chavannes. Cet artiste est par excellence l'homme des bonnes intentions, je dirai même des grandes intentions et des vastes pensées. Depuis plus de vingt ans, il se promet et nous promet un chef-d'oeuvre qu'il n'exécutera jamais, car il ne sait ni peindre ni dessiner, et il promène fièrement dans tous les coins du domaine de l'art une ignorance encyclopédique. Le défaut d'instruction première est malheureusement sans remède; ni le courage, ni la persévérance, ni même une certaine élévation d'esprit ne feront produire un poème épique en douze chants au rêveur qui n'a pas fréquenté l'école primaire et qui manque non seulement de prosodie, mais de la plus vulgaire orthographe." E. About, "Le Salon de 1883," *Le XIXe Siècle*, May 6, 1883; quoted also by Whiteley, *op. cit.*, pp. 28, 36.

[19] See D'Argencourt, Foucart et al., *op. cit.*, no. 138.

[20] Lent by Wolff to Puvis's 1887 retrospective at the Durand-Ruel Gallery in Paris.

[21] At the time the city was negotiating for Puvis's murals, so this thrashing may not be coincidental; see A. Brown Price's essay, "Puvis de Chavannes and America," in this catalog.

[22] *The Boston Evening Transcript*, January 7, 1892, p. 8.

[23] C. Naubert-Riser, "La Critique des Années 1890. Impasse Méthodologique ou Renouvellement des Modèles Théoriques?" in *La Critique d'Art en France 1850–1900*, Clermont-Ferrand, 1987, pp. 193–204, writes on the explosion of criticism which she recommends be systematically studied; see also M. Ward, "From Art Criticism to Art News: Journalistic Reviewing in Late-Nineteenth Century Paris," in M. Orwicz, ed., *Art Criticism and Its Institutions in Nineteenth Century France*, Manchester, 1994, pp. 162–81, writes of the proliferation of writers and paucity of ideas.

[24] See his *L'Art moderne* quoted in C. Chassé, *Le Mouvement symboliste dans l'art du XIXe siècle,* Paris, 1947, p. 40; also J. Feydy, "Autour du 'misérabilisme' de Chateaubriand à Bernard Buffet," *L'Information Culturelle Artistique*, I,

no. 1, 1955–56, pp. 19–20; and Prince Bojidar Karageorgevitch, "Puvis de Chavannes," *Magazine of Art*, XVII, 1894, p. 74.

[25] "Je finirais, Dieu me pardonne, si je devais encore parcourir deux salle bondées de tableaux semblables à ceux-là, par éprouver une admiration déraisonnable pour l'oeuvre de M. Puvis de Chavannes! Il est certain qu'en face de ces ennuyeuses pasticheries, *L'Enfant prodigue* et les *Jeunes filles au bord de la mer* sont de vraies merveilles. C'est toujours le même coloris pâle, le même air de fresque, c'est toujours anguleux et dur, ça agace, comme d'habitude, aves ses prétentions à la naïveté et son affectation du simple; et cependant, si incomplet qu'il puisse être, ce peintre-là a du talent . . . et il atteint même . . . une certaine grandeur. On admire ses efforts, on voudrait l'applaudir; puis on se révolte. . . ." On works in the 1879 Salon: J.-K. Huysmans, *Oeuvres complètes de J.-K. Huysmans*, vol. VI, *L'Art moderne*, Paris, 1929, pp. 18–19.

[26] "voyons l'étrange panneau de M. de Chavannes. . . . C'est une peinture crépusculaire . . . c'est sec, dur, affectant comme d'habitude une raideur naïve. . . . Devant cette toile, je hausse les épaules, agacé par cette singerie de grandeur biblique . . . puis, je me sens quand même pris de pitié et d'indulgence, car c'est l'oeuvre d'un dévoyé, mais c'est l'oeuvre aussi d'un artiste convaincu qui méprise les engouements du public et qui, contrairement aux autres peintres, dédaigne de patauger dans le cloaque des modes. En dépit des révoltes que soulève en moi cette peinture quand je suis devant, je ne puis me défendre d'une certaine attirance quand je suis loin d'elle." J.-K. Huysmans, "Le Salon Officielle de 1881," in *op. cit.*, pp. 197–98.

[27] ". . . ne dessine ni ne peint; il compose, c'est là sa spécialité"; quoted by A. Michel and J. Laran, *Puvis de Chavannes*, Paris, 1911, p. 48; see also G. Kahn, "Chronique: L'Art français à l'Exposition," *La Vogue*, IV, August 1889, p. 137. On Castagnary's criticism see Goldwater, *op. cit.*, pp. 34–35.

[28] On the painting and its formulation see A. Brown Price, "*The Poor Fisherman* A Painting in Context," in Brown Price, *Pierre Puvis de Chavannes, op. cit.*, pp, 45–53.

[29] "Remember that a painting—before being a warhorse, a nude woman, or some anecdote—is essentially a planar surface covered with colors organized in a certain order." This first appeared under Denis's pseudonym Pierre Louis, "Définition du Néo-Traditionnisme," *Art et Critique*, August 23 and 30, 1890, p. 540. I discussed this connection in Brown Price, *Pierre Puvis de Chavannes, op. cit.*, p. 49, and note that other art historians since, usually citing my work (for example J. H. Robinson, "Aimée Brown Price, *Pierre Puvis de Chavannes*," *Studies in the Decorative Arts*, III, Fall-Winter 1995–96, pp. 79–82), have also pointed it out.

[30] See J.U. Halperin, *Félix Fénéon and the Language of Art Criticism*, Ann Arbor, 1980.

[31] As in "Puvis de Chavannes et son Esthétique," *L'Ermitage,* March 1891, pp. 140–44; on Germain see Naubert-Riser, *op. cit.*, pp. 197–200.

[32] J. Simpson, *Aurier, Symbolism and the Visual Arts*, Bern, 1999, pp. 96, 99, 142.

[33] Aurier and Puvis are discussed in M.A. Marlais, *Conservative Echoes in Fin-de-Siècle Parisian Art Criticism*, University Park, 1992, pp. 132–39; the taxonomies proposed are not particularly helpful in furthering our analysis.

[34] For Geffroy's evaluation of Puvis see his *La Vie artistique*, 8 vols., Paris, 1892–1903, *passim*; Bibliothèque Nationale, *Gustave Geffroy et l'art moderne*, exh. cat., Paris, 1957; B. Petrie, *Puvis de Chavannes*, ed. with a preface by Simon Lee, Aldershot (Eng.) and Brookfield (Vt.), 1997, p. 140; J. Paradise, "Gustave Geffroy and the Criticism of Painting," Ph.D. diss. (Stanford University, 1982), pp. 151–72.

[35] Geffroy, *op. cit.*, vol. 3, pp. 331, 375.

[36] Geffroy, *op. cit.*, vol. 1, pp. 142, 248.

[37] Dario Gamboni wants to systematize criticism and evaluate its relative worth and has proposed a typology of literary, scientific, and journalistic criticism; see his "The Relative Autonomy of Art Criticism," in Orwicz, ed., *op. cit.*, pp. 182–94.

[38] Naubert-Riser, *op. cit.*, p. 197.

[39] M. Marlais, "Puvis de Chavannes and the Parisian Daily Press," *Apollo,* February 1999, pp. 3–10, proposes that (as one might expect) critics expounded their own artistic and political agendas.

[40] "vraiment, il faudrait en finir avec la blague Puvis de Chavannes. Ce *Bois sacré* a l'air d'être habité par des personnages fabriqués en planches découpées. Oh, la peinture idéaliste!" E. and J. de Goncourt, *Journal. Mémoires de la Vie Littéraire*, ed. R. Ricatte, Paris, 1956, vol. II, p. 1082; entry of June 16, 1884.

[41] "Qu'est-ce qui peut charmer chez Puvis de Chavannes? Est-ce cette triste couleur de vieilles *verdures* passées? Est-ce dessin sans esprit, sans accent, sans ressentiment . . . ce dessin . . . le plus bête de tous les dessins que j'aie vus? Est-ce l'imagination du compositeur, une imagination pour l'illustration pour complaintes antiques? Non, je crois que la critique n'ai jamais gobé pour un vrai peintre un homme aussi dénués de toutes les qualités picturales et aussi laborieusement ingénu et aussi idiotement plagiaire du passé." De Goncourt, *op. cit.*, vol. III, p. 1249.

[42] "Ce Puvis, penser qu'il y a tant de belles places blanches dans nos monuments publics qui sont condamnées à être salies par ces tristes grisailles, si mal, pis que cela, si bêtement dessinées. Je ne connais pas, depuis que la peinture existe, un peintre qui ait en le dessin aussi rondouillard." De Goncourt, *op. cit.*, vol. III, p. 46.

[43] On March 10, 1895; but a number of caricatures were made of Puvis and his painting.

[44] The pseudonym for the Comte Amédée de Noé.

[45] "reconnu comme manifeste de la génération symboliste, devient surtout *cher aux menuisiers* pour Karlutain. . . ." see L. Abélès, *Arts incohérènts. académie du dérisoire*, Paris, 1992, pp. 65–66.

[46] *Ibidem.*

[47] W. H. Low, *A Chronicle of Friendships*, New York, 1910, p. 442.

[48] Letter of March 30, 1884, to his family, private collection, France.

[49] This is a real problem in an analysis based on the criticism of Puvis's *Summer* for the Paris Hôtel de Ville, cornerstone of J.L. Shaw, "Imagining the Motherland: Puvis de Chavannes, Modernism, and the Fantasy of France," *Art Bulletin*, LXXIX, December 1997, pp. 586–610. The Salon reviewers' perceptions are mixed and melded with the author's discussion of the mural *in situ*; discussion of the mural in relationship to its pendant, *Winter*, its opposite, which would countermand much of what the author claims about its significance, is entirely omitted.

[50] G. Kahn, *Silhouettes littéraires*, Paris, 1925, p. 112.

[51] Indeed, many if not most commercial reproductions of the murals omit the borders.

[52] J.-E. Blanche, *Correspondance Jacques-Emile Blanche—Maurice Denis (1901–1939)*, ed. G.-P. Collet, Geneva, 1989, p. 26.

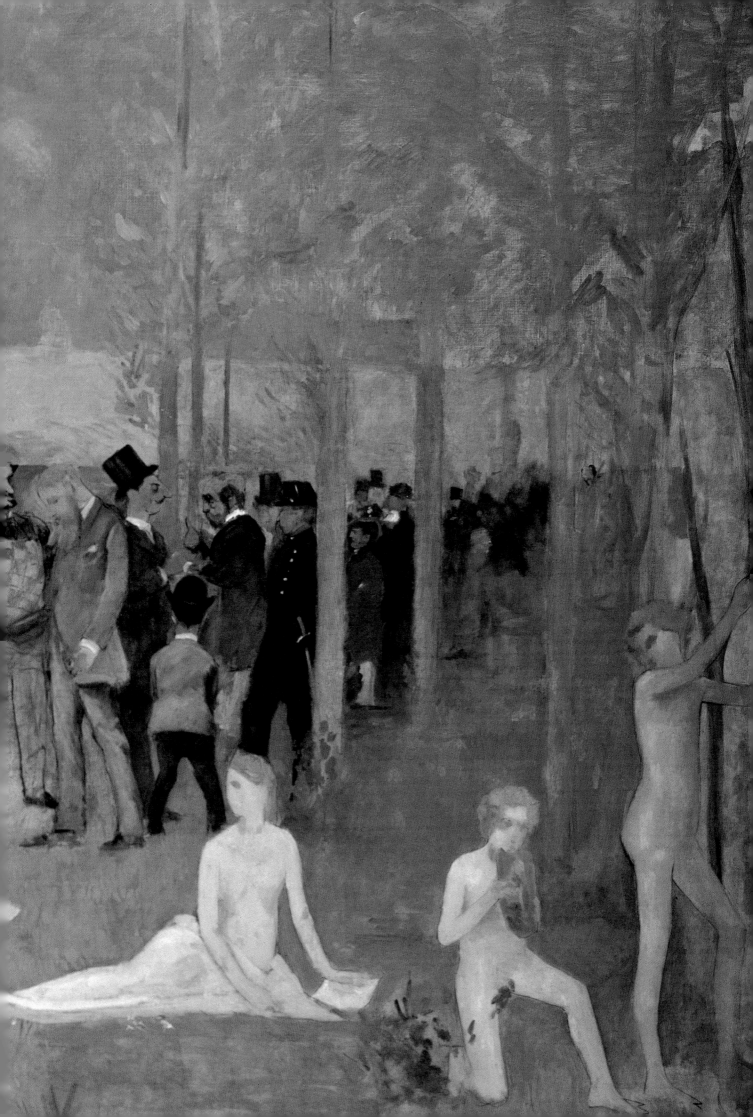

Monique Nonne

Puvis de Chavannes and the "Petit Boulevard" Painters: Emile Bernard, Paul Gauguin and Vincent Van Gogh

In Paris during the decade of the 1880s, the number of group exhibitions with no connection to the official Salon steadily increased. At the Salon, there were more and more works exhibited on the walls. Some 4942 were shown in 1881, then 4665 in 1884, the year of the creation of the Société des Artistes Indépendants, and 5416 in 1886. Because of the originality of his own very personal style, Puvis de Chavannes successfully attracted the attention of an entire generation of artists who were moving away from academic teachings as they made their way towards the invention of a fresh new avant-garde. It is interesting to investigate the basis of this esteem and to measure to what extent Puvis's work contributed to the creation of the highly original and very modern works of artists who were not strictly speaking his "disciples." Van Gogh studied for a while in the atelier of Cormon, which at this time was an incubator for young talents. He met Bernard, then Gauguin, his closest friends among the artists of the "Petit Boulevard." They all worked together before going their separate ways. Puvis's work enabled them to discover the solutions that implemented their progress toward a new art.

Puvis de Chavannes: a Highly Regarded Painter
While Puvis worked independently, he nevertheless sought recognition from his fellows as well as from the public. Therefore he took great care in the management of his career. He encouraged official clients and when the state purchased *Peace* at the Salon of 1861 where his entry was awarded a medal, he unhesitatingly offered it its pendant *War*.[1] Puvis conscientiously exhibited his compositions at each Salon, even though his relative audaciousness was not always to the Academy's taste.[2] There he exhibited the decorations that he conceived for public buildings before they were definitively installed—the large cartoons, sketches of the whole or studies of details, as well as reductions. The easel paintings were often exhibited several times—four times in ten years for the *Young Women by the Sea*.[3] Beginning in 1873, he was in contact with the dealer Paul Durand-Ruel who purchased his works and showed them in his gallery.[4] He affirmed his decorative tendency, sending the canvases and the studies for the Musée de Picardie to the *Exposition de Peinture et Sculpture Moderne de Décoration et d'Ornement* organized at the Musée des Arts Décoratifs in 1881. He also exhibited with the Pastellistes Français in 1888, 1889 and 1892. His entries never went unnoticed and his student Baudouïn later recounted that the painter "... could never enter into one of the rooms in which his work was shown without hearing himself insulted."[5] However from the very beginning his admirers, like Théophile Gautier, defended him in ever growing numbers.

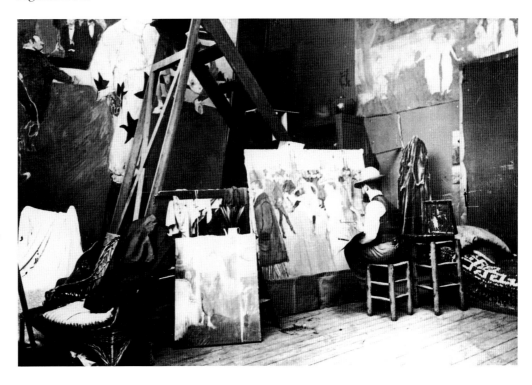

2. Henri de Toulouse-Lautrec painting in his studio.
On the upper right, *Parody of Puvis de Chavannes's "Sacred Wood."* Albi, Musée Toulouse-Lautrec

opposite page
1. Henri de Toulouse-Lautrec, *Parody of Puvis de Chavannes's "Sacred Wood,"* detail, 1884.
Princeton University, The Art Museum, Henry and Rose Pearlman Foundation

3, 4. Pierre Puvis de Chavannes, *Peace* and *War*, 1867. Philadelphia Museum of Art

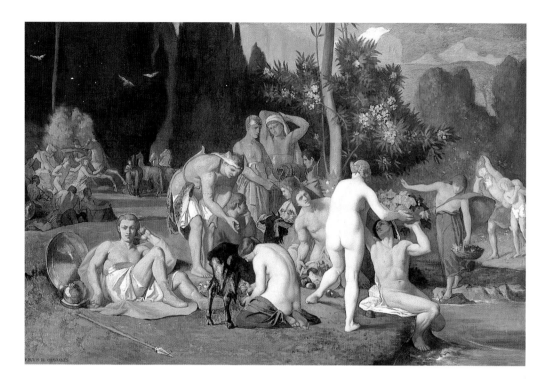

Puvis also scrutinized the reproduction of his works. He closely followed the fabrication of the lithographs, never hesitating to interrupt engravers and publishers alike.[6] The year after their first meeting, his dealer Paul Durand-Ruel[7] had an etching engraved after *Hope*[8]—perhaps the most often reproduced of his works. The Maison Goupil[9] also played an important role in the dissemination of his works. While only rarely the object of an entire album of plates, many were included in the volumes that the company published each year on the occasion of the Salon. Thus *Summer* was published in 1873[10] and *Saint Genevieve* in 1876.[11]

During the decade of the 1880s, the artist's notoriety constantly grew. Reproductions of his work multiplied. In 1884 Boussod, Valadon & Cie, successor to Goupil, devoted a major part of the series *Grands Peintres Français et Etrangers*[12] to him, and gave him the choice place in the luxurious magazine *Les Lettres et les Arts* launched in 1886. The specialized press, the popular magazines, as well as the major dailies used these same images to illustrate their ever more numerous commentaries on his work. Puvis de Chavannes's creations were seen everywhere and by everyone.

The "Great Knight of the Ideal"[13] and the Young Artists in the Ateliers
There were lively debates about Puvis's works among the students in the free ateliers directed by the masters of the time. This was especially true in Cormon's[14] studio where several students seeking out the new tendencies often went to "Durand-Ruel's shop,"[15] a shrine of Impressionism and also Puvis's dealer. The visit to the Salon where certain of their colleagues already exhibited[16] was an imperative. On May 20, 1884, Toulouse-Lautrec, Anquetin and Edouard Dujardin[17] went to the Palais des Champs-Elysées where Puvis de Chavannes exhibited *The Sacred Wood*,[18] which won a *médaille d'honneur*. It provoked ". . . heated discussions among Cormon's students. Some saw in this decoration the dream of a poet, the calm serenity of art surpassing the material, while others jeered at the flat tones and the dark outlines which isolated figures from the landscape, mocking the simplification of the drawing. 'It is too easy,' they said. As proof of the facility, they spent two afternoons making a caricature of the painting!"[19] (fig. 8) Toulouse-Lautrec signed it for them all. "We made it . . . at Cormon's, for our own amusement, part of the workshop painted it," recounted later his friend Gauzi[20] who ended his account by saying, "At any rate, this parody of the *Sacred Wood* was merely done for our entertainment, and was as much an homage as a criticism." Toulouse-Lautrec nailed the canvas onto the wall of his studio on the Rue Tourlaque "facing the window, all the way up high"[21] where his friends, the regulars of "his Saturdays" like Louis An-

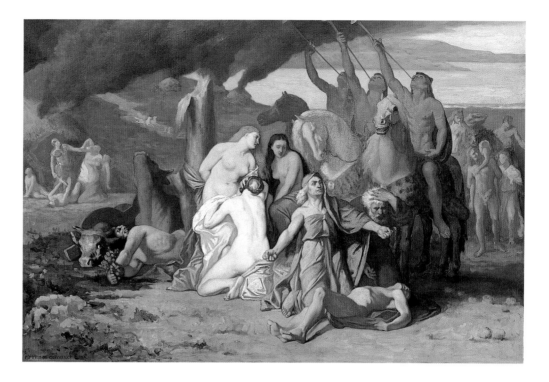

quetin and Maximilian Luce, could see it.[22] Numerous caricatures attest to its popularity. In the Salon International des Arts Incohérents in the same year of 1884 Emile Cohl presented *The Poor Fisherman in Need* and a certain Karlutain, *The Sacred Wood Dear to the Muses and Especially Woodworkers.*[23] The famous cabaret *Le Chat Noir,* meeting place for poets, musicians, critics and writers, sculptors and painters—which Puvis de Chavannes seems to have frequented[24]—was decorated with, among other things, tapestries, deer antlers, prints, a painting by Degas, and a work that was laughingly attributed to Puvis.[25]

At the end of 1887, these young artists were ready to face the public. Away from the prestigious galleries of the Boulevard Montmartre and the Rue Laffitte where their hardiness was not appreciated, Vincent Van Gogh organized with his friends—the "Peintres du Petit Boulevard" [Painters of the Lesser Boulevard] as he called them—an exhibition held on the Boulevard Rochechouart, at the Restaurant du Chalet. His fellow students from the Cormon atelier, Emile Bernard, Louis Anquetin, and Toulouse-Lautrec, all participated. Seurat paid them a visit, as did Paul Gauguin, John Peter Russell, and Camille and Lucien Pissarro. At the same time, Paul Durand-Ruel presented a major exhibition of Puvis which included 84 works.[26] The painters of the "new school" enthusiastically flocked to see it.

Vincent Van Gogh evoked certain canvases that particularly affected him, when he visited this exhibition, undoubtedly accompanied by his friend Alex Reid.[27] This amateur painter was the employee of Theo Van Gogh at Boussod, Valadon & Cie. In his notes for an unpublished article which refers to the discussions between friends, the young Scottish art dealer described Puvis as "the greatest French artist" and reported a supposed interview with a *camarade.* "In the course of conversation one day with one of the chiefs of the new school, sworn enemy to the allegories of former times . . . [he declared] his works enchant me all the same."[28] Other young members of this group have left written evidence confirming the admiration Puvis inspired within their circle. The Australian painter Russell wrote to his compatriot Roberts, "There is a fine exhibition of work by Puvis de Chavannes. Some really splendid work and I feel more inclined than ever to give him top place in French art today." Even though the master's influence was not very evident in his work, Russell nevertheless admired him: "Then in decorative art there is Puvis de Chavannes!! What music in the name."[29] At the Salon of this same year of 1887, Toulouse-Lautrec and Gauzi were indignant about where the *Cartoon of the Painting Destined for the Great Amphitheater of the Sorbonne* was placed. It was hung "in the stairway . . . instead of being given a space in the rooms reserved for 'Important Painting.'"[30] Toulouse-Lautrec wrote, with his accomplice Tristan Bernard, a humoristic critic of the Exposition Universelle two years later, "Puvis de Chavannes. Five minute stop-off. The time to show a sincere admiration and to empty a half a bottle. . . . That's good. Let's go on."[31] Puvis remained a model for Charles Angrand as can be seen in his correspondence with Signac.[32] That Charles Laval's canvases were influenced by Puvis was indicated in Fénéon's commentaries about the "bathers" hung in the Café Volpini in 1889,[33] which he qualified as clumsy imitations of Puvis.[34]

1888–90: Vincent Van Gogh, Emile Bernard and Paul Gauguin: the Search for a Modern Aesthetic

The Model. Vincent Van Gogh, Emile Bernard and Paul Gauguin shared the same interests as their fellow artists for folk art, Japanese art, stained glass, Greek antiquity, early Italian, German and Flemish Renaissance painting. They spent time in the Louvre and discussed the merits of the Old Masters, and the value of their art in these final years of the nineteenth century.

For this Puvis offered them a model which Bernard emphasized in his writings when he confirmed the freedom of the artist, and his independence when faced with academic dogma as a condition of creation. Puvis, and Delacroix before him, had come from free ateliers, and museums played an important part in their training. "These geniuses were the consequence of other geniuses, and nevertheless they owed everything to themselves since to understand is to be equal, had declared Raphael."[35] Responding to a critic, Bernard replied, "it is a bit hasty to accuse of imitation whoever draws his inspiration from a master; since do we not constantly see masters discussing masters and aspiring to look like them? Puvis himself, whom you unreservedly admire, did he not take his art from earlier sources? . . . Every artist has his ideal and his models. . . . There is therefore nothing criminal about a young artist resembling (in his own personal manner) the work he cherishes."[36]

Vincent was at the center of a group of "pals" as he put it. He worked with Bernard from the end of 1886 and joined Gauguin a year later. His brother Theo exhibited Gauguin's works in the mezzanine of his gallery.[37] Gauguin and Bernard painted together at Pont-Aven during the summer of 1888. It was the most constructive period in their relations, marked by a fruitful correspondence between Pont-Aven, Paris and Arles, where Vincent settled in February 1888. All three freed themselves from Impressionism, seeking alternatives in Neo-Impressionism. Bernard had a definite talent for conceptualizing the ideas of the moment. His vast culture and powers of synthesis and assimilation made him the theoretician of the group. He affirmed before them the superiority of synthesis over analysis, of the idea over observation. During the time of a summer, Gauguin agreed with him and provided the answers to his questions. Van Gogh took an active part in the discussions, even if his work remained tied to the real. Soon, however, rivalry took precedence over the exaltation of the exchanges, discoveries and progress realized together. Their solidarity disintegrated. Reciprocal esteem was replaced by doubt, and in the confrontation of personalities, Bernard and Gauguin broke off from each other. The death of Van Gogh in 1890 brought this important period in their careers to a close.

Puvis's Place in the Aesthetic Reflection of Three "Pals"

From the very beginning, Bernard admired Puvis, and went to visit him one day. "He opened the door of his atelier on the Place Pigalle. It was morning and he had a towel in his hand. I had been told that he was distrustful, I found him agreeable and gracious. His face reflected the serene integrity of his creations."[38] When he published, for the first time, a review of an exhibition in 1889, Bernard expressed himself in extravagant terms, praising the "prodigious" "chefs d'œuvre" by the master, and was indignant that so few were exhibited.[39] Bernard felt that Puvis had played a fundamental role in the development of this new aesthetic, for which Bernard loudly proclaimed his own precedence over Gauguin. For Bernard, Puvis was the "veritable creator of Symbolism and of Synthetism" since "he showed the path for all the innovations in poetry and the decorative arts. The harmony between line and color was conjugated through his summary expressions with Impressionism and it was out of this harmony that the Pont-Aven school was born." He concluded, "Symbolism should not be any other than an obstinate search for abstraction and style, transmitted by Puvis, continuing from the

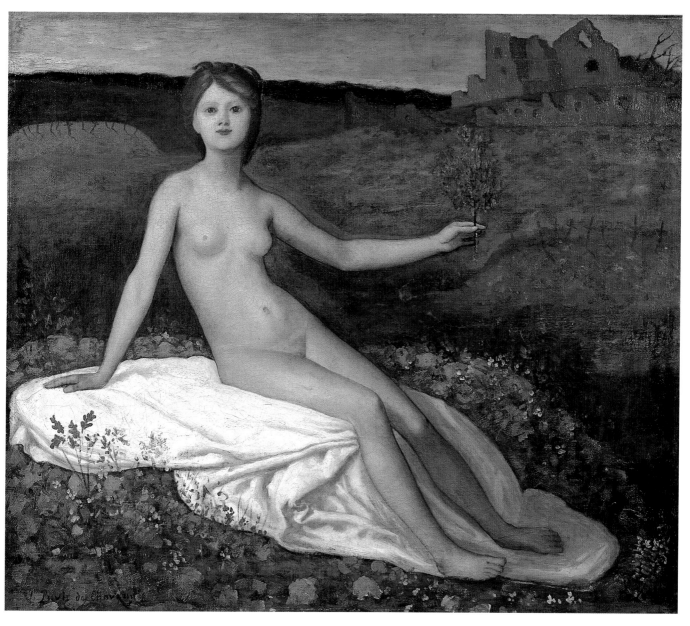

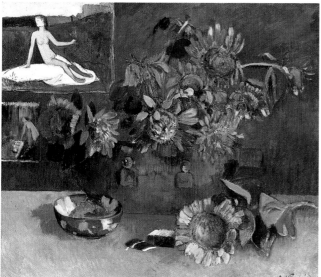

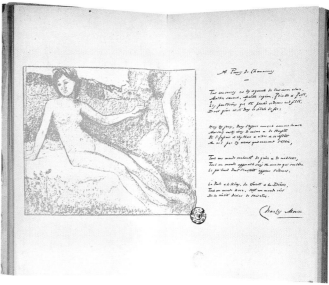

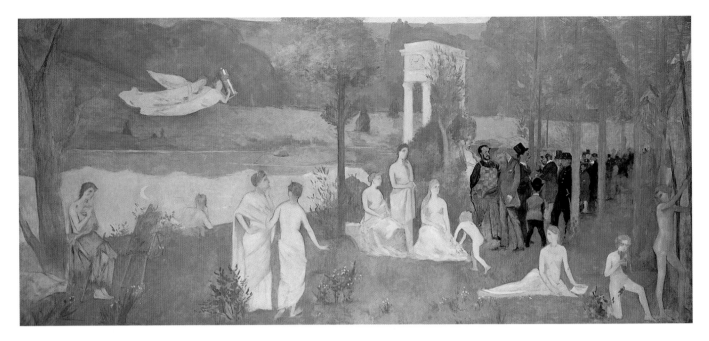

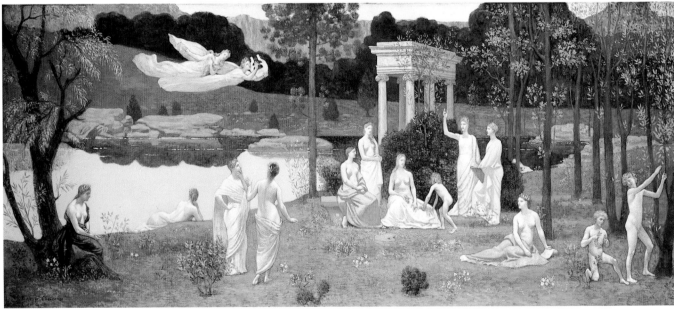

8. Henri de Toulouse-Lautrec,
*Parody of Puvis de Chavannes's
"Sacred Wood,"* 1884.
Princeton University,
The Art Museum,
Henry and Rose Pearlman
Foundation

9. Pierre Puvis de Chavannes,
The Sacred Wood, 1884.
Chicago, The Art Institute,
Potter Palmer Collection

mechanical procedures of Neo-Impressionism, those of Cloisonnism and the flat colors of the Pont-Aven school."[40]

Gauguin, who in this period of maturation of his aesthetic, was close to Puvis, among others, did not deal with this question. Addressing Huysmans, who in 1889 published without much conviction a portrait of Puvis, he wrote: "Puvis de Chavannes does not please you; his impulsive gestures do not please you. The simplicity, the nobility belong to another epoch. If this is not on our planet, it will be on another more disposed to beautiful things. . . ."[41] thus defining what attracted him in Puvis's work.

The discussions among the artists sojourning in Pont-Aven which induced Bernard and Gauguin to reorient their work, seemed to have found a favorable echo in Van Gogh, judging by the answer Gauguin addressed to him. "I totally agree with you about how unimportant precision is to art. Art is an abstraction, unfortunately we are becoming less and less understood. . . ."[42] Van Gogh declared himself in favor of this "true and grandiose renaissance of art" in the making. However, when Gauguin joined him in Arles at the end of the autumn of 1888, their conceptions of painting proved different. Gauguin took Bernard as his witness to this disagreement. "It is curious that Vincent has Daumier in mind to do here while I, conversely, see a colored Puvis mixed with Japan. Here the women with their elegant hairdos, their Greek beauty, their shawls draped as in early Renaissance painting, are, I would say, Greek processions. . . . At any rate there is here a source for beautiful *style moderne*."[43]

Urged by Gauguin to move away from the subject in order to let his imagination take over, Van Gogh made several attempts that led nowhere. If their points of view diverged, in particular as far as Puvis was concerned, Van Gogh nevertheless greatly admired the painter of *Pleasant Land*.

Van Gogh and Puvis

Unlike Bernard and Gauguin, Van Gogh only rarely wrote with an historical perspective. However, in a letter to the Dutch art critic Isaacson, that he wrote in French, Vincent underlined the relationship between Delacroix, Puvis and modern art. He took his arguments from his discussions with his friends.[44]

Vincent was already aware of Puvis before his sudden arrival at his brother's at the end of February–beginning of March 1886. When Vincent was in Paris in 1875,[45] he could have seen the *Fisherman's Family*[46] at the Salon. Edma Morisot wrote about it, "your eyes are drawn to it as soon as you enter the room."[47] Its subject corresponded to his preoccupations. But it was above all through reproductions that Vincent knew Puvis's work and could thus discuss it with his brother Theo, who was already in contact with the painter, even though Durand-Ruel's position as his dealer left little room for Theo to sell his paintings.[48] In May 1884 Vincent received a letter from Theo in which he discussed the colors in the *Sacred Wood*, and several months later, Theo sent him an issue of *L'Illustration*[49] with the reproduction of the large canvas.[50]

While Van Gogh copied Rembrandt, Delacroix, Millet and Daumier, there is little evidence of the direct influence of Puvis's painting in his work. There is certainly an allusion to *Hope*[51] (fig. 5), the painting he admired so much, in certain portraits of women he represented with flowers in their hands, like *The Italian Woman*[52] and *La Mousmé*.[53] He also remembered the portrait of Benon[54] (fig. 10), equally exhibited at Durand-Ruel in 1887. This was the painting which inspired a still life of books, with a rose.[55] Later in Auvers, he used the same accessories—book, vase with flowers—for his portrait of the Doctor Gachet[56] (fig. 11). He wrote of his admiration for this portrait to Bernard, as well as to his brother. "An ideal . . . figure to me . . . an old man reading a yellow novel, and beside him a rose and some watercolor brushes in a glass of water. . . . These are consoling things, to see a modern life as something bright, in spite of its inevitable griefs."[57]

For Vincent, Puvis was most importantly the painter of the *Pleasant Land*, of harmony and serenity. Vincent found there the peacefulness which he lacked and when he settled in Auvers, he noted that "there is much so well-being in the air . . . a quiet like a Puvis de Chavannes."[58] In May 1890, he shared with Wilhelmina his feelings before Puvis's painting which he sketched. "There is a superb picture. . . . All of humanity, all of nature simplified . . . one gets the feeling of being present at a rebirth, total but benevolent, of all the things one should have believed in, should have wished for—a strange and happy meeting of very distant antiquities and crude modernity."[59] Puvis was also the painter who reconciled the past with the present.

The Careers of Bernard and Gauguin, the Separation of the Friends
Emile Bernard

Bernard left France in 1893, spent time in Italy and then settled in Egypt for more than ten years. Early Italian Renaissance painting and Byzantine art were all important sources for him, but Puvis remained a model since he gave a "grand art," mural decoration, a new impetus. "Others like Puvis de Chavannes, to our great joy, conquered all the barriers and inscribed their names in divine capital letters on monumental walls."[60] He admired the painter's aristocratic attitude, his disdain for both the Academy and the overly bourgeois art of a "realist and banal" epoch of " spiritual collapse." "His capacity for idealization places him above our greatest masters, on the level of those geniuses whose intellectual universality can be summed up in one word: A Poet," he added. He also found in Puvis his own absorption with art in the service of the true faith—the original—that of the first Christians.[61] Bernard noticed a concordance with his new orientations. "His work is an attempt at the union of antique beauty with the primitive qualities of Giotto. It is a genuine vision of tradition." Bernard could also be critical, qualifying his work as "modern caricature of the ideal," he added, "there is beauty and ridicule in this work," before concluding, "in Puvis, the excess of the determination diminishes the spirit."[62] At the end of his life, he continued his work as an historian by situating his own evolution towards a new classicism in progress in relation to prior investigations. "First there were the Gauguinists and the Cézannians, then came the Neoclassicists who placed themselves in the renovated tradition. . . . We sought to reestablish the palette, order, qualities in the pictorial elements. . . . We went from Cézanne to Titian and to Rubens. Classicism was reborn, the union reestablished by the renovators attempting to reunite the ideal to the form. We once again discussed Beauty."[63]

Paul Gauguin

Paul Gauguin exhibited at the same time as Puvis de Chavannes at the exhibition of the Libre Esthétique in Brussels in 1894. This event once again stimulated his admiration. "Puvis de Chavannes's prodigal son magnifies this exhibition with a royal touch. . . ."[64] Gauguin never missed a chance to defend Puvis. "I remember when the public criticized the draftsmanship of Puvis de Chavannes's cartoons, while at the same time conceding to Puvis great compositional gifts, and declaring that Puvis de Chavannes did not know how to draw. Everyone was astonished when one fine day, at Durand-Ruel, he presented an exhibition devoted exclusively to charcoal and red chalk drawings and studies."[65] For a certain time they both exhibited at the same gallery—Durand-Ruel—and published in the same collections of engravings—*L'Estampe Originale,*[66] then in Dumont's *L'Epreuve Album d'Art.*[67] In his engravings Puvis once again used a procedure frequently seen in Japanese prints and which Gauguin and Bernard often practiced in Pont-Aven, that of a dominant foreground as in *Normandy.*[68] They seemed to have good relations and when Gauguin tried for a position as *Inspecteur du dessin* in the *Lycées*, he expected Puvis to come to his aid. "Puvis de Chavannes who belongs to the Institute (and it is the Institute that names these inspectors) is in favor of me."[69] He had confidence in his judgment and planned to invite him when he envisioned an exhibition for the group of canvases he sent to Paris in July 1898.[70] But beyond their personal relationship, Gauguin borrowed from Puvis just as he borrowed from Manet, Degas, antique Greece, Egypt, Asian art, Japanese prints, and the reliefs of Borobudur.[71] This caused Pissarro to write in exasperation, "He is always poaching on someone else's territory."[72] While Gauguin withdrew several times from a civilization he rejected, in order to resource himself in more primitive places, whether it be in Brittany, Madagascar or in Polynesia, he never left behind the images which stimulated him in the process of creation. At Pont-Aven his room "was decorated with Manet's *Olympia,*" as well as Botticelli, Fra Angelico and "Utamaro's prints seem to smile before the serious Puvis de Chavannes."[73] When he bade farewell to his friend Odilon Redon to go and rough it in Martinique, he explained, "I am taking in the form of photographs and drawings a whole little world of *camarades* who will chat with me every

10. Pierre Puvis de Chavannes,
Portrait of Eugène Benon, 1882.
Private collection

11. Vincent Van Gogh,
Portrait of Doctor Gachet, 1890.
Private collection

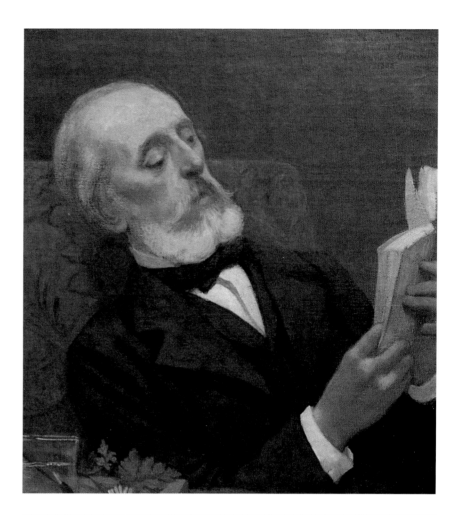

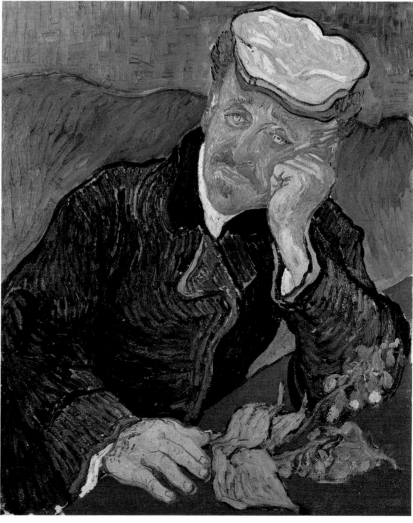

12. Emile Bernard,
Bathers, c. 1889.
Private collection

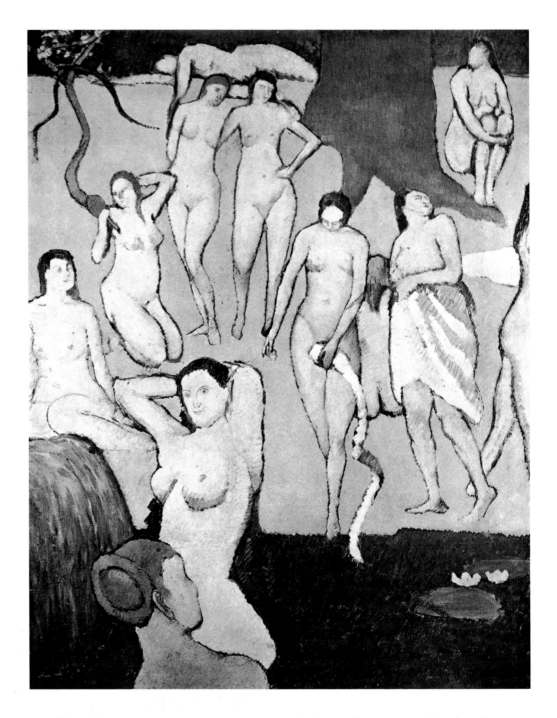

day."[74] Upon his return to Paris in 1893, Gauguin held open house on Wednesday afternoons for his friends in his atelier on the Rue Vercingétorix. The daughter-in-law of his neighbor, the musician William Molard, remembered the setting. "Cheap, light chrome yellow wallpaper framed with saffron orange bands. . . . The walls were covered from top to bottom with paintings of Tahiti, plus the *Yellow Christ*, the portrait of his mother, Cézanne's apples, a Puvis de Chavannes: a very young girl sitting in the grass with a slightly stiff gracefulness."[75] Gauguin himself described his "tropical atelier": "In my hut, there are things that are bizarre since atypical: Japanese prints, photographs of paintings by Manet, Puvis de Chavannes, Rembrandt, Raphael, Michelangelo, and Holbein. After these names, nothing by me: (I wouldn't dare)."[76] *Hope* (fig. 5) particularly affected Gauguin. When in January 1895, a dinner was organized to commemorate Puvis's seventieth birthday,[77] Gauguin illustrated with a drawing a poem by Charles Morice published by the *Mercure de France* (fig. 7). This figure of peace fascinated Gauguin for its theme, but he unhesitatingly disavowed Puvis's symbolism when he mod-

13. Paul Gauguin,
Bathing (Two Bathers), 1887.
Buenos Aires, Museo Nacional
de Bellas Artes

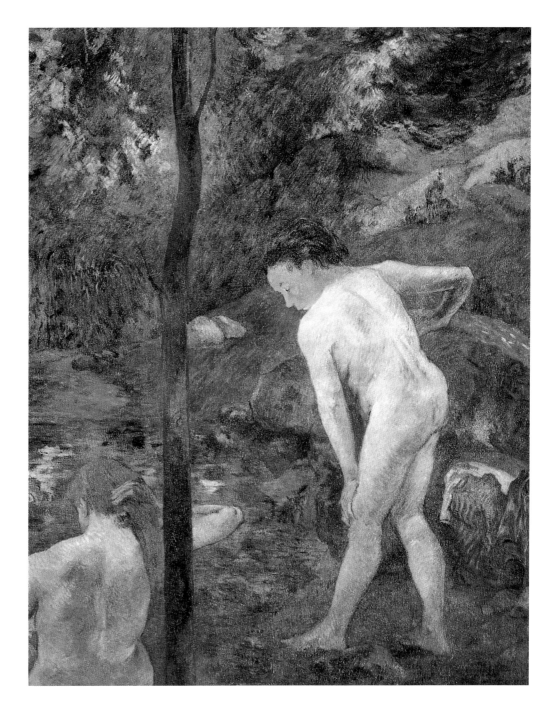

eled Cleopatra in the pose of the chaste girl for a terra-cotta vase.[78] The way in which Puvis painted the face from the front, the upper part of the torso slightly turned and the legs in profile, thus achieving a timeless hierarchical icon, interested Gauguin in *Vairaumati She Called Herself*, and then in *The Seed of the Areoi*—a new allegory of hope, that of the life contained in the seeds of the mango flower that she is holding in her hand.[79] He once again paid homage to *Hope* in the *Still Life with Sunflowers* where the painting was reproduced in the background along with a monotype by Degas, another artist he admired. In 1896, he openly took his inspiration from the subject of the *Poor Fisherman*, going so far as to inscribe the title under his signature in the small version.[80] He developed the theme in a horizontal format with a colorful and peaceful family scene, far removed from the atmosphere of misery in Puvis's canvas.[81] *Tahitian Women on a Beach*,[82] after first being modified and placed in a completely different atmosphere, reproduced the triangular pattern of the *Young Women by the Sea*[83] where Puvis had represented his figure from several points of view—from the back, the front and

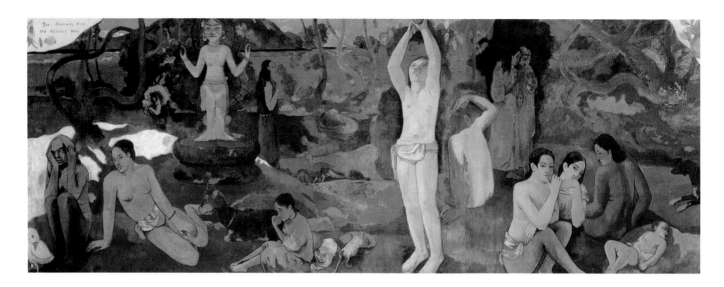

14. Paul Gauguin,
Where Do We Come from?
What Are We? Where Are
We Going? 1897.
Boston, Museum of Fine Arts

in profile. This layout can be found in a number of his compositions like *The Sacred Wood*, or the decoration for the Musée de Rouen. Gauguin also included in his repertory poses derived from the supplicant seen from the back in *War*[84] (fig. 4), and taken up again in *Bathing* (fig. 13) and then in *Women in the Waves (Ondine)*[85] (fig. 16) with variations. As Puvis repeated himself, like Gauguin, sometimes in several canvases, it can be supposed that these two paintings presented a repetition of the posture of the woman on the right in *Autumn*.[86] There are abundant examples of these analogous dispositions in the works of both painters. It is definitely in the major compositions of his last period, in which he explored the themes of life and of death, that Gauguin came the closest to Puvis. This is particularly true of his key work, *Where Do We Come from? What Are We? Where Are We Going?*[87] Before the paintings arrived at their destination, he wrote to his friend Monfreid, "No! it is definitely not a canvas created like a Puvis de Chavannes: study after nature, then preparatory cartoon, etc. It was all made without a model, straight from the brush, on a rough and uneven sack cloth."[88] He emphasized his difference: "Puvis explains his idea, certainly, but he does not paint it. He is Greek while I myself am a savage, a wolf in the woods without a collar."[89]

When the paintings he had sent were exhibited at Vollard's in November 1898,[90] the art critics did not fail to mention Puvis. Gauguin gave a long explanation of his intentions, "I tried in a suggestive decor to translate my dream without any reference to literary means, with all the simplicity possible to the craft—a hard task. Accuse me of having been inadequate, but not of having tried to do it, suggesting that I change objective and concentrate on other, already accepted, consecrated ideas. Puvis de Chavannes is the best example. Certainly Puvis crushes me with his talent, and the experience which I do not have. I admire him as much and more than you but for different reasons. (Do not be angry about it, with full knowledge of the facts)."[91] The dialogue with Fontainas continued: "You give me the pleasure, *a great pleasure*, of admitting that you had *wrongly* believed that my compositions like those of Puvis de Chavannes took as their starting point an idea, preferably abstract, that I sought to vitalize through a structural representation . . . and which my letter to some extent explained to you."[92] This misunderstanding had existed for several years and already in 1895, when, before leaving for Tahiti, Gauguin organized a sale of his works at the Hôtel Drouot (February 18), he published as preface to the catalog, a letter from Strindberg, in which the Swedish playwright and painter had already examined the question of the relationship between Puvis de Chavannes and Gauguin, but concluded with his originality as creator. "No, Gauguin was not shaped from Chavannes's rib, nor from that of Manet nor of Bastien-Lapage!"[93] Gauguin, the savage, had proven the originality of his aesthetic universe.

"Beginning in 1890, the victory was definitively secured and the triumph began. It is now that the breadth and the scope of his work can be measured. . . . He is almost seventy years old. It is the new generation which rushes toward him, surrounding him with admiration and

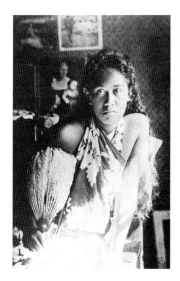

15. Young native woman in Paul Gaugin's studio on the Island of Atuana (1901).
On the wall, reproductions of *Hope* by Puvis de Chavannes and other works by Degas and Holbein

enthusiasm," art critic Arsène Alexandre wrote about Puvis in his obituary.[94] Attracted by the simple and elegant images, a plain, refined style, a harmonious universe, these artists studied Puvis each through his own awareness. The unanimity surrounding his name did not produce the same results among the painters—each found what he was expecting. Emile Bernard lived almost a half century longer than his friends and witnessed their posthumous successes, while his own art did not obtain recognition. He utilized in his numerous publications the celebrity of Puvis as a guarantee of the validity of his own approach and attempted to sanction his own painting by placing himself among Puvis's followers.

As for Vincent Van Gogh, he essentially remained in the realm of feeling. He sought in his work the harmonies which he perceived in nature and which evoked the art of Puvis like the softness of the rose laurel. Gauguin was certainly the artist who had the most complex relations with the master, so much was his art caught in the dense network of artistic and literary references. Aurier nevertheless situated him among the great decorators, "Gauguin, it must be repeated . . . is, above all a decorator . . . we only have, in our dying century one single great decorator, perhaps two, counting Puvis de Chavannes. . . ."[95]

[1] *Bellum*, Salon catalog no. 2622; The French state paid 7000 francs for *Peace* or *Concordia*, Salon catalog no. 2621; Amiens, Musée de Picardie. *Puvis de Chavannes, 1824–98*, exh. cat., L. d'Argencourt and J. Foucart eds., Grand Palais, Paris, National Gallery of Canada, Ottawa, 1977, p. 60.

[2] In 1872, the jury refused *Death and the Maiden* (Williamstown, Sterling and Francine Clark Institute). As irony would have it, although Puvis was elected for the first time as supplemental juror this particular year, he was not able to take part in the deliberations; see G. Lacambre, "Puvis de Chavannes and the Artistic Establishment of His Day," in A. Brown Price, *Pierre Puvis de Chavannes*, exh. cat., Van Gogh Museum, Amsterdam, Waanders Uitgeveres, Zwolle, 1994, p. 37 and note 5, p. 42.

[3] *Ibidem*, p. 40. At the Salon of 1879, catalog no. 2489, Exposition Nationale of 1883, no. 590, at the Durand-Ruel gallery in 1887, no. 17, then at the Centennale de l'Exposition Universelle in 1889, no. 560.

[4] A year after its refusal at the Salon of 1872, he exhibited *Death and the Maiden*.

[5] P. Baudoüin, "Mes Souvenirs," *Gazette des Beaux-Arts*, May 1935, pp. 295–314, p. 30.

[6] On January 14, 1884, Puvis interceded with the publisher Quentin because he felt that the engraver in charge of his works was hostile to him, then in 1887 he interceded on behalf of Georges-William Thornley (1857–1935) whose work he appreciated. Private archives.

[7] L. Venturi, *Les Archives de L'impressionnisme*, Durand-Ruel, éditeurs, Paris, New York, 1939, vol. 2, part II: "Mémoires de Paul Durand-Ruel," p. 192.

[8] Galerie Durand-Ruel, vol. 1 of *Recueil d'Estampes Gravées à l'Eau-Forte*, preface by A. Silvestre, Paris, 1873, 3 vols., pl. 6.

[9] This information was given to me by Pierre-Lin Renié, Musée Goupil, Bordeaux.

[10] *Summer*, Paris, Musée d'Orsay, reproduced by photography in the oversized folio of the *Salon de 1873*.

[11] *Saint Genevieve*, Paris, Panthéon, reproduced by means of photoengraving in the volume *Salon de 1876*, with a sonnet by Adrien Dézamy.

[12] E. Montrosier, "Puvis de Chavannes," *Grands Peintres Français et Etrangers*, Paris, H. Launette & Cie and Goupil & Cie (photoengravings), 7ème partie, 1884, pp. 321–36.

[13] H. Durand-Tahier, "Puvis de Chavannes," *La Plume*, no. 138, January 15, 1895, p. 34.

[14] Fernand-Anne Piestre, called Cormon (1845–1924) directed a free atelier at 104 Boulevard de Clichy beginning in the spring of 1882. At the end of 1882, Toulouse-Lautrec, Anquetin, Henri Rachou entered, at the end of 1884 Emile Bernard and John Peter Russell, in October 1885, François Gauzi, in autumn 1886, Vincent Van Gogh. See F. Destremau, "L'atelier Cormon (1882–1887)," *Bulletin de la Société de l'Histoire de l'Art français. 1996*, Paris, 1997, pp. 171-83.

[15] "As soon as I entered the atelier the wind of revolution was stirring up the theories in place. It came, so it was said, from 'Durand-Ruel's shop' where Anquetin and Lautrec were frequent visitors." E. Bernard, "Louis Anquetin, Artiste Peintre," *Mercure de France*, November 1, 1932, pp. 590–607, quoted in vol. 1 of *Propos sur l'art*, A. Rivière ed., Séguier, Paris, 1994, 2 vols., p. 261.

[16] See Destremau, *op. cit.*, p. 174.

[17] Edouard Dujardin (1861–1949) writer, founder of *La Revue Wagnérienne* and *La Revue Indépendante* who invented the term "Cloisonnisme" for his friend Anquetin, the writer Maurice Barrès (1862–1923) and Gustave Kahn (1859–1936) writer, founder and contributor of *La Révue Indépendante* undoubtedly accompanied them. *Ibidem*, p. 174 and note 22, p. 182.

[18] *The Sacred Wood Dear to the Arts and Muses*, 1884, decoration for the new staircase in the Palais des Arts in Lyon.

[19] Oil on canvas, 172 x 380 cm, The Henry and Rose Pearlman Foundation, Inc. (L. 1988, 62–13); see A. Roquebert, "Toulouse-Lautrec et la Vie Artistique: Ses Expositions (1883–1902)," in *Toulouse-Lautrec*, exh. cat., Hayward Gallery, London, Galeries Nationales du Grand Palais, Paris, 1992, pp. 40–41 and entry 23, pp. 122–25.

[20] F. Gauzi, *Lautrec et son temps*, Paris, 1954, pp. 116–17. François Gauzi (1861–1933) was a friend of Toulouse-Lautrec. According to tradition, he had been encouraged by Puvis; see G. Guitard, "François Gauzi, peintre et ami de Toulouse-Lautres," *L'Auta*, Nouvelle série, no. 577, June 1992, p. 168.

[21] Gauzi, *op. cit.*, p. 117.

[22] La Palette, "Puvis et Lautrec," *Gil Blas*, Saturday, December 27, 1913, p. 4.

[23] *Catalogue Illustré de l'Exposition des Arts-Incohérents*, Paris, 1884, nos. 54 and 120.

[24] Cabaret founded in December 1881, 84 Boulevard Rochechouart. Puvis was second on the list of founding members, *Chat Noir Guide*, edited by *Le Chat Noir* and illustrated by H. Somm, around 1886–87, Paris, Musée du Louvre, Département des Arts Graphiques, Fonds du Musée d'Orsay, RF 41435.

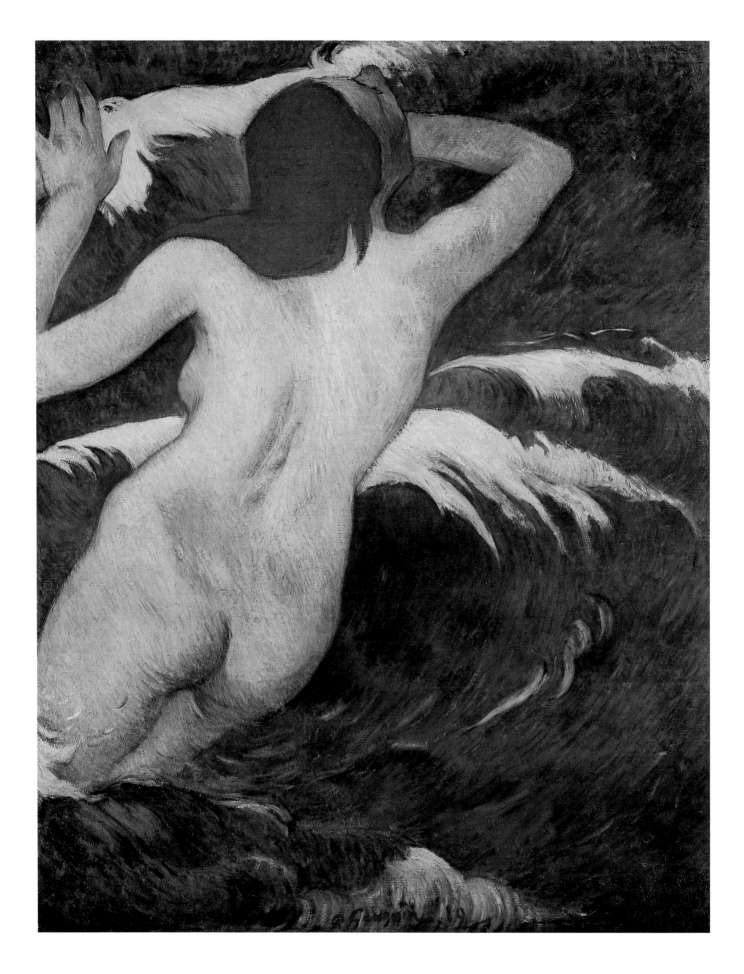

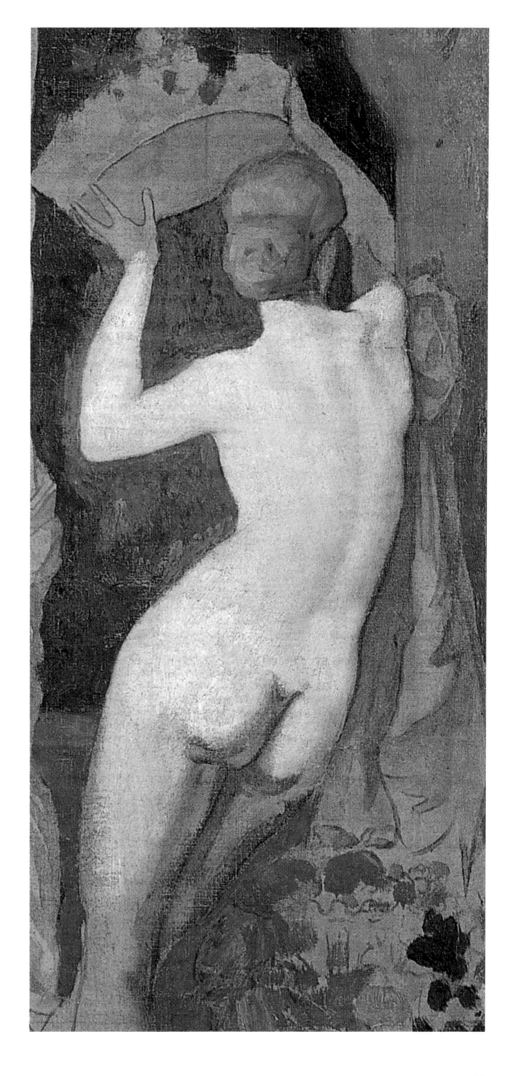

17. Pierre Puvis de Chavannes,
Autumn, detail, 1863–64.
Washington D.C., National
Museum of American Art,
Smithsonian Institution

opposite page
16. Paul Gauguin, *Woman
in the Waves (Ondine)*, 1889.
The Cleveland Museum of Art

[25] J. Grand-Carteret, *Raphaël et Gambrinus ou L'Art dans la Brasserie*, Paris, [1886], Champion–Slatkine, Paris–Geneva, 1984, p. 96.

[26] *Exposition des Tableaux, Pastels, Dessins par Puvis de Chavannes*, Paris, Galerie Durand-Ruel, November 20–December 20, 1887.

[27] Alexander Reid (1854–1928) lived with the two brothers from autumn 1886 until spring 1887. He was friends with Puvis. McNeill Reid, unpublished notes for the biography of the art dealer, National Library of Scotland, Acc. 6925, quoted by F. Fowles, *Alexander Reid in Context: Collecting and Dealing in Scotland in the late 19th and early 20th Centuries*, unpublished Ph.D. diss., University of Edinburgh, 1993, p. 25 and note 25, p. 188. Reid tried to introduce Puvis's work in Great Britain. On March 1, 1888, he purchased from Durand-Ruel for 5000 francs, *Spear Throwers* (Baltimore, The Walters Art Museum) which he exhibited at the Glasgow International Exhibition in May 1888, no. 1654. In January 1892, Reid organized an exhibition of French art in London, which he exhibited, in addition to the works by Puvis, in February at the McLellan Galleries in Glasgow, without much success (*ibidem*, vol. 1, p. 40). *A Man of Influence: Alex Reid, (1854–1928)*, exh. cat., The Scottish Arts Council, Edinburgh, 1968, catalog compiled by R. Pickvance, p. 9; Fowles, *op. cit.*, vol. 1, pp. 25–26 and notes 20–23, p. 188.

[28] See Fowles, *op. cit.*, appendix 6.

[29] John Peter Russell to Tom Roberts, winter 1887–88, letter VIII, Tom Roberts Papers, vol. III, Mitchel Library, Sydney, quoted in *The Art of John Peter Russell*, exh. cat., A. Galbally ed., Rijksmuseum Vincent van Gogh, Amsterdam, University Art Museum, Brisbane, National Gallery of Victoria, Melbourne, Art Gallery of New South Wales, Sydney, 1978, pp. 27–28 and notes 11 and 12, p. 66.

[30] Gauzi, *op. cit.*, p. 39.

[31] T. Bernard and Toulouse-Lautrec, "Le Salon du Chasseur de Chevelures Illustré," *La Revue Blanche*, vol. VI, 1894, p. 578. Puvis de Chavannes exhibited at the Salon of the Société Nationale des Beaux-Arts the entire decorative cycle for the staircase of the Préfet, Hôtel de Ville in Paris, no. 934 of the Salon catalog.

[32] F. Lespinasse, *Charles Angrand. Correspondances 1883–1926*, Rouen, 1988.

[33] *Exposition de Peintures du Groupe Impressionniste et Synthétiste*, Paris, Champ-de-Mars, Café des Arts [Café Volpini], June-October 1889.

[34] F. Fénéon, "Un Autre groupe Impressionniste," *La Cravache*, July 6, 1889, reprinted in F. Fénéon, *Oeuvres plus que complètes*, J.U. Halperin ed., Geneva-Paris, 1970, p. 158.

[35] E. Bernard, "Les Ecoles," *Mercure de France*, February, 1895, reprinted in *Propos…*, *op. cit.*, vol. 2, p. 34.

[36] E. Bernard, "Lettre ouverte à M. Camille Mauclair," *Mercure de France*, June 1895, reprinted in *ibidem*, vol. 2, pp. 332–29.

[37] Beginning in 1881, Theo Van Gogh (1857–91) directed the Boulevard Montmartre branch of Goupil & Cie which became Boussod, Valadon & Cie in 1884. Perhaps he knew Puvis through Georges-Willem Thornley who reproduced eighteen of his works in lithography, or through Michel Manzi, who directed Goupil's reproduction factory in Asnières. See *Theo van Gogh, Marchand de tableaux, collectionneur, frère de Vincent*, exh. cat., Amsterdam–Paris, 1999–2000.

[38] It is difficult to know exactly when this meeting took place, since fifteen years later Bernard gave a slightly different version. E. Bernard, "Puvis de Chavannes," *L'Occident*, December, 1903, pp. 273–80, reprinted in *Propos…*, *op. cit.*, vol. 1, p. 61; E. Bernard, "Le Symbolisme pictural, 1886–1936," *Mercure de France*, May 1936, reprinted in *ibidem*, vol. 1, p. 288.

[39] E. Bernard, "Au Palais des Beaux Arts. Notes sur la Peinture," *Le Moderniste Illustré*, no. 14, July 27, 1889, pp. 108 and 120, reprinted in *ibidem.*, vol. 2, pp. 12–13.

[40] E. Bernard, "Le Symbolisme pictural…," *op. cit.*, pp. 287–88.

[41] Upon the publication of the book by Georges Charles, called Joris-Karl Huysmans, *Certains*, Paris, 1889, Gauguin drafted a response which was never published during his lifetime; J. Loize, "Un inédit de Gauguin," *Les Nouvelles littéraires*, May 7, 1953.

[42] Paul Gauguin to Vincent Van Gogh, Pont-Aven, July 24 or 25, 1888: *Correspondance de Paul Gauguin*, V. Merlhès ed., Fondation Singer-Polignac, Paris, 1984, 158, p. 200.

[43] Paul Gauguin to Emile Bernard, Arles, late October or early November 1888: *ibidem*, 176, pp. 269–70.

[44] Vincent Van Gogh to Jozef Isaacson, May 1890: *Correspondance complète de Vincent Van Gogh, enrichie de tous les dessins originaux,* trans. by M. Beerblock and L. Reelandt, introduction and notes by G. Charensol, Paris, 1960, 614a, pp. 457–58. At the time Isaacson published a series of articles about Impressionism in the Netherlandish magazine *De Portefeuille.*

[45] Vincent Van Gogh worked for the Parisian branch of Goupil & Cie from October to December 1874 and then from mid-May 1875 until March 31, 1876.

[46] Destroyed, catalog no. 1689. Puvis also exhibited the decoration for the staircase of the Hôtel de Ville in Poitiers.

[47] Edma's letter to Berthe Morisot, June 9, 1875: Denis Rouart, *Correspondance de Berthe Morisot*, Paris, 1950, p. 84, quoted by D'Argencourt in *Puvis de Chavannes…*, *op. cit.*, p. 131.

[48] Puvis de Chavannes to Theo Van Gogh, April 28, 1890, Amsterdam, Van Gogh Museum, Vincent Van Gogh Foundation, b 1185 V/1962. Puvis asked Theo to come and see a drawing, perhaps to reproduce it. He signed "Cordially yours." Theo only sold one painting by Puvis, *The Blue Dream*, bought by Albert Wolff on November 23, 1888 (24.5 x 46.5 cm) and resold November 22, for 1800 francs to Errazuris. It is possible that in his stock were pastels and drawings that were not listed in the account books of Boussod & Valadon.

[49] *The Sacred Wood Dear to the Arts and Muses*, which Vincent had remarked is reproduced: vol. LXXXIII, May 3, 1884, no. 2149, p. 289. Undoubtedly, the young painters in Cormon's atelier had this type of reproduction when they painted their large parody.

[50] *Correspondance complète de Vincent van Gogh…*, *op. cit.*, vol. 2, letters 368 (May 1884), pp. 343 and 394, (February-March, 1885), p. 405.

[51] Paris, Musée d'Orsay, exhibited for the first time at Durand-Ruel in 1887, no. 30 of the catalog.

[52] 1887, F381, Paris, Musée d'Orsay.

[53] 1888, F431, Washington, D.C., National Gallery of Art.

[54] *Portrait of Eugène Benon*, 1882, private collection, see A. Brown Price, "Two Portraits by Vincent van Gogh and Two Portraits by Puvis de Chavannes," *The Burlington Magazine*, 117, 1975, no. 872 and R. Wattenmaker, "Vincent Van Gogh et Puvis de Chavannes," *Vie des Arts*, 26, 1981, no. 104.

[55] *Still Life with Books (Parisian Novels)*, Winter, 1887–88, F 359, Perth, The Robert Homes at Court Collection; *Vincent van Gogh*, exh. cat., Rijksmuseum Vincent van Gogh, Amsterdam, 1990, no. 29, pp. 88–89.

[56] *Portrait of Doctor Gachet*, May-June 1890, F 753, private collection; *Vincent van Gogh…*, *op. cit.*, no. 122, pp. 268–69; Brown Price, "Two Portraits…," *op. cit.*, pp. 714–17; Wattenmaker, *op. cit.*, pp. 62–66.

[57] December, 1889, *The Complete Letters of Vincent Van Gogh*, New York Graphic Society, Greenwich, Connecticut, 2nd edition, 1959, vol. 3, p. 238.

[58] Vincent Van Gogh to his brother Theo, June 1890: *The Complete Letters…*, *op. cit.*, p. 275.

[59] Vincent Van Gogh to his sister Wilhelmina, June 1890: *ibidem*, p. 471.

[60] 1895: "Les Ateliers," *Mercure de France*, February 1895, reprinted in Bernard, *Propos…*, *op. cit.*, vol. 2, pp. 194–205.

[61] E. Bernard, "Puvis de …," *op. cit.*, p. 290.

[62] E. Bernard, *Sur l'Art et sur les Maîtres*, Edition de la Douce France, Paris, 1922, reprinted in *Propos…*, vol. 2, p. 292.

[63] E. Bernard, "Le Symbolisme Pictural…," *op. cit.*, p. 290.

[64] P. Gauguin, "Exposition de La Libre Esthétique," *Essais d'Art Libre, Revue Mensuelle,* vol. V, February-October, 1894, pp. 30–32, reprinted in *Essais d'Art Libre*, Slatkine reprints, Geneva, 1971.

[65] P. Gauguin, *Avant et Après*, Editions Avant et Après, Tahiti, n.d., pp. 161–62.

[66] Gauguin published in the Album VI (1894), Puvis in the Albums IV (1893) and IX (1895); D.M. Stein and D.H. Karshan, *L'Estampe originale. A Catalogue raisonné*, The Museum of Graphic Art, New York, 1970, pp. 25 and 32.

[67] See A. and A. Bonafous-Murat, "Répertoire des Estampes Publiées dans *L'Epreuve Album d'Art*," Paris, 1991, pp. 63–86.

[68] G. Lacambre, "Sources du Japonisme au XIXe siècle," in *Le Japonisme*, exh. cat. Paris–Tokyo, 1988, pp. 28–29.

[69] Gauguin thought that at the height of his glory Puvis was a member of this prestigious institution, which was not the case. Paul Gauguin to his wife, Mette, Tahiti, early April 1893: M. Malingue, ed., *Lettres de Gauguin à sa femme et à ses amis*, Paris, 1946, (Engl. trans. H.J. Stenning, London, 1946), CXXV, p. 239.

[70] Paul Gauguin to Daniel de Monfreid, July 1898: A. Joly-Segalen, ed., *Lettres de Paul Gauguin à George-Daniel de Monfreid*, Paris, Plon, 1930, XLIV, p. 103. The exhibition would be held before the end of the year at Vollard's (see note 90).

[71] B. Dorival, "Sources of the Art of Gauguin from Java, Egypt and Ancient Greece," *The Burlington Magazine*, vol. XCIII, no. 576, March 1951, pp. 118–22; R.S. Field, "Gauguin plagiaire ou créateur," in *Gauguin*, Paris, Librairie Hachette, 1960, pp. 140–69; A. Schneider "Denken Sie immer an die Perser, die Kunst der Kambodschaner…," in *Paul Gauguin. Das verlorene Paradies*, exh. cat. Museum Folkwang, Essen, Staatliche Museen zu Berlin, 1998–99, pp. 86-101.

[72] Camille Pissarro to his son Lucien, Paris, November 23, 1893: J. Bailly-Herzberg, *Correspondance de Camille Pissarro*, vol. 3, 1891–94, Paris, 1988, 962, p. 400.

[73] A. Seguin, "Paul Gauguin," *L'Occident*, no. 16, March 1903, p. 165.

[74] Letter of Gauguin to Odilon Redon, n.d., quoted by R. Bacou, *Odilon Redon*, Pierre Cailler ed., Geneva, 1956, vol. 1, pp. 186–87.

[75] J. Gérard, "Den lilla flickan och gengangaren," in Gerda Kjellberg, *Hänt och Sant,* Stockholm, 1971, pp. 53–74; unpublished French translation, "La Petite Fille et le Tapapau," p. 5, Archives Danielsson. J. Leclercq also gives a description of the atelier in "Exposition Paul Gauguin," *Mercure de France*, vol. XIII, 61, January, 1895, p. 121.

[76] P. Gauguin, *Diverses Choses*, 1896–97, manuscript, Paris, Musée du Louvre, Département des Arts Graphiques, Fonds du Musée d'Orsay, RF 7259, folio 133 recto, p. 257.

[77] Organized by the artists of the Société Nationale des Beaux Arts, January 16, 1895, at the Hôtel Continental. Gauguin attended, as did Signac, Angrand, Pissarro, etc. Upon this occasion *La Plume* published a special issue, abundantly illustrated, no. 138, January 15, 1895, pp. 27–63.

[78] *Vase with "Hope"* or *Cleopatra Vase*, Amsterdam, Van Gogh Museum (Vincent Van Gogh Foundation), in Brown Price, *Pierre Puvis…*, *op. cit.*, no. 146, pp. 237–38.

[79] *Vairaumati tei oa,* 1892, W450, Moscow, Pushkin Museum; *Te aa no areois*, 1892, W451, New York, Museum of Modern Art, The William S. Paley Collection and *Vairaumati She Called Herself,* 1892, W450, Moscow, Pushkin Museum. See William Rubin, "Paul Gauguin, *The Seed of the Areoi* (*Te aa no areois*), 1892, (cat. 24)," in W. Rubin–M. Armstrong, *The William S. Paley Collection*, New York, The Museum of Modern Art, 1992, pp. 50–55.

[80] Oil on canvas, 76 x 66 cm, 1896, W545, São Paulo, Museu de Arte.

[81] Or *The Pirogue*, oil on canvas, 95.5 x 131.5 cm, W544, Saint Petersburg, Hermitage Museum.

[82] Oil on canvas, 109.9 x 89.5 cm, 1892, W462, New York, The Metropolitan Museum of Art, Robert Lehman Collection.

[83] Paris, Musée d'Orsay.

[84] *War*, Amiens, Musée de Picardie, was exhibited at the Salon of 1872 (see above), a smaller version was presented at the *Exposition de Peinture et Sculpture Moderne de Décoration et d'Ornement*, Musée des Arts Décoratifs, 1881, then at Durand-Ruel in 1887 with no. 49. "Monumental figures corresponding to the painting *War*, Musée d'Amiens (drawing)."

[85] *Bathing*, 1887, W215, Buenos Aires, Museo Nacional de Bellas Artes; *Woman in the Waves (Ondine)*, 1889, W336, Cleveland Museum of Art.

[86] Before this date, the larger version, in the collection of the Musée des Beaux-Arts in Lyon, was exhibited at the Salon of 1864, a variation at the Salon of 1885, and a smaller version with a variation at Durand-Ruel in 1887.

[87] Oil on canvas, 139 x 374.5 cm, 1897, W561, Boston Museum of Fine Arts.

[88] Paul Gauguin to Daniel de Monfreid, February 1898: Joly-Segalen, *op. cit.*, XXXIX, p. 91.

[89] Paul Gauguin to Charles Morice, 1898, quoted by C. Morice, *Paul Gauguin*, Paris, H. Floury éditeur, 1920, pp. 122–23.

[90] From November 17 until December 10, 1898, Vollard exhibited *Where Do We Come from?* and eight paintings related in size and subject. André Fontainas reviewed them in "Art Moderne," *Mercure de France*, January 29, 1899, pp. 235–42.

[91] Paul Gauguin to André Fontainas, Tahiti, March 1899: Malingue, *op. cit.*, CLXX, p. 289.

[92] Paul Gauguin to André Fontainas, Tahiti, August, 1899: *ibidem*, CLXXII, p. 293.

[93] August Strindberg to Paul Gauguin, February 1895: P. Gauguin, *Avant et Après*, Editions Avant et Après, Tahiti, n.d., p. 33.

[94] A. Alexandre, "Puvis de Chavannes—l'Artiste et l'Oeuvre," *Le Figaro*, Tuesday, October 25, 1898.

[95] G.-Albert Aurier, "Le Symbolisme en Peinture—Paul Gauguin," *Mercure de France*, March, 1891, p. 165.

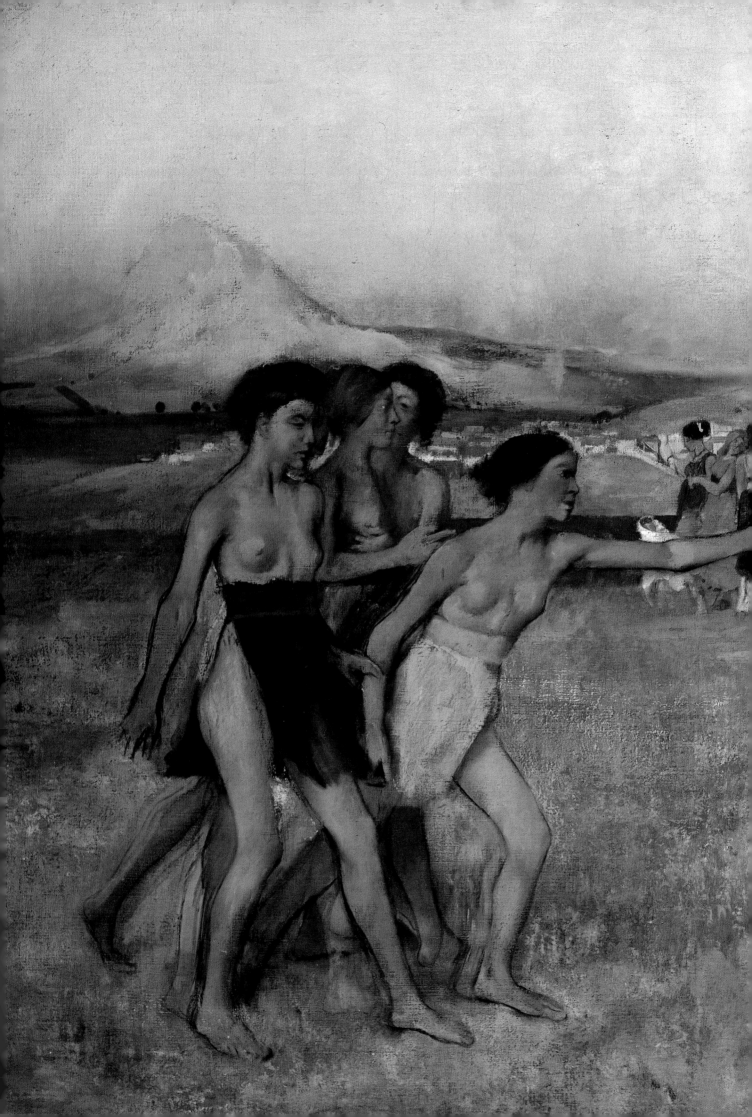

Two years before his death in 1903, just before he left Tahiti for the Marquesas Islands, Paul Gauguin painted a still-life, *Still Life with "Hope"* (1901, Chicago, Nathan Cummings Collection) in which he paid homage to three of the artists who had been his mentors.[1] The composition is dominated by a bouquet of large, heavy sunflowers, clearly an acknowledgement of his brief, turbulent friendship and collaboration with Vincent Van Gogh who had died eleven years before. On the wall behind is a photograph that Gauguin owned of Puvis de Chavannes's *Hope* (1871, Paris, Musée d'Orsay) a symbolic composition showing the figure of a naked young girl in a landscape, which Puvis had painted after France's humiliating defeat in the Franco-Prussian War. At the lower left is a less discernible image of a nude—probably a monotype—by Degas.

Gauguin is Puvis de Chavannes's most obvious heir. His Tahitian idylls with their flat, decorative style and matte, opaque surfaces demonstrate clearly the legacy of Puvis's timeless arcadias. But Gauguin was only one of a large band of artists at the *fin-de-siècle* for whom Puvis was an inspiration and a guide. The Swiss painter Ferdinand Hodler, the Norwegian Edvard Munch, many other artists in the Symbolist movement as well as the Nabis—Edouard Vuillard, Maurice Denis, Pierre Bonnard and Félix Vallotton—all found in Puvis de Chavannes's mural paintings a model for their own ambitions to create a new kind of monumental, decorative painting which could express the universal truths that they felt had been excluded from the more earthbound repertory of the Realists and then the Impressionists.

By the 1890s, Puvis de Chavannes had attained a unique position. At first critics had been puzzled by his style, which was clearly grounded in past traditions yet, at the same time, too original to be fitted into a school, but after 1859, his works began to be appreciated and appeared regularly at the Salon. The way Puvis could fuse a traditional classicism with a peculiarly modern vision eventually earned him the respect not only of the official art world but also a whole generation of younger artists, who could readily identify with this older artist who, like them, had endured the hostility of the establishment but who, when eventually honored by it, did not sacrifice his individuality. Puvis was, in fact, unusual among more academic artists for his friendships with a wide range of younger, avant-garde artists and for his willingness to be exhibited alongside them.

The enormous respect and admiration in which Puvis de Chavannes was held at the end of the century is demonstrated by the lavish banquet arranged to honor his seventieth birthday by the magazine *La Plume*. Rodin was the principal organizer, Renoir and Monet were on the committee, and Zola, Gauguin, between his two visits to the South Seas, Signac, Boudin, Bourdelle were among the 550 distinguished guests from the worlds of art, music and literature who sat down to the splendid banquet at the Hôtel Continental on January 16, 1895. Curiously, though, no record of Degas's presence has come to light.

There is no question, however, that Edgar Degas admired Puvis de Chavannes. It is true that, in his typical caustic style, he had poked fun at Léon Bonnat's bombastic portrait of Puvis shown at the 1882 Salon: "Chavannes, noble, a bit of a rehash, has the bad taste to show himself perfectly dressed and proud, in a large portrait of himself, done by Bonnat, with a fat dedication in the sand where he and a massive table, with a glass of water are posing (style Goncourt)."[2]
However, on a more serious level, he is known to have had a profound respect for Puvis, but for different reasons than his contemporaries among the Symbolists and the Nabis. For Degas, the arcane world of dreams in which the Symbolists sought escape was an anathema.
Throughout his mature career, Degas was entirely a realist, basing his art on the most acute observation of what he saw around him. Yet his art was rooted in the traditions of a classical past and even in his most modern subjects, there is always an underlying sense of classical equilibrium. He surely admired the way that Puvis de Chavannes's dreamscapes were based on tradition but not shackled by its academicism.

1. Edgar Degas, *Young Spartans Exercising*, detail, 1860–62. London, National Gallery

2, 3. Pierre Puvis de Chavannes,
Studies of Nudes,
Paris, private collection

The relationship between Degas and Puvis de Chavannes is difficult to assess. Probably they knew each other well, but from the scraps of evidence that exist we can, at best, piece together only a fragmentary collage of their connections. The known facts can be quickly sketched in. Puvis was ten years Degas's senior, and both artists came from the same *haut-bourgeois* background and this must have provided a certain common ground. They shared the conservatism and patriotism typical of their class, qualities that found their most unappealing manifestation in the anti-Semitism that both displayed at the time of the Dreyfus Affair in the 1890s. They had probably first got to know each other in the 1870s in the circle that revolved around the talented Morisot girls, the well-known Impressionist Berthe and her two painter sisters, Yves and Edma, daughters of a distinguished civil servant Tiburce Morisot.

Among the guests who were regularly entertained in their charming bohemian house with its garden studio in the Rue Franklin were Manet, whose brother Eugène married Berthe, Corot and Fantin-Latour. A brief note written by Manet to Degas inviting him to a dinner with "the Stevenses and the Puvis de Chavannes" suggests frequent social contact within this circle.[3] Other details from this fragmentary history of contacts between Puvis and Degas that are worth recording include the fact that Degas and Puvis were both present at the landmark first exhibition of Cézanne's work given by Ambroise Vollard in 1895. And Félix Fénéon recorded Chavannes's and Degas's presence at a soirée at the studio of the painter Henri Gervex in the 1890s.[4]

Puvis and Degas sometimes shared the same models. Emma Dobigny, whom Degas painted on a number of occasions, notably in *Sulking* (c. 1869–71, New York, Metropolitan Museum of Art), and who also posed for Corot, was the model for Puvis de Chavannes's *Hope* (1870, Paris, Musée d'Orsay). Another of Puvis's models, the artist Suzanne Valadon, was a close friend of Degas who admired her drawings and referred to her affectionately "la terrible Maria." Valadon was an habituée of Montmartre, the bohemian, artistic quarter of Paris where Degas lived on the Rue Victor Massé in a large three-story apartment building, only a stone's throw from Puvis's studio on the Place Pigalle. Here, Puvis held a sort of open house welcoming artists of many kinds. Since Degas, it seems, was not the total recluse, as has traditionally been thought, he also received a number of visitors in his studio, and it is more than likely that in this artistic *va-et-vient* Degas and Puvis must have called on each other from time to time.[5]

Another link between the two artists was through Paul Durand-Ruel, the Impressionists' principal champion and Degas's dealer. Durand-Ruel was also a long-time supporter of Puvis de Chavannes, buying his work since 1873, commissioning a number of smaller replicas of his mural compositions and giving him his first one-man exhibition in 1887. In the same year, Durand-Ruel showed works by Puvis together with the Impressionists. In1893, we find Puvis de Chavannes and Degas as joint witnesses at the successive weddings of the dealer's two daughters, in May and September.[6]

The 1890s when Degas, to judge from the incidental facts recorded above, seems to have encountered Puvis de Chavannes quite regularly, were also the years when he was building up his remarkable collection of works by Ingres, Delacroix, Corot, Daumier, Gauguin and others. Surprisingly, perhaps, he owned only two modest works by Puvis de Chavannes, both studies of the female nude in black chalk, squared in the academic manner, one of which hung in his bedroom.[7] Degas possessed both these drawings before 1887 since he lent them to the retrospective exhibition of Puvis's work held at Durand-Ruel in that year. According to Degas's biographer and the author of the catalogue raisonné Paul-André Lemoisne, Puvis owned a work by Degas, a version of the striking charcoal and pastel figure of a woman gazing through field glasses.[8] Probably, as has been suggested, these works were an exchange between the two artists.[9] One wonders why Degas did not acquire more substantial works by Puvis, the small-scale replicas of the mural compositions that were on sale at the 1887 exhibition for example, but no explanation for this lacuna has come to light.

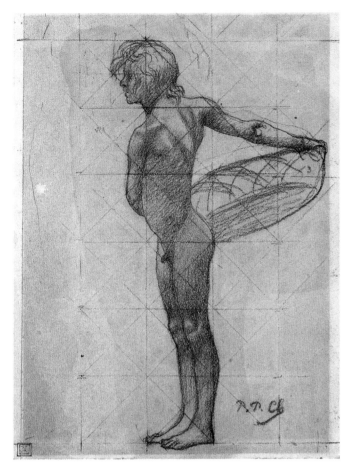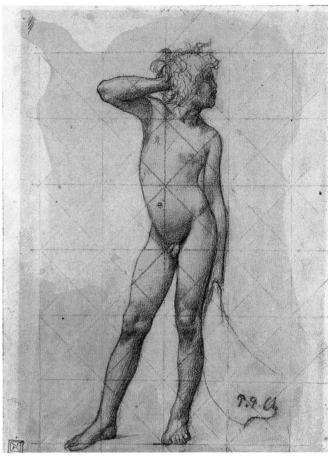

In terms of their artistic formation, Degas and Puvis had much in common. Both were virtually self-taught. For both youthful travels in Italy were an important part of their early formation and they shared an enthusiasm for the great fresco cycles of Giotto and Piero della Francesca.

Puvis visited Italy in 1847 and returned to spend a year there in 1848, a few years before Degas's extensive travels in the late 1850s. Puvis studied momentarily under Thomas Couture and then Delacroix, claiming to have learned little from either. It was the work of Théodore Chassériau, to which he was particularly responsive between 1854 and 1858, that proved far more valuable, especially in teaching him to reconcile Ingres's line with Delacroix's color. Degas shared a passion for these two opposing giants of the earlier nineteenth century. From his earliest work one sees him perfecting Ingres's purity of line—in the preparatory drawings of *Sémiramis Building a City* (c. 1860–62, Paris, Musée d'Orsay) for example—and experimenting with Delacroix's sonorous palette—in *The Daughter of Jephthah* (c. 1869–61, Northampton, Massachusetts, Smith College Museum of Art). Degas studied briefly under the academic painter Louis Lamothe, a pupil of Ingres; this was followed by a brief stint at the Ecole des Beaux-Arts. But, like Puvis, his real training came from studying the great masters of the past in the Louvre and during the years he spent in Italy.

For both Degas and Puvis, the academic practice of drawing was an essential part of the creative process of making art. Puvis always adhered to the practice of making preparatory drawings for paintings, sometimes framing and displaying them separately. Degas was a prodigious draftsman and drawing was always fundamental to his creative process. Even after he had abandoned academic subjects, he continued to conceive even his most assertively modern subjects in a traditional, academic way, exploring pose and gesture in preparatory drawings which would then reappear, often years later, in a different work. It is this that separates Degas from a number of his Impressionist colleagues—Monet and Sisley, for example—who completely rejected academic methods in favor of working *alla prima*.

The four major history paintings with which Degas made his debut—*The Daughter of Jephthah* (c. 1859–61, Northampton, Massachusetts, Smith College Museum of Art), *Sémiramis Building Babylon* (c. 1860–62, Paris, Musée d'Orsay), *Young Spartans Exercising* (c. 1860–62, London, National Gallery), *Scene of War in the Middle Ages* (c. 1863–65, Paris, Musée d'Orsay)—are a masterful display of his early visual erudition. And each, in a different way, evokes a connection with Puvis. Although it must be stressed that this is not simply a matter of influence so much as evidence of certain parallel and reciprocal aims that the two artists shared. After all, Puvis was only developing his own mature style in the early 1860s.

Degas especially admired Puvis's instinct for placing figures in a composition.[10] Much of the force of Puvis's gift for theatrical narrative—his compositions unfold like the action on a stage—derives from his innate sense of the placing of figures within a space. Degas's four early paintings share this highly developed sense of *mise-en-scène*—the placing of the figures in the compositional framework that is as precisely articulated as in a landscape by Poussin. Degas's innate sense of choreographic placement is evident in the dramatic composition of *The Daughter of Jephthah* even though this work is more obviously indebted to Delacroix's turbulent narratives. *Young Spartans Exercising* exemplifies Degas's Neoclassical interests which can be compared not only to Puvis, but also to David's austere compositional confrontations. *Scene of War in the Middle Ages* was met with silent incomprehension when it was exhibited at the Salon of 1865, probably because of its strange subject. According to Lemoisne, however, Puvis particularly complimented Degas on it.[11] Both artists were wrestling with the problem of giving the long-established genre of history painting a new relevance for the mid-nineteenth century. Probably he responded to the modernity of its strange, dislocated mood and the way in which the odd placement of its anguished figures worked both with and against traditional conventions. Four years before Puvis himself had painted his *War* (1861, Amiens, Musée de Picardie), a work in which one can sense a strong affinity with Degas's painting not only in the subject but also in the tight group-

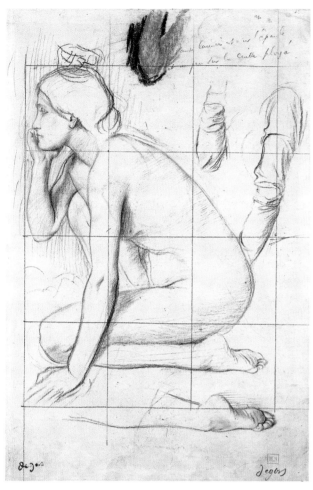

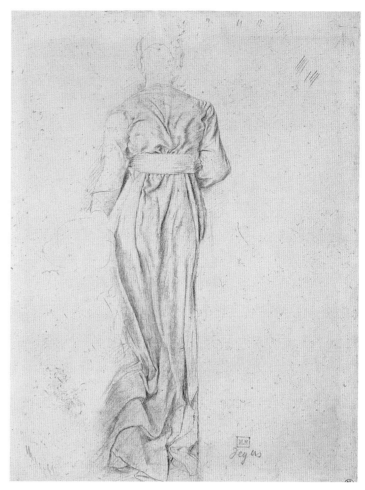

4. Pierre Puvis de Chavannes,
Study of Crouching Female Nude
for "Sémiramis," 1860–62.
Paris, Musée du Louvre,
Cabinet des Dessins

5. Pierre Puvis de Chavannes,
Study of Standing Female Nude
for "Sémiramis," 1860–62.
Paris, Musée du Louvre,
Cabinet des Dessins

6. Edgar Degas, *Young Spartans Exercising*, 1860–62. London, National Gallery

ing of the figures dispersed throughout the dun-colored landscape. However, the work that seems closest in spirit to Puvis is *Sémiramis.* Of all the early history paintings, it is the one that in its matte surface most closely resembles the effect of fresco that Puvis sought in his decorations. Its vaguely Middle-Eastern exoticism is indebted to Degas's friend and mentor from his early years in Rome in the 1850s, Gustave Moreau, who himself shared many of Puvis's aims. Inspired by Rossini's opera of the same title, it exudes a theatrical aura of enchantment. This together with the archaic amplitude that unfolds through the frieze-like format—redolent of the reliefs of antiquity—evoke Puvis's dream-like idylls.

Both Puvis and Degas loved the opera. Degas had a particular admiration for the *diva* Rose Caron and in 1885 attended nearly all the performances of the opera *Sigurd* in which she took the lead role. Back in his studio, he would apparently hum Rose Caron's arias and imitate her slow, majestic gestures.[12] He made a number of drawings of the opera and explained in a letter to his friend Bartholomé: "Divine Mme Caron, I compared her, speaking to her in person with the figures [in the paintings of] Puvis de Chavannes, which were unknown to her. The rhythm, the rhythm. . . ."[13]

Degas's respect for Puvis's sure sense of compositional design stayed with him throughout his career. As he moved away from history painting at the end of the 1860s, rejecting the seductive illusions of permanence in favor of the absolutely here-and-now, he adjusted his technique and his composition to accommodate his new program of modern life subjects. Although he now drew from a range of different sources—the compositional formats of popular caricature and Japanese prints, for example—to heighten the immediacy of his vignettes of backstage life at the opera or the corner of a café-concert, which he captured with such vivid acuity, it is perhaps not farfetched to suggest that in his highly developed

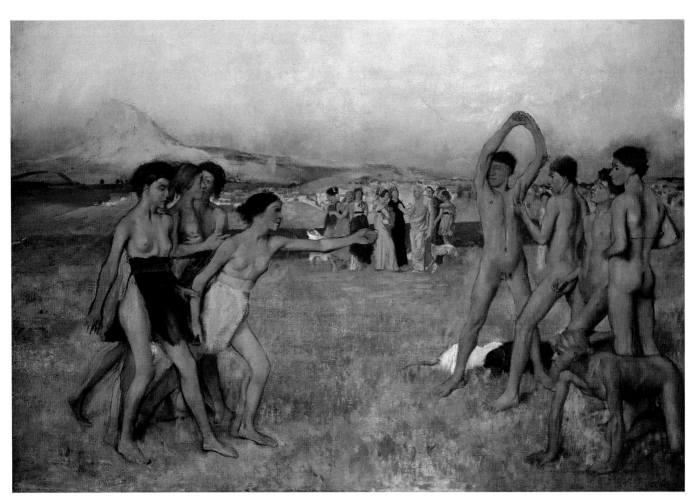

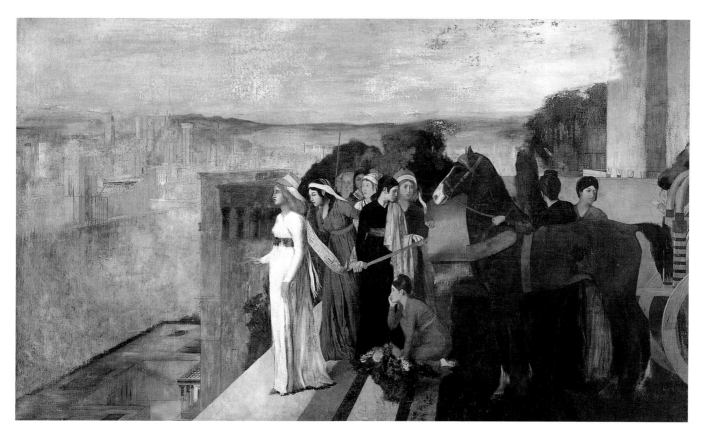

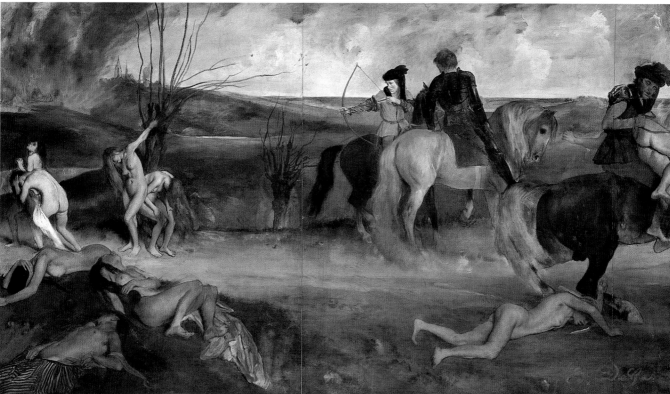

7. Pierre Puvis de Chavannes,
Sémiramis Building Babylon,
1860–62.
Paris, Musée d'Orsay

8. Pierre Puvis de Chavannes,
Scene of War in the Middle Ages,
1863–65.
Paris, Musée d'Orsay

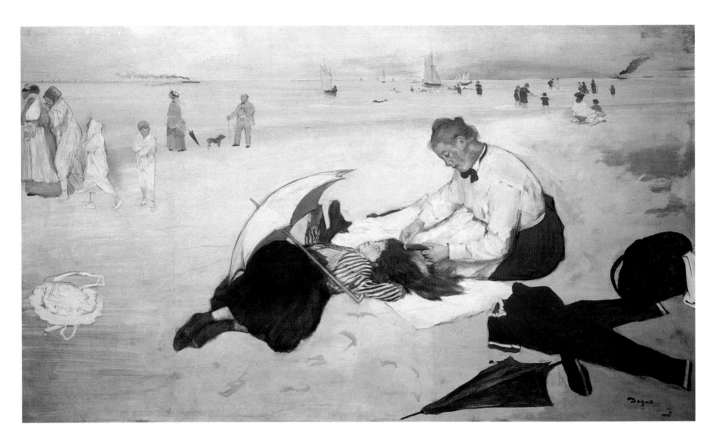

9. Edgar Degas, *On the Shore of the Beach,* 1869. Paris, Musée du Louvre, Cabinet des Dessins

sense of design, his unerring instinct for the *mise-en-page*, there lingers more than a residue of his admiration for the classical structure of Puvis's compositions. Equally pervasive, perhaps, was the example of Puvis's classical pose and gesture, which underlies Degas's work in unexpected ways. Degas's obsession with the rendering of movement undoubtedly lay behind his fascination with the dance. Once when asked why he painted dancers so much, he replied, rather enigmatically, that they reminded him of the movements of the ancient Greeks. In his sense of the composure and interval of classical movement, one can find a connection not only with Puvis de Chavannes but also with that great seventeenth-century exemplar of the theatrical sense of gesture and *mise-en-scène*—Nicolas Poussin—who was the subject of a widespread vogue in the late nineteenth century and whom Degas admired, being especially interested in the way he experimented with the placement of his figures by using small wax figurines.

In terms of subject matter, however, there was little correspondence between Degas and Puvis during the 1870s and 1880s, save for one exception. There is a striking affinity between Degas's *Women Combing Their Hair* of c. 1875 (Washington, D.C., Phillips Collection) and Puvis's *Young Women by the Sea* that was shown at the Salon of 1879. Although Degas's work precedes Puvis's, it seems, in many respects, an updated version of Puvis's classicizing seashore idyll. The classical tunics have been replaced by more contemporary shifts and the figures are less statuesque. But there is nevertheless an obvious similarity in the composition—three female figures in a landscape, the hairstyles, and the curiously detached mood. Could Puvis have seen the work in Degas's studio or in the home of the collector Henri Lerolle who bought the painting in 1878? We do not know. There is no doubt that the theme of a woman grooming her long, luxuriant tresses was popular with many artists in the late nineteenth century and it amounted to an obsession with Degas. It is the subject of numerous works from his most intimate monotypes and lithographs to the powerful charcoal drawings and pastels that are a striking aspect of his late work.

Degas is exceptionally renowned for his experimental approach to technique. Puvis too

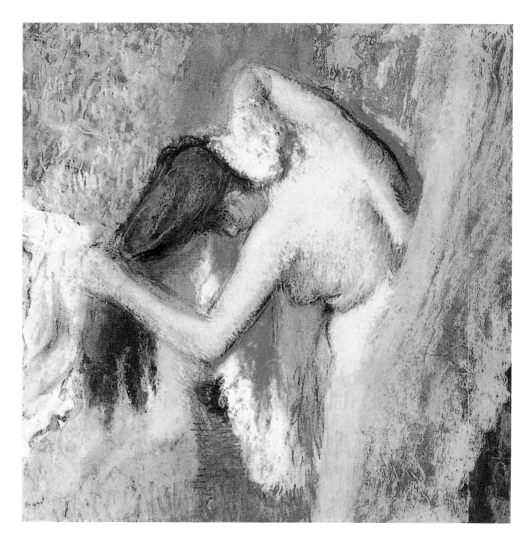

10. Edgar Degas, *Woman Drying Her Hair,* 1903. Chicago, The Art Institute

11. Edgar Degas, *After the Bath. Woman Drying Her Neck,* 1898. Paris, Musée d'Orsay

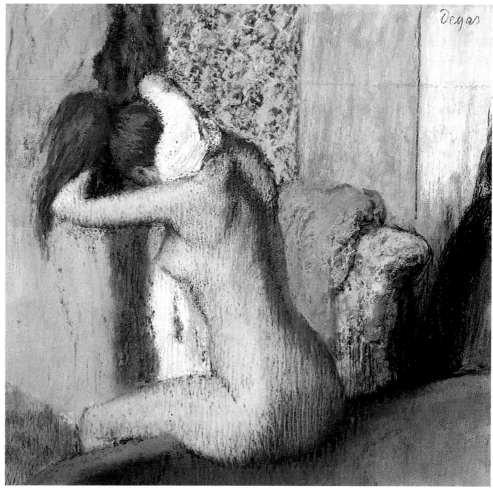

was a persistent experimenter. He evolved a technique of mixing oil paint with wax to emulate the matte textures of fifteenth-century frescoes. Both artists were preoccupied with the techniques of the Old Masters, especially the Venetian painters of the Renaissance, studying their method of achieving rich color through glazing successive layers of paint. Degas adapted this technique to his work in pastel as well as in oil. After 1880, both Degas and Puvis began to use pastel more than previously. But for Puvis pastel always remained secondary to oil paint, and never the primary medium that it became for Degas who succeeded in investing this traditionally somewhat genteel medium with a new expressive vigor. Both Degas and Puvis were experimental in their drawing techniques. Like Degas, Puvis regularly used tracing paper to transfer an image from paper to canvas, and would sometimes glue extra strips to a sheet he was working on as a drawing evolved and expanded.

Although drawing from the model remained fundamental to both Puvis and Degas, they both also believed in the distancing power of memory. Much of the dreamy poetry of Puvis's compositions derives from their being "recollected in tranquillity" rather than directly observed. Although the starting point for Degas was always observation—the works themselves were produced in the studio, a final fusion of sketches made on the spot, motifs preserved in earlier works that Degas kept in his studio, and memory.

One unexpected way in which memory functioned for both Puvis and Degas is worth mentioning, and that is their approach to landscape. Landscape was never a major part of Degas's output, but from 1890 to 1892 he produced a remarkable group of poetic, virtually abstract landscapes in color monotype, sometimes heightened with pastel, that were inspired by a vague recollection of the countryside seen from a moving train while on holiday in Burgundy in the autumn of 1890. By a curious analogy we learn that the melancholic, quiet-toned landscapes in which Puvis's classicizing idylls unfold are based on his recollections of the flat plains of Picardy which he had absorbed on several train journeys across that region.

Finally, in a group of late pastels in which Degas explores the theme of the figure in the landscape, one wonders if Degas was not thinking of Puvis. Although it is true that in taking on this challenging subject, Degas was part of a larger late nineteenth-century trend, which also embraced Renoir and Cézanne, of artists seeking to situate themselves in the classical tradition. But perhaps the note of displacement combined with sensuousness that infuses Puvis's remote Arcadias is also present in Degas's detached observations of women bathing.

The connections between Puvis de Chavannes and Degas, both as friends and as artists, remain fragmentary and elusive. The differences between them were great. Puvis never explored subjects outside the archaic realm he created, while Degas was exclusively concerned with the contemporary for much of his career. Yet, as this short study has attempted to demonstrate, there was clearly a profound reciprocity between the two artists. This is to be found not so much in the detail of a composition or a motif but more broadly in their shared reinvention of the classical tradition in a modern idiom. Perhaps it was Van Gogh who best put his finger on this paradox. On seeing Puvis's *Inter Artes et Naturam*, at the 1890 Salon he admired its "strange and happy meeting of far distant antiquities and the crude modern age."[14]

Research compiled by Emilie Augier

[15] G. Wildenstein, ed., *Gauguin, sa vie, son oeuvre*, Paris, 1958, no. 604.

[16] "Chavannes, noble, un peu resucé, a le tort de se montrer parfaitement mis et fier dans un grand portrait de lui qu'a fait Bonnat, avec grosse dédicace sur le sable où lui et une table massive, avec un verre d'eau *posent* (style Goncourt)." *Lettres de Degas,* recueillies et annotées par Marcel Guérin, Paris, 1945, no. XXXIII, p. 62. *Letters of Degas*, Marcel Guérin, ed. and trans. by Marguerite Kay, Oxford, 1947, no. 42, p. 65.

[17] See *Degas*, exh. cat., Galeries Nationales du Grand Palais, Paris, Musée des Beaux-Arts du Canada, Ottawa, The Metropolitan Museum of Art, New York, 1988–89, p. 140.

[18] "Souvenirs sur Manet," in F. Fénéon, *Oeuvres plus que complètes*, J.U. Halperin ed., Geneva-Paris, 1970, p. 377.

[19] See R. Kendall, "37 rue Victor Massé, *Degas's Last Decades*," in *Degas Beyond Impressionism*, exh. cat., National Gallery, London, and Art Institute of Chicago, Chicago, 1996–97, p. 14.

[20] *Degas, op. cit.*, p. 488.

[21] *Catalogue des tableaux moderns et anciens, aquarelles, pastels, et dessins composant la collection Edgar Degas*, Paris, Galerie Georges Petit, March 26–27, 1918, nos. 236 and 237.

[22] P.-A. Lemoisne, *Degas, L'Art de Notre Temps*, 1912, p. 64. The work is now in a Swiss private collection, see also P.-A. Lemoisne, *Degas et son oeuvre*, 4 vols. [1946–49], no. 269.

[23] See *Puvis de Chavannes and the Modern Tradition*, exh. cat. Art Gallery of Ontario, Toronto, 1975, p. xxi.

[24] See P. Bade, *Degas*, London, 1991, p. 10. I am indebted to Patrick Bade for a number of suggestions made in connection with this essay.

[25] See H. Loyrette in *Degas,* 1988–89, p. 107.

[26] H. Loyrette, *Degas*, 1990, p. 547.

[27] *Letters of Degas*, 1947, no. 93, pp. 107-08. *Lettres de Degas*, 1945, no. LXXXIV, p. 108.

[28] Letter from Vincent Van Gogh to the Dutch painter Joseph Isaacson, 25 May, 1890, in *The Letters of Vincent Van Gogh*, ed. Ronald de Leeuw, trans. Arnold Pomerans, London, 1996, p. 489.

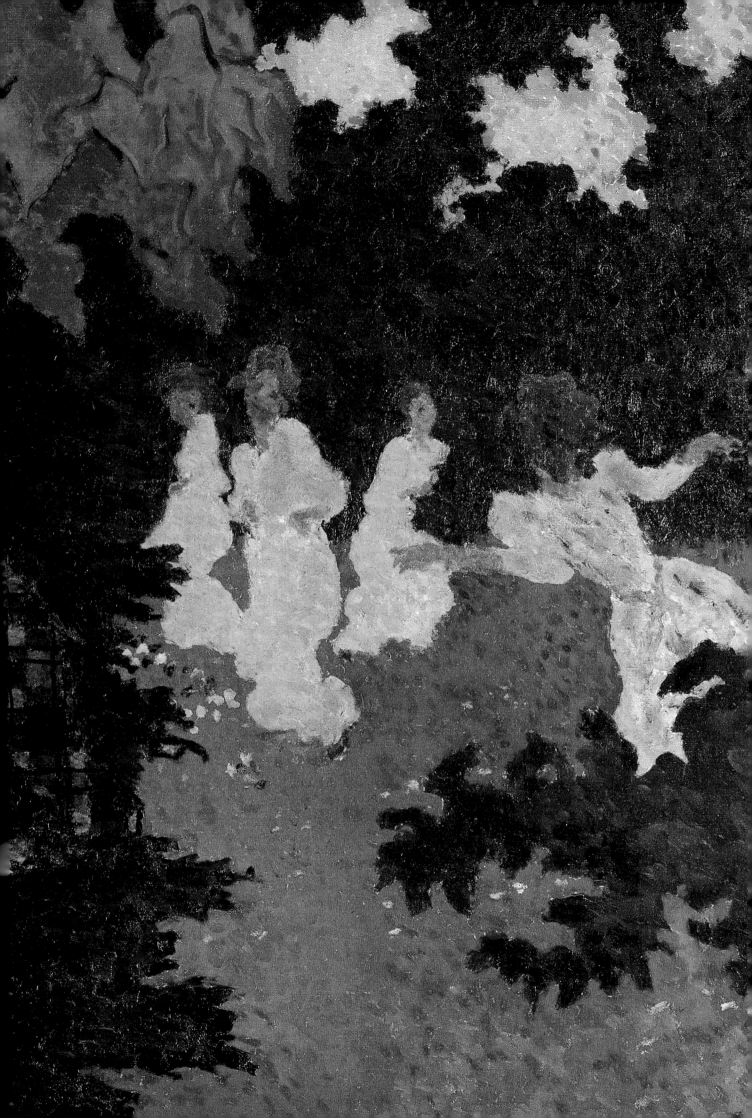

We are used to placing the Nabi movement under the aegis of Gauguin, so to say its official patron. According to Maurice Denis, who is our main witness, it was when Sérusier returned from Pont-Aven in October 1888 and showed his young friends at the Académie Julian the landscape he had painted there under Gauguin's guidance, later bequeathed to Denis and titled *The Talisman* (Paris, Musée d'Orsay), that the group was founded.[1] That story and even the title given to that small painting are probably in part fantasy: Gauguin's influence did not appear in Denis's work until the exhibition of the latter's works at the Café Volpini at the time of the 1889 World Fair, and became particularly conspicuous in 1890 (*Sun Spots on the Terrace*, October 1890, Paris, Musée d'Orsay). Later on, Denis himself would acknowledge Cézanne's supremacy. But on looking at his works, Puvis is really the one who should be placed in the foreground from the very beginning, for Denis much before Gauguin.

Denis

Indeed we should start with Denis: the theorist of the group along with Sérusier, and the author of what we can be considered its manifesto, the article titled "Definition of neo-traditionism" that appeared in August 1890 in the review *Art et Critique*.[2] At that date, Gauguin was mentioned of course, as was Puvis: *The Poor Fisherman* (1881) is cited in the second chapter, his nudes praised in the thirteenth, and the twentieth presents a vibrant tribute to the decoration of the Sorbonne hemicycle (*Letters, Sciences and Arts*, completed in 1889), whose formal organization Denis extolled, much to our enlightenment, over and above the iconography: "And the intensity of our emotion springs from the adequacy of those lines and those colors to provide their own justification, as merely beautiful and divine in their beauty." Here for the first time we have a purely formalist approach to Puvis's work, which helps explain its immediate integration in the Nabi aesthetics, as defined elsewhere by Gauguin's painting (partitioning, flat tints, bright colors, rejection of realism). For Denis, however, we should go back to the year 1887. He was only 17, and yet he already believed in his vocation as a Christian painter, dating back in particular to his contemplation of the *Crowning of the Virgin* by Fra Angelico in the Louvre (*Diary*, August 20, 1885). On December 18, 1887, his visit to the Galerie Durand-Ruel was no less a revelation, and confirmed his first one: "I found the decorative, tranquil and simple appearance of these paintings very beautiful: admirable mural color: there are wonderful harmonies of pale tones. . . . The measured, large, ethereal composition amazes me: it must be prodigiously learned. It is probably what produces that sweet, mysterious impression on the soul that calms and elevates. . . . Puvis reminded me of Flandrin, of Botticelli, of Angelico: he also reminded me of my bygone dreams." (*Diary*, December 18, 1887).[3] A painting at once decorative and expressive: the very principles of the Nabis' painting. Denis was to sum up their endeavors in 1895, when the group was about to dissolve: "In their works they preferred to seek expression through decoration, the harmony of forms and colors, and the material employed, rather than through the subject. They believed that every emotion, every human thought, had a plastic, decorative equivalent, a corresponding beauty."[4] And indeed they owed that to Puvis, "all the more expressive than he is ornamental," as another text of the same year claimed.[5]

That revelation of Puvis can be easily detected in several of Denis's early works which verge on the pastiche, such as the peculiar *Homer Walking in the Countryside*, that was certainly prior to his discovery of Gauguin, and that borrows the motifs, the verticality, and even the colors of Puvis's *Prodigal Son* (1879, exhibited at the Durand-Ruel gallery in 1887) and his *Childhood of Saint Genevieve* in the Panthéon decoration (1878); and, in August 1889—that is, this time after his discovery of Gauguin—in that portrait of the musician Raphaël Lemeunier that nearly caricatures the tendency to associate a tree trunk with the human figure, insisting on verticality and planarity, and to have the latter lean on the former on the left, like the sleeping figure in *The Dream* by Puvis (1883, shown at Durand-Ruel in 1887), and in front of the same bare landscape closed on the horizon by the undulating hills behind the parallel planes.[6]

But as soon as Gauguin's mark was truly imposed, and Denis's own themes took over in his painting, the assimilation grew deeper, without becoming an obstacle to his most personal expression, as can be seen in the years 1892–94 which were probably the height of the painter's Nabi period. The *Procession under the Trees* of 1892 (private collection) or the *Landscape with Green Trees* of 1893 are like an archetype; the association of the human figure with the tree trunks directly derives from Puvis and is found in all the painters of the group at the time. But, in the first, the procession of the communicants (or duplicated brides) with the kneeling nuns, and, in the second, the same procession and the angel greeting the only "elect" in the world of "hereafter" or "fulfillment" (that of Marthe, Denis's young bride) are as telling of the artist's deep faith as of his belief in the necessity of a "sanctification of nature," according to the definition he gave to art in his essay of 1890. More than a tribute to the Titian of *Sacred and Profane Love*, the *Nude with Bouquet of Violets* of 1894 is a quotation of the nude version of Puvis's *Hope* (1872), which it appears to match (Denis will again mention it in 1939 as "the loveliest image of the soul longing for a bliss that is not of this world"[7]). It is content to borrow its decorative frontality, raised horizon and the pose of the main figure, while ignoring the allegory completely, replacing it with the entirely personal elements of that portrait of Marthe: The beloved is in her "Florentine" closed garden, where her husband, a knight galloping along the path in the background, is about to rejoin her. In 1892, the famous panel *April*, with its zigzag cutout, obviously based on the decorative scheme of the *Poor Fisherman*, creates a sort of "positive" reverse image of it (by its left-to-right reading, its color, and the optimistic theme of that procession of youthful maying gatherers on their way to a life of bliss). The pairs of young girls that are so typical of Denis (often countless variations of Marthe and her sister Eva) can only refer to the two figures on the right of Puvis de Chavannes's *Death and the Young Maidens* (1872), here in a less gloomy version, despite the same descending pattern.

There are numerous other examples from the same period. Like most of his peers, Denis obviously yielded to the fascination of the *Young Women by the Sea* (1879, shown in 1887 at Durand-Ruel and in 1889 at the *Centennale de l'art français*). His famous 1891 *Trinitarian Evening* certainly betrays its influence, as do his 1892 *Triple Portrait of His Fiancée Marthe* (Saint-German-en-Laye, Musée Maurice Denis) and *The Orchard of the Wise Virgins* of 1893, in the pleating of the white dress in the foreground; and even more so his large *Portrait of Yvonne Lerolle in Three Poses* in 1897, with its gradual unfolding in space of the different moments in a day or in a lifetime. In 1893, his *Saintly Women at the Tombs* returns to those symmetrical layouts, those facing figures and sequences of parallel planes that we can find for instance in Puvis's *The Spring* toward 1869 (however the work had apparently not yet been exhibited) or in *The Sacred Wood Dear to the Arts and Muses* (the raised arms of the figures on the left) on the staircase in Lyon (installed in 1884, but whose reduced version currently at the Chicago Art Institute, may have been shown at the 1889 World Fair).

However, the painting that most epitomizes Puvis's presence is certainly one of Denis's most ambitious ones of that period: *The Muses* of 1893. It is a reference and a tribute both to the Sorbonne hemicycle glorified in his 1890 article and to the *Sacred Wood* in Lyon: it avails of a single motif—that of female figures dialoguing with the tree trunks of a forest—its decorative character emphasized by the carpet-like design of the leaves on the ground. Yet it was all the while a highly intimate work; Marthe's figure is tripled in the foreground, an incarnation of the "Holy Trinity" of Art, Love and Religion that underlies Denis's work and reflection. The artist's unique, true "muse," is again multiplied by her strolling sisters to the "tenth muse" in the center background who rests against a transparent sky (indeed the ten female figures reject and belie a mere allegorical illustration of mythology).

From then on Puvis would never leave Denis's side, and would easily merge through a general process of assimilation inherent to him, with others who would subsequently enrich Denis's painting: Gauguin, Cézanne, Raphael, Ingres, Renoir, Delacroix, Corot. . . His name appears regularly in the *Diary,* and Denis would always seize the opportunity for a visit and a careful examination of his work. In 1896, he claimed him as one of the founders of the revival of the Byzantine spirit in Christian art ("by restituting to painting, with their daring and genius, the logic of its essential rules, they brought the Christian tradition back to life"[8]). After the turning point of 1898, when he discovered Raphael's works in Rome,

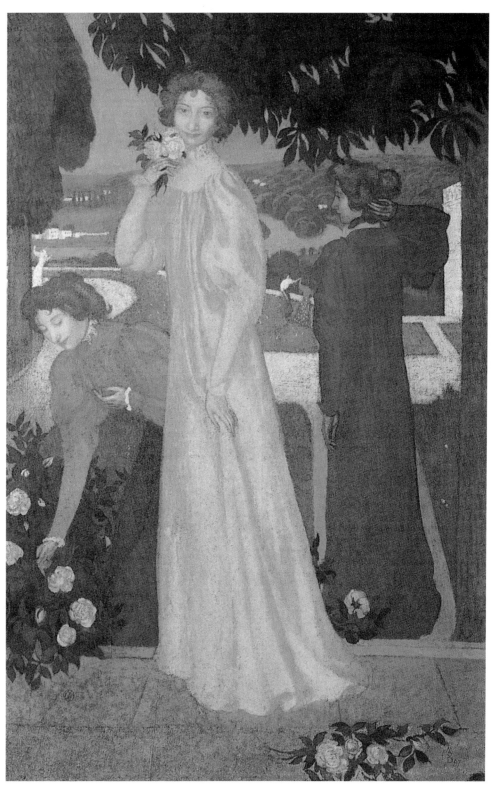

2. Maurice Denis, *Portrait of Yvonne
Lerolle in Three Poses*, 1897.
Private collection

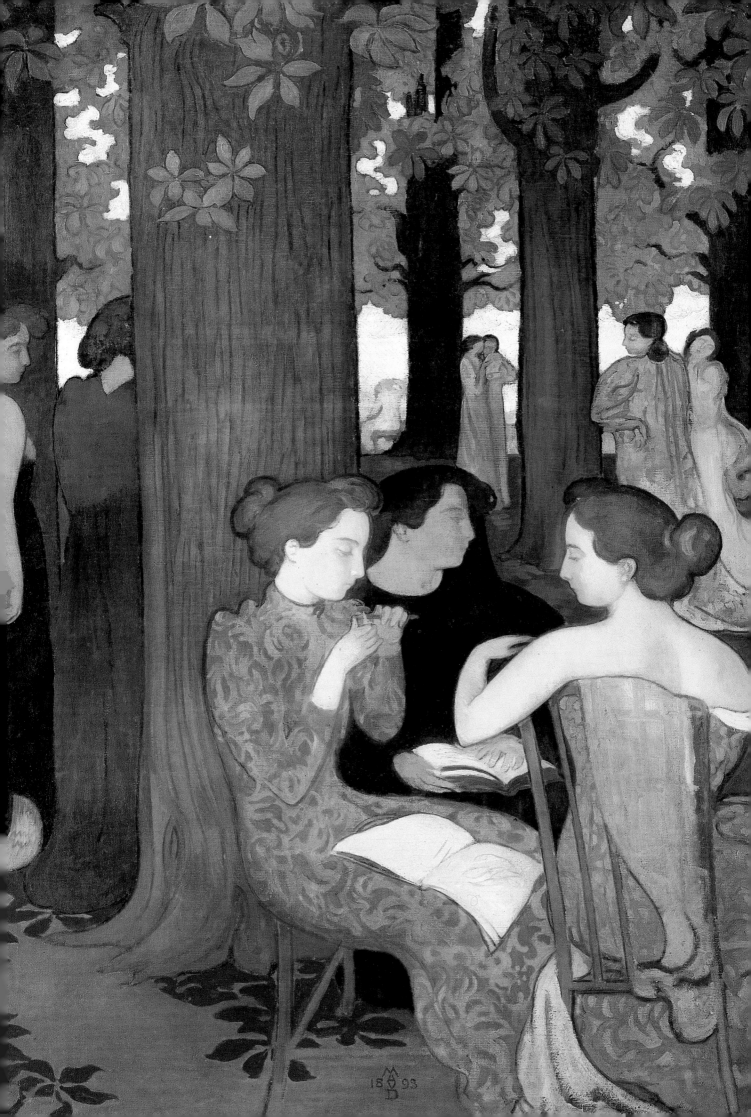

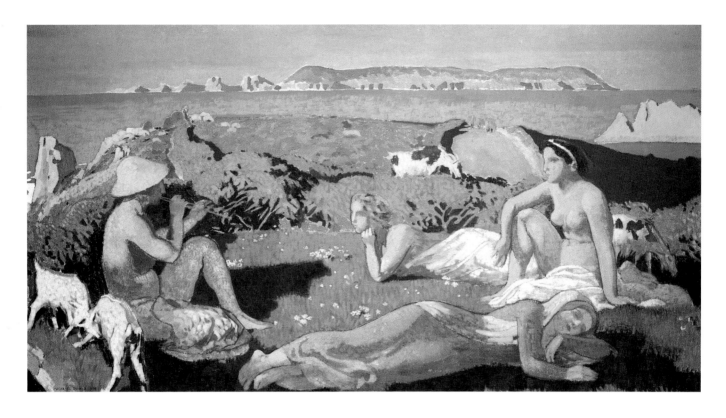

4. Maurice Denis, *The Shepherds*,
1909. Moscow, Pushkin Museum

he looked once again to Puvis among the moderns: a fine quotation of his opens the chapter "Classical Art" in the article that sums up the principles of this new theoretic approach: "I am convinced that the best-ordered composition is at the same time the most beautiful. I love order because I have a passionate love of clarity."[9]

The nudes of that same year, which have perhaps been too exclusively compared to Italian models, are also indebted to Puvis de Chavannes. This is the case of his important panel of 1898, *Women with Lilacs* (Neuss, Clemens-Sels Museum), a reference to the composition of the Boston *Virgil* (shown in Paris in 1896 at the Salon du Champ-de-Mars), introducing the nude in front and rear view as in *Autumn* of 1864, that Denis might have seen in 1889 at the *Centennale de l'art français*. Likewise *The Monotonous Orchard* of the same year, so akin to Vuillard's *Public Gardens* (1894), depended like them on the *Sacred Wood*. The following year Denis attended the new Puvis exhibition at the Galerie Durand-Ruel, that inspired new resolutions in his *Diary* (March 1899): "Exhibition of sketches by Puvis de Chavannes—You should not proceed by trial and error on a large surface: decide, specify the main lines and color schemes. Great importance of the melodic line in the decoration. Find it, sure and pure, and stick to it unreservedly." In December 1900, he lingered in front of the Puvis of Amiens (1861–82), then in front of the *Inter Artes et Naturam* of Rouen (1890): "Such ideas, such female forms! Such a clear imagination!" His large religious painting *Let the Children Come to Me* reflects (more immediately visible in the sketches), in its rigorous geometric composition on a square format, a desire for order and greatness which, from the parallel planes to the closing of the background, owes a great deal to Puvis's murals in general and specifically to the one in the Musée de Rouen, shown at the Salon of 1890.

It was at that time that Denis first undertook his own decorations, after the cycle of *The Legend of Saint Hubert*, the 1897 canvas panels, had already largely availed of the Puvis-esque model.[10] But his easel paintings present the same features. The 1900 *Badminton Game* (also called *Sacred Grove!*) (Paris, Musée d'Orsay) is a direct tribute to the central panel of Lyon and to the *Ludus pro Patria* of Amiens (1882), just as does *Figures in a Spring Landscape* of 1892, presently at the Hermitage Museum (again *The Sacred Grove*, the title given this time by the collector Shchukin, the buyer of one of the sketches of *Poor Fisherman*). His first beach scenes, in particular *Bathers, the Beach at Pouldu* of 1899, are always set

opposite page
3. Maurice Denis, *The Muses*, 1893.
Paris, Musée d'Orsay

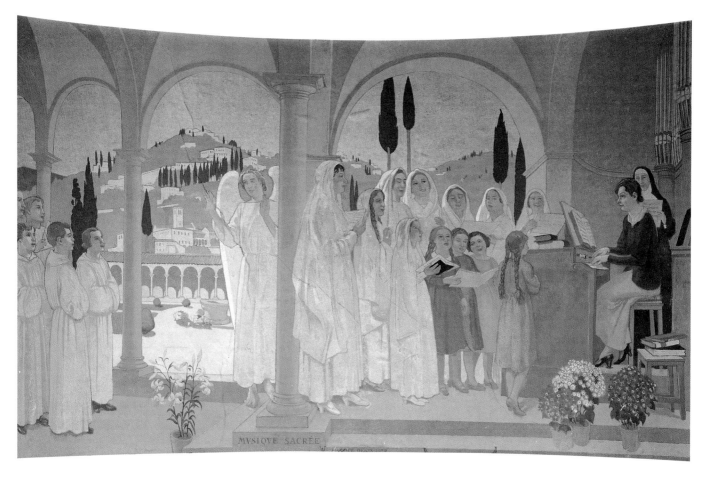

5. Maurice Denis,
The Sacred Music, 1937.
Paris, Palais de Chaillot

by a sea reminiscent of the Lyon decoration and the *Poor Fisherman*, but especially the *Pleasant Land* belonging to Bonnat (about 1882), the reduction of which had also been shown at the Durand-Ruel gallery in 1887: They borrow from it the very detail of their motifs, their order, serenity, and finally their symbolism, in the Puvisesque sense of the word. All these features would be emphasized in the coming years and would climax in the important *Great Beach* of the Viau collection (1903, destroyed) and *Beach with a Small Temple* of 1906 at the Musée de Lausanne.[11]

After 1900, Puvis did not disappear from Denis's work, although other references came to the fore: above all Cézanne, with his visit to the Aix painter in 1906 and the long theoretic article he devoted to him in 1907.[12] That same year, *Springtime in the Forest*, initially drawn from Cézanne's *Bathers*, which Denis saw as a revival of the classical theme par excellence of the nude in a landscape, was gradually rectified in the course of its lengthy execution, recurring to Puvis in order to put Cézanne's brushstroke back in its initial place, and to his color, as well as to reintroduce the line, and increase the number of figures to underpin the frieze-like composition. The final result was a decorative panel that was not as close to the *Big Bathers* as it was to Puvis's *Shepherd's Song* (1891, exhibited at Durand-Ruel and sold by him in 1906) or the *Antique Vision* of the Lyon stairway or his *Sacred Wood.* Denis was in fact in Lyon in 1904, and Puvis was the first thing he saw on his visit to the museum ("In the museum, Chavannes, especially *Christian Inspiration. . . .*" *Diary*, February 6, 1904).

It would be interminable to follow the constant subtle traces of those major works throughout the rest of Denis's career: in his mural decorations of course, such as the dome of the Théâtre des Champs-Elysées (1913), one of his masterpieces (*Diary*, June 1910: ". . . strive toward the unity of place, as Chavannes understood it [Sorbonne]"), or the great *Glorification of Saint Louis* in the church of Saint Louis of Vincennes (1927), with its conveniently forest serving as a reception hall for the king-saint, an opportunity to paint a *Sacred Grove* all over again. Traces also exist in his easel paintings, for instance the 1909 *Shepherds*, a

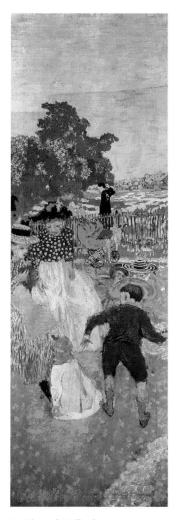

6. Edouard Vuillard,
Under the Trees, 1894.
The Cleveland Museum of Art

variation of *Antique Vision*, with the same figures in profile arranged on parallel planes, and the rocky reliefs set against the horizon above the blue sea, which also refers to the 1869–72 *Massilia, Greek Colony* (shown in 1887 and 1889 at Durand-Ruel) and the 1882 *Pleasant Land* in its overall conception and the woman seated on the right. In 1925, the portrait of Puvis naturally took first place in *The History of the Arts in France*, and was chosen as a subject for the decoration of the Dutuit stairway dome, in the Petit-Palais in Paris. Furthermore, in 1937, *The Sacred Music*, one of the two decorative panels of the Palais de Chaillot, borrows, certainly with full cognizance, the arcades through which the Italian landscape unfolds, as well as the same light, airy space in *Christian Inspiration* of Lyon that he had seen in 1920 (*Diary*, August 22, 1920: "Puvis is at his best in *Christian Inspiration*, a more compact, less arbitrary, and non academic subject featuring nature tones, fine white, pinks of the walls"). Again in 1934, Denis noted: "I can learn from Puvis, ruthless with nondescript details. . . ." (*ibidem*, November 1934), and in a retrospective article he recalled how much the painter had meant to the avant-gardes of his youth: " . . . we thought most of all . . . of Puvis de Chavannes, the Puvis of *The Poor Fisherman*, the great forgotten master, whose immense influence in the late nineteenth century cannot be overestimated."[13] The following year, he was struck with amazement, once again, before *Summer* and *Winter* of the Salon du Zodiaque in the Paris Hôtel de Ville (1891–92): "since Delacroix, our great Puvis is the best of all." And, after one of the last articles paying tribute to one of the "great geniuses" who "lit that uneven course" of nineteenth-century painting,[14] the very last lines of his *Diary* end again in 1943, precisely, on the notes made in Lyon, with his regret and hope to draw another lesson—at the age of 73!: "I didn't get a chance to see the Puvis; they would have taught me so much! A glimpse of the *Sacred Wood*: solidity."

We started off with the Nabis, and with the decisive yet relatively short moment in the formation of those young painters that preceded their long, rich careers: we have found constant loyalty to a major master whose lesson went beyond fashions and generations, and since then so many others have sought answers from the Lyon painter.

Yet the issue is not as cut and dried with the other members of the group, and Puvis's presence with each one of them assumes different forms and importance. Roussel and Vuillard worked with Denis on the decorations of the Palais des Nations in Geneva in 1936 and the Palais de Chaillot in Paris in 1937: they are the first to be examined, given their persistent interest in mural decoration.

Vuillard and Roussel

Vuillard, today praised above all for his small panels and the warmth and refinement of his intimism, was perhaps the first to see in large and monumental terms, with Puvis foremost. In the Nabi years, the speckled brushstroke, the color saturation of the motif and its repetitive fragmentation, resembling *mille fleurs* tapestries, the rich, warm harmonies that seem the opposite of Puvis's manner (except in the subdued colors of *In bed*, 1891, Paris, Musée d'Orsay, which, for that matter, is a work apart) should not mislead us: they are meant to adhere to large, light compositions, enhancing them without concealing them, where the frontality, outspoken planarity and the overlapping planes derive from the Panthéon master, for whom Vuillard constantly expressed admiration. After his modest attempt in 1892 that was already in the same spirit, with the panels (private collection) for the Desmarais, cousins of the Natansons, the nine panels of the 1894 *Public Gardens* executed for Alexandre Natanson's dining room on avenue Foch are obviously key works in this respect. The open air scene, unusual at the time for Vuillard (its form here owing a great deal to Monet) makes the analogy all the more apparent, and is particularly striking in *The Two Pupils*, with the even strip of foliage and slender rising, close-set tree trunks where the figures are distributed—a scheme previously quoted in particular by Emile Bernard in his *Madeleine in the Wood of Love* (1888), Sérusier in his *Spell* (c. 1891) and, above all, Denis in *The Muses* of the year before: a direct echo of *The Childhood of Saint Genevieve* in the Panthéon and, even more so, of the Sorbonne hemicycle, where the foliage laid out horizontally above a comparable strip of sky. The panels, executed for Dr Vaquez in 1896, are somehow a variant of it turned inward, and also accentuate the reference to Puvis by the greater immobility and hieratic quality of the figures, the silence, a certain timelessness de-

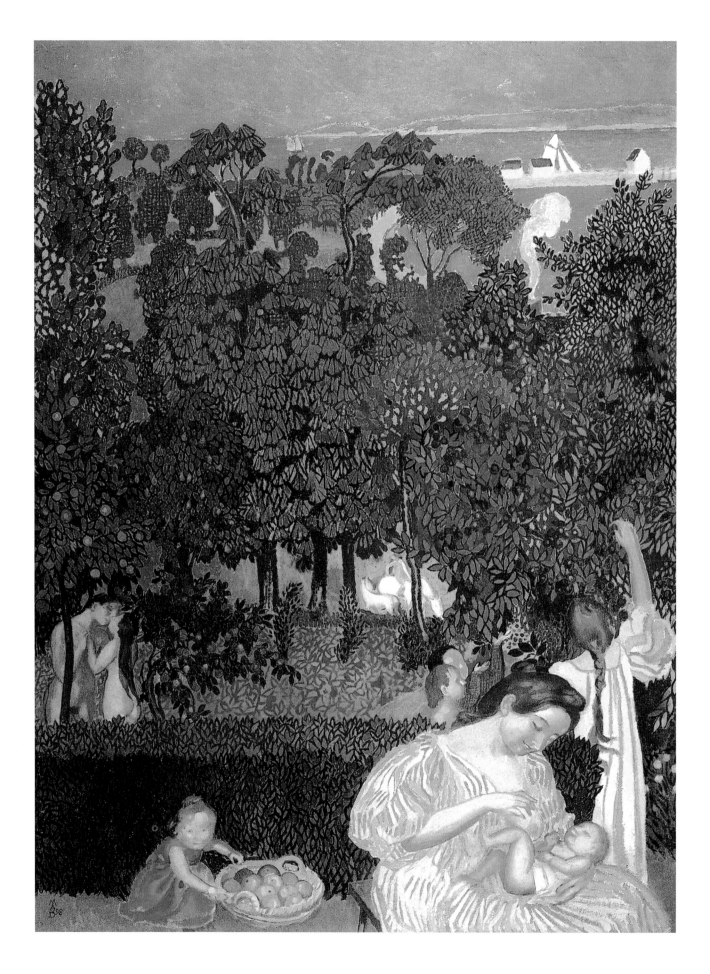

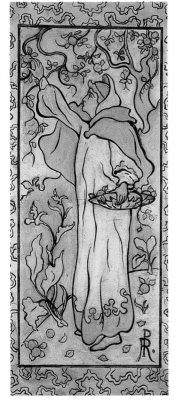

spite the contemporary furniture and attire, and an even greater emphasis, this time in all the panels, of the orthogonal squaring and the underlining of the horizontal strips. Traits that were also akin to the *Ludus pro Patria* of Amiens, the *Inter Artes et Naturam* of Rouen or again *Saint Genevieve Supplying Paris* of the Panthéon that Puvis was painting at the very same time. In 1899, in his *Landscapes of Ile de France* painted for the Natansons' father (Pasadena, The Norton Simon Foundation and The Art Institute of Chicago) near L'Etang-la-Ville, where Roussel had just moved, Vuillard would introduce, along with more muted tints, the ornamental borders that Denis would admire a year later in Puvis's first Amiens decoration: another indication of a "classicizing" closeness to the master who, after his death in 1898, was unanimously praised.

The same year, when he turned classical, Denis would reproach Vuillard for limiting himself to an insufficiently thought out vision of the instantaneous that reflected Thadée Natanson's "sensualism." And Vuillard, in their February 1898 correspondence, presented a weak defense, merely invoking his inclination for immediate pleasure. This is certainly evident in the *Gardens* which is surprising in its random poses and snatches of conversation. After 1900, Denis would have a clearer view of the essential coinciding with his own evolution: "Longing to do something big, with broad tints and outlines around a solid drawing. Vuillard's large panels. . . ." (*Diary*, October 1904). Whereas *The Two Pupils* (and *Under the Trees*, its pendant of the other panels, The Cleveland Museum of Art) derive directly from Puvis through Denis's *Muses* of the year before, the latter's *Monotonous Orchard* again renews the dialogue in the year 1898—before a quasi quotation of both appears in Klimt's landscapes after 1900, he being another less cited actor in Puvis's filiation who ought to be mentioned (*Pear Tree*, 1903, Cambridge, Mass., Fogg Art Museum). Denis's and Vuillard's aesthetic convergence in the large decorations of the 1930s comes as no surprise: it testifies to a fundamental continuity essentially due to Puvis under their apparent changes of style.

The same thing can almost be said about Roussel, who was working with them at the time. At first his admiration was nearly naïve, and perhaps more immediately transcribed than the other Nabis—yet the famous lithograph of *Dog's Education*, in 1893, with its scolded puppy and the two gossips in front of the trees of a new "Bois Sacré" seem to suggest an awareness, and an ironic distance. His small *Composition in the Forest* of the very early 1890s with the figures inserted amid the trees, and his pensive *Virgin on the Path* of the same period (private collection) with its pale, delicate harmonies—which undoubtedly derived from the *Young Women by the Sea* he had seen at the 1889 *Centennale*, and at the same time also faithfully refer to Denis—are a clear enough indication. But we can see it even more in his first decorative panels, *The Seasons of Life* or *Terrace at the Tuileries*, in all likelihood projects for an unexecuted decoration of a town hall: frieze-like compositions and female figures in conversation with the landscape, its trees and architectures. . . The critics made no mistake, Aurier being the first, thereby gaining recognition as the critic of Symbolism in painting: "If he fulfils the promises of his first studies, with their perfect style, their utterly simple, peaceful, grand vision, where we glimpse a sort of intellectual closeness with Puvis de Chavannes, he will become a wonderful decorator."[15] The prophecy was accurate, and perhaps more so after 1900 than for the 1897 pastels (Roger Marx in *La Revue encyclopédique*, no. 202, in 1897: "Roussel, whose tender pastel evocations blend the greatness of Puvis with the charm of Fantin"), when Roussel, imitating Denis (and going with him to Cézanne's in Aix in 1906), also turned classical and undertook big decorations, joining up with Vuillard and Denis in 1913, 1936 and again in 1937. There again, even though his manner changed considerably and moved away from that of Puvis, it achieved a superior and more profound assimilation: Puvis's true children, in Roussel, are the mythological scenes subsequent to 1900, beginning with the *Triumph of Bacchus* for the stage curtain of the Comédie Hall, at the Théâtre des Champs-Elysées in Paris in 1913, one might say a baroque version of the *Sacred Wood* on which he bestowed the colors of the Mediterranean.

Ranson, Sérusier and Lacombe

With Ranson and Sérusier, who can be associated, given their philosophical, theosophical and mystical concerns, another aspect of Puvis de Chavannes surfaces. For as far as Pu-

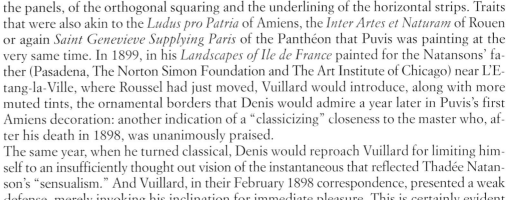

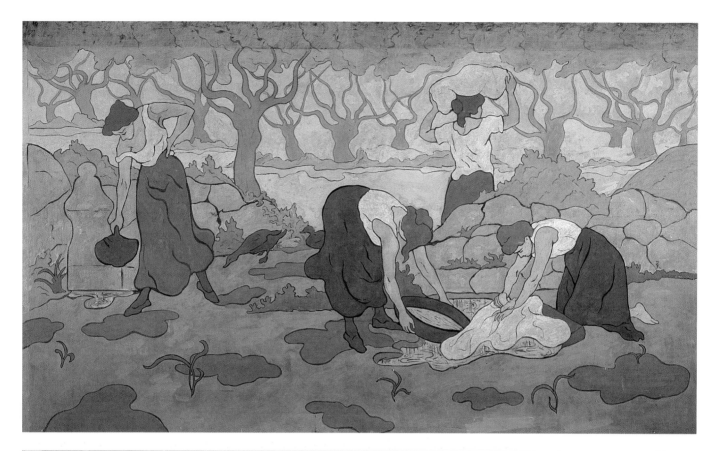

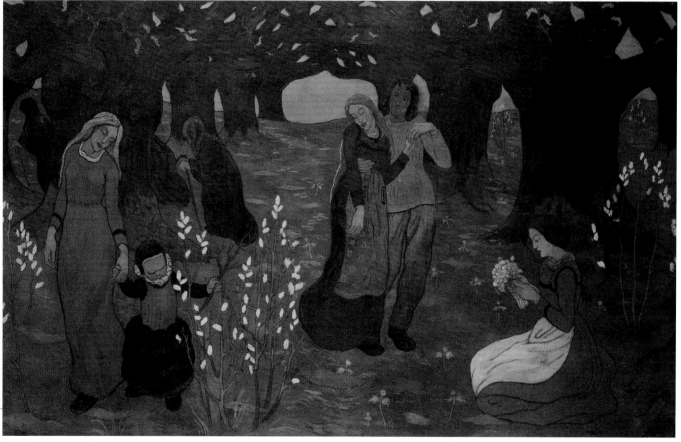

9. Paul-Elie Ranson,
*Four Women at the
Fountain*, c. 1895.
Saint-Germain-en-Laye,
Musée Maurice Denis

10. Georges Lacombe,
The Ages of Life (Spring),
1893–94. Geneva, Muséé
du Petit Palais

vis the decorator also left his mark on them, as we can clearly see in the former's decorative artworks, which are more considerable than those of the other Nabis, and rather well epitomized in the cartoons of stained-glass windows and tapestries of the 1890s: for instance in *Women Picking Apples*, 1894–95, where we find Puvis's isolated female figures, from *Autumn* of 1864 to the *Young Women by the Sea* (their composition directly underpins his curious *Hippogriffe* of 1891, private collection, whose inspiration is entirely different anyway), passing through *The Balloon* and *The Pigeon* of 1870 and 1871, where, along with the motif of the raised arm, the ornamental trimming is also found. The dining room panels that Henry van de Velde executed for Siegfried Bing's *Art Nouveau* in 1895 offer the most accomplished version, in which the composition, and even the motif of the women at work (*Four Women at the Fountain*) openly acknowledge their debt—especially to the Rouen *Inter Artes et Naturam*. The easel paintings instead reveal other concerns that would only become greater. In *The Explanation* of 1896, the unquestionably "*à la* Puvis" landscape recedes, concentrating on a tense, dramatic action that on the other hand is entirely unlike Puvis de Chavannes.

Despite his privileged ties with Gauguin, in his early days Sérusier again revealed the strong impact the Puvis exhibitions of 1887 and 1889 had had on him. The *Three Girls at Pouldu* of 1889–90 (private collection) is a direct quotation, and not without humor, of the *Young Women by the Sea* of 1879 that had been shown again at the second exhibition. In 1892, Sérusier was proud to have been complimented by Puvis himself, as well as by Mallarmé and Redon, for his exhibition with the Nabis at Le Barc de Boutteville (letter to Verkade of January 21[16]). Toward 1891, his *Eve Bretonne* or *Melancholy* (Paris, Musée d'Orsay) owes less to his summer stay in 1891 at Huelgoat and the Brittany heath or to the anecdote about the supposed local customs,[17] than to the 1879 *Prodigal Son* shown in those two exhibitions, from which it borrows, in reverse, its exact composition with the off-center figure and the trees in counterpoint on the other side, the high horizon, and above all, the sense of desolation and repentance arising from the sole refined use of those plastic means combined with Gauguin's color. Concurrently, the triptych of *The Apple Harvest* (private collection) clearly bears the mark of the *Inter Artes et Naturam*, just like Ranson's panels some time later. But the difference is all the more apparent here, between the nearly literal borrowing of certain motifs (the gathering of fruit, the tree at the top of the composition, the expanse of water in the background of the painting. . .) and the execution that profoundly alters its meaning, with the non-realistic, narrow space, the sequence of arabesques, the flat tints, and that intense color, all of which now look to the future: toward Gauguin's *Where Do We Come from? What Are We? Where Are We Going?* (1897), a final avatar as well of Puvis de Chavannes's panel. Later Sérusier's small easel paintings reveal another direction, where the concern for "content," marked at the time by his interest in theosophy, prevails over what remains of his Puvis de Chavannes recollections, as in *The Spell* for instance, and its magic ritual, or even those "bearers" (of water and of laundry) at the Musée de Brest that come from the collection of Georges Lacombe, the "Nabi sculptor" to whom Sérusier and Ranson would grow especially close. The latter adopted the same patronage during that short period, as we can see in his very similar *Forest with Red Soil*, that is also a response to Denis's *Green Trees*, and even more so in his only important decorative ensemble of which remains *The Autumn* or *The Chestnut Pickers* (1892, Pasadena, The Norton Simon Art Foundation) and *The Ages of Life* or *Spring* (1893–94) that compellingly remind us of Ranson.

Yet after Gauguin left for Tahiti, the evolution of Sérusier's painting toward "a grander art, more severe and sacred" and "hieratic," as he wrote to Jan Verkade in 1896,[18] which on the latter's insistence, could still benefit by Puvis's example, in particular in the use of subdued tones, was mostly a result of his mathematical investigations of the "Holy Proportions," for which Sérusier sought his friend's advice at Beuron (the *Portrait of Jan Verkade* was executed there, in 1903, in that spirit) and in that respect owes very little to Puvis.

Bonnard and Vallotton
Practically the same could be said about the two other leading Nabis yet to be discussed: Vallotton and Bonnard. They who might be called the "ironists" of the group, as they were

in complete contrast with the gravity and spiritual concerns of the Denis, Sérusier and Ranson trio, at first appear to have little to do with Puvis. Did Bonnard with his satirical, subtle bent, and who was particularly close to the Jarry of *Ubu Roi*, have anything to learn from Puvis's gravity, or could he even be interested in him? Without even considering the other aspect of the Panthéon master—that is, his biting caricatures (appearing in *Le Rire* as of 1895) that might have entertained the author of the *Deux Caniches* of 1891 and the *Nib Carnavalesque* lithograph of 1895—Bonnard could not help but be attracted to the mural artist's decorations in his first very earnest, even plodding, attempts to absorb the new aesthetics that Denis and Sérusier extolled. In the big, ambitious *Twilight or The Croquet Game* of 1892, mostly a pretext for a decorative layout, we can clearly discern, along with the influence of the arabesques and puzzle-like flat tints of Japanese etchings (that, with Ranson, he would emulate even more than his friends and earn him the nickname "Nabi Japonard"), Puvis's mark on the flatness of the support, and the human figures blended with the element of nature. With the small opening in the sky, the contrast between the group in the foreground clinging to the foliage and the dancing women in the background, the painting still broadly refers to *The Sacred Wood*, but even more to the 1864 *Autumn*, with its crown of light leaves, cut off by the frame, standing out against dark masses, and its remote group of figures—without even going back to the reduced version (1867) of *Peace* of Amiens (1861) shown in 1887 at the Durand-Ruel exhibition that is a model for the composition scheme.

It would seem then that Bonnard moved in another direction, toward the playfulness of etching, the decorative arts, and a sharp, amused observation of Parisian life. But this would imply overlooking the decorator, who reappeared after 1900, without real interruption, no more than was the case for Denis and Roussel. Like them, he had not forgotten Puvis. Indeed, he was the first source for the masterful monumental triptych decoration, *Mediterranean*, executed for the stairway of the Morosov mansion in Moscow in 1911 (where Denis had used the same even more marked reference for his large *Story of Psyche* of the Music Room in 1908), for which Puvis's decoration obviously comes to mind for the Lyon stairway (especially the panels of the Saône and the Rhône), despite the difference in the execution and the treatment of color.

Vallotton, too, undertook very large format paintings between the two wars, without particularly alluding to Puvis it would appear (his *Diary*, between 1914 and 1921 unlike Denis's, does not mention him), even if his painting, voluntarily flat and cold, and his "sweeping, Puvis-like style" as Louis Vauxcelles wrote in the *Gil Blas* of October 5, 1906, obviously bear his indelible mark, especially the landscapes. Instead in the early 1890s, when he joined up with the Parisian Nabis (1892), he became as unconditional an admirer as his new friends, as we see in his chronicle of the day for the *Gazette de Lausanne* (June 8): the Salon de la Nationale des Beaux-Arts "contains first–rate things, several of which, like Puvis de Chavannes's *Winter*, would qualify to make this a good year."[19] That same year he began his outrageous, fascinating *Bathing on a Summer Evening*, which signaled his breakthrough into a truly modern art and was unfavorably received at the 1893 Salon des Indépendants. It was a singular expression of what might be called a sort of love-hate for Puvis—as well as a desire to cast a sarcastic glance on the female society of his day. *Winter* of the Salon du Zodiaque at the Paris Hôtel de Ville is not especially alluded to, but *Summer* alongside it, shown at the Salon of the year before, certainly is: the same subject, similar female figures, their positions and gestures comparable, a nearly literal quotation in reverse of the rear view of the nude woman in the left foreground, an identical accented overlap of horizontal parallel planes—and, initially, the same title in the exhibitions and the painter's record book (*Summer, Women Bathing in a Tiled Pool, Outdoors*). . . At the same time, the work does have an obvious caricatural side to it ("It's great fun!" Félix Fénéon wrote in 1893, and he should be taken seriously), one that is carried even further than the famous parody of *Sacred Wood* by Toulouse-Lautrec when he was a Cormon student (1884, The Henry and Rose Pearlman Foundation), he too being torn between admiration and the sense of a much-needed liberation. It is certainly significant that Puvis would resurge twenty years later (this time like the return of an inhibition!), in 1912, in a monumental painting with the same title (Lausanne, Musée Cantonal des Beaux-Arts), with

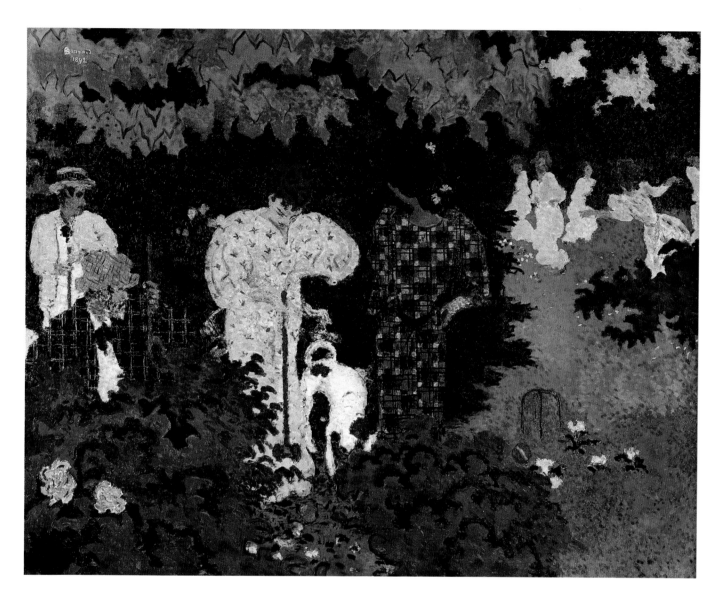

11. Pierre Bonnard, *Twilight*
(The Croquet Game), detail, 1892.
Paris, Musée d'Orsay

an accuracy that almost explains the reference to Puvis at the same time as to the 1892 work
(*Summer: Landscapes with Seven Nudes Reclining and Standing, at the End of the Seine Estuary*). We can easily recognize the reference to the panel of the Paris Hôtel de Ville, its standing or reclining women, nude or half-dressed, posing in a frieze in the serenity of a wooded landscape on the horizontal background of the stretch of water: just like Denis, Vuillard, Roussel and Bonnard, Vallotton certainly carried over into the post-1900 era the best of Puvis's teaching.

Maillol

Last of all Maillol, who joined the group of Nabis much later (1896) and more informally just when their aesthetic compactness and bonds of friendship were beginning to dissolve, but who nonetheless followed a comparable course earlier, particularly with respect to Puvis. In this regard, he was especially close to Denis, with Gauguin as his main reference, until what by 1904 was to become a strong friendship and an aesthetic proximity:[20] "Puvis! It is to him that we owe the greatest emotions of our youth," he was to confide to Judith Cladel, when she interviewed him for her monograph (1937). A copy of the *Poor Fisherman*, an *The Prodigal Son* that borrows the motifs of Puvis's work seen in 1887 at Durand-Ruel (including the famous pig) testify to that admiration. Such is the case, albeit more subtly, of the first large paintings, particularly the famous, monumental *Woman with Umbrella*, c. 1890, a variation, after all, of the *Young Women by the Sea*, which develops

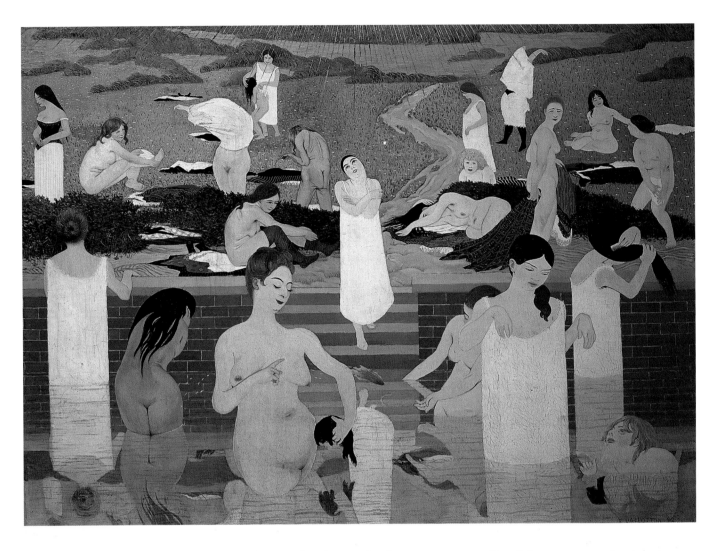

12. Felix Vallotton, *Bathing on
a Summer Evening*, 1892–93.
Zurich, Kunsthaus, on deposit from
the Gottfried Keller Foundation

the sea background and turns the three-quarters profile of the woman on the right into an
outright profile—while we should point out that that manner, typical of Maillol's portraits
at the time, is often to be found in Puvis, and its source is not only fifteenth-century portraits, as has perhaps been written too often. Between 1895 and 1898, *Mediterranean, The
Côte d'Azur* or *Two Nudes in a Landscape* (Paris, Petit Palais, Musée des Beaux-Arts de la
Ville), with their female figures clinging to soaring tree trunks whose tops are out of sight,
clearly acknowledge, along with their references to Denis and Gauguin (the rippling waves
in the background, in the first painting), their debt to *Autumn* of 1864 (especially the woman
in rear view on the left in the second, a near-quotation) or to the figures of *Sacred Wood*
and more generally to the *Pleasant Land* painted for Bonnat—whereas the third major picture of the period, the famous *Wave* (*ibidem*), alludes exclusively to Gauguin (his *Woman
in the Waves* or *Ondine* in The Cleveland Museum of Art, 1889).
But after 1900, Gauguin drew away, and Maillol joined with Denis in the new classicism
he was establishing theoretically, in particular in an important article he dedicated to his
friend in 1905, mentioning his "classical gift": "The ideal of art is to condense, to use a
few clear and concise forms to summarize the infinity of varied relations that we perceive
in nature"[21]—a formula that could immediately be applied to Puvis, and even be his own.
Puvis was one of the mainstays of their common action, as Maillol's comment at the time
of the completion of Denis's dome for the Théâtre des Champs-Elysées indicates: "I know
it is a thing of beauty and a work that no one—after Chavannes—could have undertaken
and carried out so boldly" (letter to Denis, published in his *Diary*). *Mediterranean*, whose
plaster presented at the Salon d'Automne won Denis's admiration ("amazing combinations
of planes and curves, a perfect understanding of the relative importance of the volumes,

a rich modeling and breadth throughout," he wrote in the article of 1905 quoted above), marked the end of four long years of effort. In particular, beginning with the *Women at Her Toilette* of 1883, shown at Durand-Ruel in 1887, and even more recently with his first studies, at the Centennial of the 1900 World Fair, Maillol got rid of what remained of the anecdote, and created an eternal figure that, closed up in a near-perfect cube, would become the cornerstone of a new indeed Mediterranean humanism (the title of what at first was just a *Crouching Woman* came later, but was introduced as a sort of confirmation of the intuited meaning, that Denis had clearly discerned, in 1905 when he insisted on the Mediterranean character of that classicism), on the threshold of the new century—whose share of utopia the war was soon to dash.

Conclusion

Puvis's presence is obvious from the start in an overall approach of the Nabi group: even more than Gauguin's, it is a decisive factor. Although less noticed later on, that presence remained however, in the most important members, after the group broke up and their aesthetics took a different turn. It continued to prevail especially in the large decorative works several of them would undertake after 1900, and even later on between the two wars, up to the 1930s, in what in many respects, and contrary to the widespread preconceived notion, may be considered their greatest achievement.

As a result, that lasting quality is an incentive for us to alter the usual way of approaching the issue: to speak of "Puvis and the Nabis," is to first evoke, for a rather limited period, and all too often incidentally, what concerns a far wider fundamental movement that lasted much longer. Recently, we have begun to recognize that the Bonnard of the 1930s was actually no more "irrelevant to the times" than the strictly contemporary Matisse or Picasso, who supposedly would have "come after" the Nabi generation—in particular for another use of Puvis. And some day the same may be said for the other "former Nabis": Vuillard, Roussel and Denis. Indeed the latter, whose greater loyalty to Puvis was deeper, more constant and better attested in his work than in his writings, is our best guide for following that unbroken trajectory. He has shown that beyond the appropriations or reminiscences that can be detected, what matters first of all is the *functioning* of a "Puvisesque model," that represents a key moment in the history of French art in the second half of the nineteenth century, and then, uninterruptedly, during the first half of the twentieth, the main components of which we can briefly outline.

The most obvious naturally concerns everything that has to do with mural decoration, its justification and its role, and the consequences that can be drawn from it for dealing with the flatness of the support. But this goes far beyond any mere question of form. Mural decoration, whose lesson Puvis expresses anew with such vigor, raises the more general question of the place of art in contemporary society on the whole. In 1891, Aurier ended his article-manifesto on Gauguin and "Symbolism in painting" by asking for walls for painters to decorate (". . . you have in your midst a brilliant decorator: walls! Walls! Give him walls!"). That appeal would first be heard by his disciples, the Nabis, as Verkade later wrote in his recollections of 1923, and was to become the "war cry!" in the early 1890s: "The painter's job begins where the architect sees his as over. Walls, walls to decorate! Down with perspective! The wall should remain a surface, and not be perforated by the representation of endless horizons. There is no such thing as a painting, there are only decorations!"[22] Puvis was obviously the best guide, and the Nabis in following those instructions went well beyond their master. But the space of the wall is naturally a social space as well, so we should look more closely at the articulation of what regards the public sphere and the Nabis' space, which is perhaps too hastily and too exclusively called "intimate." The latters' "murality," whether public or private, is a part of the great undertaking of the "new" wall, with its social ambition: in the very sense of Siegfried Bing's *Art Nouveau*, an initiative most of the Nabis were closely associated with (the mural decorations by Denis and Ranson for the opening of the permanent Salon on Rue de Provence particularly reflect this sense).

Then, the very form and doctrine of the "flat surface," like the determination of a "certain order" of the colors assembled upon it—to go back to the basic definition Denis gave in 1890—is indebted first to Gauguin, through Sérusier, and goes beyond Puvis's immediate message. But it extends it, and it is fascinating to see how its interpretations result in a "formalization" of the way of looking at the master of the Panthéon and the Sorbonne ("The adequacy of these lines and these colors provide their own justification," as Denis wrote in 1890), despite his concern for the choice and meaning of his subject matter. However, the very content of Puvis's works, and especially his iconography, also played a major role. Fewer details of this or that motif than in the overall conception: the human body and nature in dialogue as in the classical tradition, but freed of the weight of mythology or allegories. As the father of modern Arcadias, who looks toward the future (hope and serenity), Puvis is more the father of the Symbolist Arcadias, of which the Nabis offered the purest expression. And it is in their special form of their "Symbolism" that it is striking to see Denis—whom we know rejected the term for a long time (along with Aurier's "neo-Platonism")—quote the Panthéon master's famous statement on the subject: "For each clear idea . . . there is a plastic notion that expresses it. . . . A work springs from a sort of vague emotion in which it is contained like the animal in the egg. The thought dwelling within that emotion, I mull over and over until it is elucidated for me with all the possible clarity. Then I try to find a scene capable of accurately expressing it. That may be symbolism, if you say so. . . ."[23]

On quoting that formula in his 1898 article to define the "Symbolism" of the Nabi years that had just ended and, at the same time, the new classicism to come, Denis, who would return to that quotation in 1916 and in 1918, helps us understand that it was Puvis, and Puvis alone, who allowed for the uninterrupted transition from one to the other, by keeping alive, through form, the Symbolist "emotion" in the classical language of clarity and "accuracy." Thus he allows us to envisage a logical, coherent trajectory that goes way beyond the reductive partitioning of the usual stylistic categories. So we shall risk this paradoxical proposal: the true achievement of the Nabis' "Puvism" was their late-comer companion Maillol's *Mediterranean* in 1905, insofar as it overcomes the confusions and tentative essays of the Nabi period proper, and introduces the new classicism that Denis, Vuillard, Bonnard and Roussel, not to mention Maillol himself, would, in the years between the two wars, make live so ardently and not like someone at the point of death who is artificially kept alive: *Puvis semper vivat.*

[1] "L'influence de Paul Gauguin," 1903, last reprinted in the critical anthology, M. Denis, *Le Ciel et l'Arcadie*, Paris, Hermann, 1993, p. 73ff. (the articles by Denis quoted below follow that abridged edition: *Le Ciel et...*). Denis adds, to describe the penchant for the past he observed around him: "The most daring among the young artists who attended the Académie Julian around 1888 . . . spoke of Puvis with respectful indifference, harboring a sincere suspicion that he didn't know how to draw."

[2] *Le Ciel et...*, *op. cit.*, p. 5ff.

[3] M. Denis, *Journal 1884–1943*, 3 vols., Paris, La Colombe, 1957–59, quoted below by the entry date.

[4] *Le Ciel et...*, *op. cit.*, p. 28.

[5] M. Denis, "A propos de l'exposition d'A. Séguin," 1895, reprinted in *Théories 1890–1910. Du Symbolisme et de Gauguin vers un nouvel ordre classique*, Paris, 1912, p. 22.

[6] All the works by Denis quoted are commented more fully in J.P. Bouillon, *Maurice Denis*, Geneva, Skira, 1993. The wall decorations of the four Nabis were recently studied by Gloria Groom in the exhibition catalog *Beyond the Easel, Decorative Painting by Bonnard, Vuillard, Denis and Roussel*, The Art Institute of Chicago (February 25–May 16, 2001).

[7] M. Denis, *Histoire de l'art religieux*, Paris, Flammarion, 1939, p. 275, where Puvis is presented at once as a "poet of the soul" and "a spirit of the filiation of Poussin," and illustrated by *The Poor Fisherman, Saint John the Baptist* at the Louvre, and two frescoes from the life of Saint Genevieve at the Panthéon.

[8] *Le Ciel et...*, *op. cit.*, p. 47.

[9] *Ibidem*, p. 58.

[10] See J.P. Bouillon, "L'Expérience de La Légende," in *Maurice Denis. La Légende de saint Hubert 1896–1897*, exh. cat., Saint-Germain-en-Laye, Musée Maurice Denis, and Paris, Musée de la Chasse et de la Nature, 1999, p. 27ff.

[11] See J.P. Bouillon, "Le Denis des Plages," in *Lumières de Sable, Plages de Maurice Denis*, exh. cat., Saint-Germain-en-Laye, Musée Maurice Denis, 1997, p. 14ff.

[12] *Le Ciel et...*, *op. cit.*, p. 129ff.; see the essay by J.P. Bouillon, "Le modèle cézannien de Maurice Denis," in *Cézanne aujourd'hui*, Paris, Réunion des Musées Nationaux, 1997, p. 145ff., which led to a few temporary reservations about Puvis: *Le Ciel et...*, *op. cit.*, p. 137 and note 99.

[13] *Ibidem*, p. 207; further on, Denis speaks about "our passion for Puvis de Chavannes" (*ibidem*, p. 213). In 1909, he already said of the Nabis that they had "from the start manifested the greatest esteem for those who had shown them the way: not just Camille Pissarro and Cézanne, and Degas, and Odilon Redon, but also Puvis de Chavannes, whose official glory might have nonetheless lacked appeal for their youthful intransigence" (*ibidem*, p. 158).

[14] *Le Ciel et…*, *op. cit.*, p. 221 (1943). In 1924, he published a short article on Puvis in *La Revue hebdomadaire*, vol. XII, no. 49, December 6, pp. 8–9.

[15] A. Aurier, "Les Symbolistes," in *La Revue encyclopédique*, April 1892, p. 485, reprinted under the title "Les peintres symbolistes" in *Oeuvres Posthumes*, vol. 3, Paris, 1893 (2nd edition, Paris, 1995, p. 109).

[16] Correspondence published in the 2nd edition of his *ABC de la peinture*, Paris, Floury, 1950, p. 57.

[17] *Nabis*, exh. cat., Paris 1993, p. 254.

[18] *ABC de la peinture…*, *op. cit.*, p. 72.

[19] Reprinted in *Félix Vallotton. Documents pour une biographie et pour l'histoire d'une oeuvre*, vol. 1, Lausanne, La Bibliothèque des Arts, 1973, p. 83.

[20] See J.P. Bouillon, "Maillol et Denis, fraternité artistique et moment historique," in *Aristide Maillol*, exh. cat., Lausanne, Musée Cantonal des Beaux-Arts, 1996, p. 127ff.

[21] *Le Ciel et…*, *op. cit.*, p. 101.

[22] J. Verkade, *Le tourment de Dieu, Etapes d'un moine peintre*, Fr. trans. with preface by Maurice Denis, Paris, Rouart et Watelin, 1923, p. 94.

[23] *Le Ciel et…*, *op. cit.*, p. 64.

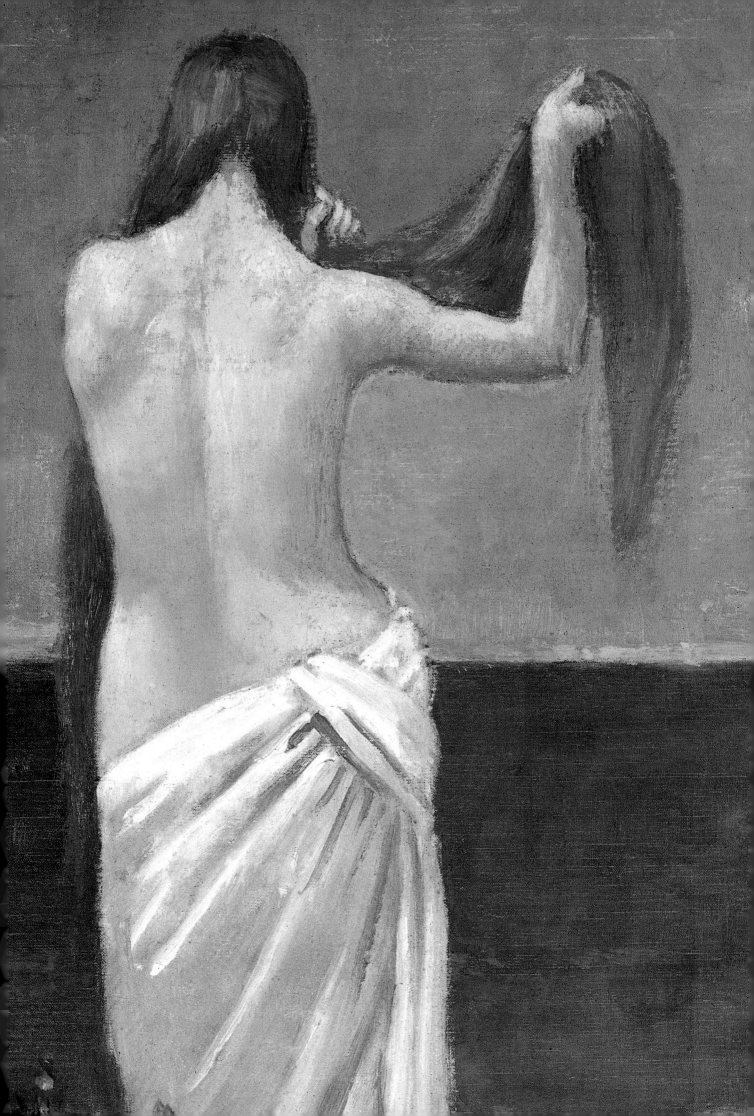

Françoise Cachin

The Neo-Impressionists and Puvis de Chavannes

"All those, from Seurat to Gauguin, who sought to recapture the harmony of form and atmosphere, even through dazzling technical illusions, even in a voluptuous, barbaric exile, far from the Latin sea and the mild autumns of the Gauls, admired and meditated on the art of Puvis de Chavannes,"[1] discerningly commented Henri Focillon between the two World Wars, at a time when Puvis was generally regarded as a stuffy academic painter, a decorator of provincial museum walls, a creator of pictures for history textbooks. That view was to persist for many years in France, at least up to the retrospective held in Paris and Ottawa in 1976.[2]
Yet in a way that might seem surprising, he had been a model for an entire generation of late nineteenth-century artists who thought of themselves as innovators. Each in his own way appreciated, in some instances, his decorative ambitions, since they deemed easel painting to be "bourgeois"; others, his moral quality, his refusal of facile effects; again others, his transparent and sometimes vivid color, applied in smooth layers. We are familiar with Van Gogh's perfect comment on Puvis de Chavannes, one that echoes the feelings he shared in Paris with his "Petit Boulevard" kindred spirits in 1886–87:[3] ". . . one gets the feeling of being present at a rebirth, total but benevolent, of all the things one should have believed in, should have wished for—a strange and happy meeting of very distant antiquities and crude modernity."[4]
Today we do not quite grasp Puvis's *crude* modernism, but we should look at his painting with eyes that at the time were used to the finished, polished painting, or filled with fitful brushstrokes, whether in official painting or in that of the Impressionists. In the 1880s, Puvis's aspirations to greatness in simplicity appealed to a generation longing to rise above the commonplace and sheer sensation.
The Symbolist poets were fond of Puvis's painting, where they could feel "the call of the grand dream" (Laforgue) lying "beyond the exiguity of impressions" (Moréas).[5] Thus, Félix Fénéon, the future champion of the Neo-Impressionists and inventor of their name, had expressed his admiration for Puvis before meeting Seurat, and had already defined his originality, with regard to the Impressionists, as well as to official painters: "It is fashionable to make fun of Puvis de Chavannes, whose work is repulsive to painters who undertake to produce beautiful workmanship and whose name rouses the bourgeois to give vent to more or less facetious puns. Let us not ask Puvis for what he deliberately ignored—I mean photographic accuracy and chronological specialization. His conception of painting is decorative: hence his subdued color scale blends perfectly with the architectural lines of buildings, but is out of place in easel painting. . . . His work—hermetic and symbolic, intelligible only to intellectuals, entirely executed in a superbly simplistic style that resumes the tradition of the great primitives Buffalmacco, Benozzo Gozzoli and Gaddo Gaddi—is bound to become one of the glories of this century."[6]
A few months later, in May 1884, that youthful writer and critic of the Symbolist generation discovered Seurat, the man, and *Bathers at Asnières*, the work, at the first Salon des Indépendants. It was not until two years later that he would write about him, defending his and his friends' technique in his celebrated piece "Les Impressionnistes en mai 1886" where he discerned especially in *La Grande Jatte*, "a modernist Puvis."[7] Lengthy conversations with Seurat, Signac and Pissarro had led to his defense and illustration of the new movement. Puvis's name must have come up often.
Seurat had already known and admired him for several years. Puvis's sway on him dates to before the *Grande Jatte*; *Bathers at Asnières* (1883–84), for instance, has often been compared[8] to his elder's *Pleasant Land* (1882), a painting that Seurat had doubtless carefully examined at the 1882 Salon which displays the same landscape composition and the same position of some models (a seated, almost reclining, woman, with her arms around her knees, and a bare-chested boy in the same position, both on the left, the same small triangular sail, on the right, etc.). Of course, this timeless representation of dreamy women and children by a sea that recalls the classical Mediterranean is repeated in a popular bathing spot in a suburban landscape, and perfectly dated by the apparel and the factory smokestacks.
A "sketch" of 1881 (cat. De Hauke no. 6) reproducing the *The Poor Fisherman* in a landscape that he had probably just seen at the Salon, already revealed Seraut's interest in Puvis's work.
It may well be that he met him personally at the time, and visited his studio with his friends Aman-Jean and Ernest Laurent, but this is by no means certain,[9] and besides it hardly mat-

1. Pierre Puvis de Chavannes,
Young Women by the Sea,
detail, 1879.
Paris, Musée d'Orsay

119

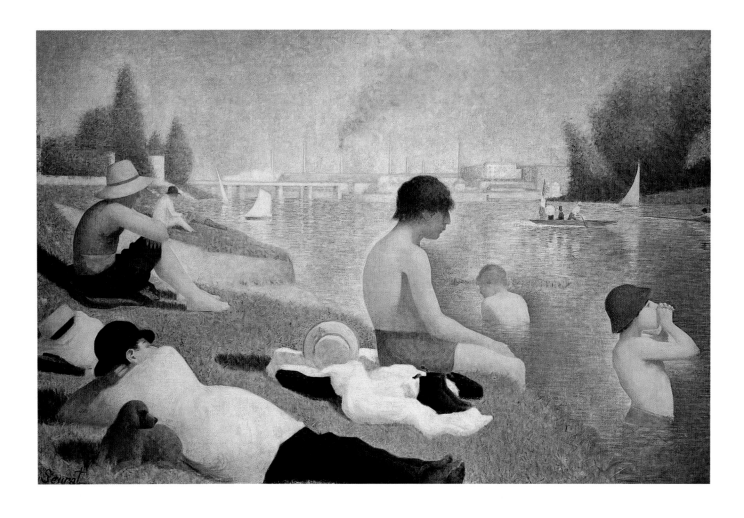

2. Georges Seurat,
Bathers at Asnières, 1883–84
London, National Gallery

ters, since Puvis's work was well-known and widely exhibited. Everything leads us to assume that Seurat went to Amiens to see Puvis's large decorations; or had at least seen the large copies at the Musée des Arts Décoratifs exhibition in 1881.

The only known meeting between Seurat and Puvis proved to be a disappointing experience for the younger of the two. Signac recalled it several years after Seurat's death: "Angrand tells me that when sitting on a bench in the back of the room with Seurat at the Indépendants [1890], they saw Puvis de Chavannes come into the exhibition in the company of a petite woman who looked like a model. While Puvis was going through the first rooms, Seurat said to Angrand, 'We'll see Puvis's expression when he stops in front of my *Chahut* . . . he'll be sure to grasp the directions, the arrangements of lines I sought . . . he'll see that I wanted this, that I did that . . . he's sure to be interested.' But Puvis walked past *Le Chahut*, which, however, was the largest and most attractive picture in the room without even glancing at it . . . . He just stopped in front of some small drawings by Maurice Denis."[10] It must have been a blow for Puvis's young admirer. Ever since *The Bather*, Puvis's shadow was to be descried behind nearly all of Seurat's large compositions, first and foremost *La Grande Jatte*.

We are familiar with the parody Toulouse-Lautrec made of *The Sacred Wood* that Puvis had shown in the 1884 Salon, before it was hung in the museum in Lyon. It would be unjustified to call *La Grande Jatte* a parody of *The Sacred Wood*, yet a number of elements, updated with a touch of humor, point to the latter as one of the sources of the Chicago painting: the overall composition (the triangle of the water is placed likewise on the left in the landscape), the even rows of tree trunks on the upper right, and the tree on the left placed by itself. Of course these modern muses have parasols and bustles, and the temple pillars are replaced by two narrow, long, parallel shapes formed by the full-face female passer-by in the center and the tree trunk on the right. Without going too far, Fénéon's intuition seems fully justified: this naturalist Sunday afternoon in the suburbs is a northern and sarcastic con-

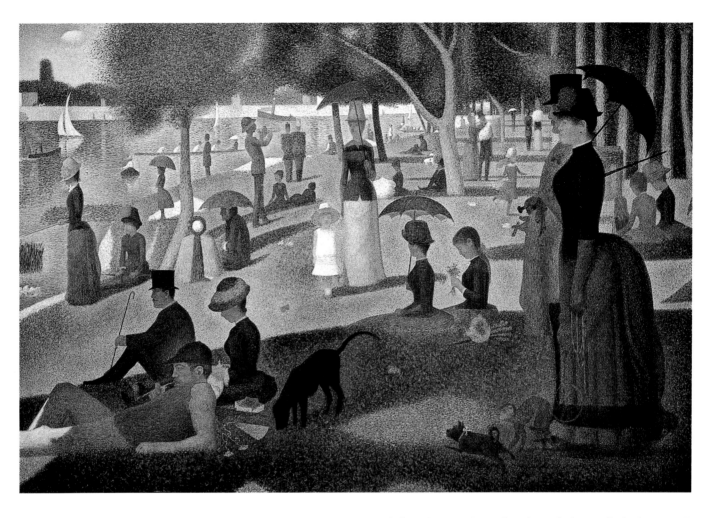

3. Georges Seurat,
*Sunday Afternoon on the Island
of La Grande Jatte*, 1884–86.
Chicago, The Art Institute

temporary version of the classical idyll in the woods, and perhaps laden with the same stiff ennui.

Would it be going too far as well to think that with his *Models*, Seurat repeated the ternary rhythm of the *Young Women by the Sea* (that he had seen twice, in 1879 and 1883[11]), systematically reversing the positions of the women: the center nude seen from behind in Puvis, and full-face in Seurat, the one on the left, full-face in the one and from behind in the other, and the third, instead, facing right in both cases?

Seurat's long thought-out large compositions are perhaps the part of his work that meant the most to him. After his death, Signac was therefore outraged that Octave Maus was not willing to organize a comprehensive Seurat retrospective in Brussels in 1904, owing to the difficulty of shipping large-format works, claiming: "It is foolish . . . to have left out the figure-painter and decorator. . . . It is only Seurat's large works that allow us to measure his contribution to contemporary art. He himself held his seascapes and landscapes to be mere exercises, and took pride in his compositions."[12]

Two other features allow us to compare the two artists. They both prepared their compositions in the traditional way, by painting their sketches and drawings. But in each case, the sketches were more highly colored than the resulting large canvases: the tiny dots Seurat made to obtain a purer color produced a certain pale effect, when seen from afar, a grayness that somehow recalled Puvis's painting. Furthermore, one may well wonder if Seurat's notion of large painted frames did not stem from the device of Puvis, who made a complete break with easel paintings which were framed by the dealer, and returned to the grand tradition of decorative painting and tapestry, in which the artist's invention extends beyond the very edge of the work.

As we shall see, among the "neos," Seurat is, along with Cross, the one who was the most influenced by Puvis. That is not the case with the "patriarch" of the movement, Camille Pis-

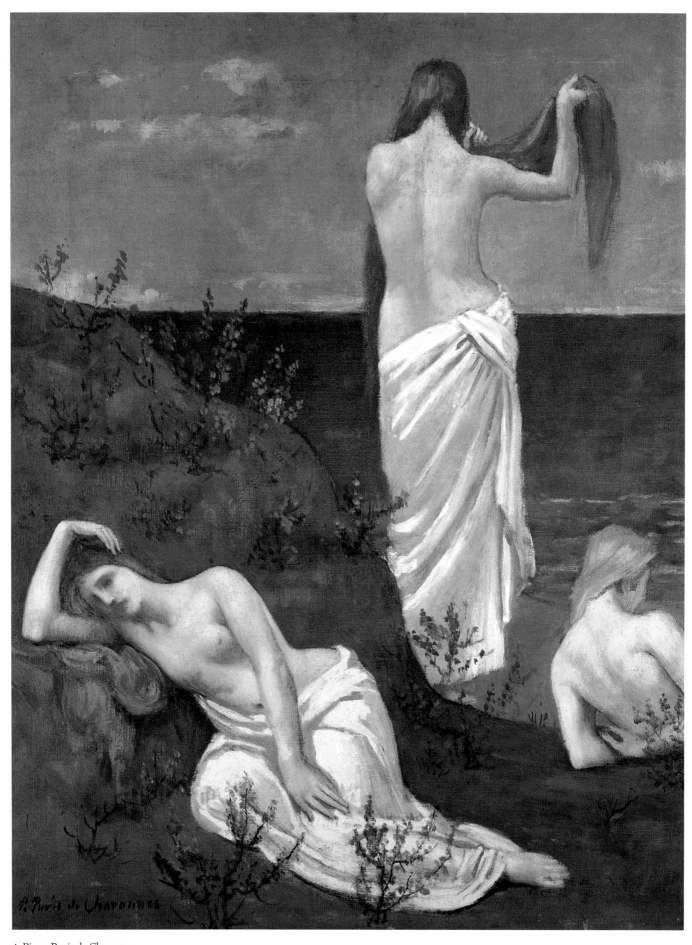

4. Pierre Puvis de Chavannes,
Young Women by the Sea, 1879.
Paris, Musée d'Orsay

sarro. The latter's attitude in his Neo-Impressionist period is revealing. His correspondence shows his admiration for Puvis de Chavannes throughout his lifetime, however, with two reservations. One is strategic. When, in 1887, Gustave Kahn wanted to reproduced a drawing of Puvis in *La Vogue* he wrote: "Even Puvis de Chavannes should not override. Why not? Because he is the opposite of us in art, whatever his talent may be. . . . He . . . will make art go backward and delay our Impressionist evolution."[13] It is obvious that Pissarro distrusted Symbolist criticism and the overall role of writers—in this instance, Kahn and Fénéon—who defended them. His sensibility remains Impressionist, and his infatuation with Seurat's method is only envisioned as a perfection of his earlier style. Besides, he was soon to give it up. Despite this passing, strictly circumstantial reservation, and the absence of influence on his own painting, his admiration for Puvis remained undimmed. For instance, ten years later we have him in Lyon, describing ". . . the magnificent decorations by Puvis de Chavannes. The famous *Sacred Wood* creates a superb effect."[14] Thus the second reservation was his deep mistrust of "literary," intellectual painting, of which Puvis might be an example, as he was in part for Gauguin, the Symbolists and the Nabis.

Puvis's moral and intellectual ambitions counted as much as his formal achievements for Signac and Cross. His way of illustrating a republican idealism, nourished by the classics, his iconographic interest in representing the lower classes, could not but appeal to those anarchistic moralists. And then, Puvis was the only artist who had resigned from the jury of the 1873 Salon, when Courbet was banned for having taken part in the Commune, and this made him immensely popular with the entire younger generation. "He created the moral landscape that suited the thoughts, the admirations, the fine melancholies, the tender-hearted optimisms of the last two generations. He compelled recognition from the painters themselves," Arsène Alexandre claimed at the time of his demise, in 1898.[15]

Indeed it was in the 1890s, the years of all the anarchist expressions ranging from violence to utopias, when Cross and Signac founded their solitary retreat in southern France, in an attempt to take their painting back to its sources far from Paris, that Puvis's influence would be the most intense for them. Signac's admiration would never wane, as his diary and letters largely prove. But it was when he decided to paint large compositions that he really turned to him. In the fall of 1892, he began a picture that above all was meant to be decorative—*Women at the Well* (Paris, Musée d'Orsay), its full title actually being *Young Provençal Women at the Well (Decoration for a Dimly-lit Panel)*. His intention is clear, as are the various references to Puvis: the slope of the hill, its top cutting across the sea on the horizon, is, in reverse, that of the *Young Women by the Sea*; and the two women by the well repeat[16] the composition of *At the Fountain* (large version, Boston, small version, Reims), paintings he had been able to see at the Puvis exhibition in 1887. A few months later, in the summer of 1893, he was contemplating his most ambitious decorative project, *In the Time of Harmony* (Montreuil, Hôtel de Ville) which would be executed in 1894 and 1895.[17]

We should also include here Paul Signac and Henri Edmond Cross, the author of *Evening Breeze* (Paris, Musée d'Orsay) that same year of 1894, in these "Puvisesque" undertakings. "We should paint large-scale" the former wrote the latter, recalling Puvis's and Seurat's examples. "All the same, how wonderful those Puvis are, don't you think? . . . When will he come, the great modern decorator: Giotto, Delacroix. . . . Since Seurat was closer to third position than Puvis . . . shouldn't we try looking in that direction? . . . Since we are both familiar with and love this sunny land,[18] why not try to raise a decorative monument to it together . . . encouraging each other with our mutual advice. . . . It would be quite a handful!"[19] They reported on the progress of their paintings to each other, and Puvis was constantly present in their letters. They sent each other reproductions of his works, sharing their enthusiasm: "Last Thursday I went to see his decoration of the main hall of the new Sorbonne. Have you seen it? My friend, it is overwhelming, admirable. I have never seen anything of his more beautiful. I am still very moved by it," Cross wrote Signac.[20] In *Evening Breeze*, his female figures have the same quality, at once *fin-de-siècle* and classicizing, as in Puvis, and their floating presence in a seascape, contrasting with the parallel verticals of the tree trunks and repeating the branches at the top of the canvas, obviously remind us of Puvis's compositions such as *Inter Artes et Naturam*, which decorated the museum of Rouen, and which he and Signac had doubtless seen at the Salon du Champ-de-Mars in 1890.

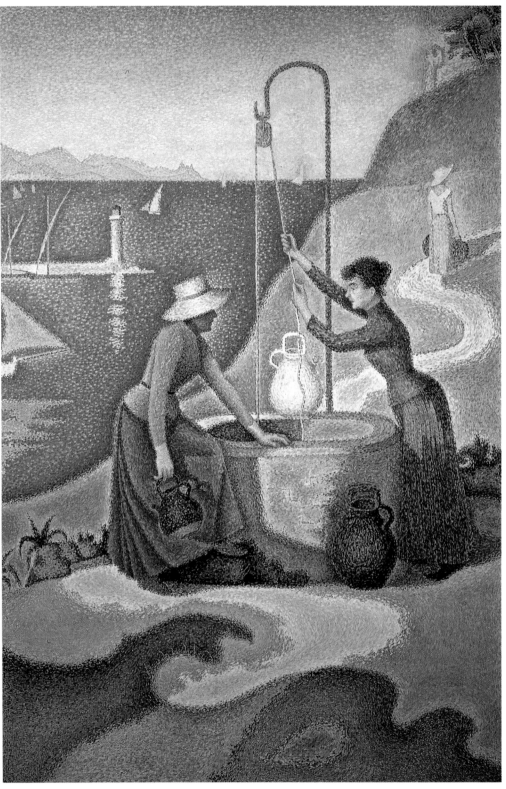

5. Paul Signac,
Women at the Well, 1892.
Paris, Musée d'Orsay

opposite page
6. Paul Signac,
In the Time of Harmony, 1894,
Montreuil, Hôtel de Ville

7. Henri Edmond Cross,
Evening Breeze, 1893.
Paris, Musée d'Orsay

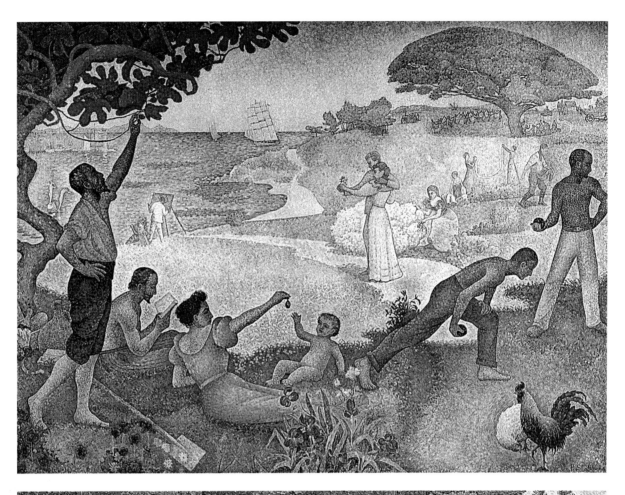

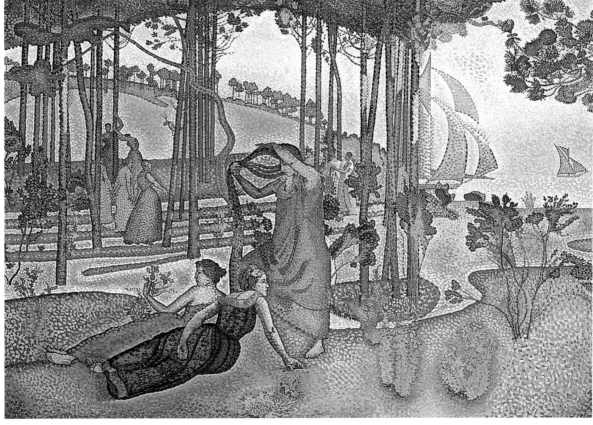

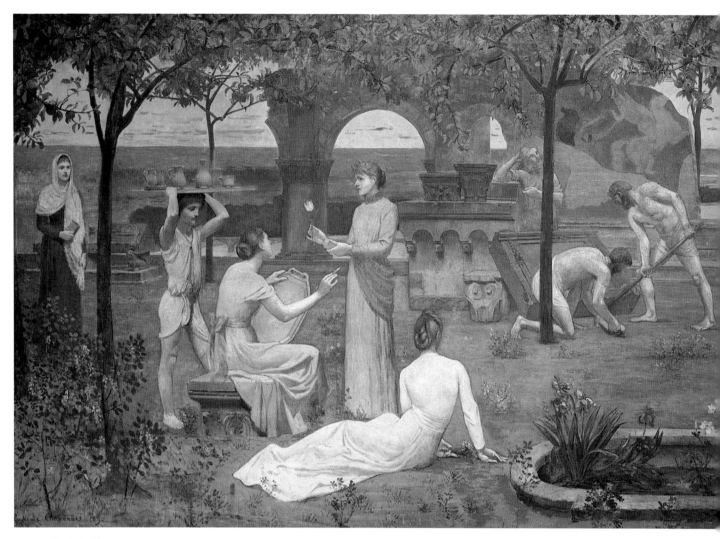

8. Pierre Puvis de Chavannes,
Inter Artes et Naturam, 1890.
Rouen, Musée des Beaux-Arts

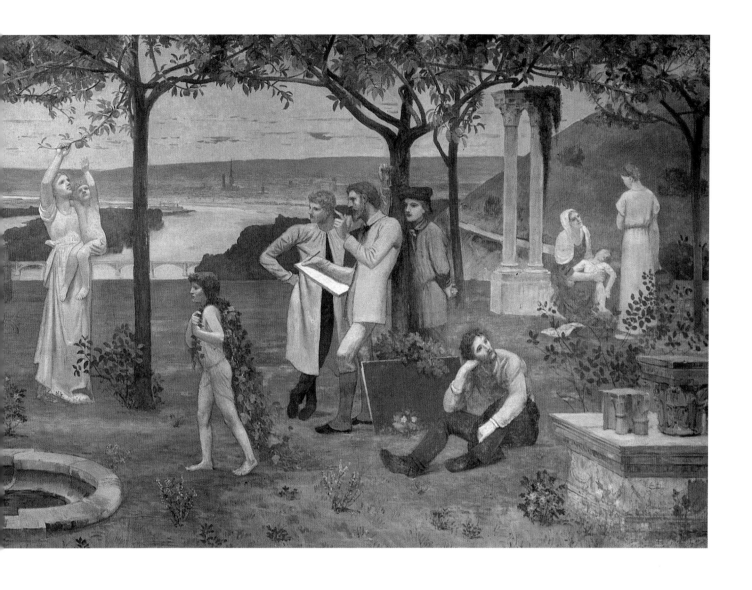

following pages
9. Pierre Puvis de Chavannes,
Marseille, Gateway to the Orient,
1869. Marseille,
Musée des Beaux-Arts

127

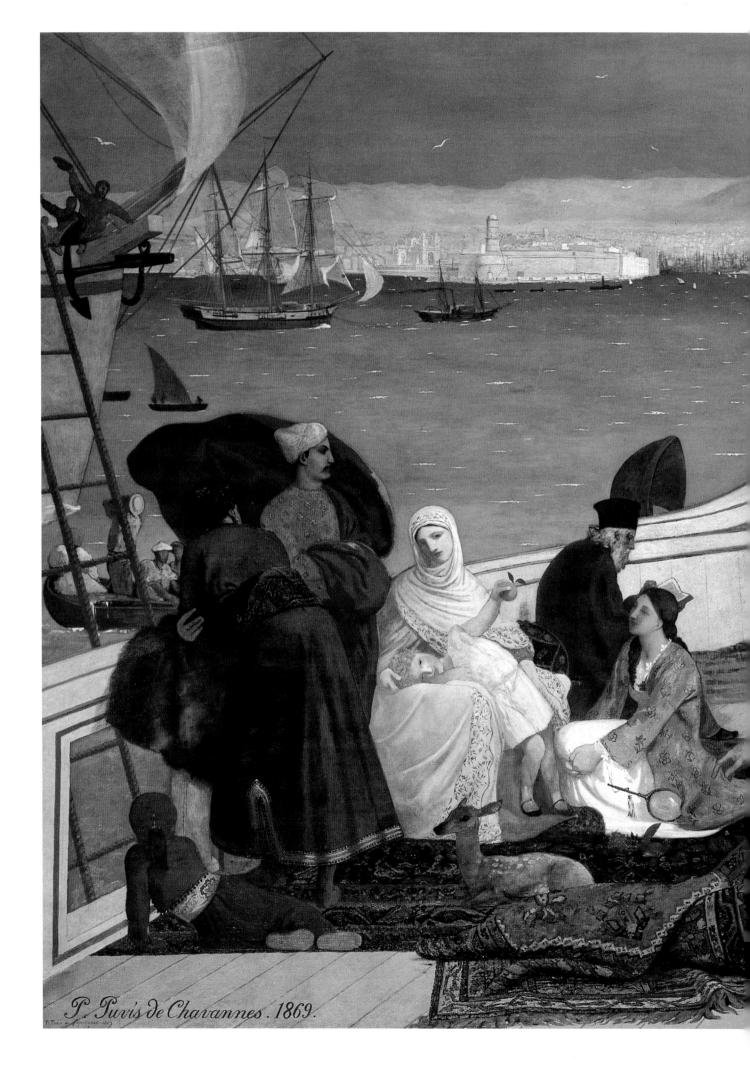

P. Puvis de Chavannes. 1869.

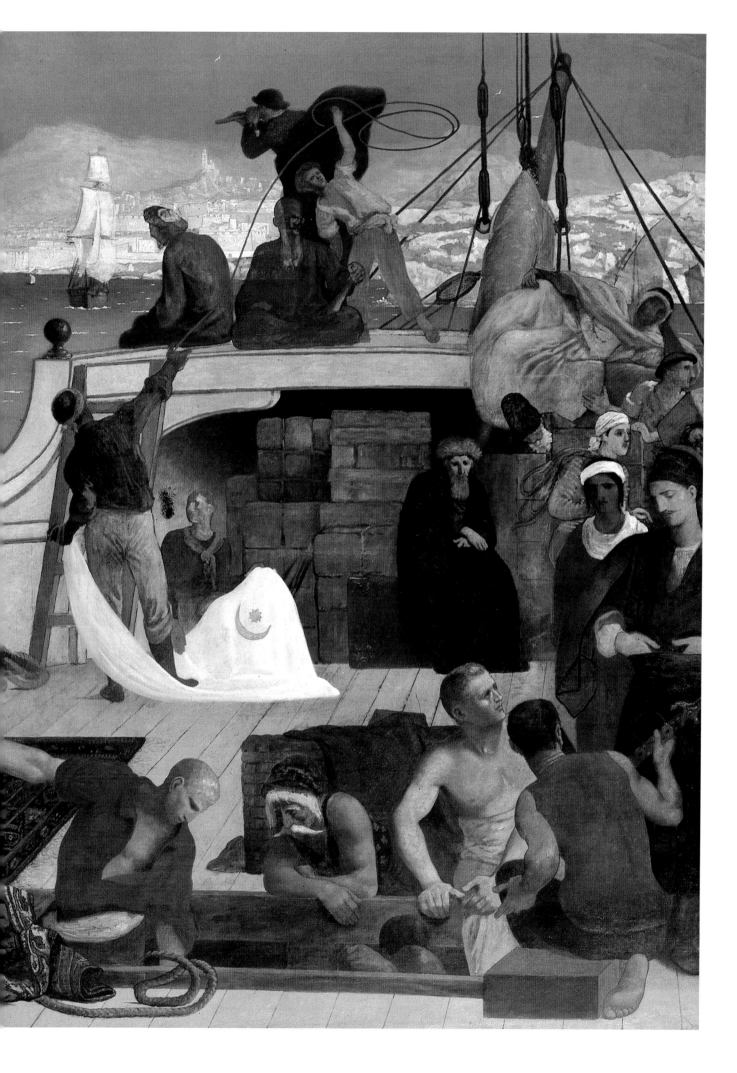

"Great news!" Signac announced to Cross, "following your advice I am about to try out a large canvas! . . . This is it: Repose, calm, happiness! The bowl player becomes an episodic figure of *In the Time of Anarchy* (title not yet definite). In the foreground a group at rest . . . man woman child . . . under a tall pine tree an old man is telling stories to some children . . . on a hillside . . . the harvest: the machines are smoking, working, getting the job done; and around the haystacks . . . a farandole of harvesters . . . in the center a young couple: free love! And so on. But it is still all jerky, confused, dull. I am writing you so we can talk about it when I come to stay at Cabasson. It will be a great help to have your advice."[21]

"Au temps d'anarchie" was to become "Au temps d'harmonie," a large utopian worker-peasant idyll, in a Saint-Tropez décor. References to Puvis are countless. The overall composition recalls *Pleasant Land*, the man's raised hand picking fruit repeats the same gesture of the central figure of *Inter Artes et Naturam*, and the grouping of the seated and standing figures under the trees is the same. At the same time he was planning his painting on the way back to Paris from Saint-Tropez, Signac spent "a supremely blissful afternoon" in front of Puvis's decoration in Lyon.[22]

Puvis's influence on Signac would dim in the late 1990s when the latter gave up big mural decorations and large formats in general. Cross, instead, referred to him often, for instance when pondering about introducing a figure in a landscape. Thus, writing in 1896 about the *Provençal Fisherman*,[23] he recalled: "As Puvis used to say to one of my friends, you can never have too clear an idea about a picture before starting it, and even when you think you have taken the most careful precautions, there always comes the time, in the course of the execution, when an unwanted wolf shows its teeth!"[24] So what Puvis's work brought to his mind was preliminary thought, and reflection prevailing over impression.

The other Neo-Impressionists were scarcely influenced by Puvis, except, indirectly, Theo Van Rysselberghe, when he painted *The Blazing Hour* (1897–98), a large-format picture of swimmers by the sea shore, like nymphs in a décor (Weimar Museum). But in that case it was more of a return to antiquity and classicism, in a Post-Impressionist style.

Of course, Matisse's celebrated *Luxe, calme et volupté* belongs to this post-Puvis and Neo-Impressionist tradition, even if it is already very much Matisse. The title is a quotation from Baudelaire—it may well be that Signac himself introduced him to *Les Fleurs du mal*, of which he had a precious edition in his house of La Hune. And then, how can we forget the first title Signac had thought of ten years earlier in beginning the conception of his own painting: *Du repos, du calme, du bonheur* [Rest, Calm, Happiness]![25]

Several years later, when seeking the squaring of the circle—that is, more freedom in his painting, while sticking to his practice of the divided brushstroke—Signac referred to Puvis again. He mentioned "the perpetual beauty of his landscapes, where he could comfortably synthesize, without being disturbed by studies of the motif," and admired in *Gateway to the Orient*, a decoration in Marseille, the fact that the vessel's shrouds rise outward, whereas observation and common sense would have them rise in an other direction in order to be attached to the top of the mast. "But it does not matter in the least, because the drawing is more harmonious," and he added: "For me, painting from nature is a kind of slavishness, a lack of creative power (painting from your window . . . it's senile!)."[26] In short, it is paradoxical, at the beginning of the century, to discover lessons of freedom in Puvis's draftsmanship. Indeed, Puvis had been a master of draftsmanship for Cross and for Signac himself who, unlike Seurat, had no academic training. An example: when Signac was working on his *In the Time of Harmony*, in 1893–94, "every morning, a half-hour of exercise: sketches from Raphael, Puvis, Andrea del Sarto, Mantegna. An excellent treatment."[27]

Had those young artists read the article on Puvis written by the Provençal painter Paul Guigou in 1892? As the painter himself clearly said: "I strive for my art to be synthetic, but I try as hard as I can to avoid it becoming abstract. . . . I do not depart from nature, but I make a selection from it. Art is a parallelism of nature. . . . [It] contains everything, but in a confused way; we must introduce order in this chaos. How? By abbreviation and simplification."[28] This perhaps explains why Puvis, the rather gray painter of Parnassian decors for official walls, caught the attention of so many artists who, in the Neo-Impressionist movement or not, were seeking at the turn of century to establish modernism in painting.

[1] H. Focillon, *La peinture du XIXème et XXème siècles, du réalisme à nos jours,* Paris, 1928, p. 230.

[2] That took place soon after Richard Wattenmaker's exhibition, *Puvis de Chavannes and the Modern Tradition,* exh. cat., Art Gallery of Ontario, Toronto, 1975.

[3] That is, Bonnard, Gauguin, Pissarro, father and son, Seurat, Signac, Lautrec, etc.—as opposed to the recognized modern painters who exhibited in the galleries of the "Grand Boulevard": the Impressionists. See the exhibition *Vincent Van Gogh and the Painters of the Petit Boulevard,* Saint Louis Art Museum and Städtisches Kunstinstitut Frankfurt, February–September, 2001.

[4] Vincent Van Gogh to his brother, June 1890, as cited in *Correspondance complète de Vincent Van Gogh, enrichie de tous les dessins originaux,* trans. by M. Beerblock and L. Roëlandt, introduction and notes by G. Charensol, Gallimard, Paris, 1960, vol. III, p. 703.

[5] See introduction by F. Cachin to F. Fénéon, *Au-delà de l'impressionisme,* F. Cachin ed., éditions Hermann, Paris, 1966, p. 15.

[6] In "L'Exposition Nationale des Beaux-Arts," *La Libre Revue,* October 1883, reproduced in *ibidem,* p. 38.

[7] *Ibidem,* p. 67.

[8] See the excellent "Seurat et Puvis de Chavannes," by R.L. Herbert, *Yale University Art Gallery Bulletin,* October 1959, vol. 95, no. 2. Before him—and after Fénéon!—Puvis's role in Seurat's art had been pointed out for some time, for instance by D. Catton Rich, *Seurat and the Evolution of La Grande Jatte,* Chicago, 1935, and by W. Homer, "Seurat's formative period," *Connoisseur,* 142, no. 57, 1958, etc.

[9] See Herbert, *op. cit.,* p. 29. Aman-Jean's son claimed instead that his father and Seurat had frequently been to Puvis's studio in the late 1870s and early 1880s. See F. Aman-Jean, "Souvenir d'Aman Jean," Musée des Arts Décoratifs, 1970, p. 18, and Wattenmaker, *op. cit.*

[10] Unpublished extract from Paul Signac's diary, January 10, 1896.

[11] At the Salon, then at the Exposition Nationale des Beaux-Arts. Meyer Shapiro had already compared the two works. See as well my catalog entry in *Great French Paintings from the Barnes Foundation,* New York, 1993, and Paris, 1994, pp. 174–77.

[12] Signac to Van Rysselberghe, 1904, unpublished letter, Getty Archives.

[13] Letter to Lucien, January 8, 1887, in *Correspondance de Camille Pissarro 1866–1890,* introduction by J. Bailly-Herzberg, vol. II, Valhermier éd., Paris, 1968, p. 98.

[14] *Ibidem,* vol. IV, p. 498.

[15] Obituary, *Le Figaro,* October 25, 1898.

[16] See C. Fréches, "Paul Signac, acquisitions récentes," *Revue du Louvre,* 1983, p. 37.

[17] See M. Ferretti-Boquillon, entry no. 75 of the *Signac* exhibition catalog, Paris, Amsterdam, New York, 2001.

[18] Signac is at Saint-Tropez, Cross at Cabasson, near Le Lavandou. See *Méditerranée. De Courbet à Matisse,* exh. cat., Paris, 2000.

[19] P. Signac to H.E. Cross, Signac Archives, n.d., quoted in M. Ferretti-Boquillon, ed., *Signac et Saint-Tropez: 1892–1913,* exh. cat. Musée de l'Annonciade, Saint-Tropez, Musée des Beaux–Arts, Reims, Saint-Tropez, 1992, p. 52.

[20] H.E. Cross to P. Signac, unpublished letter, Signac Archives, n.d. [1893].

[21] P. Signac to H.E. Cross, Signac Archives, n.d. [spring or summer 1893], partly quoted in Ferretti-Boquillon, *op. cit.,* p. 52.

[22] Signac Archives. Quoted in Ferretti-Boquillon, *op. cit.,* p. 57.

[23] Compin catalog no. 58, Allen Memorial Art Museum, Oberlin, Ohio.

[24] Cross to Theo Van Rysselberghe [1896], unpublished letter, Getty Archives.

[25] See note 21.

[26] Signac to Van Rysselberghe (1902), unpublished letter, Getty Archives.

[27] Signac to Van Rysselberghe (1893), unpublished letter, Getty Archives.

[28] Paul Guigou, "Puvis de Chavannes," *La Revue du siècle,* January 1892, no. 56.

I should like to thank the Getty Research Institute, Special Collections, for giving me permission to reproduce the unpublished excerpts from the Signac–Van Rysselberghe correspondence (notes 12, 24, 26, 27).

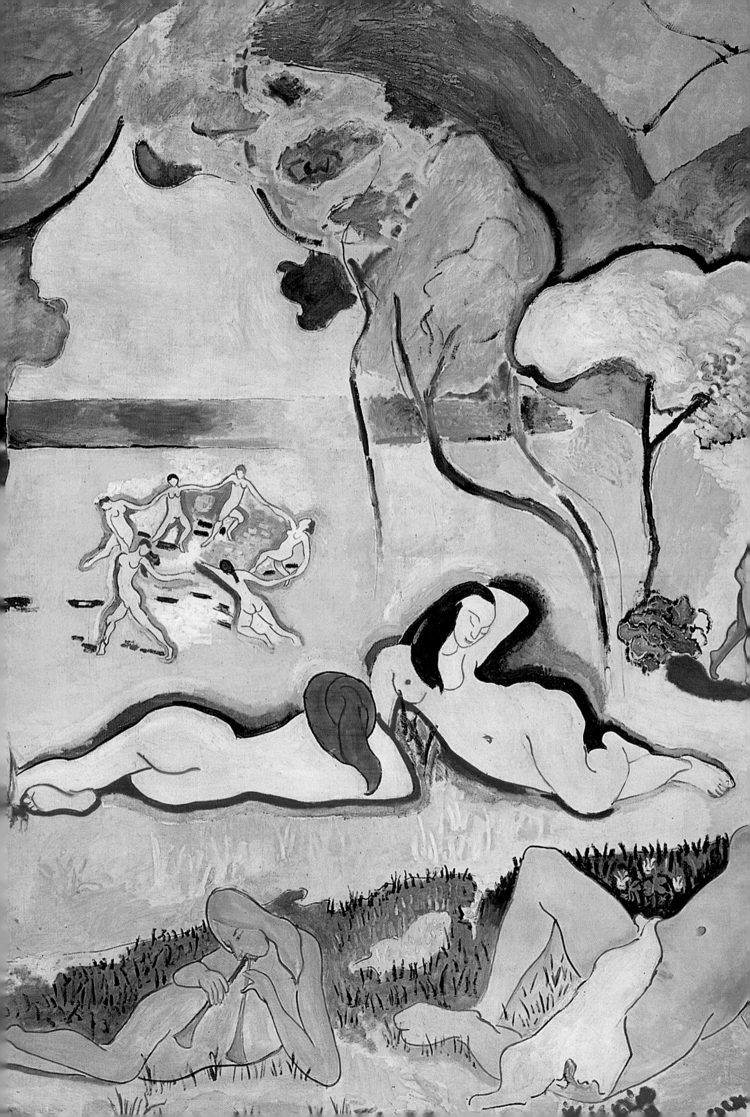

Rémi Labrusse

Matisse and Puvis de Chavannes:
Four Convergences Plus a Divergence

Paris, May 1896
Puvis de Chavannes is president of the Société Nationale des Beaux-Arts for the fifth year, and, in that quality he writes to inform Matisse he can exhibit five paintings of his choice at the Salon of the Champ-de-Mars out of the eleven he has sent.[1] For a twenty-seven year old painter, still enrolled in the Ecole des Beaux-Arts in Gustave Moreau's *atelier*, it was a considerable success, soon enhanced by the fact that two of the paintings finally shown were purchased by the state and that at the close of the Salon, Matisse was elected associate member of the Société, upon the direct intervention of its president: "In the vote of admissions for membership, Puvis de Chavannes put my name forward and Jean Béraud objected; this led to a small altercation that was reported to me. I was appointed associate member."[2] So, symbolically, however not without some commotion, Puvis was behind the first serious public success in Matisse's artistic career.

Yet the latter had not met his intercessor: Puvis, by then an old man, shied away from the social functions connected with his position,[3] and Matisse, on his behalf, never felt any urge for that kind of meeting, even with those he most admired.[4] The episode of the Salon of 1896 is more an illustration, among others, of what Marius Vachon was to write a year later about Puvis: that the old master's "public and private likings" went "to the Impressionists, the *Indépendants*, the Symbolists, etc., who are derided and thwarted; to artists seeking originality, the ones who pursue chimeras; brave, energetic innovators, struggling their way through indifferences or hostilities."[5] Instead, we have no indication that he felt particularly drawn to the manner of a young man belonging to a well-identified group, that of Gustave Moreau's pupils, even if, in the midst of that "hub of revolt," as Roger Marx described it that same year,[6] Matisse seemed to stand out by his qualities of measure—his "bourgeois Impressionism,"[7] his delicate science of grays[8]—that might have been to the liking of the decorator of the Panthéon (figs. 2–3) and the Boston Library (his last major project, of which the canvases had just been shown in Paris, before being sent to America, in 1895 and 1896[9]).

Then everything came to a halt: Puvis, like Moreau, died in 1898, and Matisse, left on his own, firmly believing he had not yet mastered his aesthetic, undertook an investigation of his own means that was to last nearly ten years, completely breaking with the prospect of a quiet success that the Salon of 1896 had seemed to forecast.

Collioure, July 1905
Matisse writes to Signac, about *Luxe, calme et volupté* (fig. 4), his large painting executed in the Neo-Impressionist manner the year before, after spending the summer with Signac at Saint-Tropez, and shown at the Salon des Indépendants in the spring: "Painting, especially the divided brushstroke, destroys the drawing whose eloquence comes from the contours. Just remember the cartoon of the picture and the canvas, and you will observe, if you have not already done so, their plastic discrepancy. To color the cartoon, all you have to do is fill in its compartments with flat colors, in the manner of Puvis for instance."[10] A second time, in other words, posthumously, Puvis played the intercessor: he helped Matisse, in this case, to rid himself of the "yoke of Divisionism"[11] and to raise the suggestion that flat colors might be as, or even more useful to him, to achieve his purpose, than the doctrine preached by Signac. Just what was that purpose? That, he claimed, still tentatively, of a decorative painting; a "decoration of walls," as Signac too would write after buying the canvas for his Saint-Tropez house.[12] There again, Puvis is not far away: he embodied that notion of monumental decoration in such an ample, determined and personal a manner for over fifty years, that no one, less than ten years after his death, could avail of it without thinking of him.[13]

Notwithstanding, in that key period of the first Fauvism the situation was far more complex for Matisse than it had been in 1896, when he could boast of having attracted the great decorator's attention. On the one hand, Matisse was much more familiar with Puvis's work: Aside from the large public decorations in Paris—the Panthéon, the Hôtel de Ville—and the Boston ones shown in 1895–96, he had had other opportunities to see him in private collections like

1. Henri Matisse,
Le Bonheur de vivre,
detail, 1905–06.
Merion, The Barnes Foundation

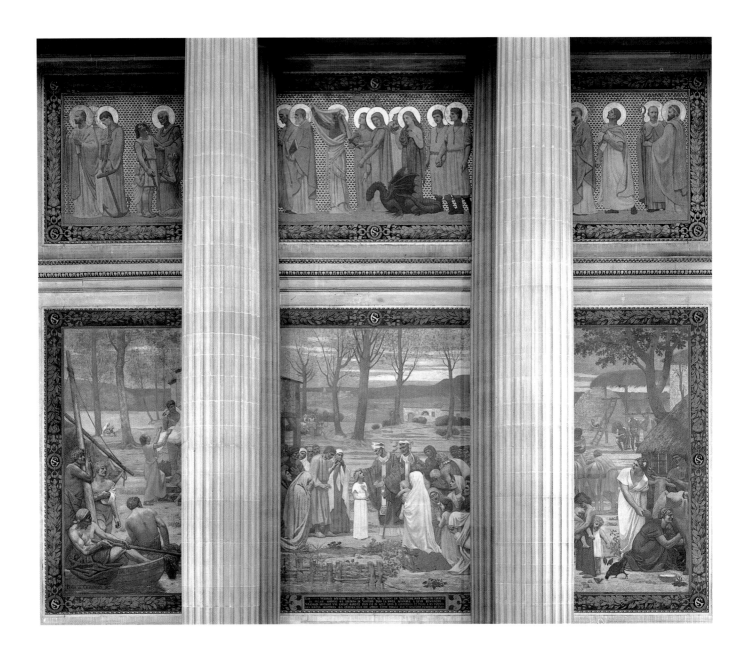

2. 3. Pierre Puvis de Chavannes,
The Childhood of Saint Genevieve,
and *Saint Genevieve Supplying
Paris*, 1893–98.
Paris, Panthéon

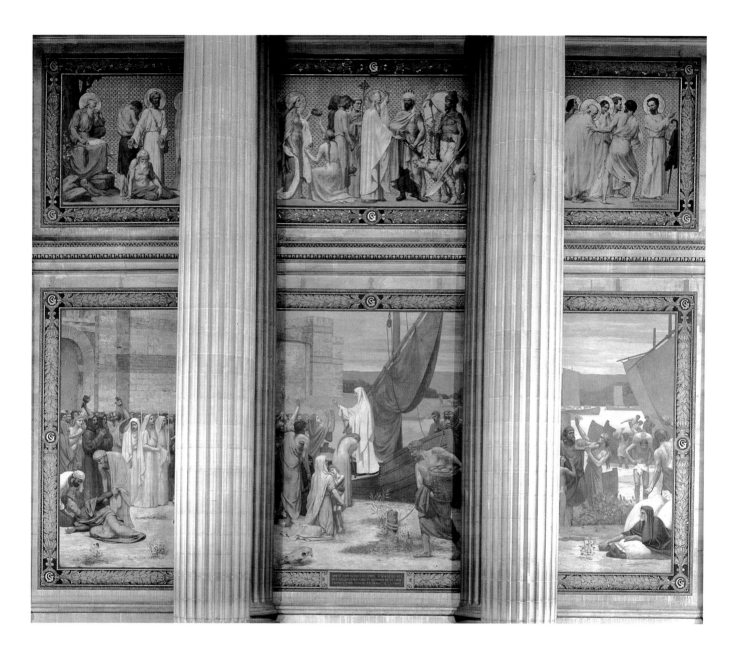

that of Henri Rouart, that he went to see around 1900,[14] at the 1900 World Fair, and especially on the occasion of the retrospective devoted to Puvis in 1904 at the second Salon d'Automne, of which Matisse was a member. Matisse showed fourteen pictures there that he could compare to the prestigious ensemble of easel paintings, decorative schemes, drawings and caricatures assembled in the Puvis room. Moreover, on an aesthetic level, one of the major conceptual debates since the 1890s, not to say the essential notion firing discussions on avant-garde painting, was the idea of decoration[15]: Through the reference to Gauguin, but to Puvis as well, the word came back so regularly in the writings of Matisse's kindred spirits—Roger Marx, Charles Morice, Signac, etc.—that Maurice Denis, in 1903, considered it the "pet theme" of "discussions among artists."[16] Nobody exactly knew what was meant by it, but at least one thing was clear, and that was that, in those discussions, Puvis's name far from acting as a foil, was very often called upon to back up the battle or battles for a new use of painting.

So that, for Matisse, early in the summer of 1905, betting Puvis against Signac was a clever ploy, since for a long time Signac himself had professed his admiration for the Amiens decorator.[17] In referring to him to formulate his own doubts, Matisse could hope to find a smooth way out of Divisionism, an exit that his Fauve paintings would begin to confirm over the summer. Several months later, during the winter, he painted *Le Bonheur de vivre* (fig. 5), that bore out the break by the systematic use of flat colors outlined by linear contours. This time, the painting was visibly conceived as a war machine against Neo-Impressionism: Its size, its ambitious iconographic program (that, not without irony, simultaneously echoed *Pleasant Land* by Puvis and Signac's large panel, *In the Time of Harmony*[18]), his ample references to the tradition of museums, all converged to make it the manifesto of a leader, no longer of a disciple. So in all, Puvis de Chavannes perfectly played the part Matisse had assigned him: By embodying the idea of painting in flat colors, he had come to the rescue by keeping the Fauve painter from assimilating Divisionist technique and decorative aesthetic. A few months later, this step was confirmed, among others, by the emphatic use of "flat colors" in the second version of *Luxe*, a painting whose dimensions and theme again called attention to its decorative purpose.

Besides, contemporary critics had often noticed—and were either pleased or anxious—that allusive presence of Puvis in Matisse's winning of his own aesthetic. By the fall of 1905, in his review of the Salon d'Automne, Maurice Denis placed the two artists in the same line, that of the modern artists who, by reacting against the fossilized tradition of the Ecole des Beaux-Arts, were guilty of the opposite sin, "the excess of theories," thus turning to "painting *per se*, the pure act of painting": "However original Matisse's endeavors may be, they stem from a systematic approach that is far from new. In Van Gogh's days, a great number of the same kind of investigations led to identical results. If, looking further back, I compare a painting by Puvis de Chavannes to a painting by Poussin, I can already see, through rather similar qualities, this deep difference: that the latter hides the firm awareness he has of his means beneath embellishments borrowed from the rhetoric of his day and beneath the charms of his sensibility; whereas the modern master lays bare everything artificial and intentional in his work."[19] Puvis as a scout, in other words, on the perilous path of modernism in painting, Puvis as the initiator of an intellectualism that Matisse would carry to its paroxysm. In the same vein—but this time favorably—Mécislas Golberg, who had published a long essay glorifying Puvis de Chavannes in 1901,[20] that is, just when he met Matisse, got in touch with him again in 1907 to ask him to write a text—"explaining [his] aesthetic, stating its case and supporting it with reproductions."[21] The critic's premature death at the end of the year would prevent that project from being carried out, but the notes Mécislas Golberg had taken would be used again by Apollinaire in his interview with Matisse in December 1907 in *La Phalange*[22]—the first text where Matisse publicly expressed himself—and we will find them echoed again in the *Notes d'un peintre*, Matisse's major theoretic text, published at last in December 1908, where several formulations, as Roger Benjamin has pointed out, cannot be understood without referring to Puvis de Chavannes.[23] Finally, several months later, when Charles Estienne collected Matisse's comments, he in turn

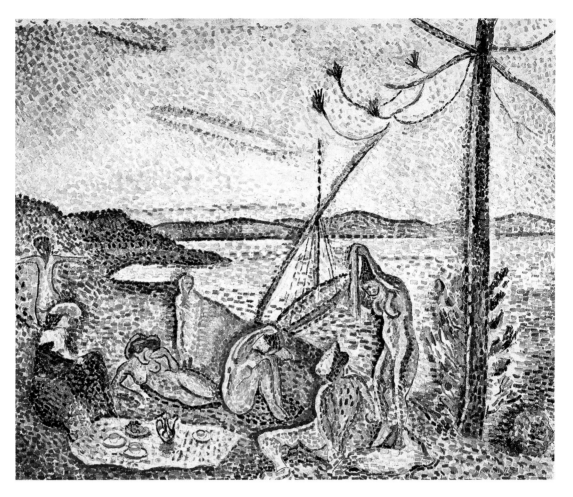

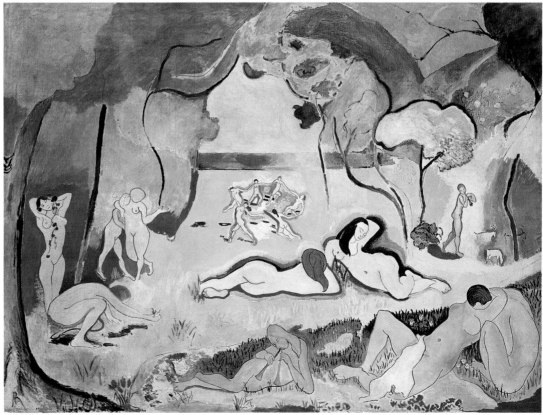

observed that "he talks like Puvis de Chavannes; for him painting is an appeal to contemplation, serenity, it should be restful."[24] Here again we have strategic statements, to defend a painting that seeks less to inspire contemplation than to make the eye bounce off the surface, and in doing so has already given the notion of decoration, right then, a vehemently new meaning.

Issy-les-Moulineaux, November 1910
Matisse, who had settled the year before in his studio in the Paris suburb, received a letter from the Bernheims, his dealers, on November 3, announcing that: "Removed by an automobile with a trailer, Puvis's canvas will reach Paris at midnight and be at your place tomorrow Friday by ten or eleven o'clock. Would you be so kind as to let us see the canvas there between one and two o'clock?"[25] According to Matisse's own words, it was a "monochrome copy of Puvis de Chavannes, a mechanical reproduction of the decoration of the Boston Library,"[26] *The Inspiring Muses Acclaim the Spirit of Light*, purchased by the Bernheim brothers from the artist's widow and that they were about to sell to the Russian collector Sergei Shchukin: Because of its size—fifteen meters long—the studio Matisse had just built in the garden of his villa was the only place where it could be easily displayed, for the dealers and their buyer to appraise it. So of that major masterpiece by Puvis, which Matisse had seen at the Salon du Champ-de-Mars fifteen years earlier, here was the "replica" installed at his place: Puvis at Matisse's, Puvis in front of Matisse, Puvis *against* Matisse, who at the time was facing the critical uproar caused by his two "decorative panels," *Dance* (fig. 10) and *Music* (fig. 9), exhibited at the latest Salon d'Automne. Events then followed one upon another over a week in a very tense atmosphere. First of all, Shchukin, who had commissioned Matisse for the two panels, reneged on their purchase with the excuse that the panels featured nudes that might shock the girls of his family; or rather, he asked the painter to make two reduced copies of them that he might then discreetly put in his own bedroom. Matisse categorically refused: "I said it was impossible to make a reduced copy of those large, four-meter panels, conceived in their dimension."[27] The opposite of Puvis's decorations, of which the latter executed "mechanical replicas," it was unthinkable for Matisse that his own might be reproducible, since the very rhythm of their creation was meant to remain alive in the final work and prevent the closing of the image upon itself.

At the same time, Shchukin, who had loved and collected works by Puvis by the end of the preceding century,[28] mulled over the purchase of the Bernheims' large panel: should it replace Matisse's or be added to them? It is unclear. The fact is that on November 7 or 8 he left for Moscow, after having bought the Puvis he had seen in Matisse's own studio, and refused the Matisses. As for the latter, discouraged, he left for Spain, while the Bernheims somehow "made it up to him," by offering him a small painting by Bonnard.[29] Then, a complete turnabout occurred: Once in Moscow, Shchukin changed his mind, accepted Matisse's two panels such as they were, sent Puvis's huge decoration back to Paris, trading it for a small painting by Matisse, with a loss of 10 000 francs. The letters he then wrote the painter reflect his turmoil: First, November 11, "In Paris, when I saw the Puvis, I was still under the influence of memories of my youth, when I was so carried away by Puvis. Back here, in another atmosphere, I can see the panel, although very handsome, is a bit flabby in the draftsmanship and even a bit (just a tiny bit) 'pompier' in style. So all I regret is the loss of money. By working, I hope to recover the lost amount. If the Bernheims refuse all offers, then I ask you to keep Puvis's panel in your studio until my death";[30] then, November 27, "I thank you so much for all the trouble over the Puvis and I am very pleased the Bernheims accepted the trade. I am more and more convinced that your course is the right one. Since I left Paris three weeks ago, I distinctly recall your paintings alone, which are engraved in my memory. All the rest is forgotten";[31] lastly on January 5, 1911, "the great project I now am proposing you is to decorate an entire room in my house (it's the room where I wanted to put the Puvis)."[32] That last plan remained in limbo, but nonetheless, in those early days of the year 1911, Matisse *cancelled out* Puvis after the crisis in the mind of the collector on the walls of his Moscow palace, exactly as Puvis had cancelled out Matisse on the walls of the Issy studio a few weeks before.

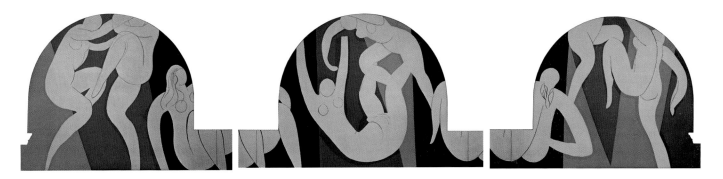

6-8. Henri Matisse,
Dance, 1932–33.
Merion, The Barnes Foundation

A decoration and its opposite: The theoretic confusion over the concept of what is decorative, typical of the years of the turn of the century and up to 1905, gave way to a clear opposition between two worlds, by the strength of painting alone. Matisse might well repeat "Puvisesque" formulations in his essays, like the old master he might call his major canvases[33] "decorative panels," he might, last of all, delight in their "mural signification" when he saw them appropriately hung on the walls of the Salon d'Automne[34]; henceforth the works performed on an altogether different register. Looking at them seriously, as Shchukin had after some hesitation, meant *no longer being able to look* at Puvis, who was all of a sudden cast into the past. That is what a fellow countryman of Shchukin's, Yakov Tugenhold, had already pointed out after seeing *Dance* and *Music* for the first time at the Salon d'Automne: "Matisse 'Americanizes' colors, turns the panel into a raucous poster you can see a mile away, forgetting that mural painting has its own *traditions*. The modest Puvis de Chavannes remembered them; Matisse doesn't care to and besides doesn't have time to grasp them."[35] As to whether Matisse had *forgotten* traditions, nothing could be less certain; but that, extended to non-European worlds, they had been fused in a new melting pot and cast into the unknown—beyond the paths that had been traced by the tradition of mimetic representation in the West since the Renaissance—was in all probability the reason behind Shchukin's choosing the two panels rather than that of Puvis.

Nice, May 1933
Matisse had just completed the second version of *Dance* (figs. 6–8) for the Albert Barnes Foundation at Merion, Pennsylvania, a project he had been working on for nearly three years, and one that gave a new, decisive impulse to his work, after having been under the threat of a crisis, and even sterility in the late 1920s. The huge panels, practically fifteen meters long in all, were about to leave for America. At this time, the painter received Dorothy Dudley and explained to her what had guided him in his work: "It is a room for paintings: treating my decoration like one more painting would have been a mistake. My aim was to translate painting into architecture, to make the fresco the equivalent of cement or stone. I believe no one does that very often anymore. Nowadays, the mural painter does paintings, not mural paintings.—And Puvis de Chavannes? I asked—Yes, he comes close, but does not achieve perfection in that sense. The walls of the Panthéon, for instance, are stone. Puvis's paintings are too gentle in feeling to produce the equivalent of that material. If you had a diamond, you would set it in metal and not in rubber."[36]

It must be said this time that the comparison with Puvis suggested by Dorothy Dudley appears nearly unavoidable. First, the latter's work had been reappraised in the world of postwar contemporary art, and first of all by Picasso who explicitly used it, at a time when he was asserting himself more than ever as Matisse's great rival. Then, from a historical point of view, Matisse's work for Merion singularly recalls the one Puvis had done for Boston; at forty years distance, two French painters at the height of their respective careers were given major decorative commissions from across the Atlantic, and they both recapitulated on those occasions, in order to transform the achievements of several decades of investigations. In Matisse, that determination for an active synthesis is particularly apparent, if only in the iconography that returns to that of *Bonheur de vivre* and the Moscow *Dance*. In Puvis as well, the large panel at the top of the stairway of the Boston Library, that had been so familiar to

9. Henri Matisse,
Music, 1910.
Saint Petersburg, The Hermitage
Museum

10. Henri Matisse,
Dance, 1909–10.
Saint Petersburg, The Hermitage
Museum

Matisse since 1895, and that may be considered the painter's masterpiece, displayed a degree of simplification he rarely attained, such a "need for the synthesis," as he said,[37] that the importance of its discursive content tended to be reduced to the benefit of a pure orchestration of its forms. Last of all, the reference to Puvis was all the more evident in that Matisse, for the first time in his career, was undertaking a decorative work proper on a large scale for a place having a public destination. The idea of the decorative that he had conceived since 1905, as a war machine in the tradition of easel painting, was thus dangerously actual in a context where the painter would have to mark the difference between the paintings exhibited in the rooms of the Foundation at Merion, and his own decoration that, he claimed, was to be incorporated in the architecture, that is, enliven the space while disappearing at the same time. Indeed, nothing could be more contrary to Matisse's aesthetic than such a distinction between picture and decoration: In all his work since 1905, whatever the destination might have been, he sought instead to challenge the frontiers between major art and minor arts, just like those between monumental art and "intimacy painting."[38] Hence, the ambiguities of the Merion project as well, the main merit of which was undoubtedly to stimulate the painter's plastic reflection.

His anxiety caught up with him, indeed, his need to redefine the grounds of his aesthetic, and it was with that in view, as though he were going back in his mind to his great conflicting years between 1905 and 1910, that he used Puvis as a foil. With a prudence that has much to say about his fears regarding the reception of his own work by the American public, he contested the "decorator" of the Panthéon's "perfection" which, *al contrario*, we can imagine he sought. Contrary to Maurice Denis, at the same time, and to many who sustained a toned-down modernism in the 1930s, he refused to acknowledge Puvis as an inspiring master, and merely looked to him as a remote predecessor who, despite his merits, had been unable to break the chains of painting bequeathed by the nineteenth century, so as to make it irradiate like an architecture. Moreover, when Matisse, who was pleased to see his decoration finally put in place, spoke to his family, he was not reminded of Puvis de Chavannes but of dazzling Gothic stained-glass windows: "The radiance of the canvas descends to the bottom of the wall. Seen from the ground floor, you have the impression you're in a cathedral."[39]

Here and Now
Can we compare Puvis and Matisse after all by simply looking at their works, apart from any historical consideration? The answer is: No.

Of course, such a comparison has already been made more than once.[40] Of course these comparisons are based on a form of filiation: historical elements, on the one hand, that in a number of crucial moments in Matisse's life prove his real knowledge of his predecessor's oeuvre; and a critical reception, on the other hand, where the reference to Puvis de Chavannes often appeared, particularly in the budding years of Matisse's career, like a way to approach the Fauve painter's research, by integrating it in a recognized historical development and thus minimizing the break that had taken place. Of course, lastly, a curious eye may occasionally enjoy pointing out certain formal echoes in the economy of means, in particular, in the simplification of the fields of the painting in flat colors, where the figures create a solidly composed rhythm on a background practically reduced to the juxtaposition of two areas of flat painting; from that point of view, the Bernheim brothers were quite clever when, in 1910, they sought to guide Shchukin away from Matisse's *Dance* in favor of the Boston decoration by Puvis.

Given all this, it is still clear that the dialogue between Matisse and Puvis never acquired a major aesthetic signification, as regards the development of the former's oeuvre. Nothing comparable, for instance, to the formidable devouring of Puvis achieved by Picasso in the same period. If the single word, decorative, linked Matisse and Puvis, it was probably strategically at certain crucial moments, but exterior after all, and with such great and obvious divergences that we can scarcely speak of dialogue or confrontation, but rather—and very simply—of two worlds extraneous to one another. Although Maurice Denis defended Puvis's modernism in

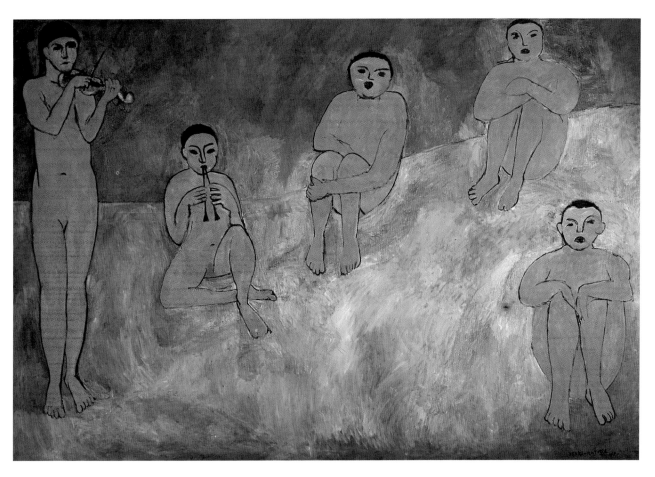

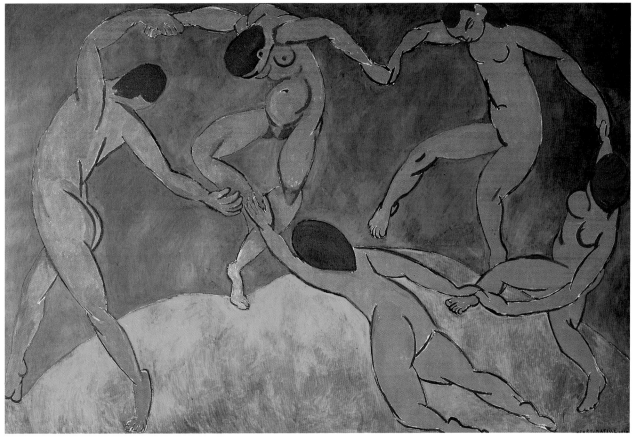

11. Henri Matisse,
*Girl with Tulips
(Jeanne Vaderin)*, 1910.
Saint Petersburg,
The Hermitage Museum

1890 by saying that "the adequacy of those lines and those colors provide their own justification,"[41] he declared that Puvis's painting is grounded in speech: It speaks—its "first principle," as Puvis told Marius Vachon, is that "the painter must paint only when he has something to say"[42]—and when it presents itself as "decorative," it is first of all in the sense that it wants to make the monument *speak*, by illustrating it with scenes whose aim is to establish its signification. It is that fundamentally discursive dimension that makes these works reproducible by their author himself (as we can repeat a speech), which Puvis always did and Matisse always condemned. Again that is what explains Puvis's so oft-quoted words, about the mental character of the process of his creation: "My way of working is interior, if I may say so; before executing anything, my creation is nearly always entirely accomplished in my head."[43] There again, Matisse replied nearly fifty years later, resolutely marking the difference between them; although a knowledge of Puvis had stayed with him all his life and helped him define himself, basically it did not touch him, nor profoundly alter him: "A work of art to be created is never accomplished ahead of time, contrary to what Puvis de Chavannes thought who claimed that you could never have too clear a view beforehand of the painting you wished to do. There is no break between thought and the creative act. There is union and unity."[44] There lies the main utopia behind Matisse's research, therein so utterly extraneous to Puvis: that the work be at once critical and decorative, at once a challenge and a construction, at once a doubt and a gift.

After all, it is up to the eye: we do not look at a Puvis the way we look at a Matisse. One aspires to be read while the other asks to be experienced. One, at the very end of the tradition of the grand monumental iconographic programs of the modern West since Giotto, unfailingly inclines the spirit toward a learned contemplation, where the surroundings, the wall, the building seem to be mentally projected in the image (in which that intellectualism assumes a sort of spectral melancholy, a faraway detachment). The other, at war with the "theater" of tradition of representation,[45] and with a strong idea of the decorative that does not identify with decorations *stricto sensu*, but wants to provoke in the viewer a dazzling opening of the eye and the spirit that are imperiously guided by the image beyond the image (as if it were consumed just when the eye, on touching its light, bounces off).

[1] Form-letter dated May 1896 and signed "P. Puvis de Chavannes," Paris, Henri Matisse Archives.

[2] *Conversations avec Pierre Courthion*, 1941, 3rd conversation (typescript copy, Paris, Henri Matisse Archives).

[3] See his letter dated precisely 1896: "This presidency [of the Champ-de-Mars] gives me additional calamities that so overlap they take up everything that used to seem a rest, an enjoyment. I have to constantly put in an appearance, when my life used to be so quiet!" P. Puvis de Chavannes, "Lettres (1888–1898)," *Revue de Paris*, February 1, 1911, p. 471.

[4] "I didn't particularly try to arrange to meet the painters I admired. Their work alone was enough." *Conversations…, op. cit.,* 4th conversation.

[5] M. Vachon, *Puvis de Chavannes*, Paris, Lahure, Braun, Clément et Cie., 1895, p. 21.

[6] R. Marx, *Revue encyclopédique*, April 25, 1896, quoted in R. Benjamin, *Matisse's "Notes of a Painter": Criticism, Theory and Context, 1891–1908*, Ann Arbor, UMI Research Press, 1987, p. 258.

[7] R. Bouyer, "L'Art et la beauté aux Salons de 1898," *L'Artiste*, 1898, quoted in *ibidem*, p. 262. In the same text, the critic explicitly opposes the painters connected with Moreau with those connected with Puvis: "Moreau's pupils exalt color and easel painting, whereas at the Champ-de-Mars, Puvis de Chavannes's followers preserve the eurythmy of the pale fresco."

[8] On March 12, 1896, Henri Evenepoel wrote his father that his friend Matisse was a "subtle painter, learned in the art of grays." H. Evenepoel, *Lettres à mon père*, ed. D. Derrey–Capon, Brussels, Musées Royaux des Beaux-Arts de Belgique, 1994, vol. 2, pp. 34 and 36. Compare Puvis de Chavannes's letter to Mme. Belly in 1861: "a large veil of a delicate gray, as delicate as the wings of the birds you mention, a gray that preserves the slightest plant's color, every object its value—such a gray is the sweet, lasting accompaniment that lets everything sing, is the wonder of wonders." P. Puvis de Chavannes, "Lettres (1861–1876)," *Revue de Paris*, December 15, 1910, p. 682.

[9] *The Inspiring Muses Acclaim the Spirit of Light* was exhibited at the 1895 Salon; at the 1896 Salon five other panels for the stairway were shown and the three last at Durand-Ruel's in September.

[10] Letter from Matisse to Signac, July 14, 1905, quoted in P. Schneider, *Matisse*, Paris, Flammarion, 1986, p. 98.

[11] "Fauvism shakes off the yoke of Divisionism," (to Tériade, 1929); quoted in H. Matisse, *Ecrits et propos sur l'art*, ed. D. Fourcade, Paris, Hermann, 1972, p. 94.

[12] Letter from Signac to Matisse, autumn 1905, quoted in R. Labrusse, *Matisse. La Condition de l'image*, Paris, Gallimard, 1999, p. 30.

[13] See, among many other examples, what Puvis confided to Marius Vachon: "The true role of painting is to bring walls to life." Vachon, *op. cit.*, p. 33.

[14] "Over forty years ago, I went to visit the Rouart collection. I was with one of my cousins, an art dealer." *Conversations…, op. cit.* The collector owned in particular the second version of Puvis's *Hope* (1872, oil on canvas, 70,7 x 82, Paris, Musée d'Orsay).

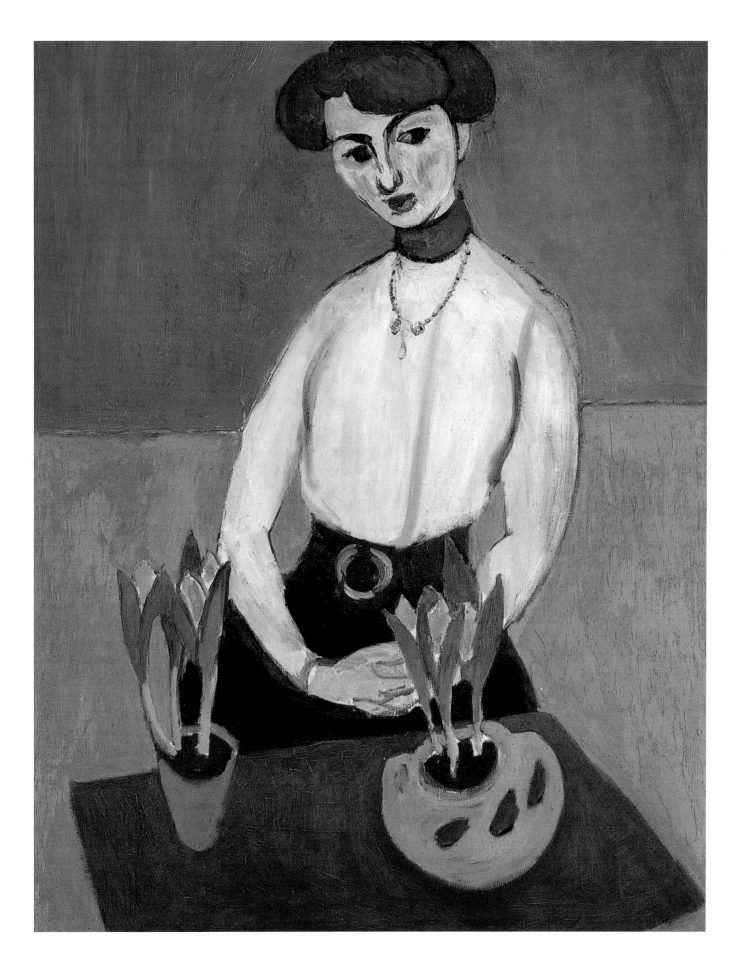

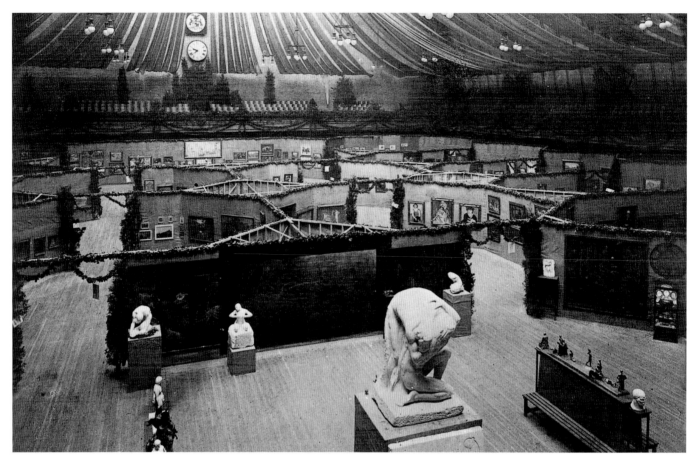

12. The Armory Show, New York 1913. Matisse's paintings were exhibited next to those of Puvis de Chavannes in the first room on the right.
Washington, D.C., Smithsonian Institution, National Archives of American Art

[15] One of the starting points being the famous conclusion of Albert Aurier's article on Gauguin in 1891: "So indeed! In our expiring century, we have but one great decorator, maybe two counting Puvis de Chavannes, and our imbecillic society of bankers and polytechnicians refuses to give this exceptional artist the smallest palace, the tiniest national hovel to hang the gorgeous cloaks of his dreams!" "Le Symbolisme en peinture, Paul Gauguin," 1891, in A. Aurier, *Textes critiques, 1889–1892*, Paris, ENSBA, 1995, p. 38.

[16] M. Denis, "L'influence de Gauguin," 1903, in *Théories, 1890–1910. Du Symbolisme et de Gauguin vers un nouvel ordre classique*, Paris, Rouart et Watelin, 1920 (1st ed., 1912), p. 170.

[17] In *D'Eugène Delacroix au néo-impressionisme*, that Matisse had read when it came out in 1898–99, Signac mentions "four admirable compositions by Puvis de Chavannes" in the museum of Amiens, although he adds that their position between the windows makes them invisible, whereas the use of a divided brushstroke would have enabled them to withstand being seen against the light. P. Signac, *D'Eugène Delacroix au néo-impressionisme*, ed. F. Cachin, Paris, Hermann, 1978, p. 125.

[18] In 1897, Roger Marx referred to Puvis's oeuvre in terms directly echoing themes developed by Signac and anticipating Matisse's in *Luxe, calme et volupté* and in *Bonheur de vivre*: "[Puvis de Chavannes's oeuvre] . . . contrasts to the overall pessimism the comforting vision of another world, a better world, inhabited by beings who are like us as brothers. There, according to the poet's wish, '*Là, tout n'est qu'ordre et beauté.*' From this new Arcadia, all violent ideas, emotions, motions, light are banned. Before the vision of such peace and harmony, our soul was constrained to rediscover the secret of the lost quietude, and in a dupe of the mirage, was again caught up in the illusion of a possible joy of life." R. Marx, "Puvis de Chavannes" [1897], in *Maîtres d'aujourd'hui*, Paris, Calmann-Lévy, 1914, pp. 171–72.

[19] Denis, "De Gauguin, de Whistler et de l'excès des théories," November 15, 1905, in *Théories…, op. cit.*, pp. 208–09.

[20] M. Golberg, *Puvis de Chavannes, Cahiers mensuels de Mécislas Golberg*, March–April 1901, Paris, Wolff, 1901.

[21] Letter of summer 1907 (Paris, Henri Matisse Archives). Golberg had met Matisse at the beginning of the century in Bourdelle's studio ("You may still remember me from the time we met at Bourdelle's"). In 1902, Bourdelle had shown a *Buste de Golberg* in the Salon (Paris, Musée Bourdelle).

[22] See on the subject, *Mécislas Golberg, passant de la pensée (1869–1907). Une anthropologie politique et poétique au début du siècle*, ed. C. Coquio, Paris, Maisonneuve et Larose, 1994.

[23] See Benjamin, *op. cit.*, pp. 198–99.

[24] Matisse, *op. cit.*, p. 62.

[25] Paris, Henri Matisse Archives.

[26] *Conversations…, op. cit.*, 8th conversation.

[27] *Ibidem.*

[28] See B. Whitney Kean, *French Painters, Russian Collectors. The Merchant Patrons of Modern Art in Pre-Revolutionary Russia*, London, Hodder and Stoughton, 1994, p. 133.

[29] See the letter from Fénéon, in charge of contemporary painting at the Bernheims', to Matisse, November 8, 1910: "As long as M. Sergei Shchukin was still in Paris, we would not have said the following, so as to leave to your so obliging

intervention between him and you its merely cordial character. Now that he is gone, would you allow us to offer you the Bonnard 18316, *Coquelicot sur fond noir et bleu* you were especially fond of?" Paris, Henri Matisse Archives.

[30] A. Kostenevich and N. Semionova, *Matisse et la Russie*, Paris, Flammarion, 1993, p. 167.

[31] *Ibidem.*

[32] *Ibidem*, p. 169.

[33] In the catalog of the 1910 Salon d'Automne, *Dance* and *Music* are designated under the rubric "decorative panel" (*Catalogue des ouvrages de peinture, sculpture, dessin, gravure, architecture et art décoratif exposés au Grand Palais des Champs-Elysées du 1er octobre au 8 novembre 1910*, Paris, Kugelmann, 1910, nos. 536 and 537, p. 109).

[34] "I had them raised to a height of five or six meters in the Grande Salle, on the wall facing the main stairway, where they took on their mural signification and set their ardent rhythm free." *Conversations…, op. cit.*, 8th conversation.

[35] Y. Tugendhold, *Apollon*, 1910, no. 12, quoted in Kostenevich and Semionova, *op. cit.*, p. 117.

[36] D. Dudley, "The Matisse Fresco in Merion," January–March 1934, in Matisse, *op. cit.*, p. 140.

[37] Vachon, *op. cit.*, p. 27.

[38] That was, in particular, how he put Islamic art to use: " With its accessories, that art suggests a larger space, an authentic plastic space. It helped me break away from intimacy painting." (to Gaston Diehl, 1947, quoted in Matisse, *op. cit.*, p. 203).

[39] Letter to his wife, March 17, 1933, quoted by J.D. Flam in *Autour d'un chef-d'oeuvre de Matisse. Les trois versions de la Danse Barnes (1930–1933)*, Paris, Réunion des Musées Nationaux, 1993, pp. 75–76.

[40] See R.J. Wattenmaker, *Puvis de Chavannes and the Modern Tradition*, exh. cat., Toronto, Art Gallery of Ontario, 1975, p. 27.

[41] Denis, "Définition du néo-traditionnisme," August 1890, in *Théories…, op. cit.*, p. 8.

[42] Vachon, *op. cit.*, p. 28.

[43] Quoted by E. Bernard in "Puvis de Chavannes," *L'Occident*, no. 25, December 1903, p. 278.

[44] To André Verdet, 1952, in Matisse, *op. cit.*, p. 47.

[45] See, for instance, Matisse's conversation with Friar Rayssiguier, January 14, 1950: "on the subject of the Michelangelo of the Sistine Chapel: 'it is theater, they are all performing' and he gravely adds: 'To think I once liked that'" (*La Chapelle de Vence. Journal d'une création*, ed. M. Billot, Paris, Cerf, 1993, p. 291).

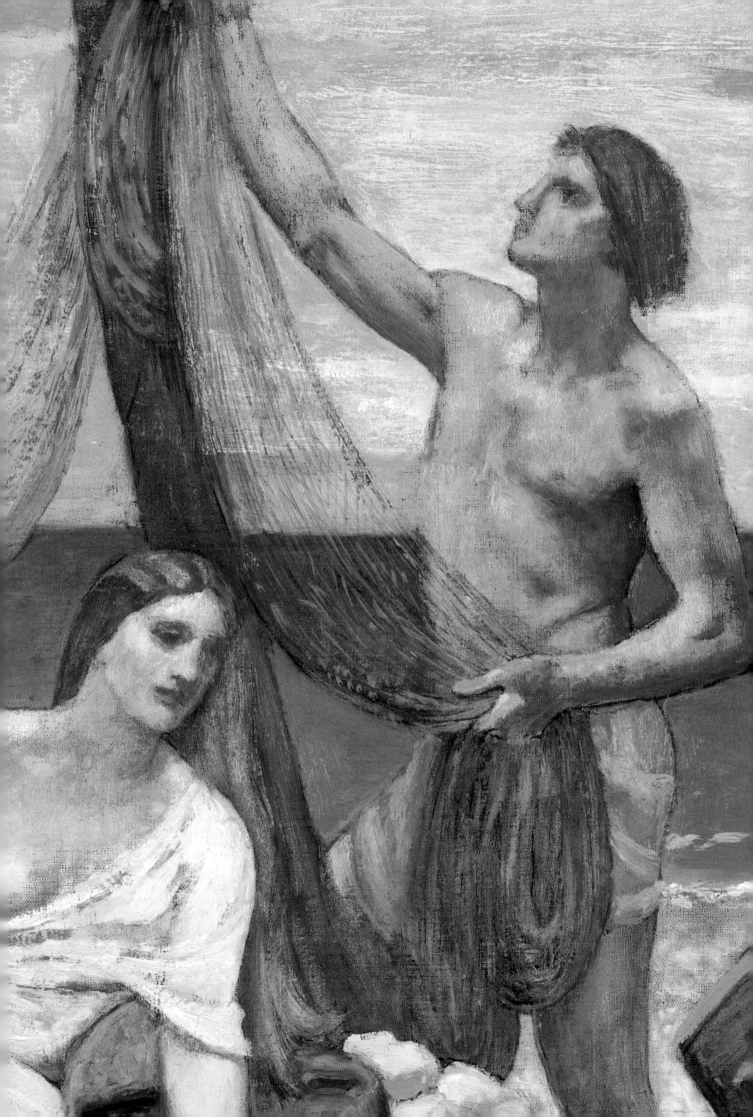

Anne Baldassari

From Puvis de Chavannes to Picasso, "To Turn Abstraction into the Forge of Signs"

"Led by the inexplicable clear-sightedness of their art, creators turn abstraction into the forge of signs," wrote Mécislas Golberg in April 1901,[1] going on to observe: "this is how Puvis de Chavannes arrived at the peak of his art. His figures, his colors and the whole tonal range of his pictorial vision, blended together in a serene and accomplished oeuvre. Such works remain where destiny places them, that is to say, at a cross-roads. However, in spite of this fate, the generations to come can draw precious pointers from them."[2] In the same year as these comments were written, the twenty-year-old Pablo Picasso held his first exhibition in Paris, at the Galeries Vollard. From the very beginning, Max Jacob would place Puvis among that body of eclectic influences against which the young painter, who already "imitated everyone a bit,"[3] was measuring himself.

While Picasso's *Ingrisme* soon became a subject of study and discussion, the first systematic analysis of the influence of Puvis de Chavannes on "the modern tradition" would not come until 1975, in a work by Richard J. Wattenmaker.[4] Since then, historians of Picasso's work[5] have discussed his debt to Puvis in the paintings of the Blue Period, the early "Classical" period of the years 1905–06, and the classical-style compositions of 1919–25, identifying such similarities as: the handling of figures and groups, the simplified organization of space, a reduced palette range, a tendency to the monumental format, etc. However, one must go beyond a simple list of the formal or iconographical links between the two artists, and try to see their connection within the complex relationship that Picasso established with the master artists of the generations who preceded him. This relationship was even the subject of a game which André Salmon tells us was played by the circle of artists and poets that had gathered around the young painter: "One of us would suggest: 'Let's do Degas!' . . . And so, one of us would be Degas, a famous old grumbler, popping in to visit Pablo and judge his work. But the Degas might not be Degas exactly, he could be Puvis de Chavannes, or Bonnat, or Bouguereau or Courbet, or even Baudelaire writing on a *Salon*. Picasso laughed to find himself on the receiving end of such stiff comments because—as I've already said—we didn't mince words with each other in those days."[6]

The same humor can be found in a postcard sent by Apollinaire, on which the poet faked the signatures of his artist friends and a number of other well-known painters, including Puvis de Chavannes.[7] And here it is worth remembering that the latter was not only the hallowed creator of works celebrating national and religious virtues; he was also known to his friends as a fierce caricaturist,[8] and a man of an ardent physical temperament that was regularly the subject of jokes that did the rounds of the Paris studios. Picasso himself would involuntarily echo these when, in 1902, he remained true to his Spanish pronunciation in labeling one of the sketches he had done in the Panthéon[9] "De *Pubis* en el Panteon"; and the older artist's legendary virility was also the subject of a comment Braque made to Picasso in 1912, when the first *Triennale d'Art Français* exhibited Puvis de Chavannes "among the great dead of the contemporary French School" who are summoned to take their place "amid the work of living artists."[10] "The model was sacred for Puvis," Braque joked. "And when he couldn't resist it any longer, he stepped on his own, into an improvised boudoir. 'I am beating down Nature,' the master would say jovially."[11] And just as this comment seems to reveal an almost affectionate mix of mockery and respect, so do the references to the Old Masters in Picasso's own paintings seem to be both a quotation and a holding at a distance. They are references which only have form and meaning due to their juxtaposition with a multiplicity of other visual material, and through the constant process of reformulation to which Picasso submits the plastic language of his art. Thus an understanding of the role played by Puvis's oeuvre in Picasso's own work depends on an understanding of that "abstraction of signs" which was a constant in the latter's own artistic project—a project that was pursued through all the subsequent phases of his own great oeuvre.

Up to now, art historians have restricted themselves to the first three decades of the twentieth century in an attempt to understand the influence of Puvis de Chavannes on Picasso; however, we will have to look further afield for the more decisive encounters with the rhetoric of the earlier artist's work—encounters that occur on those rare occasions when Picasso brings to bear on a full scale the challenge represented by monumental painting.

"Let's Do Puvis!" Picasso and Quotation in Painting

Wattenmaker showed how the young Picasso could have been introduced to the work of Puvis de Chavannes thanks to the Catalan Symbolist circles in which it was well known (the im-

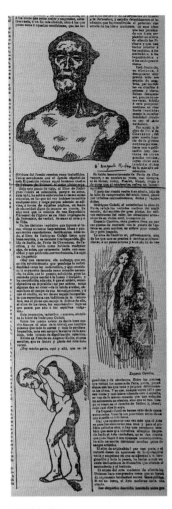

2. Pablo Picasso,
Man Carrying a Sack
(*El Liberal*, August 10, 1903).
Arxiu Historic
de la Ciutat de Barcelona

portant figure here was the writer and painter Santiago Rusiñol[12]). The scholar was also the first to draw attention to two drawings dating from Picasso's first years in Paris—*Man Carrying a Sack*[13] and *Three Figures*[14]—and to argue a connection with the Panthéon triptych *Saint Genevieve Supplying Paris*.[15] He also suggested that the mural of the Sorbonne could have served as a "mine of poses and gestures used in the draped figures of the Blue Period,"[16] a claim that may be confirmed by the fact that the Picasso Archives contain four postcards dating from the beginning of the century which show details from this vast panel. However, following Anthony Blunt and Phoebe Pool,[17] Wattenmaker claims that Picasso's most extensive exposure to the work of Puvis de Chavannes only came with the exhibition that was part of the 1904 Salon d'Automne, and that it was this show that accounts for the more resonant echoes of Puvis which can be found throughout the Pink Period.[18] Nevertheless, one should not underestimate the importance of the "contact" established between the two artists at the turn of the century—even if it was a contact *in absentia*.

Picasso arrived in Paris for the first time in October 1900—that is, only two years after the death of Puvis de Chavannes and the completion of the second cycle of paintings at the Panthéon, which the older artist had intended as his "last will and testament."[19] In spite of the generational gap between the two painters, the *Saint Genevieve Watching over Paris* panel, with its nocturnal blue, its draped figures and the pure geometry of its architecture, is not very much earlier than such Blue Period works as *Two Sisters*[20] and *The Fisherman's Goodbye*.[21] What is more, the reason for Picasso's first visit to Paris was the Universal Exposition, where his painting *Last Moments* was part of the official Spanish exhibit[22] ("The Exposition will close soon, and we have only seen the painting section," the artist wrote on October 25[23]). This visit to the Grand Palais gave him the chance to see the ten-year Exposition that included his own picture, and the Centenary Exposition of French Art, which included four paintings by Puvis de Chavannes which would later find an echo in Picasso's own work: *Vigilance* (1866), one of the panels painted for the Paris home of the woman writer and sculptor, Claude Vignon; *Young Picards Practicing the Javelin* (1880), one of the studies for the decoration of the Amiens museum; *The Toilette* (1883) and *The Fisherman's Family* (1887).[24] In Paris that year the young Spanish prodigy was representing his country with a painting that was still imbued with academic sentimentalism, thus near to the works of the recently-deceased master of monumental painting. What is more, Picasso would choose works by Puvis de Chavannes, Rodin and Carrière as illustrations for the article Carles Junyer-Vidal wrote on the Exposition for the newspaper *El Liberal* (published August 10, 1903).[25] He would also re-use his own sketch *Man Carrying a Sack*[26] for this purpose.

From its very beginning, the art of the Blue Period, with its subdued palette and its figures representing various allegories of wretchedness, might be seen as reflecting the work of Puvis de Chavannes. The description Max Jacob has left us of the room Picasso occupied at the Hôtel du Maroc, Rue de Seine, in 1902, comments on the iron bed "covered with drawings recalling those of Puvis de Chavannes . . . [which] nobody wanted."[27] Early in 1903, the painter told the poet that he intended "to do something for the Salon."[28] This was when, in a highly symbolic gesture, he decided to paint over *Last Moments* with that enigmatic allegory which would be entitled *La Vie*.[29] His next letter to Max Jacob[30] would be illustrated with several sketches of a seated woman with open arms, echoing the tutelary gesture seen in Puvis de Chavannes's *Generosity* in the new Hôtel de Ville (1894).[31] On August 6, 1903, Picasso would announce to Max Jacob that he was "thinking of doing a painting of three meters [two illegible words] sailors on a small boat,"[32] a project which may have been foreshadowed by the drawing *Farewell to the Fishermen*[33] that so clearly echoes the 1887 *The Fisherman's Family*.[34] However, it would be impossible to underestimate the extent to which Picasso holds Puvis's pictorial language at a distance at the very same time as he is borrowing from it. Various Blue Period paintings[35] have been linked with the 1881 *The Poor Fisherman*, an iconic work by Puvis[36] that mixes together social pity, an indeterminate historical setting and the Christian image of *Ecce Homo*.[37] These same features can undoubtedly be seen in the 1902–03 paintings mentioned here. However, while figures with their arms held tightly to their sides recur constantly in the paintings of the outcasts that Picasso was producing during these years,[38] the pose is not drawn solely from the work of Puvis (as one can see from the artist's archives, another source for this image of pathos was an old photograph of a deposed "prince" of an Amer-Indian tribe[39]). Indeed, the gesture com-

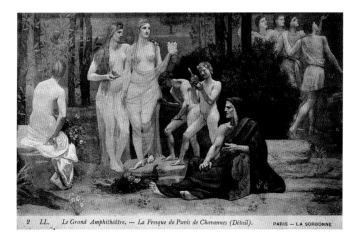
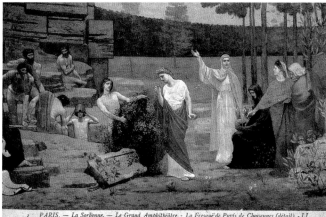
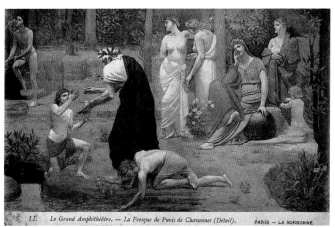
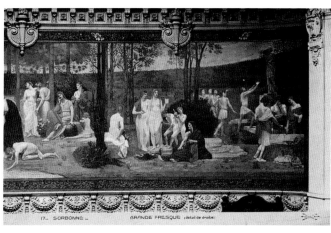

3-6. Four postcards reproducing sections of Puvis de Chavannes's mural at the Sorbonne. Paris, Musée Picasso

municates not only a sense of being overwhelmed by adversity but also a certain obstinate defense of one's human dignity. Similarly, while they may be as vague as in *The Poor Fisherman*, the shorelines and horizons in the Blue Period works showing the sea can easily be read as depicting the outskirts of Barcelona, which is taken as archetypical of the grind and misery of the contemporary metropolis.[40]

In the same way, the works that draw on the two Saint Genevieve cycles reveal a clear shift in symbolism, away from the religious message that was integral to the iconographic program laid down by the Marquis de Chennevières for Puvis de Chavannes. In spite of its nudity, the sketched figure of *Man Carrying a Sack* has more the air of a modern porter than of the figure wearing a tunic and bearing a biblical-looking vase in the Panthéon mural. Similarly, while the composition of the 1905 *Acrobat on a Ball*[41] is taken from the mural *Saint Genevieve in Prayer*, it replaces the child demonstrating "signs of ardent piety" with the slim and secular body of a young acrobat, directly inspired by a vignette in the illustrated magazine *Blanco y Negro*, which Picasso had been familiar with since his childhood.[42] The gap is even wider between *Saint Genevieve Watching over Paris* and one of its Picasso counterparts, the draped woman reproduced on the front page of *El Liberal* (October 5, 1902) on the occasion of the Fiesta de la Merced, which was particularly significant that year, coming as it did after the bloody repression of the general strike called on February 17. The wretchedness depicted by Picasso has, in these circumstances, been taken as revealing a "relatively a-political" resignation.[43] However, one should note that the woman with the children turns away from the other participants at the Fiesta who are dressed up in their Sunday best. Physically and symbolically detached from the parade, the figure might well have the contradictory meaning that has been read into the silent figures of the Blue Period, who have been described as "self-absorbed and socially isolated, backs often turned to the viewer, [they] resist incorporation into the politics of bourgeois reform."[44] A simple contrast of titles ("*Paris Besieged*" in the Puvis de Chavannes cycle; "*Barcelona Triumphant*" in the editorial illustrated by Picasso) vividly encapsulates how Picasso undermines the sublimity of Puvis's image, with a clear shift in historic perspective (from religious tradition to social modernity).

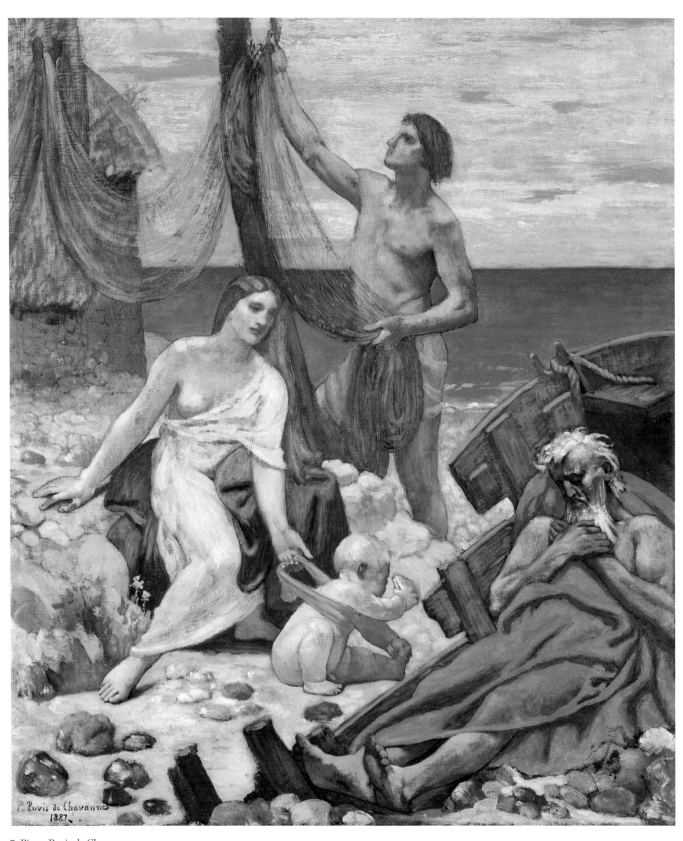

7. Pierre Puvis de Chavannes,
The Fisherman's Family, 1887.
Chicago, The Art Institute

8. Pablo Picasso,
Farewell to the Fishermen, 1903
Paris, Musée Picasso

9. Pablo Picasso, *Bearded Man
with Arms Crossed*,
Paris, Musée Picasso

10. Prince Gougou
of the Mic-Mac photographed by
Paul-Emile Miot in 1859
in Newfoundland.
Paris, Musée Picasso

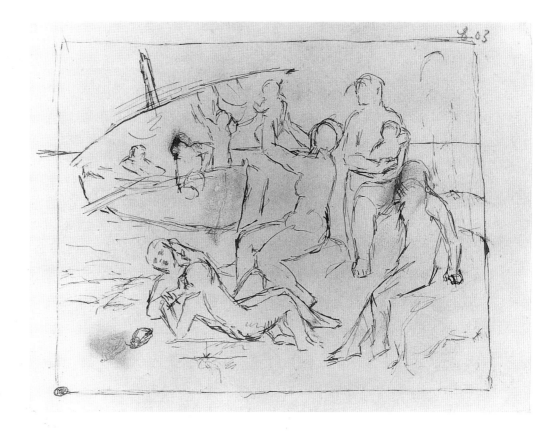

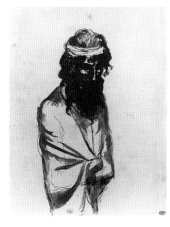

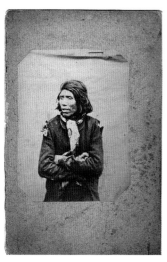

With regard to the works of 1919–25, Kenneth E. Silver has shown how the references to Puvis de Chavannes are to be seen in the context of ideas calling for a "return to order." The scholar reads a number of paintings from the early 1920s[45] as discreet patriotic allegories, which echo the contemporary post-war climate in the same indirect way as Puvis's *Hope* (1877) echoed the climate after the debacle of 1870.[46] The champions of the "classical tradition"[47] then rediscovered the man who would "restore the full dignity of French art."[48] In 1920, with all the ardor of a turncoat, Emile Bernard had used Puvis de Chavannes as an unflattering parallel designed to denigrate Cézanne: "For one, everything is grand; for the other, everything is complex, small and difficult;"[49] conversely, in 1913 Maurice Raynal had contrasted the art of Cézanne to the simple "skill in effects" that he saw in Puvis.[50] Far from responding to these sharp Manichean admonitions, Picasso at this point would then develop his painting simultaneously in two different ways, extending Cubism or referring to the great tradition of Western painting. Thus, in summer 1921, in his Fontainebleau studio he would paint the two versions of the *Three Musicians*[51] and the *Three Women at the Spring*,[52] materializing the vis-à-vis of these male and female compositions somehow defining the field of force within which Post-Cubism measured off against Neoclassicism.[53] According to Rosalind Krauss, throughout this period these two "equally unauthentic"[54] techniques of pastiche were simply an expression of Picasso's horror at the "serialization of art"[55] inherent in Cubism. And anticipating questions that would be raised by his stylistic turnabout, the artist himself suggested that the two manners of painting reflected each other like "two mirrors facing each other," forming "the same images, only against different planes."[56] His taste for parody, however, was not without its tactical side or elements of self-parody—something that Henri Matisse would bear witness to during World War II: "As early as 1914 Picasso had, with an eye to the future, done some drawings in Ingres's style in soft half-tones. He even had a funny story on the subject: since all his followers imitated him—something he found exasperating—he commented to Juan Gris, when the latter was praising the drawings, 'I do that stuff when I want to give myself a good clean-out!'"[57] Passing from Ingres to Puvis de Chavannes in the summer of 1918, his *Bathers*[58] would effect a transposition of the 1879 *Young Women by the Sea*;[59] however, not only did Picasso introduce "numerous droll changes,"[60] he also forged an "unthinkable" cultural partnership (the multi-colored swimsuits and the gaucherie of the girls are as direct an evocation of Douanier Rousseau's *Football Players* as the ethereal figures of the

11. Pablo Picasso, *Merced Festival*
(*El Liberal*, October 5, 1902).
Arxiu Historic de la Ciutat
de Barcelona

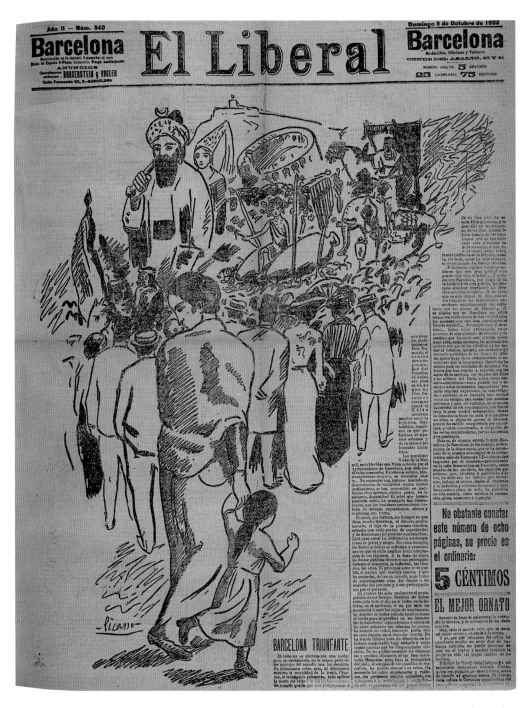

great master). And even when it lost its bizarre character, irony was always present in these displays of Picasso's "Neoclassicism."[61] Thus, the latter should be seen in the context of a more long-
term development, which had started in 1905–06 with the artist re-reading the work of Puvis
de Chavannes and of Cézanne in terms of the abstraction of the form and the figure and background relationship—that would make it possible to formulate the principles of Cubism. In 1921,
Picasso would return to where he had left things with his *Two Nudes* of 1906,[62] only this time
he used the "classical" idiom to subject the figures to that process of dismemberment and fetishis-
tic segmentation that would reach its peak in his Surrealist period.

"A Deliberate Appeal to the People" Picasso and the Challenge of the Monumental
Attention should also be drawn to how the influence of Puvis de Chavannes makes itself felt in
what is the earliest Picasso mural still extant. Nothing now remains of the strange decor he painted for his Riera de San Juan studio, for the apartment in calle de la Consulado in Barcelona or

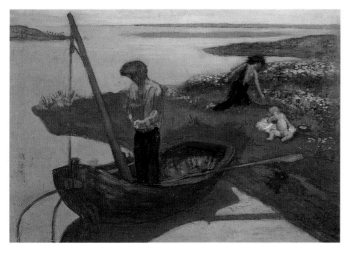

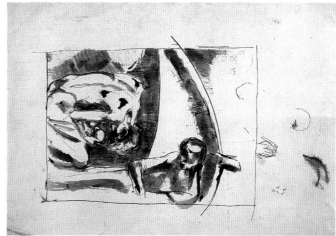

12. Pierre Puvis de Chavannes,
The Poor Fisherman, 1881.
Moscow, Pushkin Museum

13. Pablo Picasso, *Man, Woman
and Child in a Boat,* 1902.
Paris, Musée Picasso

for the *Zut* in Montmartre.[63] All created in the early 1900s, these were improvised works that Picasso painted "with the tip of his brush dipped in blue,"[64] the same procedure he would follow in the summer of 1918 when producing the decoration for the Biarritz villa of Madame Errazuriz. Still extant, this decorative scheme consists of a number of mythological scenes—*Venus, The Abundance, The Three Graces, Bacchanal* and *Bathing Nymphs*—completed with a calligraphic inscription of the first quatrain of Apollinaire's *Saisons* and a star-dusted ceiling. While one can see numerous echoes here of the work of Puvis de Chavannes,[65] the most decisive influence was the latter's sole private commission, the cycle for the Hôtel Vignon (of which Picasso definitely knew *Vigilance* exhibited in 1900, and *Fantasy* shown at the 1904 Salon d'Automne[66]). Both commissioned by female patrons who were also friends of the artist, these two schemes consist of a series of different sized panels decorated with allegorical female figures. The elongated arabesques of the bodies and the pale blue monochrome of the palette in the Puvis de Chavannes cycle in some way foreshadow the goddesses in the Chambre Bleue in Biarritz. Silver's prejudice against a work which he sees as marking Picasso's new acceptance by the "rive droite"[67] leads him to ignore the exceptional freedom with which the decorative line occupies the surface of the wall (left a simple white); the curves and twists of the draftsmanship here reveal a cheerfulness that is rare in Picasso's work.

This link with the mural decorations produced by Puvis de Chavannes suggests a new reading of the monumental and allegorical works that Picasso would paint in the decades to come.[68] Another important milestone here is the 1917 stage curtain for *Parade,*[69] whose debt to the juxtaposition of Pegasus, broken classical arches and modern dress in *Inter Artes et Naturam* has been well described by Wattenmaker.[70] This was the first project on this scale that Picasso ever finished. For example, a large Arcadian composition of 1906—which echoed the work of Puvis de Chavannes and Gauguin, as well as Matisse's *Bonheur de vivre*—did not get beyond the watercolor *Bathing Horses,*[71] even if it did influence a number of Pink Period works (for example, *Boy Leading a Horse*[72] takes up the central figure in that study). As for the 1910 commission for the decoration of Hamilton Easter Field's library, it would lead to the production of several paintings over the following years but the artist had to deal with the contradiction between large-format works and the analytical language of Cubism.[73] In 1935, the artist reiterated his abhorrence of the fact that the Old Masters had submitted to "decoration," "nothing but ornaments for churches and palaces. . . ."[74] Nevertheless, he assumed full responsibility for the propagandistic intentions behind his *Guernica*—"a deliberate appeal to the people"[75]—and compositions such as *Massacre in Korea* (1951) and *War* and *Peace* (1952)—"I would like my work to be able to help men to choose. . . ."[76] And when the 1937 exhibition unveiled its vast program of public art, Claude Roger-Marx could actually talk of a "return to Puvis de Chavannes," underlining his "especial contemporary relevance at a time when so many artists who have called for large surfaces to paint have been put 'up against the wall.'"[77] In Picasso's own political works one can see something of that determination to express civic and patriotic virtues which was the main driving-force behind the vast compositions in Amiens and the Sorbonne. What is more, real par-

14. Pablo Picasso,
Three Women at the Spring, 1921.
Paris, Musée Picasso

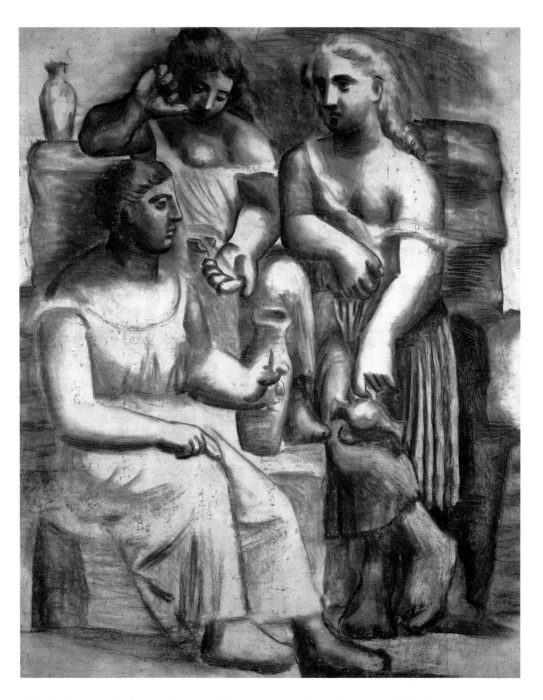

allels in dramatic rhythm can be traced between *Guernica* and an "unpublished cartoon," *Ludus pro Patria,*[78] which was made public in 1895 and shows Puvis de Chavannes recycling two studies—*The Seated Warrior* and *Man Throwing a Stone*—that were supposedly produced when he was still in a state of shock at the outcome of the 1870 Franco-Prussian war.[79] Whether or not Picasso knew the issue of *La Plume* in which this study was first published—though it seems very likely that he did—both that work and Picasso's famous 1937 painting could be described using Golberg's observation regarding the Amiens murals: "all the movements of the figures converge towards one goal and lose their individual character."[80] In both cases, the tangled pyramidal composition creates a vertical contrast between brute force above (the wielded stone, the horse's head) and destruction below (the corpse stretched diagonally, the weapons abandoned on the ground); at the same time, one moves from right to left, from the victim, through the sentry or the interceding woman, to the witness. Thus one gets a measure of how, through its Post-Cubist plastic language, the 1937 painting continues to employ the visual rhetoric that was part of the tradition of large-scale allegorical painting.

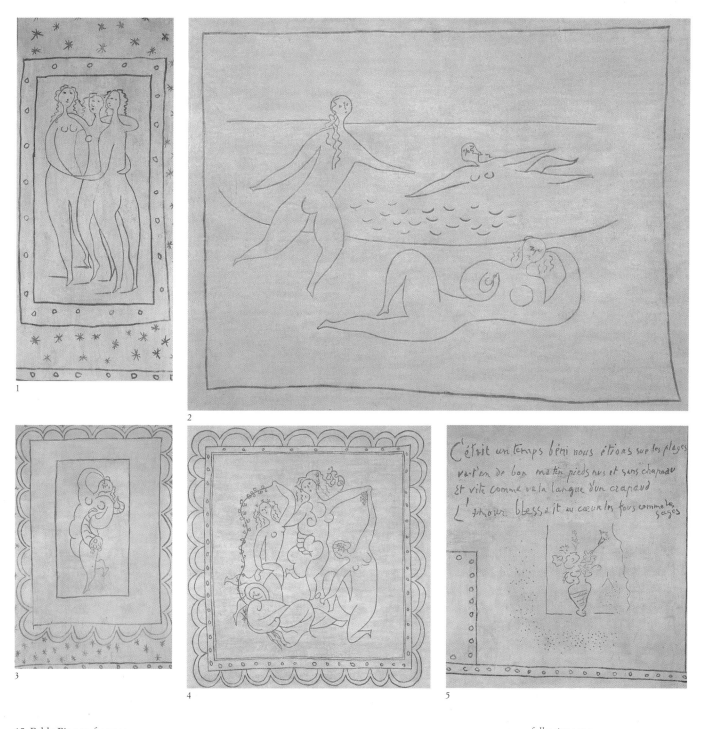

1

2

3

4

5

15. Pablo Picasso, frescoes
for the La Mimoseraie
in Biarritz, 1918:
1. *The Three Graces*
2. *Bathers*
3. *The Abundance*
4. *Bacchanal*
5. *Untitled*

following pages
16. Pierre Puvis de Chavannes,
Concordia, 1861.
Amiens, Musée de Picardie

pages 158–159
17. Pierre Puvis de Chavannes,
Bellum, 1861.
Amiens, Musée de Picardie

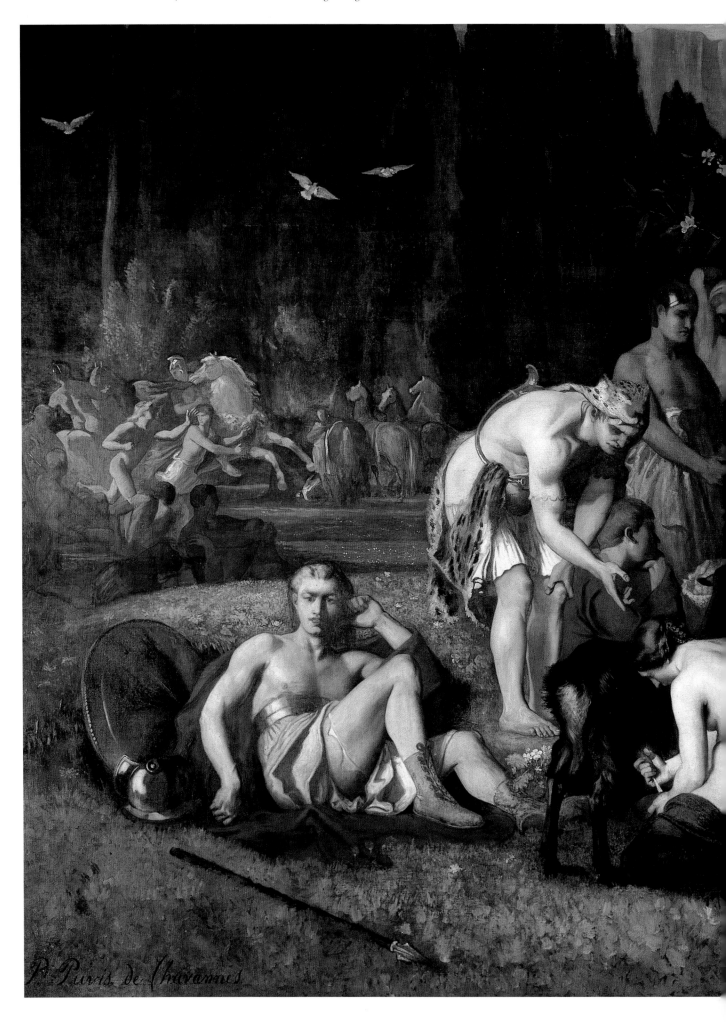

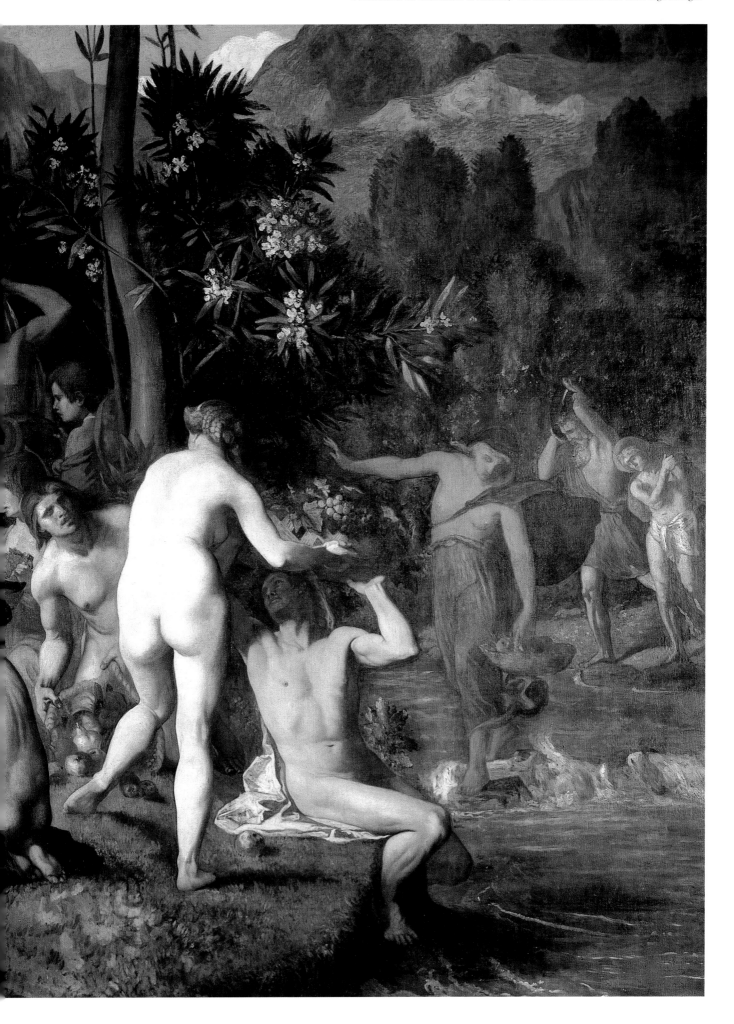

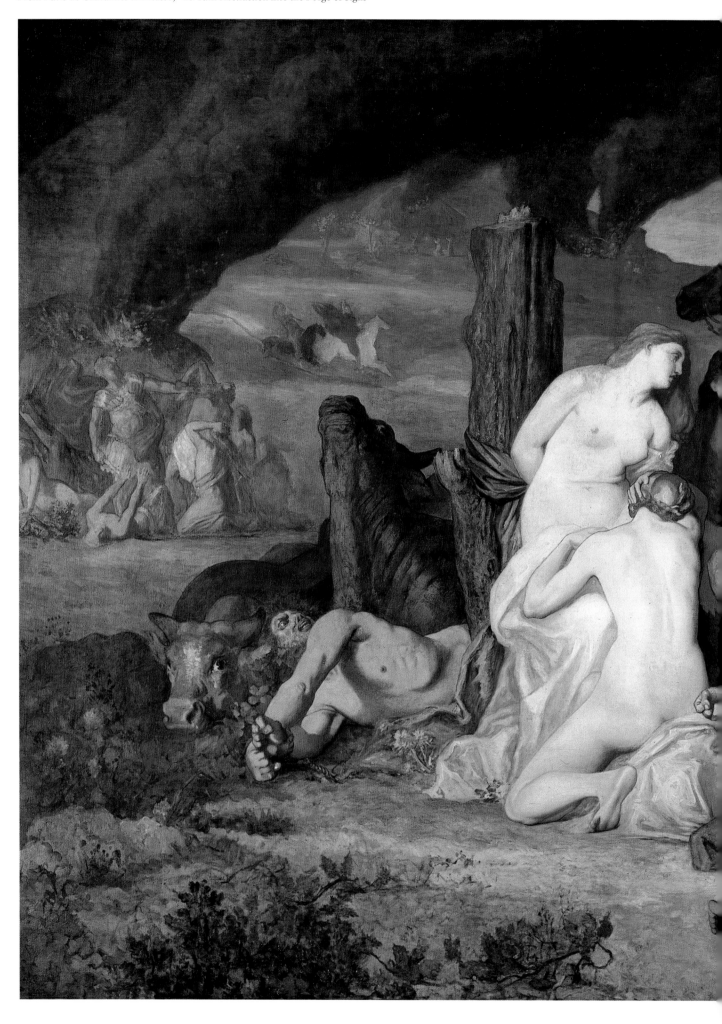

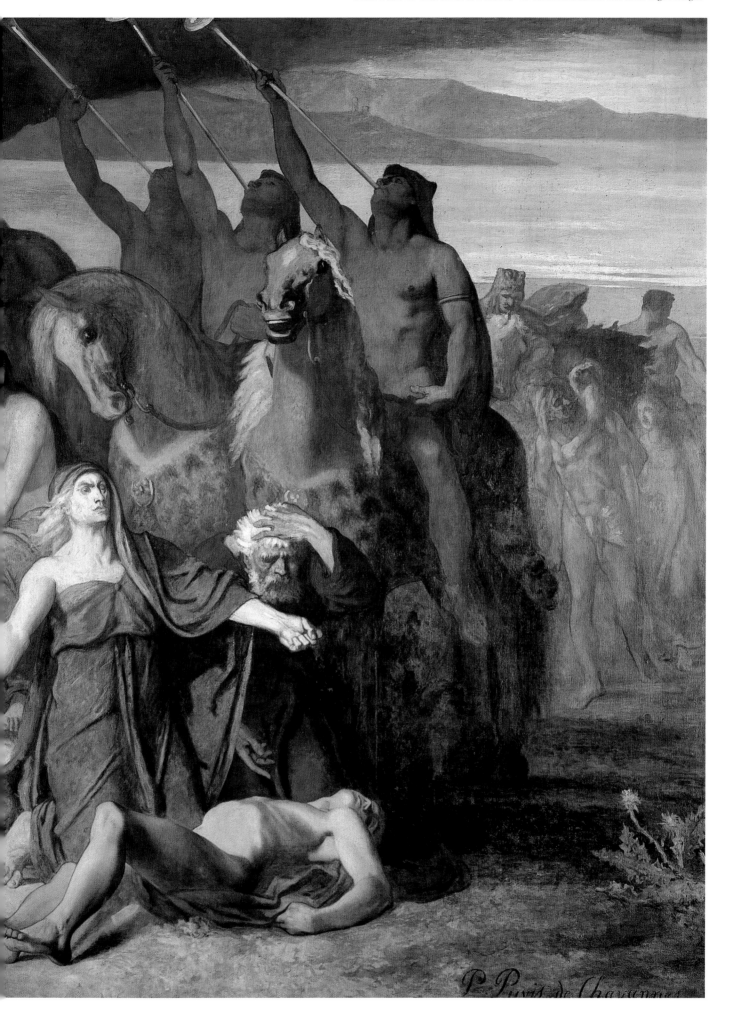

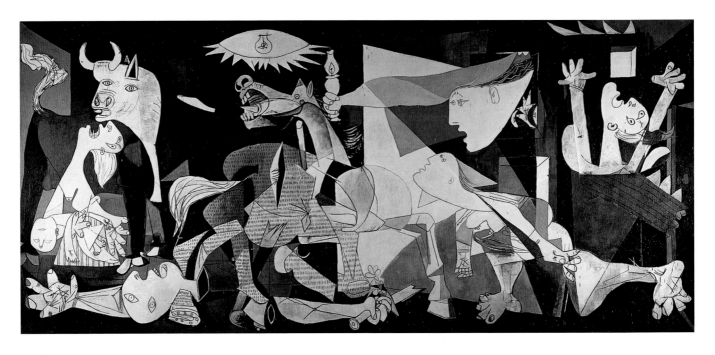

18. Pablo Picasso, *Guernica*, 1937. Madrid, Casón del Buen Retiro

The action of war is depicted in the mural panel *Pro Patria Ludus* in the very attenuated form of javelin-throwing. In his *Massacre in Korea*[81]—the academic re-working of *Guernica*—Picasso (who had first encountered this motif in Puvis's work thanks to *Young Picards* shown at the 1900 Exposition) would not only take the organization of the men carrying machine-guns directly from that earlier work, but would also follow the Amiens panels in his landscape background and his depiction of the group of women and children. The face-to-face encounter of victims and aggressors is here rendered by using the linear narrative of the cartoon strip,[82] further simplifying the "frieze principle"[83] Puvis had adopted in organizing his three groups—embodying the virtues of family, country and work—on a single horizontal plane.[84]

And it was again from Puvis de Chavannes—this time from the very first of his monumental works, the diptych *Bellum* and *Concordia*[85]—that Picasso would borrow in 1952 when at Vallauris he set about producing a secular response to Matisse's chapel at Vence. This project might well be described using the Explanatory Notes that accompanied Puvis's diptych at the 1861 Salon, citing the contrast between "the terrible consequences of war: murder, pillage, fire and desolation" and "all the advantages of concord: tranquillity, repose, unstrained labor richly rewarded by abundant harvests."[86] One can trace a link, via the stage curtain for *Parade*, between Picasso's *Peace* and Puvis's *Inter Artes et Naturam*, while the bucolic sport of women and children recalls the elegiac atmosphere of the 1882 *Pleasant Land*. Similarly, in *War* as in Puvis's *Bellum*, the horses are used to depict power on the march, with the raised trumpets corresponding to the raised arms bearing spears and swords. As for the soldier protecting himself from an aggressor with a shield decorated with the dove motif, he recalls the gesture of hope and warning to be seen in the female figure of *The Carrier Pigeon*.

From the Paris siege of 1871 to the Cold War, the same repertoire of "signs" tending towards "abstraction" unfolds, and is apparent even at this *point d'orgue* within the long relationship between Picasso and the art of Puvis de Chavannes—an art which, in Golberg's words, "attempts to rebuild the concept of universal amity by seizing on large gestures and life-enhancing events: work, thought, sacrifice"[87] in order to "recreate the common man, the social being."[88]

[1] M. Golberg, "Puvis de Chavannes," *Les Cahiers de Mécislas Golberg*, nos. 5–6, March–April, 1901, Paris, Albert Wolff, p. 43.

[2] *Ibidem.*

[3] *Verbatim* from a lecture by Max Jacob (1935–37), as cited in H. Seckel, *Picasso et Max Jacob*, Paris, Réunion des musées nationaux, 1994, p. 243.

[4] R.J. Wattenmaker, *Puvis de Chavannes and the Modern Tradition*, exh. cat., Art Gallery of Ontario, Toronto,1975, pp. 168–77.

[5] See, in particular, A. Brown Price, *Pierre Puvis de Chavanne*, exh. cat., Van Gogh Museum, Amsterdam (February 25–May

19. Pierre Puvis de Chavannes,
Ludus pro Patria
(*La Plume*, 1895)

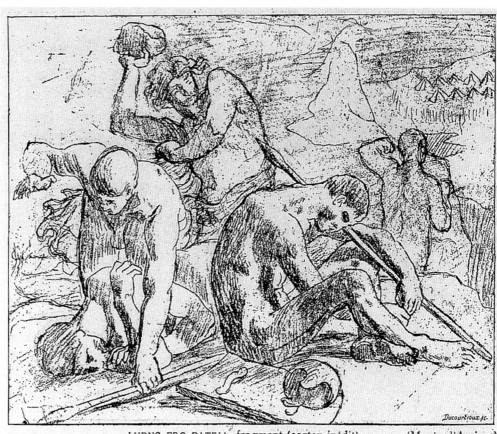

LUDUS PRO PATRIA, fragment (carton inédit)　　　(Musée d'Amiens)

29, 1994), Amsterdam, Waaders Uitgevers, 1994; and K.E. Silver, *Vers le retour à l'ordre. L'Avant-garde parisienne et la Première Guerre mondiale*, Paris, Flammarion, 1991.

[6] A. Salmon, *Souvenirs sans fin, deuxième époque (1908–1920),* II, Paris, Gallimard, 1956, pp. 199–200.

[7] Postcard from Guillaume Apollinaire to Pablo Picasso, Chatou, 1907.

[8] Several of his caricatures were published in 1895 (*La Plume*, special issue, January 1895) and 1906 (M. Adam, *Les caricatures de Puvis de Chavannes*, Paris, 1906).

[9] *Three Figures*, MPB 110-468.

[10] *La Triennale, Catalogue des ouvrages de peinture, sculpture, dessin, gravure, architecture et art décoratif exposés à la salle du Jeu de Paume* (July 1–31, 1912), Paris, Imprimerie Kugelmann, 1912, p. 56. Puvis de Chavannes was represented by his *The Grape Harvest* (no. 221) and a *Pietà* (no. 222).

[11] Georges Braque, postcard to Pablo Picasso, June [21] 1912. Picasso Archives, Paris. F. Thiébault-Sisson ("Puvis de Chavannes d'après des souvenirs personnels," *Feuilleton du Temps*, January 11, 1925, n.p.) attributes a "love of womanizing" to Puvis de Chavannes, while J. Buisson ("Puvis de Chavannes, intime et sentimental," *Gazette des Beaux-Arts*, July–September, 1899, p. 210) speaks of "the implacable virility of this extraordinary male . . . resolute in his pursuit of virile pleasures until he was well into old age . . . like another Baron Hulot."

[12] In Paris he had been an associate member of the Société Nationale des Beaux-Arts, founded in 1890 by Puvis de Chavannes and Meissonier; he was also present at the banquet held in 1895 to celebrate Puvis de Chavannes's seventieth birthday.

[13] MPB 110-331. In relation to this Panthéon triptych, see also MPB 110-439, 481 and 492.

[14] MPB 110-468. J. Richardson (*Vie de Picasso, volume I 1881-1906*, Paris, Chêne, 1992, p. 257) sees this sketch as one of the sources for the 1902 painting *The Soup* (Z. I, 131; D.B. VII, 11), in which the pleading gesture of the arms is, moreover, directly taken from a figure in the left panel of *The Childhood of Saint Genevieve* and in some studies published in 1895 (*La Plume*, special issue, January 1895, p. 45; M. Vachon, *Puvis de Chavannes*, Paris, Braun, Clément et Cie, 1895, p. 28). See also the drawing MPB 110-463.

[15] On the other hand, Brown Price (*op. cit.*, pp. 249–50) sees a relation between the drawing *The Golden Age* (MPB 110-546) and the panel *Saint Genevieve as a Child in Prayer* and identifies the Puvis de Chavannes sources for the 1902–03 drawings now in the Picasso Museum in Barcelona (MPB 110-447, 468, 469, 492, 493).

[16] Wattenmaker, *op. cit.*, p. 170.

[17] A. Blunt and P. Pool, *Picasso, The Formative Years, A Study of his Sources*, London, Studio books, 1962, p. 26.

[18] From the 1905–06 years, Wattenmaker analyzes Puvis's influence in *The Family of Saltimbanques* (Z. I, 285; D.B. XII, 35), *Acrobat on a Ball* (Z. I, 290; DB XII, 19). *La Toilette* (Z. I, 325; D.B. XV, 34), *Young Girl with a Basket of Flowers* (Z. I, 256; D.B. XIII, 8), *The Two Brothers* (Z. I, 304; D.B. XV, 9) and *Boy Leading a Horse* (Z. I, 264; D.B. XIV, 7).

[19] Buisson, *op. cit.*, p. 13.

[20] 1901, Z. I, 163; D.B. VII, 27.

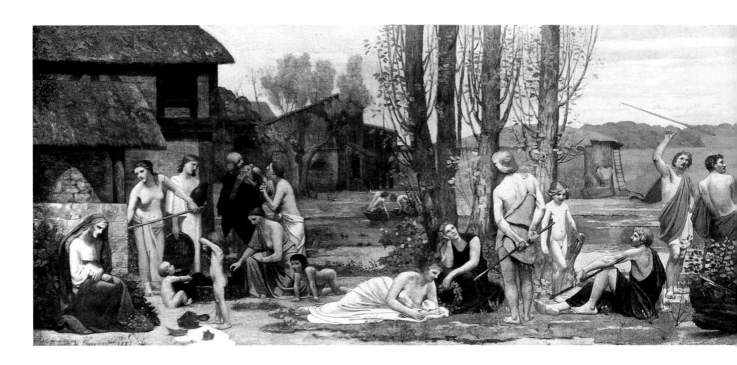

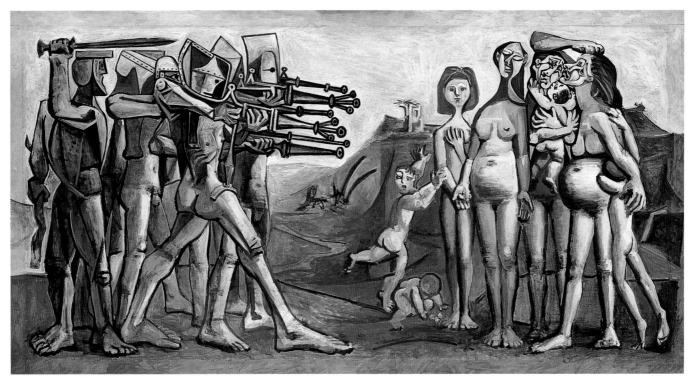

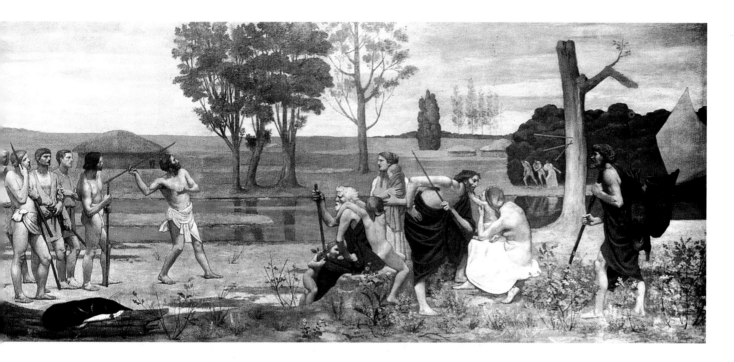

20. Pierre Puvis de Chavannes,
Ludus pro Patria, 1881–82.
Amiens, Musée de Picardie

21. Pablo Picasso,
Massacre in Korea, 1951.
Paris, Musée Picasso

21 1902, Z. XXI, 363; D.B. VII, 191.

22 *Exposition Décennale des Beaux-Arts*, Spain, no. 79. See the study MPB 110-797.

23 Letter from Picasso and Carles Casagemas to Ramon Revento (October 25, 1900). J. Palau i Fabre, *Picasso vivant, Enfance et première jeunesse d'un démiurge, 1881–1907*, Könemann, 1981, p. 513.

24 Respectively nos. 538bis, 538, 536 and 537 of the *Official General Catalogue*. In his 1906 *La Coiffure* (Z. I, 313; D.B. XIV, 20) Picasso borrows fairly explicitly from *The Toilette*. His interest in this painting is further confirmed by the discovery in his archives of a reproduction of the work found in a bundle of letters dating from 1922—perhaps linked with the Charles Haviland sale (Drouot, December 7, 1922).

25 The article is an account of the work by Rodriguez Codolà, *La pintura en la Exposicion universal de Paris en 1900*. De Chavannes is defined as a "revolutionary of contemporary painting."

26 The version published by Wattenmaker is moreover the reinterpretation produced for the engraving of a drawing made earlier in Paris (MPB 110-331). Both versions are published in Palau i Fabre, *op. cit.*, figs. 908 and 909.

27 M. Jacob, "The Early Days of Pablo Picasso: A Memoir of the Celebrated Painter by a Friend and Contemporary," *Vanity Fair*, May 1923, translated and cited in Seckel, *op. cit.*, p. 192. Speaking of the years 1903–04, Max Jacob would confirm that "there was a tendency towards Puvis de Chavannes in his drawings" (M. Jacob, "Souvenirs sur Picasso contés par Max Jacob," *Cahiers d'art*, vol. II, no. 6, 1927).

28 Letter of March 1903 (Barcelona), in Seckel, *op. cit.*, p. 18.

29 Z. I, 179; D.B. IX, 13. See the interpretation recently put forward by W.H. Robinson in "The Artist's Studio in 'La Vie,' Theater of Life and Arena of Philosophical Speculation," in M. FitzGerald, *Picasso, The Artist's Studio*, New Haven, London, Yale University Press, 2001.

30 Letter of May 1, 1903, in Seckel, *op. cit.*, cat. 27 verso, p. 18. There are also similarities to the 1869 *Saint John the Baptist* and the 1887 *Maternity* and *Pity* (and related studies); see Brown Price, *op. cit.*, nos. 108 to 111.

31 This same figure could well have inspired the drawings of May 1902 (MPB 110-522 and 523), in which a winged figure opens its arms wide above a nude couple. Robinson (*op. cit.*, p. 66) points out that X-rays have revealed a similar figure sketched in at the center of the 1903 painting, *La Vie*.

32 Letter to Max Jacob, quoted in Seckel, *op. cit.*, p. 23.

33 January 1903, Z. XXI, 354, MP 449.

34 In relation to this painting, also see the 1902–03 drawings, Z. VI, 472 (MP 463) and MPB 110-444, 444R and 493.

35 Notably, *Woman and Child by the Sea* (Z. VI, 478; D.B. VII, 20) and *The Tragedy* (Z. I, 208; D.B. IX, 6). One could also add the illustration *Ser o No Ser*, published in Barcelona in *Joventut* (August 16, 1900) and the 1902 drawing *Man, Woman and Child in a Boat* (Z. XXI, 389; MP 475).

36 See "The Poor Fisherman. A Painting in Context," in Brown Price, *op. cit.*, pp. 45–53.

37 Subject treated by Puvis de Chavannes himself in 1858.

38 Notably, *The Absinth Drinker* (Z. I, 100; D.B. VI, 25), *Man in Blue* (Z, I, 142; D.B. VIII, 1), *The Tragedy* (Z. I, 208; D.B. IX, 6) *Acrobat and Young Harlequin* (Z. I, 297; D.B. XII, 9) and the drawings MPB 110.451 and *Beared Man with Arms Crossed* (Z. XXII, 9; MP 472). In Puvis, the same gesture can be found in *The Prodigal Son* of 1879.

39 This figure is prince Gougou of the Mic-Mac, photographed by Paul-Emile Miot in Newfoundland in 1859. This identification was first presented in A. Baldassari, *Picasso e la fotografia, Lo specchio nero*, Paris, Flammarion, Florence, Alinari, 1998.

40 An elegiac reading of Puvis's figure of *The Fisherman* can be found in *Bathers* (Z. II*, 66), a "proto-papier collé" (P. Daix, *Dictionnaire Picasso*, Paris, Robert Laffont, 1995, p. 80) created in 1908 using the cardboard of a box from the Grands Magasins du Louvre department store. The triangular composition is borrowed from Manet's *Déjeuner sur l'herbe*; but the man in the background—drawing the nets into his boat—takes up a motif that runs through the entire oeuvre of Puvis de Chavannes (see M.C. Boucher, *Catalogue des dessins et peintures de Puvis de Chavannes*, Paris, Petit Palais, Mu-

22, 23. Pablo Picasso,
War and *Peace*, 1952.
Paris, Musée Picasso

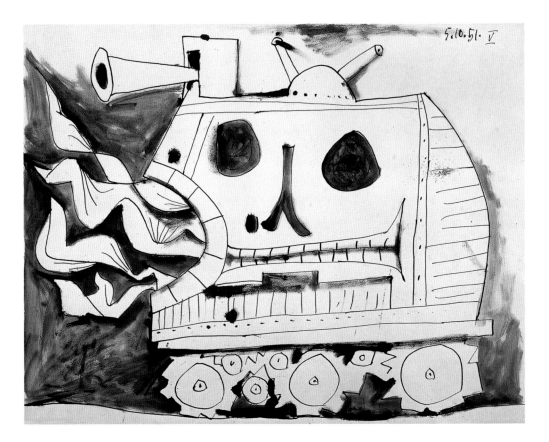

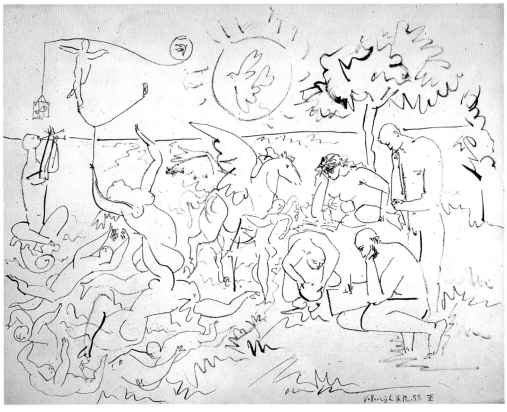

sée des Beaux-Arts de la Ville, 1979, nos. 3, 4 and 28 and the right-hand side of *Ave Picardia Nutrix*).

[41] Z. I, 290; D.B. XII, 19.

[42] On this subject, see A. Baldassari, *Picasso Working on Paper*, London, Merrell Publishers, Dublin, Irish Museum of Modern Art, 2000, pp. 14–30, and especially fig. 17.

[43] T. Kaplan, *Red City, Blue Period, Social Movements in Picasso's Barcelona*, University of California, 1992, pp. 61–74.

[44] R.S. Lubar, "Barcelona Blues," in *Picasso, The Early Years, 1882–1906*, ed. Marilyn McCully, Washington, National Gallery of Art, 1997, p. 97. See also Baldassari, *Picasso Working on Paper*, *op. cit.*, pp. 30–31.

[45] Especially *Woman in White* of 1921 (Z. V, 1).

[46] Silver, *op. cit.*, pp. 254–56.

[47] See especially C. Mauclair, *L'Avenir de France*, Paris, 1918.

[48] A. Michel, "L'Art français après la guerre," *La Revue hebdomadaire 26*, no. 11, March 17, 1917, p. 328.

[49] E. Bernard, "La méthode de Paul Cézanne," *Mercure de France*, no. 521, March 1, 1920, pp. 300–01.

[50] M. Raynal, "Esthétique des arts plastiques. Puvis de Chavannes," *Montjoye!, Organe de l'impérialisme artistique français*, March 14, 1913, pp. 5–6.

[51] Respectively Z. IV, 331 and 332.

[52] Respectively Z. IV, 322 and MP 74.

[53] On this subject, see Baldassari, *Picasso e la fotografia…, op. cit.*, pp. 174–77.

[54] R.E. Krauss, "Picasso / Pastiche," in *The Picasso Papers*, London, Thames and Hudson, 1998, p. 202.

[55] *Ibidem*, p. 194.

[56] P. Picasso, "Picasso Speaks, A Statement by the Artist," ed. Marius de Zayas, *The Arts*, no. 5, February 1923, p. 319.

[57] Henri Matisse to Pierre Matisse, December 2, 1940, Pierre Matisse Archives, Pierpont Morgan Library, New York.

[58] Z. III, 327, MP 61.

[59] Silver, *op. cit.*, pp. 213–14.

[60] *Ibidem*, p. 214.

[61] Silver, (*op. cit.*, pp. 239–48) analyzes the de Chavannes origins of the classical style compositions *Three Women at the Spring* (1921, Z. IV, 322) and *The Pipes of Pan* (1923, Z. V, 141; MP 79). One might well add here the relation that could be established between *The Reading of the Letter* (1921, MP 72) and Puvis's *Man Reading* or the other male figures shown reading, which have been discussed by Brown Price (*op. cit.*, no. 128, pp. 210–12).

[62] Z. I, 366; D.B. XVI, 15.

[63] J. Sabartés, *Picasso, Portraits et souvenirs*, Paris, Louis Carré et Maximilien Vox, 1946, pp. 86–87.

[64] *Ibidem*, p. 103. Wattenmaker (*op. cit.*, p. 169) also mentions other attempts at frescoes in 1901–02, giving as his only reference a vague allusion by Alfred H. Barr.

[65] In addition to the *Young Women by the Sea*, such works as *Autumn* (1863–64), the bathers in *Ave Picardia Nutrix* (1864), the group of dancers in *Death and the Maidens* (1872) and the winged Muses in the Boston Public Library (1895).

[66] No. 6 in the Salon catalog. The decoration of the Hôtel was completed with pictures of *History* and *Meditation*.

[67] Silver, *op. cit.*, p. 124. On this decor scheme see also P. Daix, "Pablo Picasso—Le Bonheur parfait à Biarritz," in *Picasso, La Villa Mimoseraie*, Cologne, Galerie Gmurzynska, 1993.

[68] Van Gogh would see in this "a strange and happy meeting of very distant antiquities and crude modernity" (letter with sketch, June 1890: Brown Price, *op. cit.*, no. 147, pp. 239–40).

[69] Z. II**, 951.

[70] Wattenmaker, *op. cit.*, p. 176.

[71] D.B. XIV, 16.

[72] 1906, Z. I, 264; D.B. XIV, 7.

[73] See the detailed study of this project in W. Rubin, "Appendix. The Library of Hamilton Easter Field," in *Picasso and Braque Pioneering Cubism*, exh. cat., The Museum of Modern Art, New York, 1989, p. 63–69.

[74] D.H. Kahnweiler, "Picasso: 'Ours is the only real painting,'" *The Observer*, London, December 8, 1957, pp. 8–9.

[75] J. Seckler, "Picasso explains," *New Masses*, March 13, 1945, French edition in *Fraternité*, September 20, 1945.

[76] A. Trombadori, "Un invito al sogno per capire la realtà," interview with Pablo Picasso, in *Vie Nuove*, Rome, January 25, 1953.

[77] C. Roger-Marx, "Retour à Puvis," *Les Nouvelles littéraires*, January 26, 1937.

[78] *La Plume*, special issue, January 1895, p. 34.

[79] Unlike Brown Price (*op. cit.*, pp. 135–37), L. d'Argencourt (catalog of the works, in *Puvis de Chavannes, 1824–98*, exh. cat., Grand Palais, Paris, National Gallery of Canada, Ottawa, 1976, p. 94) dates them around the 1860s.

[80] Golberg, *op. cit.*, p. 36.

[81] January 18, 1951, Z. XV, 173; MP 203.

[82] D.H. Kahnweiler ("Huit entretiens avec Picasso," in *Le Point*, Mulhouse, 1952, p. 27) suggests that the Ivanhoe series then published in *L'Humanité* was the inspiration for the painting *Jeux de pages* (Z. XV, 184; MP 204) produced at the same time as *Massacre in Korea*.

[83] D'Argencourt, *Puvis de Chavannes…, op. cit.*, p. 168.

[84] See D. Viéville, *Les peintures murales de Puvis de Chavannes à Amiens*, Amiens, édition Musée de Picardie / Ville d'Amiens, 1989, p. 28.

[85] Exhibited at the 1861 Salon, these panels were the starting-point for the cycle Puvis would produce for the Amiens museum.

[86] Quoted in d'Argencourt, *Puvis de Chavannes…, op. cit.*, p. 61.

[87] Golberg, *op. cit.*, pp. 38–39.

[88] *Ibidem*, p. 38.

NB. The references to Picasso's works are from the catalog edited by Christian Zervos (Z), Pierre Daix and Georges Boudaille (D.B.), the Musée Picasso in Paris (MP) and the Picasso Museum in Barcelona (MPB).

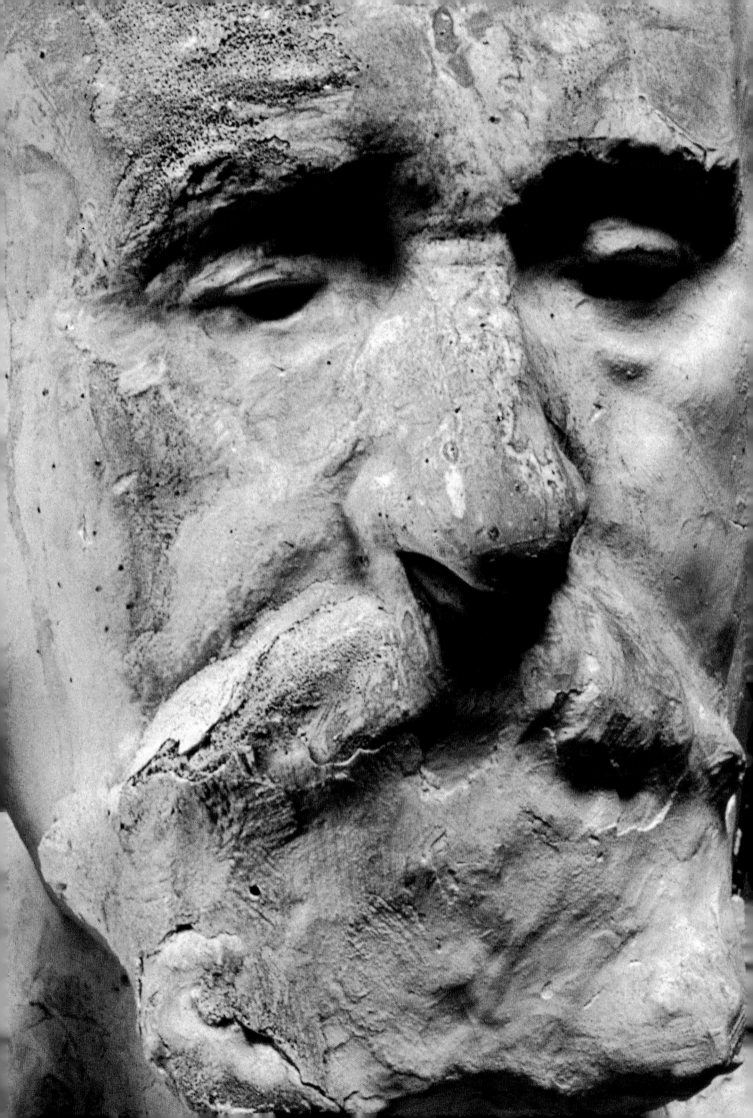

"To think he lived among us. . . . To think that genius worthy of the most glorious periods of art spoke to us, to think I shook his hand. For me it is as though I had shaken hands with Nicolas Poussin," Rodin intimated to Paul Gsell.[1] At the very end of his life, the sculptor reasserted his admiration for the painter: "And some say Puvis de Chavannes's work is not beautiful," he murmured before dying.[2] An expression of that admiration can be found in two busts of which there are several versions, and in the project for a monument.

We do not know exactly when the two artists met, but both were founding members of the Société Nationale des Beaux-Arts in 1890, and both were pleased that in a decree of July 18, 1890, Rodin was commissioned to make a marble bust of the painter, intended for the museum of Amiens, where Puvis's monumental paintings had just been unveiled to the public. Even before the commission became official, the latter expressed his joy to Rodin:

"My dear Rodin,

I am delighted about what you have told me. My head is yours. When do you want to start? Personally, I would like it to be as soon as possible since I am anxious to see a masterpiece emerge from your hands. If it suits you, I suggest nine o'clock in the morning on the day you say. Will it be on Rue de l'Université?

Yours with affection and sincere admiration."[3]

The execution of the bust proceeded swiftly. "I believe," Puvis wrote on October 25, "that it is in our common interest to work uninterruptedly until it is completed." A plaster model was presented at the second Salon de la Société Nationale des Beaux-Arts in May 1891 (no. 1364), at the time that Victor Peter began work on the marble. Exhibited at the next Salon (no. 1572), it was sent to Amiens in 1893 where it was unveiled in the Salon du Dôme on November 10, 1895 (fig. 2).

The portrait had gradually become more accurate during the countless sittings, and influenced by the sitter's observations. A sketch in the *New York World* on May 31 and comments in the press describing the bust shown in 1891 as a "piece" or even a "small piece," imply that it was the simplest, shoulderless version. Yet it would seem that Rodin had first thought of giving Puvis an image akin to that of *Jules Dalou* (1883) whose nude, cut off "Florentine-style" torso emphasized the accurate psychological analysis of the face. But Puvis had just been appointed president of the Société Nationale des Beaux-Arts and such a timeless vision did not appeal to him. "I often think about all the fine things I have seen at your place, and of course about my bust. On the subject I would like to humbly make the following suggestion: it seems to me that while my modern beard shows me as a man of my time, my shoulders and chest look too bare. It is an anachronism somehow. What do you think?"[4] According to the journalist Emile Michelet, it was not until the very morning of the unveiling that "Rodin applied some plaster and with two or three thumb marks gave the bust a frock coat that horribly mars this fine work."[5] We can thus imagine that following Puvis's remarks, Rodin had only kept what was needed to support the head of the originally nude torso, and that, at the last minute, he let himself be persuaded to add a hint of a coat collar. For the execution of the marble, he probably started off from this version: indeed the Musée Rodin possesses the plaster model used for the final version (fig. 3) in which we recognize the 1891 bust, enclosed in a sort of wire and plaster construction simulating the final bust, with shoulders, and dressed in a frock coat featuring a highly visible rosette of the Légion d'Honneur! As was his custom, Rodin had not felt the need to make a perfect model. But in the case of a state commission, the model belonged—like the finished work—to the Direction des Beaux-Arts. Therefore the artist was requested to send it to the museum of Lyon,[6] where Puvis de Chavannes had made a large decoration. As a result, Rodin modeled a bust with shoulders whose rapidly roughed out attire contrasts with the well-defined contours of the face.[7] That plaster model was delivered to Lyon in 1896 and used for casting at least six bronzes, among which the one shown here,[8] as well as for the marble replica meant for the Panthéon, commissioned from Rodin in February 1911. For the latter, Rodin first executed a very free portrait with the head rising from a huge block of uncut marble (fig. 4). He then returned to the earlier shouldered version, eliminating the details of the frock coat, and roughing out the mass so that the arms were barely distinct from the torso (Paris, Musée Rodin, S. 1387).[9]

Rodin had given in for the attire, but remained inflexible about the angle of the face which was slightly thrown back in order to receive more light, according to the principle of Greek

1. Auguste Rodin,
Bust of Pierre Puvis de Chavannes, detail, 1911–12.
Paris, Musée Rodin

2. Auguste Rodin,
Bust of Puvis de Chavannes, 1892.
Amiens, Musée de Picardie

3. Auguste Rodin,
Bust of Puvis de Chavannes, 1891.
Paris, Musée Rodin

4. Auguste Rodin,
*Bust of Puvis de
Chavannes*, 1911–12.
Paris, Musée Rodin

sculpture as he himself had analyzed it. However, right after the opening of the 1891 Salon, Puvis had written him to ask for "a favor . . . a very pressing favor, that is, to put my bust back in its original position, without that backward motion that gives me an arrogant look, and is the opposite of my rather concentrated nature, I believe. All our friends were struck by it, as well as by the lack of fullness of the body. In this regard, I think that since, as you have told me, you cannot remedy such an essential point of the likeness for the time being, it would be better to just deal with the head. You know how much I admire you and I am sure enough of your friendship to insist on this modification."[10] But Rodin refused to retouch the bust and on several occasions exhibited the shoulderless version. Furthermore, the public generally approved of the portrait, admiring the sensitivity and carefully rendered expression, even if some viewers deemed it "stiff" and "dry." "The head is a wonder. It is proudly thrown back in the attitude of a man who looks at people squarely and is conscious of his worth. The eyes shine like steel, the mouth has something haughty and disdainful, in short, the bust is the man."[11]

Puvis de Chavannes, instead, never liked his bust, although he did write in 1894 that he "had seen it again with great pleasure."[12] "It was one of the disappointments of my career," Rodin claimed. "He felt I had caricatured him. And yet I am sure I expressed all the enthusiasm and veneration I felt for him in my sculpture."[13] This disagreement however did not alter the two artists' friendship. In October 1893, the painter warmly thanked the sculptor for recommending a model to him. "She is indeed charming and makes one want to draw. The area around her eyes is especially lovely;"[14] on January 16, 1895, Rodin planned and presided over the banquet given for Puvis's seventieth birthday, and in 1896, when the two artists exhibited together in Geneva, the bust appeared—the one that bears the first number in the section devoted to Rodin (no. 95)—together with a preparatory sketch for one of the paintings of Amiens, *Ludus pro Patria*, that belonged to Rodin (no. 6). Dedicated to "the sculptor Rodin, his admirer, his friend P. Puvis de Ch.," this drawing (fig. 5) had probably been given to him by the latter on the occasion of the January 1895 banquet, an event that had deeply moved Puvis, as we see in his very refined letter in which he wrote to Rodin, "to you who, with the generous heart of a great artist and friend, conceived that celebration, my ardent, desire to express, if possible, my gratitude for the acknowledgment I have received."[15]

Just as the two artists were planning another exhibition together, Puvis de Chavannes died on October 25, 1898, so Rodin exhibited alone for the first time. The exhibition that opened on May 9, 1899, in Brussels featured a new, and probably recent work, the small *Funerary Genius*, presented as a "project for the monument to Puvis de Chavannes" (no. 23). The committee, presided over by Carolus-Duran, that had been formed in the Société Nationale des Beaux-Arts after Puvis's death for the execution of a monument, had naturally decided to have Rodin do it, undoubtedly recalling the success of the *Monument to Victor Hugo* at the 1897 Salon, and not the problems that had arisen over the statue of *Balzac* in 1898. Rodin was awarded the official commission on March 24, 1899,[16] and he soon announced his intention to return to the 1891 bust "to amplify it, and give it an heroic appearance appropriate for outdoor works. I shall place the figure of a woman beside it. Chavannes had the sense of female beauty. I shall strive to express that with my marble figure."[17] Yet a few weeks later, the woman had become a genius. What had happened? Had Rodin changed his mind and specially modeled a male figure for the monument, as he would do in 1905–06 with the monument to Whistler *Muse Climbing the Mountain of Glory*? Or else, and this seems more likely considering the short lapse of time between the commission and the Brussels exhibition, did the *Genius* already exist? Whatever the case may be, its "enlargment" appears in Henri Lebossé's accounts[18] as early as the month of June, and both the large and small models were presented at the Pavillon de l'Alma in Paris the following year.[19] At that date, the monument was sufficiently advanced, at least in Rodin's mind, to be described: "Puvis de Chavannes's bust rests upon a low stele, on which leans a genius who, his head bowed over his bent arm, falls asleep in peace, in glory. Glory is symbolized here by a delicate laurel bush . . . the symbolic figure, that rests on a base, will be bronze, the bust marble. As for the stone stele, it will have a classic simplicity, M. Rodin refusing to call upon the embellishments of architecture to add grace to his work."[20] At the end of 1902, the press announced that the maquette of the monument was completed; yet it continued to develop in the following

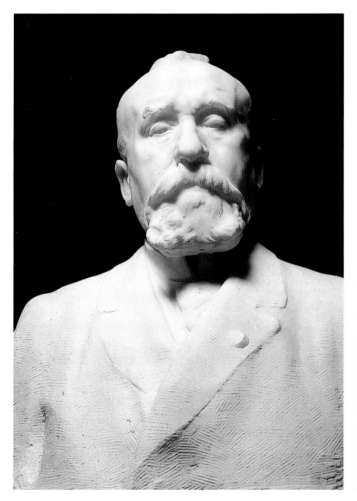

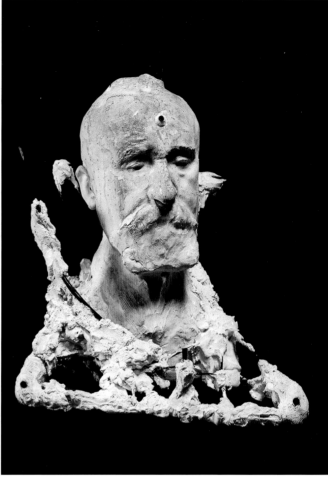

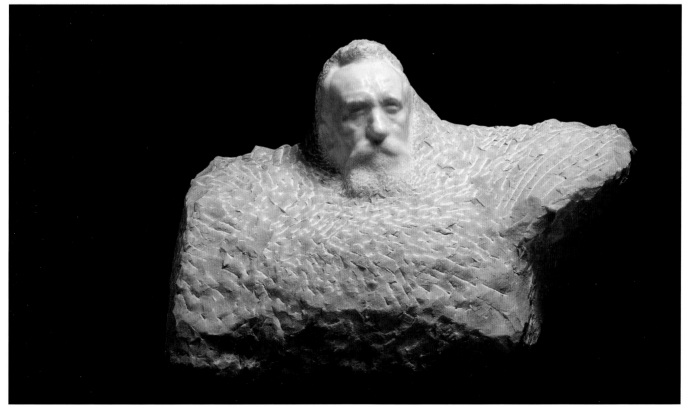

5. Pierre Puvis de Chavannes, *Study for "Ludus pro Patria,"* c. 1889. Paris, Musée Rodin

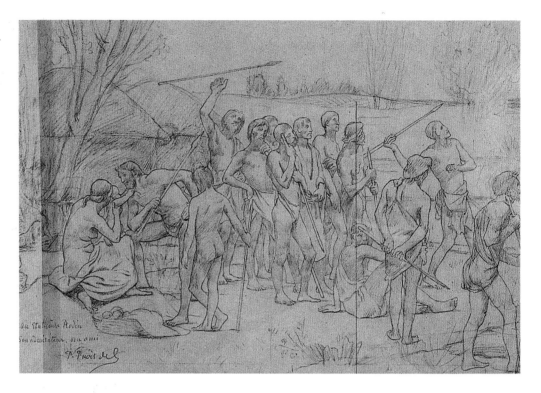

months, and early in May 1903, the committee, represented by Carolus-Duran, Montenard, Jean Béraud, Dubufe and Jordan, went to Rodin's studio to see the model: "Carolus-Duran had spoken to me with extraordinary enthusiasm about your monument to Chavannes," Arsène Alexandre wrote. "I'm told it is as moving and as beautiful as the most admirable works we've ever seen. That does not surprise me. But I would certainly like to see it, and perhaps write a piece about it."[21]

While in one way, Rodin had returned to a more traditional conception of the monument than for his *Balzac*, adding to the portrait an allegorical figure, the latter is as impersonal as possible. Indeed, given his reservations about allegory, he always kept from giving it too precise a meaning. So, more than a reference to his career, the *Genius* represents an attitude toward the life of a man about whom Rodin used to say: "I love his serenity, his meditative tranquillity."[22] Described in 1900 simply as "one of his latest works, possessing an intense melancholy, a penetrating, funereal grace, it is meant to be a a commemorative monument."[23] Indeed its title is the same as that of the antique statue that visibly inspired it, *Sleep* or *Genius of Eternal Rest*, that arrived in the Louvre during the Revolution (MA 435), which was engraved several times and reproduced in drawings. The discussions in the *dépôt des marbres* studio must certainly have been lively: Was the figure to represent painting? Was it necessary that it hold a palette? It was most probably then that Rodin declared, referring to the young Englishman who was collaborating on the monument—the animal sculptor Watson: "young people do not know how to make sacrifices (they want to put in everything)."[24] He felt strongly about this, for we find it echoed in Judith Cladel at the same time: "In art, you have to be able to make sacrifices."[25] Three years later it led him to eliminate the allegorical figures in his *Monument to Victor Hugo*.

Nonetheless, while Rodin was stripping away superfluous accessories, he increased the significance of the monument by suggesting with a realistically represented apple tree, the mood of Puvis's painting, that Arcadia which constitutes its background. By striving to "[go further] by suggesting the figure depicted and [make] it part of a whole that the imagination gradually recomposes,"[26] to give it its deepest meaning, he ran counter to the traditional, didactic conception of the public monument: "[*Balzac*] was a rock, this one is an orchard," discerned Arthur Symon, one among those who best grasped the symbolism of Rodin's work.[27] Indeed the artist had created an extremely daring ensemble (fig. 6) constituting an "authentic 'installation,' in the most contemporary sense of the word,"[28] even if the compositions exe-

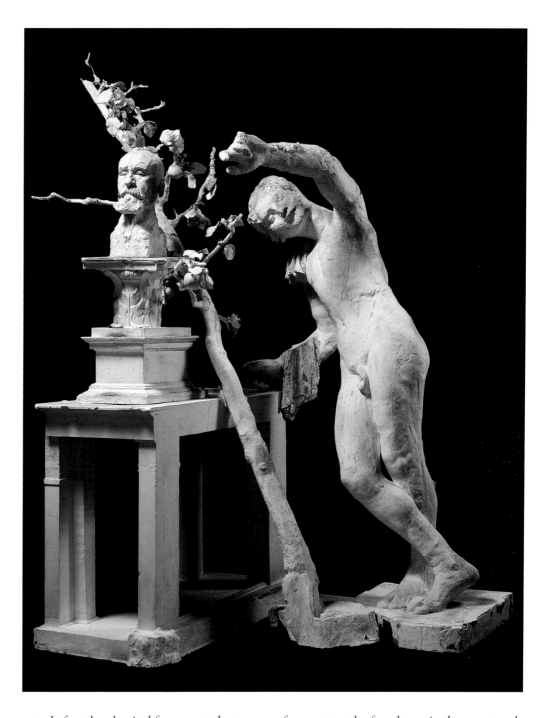

cuted after the classical fragments that were so frequent on the façades or in the courtyards of Roman palaces may have given him the idea for it. The monument includes various elements without any real unity: some of these are everyday objects that he thought of diverting from their normal use long before the Surrealists. The stele had actually been replaced by a kind of small family altar formed by a Corinthian capital placed askew on a plaster base, on which sat the *Puvis de Chavannes* bust. On one side the *Genius of Eternal Rest* leaned, seemingly picking apples from a fruit-laden tree, the ordinary laurel having been turned into an apple tree; it was a more direct reference to the painter, perhaps that had been suggested to Rodin by the rolling apples at the center of one of the Amiens pictures, *Concordia* [Peace]. The leaves and the fruit were cast like the table and the capital, since Rodin never wasted time modeling anything that already existed.

Similarly to its exact contemporary *Man Walking*, the *Monument to Puvis de Chavannes* marks a key moment in the evolution of early twentieth century sculpture. It has become an intel-

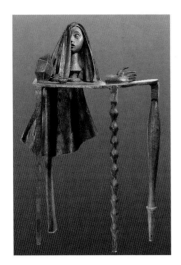

7. Alberto Giacometti, *Surrealist Table*, 1933. Paris, Musée National d'Art Moderne, Centre Georges-Pompidou

lectual construction in which the artist's hand no longer directly intervenes, having been replaced by operations of a mechanical nature, casting, assembly, enlargement, and even more daringly, by randomness. While the *Genius* directly emulates a classical marble, Rodin distances himself from his model by increasing the angle of the torso to its right until it is unbalanced, and by lengthening the forms. The presence of a very visible crack at the height of the waist, as well as a discrepancy in the assembly of the left leg, leads us to think that there had been an earlier clay version, at first perfectly vertical like the classical piece, then bent over so far as to break the figure at waist height. As always, Rodin refused to erase the traces of the accident, so that they were incorporated into the work and reproduced at the time of the enlargement.

In 1903, the monument seemed near completion. It was photographed[29] and Rodin returned to the *Genius* at the end of the summer of 1903,[30] probably to alter the arms. Several sites were suggested, Cours-la-Reine, parc Monceau—which neither Rodin nor the committee liked—Place Pigalle; but nothing was decided. However, Rodin had an estimate made for the execution of the base, table and capital in Echaillon stone, and for the apple tree in wrought iron. The bust was to be executed in bronze and the *Genius* in marble. In August 1907, a marble block was delivered directly to the chiseler Louis Mathet, and then, in 1910, removed to the studio of Louis Despiau who scarcely touched it before he was drafted in 1914, leaving a very rough version of the figure (Paris, Musée Rodin). Was Rodin still satisfied with the project at that date? Maybe not. Indeed the model had been dismantled before 1912: "Chavannes, in pieces, lies there in a corner waiting for its hour to come—if it ever does—when Rodin after his final thumb mark or fist blow, will say: 'It's done!'"[31] By then, however, the artist was thoroughly unable to complete so important a project, and at his death, in 1917, the monument had still not been executed.

After the war, some time before the hundredth anniversary of Puvis's birth, Albert Bartholomé relaunched its execution: the bust Rodin had made, slightly enlarged, was completed this time by a female figure, *Painting,* who was easy to recognize by the palette in her hands. It was the work of Jules Desbois, Rodin's former assistant, who had returned to the old language of allegory.

The monument was unveiled on December 20, 1924, in Paris, in Place Paul Painlevé, near the Sorbonne, on the occasion of the celebration of Puvis de Chavannes's hundredth birthday.[32] The following year, at the exhibition of the Arts Décoratifs, Despiau showed the stone enlargement of the *Enchantress* of 1910–12 under the title *Female Faun* (today at St. Nazaire); its composition is the same as that of the *Genius of Eternal Rest*, once again vertical with its arms reversed. But Rodin's true posterity is to be sought neither in Desbois nor in Despiau, but rather in Giacometti: the latter may well have been told about Bourdelle's *Monument to Puvis* at La Grande Chaumière,[33] and he made a striking tribute to his elder with his 1933 *Surrealist Table* (fig. 7) on which various objects are placed, apparently at random, two of which at least, the hand and the veiled bust, are a direct reference to Rodin's world.

[1] A. Rodin, *L'Art. Entretiens réunis par Paul Gsell*, Paris, Bernard Grasset, 1911, p. 184.

[2] J. Cladel, *Rodin, sa vie glorieuse, sa vie inconnue*, Paris, Bernard Grasset, 1936, p. 415.

[3] P. Puvis de Chavannes to Rodin, [July 11, 1891], Paris, Musée Rodin Archives.

[4] P. Puvis de Chavannes to Rodin, March 23 [1891], Paris, Musée Rodin Archives.

[5] E. Michelet, *La Revue indépendante*, June 1891, Paris, Musée Rodin Archives.

[6] H. Marraud, "Catalogue des sculptures au musée des Beaux-Arts de Lyon," in *Les Métamorphoses de Mme. F. Auguste Rodin, Maurice Fenaille et Lyon, Bulletin des musées et monuments lyonnais*, 1998, nos. 2–3, p. 110.

[7] It was probably at that time that the small wax was made, now at the Fogg Art Museum, which was most likely a reduced version for an edition rather than a preliminary study.

[8] Cast by Alexis Rudier in March 1914 and part of Rodin's donation to the French state in 1916.

[9] N. Barbier, *Marbres de Rodin. Collection du musée*, Paris, éditions du Musée Rodin, 1987, nos. 22 and 23.

[10] P. Puvis de Chavannes to Rodin, [May 16, 1891], Paris, Musée Rodin Archives.

[11] Anonymous, *Le Progrès*, Lyon, May 18, 1891.

[12] P. Puvis de Chavannes to Rodin, [May 4, 1894], Paris, Musée Rodin Archives.

[13] Rodin, *op. cit.*, p. 187.

[14] P. Puvis de Chavannes to Rodin, October 6, 1893, Paris, Musée Rodin Archives.

[15] P. Puvis de Chavannes to Rodin, Paris, January 22, 1895, Paris, Musée Rodin Archives.

[16] D., "Monument Puvis de Chavannes," *Le Gaulois*, April 4, 1899.

[17] "A travers la presse. Chez M. Rodin. Du *Figaro*," *Le Corrézien*, March 28, 1899.

[18] See *Relevé de comptes 1898-1899*, and Henri Lebossé to Rodin, August 2–September 8, 1899, Paris, Musée Rodin Archives.

[19] See *Rodin en 1900. L'exposition de l'Alma*, exh. cat., Paris, Musée du Luxembourg, 2001, nos. 48 and 88.

[20] *Le Gaulois*, February 25, 1900.

[21] Undated: May 1903? Paris, Musée Rodin Archives.

[22] Quoted by G. Coquiot, *Rodin à l'hôtel de Biron et à Meudon*, Paris, librairie Ollendorff, 1917, p. 37.

[23] *Rodin* exhibition, Paris, Pavillon de l'Alma, 1900, no. 65.

[24] R. Chéruy, Manuscript notes, notebook 1 and 2, Paris, Musée Rodin.

[25] J. Cladel, *Auguste Rodin pris sur la vie*, Paris, éd. de la Plume, 1903, p. 15.

[26] Quoted by P. Gsell, "Propos de Rodin sur l'art et les artistes," *La Revue*, November 1, 1907, p. 100.

[27] A. Symons, *From Toulouse-Lautrec to Rodin with Some Personal Impressions*, London, John Lane the Bodley Head Ltd., 1929, p. 242.

[28] J. Vilain, exh. cat. Paris, Musée Rodin, 1995 (*Whistler*), preface, p. 12.

[29] Several photographs were taken around May 1903 at the Musée Rodin, and a very accurate drawing of the base was made as well (Musée Rodin, D. 7718).

[30] On August 14, 1903, Rodin asked Bourdelle if he knew "a male model, about fifteen years old, with rounded arms, to pose for my genius" (Paris, Musée Bourdelle Archives). According to a note in the Musée Rodin Archives, "it's the *little* Pignatelli who posed for the *génie du repos éternel* of Puvis de Chavannes's monument."

[31] A. Alexandre, "Sur un monument promis par Rodin," *Comoedia*, September 7, 1912.

[32] See P. Desachy, "Le monument Puvis de Chavannes et Jules Desbois," *Le Figaro artistique*, May 1, 1924, pp. 2–3.

[33] An ink sketch by Bourdelle of the monument is conserved at the Musée Bourdelle.

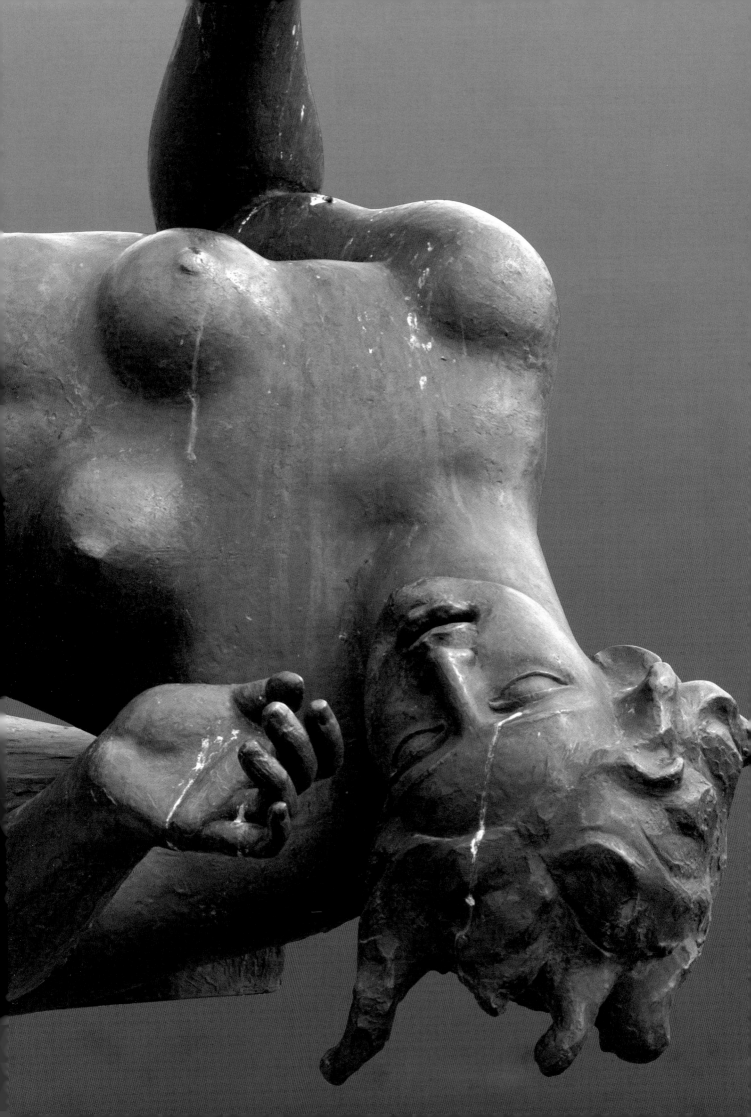

Catherine Chevillot

"Was Puvis de Chavannes a Painter?"[1]

When, around 1880, Puvis de Chavannes's cycle of paintings at the Panthéon was achieving true recognition, French sculpture was passing through a crucial period.[2] Year after year, the critics visiting the Salon de Sculpture reeled off complaints about the loss of true creativity among the practitioners of this art; commentators were simply fed up with displays of technical virtuosity and descriptive realism, and attacked the prevailing taste for anecdote and genre scenes. Statuary, one wrote, "is represented by numerous works, but most of these are far from being sculptural. They are examples of sculpted painting, with lots of face-pulling or sentimentality. The end result is almost always either strident or bland."[3] The loss of monumentality in both scale and spirit was particularly deplored, especially as this was considered one of the main, indeed, the noblest, aim of sculpture. Contemporary sculptors failed to achieve this monumentality, it was said, because "when one has to model clay, to attack solid stone, to breathe life into marble or bronze, subordinating the work to the precise rhythm of a building or an interior, one cannot get by with half-measures or approximations."[4] Buisson argued that "a symptom of the degeneration in this art is . . . the predominance of purely decorative sculpture over monumental sculpture",[5] while Paul Vitry, when faced with the *morceaux* at the Salon, decided to set them "definitely to one side, because they totally lack any serious monumental or decorative intention."[6] At the end of the nineteenth century, this loss of monumentality was taken to indicate that sculpture was no longer an embodiment of an "idea"; it no longer had that "divine"[7] role dreamed of by Winckelmann, championed by Baudelaire and inculcated into a generation of artists by Charles Blanc's *Grammaire*. Bénédite argued that sculpture had "lost its prestige and its divinity. [It] has entirely misunderstood its goal and meaning."[8] For his part, Roger-Marx spoke of "cerebral anemia" and quoted Ruskin: "sculptors have lost the use of thought."[9]

There was an urgent desire for a new universe of sculptural form. "It seems that a certain modern sculpture is yet to be created."[10] Sculptors aspired to rediscover the laws governing their art: "One must read the past, not simply imitate what it has done. One must, through a lifetime of long-frustrated effort, finally discover the laws behind it,"[11] wrote Bourdelle, who lambasted "all those who desert the laws of art."[12] Through his own work, he had learned "that sculpture depends on matter, volume and weight,"[13] and that matter is what should predominate and impose itself; yet what he discovered was that "one no longer respects marble."[14] In Maillol's sculpture, Denis emphasized "the degree [to which it reveals] a feeling for form, for the beauty of a line, for the geometrical perfection of a finished work." This was because his sole guide was an "exquisite, instinctive and uncerebral sense of form," drawing upon "the sphere and cylinder."[15] The same theme reappears in Lehmbruck's writings: "an intelligent respect for a physical law, authorizing some comparisons between air and what is heavier than air, isn't that worth more than this orgy of sentimental invention, which does not organize anything systematically and, more often than not, supposes it can even fly in the face of the ineluctable necessities of matter itself."[16] The goal to be achieved implicitly contained an ideal portrait of the artist who would save sculpture from the numerous perils besetting it. He was someone who would break the link between figuration and optical resemblance, between plastic art and artifice; who would restore the noble ambition of monumental art to form; who would succeed in breaking with the tradition of the Renaissance; who would restore matter to its rightful primacy in the construction of compositions. And where was one to find this prophet among the most famous of contemporary artists? Certainly not in Rodin's studio at the Hôtel Biron. One of the criticisms leveled at his work was precisely his tendency to subject form "to the tyranny of literary ideas, which generate illusions that are alien to the nature of plastic art."[17] Rodin may have introduced changes into the art of sculpture, but he was leading it in the direction of expressionism, and what was emerging was a powerful aspiration toward the classical. However, there was no contemporary sculptor who embodied this classical ideal. At this point, sculptors began to look to Puvis de Chavannes, who, together with Rodin, was one of the most prestigious artists of the Third Republic, both because of the aura generated by his career and the universal recognition enjoyed by his works.[18]

The Painter and the Sculptors

It was recognized that the influence of Puvis de Chavannes extended well beyond the field of painting. "He has made his mark on the general taste to a quite unexpected extent," wrote Re-

1. Aristide Maillol, *The River*, detail, 1938.
Paris, Musée National d'Art Moderne, Centre Georges-Pompidou

nan. "The sculptors, composers, poets and prose writers of a rejuvenated France, a whole galaxy of thinkers and independent lovers of art, all owe a great deal to this painter."[19] Pierre Godet thought that "a number of the great among the recent dead offer a response to that generation which is once again posing itself the problem of the classical—and one of those men is Puvis de Chavannes," who, he argued, was—together with Cézanne and Gauguin—"the initiator of this 'return to style' that is a reaction against Impressionism."[20] Puvis was considered to be the man who had restored life to a classicism "in which society as a whole recognizes the expression of its needs and the language of its instincts."[21] Writing in 1922, Bénédite said that "dominating our contemporary art, this immortal oeuvre"[22] breaks with that gesticulatory art which was so heavily criticized in sculpture (the result of the influence of the theater and its great set designers from the sixteenth century onward).[23] And for Focillon it was clear that "the artists who tried to reestablish a certain measure and cadence in pictorial composition . . . felt the dominant effect of this great example. From Seurat to Gauguin, all those who attempted to restore serenity of form and decor . . . have admired or meditated upon the art of Puvis de Chavannes."[24] And in the field of sculpture itself, the period around 1890 saw the emergence of a new generation of sculptors who in the years to come would introduce noteworthy changes into their art. In France, the most notable included Emile-Antoine Bourdelle, Aristide Maillol, Albert Bartholomé and Joseph Bernard; abroad, George Minne and Wilhelm Lehmbruck.[25] By 1905 these artists would have developed their own independent artistic language; many of them had worked under Rodin; all of them defined themselves in opposition to him.

Yet isn't the idea of Puvis de Chavannes's influence on sculpture to be dismissed a priori, given that the wellsprings of sculptural inspiration are to be found in sculpture itself? The history of art would seem to suggest so; the tradition in the nineteenth century was to treat each of the arts as a separate domain (and contemporary writers and critics do just the same). In many ways, one can hardly find fault with this approach, given that more often than not, evidence concerning the concatenations of works or the reactions provoked take precedence over links that are all in all rather marginal. However, on this particular occasion, such an approach forgets two specific facts—that the ideas of Viollet-le-Duc and the Arts and Crafts, and afterwards the Art Nouveau movement made their influence felt in all areas of artistic debate. The relation between painting and sculpture was thence modified; and as it was modified in the field of praxis (many artists were not only sculptors but also painters, ceramists or interior designers), couldn't it also have been modified in the field of influences? What is more, someone like Puvis de Chavannes was perceived by the artistic world of the late nineteenth century as much more than a painter; he was someone who had revitalized monumental art, something which was of capital importance to sculpture.[26] He had severed the Gordian knot of artistic antinomies, to such an extent that Mauclair actually asked "Is Puvis de Chavannes a painter?" only to answer a few lines later[27] that he was "above all, a thinker," and that in his work painting returns to its place "as an expression of ideas, comparable to music and poetry."[28] What is more, together with Meissonier and Rodin, Puvis had offered hope to young artists through the foundation of the Société Nationale des Beaux-Arts; and at a personal level he was always open in his support of new talent.

The direct and indirect relations between Puvis de Chavannes and a number of sculptors were far from negligible. Both Bourdelle and Maillol voiced their admiration for the painter repeatedly. In listing the artists who had influenced him before his artistic maturity, Bourdelle mentions first Barye, then "it was Dalou and his constructions created with a pair of compasses—Dalou, that forceful workman—and then Rodin, that powerful artist. Rodin was like an intimate study, a profound analysis of life. And finally there was de Chavannes, whom I admired a great deal."[29] Kémeri, who published a book on Bourdelle during the sculptor's lifetime, did not hesitate to write that no artist "apart from Puvis de Chavannes has been Bourdelle's equal in constructing and expressing purity of form . . . with a balance and harmony that verge on the monumental."[30] Linked together here are Puvis de Chavannes, a search for monumentality and a rejection of Rodin. The influence of the painter on Maillol is borne out by the latter's very beginnings in the medium of paint. "Not receiving advice from anyone," says Maillol, "I tried to find my own in the paintings of the great artists; so, while I was painting the portrait of my aunt at Banyuls, I turned to [the work of] Puvis de Chavannes for advice."[31] He mentions his copies of *The Poor Fisherman* and the *Saint Genevieve* in the Panthéon. "Puvis! It is to him that we owe the greatest emotions of our youth. . . . Even if I did not become a painter, I learned a lot from paintings."[32] (An anecdote recalls that the young artist painted the sets for the puppet theater of his friend Maurice Bouchor: "when the curtain went up, a striking old man sitting in the stalls did not fail to applaud—it was Puvis de Chavannes."[33]) Maillol did not view Puvis simply as a grand artist to whom it was natural that the young should turn for inspiration; he also considered him a figure who could save the Ecole des Beaux-Arts, and was very indignant when Puvis was turned down there as a teacher. Later, it was from Gauguin and Denis—both interested in the same plastic synthesis of composition that he found in Puvis—that Maillol drew sustenance for his own early attempts[34](Denis would play an important role in championing Puvis's ideas not only through his own artistic works but also through his critical writings).[35]

There is equally clear evidence of Puvis de Chavannes's influence on sculptors outside France. For example, the *Paris-Bruxelles* exhibition gave some measure of the place he occupied in Belgium: his works were regularly exhibited there from 1877 onward, and he was the most talked-about artist at the 1888 Exposition Internationale d'Art Monumentale in Brussels (exhibiting his *Ludus pro Patria* and the *History of Saint Genevieve*). Indeed, his style was said to "fascinate the avant-garde."[36] It was undoubtedly during the exhibition of the cartoons in 1888 that Minne made his copy of *The Childhood of Saint Genevieve*. As Robert Hoozee has shown, the works of Puvis de Chavannes "not only influenced Minne's work as a book illustrator, but also the style of certain of his sculptures." *The Prodigal Son* was exhibited at *Les Vingt* in 1894, and Minne's *Kneeling Man and Woman* of 1889 has been linked with *The Poor Fisherman*. In this period, Meunier too came under the influence of the artist.[37]

Related Ideas, Related Forms

Quite apart from the tangible relations between the men themselves, one can make out other connections. The change that occurred in sculpture around 1900 is always read as a reaction against Rodin, which is true as far as it goes. However, the notion of reaction serves to identify what was to be rejected; it does not necessarily forecast the ways in which the work of these various sculptors would converge. Obviously, the role of certain external influences—archaic sculpture, and particularly that of Egypt and of the Middle Ages—has been emphasized. However, it is reasonable to doubt that they alone serve as a sufficient explanation. There was a classical current in the French sculpture of this period, even if the hiatus between Guillaume's *The Mower* and Bourdelle's *Penelope* is clear. It is in this area that a close look at the ideas put forward by Puvis de Chavannes and at the debate provoked by his work reveals remarkable correspondences between that work and the still, at least formally, unexpressed desires of a young generation that was striving to escape from Rodinesque expressionism.

"Nature contains everything," Puvis said, "but in a confused manner; the chaos has to be sorted out. And how is that to be done? Through abbreviation and simplification. Express what is important; leave the rest to one side. That is the secret of drawing, that is the secret of composition."[38] This simplification of forms to the point of austerity, this "making a little go a long way,"[39] the reduction of the picture space to the plane of a wall or canvas—these are among the most striking features of Puvis's art. And Bourdelle? He "used his willpower and his intelligence to make himself less complex. . . . In the same way, [his] method of working led to a move from the complex to the simple; when presented to the public, a particular work is in fact his third or fourth attempt. The sculptor . . . helped his statue to grow gradually, by suppressing what was useless, reducing the ensemble to the planes and surfaces which were necessary."[40] Bourdelle himself was happy to explain that art "is undoubtedly a very simple thing. It is we who are complicated."[41] Maillol made the same point: "The ideal in art is to condense, to use a few clear and concise forms to summarize the infinity of varied relations that we perceive in nature. The aim is to reduce our most specific, detailed sensations to what is essential, to make something simple out of something complicated."[42] And, just as in Puvis, this involves a daily sacrifice: "'Art is complicated,' I used to say to Rodin, who would laugh because he felt that I was wrestling with nature. I was actually trying to simplify, while he was rendering all the outlines, all the details."[43] This sobriety naturally implied a rejection of the anecdotal. Puvis de Chavannes argued that "an insignificant detail, one that has nothing to do with the main idea, is capable of destroying the entire emotional power [of a work]."[44] This was what struck Rodin most about Maillol's work:

"In none of his works—at least, in none of those I have seen—is there anything, ever, that will seize the curious attention of the passerby."[45] This would explain the latter's rejection of movement[46] and his difficulty in finding a satisfactory manner of integrating the arms with the rest of a figure.[47] The result of all this was a special iconography common to all these artists. "One could say that Puvis de Chavannes broke with the narrow lexicon of conventional gestures, with that pretentious and mannered contortion, that academic posing, those ballet steps and tableau vivant stances that have so long perverted vision in our art schools."[48] One can see the same rupture in the work of Maillol: "The geometric bias is," argues Judith Cladel, "a resounding reaction against the gesticulatory sculpture of the nineteenth century—that very sculpture which, while claiming to draw on classicism and tradition, is actually the proof of a disorder resulting in works which are the very opposite of the classical."[49]

By exploring the destiny of man and nature, these artists sought the permanent, the universal. "I strive to see the universal in things, to see their enduring character," said Puvis.[50] This was precisely why his art was perceived "as outside place and time," and why he was able to attract the interest of young artists.[51] The attraction lay not only in the formal characteristics of his own artistic universe, but in the fact that this universe itself was one of *monumental* painting, "which presents itself with all the prestige of a survivor. Guaranteed to last as long at the building it adorns, it was conceived with neither a specific social class nor a generation in mind. It is dedicated to posterity; it addresses the universal soul."[52] And Bourdelle's work too aspired "to return to the things that are immortal . . . to see their unity in relation to the universal, in the realm of forms as in the realm of human desires, emotions and aspirations. I want to find their roots, their links with the infinite."[53] An aim that is echoed by Maillol: "The detail does not interest me; what is important to me is the general idea, because the aim of art is 'to stir in the heart of the people what is eternal in mankind.'"[54] And with regard to Minne, Verhaeren underlines that "his characters are almost beyond the possible conditions of being. They are detached from a specific milieu; they come and go toward a world beyond, which can only be inhabited by ideas."[55]

A universal language must be comprehensible to everyone; and this extreme intelligibility is the result of a formal *synthesis*, one that was so important that it would actually serve as a label for group of artists. As early as the 1880s, this formal synthesis was being held up as one of the characteristic features of the work of Puvis, who said of himself: "When I think about what I have been able to do, what I discover in it is not a striving but a need for synthesis."[56] Bourdelle in his turn, would urge his students to "tighten" their volumes: "Look for the source of outlines as if you were searching for the source of a river. . . Too much undulation! Be careful! One should not undulate like that. You have to tighten your volumes, put them in order."[57] This was what Maillol looked for in ancient sculpture: "the Greeks proceeded by synthesis, above all in their primitive sculpture, like that on Mount Olympus. . . . I have only a few main contours, and yet I think that is more than enough."[58] And when he thinks back to the time when his art was achieving its maturity: "One must be synthetic. When young, it was second nature to be synthetic."[59] In Belgium, "Minne's works reveal such a powerful synthesis of moral and plastic values that they are akin to the most venerable and essential works of sculpture that exist."[60] The means to the achievement of this synthesis was drawing, the privileged form of expression for all those artists for whom art was primarily a "mental thing." Theirs was not a drawing that aimed to be descriptive, but one that was the result of a gradual purging of an initial mental concept.[61] The logic behind the work of the hand was not to reproduce but to construct. In 1892, Guigou emphasized the importance of such constructive lines: "This concealed geometry is just as much at the heart of a decorative idea as it is at the heart of an architectural notion";[62] Rodenbach, in fact, would compare Puvis to an engineer, a surveyor.[63] Obviously construction requires putting things in order: "That which he considered as the very basis of his notion of art and which dominates the composition . . . is the above-mentioned order, an order which, in the plastic arts, rests mainly on correct proportions and relations between things."[64]

A prime concern among all the classical sculptors of the early twentieth century was the architectural structure of a work of sculpture. Fascinated by "mathematical beauty,"[65] Bourdelle corrected a work using these terms: "the framework, this vault, and the heel that touches the ground; one has to build all that. And, to build well, one must know how to add, subtract and multiply.

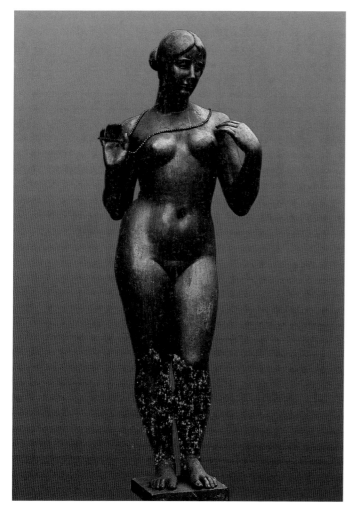

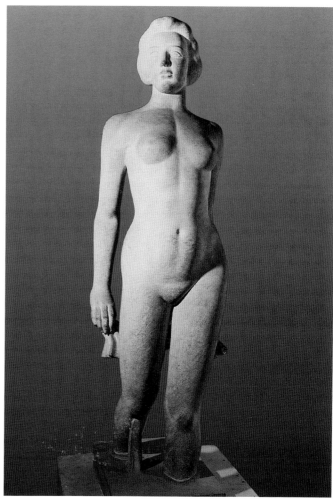

2. Aristide Maillol,
Venus with Necklace, 1930.
Zurich, Kunsthaus

3. Aristide Maillol,
L'Ile de France, 1921–25.
Paris, Musée National
d'Art Moderne, Centre
Georges-Pompidou

The good statue-maker must have all the laws of mathematics and the highest degree of geometrical knowledge at his fingertips."[66] For him, this approach was clearly synonymous with an aesthetic rupture, in which subjectivity was in opposition to the mathematical attitude that an artist must possess,[67] and like Puvis he sought a rhythm for his compositions.[68] For his part, Maillol did not hesitate to give this definition of sculpture: "[it is] architecture, an equilibrium of masses, a tasteful composition. This architectural aspect in sculpture is difficult to achieve. I try to attain it in the same way as Polycletes did. I start from a geometrical figure—square, lozenge, triangle—because these are the forms that hold together best in space. . . . My *Mediterranean* is enclosed within a perfect square; my *France* within an acute triangle." Did not the sculptor himself declare: "I am an architect?"[69] And one finds the same sort of thing in Minne: "architectonic in approach, he groups human forms in logical balanced monuments. Who has not been struck by the construction implicit in the works of this son of an architect from Ghent?"[70] And according to Lehmbruck, measure and proportion were the basis of artistic creation: "This is why," he says, "a good sculpture must be constructed, just like a building."[71] Without it, "a statue lacks the essential, that is, a monumental character."[72]

Monumental Art

The construction these artists sought was not the inner logic of a form endowed with its own autonomous life. Quite the opposite; their concern was to construct figures that could be incorporated in an ensemble (Puvis de Chavannes worked out his own ensemble compositions by juggling around the position of plaster casts). The figure became a formal component at the service of something grander: the composition in which the hierarchical distinction between the different parts disappeared, the famous "*morceaux*" of the Salon.[73] The same principle governed the ensemble of the painted surface; the first consideration was unity,[74] in opposition, wrote Godet

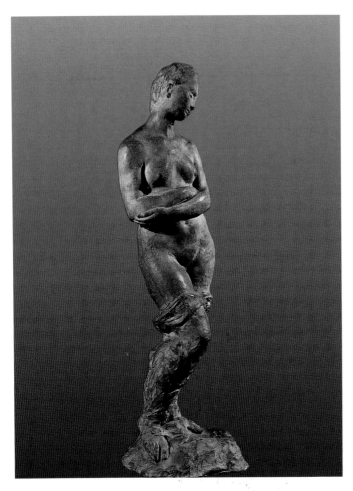

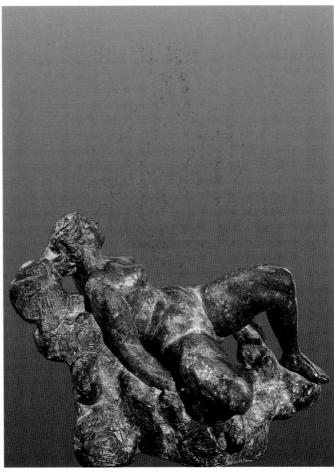

4. Wilhelm Lehmbruck,
Standing Female Figure, 1910.
Detroit Institute of Art

5. Emile-Antoine Bourdelle,
The Cloud,
Paris, Musée Bourdelle

opposite page
6. Emile-Antoine Bourdelle,
Athena Pallas as a Warrior.
Paris, Musée Bourdelle

"to an annotation by blots of multiple and fugitive appearances . . . synthesis took the place of analysis." In this area, the work of Puvis de Chavannes served as both a "benchmark and a norm."[75] Similarly, for Bourdelle every part of a composition had to be given the right weight; nothing must "overwhelm or prevail over"[76] the other parts of the composition or the relation between the latter and its environment.[77]

The ambition of these artists went beyond the mere physical limits of their work. In Bénédite's opinion, Puvis "understood the relationship between the figures and the interior of which they are a part, the implicit participation of that interior as an inanimate witness of the scene it contains—just as in the theater one feels that the actors on stage belong within their setting."[78] For Bourdelle, "the proportions of the whole, its fittingness, the calm rhythm of the ensemble lead one's thoughts beyond sculptures, beyond architecture," with the result that "the whole is harmonized with the entire universe."[79] It was now unthinkable that one should design a work without taking into consideration the site it would occupy, without "constructing it in harmony with the whole. This is not easy, however it is the essential."[80] For his part, Maillol strove to achieve volumes that were in equilibrium with external space: "more often than not, he worked out his statues in the open air, constructing and coordinating his volumes to maintain their plenitude of force in spite of the softening effect of broad daylight. . . . His search for the monumental led him toward luxuriant flesh-like surfaces which eschewed hollows and shadows."[81]

Now the monumental, as Puvis de Chavannes had reintroduced it into the art of his day, was considered to be *sculptural*. Contemporary critics never ceased to underline that everything was sculptural: the poses,[82] the line,[83] the contours.[84] Focillon would even go so far as to talk of a "style of metopes and pediments."[85] One understands nothing about Puvis de Chavannes, says Camille Mauclair, "if one for one instant forgets that he worked on walls."[86] The artist himself never forgot this, judging by a famous dictum of his that was repeated all over the place: "If you don't give a f... about the wall, then the wall will puke back on you."[87] The palette range in these paintings certainly struck the sculptors. Do not be misled, Léon Werth warned, "this neutrality is not

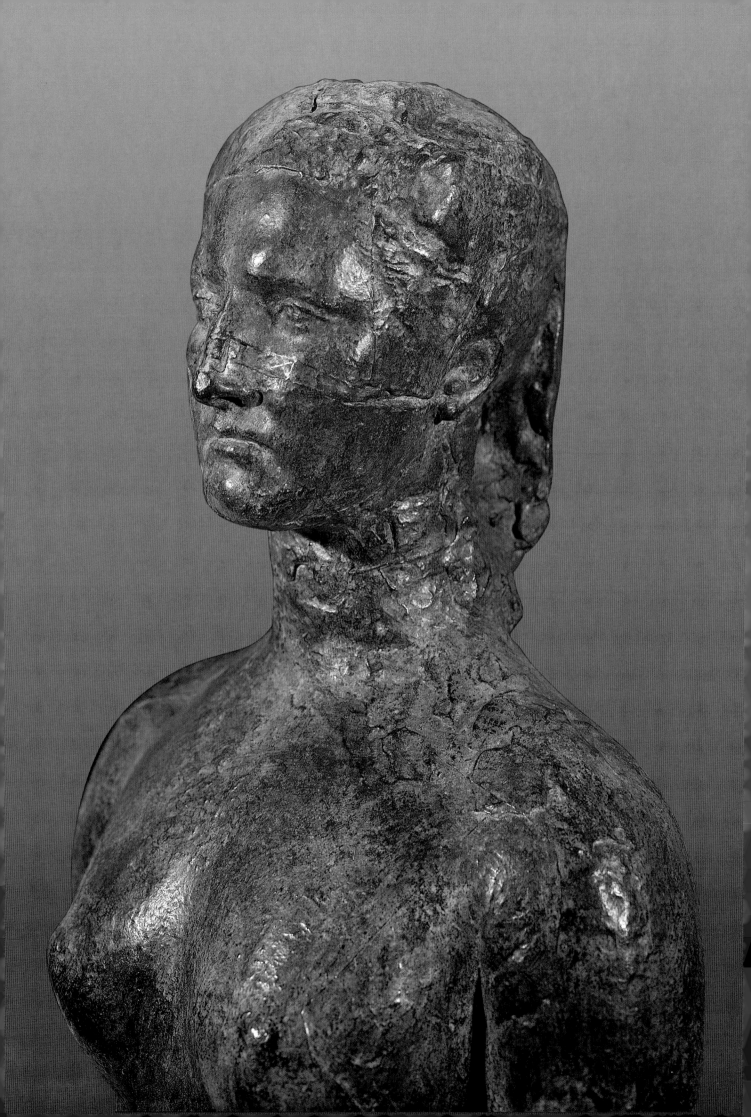

a choice; it is the elimination of color itself."[88] Of course, Puvis used light colors, so that the decor would harmonize with the stone; the choice of palette produced figures that were unusual in being stony pale—in a word, sculptural.

Likewise in sculpture, there was a forsaking of bronze for marble, stone and other new materials (concrete, reconstituted stone[89]). One need only think of Bourdelle's comment: "Come on, shake up all its shadows, all those timid gleams of frozen forms, all that penumbra."[90] Maillol himself preferred marble, and when he did have to produce a statue in metal, opted for lead in preference to bronze.[91] "Color?" he asked amazingly. "I don't know what color has got to do with sculpture. . . . I am seeking light, but I want it to fall on the sculpture simply, just as it falls across a wall. It is said that I am moving further and further toward light."[92] And when Minne gave up painting, he gave up color: "Convinced of the superiority of form over its changing vestment of light and color . . . he abandoned the paintbrush and took up the chisel."[93] He aimed for forms whose existence was an expression of plenitude; however, in striving for this he went in the opposite direction from Maillol. Chabot speaks of the terrible lighting in Minne's studio, and describes his amazement when, having mentioned it to the artist, the latter asked him to "suggest ways of making it even more worse" because, he said, if my works can stand up in this light, they can stand up in any light."[94] One is reminded of Puvis trying to paint figures that were perceptible in the penumbra of monumental halls; this very reason led him to work without color. Similarly, in 1914 Salmon would point out that "wherever you place a monument by Lehmbruck, in whatever lighting conditions, it will always be more brightly-lit than what stands around it."[95]

Paralleling Puvis de Chavannes's achievement in painting, Bourdelle is recognized as the person who freed sculpture from its tragic destiny "which is the common fate of our day: the divorce between . . . sculpture and architecture." In fact, "he respects the wall, a surface that should not be upset by some overhanging stone addition, nor penetrated by some *trompe-l'oeil* perspective. . . . He subordinated painted and sculpted decoration to the order of the building, the decoration or the landscape."[96] In some ways, he completed the tendency launched by the earlier artist; but, in the 1910s, it was pointed out that "all this seems logical, indeed, absolute; something which is almost never seen in contemporary sculpture."[97] Minne's approach to sculpture is also closely bound up with his interest in large-scale painted interiors. From 1883 to 1886 he was not studying sculpture but architecture, and then monumental painting with Théodore Canneel (in 1885 he painted his now lost mural decor *The Fall of the Rebel Angels*).[98] He would first come to sculpture in 1885, effecting a total change in his style with his *Sorrowing Mother* of 1888, the same year he made his copy of Puvis's *The Childhood of Saint Genevieve*. Undoubtedly, there were other influences at work: for example, Rodin and Gothic sculpture, but he held the former at some distance because "the rigor of his own concepts [of sculpture] inclined him toward considerations of construction and monumentality."[99] Fierens-Gewaert holds that "his sculpture only achieves its full expressive power when united with architecture."[100]

The Way Forward?
The few sculptors chosen here as representative of the debate which emerged around 1890 and of the sculptural aesthetics that developed about a decade later have certain things in common. With slight differences in the time scale, the work of each reveals a profound shift in approach. Bourdelle began exhibiting in the 1890s[101] with works that were a perfect continuation of those of his master,[102] but which reached a crisis point with the *Night* series of 1904. In 1901, Bourdelle created his *Headless Bust of Pallas Athena*, at which time "he finally turned his back on the man who had been a veritable master for him for so long."[103] There followed an homogenous group of works from 1905 to 1910 which range from the *Bather at Her Toilette* through the various versions of *Penelope* to *Fruit*.[104] Maillol's sculpture of the 1890s, on the other hand, was still heavily indebted to the decorative tendencies of Art Nouveau. Toward 1900 his style changes (with *Eve with the Apple*, *Leda* and *The Bather*) and then achieves its full breadth of expression in his *The Mediterranean* (1905). The most significant period in Minne's career is from 1888, the year he copied Puvis's mural, to 1900. The change in Lehmbruck's style is to be seen in relation to the influence of Hans von Marées, but actually coincides with his arrival in Paris in 1910 when he also began work as a painter and graphic artist (although he did pay

7. Aristide Maillol, *The River*, 1938. Paris, Musée National d'Art Moderne, Centre Georges-Pompidou

a visit to Rodin in that year, he was already breaking free of his influence and striking out in another direction).[105]

At the beginning of the century, all of these men were posing the same question: what was the way forward? In the end, all decided that the way forward was a return, as art criticism had been saying, a return to a study of the means specific to sculpture, a striving for forms that flow from the very material of sculpture and its relation with the circumambient space; a development of a new aesthetics based on form, volume and relief.[106] And in all this, a new emphasis was placed on the importance of craft.[107] "Shorn of color, landscape, and the encasing of air and light, it [sculpture] has, to its great good fortune, only to concern itself with the modeled form, to study that form amorously and let the rays of daylight play upon it."[108] That is to say, the goal was to achieve what Puvis de Chavannes had done in painting when he "restored decoration to the observance of its intrinsic laws."[109] And those laws for sculpture can be summarized in Maillol's dictum: "a statue is a study of volume in space."[110] From 1880 to 1905, Puvis's reputation and standing grew constantly: there were the exhibitions of 1887 and 1894, the foundation of the Société National des Beaux-Arts in 1891, the celebratory banquet of 1895, the attention aroused by his death, the room dedicated to his work in the 1904 Salon d'Automne[111]—all of which played an important role at the opportune moment. And 1905 was a key year in the history of sculpture: Bourdelle and Minne had their first one-man shows, and Maillol achieved real fame with the exhibition of his *Mediterranean*.[112]

Thus, the works that mark the artistic maturity of these sculptors, all of which dating from between 1890 and 1905, are in some way related to each other. Pensive figures that are absorbed in themselves, they might be expressions of sorrow (Minne), grave introspection (Bourdelle), reverie (Lehmbruck) or serenity (Maillol), and yet all show a marked preference for the solid form, in which the aim is a weighty plenitude of volume. In a number of works, the treatment

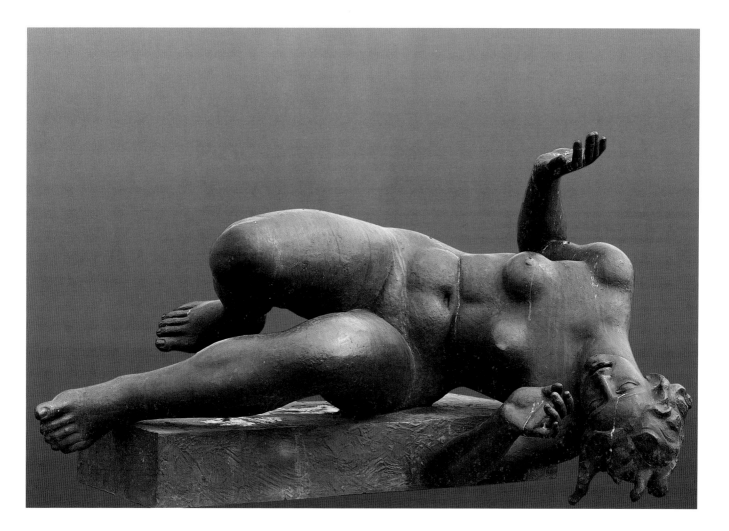

of specific themes recalls that of Puvis. This is true of Minne's 1886 *Wrestlers* and the 1897 *Man with Wineskin*,[113] and of Maillol's 1909 *Cyclist*, of his figures of children whose stark thinness recalls that in *Pleasant Land* (1882) or the 1885–89 *Autumn* or *Children in an Orchard*. Similarly, the ample proportions of the female figures in Bourdelle's *Penelope* and his *Noble Burdens* (1910–12)—works "full of the concentrated glow of mysterious expectancy, of fecund energy"[114]—carry on the taste for calm meditative compositions that can be seen in the 1873 *Summer* and the 1888–89 *Antique Vision*.[115] Or again, *Fruit* clearly echoes the leaning figure shown from the back in *Autumn* (1864); and one can trace some parallels between the severe, collected outlines in Maillol's *Mediterranean* and *Night*, or Bourdelle's *Sappho*, and the 1861 *Peace* (the seated figure on the left), the 1868 *Massilia, Greek Colony*, the 1873 *Charles Martel Conqueror of the Saracens* (figure on the lower right), the 1874–78 *The Childhood of Saint Genevieve* (right and lower-right sections), the 1891 *Shepherd's Song*, and so on. Minne's 1906 *Immortality* echoes the reclined figure in *Massilia, Greek Colony*; while Lehmbruck's 1911 *The Kneeling Woman* evokes the draped female figure in the 1863 *Rest* and in the 1869 *At the Fountain*; and Bernard's *Water Bearer* draws on the woman with the jug in the *Antique Vision* and the *Shepherd's Song*. Finally, Lehmbruck's 1914 *Three Women* is very close to the 1879 *Young Women by the Sea*.

If Puvis de Chavannes's work is characterized by "great uncomplicated emotions, by the decisive incidents of life, by centuries-old gestures that escape the passage of time"[116]—thus depicting both what is most day-to-day and what is most enduring in humanity—his artistic purpose might well be echoed in these words by Bourdelle: "the sublime is on our very doorstep; it is sitting in our homes; around me, my wife and children make the truest gestures, achieve the rarest composition of planes—just like those already discovered by the thinkers of old."[117] A visionary art of pathos was rejected in favor of an art of internalized silence, of grave and unhurried rhythm. In their attempt to achieve "tranquillity and eternal stability"[118]and thus escape from "Rodin's roughly-twisted figures; from thick cords of muscles strained to breaking-point because they are not supporting any weight, from characters who appear to be contorted in some sort of spasm," it was far from illogical for these young sculptors to look toward the great mural works of Puvis de Chavannes. Obviously, their subsequent development is not to be explained solely by his influence, but it clearly owed a great deal to the regeneration of artistic vision brought about by a man who was viewed by his contemporaries more as a thinker than a "mere" painter.

[1] C. Mauclair, *Puvis de Chavannes*, Paris, Plon, 1928, pp. 146–48. I would like to thank here Serge Lemoine, recognizing that his research project pre-dates mine. My gratitude also goes to my colleagues at the Musée d'Orsay (whose documentary archives were essential in writing this article); in particular, I would like to thank Anne Pingeot, Laure de Margerie, Véronique Gautherin and Claire Barbillon for re-reading the text. Given the lack of space, I shall cite the great figures of Bourdelle and Maillol as representatives of France, Minne as representative of Belgium and Lehmbruck of Germany. One could easily extend what I say to cover other sculptors.

[2] See " Réalisme optique et progrès esthètique," *Revue de l'Art*, 1994, pp. 22–29.

[3] E. Blémont, "Sculpture," in *L'Artiste*, 1884, I, pp. 455–72 and 465.

[4] P. Leprieur, "La sculpture décorative aux Salons," *Arts et Décoration*, I, 1898, p. 179.

[5] J. Buisson, "Le Salon de 1881," 3rd art., *Gazette des Beaux-Arts*, 81–2, 1881, pp. 223 and 231.

[6] P. Vitry, "La sculpture monumentale aux Salons," *Arts et Décoration*, 1902, II, pp. 14–23.

[7] C. Baudelaire, "Salon de 1859, la sculpture," in *Oeuvres complètes*, Paris, 1968, p. 419.

[8] L. Bénédite, "Les Salons de 1898," *Gazette des Beaux-Arts*, II, 1898, p. 133. See also A. de Lostalot, "La sculpture au Salon de 1882," *Gazette des Beaux-Arts*, II, 1882, p. 503.

[9] C. Roger-Marx, "Les Salons de 1895," in *Gazette des Beaux-Arts*, II, 1895, p. 112.

[10] A. Michel, "Le Salon de 1888, la sculpture," *Gazette des Beaux-Arts*, 1888, p. 148.

[11] G. Varenne, *Antoine Bourdelle, Ecrits sur l'art et sur la vie*, ed. J. Haumont, Plon, Paris, 1955, p. 66. See also p. 67 and J.-L. Vaudoyer, *L'Echo de Paris*, April 5, 1923, in R. Cogniat, *Hommage à Bourdelle, Documents et dessins inédits*, Paris, Plon, 1961, p. 66.

[12] E.-A. Bourdelle, "A propos de notre demain," *La Vie*, March 1915, no. 2, p. 84.

[13] P. Mille, "L'Art de Bourdelle," *Les feuillets d'art*, March 31, 1919, p. 41.

[14] Bourdelle, "A propos…," *op. cit.*, p. 84.

[15] M. Denis, *A. Maillol*, Paris, Crès & Cie, 1925, pp. 20, 23, 24. See also J. Cladel, *Aristide Maillol, sa vie, son oeuvre ses idées*, Paris, Grasset, 1937, pp. 38 and 146; and Mirbeau (1905, p. 325) as quoted in A. Romain, "Maillol," *Aristide Maillol*, exh. cat., Musée de l'Annonciade, Saint-Tropez, pp. 19–108. For him, too, matter played an equally important role: "What I cannot accept," he said, "is that a sculptor, for example, claims to be a complete artist without first and foremost being a perfect manual craftsman, that is, someone who can tame the material he works with." Mirbeau (1905, p. 340), quoted in *ibidem*, p. 58.

[16] A. Salmon, *Wilhelm Lehmbruck*, preface to the exh. cat., Galerie Levesque et Cie, Paris (June 20–30, 1914), n.p. With regard to the debate of these questions, the 1893 book *Das Problem des Form in der bildenden Kunst* by the sculptor A. Hildebrand is important. A French translation was published in 1905 (Paris, Vve Emile Bouillon, Strasbourg, Heitz und Mündel).

[17] L. de Fourcaud, "Salon des Artiste Français. La sculpture," *Revue des Arts Décoratifs*, 1898, p. 201.

[18] See L. Bénédite, *Notre art, nos maîtres*, Paris, Flammarion, 1922, p. 13.

8. Aristide Maillol,
Night, 1902.
Winterthur, Kunstmuseum

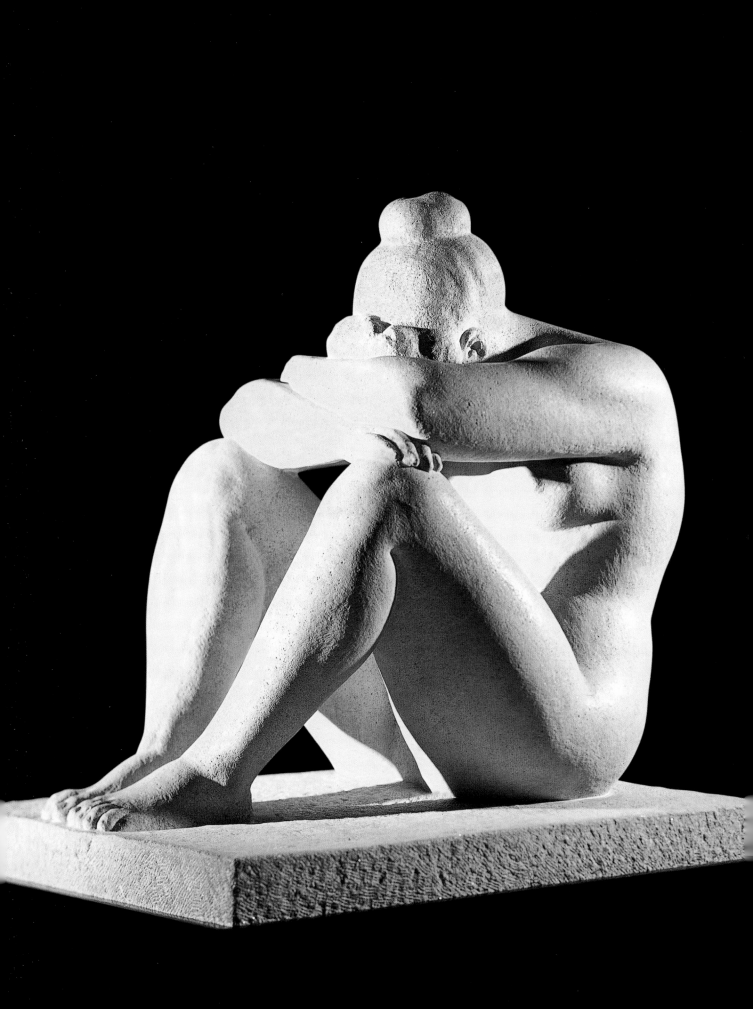

[19] E. Renan, "Puvis de Chavannes," *La Revue de Paris*, I, January 15, 1895, p. 439.

[20] P. Godet, "Puvis de Chavannes et la peinture d'aujourd'hui," *L'Art Décoratif*, January–June 1912, p. 37.

[21] *Ibidem*, pp. 47 and 49.

[22] Bénédite, *Notre art…*, *op. cit.*, p. 75.

[23] *Ibidem*, pp. 139–40. Bénédite was also Curator of the Museum of Living Artists from 1892 to 1925. On this subject, see T. Gautier, "Salon de 1861," in R. Bouyer, "Le centenaire de Puvis de Chavannes," *Le Figaro artistique*, December 11, 1924, pp. 130–34; Bénédite, *Notre art…*, *op. cit.* p. 64 and Renan, *op. cit.*, p. 447.

[24] H. Focillon, *La peinture au XIXème et au XXème siècle. Du réalisme à nos jours*, Paris, 1928, p. 250.

[25] Guillaume, Dubois, Barrias and Cordier all died in 1905; earlier had come the deaths of Chapu (1891), Cavelier (1895), Cain (1894), Jacquemart (1896), Schroeder (1898) and Dalou (1902), while a few years later came the deaths of Faiguière (1906) and Fremiet (1910). A. Bartholomé made his debut around 1887 and died in 1928; the two equivalent dates for the following artists are given in brackets: J. Barnard (1887 and 1931), Bourdelle (1885 and 1929), Maillol (1885 and 1945) and F. Pompon (1874 and 1933).

[26] L. Werth, "Puvis de Chavannes," *Portrait d'hier*, first year, no. 2, April 1, 1909, p. 61.

[27] Mauclair, *op. cit.*, pp. 146–47.

[28] *Ibidem*, pp. 28 and 148.

[29] Varenne, *op. cit.*, p. 20.

[30] S. Kéméri, *Visage de Bourdelle*, Paris, Armand Colin, 1931, p. 35.

[31] Cladel, *op. cit.*, p. 39.

[32] *Ibidem*, pp. 40–41: see also p. 155. But he always denied that his sculpture had been influenced by Gauguin (*ibidem*, p. 130).

[33] "Maurice Bouchor, who knew him, introduced Maillol: complimented on being invited to visit the famous painter's studio, the young artist 'too shy, too stupid' never dared to go." (*ibidem*, pp. 42–43)

[34] *Ibidem*, pp. 33–34.

[35] *Ibidem*, p. 66.

[36] M. Nonne, "Echanges artistiques" and "Puvis de Chavannes," in *Paris-Bruxelles, Bruxelles-Paris. Réalisme, impressionisme, symbolisme, art nouveau. Les relations artistiques entre la France et la Belgique, 1848-1914*, exh. cat., eds. A. Pingeot and R. Hoozee, Paris–Ghent, 1997, p. 45 and 533. The years 1894–97 marked the peak of his fame in Belgium: the Exposition Universelle in Antwerp (1894), the exhibition of the *Pour L'Art* Symbolist group (1895), the honorary presidency of the French section at the Exposition Universelle in Brussels (1897). Both Rodin and Puvis were invited to the Maison d'Art in Belgium in 1896, and "the death of Puvis de Chavannes left [Rodin] reigning there alone" (A. Pingeot, "Vers la sculpture moderne," in *Paris-Bruxelles*, pp. 210–16). On the influence of Puvis in Belgium, see also B. Fornari "Les Abimes," in *Paris-Bruxelles*, pp. 307 and 318.

[37] R. Hoozee and M. Tahon-Vanroose, "Minne et l'art alentours de 1900," in *George Minne*, exh. cat., Ghent, Musée des Beaux-Arts (September 18–December 5, 1982), pp. 175–81. French-language leaflet, p. 16.

[38] P. Guigou, "Puvis de Chavannes," *La Revue du siècle*, January 1892, no. 56, p. 7.

[39] Puvis de Chavannes quoted in Renan, *op. cit.*, p. 439. Bénédite, *Notre art…*, *op. cit.*, pp. 37 and 60.

[40] F. Dehérain, "A propos des oeuvres de E.-A. Bourdelle," *Idées Modernes*, May 1909, vol II, p. 304.

[41] Course held at the Grande Chaumière, January 9, 1914, in Varenne, *op. cit.*, p. 78.

[42] Denis, *op. cit.*, pp. 10–11.

[43] Cladel, *op. cit.*, p. 128. This process of elimination meant that all these artists were accused of awkwardness. Denis, *op. cit.*, pp. 10, 11 and 28. See also Cladel, *op. cit.*, p. 85. On the awkwardness of Puvis de Chavannes, see Castagnary quoted in Werth, *op. cit.*, p. 44, Mauclair, *op. cit.*, p. 129, Denis, *op. cit.*, in Romain, *op. cit.*, p. 40; Varenne, *op. cit.*, pp. 65–66; and E. Verhaeren, *Ecrit sur l'art (1881–1892)*, Brussels, Labor, 1997, pp. 378, 399, 400, 407 and 740. See also A. Alhadeff, "Minne, Gauguin et les Vingts," Ghent, 1982, French-language booklet, pp. 6–7.

[44] Puvis de Chavannes in C. Roger-Marx, "Puvis de Chavannes," *Revue Encyclopédique*, December 23, 1899, p. 1080.

[45] Rodin quoted by Mirbeau (p. 326), in Romain, *op. cit.*, p. 52.

[46] Cladel, *op. cit.*, p. 134.

[47] "If [The Venus de Milo] had arms, perhaps holding a shield, it would be less beautiful. There is a mystery there: the arms would have to be performing some explicatory gesture, something anecdotal; while in its present state, the statue is beauty in its pure form." (*ibidem*, p. 141).

[48] Bénédite, *Notre art…*, *op. cit.*, p. 130.

[49] Cladel, *op. cit.*, p. 167.

[50] Puvis de Chavannes in Guigou, *op. cit.*, p. 7. See also Mauclair, *op. cit.*, p. 39.

[51] Bénédite, *Notre art…*, *op. cit.*, p. 40. See also J. Foucart, "Preface" in *Puvis de Chavannes*, exh. cat., Paris, Grand Palais (November 24, 1976–February 14, 1977), p. 17.

[52] Roger-Marx, "Puvis de…," *op. cit.*, p. 1077; Focillon, *op. cit.*, p. 240.

[53] Notes for March 6, 1906, Varenne, *op. cit.*, pp. 25–26. See also Charles Bernard in Cogniat, *op. cit.*, p. 90; Varenne, *op. cit.*, pp. 24, 65 and 77.

[54] Cladel, *op. cit.*, pp. 127–28.

[55] Verhaeren, *op. cit.*, p. 497.

[56] Puvis de Chavannes quoted in Roger-Marx, "Puvis de…," *op. cit.*, p. 1080. Longer quote in Werth, *op. cit.*, p. 61.

[57] Kéméri, *op. cit.*, p. 102.

[58] Cladel, *op. cit.*, p. 132.

[59] *Ibidem*, p. 127.

[60] H. Fierens-Gewaert, "George Minne," *Art et décoration*, 1901, p. 109.

[61] On this question of mental images, see Bénédite, *Notre art…*, *op. cit.*, p. 141 (Puvis), Varenne, *op. cit.*, p. 96 (Bourdelle), Cladel, *op. cit.*, p. 146 (Maillol).

[62] Guigou, *op. cit.*, pp. 13–14.

[63] G. Rodenbach, "Puvis de Chavannes," in *L'Elite*, Fasquelle, 1899, p. 219.

[64] P. Vaisse "Puvis de Chavannes et l'escalier du musée des Beaux-Arts de Lyon," in *Puvis de Chavannes*, exh. cat., Lyon, Musée des Beaux-Arts (October 1–December 6, 1998), p. 47. On Minne, see P. Boyens, *L'Art flamand. Du symbolisme à l'expressionisme à Laethem-Saint-Martin*, Laethem-Saint-Martin, 1992, p. 238.

[65] Bourdelle, "A propos…," *op. cit.*, p. 83.

[66] Kémeri, *op. cit.*, p. 76; see also p. 75.

[67] *Ibidem*, p. 65.

[68] See R. Duncan, *Evangelos*, December 5, 1921, no. 10, p. 3.

[69] Cladel, *op. cit.*, pp. 148 and 123, on the subject of the third house at Marly.

[70] G. Chabot, "George Minne," *Gand artistique*, third year, no. 1, January 1, 1924, p. 9.

[71] Lehmbruck, quoted in Duisbourg, *Hommage à Lehmbruck, Lehmbruck in seiner Zeit*, exh. cat., Wilhelm Lehmbruck Museum der Stadt Duisburg (October 25, 1981–January 3, 1982), p. 42.

[72] Salmon, *op. cit.*, n.p.

[73] Roger-Marx, "Puvis de…," *op. cit.*, p. 1078; Bénédite, *Notre art…*, *op. cit.*, p. 85; Mauclair, *op. cit.*, p. 25 and p. 150.

[74] Bénédite, *Notre art…*, *op. cit.*, p. 66; A. Alexandre, "Puvis de Chavannes, l'artiste et l'oeuvre," *Le Figaro*, October 25, 1898.

[75] Godet, *op. cit.*, pp. 38 and 41.

[76] Bourdelle, quoted in Aurel, "La parole de Bourdelle," *La Vie*, no. 1, February 24, 1912, p. 26.

[77] E.-A. Bourdelle, "L'Art roman français," *L'Amour de l'art*, June 1920, no. 2, pp. 261–62.

[78] Bénédite, *Notre art…*, *op. cit.*, p. 69 (1911) and p. 75.

[79] Varenne, *op. cit.*, pp. 53 and 97.

[80] Kémeri, *op. cit.*, p. 166.

[81] Cladel, *op. cit.*, pp. 81 and 84.

[82] "The air of calm pagan sensuality given to the woman; her slow, almost tired, movements, plus an equal desire to achieve expression without displacing the line, without troubling the eurythmics of the sculptural pose." (Roger-Marx, "Puvis de…," *op. cit.*, p. 1079).

[83] "His thought is unburdened by pointless erudition; it emerges with a breadth of logical action; its embodiment may suffer from an overly-sculptural quality—but that is a fault which is due to an excess of mastery" (L. de Fourcaud, "Notes sur quelques décorateurs. Pierre Puvis de Chavannes," *Revue des Arts Décoratifs*, July–August 1888, p. 10).

[84] "The overly-simplified form reveals a striving for sculptural outlines," Guigou, *op. cit.*, pp. 1–17.

[85] Focillon, *op. cit.*, p. 246.

[86] Mauclair, *op. cit.*, p. 41. See also Rodenbach, "Puvis de Chavannes," p. 220, and A. Brown Price, in *Puvis de Chavannes 1924-98*, exh. cat., Grand Palais, Paris, National Gallery of Canada, Ottawa,1977, p. 21.

[87] In Werth, *op. cit.*, p. 55.

[88] *Ibidem*, p. 52.

[89] Lehmbruck too explored new materials, such as terracotta for his large format *steinguss* (*Lehmbruck. Durch Form zum Geist*, Bremen, Gerhard Marcks-Haus, 2000).

[90] Course at the Grande Chaumière, February 10, 1910, in Varenne, *op. cit.*, p. 59.

[91] Cladel, *op. cit.*, p. 84. See also Guilleminot, "Villégiatures d'artistes. Le sculpteur Maillol," *Gil Blas*, September 1, 1911.

[92] Cladel, *op. cit.*, p. 151.

[93] Chabot, *op. cit.*, p. 9

[94] *Ibidem*, p. 8

[95] Salmon, *op. cit.*, n.p.

[96] Mille, *op. cit.*, p. 41 and M. Pays, *Le Radical*, May 31, 1913, in Cogniat, *op. cit.*, p. 42. See also L. Gillet (1925) in *ibidem*, p. 77.

[97] A. T'Serstenvens, December 21, 1912, in Cogniat, *op. cit.*, p. 33.

[98] Hoozee and Tahon-Vanroose, "George Minne," in *George Minne*, *op. cit.*, p. 3.

[99] Boyens, *op. cit.*, p. 238.

[100] Fierens-Gewaert, *op. cit.*, p. 112.

[101] In fact, the first works he presented at the Société National des Beaux-Arts were pastels not sculpture (Rhodia Dufet-Bourdelle and Jean Selz, *Bourdelle peintre 1861–1929*, Paris, n.d.).

[102] *Léon Cladel* (1894), *The Cuirassier* (1897), *Terrors of War* (1899), *Desperate Hand* (1897–97); *Colonne Roland* (1898–1900). Following these are the comparable debut pieces during the 1880s of all his students at the Ecole des Beaux-Arts: *Saint Sebastian* (1883), *Hannibal's Victory* (1885), *Dying Love* (1886), *Adam* (1889)—all very academic works.

[103] V. Gautherin, in *Paris à la Belle Epoque*, Essen, 1994.

[104] *Bather at Her Toilette* (1906), *The Offering* (1905–06), *Bather with Crossed Legs (on a Rock)* (1906–07), *Woman Sculptress Resting* (1906–08) (and *Woman at a Fountain*), *Penelope* (1907) (various versions), *Melancholy* (1909), *Bather with Grapes* (1907–09), *Fruit*, first version (1906–11) and *Sappho* (1924, first version dating from 1887).

[105] In which he is usually said to have been influenced by Hildebrand and Hans von Marées, as well as Minne. U. Finkbeiner, *Hans von Marées als inspirations-quelle für Wilhelm Lehmbruck*, graduate thesis under Professor Graevenitz, Cologne 1994; *Hans von Marées und die Moderne in Deutschland*, Bielefeld and Winterthur, 1987–98; J. Laude, "La Sculpture en 1913," *L'année 1913*, ed. L. Brion-Guerry, Paris, Klincksieck, 1971, p. 223, n. 37.

[106] M. Hamel, "Le Salon de 1887, la sculpture," *Gazette des Beaux-Arts*, II, p. 35.

[107] G. Lafenestre, "Les Salons de 1897," *Revue des Deux Mondes*, July 1, 1897, pp. 177–91, and Leprieur, *op. cit.*, p. 179.

[108] E. Pottier, "Les Salons de 1892," *Gazette des Beaux-Arts*, 1892, II, p. 6.

[109] Roger-Marx, "Puvis de…," *op. cit.*, p. 1078; Focillon, *op. cit.*, p. 246.

[110] Puig (1965, p. 30), quoted in Romain, *op. cit.*

[111] Even more so as they were all more or less linked with Rodin; we know, through Judith Cladel, that Rodin's last words concerned Puvis de Chavannes.

[112] Perhaps inspired by Gauguin's painting *Aha Œ Feii*, see Romain, *op. cit.*, p. 80.

[113] Which he began in 1896 (*The Kneeling Boy* [1896], *The Little Bearer of Relics* [1897]).

[114] E. Faure, catalog of the exhibition *Sculptures, peintures, pastels, etc, par Emile Bourdelle*, Paris, Galerie Hébrard, 8 Rue Royale, 1905, in Cogniat, *op. cit.*, p. 24.

[115] Certain of Bourdelle's paintings may also be compared with works by Puvis de Chavannes, particularly with regard to their composition (*Stéphanie Van Parys*, *Bathers*); not to mention the frescoes for the Champs-Elysées Theater, discussed in this catalog by Véronique Gautherin.

[116] Focillon, *op. cit.*, p. 241.

[117] Varenne, *op. cit.*, p. 65.

[118] Thierry-Maulnier, *Gimond*, Monte-Carlo, 1948, pp. 12–13.

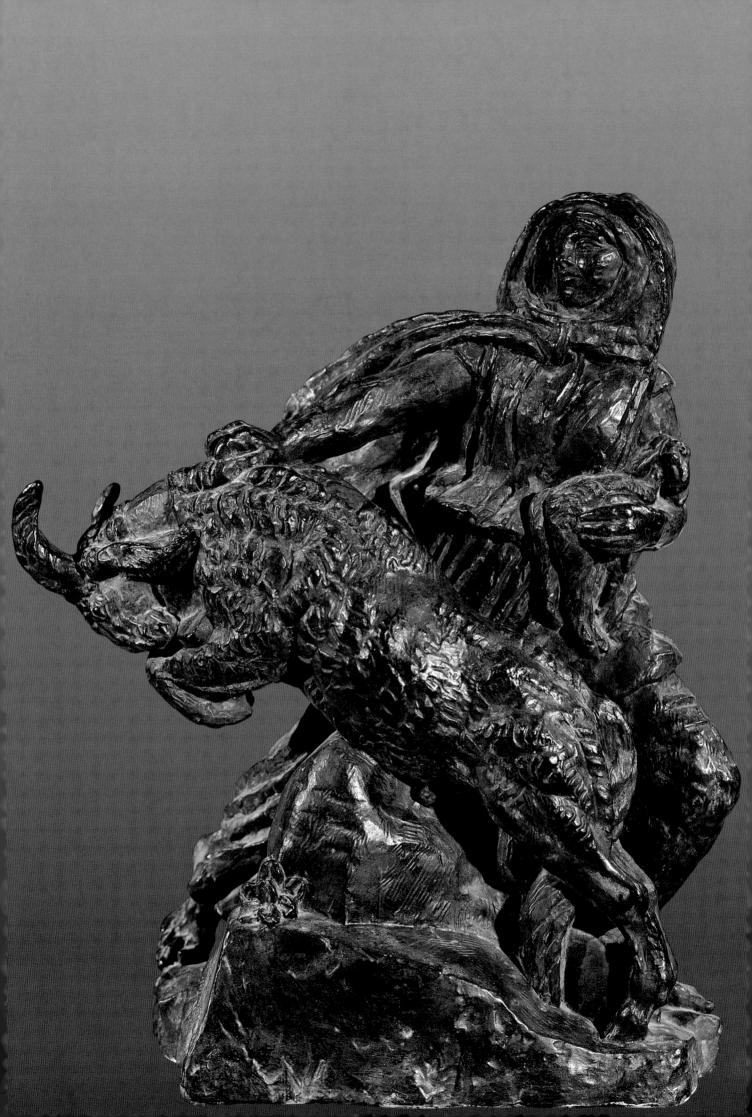

Puvis de Chavannes was more admired and studied by his contemporaries than any other turn-of-the-century artist. A whole generation of painters paid him tribute and claimed to follow him. From Gauguin to Picasso, from Seurat to Matisse, including Van Gogh who considered him a visionary prophet, they all, at one time or another, were "arrested by the lingering enchantment of his . . . allegories . . . removed from the time and places where their existences unfolded . . . in strict accordance with the essential dictates of the material,"[1] and thus anticipating the formal developments the new century would usher in. But painters were not the only ones to be drawn to the decorative aesthetic of the Lyon painter's monumental works, whose qualities stirred in them a forgotten sense of the monumental and an essentialness that the blind submission to reality vaunted by the Naturalists had—wrongly in their opinion—forced their predecessors to abandon. For a number of sculptors of the Post-Impressionist generation, the remote approach to reality that gave rise to the long processions of classicizing figures, steeped in a nostalgia-laden atmosphere, present in his timeless compositions, proved to be a determining source of reflection and maturation. It provided them with a nourishment that enabled them to direct their discipline toward a renewal that their rejection of Rodin's expressionism urged them to seek. Catherine Chevillot points out in her essay[2] the importance Puvis had for artists such as Lehmbruck, Minne or Maillol. The latter was very open about it. "We owe to Puvis the greatest emotions of our youth," he confided in his conversations. "Even if I did not become a painter, I learned a lot from painting," thus indicating that the notion of a separation of the disciplines that analysts often endorse has nothing to do with historical facts, nor with the way influences were exerted or filiations occurred.

However, Bourdelle seems to be the one who devoted the deepest, sharpest and most discerning reflection to the lessons of primitive monumentality expressed in Puvis's art, thus appearing in history as one of his most outstanding heirs. Bourdelle's debt to his elder was indeed far more considerable than has been stated, and Puvis's role, along with Cézanne's, was decisive in his evolution at the turn of the century. This lifelong debt can be appraised by the iconographic and thematic loans revealed in many affinities, in his graphic work as well as his painting. But it is even more obvious in the stylistic, formal likenesses that a careful study of his works as a sculptor establishes, in his harmonious use of rhythms and cadenzas as well as in his methodical application of strict compositional principles. An elective affinity, grounded in a fondness for allegory, synthesis and the archaistic simplification of forms, led him to instinctively look to Puvis's precursory art and ponder on it. Everything he said reveals he was steeped in it and had grasped its essence, transposing its conceptions to his own field.

We have seen that Puvis enjoyed considerable fame during his lifetime. He received numerous tributes to which Bourdelle, his ardent admirer, contributed. This vogue reached its climax on the occasion of the banquet given in his honor, for his seventieth birthday, on January 16, 1895, at the Hôtel Continental. This event of unanimous recognition, presided by Rodin, and attended by poets, painters and ministers, including Zola, Pissarro, Félicien Rops, but also Mallarmé, Gauguin and Mirbeau, was of great consequence. As we know, it was after this commemoration that Picasso, influenced by his friend, the Catalan painter Santiago Rusiñol, whom the celebration had greatly impressed, became interested in Puvis's work and, on his third trip to Paris, in 1903, copied Puvis's frescoes in the Panthéon.[3] Rusiñol deemed Puvis a modern counterpart of El Greco, for him an absolute master, and he contributed, with Manuel Cossio, the author of the catalogue raisonné of the Toledo painter published in 1908, to rehabilitate his work. Rusiñol described Puvis as "the most universal genius of his time."[4] This opinion was shared by a number of his contemporaries, and the memorable tribute was celebrated in an anthology of pieces written by Hérédia, Sully Prudhomme, Verlaine, Jarry and a hundred other poets.

Yet Bourdelle had not waited for this banquet to become interested in the art of his elder, for his contacts with the Symbolist circles had already drawn his attention to him. Archives indicate that in the years 1884–85, even before meeting him[5] in the milieu of the Salon de la Société Nationale des Beaux-Arts, of which Puvis was a co-founder, together with Rodin and Dalou, Bourdelle was familiar with his work. "Puvis is nature in an essence phial,"[6] he confided to a friend in 1886, thus paying tribute, in a poetic image, to the ethereal aesthetic of

1. Emile-Antoine Bourdelle
The Kicking Ram,
Paris, Musée National d'Art Moderne, Centre Georges-Pompidou

189

the Lyon painter, in whom he saw embodied the ideal fusion of inspiration and creation. Recalling the artists whose influence he deemed decisive after leaving the Ecole des Beaux-Arts, Bourdelle put it succinctly: "Lastly, there was Chavannes whom I admired enormously."[7]

It seems likely Bourdelle discovered Puvis's art as soon as he arrived in Paris, on the occasion of the Salon of 1884, where the *Sacred Wood Dear to the Arts and Muses* was exhibited, as a text he wrote in 1898[8] proves he had seen. Later, he had the opportunity to further this knowledge in the Salons as well as the exhibitions mounted in 1887 and 1894 by the Galerie Durand-Ruel which we presume he attended, along with the retrospective of forty-three large paintings presented in 1904 at the Salon d'Automne that we know for certain inspired a number of artists with a renewed interest in his work.

We can assume that by the 1890s Bourdelle had become very familiar with Puvis's work, and had acquired a knowledgeable insight into the essential monumental, synthetic and classical qualities it reflected, as attested by the presence in his library of a series of books on the man and his work. Bourdelle possessed Léon Riotor's biographical essay published in 1896, a copy of which—number thirty-six out of fifty-four—was dedicated to James Vibert, also the author of an essay on Puvis, and was conserved in his archives.[9] In the Symbolist and Rosicrucian circles Bourdelle mixed with for a while, the Lyon painter was the only one, along with Gustave Moreau, who was not only approved by the theoreticians of those circles, but also deemed by those intransigent doctrinaires to be an example of the "idealistic and mystical" art they called for. Now it is obvious these views not only contributed to the anti-positivist conception Bourdelle was steeped in, but also influenced him and played a role in his growing interest in the Lyon painter's work, as his friendship with Victor Koos, Puvis's collaborator and the posthumous author with Paul Baudouin of the frescoes of Saint Genevieve at the Panthéon, confirms.

An essay of 1898 in which Bourdelle relates the circumstances in which the news of Puvis's death reached him on a gloomy October day when he was not far from Paris—"mentally on the banks of the Styx," "in the soul of autumn, treading upon the dying leaves in the woods, near the royal necropolis of Versailles," recalling the profound sadness in which the news had plunged him[10]—reveals that he had indeed been a friend of the painter's helper, who had remained in obscurity. "The news reached me very quickly," he wrote, "brought with great anguish by my friend the painter Victor Koos, the practically unknown assistant of the great painter's last years."[11] Then comes a breathless tale of his rushing across Paris in the night to be with his friend, his heart oppressed by the feeling that "winter had come to the Sacred Wood."[12] This funereal evocation of "one of the purest and most symphonic" of Puvis's compositions, where the figures appear to wander among the timeless shades of an intensely pure azure, perfectly expresses the interest Bourdelle already felt for Puvis and went beyond mere circumstantial admiration.

His relationship with Mécislas Golberg at the turn of the century, which we might assume had been decisive in that regard, merely sustained him in his interest, by making him grow even more aware of the lessons he might draw from studying the painter's works, and connecting them to his own investigations. Golberg, a key figure on the Parisian scene between 1900 and 1907, had the highest esteem for Puvis de Chavannes. Bourdelle, who saw a great deal of him, must have known this. They surely discussed the subject and told one another what they felt was the singularity of his art and what made it exemplary. John Richardson, in his biography of Picasso, maintains that Golberg was largely responsible for the renewal and growth of Picasso's interest in Puvis de Chavannes. As a matter of fact, in November 1900, in the first issue of his *Cahiers mensuels*, a study on Puvis's art appeared.[13] It was followed, in the second issue of the same *Cahiers*, in January-February 1901, by notes[14] drawn from a lecture Golberg had given some time before at the Café Voltaire, on the Place de l'Odéon. The November 1900 study, reprinted in the March-April issue of the *Cahiers* the following year, was ultimately published in an octavo by A. Wolff in 1901.

Golberg was enthralled by modern displays of classicism, and saw outstanding examples in Puvis, as in Bourdelle, whose art—we note with interest—he compared to that of the painter. He drew parallels between the Lyon painter's art and that of the Sienese primitives, about whom, after further developing his reflections, he would publish a key study, three years later. Bourdelle himself viewed Puvis's aesthetics as a masterful lesson in hieratic primitivism,

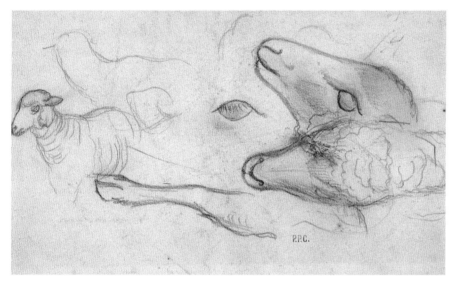

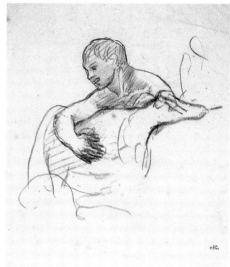

2. Puvis de Chavannes,
*Study of Sheep Head, Leg,
and Eye for "Summer,"* 1873 (?).
Paris, Musée Bourdelle

3. Puvis de Chavannes,
*Study of Young Shepherd Holding
a Lamb for "Summer,"* 1873 (?).
Paris, Musée Bourdelle

the remote posterity of Byzantine art that he admired and that would serve as a profound source of inspiration.

Through his friendship with Golberg, Bourdelle had the opportunity to reflect upon the theoretic aspect of Puvis's lessons; and his practice of an intentionally unadorned sculpture and the aesthetic project he was striving to materialize led him to draw on them.

A significant token of Bourdelle's interest in the master is the fact that he owned three of Puvis's drawings.[15] These works, purchased after the latter's death—as indicated by the estate stamp P.P.C. on them—are evidence of his lasting attachment to the art of that master of "high-painting,"[16] in whom he admired "the sense of universality"[17] and "the orderly reflection, the source of beauty."[18] The first two of these drawings (figs. 2, 3), in all likelihood the earliest, represent a child grappling with a lamb and a triple study of sheep legs and head. These preparatory sheets are to be compared to the figure of the young shepherd in the foreground of one of Puvis's very first Arcadian compositions, titled *Summer,* that was shown at the 1873 Salon and is presently in the Musée d'Orsay. The pose of the youth, as it appears in the study Bourdelle had purchased, while more suggestive of the vigor of a struggle than the impulsive ardor of play, is indeed quite different from that of the child in the foreground of the final composition of this canvas with its echoes of Poussin, yet the connection between the two figures is strong enough to leave little doubt regarding the relationship between the two works.

The third drawing that Bourdelle owned by Puvis, belonging to a later period, is a double recto-verso study of a kneeling man holding a child. This fine work coincides with a squared preparatory study for the rear-view figure in the foreground of the central panel of the *Life of Saint Genevieve* in the Panthéon, on the theme of *Saint Genevieve Supplying Paris.*

We are not aware of the circumstances in which Bourdelle purchased these sheets but they do provide stiking proof of his sense of drawing which was known to be determinative in his approach to sculpture as well as being essential to Puvis's pictorial practice. Bourdelle could only agree with this primacy granted to draftsmanship. He availed of it in the same way, since drawing was for him, as for Puvis, the means to mature and perfect his compositions. The comparisons that can be made from a typographical as well as a technical point of view between the preparatory studies, like the ones mentioned, and the group of sketches, studies and cartoons he amassed during his work at the Théâtre des Champs-Elysées, using identical compositional principles such as squaring and successive enlargements, repetitions and variations on a same motif, are particularly illuminating. This closeness might appear merely pragmatic, yet it actually reflects a far more profound intimacy, touching on the very mechanisms of the creative process in the two artists. Their approach to the idea and their way of formally transcribing it by drawing (which was their mode of writing) indeed betrays a similar manner of conceiving art as a language founded on a rhetorical and symbolic mastery of forms they were both seeking while obeying the laws of the material.

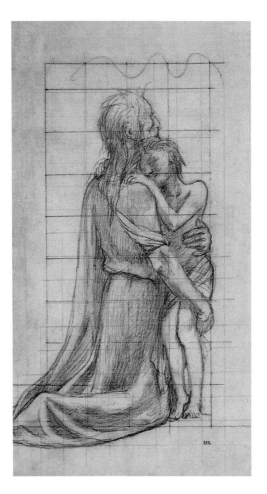

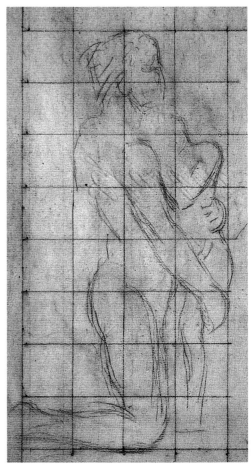

His torment and his stubborn determination, confided Bourdelle, Puvisesque at heart and an open dissident of Rodin, was for "his art to succeed in condensing in its many manifestations, the gentleness of clay, the kindliness of wood, the stillness of stone, the immutable light of marble and the gravity of bronze."[19] "If the artist is not in harmony with these natural collaborators . . . if he believes he should subject them, reduce them and not solicit, marry, fecundate them, make them blossom, then these unutterable materials, overwhelmed, exhausted, buried, lose their spirit," he wrote in another meditation early in the century. "Too much febrility, too many accidents . . . too many shocks . . . violating the admirable innocence of things and therefore equally departing from the general laws, make the work fall short . . . of beauty."[20]

To avoid those excesses and attain the exact and very Hegelian alchemical embodiment of spirit in matter, drawing, seen as an exercise in the methodical decantation of forms through simplification and gradual synthesis, was a unique means. Their common concern to permeate matter with the very essence of things to reach their universality led Puvis and Bourdelle to use drawing in the same way, performing a series of operations we can describe as mental, of a similar nature. The sequence draft-sketch-overall study-detail study-final squared study, including the systematic use of tracing,[21] inherited from academic tradition, but used for purely formal rather than narrative ends, can be found in both.

The likenesses, thematic as well as stylistic, with the art of Puvis that appear in Bourdelle's work, the result of the latter's conscious, reasoned meditation, are only rarely a word-for-word imitation of the motifs of which he was so fond. Of course, some of his early drawings show that he did emulate, by having young models pose in his studio, the poses of certain figures that return like leitmotifs in Puvis's work.

A series of sketches that we can date to 1885–86 representing a youth with medium-length hair in a series of varied postures indeed suggest—in several instances (fig. 6)—a blatant similarity with the kneeling figures, one bent slightly forward, his arm detached from his body,

6. Emile-Antoine Bourdelle,
Study of Nude, c. 1885.
Paris, Dufet-Bourdelle Collection

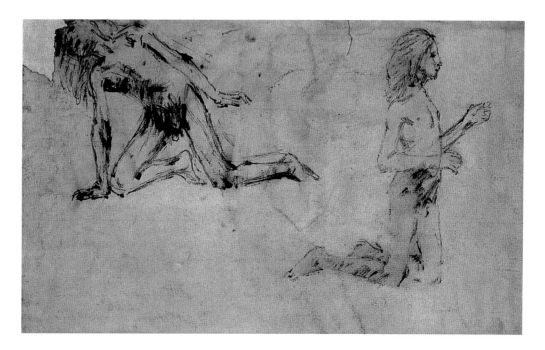

and the other resting on the ground, that we find, with slight variants, in the background of the *Poor Fisherman*, in the foreground of the *Sacred Wood*, and at center of the Sorbonne amphitheater decoration.

A fresco cartoon like the one painted on the theme of *Orpheus and Eurydice* for the Théâtre des Champs-Elysées, aside from its muted color—which would alone be worth discussing and is further proof of Puvis's influence, in this field as well, on his epigone[22]—has an obvious kinship with the figures of the Muses floating about in the golden sky of the *Sacred Wood*. And again, a composition such as that of the nine *Muses Rushing* toward the god *Apollo and His Meditation* conceived by Bourdelle to adorn the façade of the Théâtre des Champs-Elysées, visibly proceeds from a recollection of the decoration of the Boston Library stairway representing *The Inspiring Muses Acclaim the Spirit of Light* that the sculptor was familiar with, since he had seen it at the 1895 Salon where it had been exhibited.

Yet these examples are exceptions, and although we can discern latent ties between the rhythmized poses of the allegories silently inhabiting the compositions of the painter and the sculptor that might come straight out of some *Antique Vision*,[23] it is above all in the principles ruling their laws that these works can be compared. More than their poses, it is their very symbolic nature and the atmosphere they are steeped in that make them spiritual daughters.

Bourdelle never copied Puvis literally, as Picasso and others would, but assimilated his spirit and transposed it. His is indeed a transposition, that of a melody whose charm inspired him to imitate the tone rather than the harmonies.

Bourdelle's works between 1905 and 1920, especially the allegorical ones that include monumental mythological figures, such as *Penelope* and *Sappho*—whom we can compare to the meditative figure seated at the center of the *Antique Vision*[24]—but also his more modest works like the series of *Bather[s]*, *Woma[e]n Sculptress[es]* and *Woma[e]n at a Fountain*, of which versions exists with or without a capital, are the ones that most openly reveal his appropriation of Puvis's aesthetic.

A small composition like *The Offering*, in which the position of the arms is reminiscent of the invocatory one of the central figure of *Autumn*, conserved in the Fine Arts Museum of Lyon, an unfinished study of which had been exhibited at the Durand-Ruel gallery in 1894 that Bourdelle might have seen then, is typical of his borrowings, probably largely unconscious, but frequent nonetheless.

Photographs of the clay version of the *Woman Sculptress Resting* (figs. 7–8), taken at the time of its execution by Bourdelle himself, and staged so as to make it loom out of the shadow that carves its volumes with an enveloping serenity, reveal this cultivated closeness. The figure, a sister of Puvis's Muses, dwells in the same space, and possesses the same notion of eter-

7, 8. Emile-Antoine Bourdelle,
Woman Sculptress Resting,
small version, c. 1908.
Paris, Musée Bourdelle

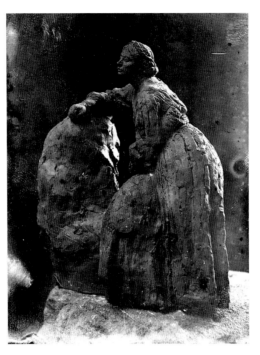 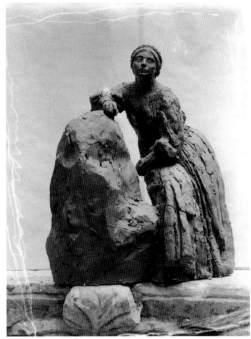

nity. An incarnation of pure form that Bourdelle, in his determination to return to style according to Hegel, sculpted as modernism was dawning. A worthy daughter of *Sappho* (whose creation—in its first form—had prefigured her twenty years earlier), she is Bourdelle's tribute to the one who, better than a sculptor, had taught him the laws of his discipline. Silent, that tribute was not heard. Once revealed, it rises like a hymn chanted by a mysterious coryphaeus that chants in the long procession of female allegories that seem to embody its modulations.

Vois, plus haut, abats les détails,
Agrandis le geste de tes lignes,
Elève l'âme des proportions,
Songe à l'équilibre des mondes,
Gronde tes yeux,
Ne crois que ta raison!
Elle voit plus sublime,[25]
Dixit sculptor.

The publication of this essay is owed to Catherine Chevillot and her attentive concern. I wish to thank her.

[1] A. Fontainas, *Mes souvenirs du symbolisme*, Paris, Editions de la Nouvelle Revue Critique, 1928, pp. 98–99.
[2] C. Chevillot, "Was Puvis de Chavannes a Painter?" critical essay in this catalog.
[3] J. Richardson, *Vie de Picasso, 1881–1906*, Paris, Editions du Chêne, 1992, p. 257.
[4] R.J. Wattenmaker, *Puvis de Chavannes and the Modern Tradition*, exh. cat., Toronto, Art Gallery of Ontario, 1975, p. 168.
[5] Bourdelle and Puvis de Chavannes knew each other, they exhibited together for nearly a decade, at the Salon of the Société Nationale des Beaux-Arts. A letter conserved in the Musée Bourdelle attests this direct connection that, however, never became a close friendship, but rather a cordial sympathy, reflecting the official exchanges between members of the Society of which they were both members. Puvis de Chavannes to Bourdelle, July 17, 1891, Paris, Musée Bourdelle, Dufet-Bourdelle Archives.
[6] Bourdelle to Emile Pouvillon, September 26, 1886, Paris, Musée Bourdelle, Dufet-Bourdelle Archives.
[7] A. Bourdelle, draft of a letter to Madame S…, January 29, 1912, quoted in *Ecrits sur l'Art et sur la Vie*, Paris, Librairie Plon, 1955, p. 18.
[8] A. Bourdelle, *Comment meurt un grand homme*, manuscript notes, Paris, Musée Bourdelle, Dufet-Bourdelle Archives.
[9] L. Riotor, *Essai sur Puvis de Chavannes*, Paris, L'Artiste, collection L'Art et l'Idée, 1896. This copy bears the dedication: "*Léon Riotor / à James Vibert / auteur d'un Puvis que / j'admire / Voici le mien / Léon Riotor*" [Léon Riotor to James Vibert / author of a Puvis I admire / here is mine / Léon Riotor]. This book, published in fifty-five numbered copies by the contemporary art magazine *L'Artiste*, was probably given to Bourdelle by Vibert himself, in unknown circumstances and on an unknown occasion. The presence in the Archives of the flyleaf of another copy of this essay that was found by the

young researcher Colin Lemoine, and on which a draft of a letter to a friend is written, seems to indicate Bourdelle already had his own copy.

[10] Bourdelle, *Comment meurt...*, *op. cit.* In this text, Bourdelle wrote: "It was, when I came home, my father who taught me the great death. . . . I quickly ate supper. My lamp seemed poignant. Over the peaceful family mealtime hour loomed a great mournful death-knoll. The forest of France, the forest of mankind had lost its loveliest golden foliage, it was indeed . . . the darkest day of autumn. . . . It was winter coming to the sacred wood. I rushed off, wrapping myself in my coat in the night."

[11] *Ibidem.*

[12] *Ibidem.*

[13] M. Golberg, in *Cahiers Mécislas Golberg*, nos. 1–2, November–December 1900, pp. 33–44.

[14] M. Golberg, in *Cahiers Mécislas Golberg*, nos. 3–4, January–February 1901, pp. 30–32.

[15] A fourth is conserved, but had probably been purchased by his son-in-law, the decorator Michel Dufet. This pencil drawing, on squared tracing paper, representing a nude woman, with a vase, resting on her elbow, is a fragment of a preparatory study for the figure in the foreground of the decoration titled *Antique Vision* of the stairway of the Musée des Beaux-Arts in Lyon. Puvis de Chavannes, *Femme nue allongée*, 1884, 23,1 x 41,8 cm., Paris, Musée Bourdelle, Dufet-Bourdelle Archives.

[16] A. Bourdelle, *Au-delà de la mort de Puvis de Chavannes*, manuscript notes, Paris, Musée Bourdelle, Dufet-Bourdelle Archives.

[17] *Ibidem.*

[18] *Ibidem.*

[19] A. Bourdelle, *Réflexions à propos d'un groupement de sculptures*, manuscript [autograph], Paris, Musée Bourdelle, Dufet-Bourdelle Archives.

[20] *Ibidem.*

[21] Puvis is known for having made an abundant use of tracing for the eurhythmic layout of his compositions and their sequences. Bourdelle, too, used it for his fresco work.

[22] Bourdelle's conceptions on the subject are very close to those of his elder. His fondness for muted tones and matte effects directly recall Puvis's precepts extolling twilight harmonies.

[23] Title of the panel on the left of the *Sacred Wood* in the Fine Arts Museum of Lyon that had been exhibited at the Salon of the Société des Beaux-Arts in 1886 and that Bourdelle had seen.

[24] The composition of this work, undoubtedly Bourdelle's most Puvisesque, whose creation dates to 1887, the year the Sorbonne decoration that may have inspired it was presented in the Salon, later revisited in 1907 and in 1924, also reminds us, except for the lines of the clothing, of the figure of the young shepherd occupying the center of the *Antique Vision* in the Lyon museum.

[25] "Look, look up, cast away details / Extend the gesture of your lines / Raise the soul of proportions / Think of the balance of worlds / Scold your eyes / Believe only in your reason! / Its vision is more sublime." A. Bourdelle, autograph manuscript, Musée Bourdelle, Dufet-Bourdelle Archives.

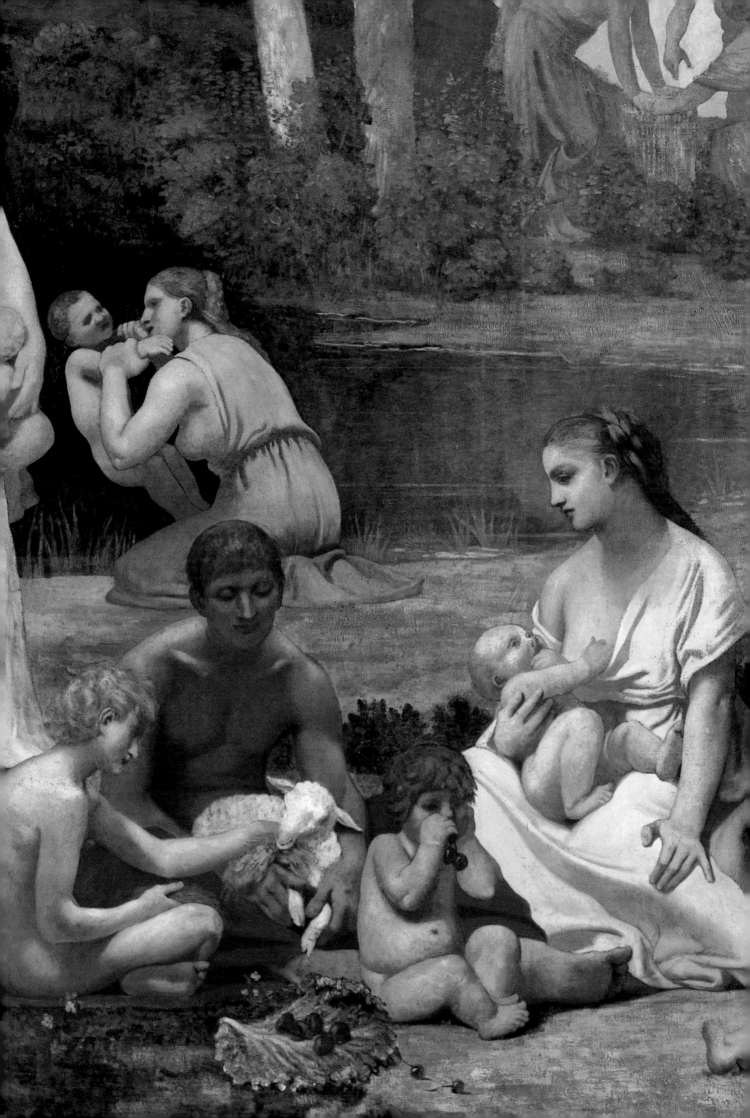

Puvis de Chavannes and America

Nowhere outside France was Pierre Puvis de Chavannes better appreciated during his life-time than in America. Aspiring American artists copied his works and endeavored to meet him. Collectors and connoisseurs (sometimes one and the same) purchased what they could—often through the entrepreneurial art dealer Paul Durand-Ruel who opened a New York outpost of his Paris gallery to be closer to his clients. Puvis's only mural cycle out-side his own country was for the grand new Boston Public Library. It served as very real inspiration for public murals in other civic buildings in the United States, part of the City Beautiful movement at the end of the nineteenth century. But even before Puvis's Boston murals were inaugurated, his monumental wall paintings were well known to the cognoscen-ti. The intense interest in Puvis de Chavannes is indicated by an anecdote about a young American art student returning to the United States after his obligatory stint in Paris study-ing art, "he diverted fifteen francs ($3) from his food budget in order to buy for [Augus-tus] Saint-Gaudens [his teacher] a fine copy of Pierre-Cécile Puvis de Chavannes's . . . *Sa-cred Wood*—one of the staircase murals for the museum at Lyon that were the art world's latest sensation."[1]

Puvis de Chavannes and American Artists

Americans who sought culture had to go to Europe for instruction—as Mark Twain indi-cated in his only partly sardonically entitled *Innocents Abroad*; or like the likable protag-onist in expatriate Henry James's *The American*, once having obtained wealth at home, he could travel to Paris to acquire culture—with which he would return.[2] Americans, with few pretensions, were often uneasy about their lack of sophistication in these matters and though sometimes wary of Europeans for their presumed superiority, wished to learn what they could by going abroad. This was especially true of young artists. If their destination was Paris, the preeminent place to study art,[3] with its considerable allure, their family might warn them about the high spirits and low morals of the French. From at least the mid-nine-teenth century they went; as Americans, they had a particular, historical affinity for France. They could study with the likes of Couture (from the 1850s through the 1870s), Gérôme (as did Eakins among others),[4] Léon Bonnat or, for only a few, Puvis de Chavannes.[5] For a time Puvis taught with Bonnat and Alfred Roll at what was called the Ecole de Dessin et Peinture,[6] its location and three professors noted in such guides as the American hand-book *The Art Student in Paris*, published in Boston in 1887.[7] More Americans would lat-er claim to be students of Puvis than was actually the case; though in some instances "stu-dent of" was meant in the most general, metaphorical sense, signifying that they had vis-ited his atelier, or took him as an example, a model, a paragon.[8]

Among those who came under Puvis's sway was Edwin Howland Blashfield (1848–1936), to be a central figure in the American mural movement,[9] and an influential teacher and lec-turer.[10] As a student in Paris he had produced his own *Copy after Puvis de Chavannes's Pan-théon Mural of Saint Genevieve* (fig. 2),[11] and he declared that he "worshipped at the shrine of Puvis's *Sacred Wood* in the Sorbonne," Puvis's great 1889 mural.[12] Several Blashfield com-positions follow those formulated by Puvis: *The Edict of Toleration of Lord Baltimore*[13] (court house, Baltimore, Maryland), echoes Puvis's Victor Hugo painting for the Paris city hall; his study for the central figure of Alma Mater (for the Massachusetts Institute of Technology, fig. 3) resembles Puvis's Alma Mater at the Sorbonne that he so admired.

Arthur Wesley Dow (1857–1922), an artist as well as an exceedingly influential teacher of modernism in art,[14] studied in Paris from 1884 to 1889 and exhibited at the 1889 Universal Exposition. When opposition arose at the prospect of having Puvis do murals for the new Boston Public Library and the project's merits were debated[15] and when his *Summer* (fig. 4) was criticized, Dow came to their defense.[16] Indeed, even a decade later, the wis-dom of having gived the commission to a foreigner or whether a native, American art would have been preferable, continued to be argued.[17] Dow reproduced his own schematized ver-sion after Puvis's *Winter* (fig. 5) in his innovative pedagogical *Composition [SYNTHESIS]* (fig. 6)[18] and called Puvis the "greatest painter of modern times . . . being abstract, spiri-tual, full of infinite meaning, [and] furthest removed from realism which is 'of the earth.'"[19]

When he was in Paris in 1886–88, Louis Eilshemius (1864–1937) must have seen Puvis's work. Back in America, he created dreamlike scenes of what look like cut and paste female

1. Pierre Puvis de Chavannes, *Summer*, detail, 1873. Paris, Musée d'Orsay

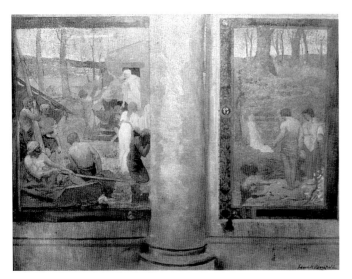

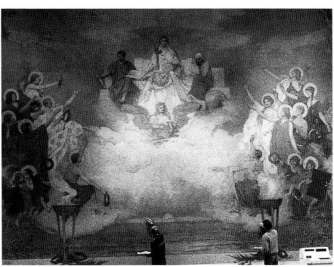

2. Edwin Howland Blashfield,
*Copy after Puvis de Chavannes's
Panthéon Mural for "Saint
Genevieve,"* after 1879.
Location unknown

3. Edwin Howland Blashfield,
Alma Mater.
Cambridge, Massachusetts
Institute of Technology

figures in a variety of poses floating over the landscape as in his 1889 *Afternoon Wind*. They
are similar to such stiff hovering figures by Puvis as in *The Dream* of 1883 (Paris, Musée
d'Orsay), that Eilshemius could have seen at Puvis's important 1887 exhibition at the Durand-Ruel Gallery. The element of gawkiness in Puvis's work, which few people knew what
to make of,[20] is magnified in Eilshemius's works with their stilted, compelling crudeness,
as if painted by an unschooled painter rather than one who turned to primitivism, presenting
qualities later cherished in so-called outsider art.

Even those not in the Puvis orbit were inspired by his work. George de Forest Brush
(1855–1941) studied with Gérôme whose work provided a model for his *Orpheus* of 1890
(fig. 7), yet its subject and austere surrounds suggest that Puvis's *Orpheus* of 1883 (fig. 8)
played a part in his severe rendering of this classicizing image.

Mary Cassatt (1844–1926), moved to Paris in 1874 and exhibited with the artists soon called
Impressionists. She famously encouraged her wealthy American friends to buy new French
art, especially Degas. Though very much her own person, when she received her first mural commission, *Modern Woman* (destroyed, fig. 9) for the Woman's Building for the 1893
World's Columbian Exhibition in Chicago,[21] she turned to Puvis de Chavannes's murals
for guidance, particularly his *Ave Picardia Nutrix* (Amiens, Musée de Picardie), and his
recent *Inter Artes et Naturam* (Rouen, Musée des Beaux-Arts), from which she borrowed
such motifs as the mounting of ladders that fill the composition's upper reaches and the
woman with a baby picking fruit. But his influence is also very much in evidence in her
tilted-up, raking landscape, the flattening and rhythmic spacing of elements, and general symmetries.

Though Mary Fairchild MacMonnies, later Low (1858–1946), sought advice on her mural *Primitive Woman* opposite Cassatt's in the Woman's Building[22] and is said to have studied with Puvis,[23] she had not; that misinterprets an account of her reciprocating a compliment that Puvis paid her (when they met in Paris). He asked who had taught her to paint
so well, and she responded, "If you see much of merit in my picture, Monsieur, I must tell
you that the one who taught me the best things, the master to whom I owe the most, is your-
self." Puvis is then gallantly alleged to have "begged as an honor to be named among the
teachers of the gifted American."[24]

During his first trip to Europe in 1893–94, Arthur B. Davies (1862–1928) was much impressed by Puvis's pictorial ideas, a palpable influence on his own. Davies's elongated, horizontal compositions often include a frieze of spaced out figures as in *Unicorns* (fig. 11).
Both Davies and Eilshemius could capture the most ineffable of Puvis qualities, something
of the awkwardness of his figures and their revery or extreme self-absorption, with no in-
teraction other than tangentialism among them—though sometimes even crowded together,
they literally pay each other no mind.

Puvis received droves of young artists informally[25] and the instruction he provided Bryson
Burroughs (1869–1934) may have been of this sort.[26] Puvisesque characteristics indelibly

4. Pierre Puvis de Chavannes,
Summer, 1873.
Paris, Musée d'Orsay

mark Burroughs's mythological and religious figurative paintings: ineluctably flat and austere, with a restrained artificiality in composition, a certain vapidness, and emphatically whitened, anemic colors is *Eurydice Bitten by the Snake* (fig. 10). Burroughs, curator at the Metropolitan Museum of Art from 1909, was a staunch advocate of Puvis's work on which he wrote[27] and lectured.[28] He must have seen to it that Puvis's works, occasionally lent by private collectors, were prominently displayed. A curator at the Boston Museum of Fine Arts, John Briggs Potter (1864–1949), also had some instruction from Puvis and produced some wonderful drawings.[29]

Puvis's murals were crucial to the solemn pacing, shallow space, and absolutely flat background of Gari Melchers's (1860–1932) murals for the 1893 World's Columbian Exhibition (*The Arts of Peace* and *The Arts of War*, now Ann Arbor, University of Michigan); at the Library of Congress, and others later. Indeed, Melchers borrowed specific motifs. According to one account, when he visited Puvis in 1895 after having become a Chevalier of the Legion of Honor but before he received the medal, "The Frenchman is said to have taken his own Cross of the Legion, presented to him years before by Napoleon III, and pinned it to the chest of the young American."[30] Puvis also dedicated a female head to Melchers (Belmont, Falmouth, Virginia) who was instrumental in having his so-called *John the Baptist*, dedicated to Marcellin Desboutin, purchased by the Telfair Academy of Art in Savannah, Georgia (present location unknown).

The charming, decorative, American Arcadias of picnics and other recreational pastimes that Maurice Prendergast (1858–1924) produced, particularly in 1913–15, are beholden to Puvis de Chavannes's pastorals.[31] Prendergast studied art in Paris from 1891 to 1894 and by 1904–05 drew a number of sprightly copies after Puvis paintings—*Pleasant Land*, *Summer*, *Young Women by the Sea*,[32] including a Boston mural.[33] Like Puvis he interlocked fig-

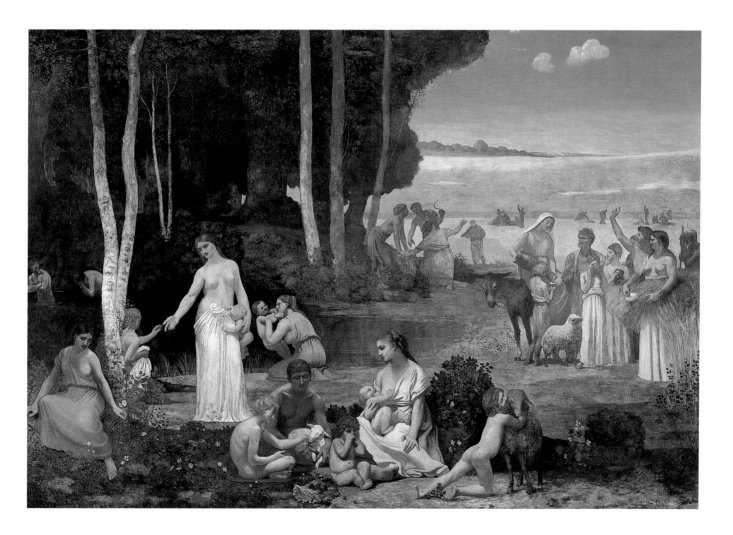

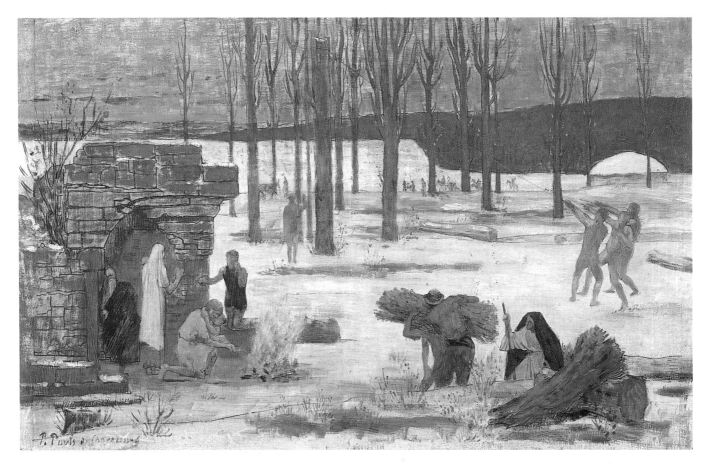

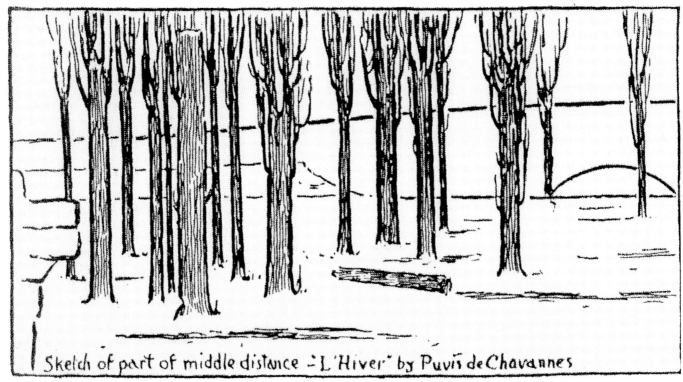

Sketch of part of middle distance – "L'Hiver" by Puvis de Chavannes

5. Pierre Puvis de Chavannes, *Winter*, 1892.
Paris, Petit Palais, Musée des Beaux-Arts de la Ville

6. Wesley Dow, *Scheme of the Intermediate Plane of Puvis de Chavannes's "Winter"* (W. Dow, *Composition Theory and Practice of Teaching Art*, 1931)

ures and landscape elements in opaque, textured, fresco-like planar compositions. They too are stationed frieze-like in often classicizing poses, but face out to the viewer. From 1908 Prendergast used the designation "decoration" for certain easel paintings—the original title for *The Picnic* was *Decoration–Summer*—an idea and aesthetic stemming from Puvis de Chavannes.

Though verging on abstraction, Augustus Vincent Tack's (1870–1949) large, non-hierarchical, flat decorations of the 1920s such as *Voice of Many Waters* (fig. 13) in their most basic aesthetic of restrained rhythmic patterns and colors (laced with gold and silver) redound to Puvis's decorations via Dow's theories.[34] Like Puvis's work they find their beauty and sumptuousness in restraint and also appealed to the great connoisseur collector Duncan Phillips, who was to have major holdings of Tack's work as well as important works by Puvis and Davies.[35]

Most American artists inspired by Puvis de Chavannes at the end of the nineteenth and in the early twentieth centuries tended to be either modernist painters—Dow, Davies, Prendergast, and later Tack—or muralists—Blashfield or Kenyon Cox, though there is some overlap.[36] Many of these artists knew each other, sometimes very well, and they were often sympathetic to a new kind of classicism and decoration. Others had an affinity for Puvis's imagery, though the list of those said to be influenced by him, as subtle and simple as their tonalist landscapes may be (a Leon Dabo, a sober and restrained Dwight W. Tryon) is overly long.

Puvis's Mural Commission for the Boston Public Library

The most important tangible manifestation of Puvis de Chavannes's relationship to the United States is his major mural cycle for the Boston Public Library. Internationally prestigious, he was the triumphant choice of a cadre of the city's distinguished intellectual and artistic elite. First approached in 1891, he was offered a fee of 250 000 francs ($50 000),[37] several times larger than he had ever received. He completed the paintings—*The Inspiring Muses*, some ten by twenty meters, and eight other panels—in 1895–96.[38] As was always the case with his public wall paintings, they were painted on canvas, exhibited at the Salon in Paris, and shipped to their destination to be installed.[39] Puvis was not unemotional about sending them far away across the Atlantic ["la grande tasse"] to cover walls he would never see.[40] The witty (and prescient) art critic Gustave Geffroy viewed them as cultural emissaries to be exchanged for technological marvels from America that would permit rapid travel to inspect them: "Nous avons déjà entendu dire, et nous l'entendrons encore, qu'il est grand dommage de voir partir ces belles peintures pour l'Amérique lointaine. Il est certain que beaucoup entre nous ne les verront plus. Mais à la réflexion, ce départ est admirable. L'art traversant le monde, s'en allant au delà des océans, chez un peuple nouveau. . . . Qu'elles s'en aillent, ces peintures, et d'autres qu'elles accomplissent leur mission. Cette mission n'est pas d'anémier et de mourir sur place. . . . Les grandes conquêtes de demain se feront comme elles se font déjà, par le livre, le tableau, la statue, le drame lyrique. Et l'Amérique, après nous avoir demandé les peintures de nos artistes, saura bien nous donner, pour aller les revoir des aérostates et des pyroscaphes [a neologism meaning fire-driven, boat-shaped vehicles], miraculeux qui nous feront, en quelques heures, traverser l'océan et retrouver notre pensée, si nous l'avons perdue."[41]

The murals were received with considerable fanfare—Henry Adams called them "the greatest things ever painted"[42]—Puvis's large-scale mural complex was to be of intense interest to American artists and enormous influence on the American mural movement. They ratified Puvis's extensive reputation in America and the continuing acquisitive taste for his work.

Collecting Puvis in the United States

During his lifetime, the goodly number of Puvis de Chavannes's paintings in American collections was in large part due to the entrepreneurial efforts of Paul Durand-Ruel. Puvis embraced critical and commercial success, but in the 1880s at least took a wary attitude toward Americans who bought for wrong-headed reasons and besides he preferred that his work remain on native soil. Having sold some paintings in France he wrote his fami-

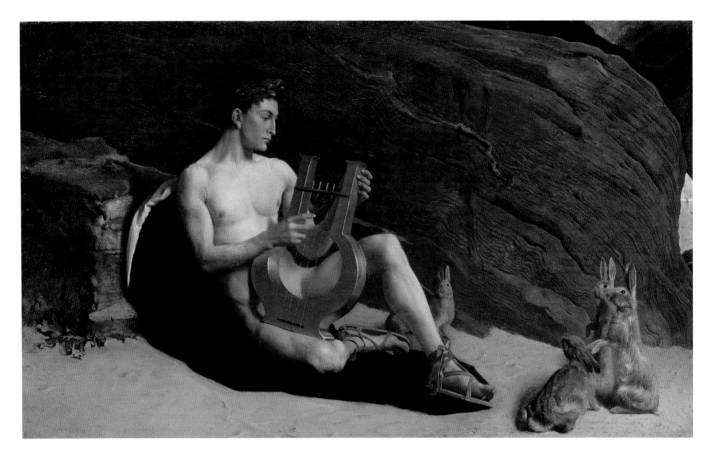

7. George de Forest Brush,
Orpheus, 1890.
Boston, Museum of Fine Arts

opposite page
8. Pierre Puvis de Chavannes,
Orpheus, 1883.
Oslo, Nasjonalgalleriet

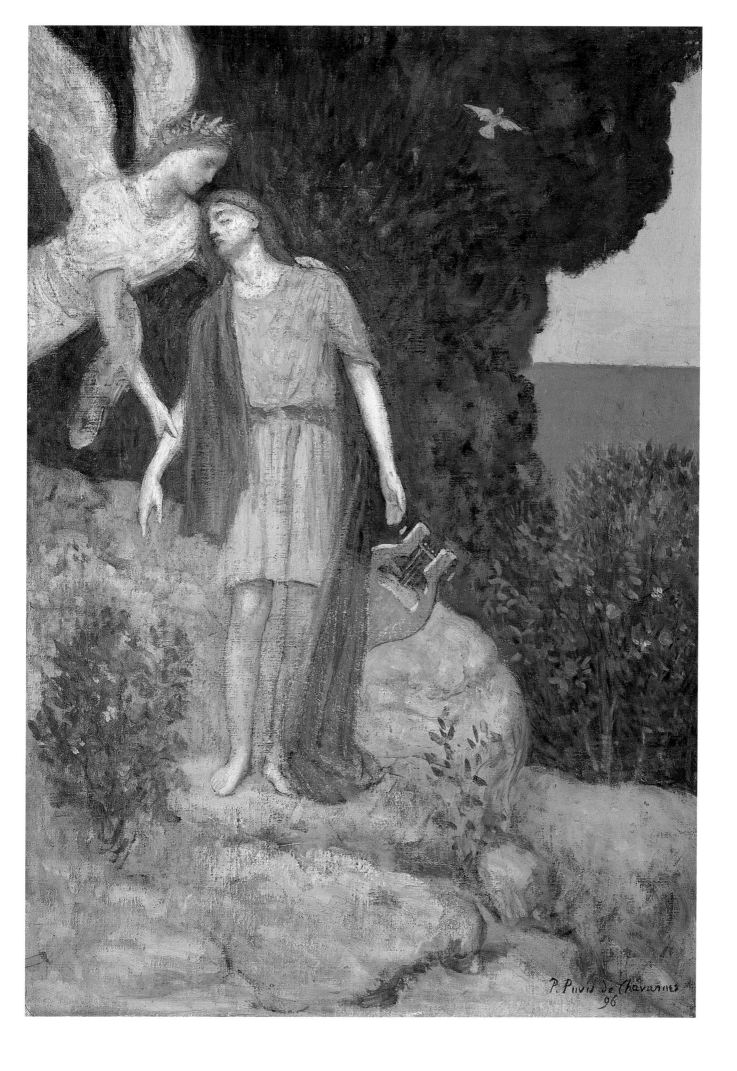

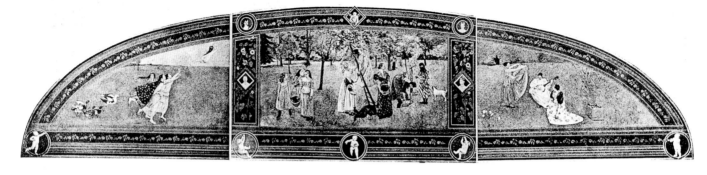

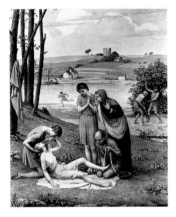

9. Mary Cassatt,
Modern Woman, 1893.
Woman's Building at the 1893
World's Columbian Exposition
(destroyed)

10. Bryson Burroughs,
Eurydice Bitten by the Snake, 1930.
New York, The Metropolitan
Museum of Art, George
A. Hearn Fund

opposite page
11. Arthur B. Davies, *Unicorns.*
New York, The Metropolitan
Museum of Art, Bequest of
Lizzie P. Bliss

12. Augustus Vincent Tack,
Allegro Giocoso, 1917.
Washington, D.C.,
The Phillips Collection

ly: "what pleases me particularly in all this is that there is no American surprise, no savage's fantasy, and that these canvases are beautiful and well from now on in the galleries of French amateurs. . . ."[43]

In 1885 Durand-Ruel was keen on showing Puvis in the United States, but Puvis demurred, stating that American museums and galleries had never shown interest in his work: "it is quite clear that my painting would not please over there. So I shall abstain, feeling that I do not want to undertake late conversions, especially at the end of the world."[44] Durand-Ruel nonetheless showed his works at an exhibition he organized in 1887 at the National Academy of Design,[45] and in 1894 exhibited thirty-two works by him at his own gallery.[46] Indeed, by 1890 Puvis's opinion of American patrons underwent a complete about face; he was hoping to "make things with dimensions fit to live with that they seem to want in *America*, for the French are Stingy in art matters, and it is beyond the ocean that the art lover [*l'amateur*] is found today."[47] His easel paintings and reduced versions after his murals were selling especially well in America and at good prices according to a list sent him by Paul Durand-Ruel.[48]

Many Americans who acquired Puvis's work were self-made millionaires, captains of industry whose lives and fortunes were intertwined with a prospering America. They avidly amassed sizable, even huge art collections, with energy and purposiveness. The same names crop up repeatedly as collectors of Puvis's work, the Impressionists, and of Degas.[49] Many were close associates and friends: John G. Johnson, lawyer and cicerone to Peter A.B. Widener of Philadelphia; the Havemeyers of New York, who built a vast art collection of often audacious taste; the Potter Palmers of Chicago, who were also adventurous in their purchases. Mrs. S.D. Warren of Boston, A.W. Kingman, Theodore M. Davis, James Jerome Hill, Mr. and Mrs. Jephtha H. Wade of Cleveland, and a number years later John Quinn,[50] the New York lawyer, and Duncan Phillips also had Puvis holdings. A not atypical though particularly ardent Puvis collector was Catholina Lambert (1834–1923), a poor émigré from England, who built a huge fortune (through silk and other industries), an immense collection of art (of sometimes only presumed Old Masters), a "castle" in Paterson, New Jersey to house it, and was forced to sell because of labor and financial problems and the 1914 liquidation of his firm.[51] Among his Puvis paintings *Death and the Maidens, Autumn, The Meeting of Saint Genevieve and Saint Germain*, the frieze *Legendary Saints of France*, and for a brief time *The Wine Press*—all now in American museums. Many of these collectors also bought, sold, and traded among themselves, doubtless bolstering each other's taste by acquiring literally the very same things, in a manner that seems less competitive than reinforcing. The museums in the cities where they lived were beneficiaries of their largesse, as Puvis's paintings at the Philadelphia Museum of Art, The National Gallery, the Metropolitan Museum of Art, the Chicago Art Institute, and the Boston Museum of Fine Arts testify.

American patrons also traveled to Paris where they could see Puvis's paintings prominently placed at the Salons or in galleries. Among the visitors to Puvis's important 1887 retrospective at the Durand-Ruel Gallery was the young Bernard Berenson, already something of a connoisseur, who went more than once and described several paintings including *Women at the Seashore* ("so simple, so sweet, so peacefull, so Greek without being classic. . . ."), *Sleep* (that recalled "'Endymion' in his undersea wanderings with its mistiness, and ooziness, and vague grandeur"; and *Hope*, that brought to mind a Cardinal Newman

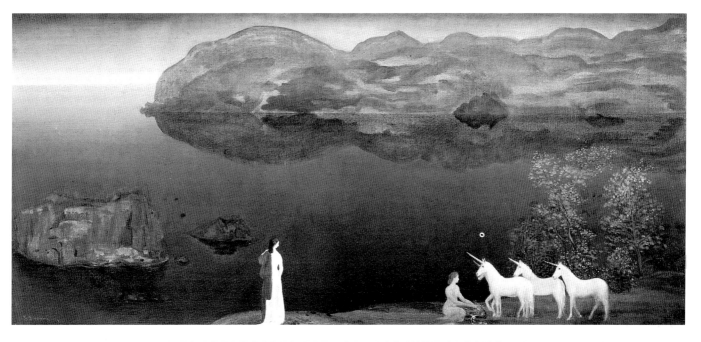

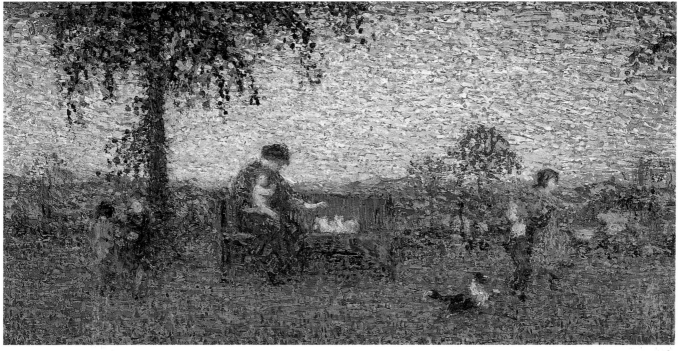

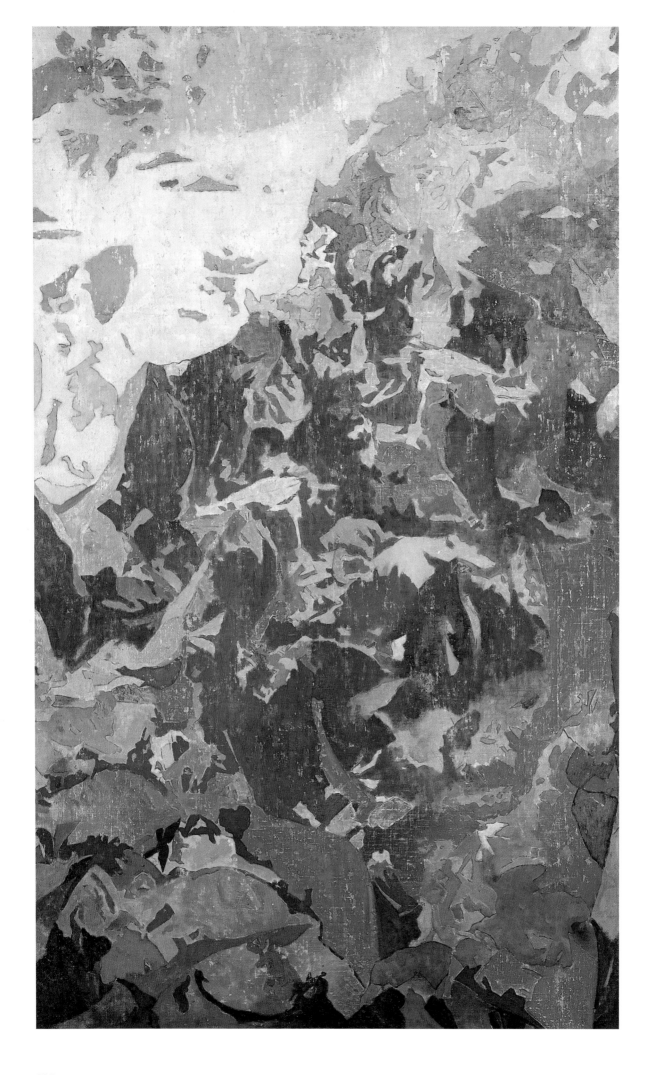

hymn he wrote Isabella Stewart Gardner.[52] His interest and hers must surely have helped pave the way for Boston to covet a Puvis of their own, that would eventuate in the public library commission.

Before the end of the nineteenth century Puvis and his work were known to a wider American public through newspapers, magazine articles (one pointed out that many of his works were in American collections),[53] a monograph, and a score of books in English that had a section devoted to him.[54] Among those who wrote most cogently about his work early on were John La Farge (1835–1910),[55] Will Hicok Low (1853–1932), Kenyon Cox (1859–1919), and Bryson Burroughs, all of whom were painters and writers. Cox remarked that Puvis's work was not for everyone, but (quoting Shakespeare's *Hamlet*) "caviare to the general."[56] Both under his own name and at least one of his pseudonyms[57] the cosmopolite Sadakichi Hartmann (1867–1944), who admired the frugal simplicity of Puvis's compositions and the rhythms of his colors, championed his paintings before an American audience.[58] He wrote in tribute "Without him, Manet, Monet and Whistler, originality in modern painting would not exist."[59] He understood Puvis's work as leading to a new art, if not beginning a new art of painting.[60]

Further exhibitions followed: the Carnegie Institute in Pittsburgh awarded his work a prestigious international prize at their second international exhibition and then acquired it.[61] Showing Puvis de Chavannes's works in the early years of the twentieth century was an earmark of distinction for museums, occasionally after having received bequests, so the Boston Museum of Fine Arts exhibited *Paintings from the Collection of the Late Mrs. S.D. Warren* in 1902. The Durand-Ruel Gallery in New York accorded him exhibitions in 1912[62] and 1930.[63] And his work was included in 1913 at the then somewhat notorious *International Exhibition of Modern Art*, better known as the Armory Show (of which Arthur Davies was a principal organizer), that introduced the latest in European painting and the most forward-looking American art to a sometimes disbelieving and outraged public.

[1]Christian Brinton tells the tale of the young sculptor "Frederick MacMonnies [1863–1937]," *Munsey's*, 34, no. 4, January 1906, p. 422, as cited in M. Smart, *A Flight with Fame: The Life and Art of Frederick MacMonnies (1863–1937)*, Madison, Conn., 1996, p. 62.

[2]S.L. Clemens (Mark Twain), *The Innocents Abroad, or The New Pilgrim's Progress. . . .* Hartford, et al., 1869; H. James, *The American*, Boston, 1877.

[3]See M. Marlais, *Americans and Paris*, exh. cat., Colby College Museum of Art, Waterville, Maine (August 1–October 22, 1990), pp. 7–35; and H.B. Weinberg, *The Lure of Paris. Late Nineteenth-Century American Painters and Their French Teachers*, New York, London, and Paris, 1991, particularly pp. 7–11, 161, 164–66; and *passim*.

[4]See H.B. Weinberg, *The American Pupils of Jean-Léon Gérôme*, Fort Worth, 1984, who also (p. 3) quotes advice from William Morris Hunt to Edwin Blashfield setting out on his career: "Go straight to Paris."

[5]Puvis's atelier and teaching practices are discussed in my forthcoming book on Puvis de Chavannes, that comprises a monograph and a catalogue raisonné of the painted work.

[6]See *Chronique des Arts*, no. 13, March 26, 1887, p. 108.

[7]Noted by Weinberg, *The Lure of Paris, op. cit.*, p. 161.

[8]So with the American Mary Fairchild MacMonnies (1858–1946), who never actually studied with Puvis, *pace* J.A. Barter, "Helping 'Fine Things Across the Atlantic,' Mary Cassatt and Art Collecting in America," in *Mary Cassatt: Modern Woman*, exh. cat., The Art Institute of Chicago, New York, 1998, pp. 87, 88, 96, 105 n. 123.

[9]Blashfield became president of the National Academy of Design, the Society of American Artists, the National Society of Mural Painters (which he helped found in 1895), and the National Institute of Arts and Letters.

[10]The Scammon lectures at the Chicago Art Institute (March 1912), about American mural painting were, as revised and enlarged, published in New York in 1913 as *Mural Painting in America*.

[11]Sale, New York, Christie's East (November 30, 1988), no. 187.

[12]Interview with DeWitt McClellan Lockman, Sherwood Studios, July 1927; typescript with Blashfield Papers, New York Historical Society, cited by L.N. Amico, Williamstown, Mass., Clark Art Institute, *The Mural Decorations of Edwin Howland Blashfield*, exh. cat. (April 1–May 7, 1978); and Weinberg, *The Lure of Paris, op. cit.*, p. 166.

[13]*The Works of Edwin Howland Blashfield*, intro. R. Cortissoz, New York, 1937, pl. 10.

[14]He taught at the Pratt Institute, Brooklyn, New York; the Art Students League (1899–1903); Ipswich; and from 1904 was the chair of the art department at Columbia Teachers College. See notes for a lecture on "modernism," n.d., Arthur Wesley Dow Papers, Ipswich Historical Society; and Dow papers, Archives of American Art.

[15]In *The Boston Evening Transcript*, January 23, 1892.

[16]It was exhibited at MIT; *Boston Evening Transcript*, May 28, 1892; see F.C. Moffatt, *Arthur Wesley Dow (1857–1922)*, exh. cat., National Collection of Fine Arts, Smithsonian, Washington, D. C., 1977, p. 141, n. 124.

[17]B. Curtis, "A Passing Note on American Mural Decoration," *Our Town, A Monthly Magazine Devoted to the Interests of the Town of Wellesley*, VI, no. 3, March 1903, p. 32; as cited by S.E. Earle, "Puvis de Chavannes and America: His Artistic and Critical Reception 1875–1920," Ph.D. diss., Institute of Fine Arts, New York, 1998, n. 64. On the later turn against Puvis and his kind of wall painting, see pp. 308–20.

[18]First published in 1899, it was subtitled *Theory and Practice of Teaching Art. A Series of Exercises in Art Structure*

for the Use of Students and Teachers; the schema was in the 1931 edition, p. 43, fig. 17 (and may be in earlier or later editions as well).

[19]Moffatt, *op. cit.*, p. 61. Dow quoted T. Child ("Some Modern French Painters"), R. Curtis (*Boston Evening Transcript*, February 10, 1893), and M.G. Van Rensselaer ("The New Public Library in Boston," *The Century Magazine,* 50, June 1895, p. 260).

[20]See the Goncourt diatribe against just these qualities in my essay on the critical reception of Puvis's work in this catalog.

[21]See "Pierre Puvis de Chavannes. The Development of a Pictorial Idiom," in A. Brown Price, *Pierre Puvis de Chavannes*, exh. cat., Van Gogh Museum, Amsterdam (February 25–May 29, 1994), Amsterdam, Zwolle, 1994, p. 23.

[22]Smart, *op. cit.*, pp. 124, 126.

[23]N. Mowll Mathews, *Cassatt and Her Circle: Selected Letters*, New York, 1984, p. 208; ". . . had trained in the Paris studio of Pierre Puvis de Chavannes," in Barter, *op. cit.*, pp. 87, 88, 96, 105 n. 123.

[24]From "About the Studios," *Chicago Inter-Ocean*, March 12, 1893, scrapbook 1, as quoted in Smart, *op. cit.*, p. 124.

[25]His atelier and relationship with young artists is discussed in my forthcoming book on Puvis de Chavannes.

[26]F.J. Mather, "Bryson Burroughs," in *The American Spirit in Art*, New Haven, 1927, p. 159, quoted in D. Dreishpoon, *The Paintings of Bryson Burroughs (1869–1934)*, exh. cat., Hirschl and Adler Galleries, Inc., New York, 1984, p. 9.

[27]"Two Paintings by Puvis de Chavannes," *Bulletin of the Metropolitan Museum of Art*, XI, 1916, pp. 12–13.

[28]"Three Lectures to Art Students," typewritten manuscript, 1915–17, Metropolitan Museum, New York, Library.

[29]See *Miss Grace Ellery Channing* of 1893 (Boston Museum of Fine Arts, 1903 03.713).

[30]J.C. Oresman, *Gari Melchers 1860–1932. American Painter*, exh. cat., Graham Gallery, New York, 1978, p. 12.

[31]Richard Wattenmaker has ably discussed linkages in *Puvis de Chavannes and the Modern Tradition*, exh. cat., Art Gallery of Ontario, Toronto, 1975, pp. 188–92; see also Brown Price, *op. cit.*, pp. 247–48; and R.J. Wattenmaker, *Maurice Prendergast*, New York, 1994, pp. 120–24, 127–28.

[32]Sketchbook, no. 46, pp. 34 and 35, Boston Museum of Fine Arts.

[33]Drawing *Dramatic Poetry*, sketchbook no. 51 (CR 1506), Boston Museum of Fine Arts.

[34]See L. Furth in *Augustus Vincent Tack: Landscape of the Spirit*, exh. cat., Phillips Collection, Washington, D.C., 1993, p. 43.

[35]The Phillips Collection, Washington D. C.

[36]Other Puvislike murals are no longer extant: so, Francis D. Millet's *Thesmophoria* of c. 1894 (Bank of Pittsburgh, destroyed); P. King, *American Mural Painting. A Study of the Important Directions by Distinguished Artists in the United States*, Boston, 1902, p. 254, repr.

[37]In 1894 Edwin Austin Abbey and John Singer Sargent were each offered $15 000 for murals for the Boston Public Library.

[38]On the commission see Brown Price, *op. cit.*, pp. 230–33, and my forthcoming book.

[39]His aide Victor Koos saw to the multiple tasks of installation.

[40]Letter of September 1896, to his niece Isabelle, private collection, France.

[41]"We have already heard it said, and shall hear it again, that it is a great pity to see these beautiful paintings leave for far away America. It is certain that many among us will not see them again. But on reflection, this departure is admirable. Art crossing the world, going beyond the oceans, to a new people. . . . These and other paintings are leaving to fulfill their mission. This mission is not to grow weak and anemic and die in their own place. . . . The great conquests of tomorrow will be made as they are already made, by books, paintings, statues, lyrical dramas. And America, after having asked for paintings from our artists, will know quite well how to give us, in order to see them again, air balloons and miraculous *pyroschapes* [a neologism meaning fire-driven, boat-shaped vehicles], which will make us cross the ocean in a few hours and regain our thought, if we have lost it." Translated into English by this author from G. Geffroy, "Le Salon de 1896," vol. 5 of *La Vie Artistique*, 8 vols., Paris, 1892–1903, pp. 148–49.

[42]Letter of September 8, 1896 to Mabel La Farge; see *Henry Adams and his Friends, a Collection of his Unpublished Letters*, intro. H.D. Cater, Boston, 1947, p. 385.

[43]"ce qui me plaît particulièrement dans cette affaire, c'est qu'il n'y a aucune surprise américaine, aucune fantaisie de sauvage, et que ces toiles sont belles et bien désormais dans des galeries, d'amateurs Français . . . ." Letter of February 1, 1884 to Valentine, private collection, France.

[44]"il est bien clair que ma peinture ne saurait plaire là-bas. Je m'abstiens donc, n'ayant aucune envie d'entreprendre des conversions tardives, surtout au bout du monde." Letter of September 24, 1885; L. Venturi, *Les Archives de l'Impressionnisme*, II, Paris and New York, 1939, pp. 93–94.

[45]*Celebrated Paintings by French Masters* had ten works by Puvis and lasted little more than a month, May 25–June 30.

[46]The exhibition, from December 15 to December 31, 1894, may have been geared for Christmas giving.

[47]"j'aspire à un peu de liberté qui me permette de travailler davantage pour moi et de faire avec des choses de dimensions logeable dont on paraît avoir envie en *Amérique*, car les Français sont Lesineurs en matière d'art, et c'est au delà de l'océan que se trouve aujourd'hui l'amateur." Letter of October 1, 1890 [1 8bre 90], private collection, France.

[48]These included some thirteen works with buyers, purchase prices, dates of purchase; private collection, France.

[49]See A. Dumas, "Degas in America," in *Degas and America: The Early Collectors*, exh. cat., High Museum of Art, Atlanta, and the Minneapolis Institute of Art, Minnesota, 2001, pp. 13–33.

[50]Quinn had some fifty-one paintings and drawings by Puvis, including the large *Beheading of Saint John the Baptist* (now in the Barber Institute of Art, Birmingham, England).

[51]The Lambert sale included 365 pictures and 27 sculptures and was held in February 1916 at the Plaza Hotel, New York; works were said to fetch about one third of their worth. Yet, Puvis's works brought considerable sums: *The Meeting of Saint Genevieve and Saint Germain* over $18 000, bought by another Puvis aficionado, the New York lawyer-collector John Quinn; one may compare a *Madonna and Child* attributed to Botticelli that went for $22 000, a Renoir *Girl Knitting* for $10 000, and Blakelocks from $5600 to $20 000.

[52]Letter of December 11, 1887, *The Letters of Bernard Berenson and Isabella Stewart Gardner*, ed. Rollin Van N. Hadley, Boston, 1987, p. 12; my thanks to Serena Stier for this citation.

[53]Anonymous, "The Atelier: Puvis de Chavannes," *Art Amateur*, 1890, n.p.

[54]Among the first, L.L. Rood, *Puvis de Chavannes, A Sketch*, Boston, 1895.

[55]J. La Farge, "Puvis de Chavannes," *Scribner's Magazine*, XXVIII, 1900, pp. 672–84.

[56]Meaning a good thing unappreciated by the ignorant; K. Cox, "Puvis de Chavannes," *Century Magazine*, LI, 1895, p. 558.

[57]As S. Allan (that he used in writing for *Camera Work*), see his "Repetition with Slight Variation," *Camera Work*, no. 1, January 1903, pp. 30–33. See also J. Green, *Camera Work. A Critical Anthology*, New York, 1973, *passim*.

[58]In, *inter alia*, his "Puvis de Chavannes," *The Art Critic*, vol. 1, no. 2, January 1894, pp. 30–31.

[59]S. Hartmann, "Art and Artists: Puvis de Chavannes," *Musical America*, vol. 1, no. 6, November 12, 1898, p. 39.

[60]*Ibidem.*

[61]Pittsburgh, Carnegie Institute, *First Annual Exhibition* (November 5, 1896–January 1, 1897); Pittsburgh, Carnegie Institute, *Second Annual Exhibition* (November 4, 1897–January 1, 1898).

[62]*Exhibition of Drawings and Pastels by Chavannes, Degas, Renoir* (December 18–31, 1912), with twenty works.

[63]*Exhibition of Drawings by Constantin Guys, Puvis de Chavannes, Degas, Cassatt, André and Others* (February 1–13, 1930), included fourteen entries.

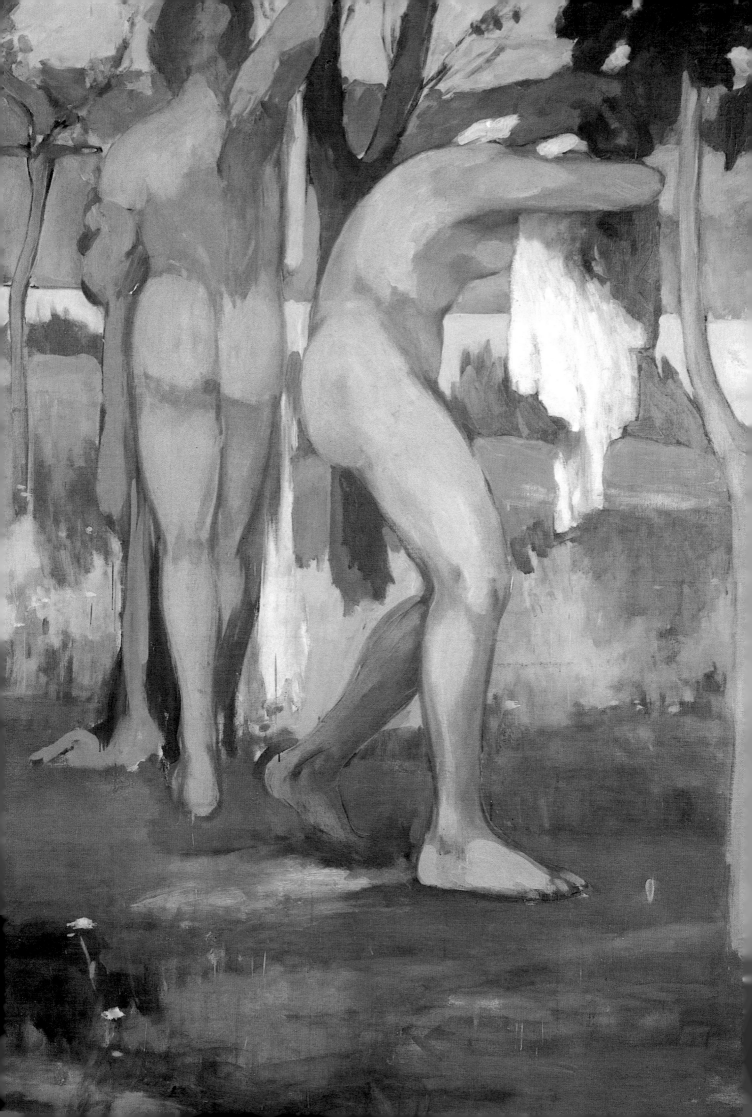

Given a career that had produced not only honors but also half-hearted praise and violent criticism, Puvis de Chavannes is hardly likely to have been disturbed by the squabbles he aroused in Italy during the last three years of his life. In 1895 "at the height of his fame" he had to be included among those backing the new Venice Biennale, and held up as an example to the younger generations because "his idealism of concept and of technique are perfectly in tune with the present-day reaction against the grimness and excess of Naturalism."[1] However, the paintings he sent to the first two Biennales did little to quell the skepticism that his work aroused in certain quarters. In defending Puvis de Chavannes's work, Giulio Aristide Sartorio showed great critical acumen in focusing on technical considerations: "The influence the artist has exerted on the present generation is immense; and his use—in both murals and pastels—of complementary colors is, interestingly enough, reflected in the techniques adopted by the Impressionists."[2] In his own defense of the French artist, Vittorio Pica resorted to the aesthetics of "suggestion" championed in a recent book by Paul Souriau, the last lines of which might well have been written with one of Puvis de Chavannes's paintings in mind: "Obtaining the maximum effect through the minimum use of material means; being sublime in concept and simple in expression; exerting authority over the soul rather than simply addressing oneself to the senses; communicating beautiful dreams from one spirit to another: this is what constitutes great art!"[3] Such concepts enabled one to render full justice to Puvis de Chavannes's "exclusive" painting, in which the artist did not so much add as subtract, while nevertheless creating works "that were nobly poetic in the archaic simplicity of their composition, the gentle paleness of their palette, and the charming suggestiveness of their skillfully synthetic draftsmanship."[4] However, both Sartorio and Pica admitted that the painter "needs to have large wall spaces to decorate if he is to express all the austere yet ingenuous grandeur of his ideas."[5] A comment echoed by Alfredo Melani, who observed: "One has to see Puvis de Chavannes in his large mural works."[6] This, of course, meant that the Puvis de Chavannes on display at Venice was, in some way, a mere abstraction of the real thing, an artist whose true achievements were confined to the surface of far-distant walls.

Between the two Biennales Puvis de Chavannes exhibited his *Beheading of Saint John the Baptist*[7] at the Festa Fiorentina dell'Arte e dei Fiori, but the result was pretty much the same. Before the opening of this Florence show, the magazine *Il Marzocco* published a piece that guaranteed a certain reputation for the artist, who was described as a symbol within the figurative arts of that rebirth of idealism championed by Ferdinand Brunetière. "And who is unaware that the young no longer turn to the likes of Courbet and Manet as their masters, but to Puvis de Chavannes, whose paintings—with their introspection and harmony of individual details, overall composition and poetic meaning—are an inexhaustible source of pleasure for the soul?"[8] The Florentine magazine would also later try to establish even closer links with Puvis de Chavannes by publishing his observations in its 1897–98 survey of Italian art and literature; however, all the French artist supplied was a disappointingly general comment.[9] And yet for all this pre-advertising, the *Beheading of Saint John the Baptist* ended up being overwhelmed by the vogue for the Pre-Raphaelites, which Anglophile critics in Florence (and elsewhere) rather blandly associated with the "love of Byzantine art" to be seen in the work of Puvis de Chavannes.[10] There were, of course, some exceptions, such as the young Ardengo Soffici, who in recalling his reaction to that painting, wrote: "A *Beheading of Saint John the Baptist* by Puvis de Chavannes interested me. I had heard about the artist, because my new friends at the Academy had mentioned him—and I had also seen some reproductions of his murals. But this painting was nothing like them. It was a picture that one felt was indirectly inspired by the Italian—the Venetian—school, in particular by the work of Tintoretto. It was also indirectly inspired by Delacroix, with his sense of color and composition, his daring and rough way of handling forms, and even something of his brushwork. The tone was warm and also rather grim; there was a rich, thick impasto that created a dense surface—and so the painting was, in a certain sense, the very contrary of what one generally associated with that artist, and what I would have expected to see."[11] Soffici wrote this many years later, so it is more than probable that he was making a few *post hoc* adjustments to his memories, in order to underline his long-standing interest in the rediscovery of a vital, corporeal "Italianness" (in his comments of Cézanne, he would again mention Tintoretto) rather than in the artificial exploitation of archaic stylistic features. Indeed, he comments: "I will add, as a parenthesis, that when, a few years later in Paris, I found

1. Ardengo Soffici, *Bathing*,
detail, 1905.
Private collection

myself in front of the Puvis de Chavannes of the Panthéon and the Sorbonne, the artist of the various paintings exhibited here and there—in short, that would-be primitive, Giottoesque de Chavannes—I couldn't help but wonder if perhaps that artist had not made a big mistake in abandoning that more natural and spontaneous manner, which was less literary and more pictorial."[12]

In fact, at the end of Puvis de Chavannes's "Italian" triennial, the prevailing opinion was the one that Enrico Thovez so forcefully argued by in the *Emporium* (rendered all the more powerful by the circulation of the publication, the authoritative standing of the writer himself, and the overall detail of his argument).[13] Richly illustrated with some fourteen plates, this 1897 publication was the most complete Italian study of Puvis de Chavannes to date; and it was written by the most determined opponent of Pre-Raphaelite art in a generally Pre-Raphaelite Italy—the man who in 1895 had written a manifesto against the "new rachitis" represented by all forms of medieval revivalism (and included the French artist among the targets of his attack).[14] The length of the *Emporium* article now gave the Turinese critic the chance to launch an attack argued in much greater detail. Introduced by a short biographical sketch, which skillfully highlighted the relatively tardy artistic vocation of a Puvis de Chavannes who had, through family tradition, been raised with "algebra and geometry,"[15] the piece then continued (in the fifth section) to define the artist's work as essentially "more intellectual than sensorial," as "nobly ideal and grandiosely synthetic." The indisputable merits of his work are discussed in these terms: "Few minds are capable of rising from the particular to the general, from the accidental to the law behind it, from an isolated phenomenon to the complete cycle of events, from the subjective limited poetry of the individual to the objective infinite poetry of nature."[16] However, from that point onward, an incessant barrage of criticism gradually adds to the picture of Puvis de Chavannes as a non-painter. According to Thovez, Puvis de Chavannes's lofty thoughts are deformed by their anachronistic expression in the forms of a stereotyped classicism, a "rigid and labored mannerism."[17] His "excessive simplifications," his "incorrect" draftsmanship, his "lopsided relief," his "poor" and muddy colors—all inevitably undermine the noble poetry of his original intention, even in what may be considered his masterpiece, *The Poor Fisherman*.[18] What is more, the much-hailed mastery of his monumental compositions is disparaged in a sequence of specific technical considerations: these grand decorations were not, as many believed, frescoes but works on canvas, painted "with thin paint and a meanness of brushstroke that may well appear to be due to the paint's absorption by the wall but is actually intended or spontaneous."[19] And in conclusion, Thovez holds Puvis de Chavannes up as a pernicious example, his painting offering an alibi to young artists: "his technical failings blaze a very easy path for the incapable or the impatient, who can use the example set by this famous artist to mask their own lack of talent or study."[20] Of course, one could not have expected anything else from a critic such as Thovez, who, among that varied array of writers championing "democratic" art, inclined to support a modern Naturalism, the heir to a tradition that in France could be traced from Courbet and Millet to Dagnan-Bouveret and Alfred Roll. And yet, for all its one-sidedness, his article seems to have had a powerful effect. For a long time to come his considerations of Puvis de Chavannes's classicism of form and theme would inhibit appreciation of his work in Italy, and prevent the perception of other qualities such as narrative density, anti-naturalism, synthetic rendering, an awkwardness, and that "harmonious simplification in the rhythms of line, surface, volume and color itself" which—as Franco Russoli would so perceptively point out—"are not the response to some sort of Neoclassical canon, but explorations of the recesses of psyche and metaphysics, and of a human condition in which it seems that the absolute and the constant can only be seized through alienating variations within the world of phenomena and existence."[21]

Announced with a few respectful obituaries, the artist's death seemed to lead to a rapid demise of his renown. However, while Pica was still desperately trying to defend the "charming suggestiveness" of Puvis de Chavannes's Symbolist art in 1900,[22] Ardengo Soffici, who was then in Paris, gave impetus to the French artist's role as a model. Again, the distance between the events themselves and the written recollection of them seems to have led to some rather significant "re-writings" of the past. In his 1954 *Salto Vitale*—written at a time of obscurantist bigotry against all forms of so-called "academic" art—Soffici's account of his visit to the paintings in the Panthéon and the Sorbonne suggests that his companion, Giovanni Costetti, reacted much

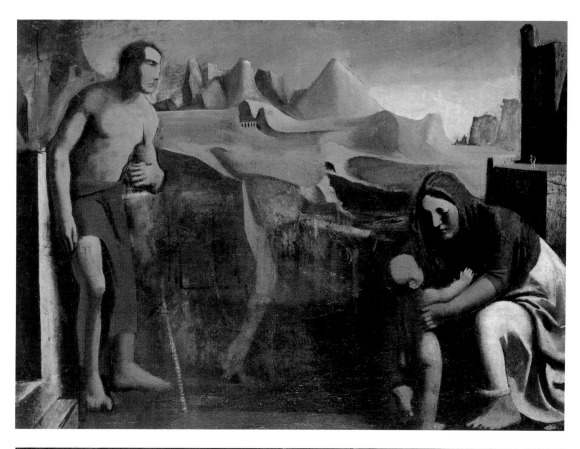

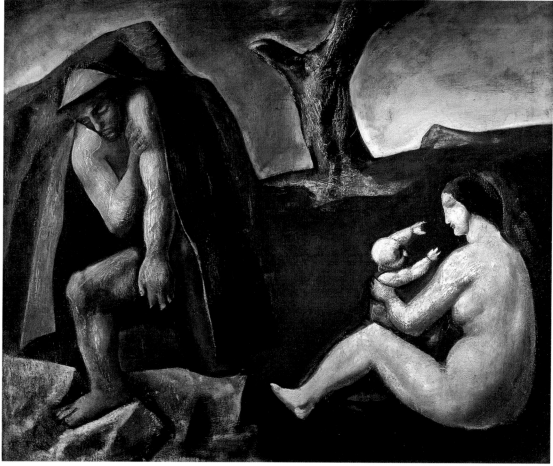

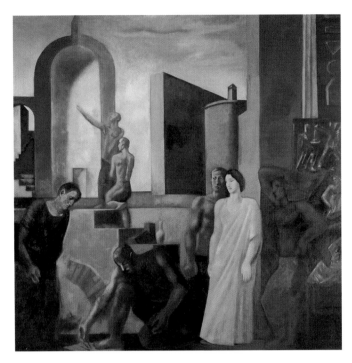
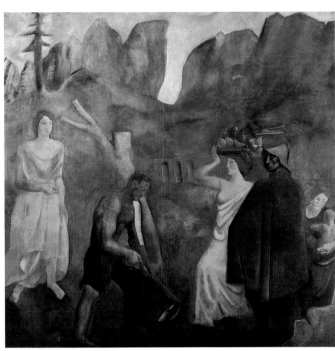

4, 5. Mario Sironi, *Architecture* and *Plowing*, 1933. Rome, Ministero delle Poste e Telecomunicazioni

more enthusiastically than he himself did. "[Costetti] took them as an example to denigrate the more modern artists we were arguing about . . . even though neither of us denied the great talent of that painter [Puvis de Chavannes] or the many beautiful things to be found in his works. I myself particularly admired the nobility, the poetic aura and even the innovation to be seen in parts of them; but I simply preferred the lyrical realism of the new school."[23] By 1954, Costetti was dead, and works that might have borne witness to a long-standing passion for Puvis de Chavannes had not survived (if they had ever existed);[24] Soffici could thus easily limit the extent of his past enthusiasm without fear of contradiction. However, in 1939, when the prevailing climate still favored contorted readings of foreign art in terms of its "Italianness," and when the Italian artists themselves were being exhorted to "bring painting back to walls," Soffici had given a rather different account.

"When, in 1900, I moved with some friends to Paris, to see how tradition might be continued with new spirit and form, French painting was shining in all its genuine splendor. All the manifestations of this art, from the great mural works of Puvis de Chavannes and Besnard, to the easel paintings of Renoir, Degas, Cézanne, Seurat, etc. . . . have a single fundamental character. For the monumental works, this fundamental characteristic was the striving for grandeur of style through the study of the Old Masters of Italian art and careful observation of contemporary daily life."[25] If the "constructive" approach of the Impressionists vouchsafed a disciplined vision of "contemporary daily life" which Puvis de Chavannes was accused of ignoring, the latter nevertheless provided an essential model for the monumental concept of a work of art—and what is more, a model which bore within itself the vital seed of the Italian figurative tradition. Furthermore, this reflection—posed in terms that were most acceptable to the regime of the day—actually conveyed an idea of Puvis de Chavannes that Soffici had expressed with great clarity many years before. For example, in 1904, the then "Stéphane Cloud" wrote a long article on the retrospective that the Salon d'Automne of that year had dedicated to Puvis de Chavannes.[26] In a tone that is quite similar to Costetti's enthusiasm, Soffici identified the ethical value of his monumental painting and his solid links with the Italian tradition as being the key to what might be learned from Puvis de Chavannes who, together with Segantini and Böcklin, was described as a "high priest" of the Mediterranean figurative tradition. "Puvis de Chavannes has restored to painting its true and original function as the embellishment of monuments, as an incitation to great actions. . . . Puvis de Chavannes's work is one of nobility and grandeur; and yet precisely because it is part of a tradition which is not that of his own country, it will—like the oeuvre of the magnificent Poussin—fail to generate a lineage." Already Soffici was complementing what he took as Puvis de Chavannes's excessive absorption in archa-

6. Mario Sironi, *Fishing*, 1931.
Private collection

ic dreams that were dissociated from the contemporary world with Cézanne's "contemporary soul": "Puvis de Chavannes was too contemplative a soul to get mixed up in the confused turmoil of life around him. . . . And the meaning of impetuous modernity escaped him; but that did not mean that his art ceased to be powerful, significant and personal. The French artist who never lost this sense of modernity is . . . Paul Cézanne."[27] Thus Soffici had shared Costetti's enthusiasm for Puvis de Chavannes to a much greater degree than he subsequently admitted. And perhaps his enthusiasm was less transitory, given that during his time in Paris he frequented the eclectic literary and artistic circles of Late and Post-Symbolism, where the figure of Puvis de Chavannes had maintained all its luster (this was particularly true of the circle associated with the magazine *La Plume*, which had dedicated a special issue to the artist in 1895). Within Soffici's own work, traces of this early passion for Puvis de Chavannes can be seen in the decoration he produced for the Hotel at the Roncegno Spa in 1905. The one extant panel—*Bathing*—is a perfect example of the complex interweave the Tuscan artist created between French and German culture;[28] the rhythm of the vast composition obviously owes a lot to Pu-

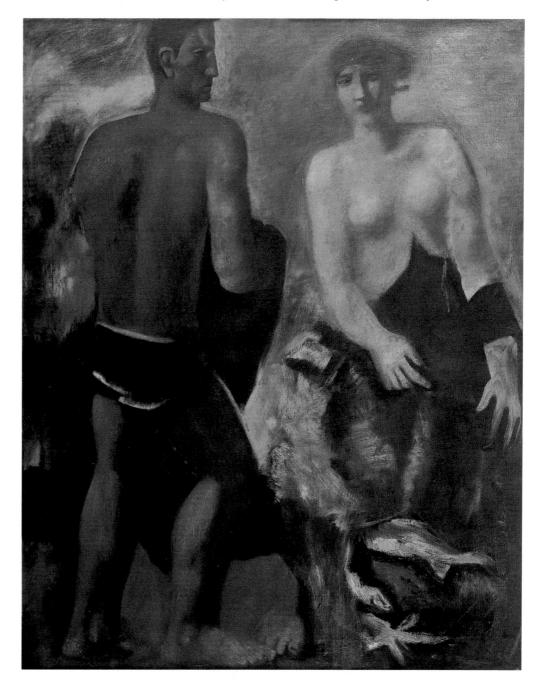

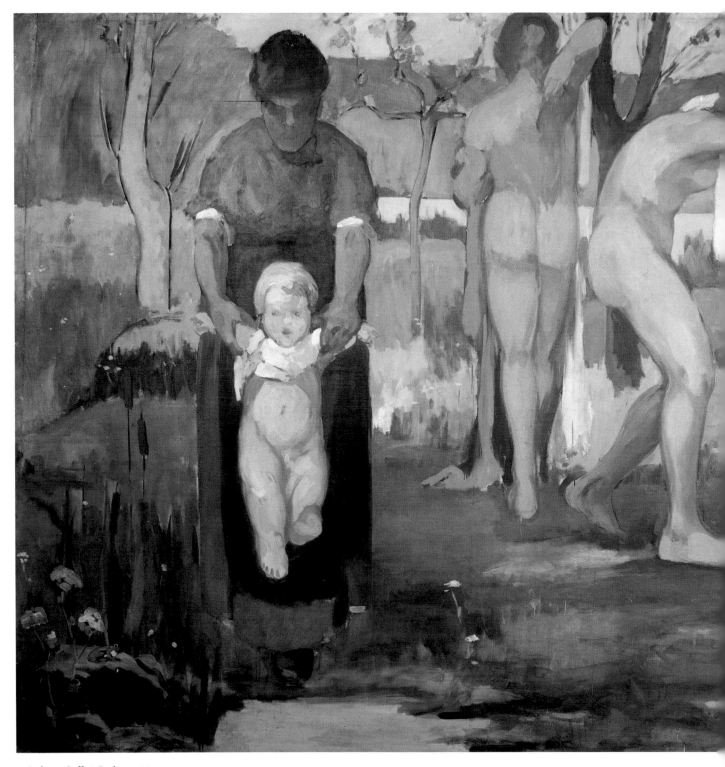

7. Ardengo Soffici, *Bathing*, 1905.
Private collection

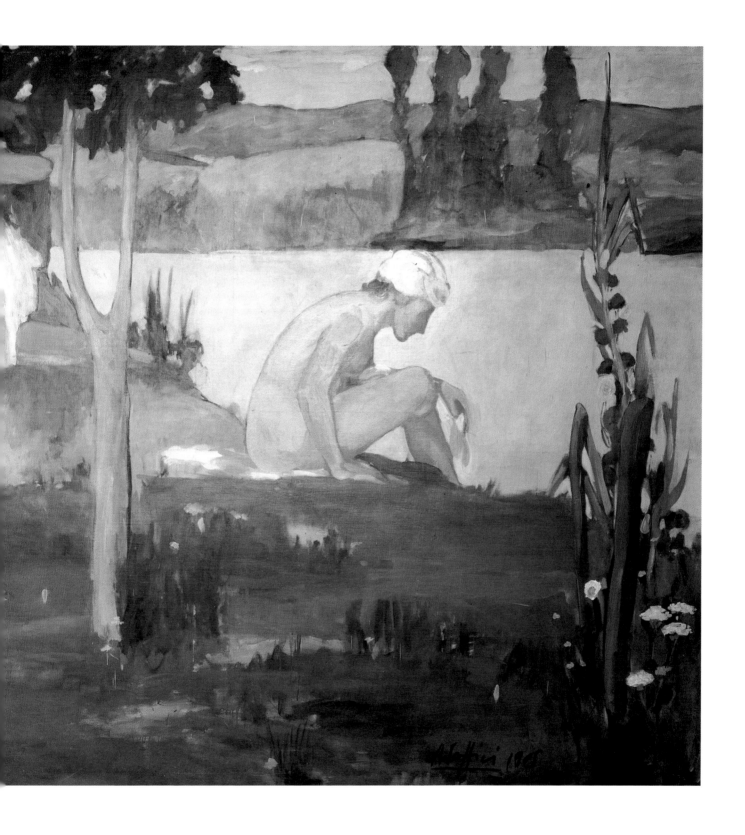

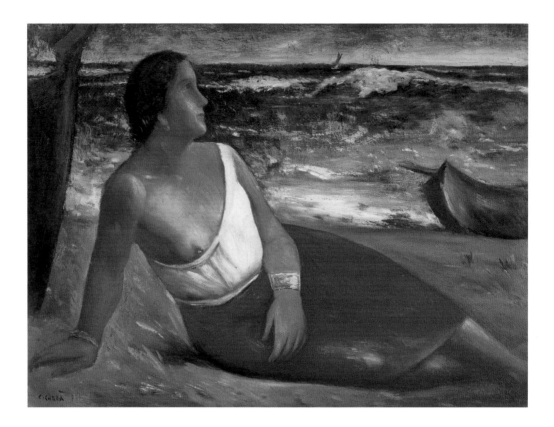

vis de Chavannes, while the plastic modeling of the whole reveals the more modern influence of the Nabi group (and of Vallotton in particular).

The different layers in Soffici's "recollections" of Puvis lead one to wonder whether the French artist also served as an example for later generations of Italian artists. One case—vaguely connected with Soffici himself through a slight acquaintanceship—is that of Lorenzo Viani. On his three visits to Paris (between 1908 and 1912), this artist lived in the very dregs of the city, an "enormous prison-house" of mud and rags, a grim coal tunnel inhabited by the beings who appeared in the worlds of Meunier and Laermans, where what color there was were the powerful but not radiant ones found in the works of Van Gogh or Van Dongen. This experience was recounted in a perhaps somewhat "rewritten" form in Viani's 1925 "novel" *Parigi*, which often draws on notes taken at the time, for example, his visit to the Musée de Luxembourg.[29] The works of Rodin and the Impressionists disappointed Viani; but he did see a brief flash of true life in Medardo Rosso, and also in another work, which he gazed upon so long that he describes the experience in an entire paragraph: "The most austere picture is by Puvis de Chavannes, *The Poor Fisherman.* This restrained artist drew his inspiration from the Italian primitives, even in his much more sizeable works, such as those at the Panthéon. However, they are more relaxed than this painting, in which it is impossible to clearly identify the line that marks the division between the leonine virtue of candor and simple poverty. The thin figures do not have clearly-defined contours; there is no burning passion within them as they are mortified by the majesty of nature. The anemic pinks, the dissipated blues, the pearl grays often draw long sighs from emaciated ladies whose consuming intellectual passions are written across their forehead: 'You know, I feel at my ease with that.'"[30] The picture clearly made an impression on Viani, despite all his contempt for the rarefied intellectual passions that were so thrilled by Puvis de Chavannes's art. Indeed, it is fair to assume that *The Poor Fisherman* left a mark on the work of the Italian artist, not only because its long-suffering humanity was characterized by desolate grandeur and religious silence, but also because of the power of certain formal characteristics (the architectural boat, the jagged rendition of human anatomy, the use of flat surfaces of paint for the sea and the earthy palette). Such works as Viani's 1914–16 *Benediction of Those Who Died at Sea* and some of his pictures of vagabonds would seem in fact to draw on this experience of Puvis de Chavannes; this is borne out perhaps by the commentary that the artist attached to the woodcut of the *Benediction*, which appears to voice the most widely preached principles behind Puvis de Chavannes's art: "Those who are truly familiar with the order and discipline that is part of my work will not be surprised to see that in these pictures I strive for a synthesis that a friend has defined as 'desperate' . . . . Since I believe that art is a phenomenon of the will, I have tried to give this work a special primitive character in the composition of the group in order to make the concept more embracing: universal!"[31] In this way, Viani completed the usual *imagine* of Puvis de Chavannes, as a painter whose work was characterized by the archaic, the monumental and the synthetically condensed, with another "expressionist" interpretation of *The Poor Fisherman*, as an unprecedented hymn to the heroism of poverty.

And, again in Soffici's day, one might point out how the *lumineuse triade* of Segantini-Böcklin-de Chavannes[32] was, in 1920, momentarily transformed into a group of *maîtres manqués.*[33] It was, of course, the avant-garde that so severely demoted them; but this hyperbolic fall from grace actually reveals that Puvis de Chavannes was a powerful presence for the agitators of Futurism. In the conference on Futurist painting held in Rome in 1911, Umberto Boccioni attacked the Italian public as backward and Italian critics as myopic. His drastic conclusion was that in Italy "since the days of Tiepolo"—with the exception of the Lombard Divisionists and a few of the Tuscan *Macchiaioli*—"there has not been one picture that measures up to even the most mediocre sketch by the artists who have flourished in France, from Manet to Gauguin, from Puvis de Chavannes to Maurice Denis."[34] This dramatic state of affairs authorized the subversive acts of the Futurists, which elsewhere might have been "almost pointless" but were strictly necessary in Italy. Three years later—in the brief book *Pittura e scultura futuriste*—Boccioni qualified his judgment, arguing it in more detail. Like d'Annunzio, Wilde, Huysmans, Moreau, Rossetti and Burne-Jones—all of whom had initially been championed by the Futurists—Puvis de Chavannes was the very symbol of cultural decadence: "One finds [in their art] elements of elegant grace, refined superficiality, cultural hypersensitivity: all uniformly rendered through a more or less evident plagiarism from the famous masterpieces of the past."[35] However, a little further on, de Chavannes is spared this criticism of *passatismo*, because of his ethical rigor when faced with a public that did not understand him and attacked him; though Boccioni then adds: "In short, one might say that even sincere artists—for example, Gaetano Previati, Henry de Groux and Puvis de Chavannes in the field of painting, in the struggles they fought with the public, betrayed our cause of a fundamental renewal of art."[36] Indeed, Boccioni acts as if Puvis (like Previati and de Groux) were still alive, and criticizes him for not standing back from tradition, and for drawing the inspiration for his own art from "the silent solemnity of museum masterpieces." And, finally, a little further on, Puvis de Chavannes reappears in Boccioni's text as an example of a negative model. The Futurists were investigating the powers of intuition, and the dynamics of the psyche, and in this research the "plastic state of mind" permits "the perfect fusion of impassive plastic power . . . and the expression of the lyrical problem of consciousness." The "plastic state of mind" is "the way out of skeptical, analytical negation; it is the exhilarating aspiration toward a future distinction and hierarchy within the discouraging equality of all plastic and emotional values that besets an overly rationalistic mind. It is the creation of a new order and a new clarity, which are in clear opposition to the classical interpretation of these terms upheld by Puvis de Chavannes. This order and clarity arise from the Futurist hatred for ancient laws and the last traces of democratic-veristic slavery."[37] Boccioni's reference is very clear and reveals significant attention to the ideas of Puvis de Chavannes, given that those two terms "order" and "clarity" were taken from a quotation of the artist that had appeared in a recently published book by Maurice Denis, *Théories*, which would play no small role in reawakening Italian interest in Puvis. In the key essay, *Les Arts à Rome ou la méthode classique*, Denis headed the section *De l'Art classique* with a quote from Poussin and one from Puvis de Chavannes—thus charting the course of French classicism as it emerged from the Italian tradition. And the comment by the latter artist provided Boccioni with his two key concepts: ". . . I am convinced that the best-ordered composition is at the same time the most beautiful. I love order because I have a passionate love of clarity."[38] What is more, a few pages later Boccioni probably read another quotation: "All clear ideas [have] a plastic thought that translates them. But our ideas often occur mixed up and jumbled together. Thus, we must untangle them if we are to hold them in their pure state before our inner eye."[39] His own thought

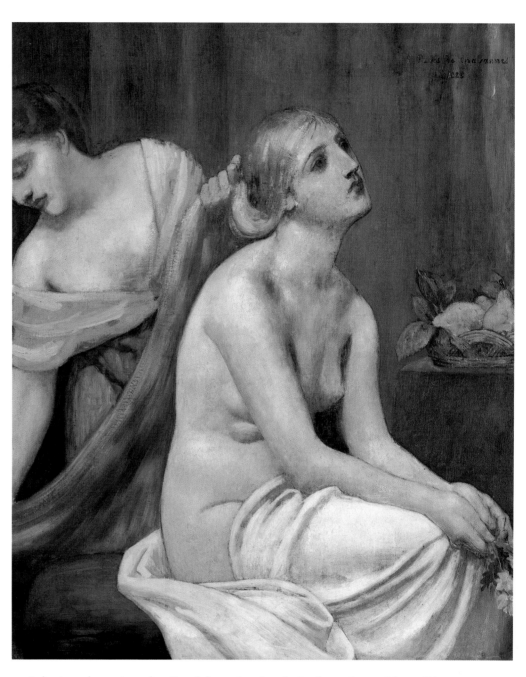

9. Pierre Puvis de Chavannes,
Young Woman at Her Toilette, 1883.
Paris, Musée d'Orsay

on "plastic and emotive values" and the rational analysis of emotions might well be seen as conceived in concise opposition to these ideas put forward by Puvis de Chavannes.

One can never know whether, having passed the acme of his Futurist fury, Boccioni reflected on the intensity of this engagement with Puvis de Chavannes in his own paintings. What is certain is that the name of the French artist was one of things "caught up" in the avant-garde whirlwind, and was constantly reemerging. For example, when—having just recently read Boccioni's book on Futurist sculpture—the young Roberto Longhi was (in 1914) embarking on his first study of Caravaggism, he could find no better example than Puvis de Chavannes when trying to draw a sharp distinction between the chromatics of the Battistello and Lanfranco frescoes in the Oratorio dei Nobili in the Naples church of Gesù Nuovo: "The work [of Battisello] is in a very clear light and rather wan in tone. However it is in perfect harmony, and if it did not suffer as a result of its being besieged by Lanfranco's figures, which have the texture of brushed velvet, one might be able to appreciate it (the juxtaposition is rather like placing a mural by Puvis de Chavannes alongside one by Delacroix)."[40] Nor should it come as a surprise that in 1913 Carlo Carrà ruthlessly argued that "the false classics, Poussin, David and Ingres (with-

10. Carlo Carrà,
Morning Toilette, 1939.
Private collection

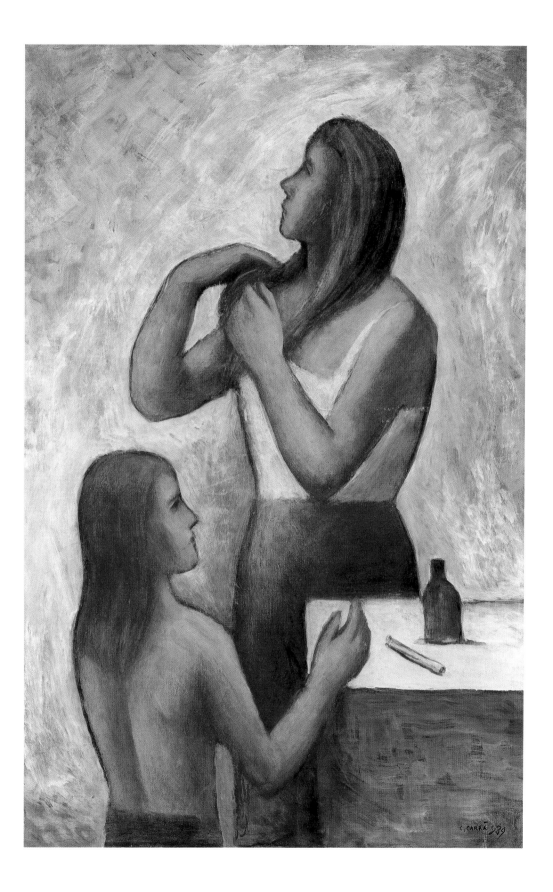

11. Massimo Campigli,
The Sailors' Brides, 1931.
Rome, Galleria Nazionale
d'Arte Moderna

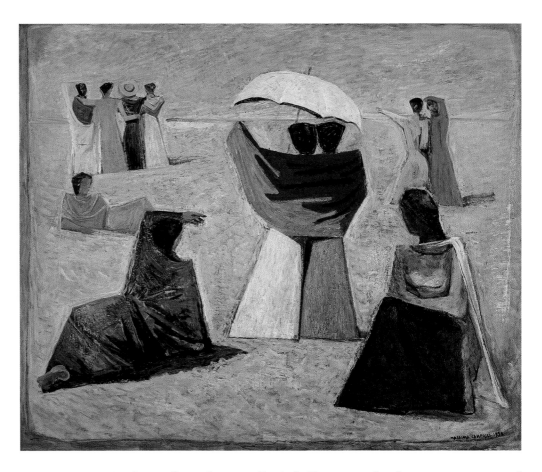

out even mentioning that mediocre decorator Puvis de Chavannes who, for a moment, appeared
to be another classic himself) bring absolutely nothing to the realization of the classical ideal.
Such artists are not to be seen as making a contribution to any period in the history of art,"[41]
but some time later in his life he held rather different views.

As has already been mentioned, the collection of Denis's theoretical and critical writings reasserted Puvis de Chavannes's standing, placing him at the center of that movement "which
is drawing French culture and French energy toward a new order."[42] The book was widely read
in Italy, and was reviewed—from rather different points of view—in *Il Marzocco* (by Carlo Placci) and *La Voce* (by Soffici).[43] Placci was an intellectual dilettante who had been introduced to
Denis by Berenson in 1907 and now emphasized the Neo-Renaissance aspects of his approach;
while not ignoring the relevance of the work to contemporary cultural questions in France, he
mainly read it in terms of his own Pre-Raphaelite preferences (preferences that were still shared
by the readers of the Florentine journal). For his part, Soffici had been close to Denis in the
days of Adrien Mithouard's *Occident* and shared many of his ideas—from the notion of a
"Mediterranean culture" to the need for the recovery of autonomous national traditions—as
well as his admiration for Cézanne. However, now he viewed him from the point of view of
the avant-garde, and saw him as a perfect counterpart to Paul Claudel—an example of intol-
erably affected archaism and Roman Catholic mysticism. These different reactions to Denis's
book indirectly affected the reputation of Puvis de Chavannes himself. The first example of
this can be seen within the context of the movement to regenerate sacred art which was promoted in Italy under the aegis of Don Celso Costantini —a movement to which Denis himself
made a solid contribution, often working alongside his fellow critics and artists Francesco Mar-
gotti and Giuseppe Grondona, both of whom worked for the magazines *Arte Cristiana* and *Vita e Pensiero*.[44]

In fact, the second monographic study of Puvis de Chavannes—by the painter Biagio Biagetti—appeared in *Arte Cristiana* in 1917.[45] Illustrated with eleven plates (of which seven, given
the main concerns of the journal, were dedicated to the Saint Genevieve cycle), the article, in
the author's own words, was a "mixture of admiration and reservations."[46] The latter were in

the same vein as those put forward by Thovez: "The limits in [Puvis de Chavannes's] representative language" led to a form that was "slipshod and lacking in mastery, even to the point of producing truly mediocre results." It was a mistake to take this lack as being essential to the charm of his work, because it would bring to pass the very danger that such painting posed—that is, the elevation of the maladroit to the level of art "because it is by accepting this fallacy that one reaches the point of accepting and applauding each anomaly and abuse of this very modern pseudo-technique. There is an attempt to replace the laws of beauty with anarchy, because the latter is easier."[47] Thus after having hinted that Puvis de Chavannes might be somewhat responsible for the contemporary "anomalies," Biagetti then goes on to sing his praises, focusing his plaudits essentially on his mural works and his two "heroic" and "hieratic" paintings *The Fisherman's Family* and *The Poor Fisherman*. Loftiness of thought, symbiosis with the architectural setting and grandeur of composition, all made Puvis de Chavannes the greatest modern example of a monumental painter. "It has been centuries since mural art has had such pure, noble and eloquent works!"[48] And here, Biagetti takes up and underlines the idea of the "Italian" Puvis de Chavannes: "he traveled frequently, especially in Italy, where the main object of his love and admiration was the work of our primitive artists: His enthusiasm for the simple and powerful works of Piero della Francesca in Arezzo is well known. . . . Thus the origins of his art are to be found in our country, where he drew simplicity from our medieval art, synthesis of line from Raphael and ease of natural movement and gesture from Giotto."[49]

Here perhaps one need only mention one of the results of Biagetti's article: upon reading the text, his exact contemporary Adolfo De Carolis, then in the middle of his work on the frescoes of the Salone del Podestà in Bologna and of the University of Pisa, wrote that same year (1917) to ask Denis for reproductions of the Puvis de Chavannes decorations of the Boston Library.[50] In the different Italy of the 1920s and 1930s, yet another Puvis de Chavannes emerges. He was still monumental and civic-minded, "primitive" and Italian, but now also human, with touches of tragedy or melancholy, and the mythical or the dream-like. From this point onwards, the artist's work would, in a certain sense, be reduced to silence precisely because it was considered to be one with that of Cézanne, Seurat and Picasso (perhaps partly because of his spare, summary and rather gauche draftsmanship, as had been illustrated by the works at the 1924 Venice Biennale).[51] Indeed, with its mission of a "return to the wall," Italian painting of the 1930s could hardly ignore the man. Mario Sironi, for example, may never have talked about Puvis de Chavannes in recorded documents, but the fact that he exhibited a *The Poor Fisherman* at the Third Rome Biennale in 1925 is a sufficiently eloquent act of homage. Similarly, the subsequent series of *Fishermen* and *Families*—and, above all, the large 1933 panels of *Architecture* and *Plowing* in Bergamo—reveal his study of the rarefied monumentality of Puvis, and of the stony isolation of the *The Prodigal Son*. After he moved beyond Metaphysical art in 1921, Carlo Carrà also began to revise his opinion of the French artist. In 1924, he wrote: "we have had a large number of artists whose art is impregnated with mysticism. I shall mention here Puvis de Chavannes and Giovanni Segantini, two of the worthiest examples. Although unbearable to a large number of people, mysticism had at times a very meritorious effect upon these two artists";[52] while in 1929 he went even further: "Of Puvis de Chavannes's work I will mention the *The Poor Fisherman* in the Musée de Luxembourg in Paris, which is, in my opinion, one of the modern paintings most powerfully imbued with pictorial mysticism."[53] And at the same time as his own painting began to strive toward a mythical representation of the worlds of nature and dream, so it began to show the influence of not only *The Poor Fisherman* but also of *Young Women by the Sea*, *Young Woman at Her Toilette*, *The Goatherd* and *The Magdalene*. At the risk of falling victim to the sarcasm Longhi expressed with regard to "a certain painter,"[54] one cannot help but find a renewed feeling for the art of Puvis de Chavannes reflected in the tighter, more muted tones to be seen in such Carrà paintings as the 1929 *Swimmers*, the 1930 *Summer*, the 1937 *Easter Eve*, the 1939 *Morning Toilette*, and even in graphic works of the 1940s as *Women at the Lake* and Quasimodo's *Odyssey*—in short, in those works that (in 1933) Raffaello Giolli spoke of in terms of an "unquiet and subtle [voice] that ranges from the tragic to the refined," at the same time referring to their "intense mystery" and "images of the eternal."[55]

From that moment on, any "echo of the heart" might well draw on the works of Puvis de Chavannes—as one can see in Libero Andreotti's silent *Affrico and Mensola*, in Arturo Martini's

13. Libero Andreotti,
Affrico and Mensola.
Rome, Galleria Nazionale
d'Arte Moderna

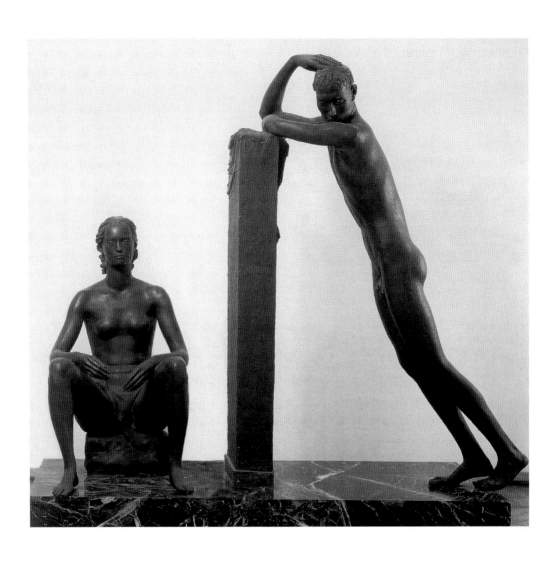

The Hospitality to the Fisherman's Wife or his dream-like *Stars*, and in Giovanni Colacicchi's brightly-mythical *Niobe*.[56] And the same might be said of all those other works that were striving to depict an island of thought and feeling.

"His influence can still be felt in our day," was the comment in the entry on Puvis de Chavannes in the 1935 edition of the Treccani Encyclopedia.[57] His was such a diffuse influence that it finally dissolved away to the imperceptible.

[1] *Prima Esposizione Internazionale d'Arte della Città di Venezia*, exh. cat., Venice, 1895, pp. 25–26.

[2] G.A. Sartorio, "L'Esposizione di Venezia," *Il Convito*, I, 1895, p. XXXI.

[3] P. Souriau, *La Suggestion dans l'art*, Paris, 1893, p. 345.

[4] V. Pica, *L'Arte Europea a Venezia*, Naples, 1895, p. 96.

[5] *Ibidem.*

[6] A. Melani, "Prima Esposizione Internazionale d'Arte della Città di Venezia," *Emporium*, I, 1895, I, p. 487.

[7] *Festa dell'arte e dei fiori 1896–1897, Catalogo della Esposizione di Belle Arti*, exh. cat., Florence, 1896, p. 72, no. 521: "Puvis de Chavannes. Paris, *Beheading of St. John*, Fr. 25 000."

[8] [Editorial], "Il rinascimento dell'idealismo," *Il Marzocco*, I, 16, May 17, 1896, p. 1.

[9] See *Il Marzocco*, II, 50, January 16, 1898, p. 2.

[10] E. De Fonseca, *Conversazione d'arte. Studio critico dell'Esposizione di Firenze 1896–1897*, Florence, 1897, p. 91.

[11] A. Soffici, *Passi tra le rovine. Autoritratto d'artista italiano nel quadro del suo tempo. II. Adolescenza*, Florence, 1952, p. 375.

[12] *Ibidem*, pp. 375–76.

[13] E. Thovez, "Artisti contemporanei: P. de Chavannes," *Emporium*, III, 1897, VI, pp. 414–37.

[14] E. Thovez, "Il nuovo rachitismo," October 16, 1895, in idem, *Il Vangelo della pittura ed altre prose d'arte*, Turin–Genoa, 1921, pp. 121–26.

[15] Thovez, "Artisti contemporanei…," *op. cit.*, p. 414.

[16] *Ibidem*, p. 416.

[17] *Ibidem*, p. 421.

[18] *Ibidem*, pp. 423, 427.

[19] *Ibidem,* p. 423.

[20] *Ibidem*, p. 435.

[21] F. Russoli, "Linguaggio e immagine nel Simbolismo," *Paragone*, 317–319, 1976, p. 223.

[22] V. Pica, "La pittura all'Esposizione di Parigi. II. Ancora la Francia," *Emporium*, VII, 1901, XIII, p. 34.

[23] A. Soffici, *Il salto vitale. Autoritratto d'artista italiano nel quadro del suo tempo. III. Giovinezza*, Florence, 1954, p. 239.

[24] See *Grafica di Giovanni Costetti (Reggio Emilia 1874—Settignano 1949)*, exh. cat., Reggio Emilia, 1976, pp. 9–10, 24.

[25] A. Soffici, *Selva. Arte*, Florence, 1943, p. 263 (note dated February 15, 1939).

[26] S. Cloud [A. Soffici], "Le Salon d'Automne. Considérations," in *L'Europe artiste*, I, 1904, pp. 333–39, republished in M. Richter, *La formazione francese di Ardengo Soffici 1900–1914*, Milan, 1969, pp. 290–96.

[27] Cloud, *op. cit.,* p. 292. Even if with rather less transport, Soffici would repeat these ideas on Puvis de Chavannes in a 1908 article on Maurice Denis: "Like that of the greater Puvis de Chavannes, [Denis's] work reveals a way of conceiving a work of art which is not common among his fellow countrymen: it derives less from his own national traditions than from qualities that are specific to the Old Masters of Italy, and especially Tuscany. . . . Every time a French painter is unwilling to follow the genius of his own race . . . Italy becomes his spiritual home; this happeend with Poussin and with Puvis." A. Soffici, "Maurice Denis," *Vita d'Arte*, II, 1909, IV, pp. 506, 508.

[28] See M. Pratesi and G. Uzzani, *L'arte italiana del Novecento. La Toscana*, Venice, 1991, pp. 55 *passim*.

[29] See L. Viani, *Parigi, 1925*, Florence, 1994, pp. 141–44, and idem, *Opera omnia, Scritti e pensieri sull'arte*, Viareggio, 1997, pp. 47–52.

[30] Viani, *Parigi…, op. cit.,* p. 144.

[31] L. Viani, *Il Martirio. Raccolta di XII xilografie originali e dirette*, Viareggio, n.d. [1915], pl. 1, Florence, Gabinetto Disegni e Stampe degli Uffizi.

[32] Cloud, *op. cit.,* p. 292.

[33] A. Soffici, "Preraffaellismo," *Rete mediterranea*, March 1920, pp. 71–76: "around Puvis de Chavannes and Böcklin there was a change in the group of the artists who had fallen into the 'trap' of archaism, with von Marées and De Carolis replacing Segantini."

[34] U. Boccioni, "La pittura futurista" (conference held in Rome, 1911), in idem, *Altri inediti e apparati critici*, Milan, 1972, p. 25.

[35] U. Boccioni, "Pittura e scultura futuriste," 1914, in idem, *Gli scritti editi e inediti*, Milan, 1971, p. 100.

[36] *Ibidem*, p. 100.

[37] *Ibidem,* pp. 203–04.

[38] In M. Denis, *Théories 1890–1910. Du Symbolisme et de Gauguin vers un nouvel ordre classique*, 1912, 3rd edition, Paris, 1913, p. 45.

[39] *Ibidem*, p. 50.

[40] R. Longhi, "Battistello," 1915, in idem, *Scritti giovanili*, Florence, 1961, p. 199.

[41] C. Carrà, "Da Cézanne a noi futuristi," May 15, 1913, in idem, *Tutti gli Scritti*, Milan, 1978, p. 14.

[42] Denis, *op. cit.*, p. VII.

[43] C. Placci, "Il neo-tradizionalismo dei francesi moderni," *Il Marzocco*, XVII, 52, December 29, 1912, pp. 1–2; A. Soffici, "Arte francese moderna," in *La Voce. Bollettino bibliografico*, January 30, 1913. See C. Pizzorusso in *Carlo Placci e l'arte francese del primo Novecento. Incontri di un dilettante fiorentino*, exh. cat., Florence, 1977, pp. 65–68.

[44] On this, see C. Zappia, *Maurice Denis e L'Italia. Journal, carteggi, carnets*, Perugia, 2001, pp. 92–95, 104–06, 150–58.

[45] B. Biagetti, "Puvis de Chavannes," *Arte Cristiana*, V, 5, May 15, 1917, pp. 130–40.

[46] *Ibidem*, p. 138.

[47] *Ibidem*, p. 133.

[48] *Ibidem*, p. 135.

[49] *Ibidem*, p. 133.

[50] See Zappia, *op. cit.,* pp. 113–15.

[51] *XIVa Esposizione Internazionale d'Arte della Città di Venezia*, exh. cat., Venice, 1924, p. 192. In the French section (curated by Léonce Bénédite and André Dezarrois) there were five Puvis de Chavannes drawings: three studies for *The Childhood of Saint Genevieve*, one study for *The Poor Fisherman* and one drawing of a female figure.

[52] C. Carrà, "Georg Schrimpf," 1924, in idem, *Tutti gli scritti*, p. 480.

[53] C. Carrà, "Misticismo e ironia," June 19, 1929, in idem, *Segreto professionale*, Florence, 1962, p. 67.

[54] "So when one hears a recent painter who is in and out of fashion claim that [in Carrà] there are not echoes of Giotto . . . but of Puvis de Chavannes, all one can do is point out that there are at least three painters of whom he knows nothing: Giotto, Puvis and Carrà." R. Longhi, "Carlo Carrà," in *XXV Biennale di Venezia*, exh. cat., Venice, 1950, pp. 70–71.

[55] R. Giolli, "Carrà," *L'Ambrosiano*, November 22, 1933.

[56] It is worth recording the comment Colacicchi made in a personal communication in 1976: "Contrary to what people say, Puvis and his group had a decisive influence on modern art. On Picasso, for example. And, in Florence, a lot of influence on Cagli. Perhaps I myself felt the influence of Puvis, whose work I first knew through reproductions, and then directly, on my last trip to Paris."

[57] Y. Obriot, "Puvis de Chavannes, Pierre," in *Enciclopedia Italiana*, XX, Rome, 1935, p. 565.

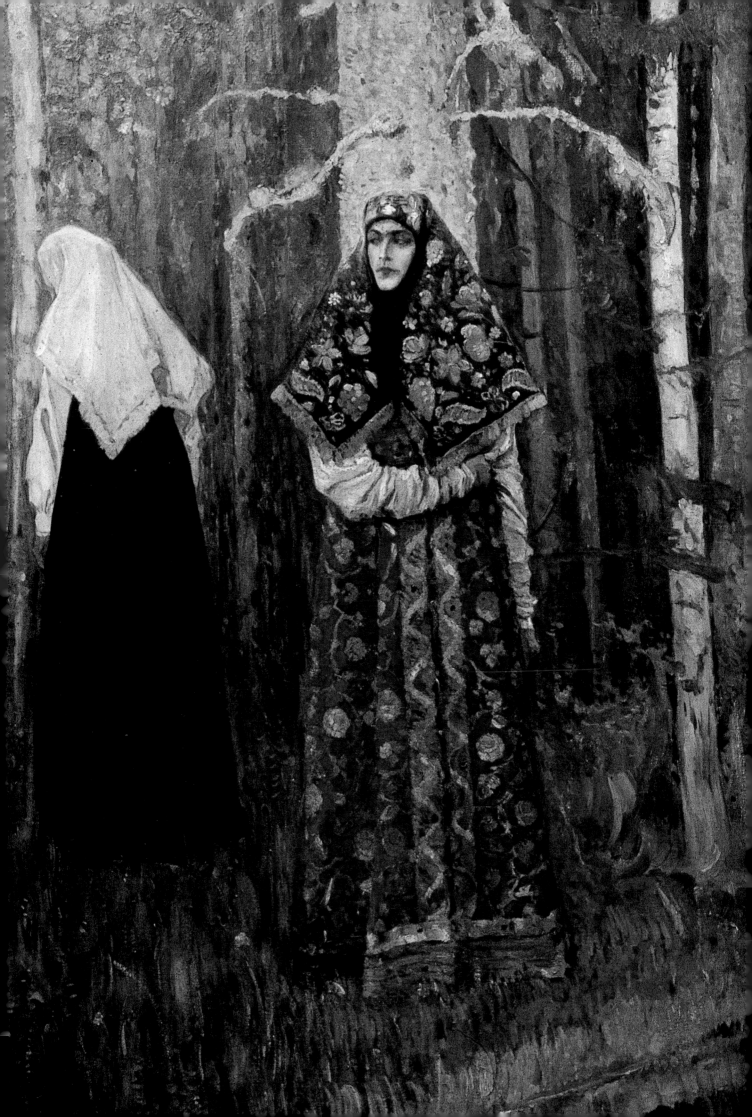

In the history of Russian painting, Pierre Puvis de Chavannes is a particularly outstanding figure. We would not be overstating it to claim that his influence on artistic life in Russia at the turn of the twentieth century is matched only by that of two other brilliant personalities of French painting: Paul Gauguin and Paul Cézanne. The reasons are easy enough to identify, if we take a look at the essential principles of Russian culture that presided over the development of painting in that period.

In nineteenth-century Russia, literature played a pivotal role in the overall culture. In a country still under a feudal regime, where fundamental civic rights were unheard of, and where serfdom, at least from a formal point of view, actually lasted up to 1861, literature was the most conspicuous platform for diffusing the most important, current or revolutionary messages. In a political system that limited the free expression of ideas, in a regime featuring quite a strict censorship, sometimes imposed by the emperor in person, writers had to speak in allegories and, emulating the figured style of Aesop's fables, seek vivid images whose significance was not immediately obvious, and instead could only be understood in the artistic, historical context of the work. First A. Pushkin, M.Y. Lermontov and N.V. Gogol, and then F.M. Dostoevsky, I.S. Turgenev, L.N. Tolstoy, A.P. Chekhov and others actually ruled the minds of several generations and even fashioned their ideology. Figurative art was deeply affected by these remarkable talents, that guided society not only in an ethical and moral sense, but an aesthetic one, according to principles inspired by a deep social awareness. Russian painting responded to the rules the writers proclaimed by creating its own form of Realism. And while being a kind of pictorial counterpart of literature, which exerted an unconditional, absolute authority, it proved itself to be admirably vital and flexible. This artistic tendency conditioned in many aspects the particular character of the evolution of late nineteenth-century Russian art, which can be deemed relatively conservative, but proved also capable of giving rise to the socially-conscious ideological avant-gardes.

The revolution broke out between the early 1880s–90s: when, in March 1881, the Emperor Alexander II (the pro-reform czar who during his reign had abolished the slavery of the serfs, granting them most of the middle-class rights) was killed in a terrorist attack, his successor Alexander III, who firmly believed it would be a mistake to introduce hasty, thoughtless reforms in such a huge territory as Russia, adopted an extremely rigid domestic policy, aimed first of all at consolidating the positive trends that had previously surfaced. The ensuing economic and social stability enabled the country to swiftly emerge from the profound crisis it had gone through at the end of the preceding emperor's rule, spurring it toward further development. Alexander III's foreign policy was also carefully thought out, and aimed at preserving the *status quo* in Europe. Alexander himself was largely responsible for the closer relations between Russia and France that coincided with the interests of both countries and safeguarded the peace, as well as strengthening the cultural ties between Russia and France.

The emperor's own aesthetic interests influenced in many ways his open Francophilia. During his many trips to Paris when he was heir to the throne, Alexander enjoyed visiting painters' studios, and purchasing paintings that appealed to his taste. A taste, in any event, that was quite conservative: Alexander III, who for years was a regular client of Durand-Ruel's, collected works by the Barbizon school artists and the most fashionable academic artists; yet not those of the Impressionists whom he indulgently called "rascals." As for Puvis de Chavannes, we can assuredly claim that the emperor was familiar with his art, and it would seem quite impressed by it. Perhaps the influence of the French master's paintings, which embodied religious and patriotic ideals, had caused Alexander III to enthusiastically embrace the idea of giving rise in Russia to a revival of religious mural art, an undertaking that would finally lead to the narrative cycles executed in several churches by artists such as V.M. Vasnetsov, M.A. Vrubel and M.V. Nesterov.

Mikhail Nesterov is perhaps the first Russian painter in whom we can clearly discern Puvis de Chavannes's strong influence. Nesterov had the opportunity to see the French master's art during his trip abroad in 1889; in the course of his stay in Paris, he visited the Panthéon and the painting section of the World Fair where several pictures by Puvis were also shown. Nesterov was impressed, but puzzled as well. In a letter from Paris, he wrote that Puvis de Chavannes "here ignores drawing and colors, but the impression is vivid."[1] In recalling the

1. Mikhail Nesterov,
Khovanshchina, detail, 1918.
Moscow, private collection

following pages
2. Pierre Puvis de Chavannes,
The Sacred Wood, 1884–86
Lyon, Musée des Beaux-Arts

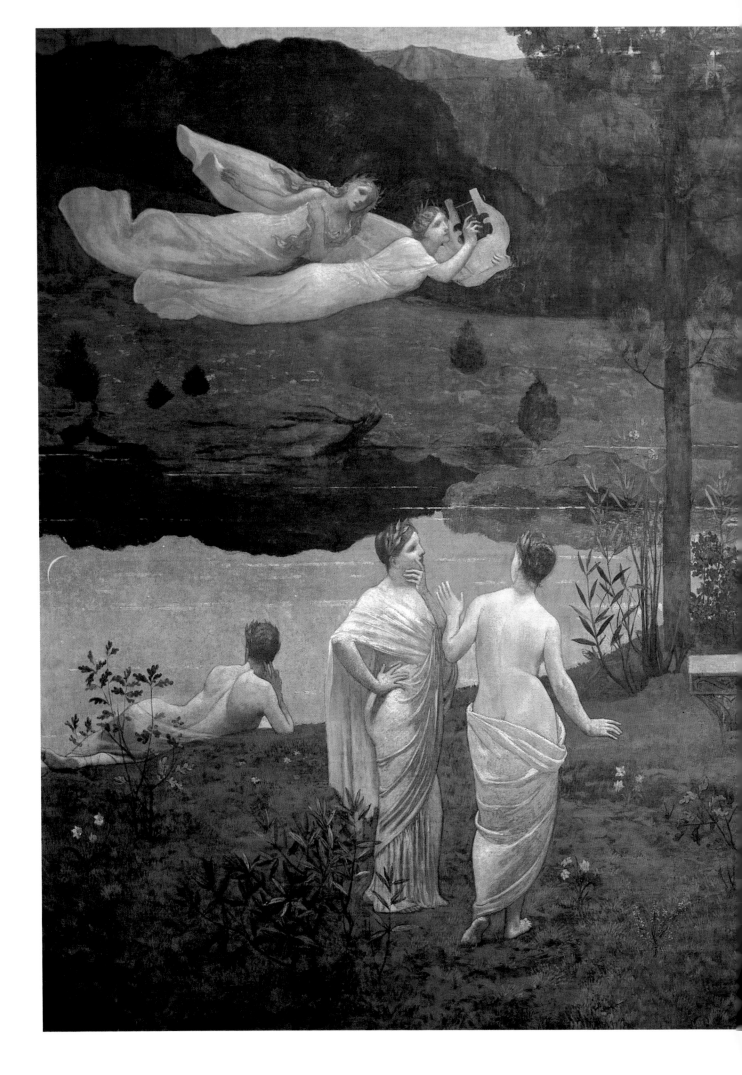

228

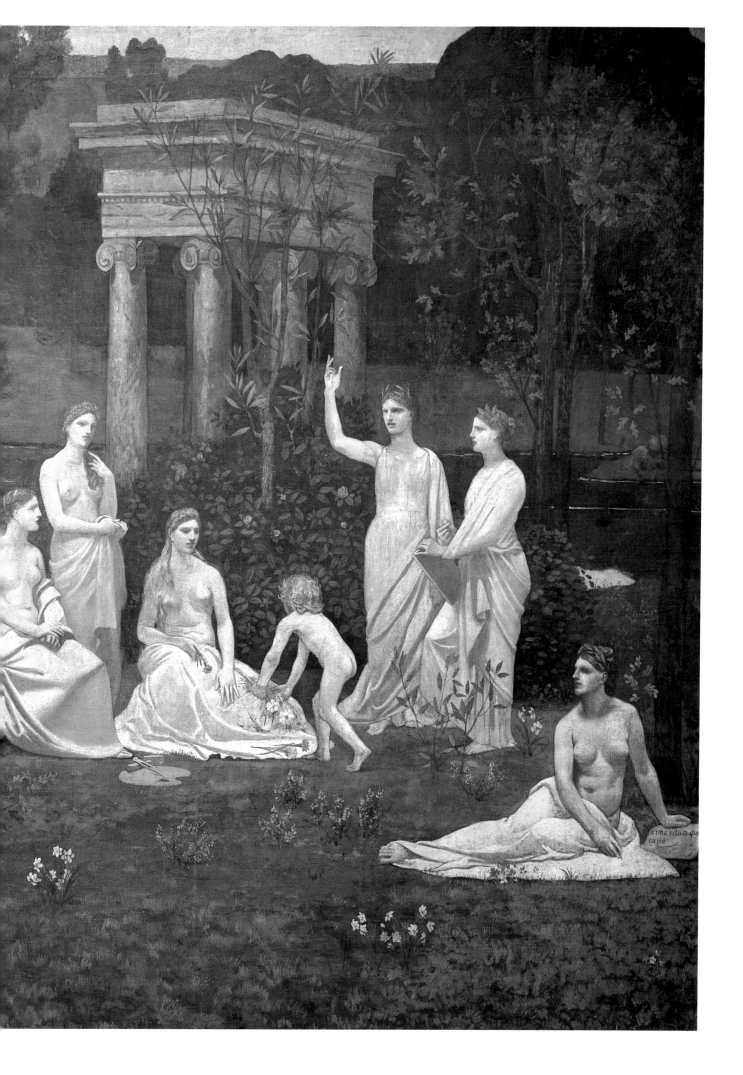

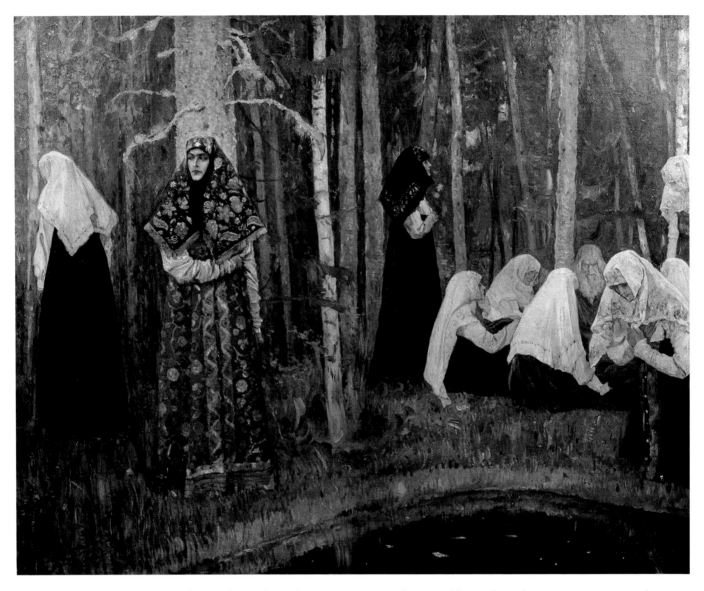

3. Mikhail Nesterov,
Khovanshchina, 1918.
Moscow, private collection

lesson drawn from that trip many years later, and his early enthusiasm—experienced on seeing the painting by J. Bastien-Lepage *Joan of Arc*—the painter wrote: "The Panthéon alone
with its Puvis de Chavannes aroused in me a new surge of intense emotions. Puvis's *Saint
Genevieve* nearly carried me back to the Florence of Ghirlandaio's frescoes. . . ."[2] And further on: "Puvis fully grasped the spirit of the Florentines of the Renaissance, adding his contribution to some of their principles, to their achievements: he added what vibrated and sang
in him, he unified everything with the modern technique and offered his homeland this wonderful gift that made him immortal."[3] His summing-up of all these reflections is also extremely
significant: "Of all the modern Western painters, Puvis and Bastien-Lepage, they alone, gave
me all that all the artists of all the other countries put together gave me, and I felt that had
I been in France for months, or even a year or two, I wouldn't have been able to gain anything more profitable for myself than what I had learned from those two so different artists.
All their characteristics were precious to me: talent, intelligence and knowledge, the great
school they came from; a very successful blend that for me placed them way above all the
others. They focused all my sympathies, and seeing them after my trip to Italy, I felt that henceforth I could deem my European training, my assimilation of Western culture, completed.
I could serenely return to my native land, and devote myself, at home, to somehow carrying
out what I had seen, and then, perhaps, something would have come out of it that would not
have been too negative for Russian art."[4]

All of Nesterov's subsequent artistic production, until the October Revolution (after which the artist could no longer openly work on the themes he had dealt with before), bears the indisputable mark of those Parisian impressions. In that sense, of particular interest is the narrative cycle devoted to the life of Saint Sergei of Radonezh, an outstanding personality in the political and religious life of old Russia, during the battles to free the country from the Tatar-Mongol yoke. The paintings *Vision of Young Bartholomew* (1889–90, Moscow, Tretyakov State Gallery), *Youth of Saint Sergei* (1892–97, same collection), *The Labors of Saint Sergei* (1896–97, same collection), *Saint Sergei of Radonezh* (1899, Saint Petersburg, Russian State Museum) and the watercolor sketch for an unexecuted painting titled *Saint Sergei Blesses Dimitri Donskoj at the Battle of Kulikovo* (1897, Moscow, Tretyakov State Gallery) offer a certain likeness with the frescoes, the episodes of the life of Saint Genevieve, executed at the Paris Panthéon by Puvis de Chavannes. We can imagine that it was precisely what Alexander III was referring to when, during an exhibition in front of the *Youth of Saint Sergei*, he suddenly stopped and began talking about the famous French artist. Furthermore, we can observe a definite kinship, especially as regards content: Nesterov's project is just as literary, patriotic and laden with symbolic meanings, and appeals to the viewer's national awareness. As for the formal aspect, as an easel painter, Nesterov proves to be closer to Bastien-Lepage and the traditions of the Russian school of Realism. In reviving the fond motifs of his homeland, expressing them in the language of plein air painting, the artist reproduced the forms of nature in a slightly stylized version, in the spirit of the modern style that had just appeared in Russia, thus introducing in his works a shade of subjectivity.

The *Vision of Young Bartholomew* was the very first work by Nesterov to be shown to the public on the artist's return to Russia. The painting, with its wonderful sense of poetry and novel way of interpreting the subject, made a deep impression on his contemporaries. The figures of the youth and the *starec*, although treated in a naturalistic style, are slightly flattened and seem to be a superimposition on the landscape: the result somewhat recalls the style of icons; and on the other hand, even the composition of the background landscape, which is stylized and consists of characteristic fragments, does not create a perspective distance from the figures. Thus, the entire picture has an unusual unitary character. *Vision*, presented at the XVIII exhibition of the Company of Wanderers (*Peredvizhniki*), became, we might say, the first public display of the modern Russian style in painting, or to be more accurate, that variant of the "new style" we might define as "the evolution . . . of the traditional style of Russian Realism in the late nineteenth century."[5] The painting was the object of heated discussion and became a sort of "litmus paper" revealing the presence of real clashes among the first-generation *Peredvizhniki* and those of the following generations, and thus lay the ground for the break that would later occur within the association.

Vision aroused an intense reaction of indignation in V.V. Stasov, the main ideologist of Russian Realism who, commenting on the art of the young member of the Wanderers, angrily wrote: "Among the newcomers there is one I do not care for at all. It is Nesterov. Not so much because the artist seems to only want to depict hermitages, monks of the strictest rule, scenes of monastic life, and so on: If such is his vocation, all right; the trouble is that he depicts all this in a hypocritical, falsely naive, and a bit sanctimonious way, affecting a certain unnatural air, a stiffness of lines, landscapes and colors, something dead and mummified. In our day in France, an entire school of these hypocrites has appeared, led by Puvis de Chavannes; recently the French brought us here one of those paintings (the *Annunciation*). Do we by any chance want to start imitating them, welcoming them with open arms? God forbid. Away with these landscapes made of trees that are as dry and haggard as street-sweepers, with faded colors, like dirty old rugs. No, I still hope Mr. Nesterov will quit this road that leads nowhere and start having to do with real life."[6]

The further evolution of Nesterov's art does not coincide with the famous critic's wishes. Early in the last decade of the century, the artist began to devote himself seriously to the decorative painting of churches. The tendency had been encouraged by Alexander III's active policy as regards church building, and also the upsurge of interest in the history and art of Rus', then undergoing a revival in society. The paintings Nesterov executed in the cathedral of Saint Vladimir in Kiev (1890–95) and the church of Saint Alexander Nevski at Abastumani (1898–1904) are further evidence that the author was familiar with the art of the medieval masters, but also of contemporary Western art, especially Bastien-Lepage and Puvis de Cha-

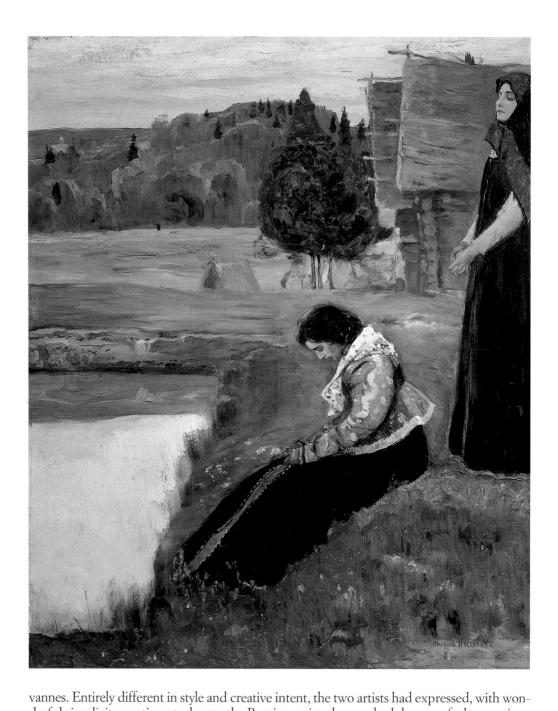

opposite page
5. Viktor Borisov-Musatov
The Emerald Necklace, 1903–04.
Moscow, Tretyakov State Gallery

6. Viktor Borisov-Musatov,
The Artificial Lake, 1902.
Moscow, Tretyakov State Gallery

vannes. Entirely different in style and creative intent, the two artists had expressed, with wonderful simplicity, sentiments dear to the Russian artist: they evoked dreams of a harmonious life, represented harmonious human beings endowed with deep faith, capable, if necessary, of joyfully accepting the crown of martyrdom. The greatest works Nesterov executed in the Kiev cathedral (*Saint Boris, Saint Gleb, Saint Barbara, Resurrection, Christmas*) and the church of Abastumani (*Vision of the Mother of God to Saint Nina, Saint Seraphim of Sarov, Saint Nina, Saint George, Annunciation* and others) might seem at first sight to embody those dreamlike qualities, even if the context in which the figures appear seems quite flimsy and ephemeral, one of precariousness and feverish expectation. Despite formal likenesses and even actual quotations, in Nesterov's works the placid monumentality that characterizes Puvis de Chavannes's frescoes is but a mere echo. The Russian artist, although rejecting the very academic traditions the famous French master had overcome, failed to do so in the execution of truly monumental images: He would always remain a lyric and an easel painter. In stylizing the landscape and the figures, the painter seems to stylize the mood permeating the images as well. The morbid exaltation typical of Nesterov's figures is an expression of his feel-

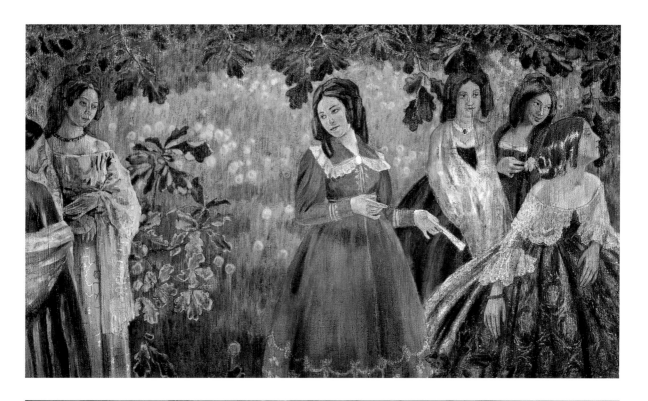

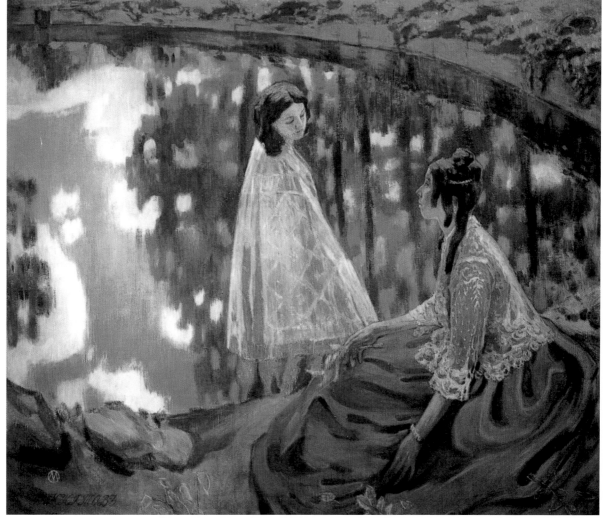

ings of devotion and his vision of the world; so the images offered to the worship of the faithful lacked the "objectivity" he had sought.

Several years after Nesterov's trip to Paris, Puvis's name and art had begun to be widely known
in Russia, while his works were shown on several occasions in exhibitions in Saint Petersburg. No longer was anyone surprised that there were artists who admired the French master, nor were they ostracized as they had once been. In 1895, Viktor Borisov-Musatov, one
of the most sensitive, poetic exponents of Russian painting, went to Paris with the firm intention of becoming his pupil. And we can imagine his disappointment when he realized he
could not carry out his plan. We read in a letter he wrote to his mother: "During the entire
journey I was afraid of arriving and discovering he had died, because he is already over seventy years old. Instead he did something worse: He got married, and just before the wedding he closed down his studio. As soon as I arrived, I sought the newly-wed's new address
and appeared at his house around nine in the morning. He greeted me attired in a pale lilac
dressing-gown; I told him about my aspiration and, while expressing his appreciation for my
intention, he told me he was no longer taking on any pupils."[7] Thus, Borisov-Musatov had
to seek his Parisian training in the studio of F. Cormon, who provided him with solid notions
of craftsmanship, but was not capable of forming his artistic personality. So Musatov's true
master was still Puvis de Chavannes, whose influence can certainly be discerned in the white-
washed tones of his paintings, in the slow, melodic rhythm of his decorative compositions.
The poetry of an era of "wigs and crinolines" and "noblemen's nests" in its declining days
permeates the Russian artist's works (*Gobelin, Artificial Lake, Emerald Necklace* [Moscow,
Tretyakov State Gallery]; *Twilight Walk, Spring* [Saint Petersburg, Russian State Museum],
and others). For Borisov-Musatov, contemplation and unison with the natural environment
were the means whereby man attains an inner harmony capable of transfiguring the world.
It is not so much a withdrawal from reality, as the representation through individual mediation of a better present, where the references to the past somehow attenuate its clearly utopian nature. Therein lies the unquestionable affinity between the perception of reality inherent to these two personalities, the Russian artist and the French master.

Precisely because of his tendency to look to the past, Borisov-Musatov appears in agreement
with the young Saint Petersburg artists who rallied around the review *Mir Iskusstva* [Russ-

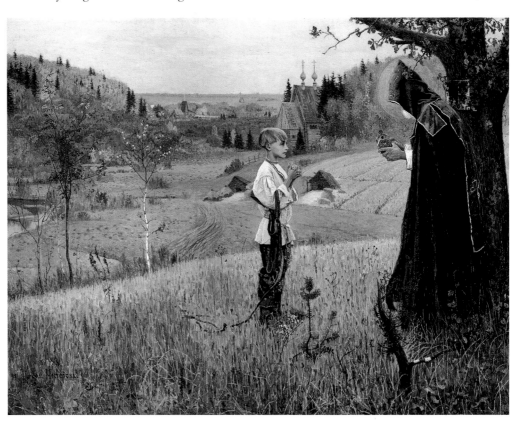

7. Mikhail Nesterov,
Vision of Young Bartholomew,
1889–90.
Moscow, Tretyakov State Gallery

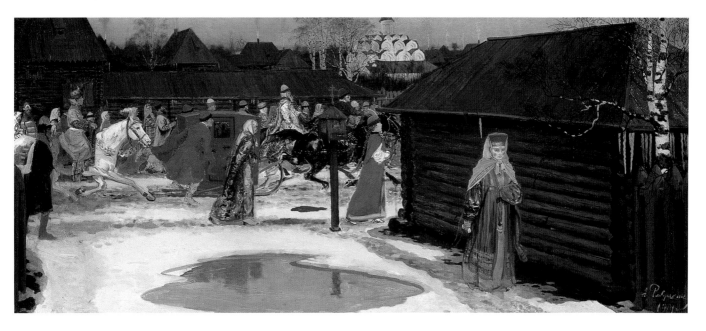

8. Andrei Petrovich Pyabushkin,
*The Wedding Procession in
Moscow*, 1901.
Moscow, Tretyakov State Gallery

ian World of Art] they had founded. For the members of the group, Puvis de Chavannes was one of their idols: it was actually what largely determined their first interest in M.V. Nesterov and V.M. Vasnetsov. When Serge Diaghilev, the soul and leader of the group, came to the West, he felt it his duty not only to acquaint himself with Puvis de Chavannes's most important works and meet the artist in person, but also to diffuse his oeuvre. We know that the future famous impresario, the organizer of the "Russian Seasons" in Paris, had placed in his studio "a splendid woman's head by Puvis de Chavannes."[8] Diaghilev deemed it indispensable to include the French master's works in the International Art Exhibition held in 1899 in Saint Petersburg [9] (one of his first large-scale projects) and furthermore to reproduce it in an issue of *Mir Iskusstva*. As in the past, V.V. Stasov expressed his opposition in every way possible, accusing the review of "an unbearable decadent spirit." But by now the criticism addressed to the French master seemed more like a cry of desperation, having lost all sense of objectivity: "What in the world could be as hackneyed, academic, stiff and boring as these temples, these women, nude or covered with draperies, of these little fake antique puttos and these angels fluttering about in the sky? My God, how they annoy and discourage my soul!"[10] At the time Stasov could not have known that a young artist who was his friend, who would often drop by to see him in the Public Library to ask him for advice and do some historical research, was to become one of Puvis de Chavannes's most faithful followers, and in 1910 would revive the *Mir Iskusstva* group. That young painter was N.K. Roerich.

Unlike Nesterov and Borisov-Musatov, Nikolai Roerich went to Paris in 1900 when Puvis was already dead: This did not prevent him from mentioning him later on as his second master, right after the landscape artist A.I. Kuindzhi, with whom Roerich had studied at the Saint Petersburg Academy. At the time, Roerich wrote, describing his impression on seeing Puvis de Chavannes's frescoes: "The more I immerse myself in the contemplation of his works, the more I hear about the way he worked, his life and habits, the more amazed I am at the great likeness there is with many factors that concern me, too."[11] The creative career Roerich was later to follow, achieving his own original pictorial and ethical-philosophical system, proves he had assimilated Puvis de Chavannes's lesson on a level that was not merely formal. The French master and his disciple the Russian artist have many likenesses, most of all in their way of approaching the issues of life and art, which is clearly seen in Roerich's pictorial practice. Like Puvis de Chavannes, Roerich sought to elevate the viewer to new spiritual heights by actively availing himself of the strong impression produced by monumental painting in decorating churches and creating cycles of decorative panels. If we look at their respective biographies and compare the two artists' statements about themselves and their art, we cannot help but be struck by the abundance of common elements. Roerich and Puvis de Chavannes both aspired to an all-embracing synthesis and sought to create symbolic, portentous

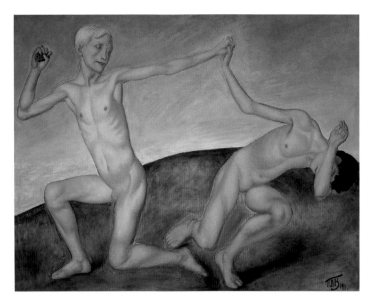
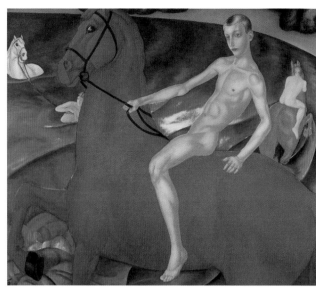

9. Kuz'ma Petrov-Vodkin,
Boys Playing, 1911.
Saint Petersburg, Russian State
Museum

10. Kuz'ma Petrov-Vodkin,
Red Horse Bathing, 1912.
Moscow, Tretyakov State Gallery

images, authentic plastic counterparts of certain ideas; they have the same views on the past, on work, the role of color and impressions drawn from nature, and the same intents with regards to creative methods.[12] Thus, for Roerich, Puvis de Chavannes was less someone who taught him his craft (like Borisov-Musatov, Roerich had also learned his technique in Paris from F. Cormon) than a spiritual guide, a sort of mirror in which the young artist saw reflected his own future image.

The last sign of interest for Puvis de Chavannes in the history of pre-revolutionary Russia occurred in the transition period between the first and second decades of the twentieth century. In those years the situation had radically changed: not only Realism, but the modern style as well had exhausted its potentials, and avant-garde trends were beginning to appear on the artistic scene. At the same time, a certain Neoclassic slant could be observed, especially among those artists who believed it could somehow be an "antidote" to the stylistic eclecticism (or what they considered a lack of style) of contemporary art. Such attitudes were shared both by recognized artists, such as V.A. Serov and L.S. Bakst, and painters of the younger generation, among whom the most gifted and representative was K.S. Petrov-Vodkin. In his works, the Neoclassic reminiscences came down to him precisely from Puvis de Chavannes himself. Compared to Nesterov or Borisov-Musatov, Petrov-Vodkin would be the one to come closest to his model. This situation was exactly the opposite of the one ten or fifteen years before: whereas in the past the slightest hint of academism provoked an instant, distinct rejection, now the young painter's works such as *Shore* (1908) and *Sleep* (1910; both in Saint Petersburg, Russian State Museum), featuring an obvious classical slant, could instead be interpreted as expressing the most advanced trends.

The stimulus for Petrov-Vodkin to create such works had arisen during his stay in Paris in 1906–08, when he had worked in several studios and shown his own works in Parisian exhibitions. It would seem that Petrov-Vodkin had turned to Puvis de Chavannes in part following the impression produced by Maurice Denis's paintings (*Polyphemus*, 1907; *The Green Beach*, 1919; both in Moscow, Pushkin State Museum of Fine Arts). At that time, Denis was trying out a neo-academic style. Both *Shore* and *Sleep* display to the same degree the painter's serious study of Puvis de Chavannes: We can see it in his treatment of the individual figurative forms, as well as in his overall approach to composition. Petrov-Vodkin did not hesitate to make actual quotations, borrowing from Puvis de Chavannes motifs or certain poses of the figures.

Besides, in the instance of Petrov-Vodkin, the fascination for Puvis de Chavannes was just an episode in the elaboration of his own original creative conception. The artist's later works, including the frescoes for the church of Vasily Zlatoverhi at Ovruc (Ukraine) dated 1910, *Boys Playing* (1911, Saint Petersburg, Russian State Museum), *Red Horse Bathing* (1912, Moscow, Tretyakov State Gallery) and *Madonna of Mercy of the Wicked Hearts* (1914–15, Saint Petersburg, Russian State Museum), reintroduce old Russian mural and icon painting as stylistic models, and even relegate his recent Parisian enthusiasms to a position of second importance. Notwithstanding, it is clear that, as in the case of Roerich, the noble spiritual content of Puvis de Chavannes's monumental art was to leave a lasting mark on the painter's entire later work.

Kuz'ma Petrov-Vodkin belongs to the group of Russian artists who, in 1917, welcomed the October Revolution and took part in the new organization of cultural life. We should mention that even prior to the revolutionary events, Puvis de Chavannes's art had aroused the enthusiasm of several leading members of the Bolshevic party who, having emigrated abroad, had on occasion visited Paris. A.V. Lunacharsky who was appointed People's Commissar for Culture after the Revolution, could make out in the works of the French artist: " a glimmer of the future, a bit of clear sky coming out of the clouds of coal smoke, the clouds of steam and the looming storm of today,"[13] as well as the prototype of a monumental art that could be created by a regenerated humanity. Equally struck by Puvis de Chavannes's painting, in which "everything was seen through the prism of a luminous dream,"[14] was V.A. Antonov-Ovseenko who later on, in October 1917, was to lead the assault on the Winter Palace, where the temporary government was assembled. So we can assume with some validity that, when it sought to execute idyllic portrayals of "Soviet reality" or the "shining future," the academic monumental painting of the Stalin era emulated to some extent Puvis de Chavannes's art that describes a world in which life was ruled by the natural laws of harmony, industry and beauty.

[1] M. V. Nesterov, *Pis'ma*, selected letters, with introduction and notes, edited by A. A. Rusakova, Leningrad, 1988, p. 56.
[2] M. V. Nesterov, *Vospominanija*, edited, with introduction and notes, by A.A. Rusakova, Moscow, 1989, p. 132.
[3] *Ibidem.*
[4] *Ibidem*, p. 133.
[5] G.Y. Sternin, *Hudožestvennaja žizn' Rossii na rubeč XIX–XXvekov*, Moscow, 1970, p. 158.
[6] Quoted in S.N. Durylin, *Nesterov v žizni i tvorčestve*, Moscow, 1976, 2nd ed., p. 141.
[7] Quoted in A.A. Rusakova, *Viktor. El'pidiforovič Borisov-Musatov*, Leningrad-Moscow, 1966, p. 40.
[8] A. Benois, *Moivospominanija*, Moscow, 1993, 2nd ed., in 5 parts: part I, II, III, p. 646.
[9] Puvis de Chavannes partecipated in the show with several sketches.
[10] V.V. Stasov, *Izbrannye sočinenija*, Moscow, 1952, 3 vols., vol. III, pp. 237–38.
[11] E.N. Poljakova, *Nikolaj Rerih*, Moscow, 1973, p. 57.
[12] For further details on the topic, see A.D. Alehin, "N.K. Rerih iPjuvi de Šavann," in *"Utrennjaja Zvezda," Naučno-hudožestvennyj illjustrirovannyjal'manah meždunarodnogo centra Rerihov*, nos. 2–3, 1994–97 (Moscow 1997).
[13] Quoted in Sternin, *op. cit.*, p. 101.
[14] *Ibidem*, pp. 227–28.

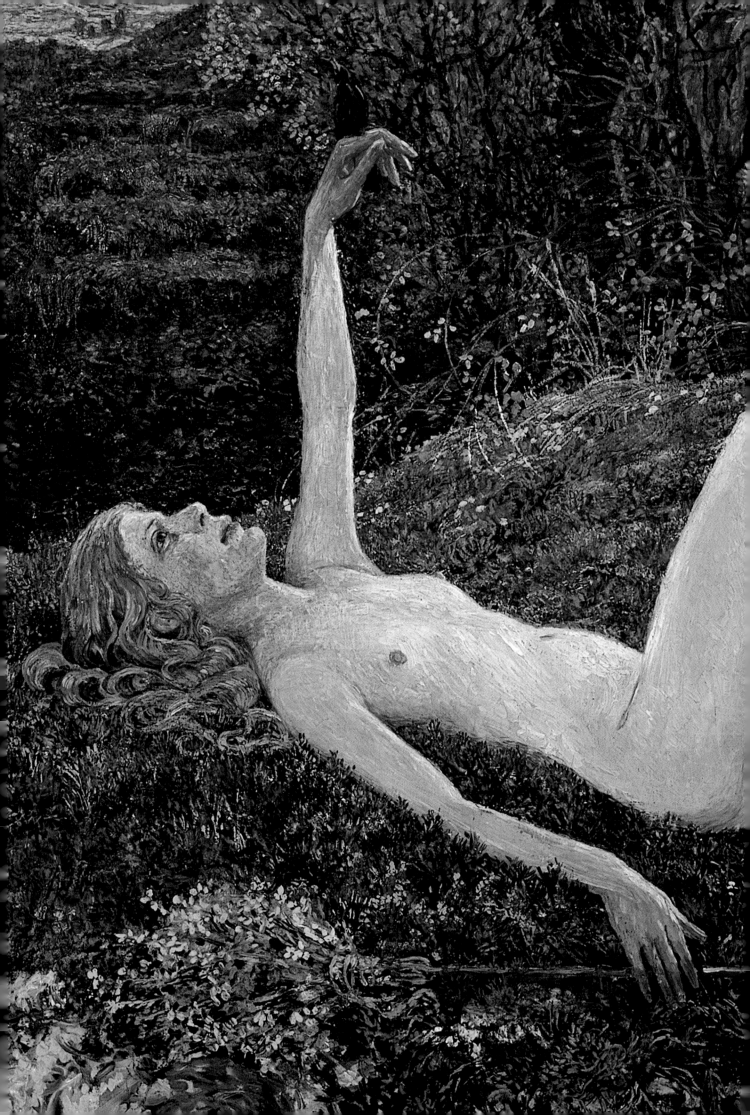

Thomas Gaehtgens

The Critic's Opinion of Puvis de Chavannes in German-speaking Countries around 1900. Artists, Critics, Art Historians.

Puvis de Chavannes as Seen by German and Swiss Artists

Both before and after 1900, German collectors were among the earliest and most significant discoverers of French Impressionism. Under the directorship of Hugo von Tschudi, the National Gallery in Berlin even acquired a number of Impressionist works—albeit in the face of determined opposition—at a time when in France the debate over the Caillebotte bequest was still raging.[1] The enthusiasm for Manet, Monet, Renoir and Degas was not, however, bound up with appreciation for another painter who in his homeland was then enjoying all the honors of fame and success: Puvis de Chavannes. While Liebermann used his art and his art collection to inspire his friends and fellow members of the Secession, the art dealer Cassirer and Hugo von Tschudi, to build a bridge between France and Germany and thus assist French modernism to make an international breakthrough in terms of recognition, only a very few works by France's leading monumental painter found their way to Germany.[2]

It is nonetheless significant that the art of Puvis de Chavannes did find its advocates in Germany. A number of artists found inspiration in his work, but above all there were art critics and historians ready and willing to defend him, sometimes strenuously. Their views reflect the fact that in the German cultural area no single approach to modernism was regarded as the one proper path. Hopes for a renewal of academic tradition were also able to identify with the model of Puvis's art. The critical reception of French art is also thus in some ways a reflection of a coming to terms with artistic tradition at home. Simplicity of line, concentration on balance and harmony, the renewal of monumental painting after the example of the early Italian Renaissance, muted tonality of color and poetic atmosphere: these were the criteria on which the positive judgment of German-speaking artists and critics was based.

German artists also reacted directly to the art of Puvis de Chavannes. Although few of his works were on view in German galleries and museums, painters could nevertheless familiarize themselves with his output through reproductions and visits to Paris. Böcklin, Marées, Thoma, Hodler, Beckmann and Hofer—to name but a few—came nonetheless from a different tradition of painting. The way they understood the French artist's work was thus conditioned by their preconceptions. They did indeed admire and perhaps were fascinated and impressed, even inspired by Puvis, but it must be recognized that in the end they went their own separate ways, absorbing his influence only to a limited extent.

Böcklin

Böcklin and Puvis de Chavannes were both convinced that the culture of the ancient world continued to hold its validity in the present day. Notwithstanding this shared belief, their art is quite distinct in character.

Although the two artists probably never met, it may be assumed on the basis of their celebrity that by the 1890s at the latest they must both have been familiar with each other's work. There is no record of any opinion on the part of Böcklin regarding Puvis de Chavannes. However, a comparison of *The Sacred Wood* (1866) with Puvis's *The Sacred Wood Dear to the Arts and Muses* makes it abundantly clear just how opposed were their approaches as painters. Böcklin attempts to draw the viewer into the picture by the magical light and power of his palette and the enticing composition of the lines of trees that open outwards. In contrast, Puvis's antique scene appears to belong to a world of art closed in upon itself, allegorical and remote from the present. While the Swiss painter dramatizes elegiac, heroic moods as the driving forces of emotional feeling, the French artist emphasizes the detachment of observer and representation through the balance of form, quietude and color. Although both tread common ground in terms of subject matter, they differ fundamentally in its treatment. Puvis continued a painterly tradition that descended to the nineteenth century from antiquity via the Renaissance and Poussin; Böcklin portrays the search for the self, for the meaning of existence and destiny, in cryptic compositions that convey Romantic, fantastic atmospheres but are expressed in naturalistic form.

Böcklin and Puvis de Chavannes were contemporaries who shared a comparable formative background and similar themes, but were separated by their distinct visions of painting.

1. Heinrich Vogeler,
Spring, detail, 1909.
Kulturstiftung
Landkreis Osterholz

Hans von Marées

Hans von Marées and Puvis de Chavannes were contemporaries, but it is unlikely that they knew each other personally; indeed we cannot even be sure whether Marées ever saw original works by Puvis. When staying in Paris in 1867, the German painter formed an impression of his French colleague's work that was anything but favorable. In a letter to Hildebrand on July 23 he wrote: "I found it very interesting to have an opportunity to see a large number of works by the modern French artists all together. There are plenty of specific things which are commendable, but I saw not a single work which showed absolute mastery, nothing which could serve one as a model. On the other, hand the gallery of Old Masters is one of the finest there is. . . ."[3] Nowhere does Marées note that he had seen works by Puvis.[4] When he returned to the French capital in 1874 he continued to be unenthusiastic about the work of his contemporaries and once again made no mention of Puvis.

Art historians have occasionally alluded to the parallels between the works of the two artists, but so far no thorough comparison of their respective œuvres has been carried out. Quite apart from whether the two artists actually met, the question of the comparability of their artistic ambitions is of some interest. Remarkably, comparisons have more frequently been made between Marées's painting and that of Delacroix, Manet and Cézanne.[5]
There are several obvious reasons for this. Firstly, Marées's work was long given consideration only from the point of view of form and decorative organization. The pictorial subject matter tended to be seen as marginal. Indeed, his having gone beyond the concrete theme in favor of the independence of artistic form was viewed as being the essence of his modernity. A timely critique of this kind of approach to Marées's painting has only recently been offered.[6] Another factor which separated the two artists was their entirely different modes of expression in paint.

In subject matter at least, a number of parallels do emerge in the work of Puvis de Chavannes and Hans von Marées. The mythological subjects of *The Sacred Wood Dear to the Arts and Muses* and *The Hesperides*, both completed in the 1880s, fall into the classical tradition of depictions of Arcadia. (figs. 2–4) But the two paintings reveal artistic approaches that could hardly be more different. Puvis places his figures in a peaceful landscape, bringing together figure and nature in a unified whole, whereas Marées wrestles with the presence of plastic form in paint. There are individual attitudes and poses in the works of both artists which are virtually equivalent, and yet it is difficult to imagine how the contrast between their different interpretations of the figures could be greater. Puvis emphasizes line and surface, adjusting his colors to a delicate overall tone, while Marées builds up a sculptural presence with magical, dramatic strong lighting.
Both artists blazed a trail toward modernism. The influence of the German was to be carried forward by Hildebrand and Lehmbruck, while the flatness of the picture surface in Puvis pointed French artists toward abstraction.

Klinger

Max Klinger spent much of the period between 1883 and 1885 in several lengthy stays in Paris. There can be no doubt that he was profoundly impressed by the work of Puvis de Chavannes. He must have known the paintings in the Panthéon; whether he already knew the murals for the staircase in the Lyon Museum, where work was in progress at the time, cannot be ascertained. On the other hand, we may take it that he was familiar with *The Sacred Grove Dear to the Arts and Muses* (1884), at least from reproductions. At all events, the work of the French artist was able to provide a decisive source of inspiration both for Klinger's monumental paintings, and for his mythological-symbolist themes. He may well have had works by Puvis in mind—for instance the monumental decorations for the Sorbonne—not only for *L'Heure bleue*, but also when he produced his own scheme for the hall at the University of Leipzig in 1905–06.[7]
The composition, symbolist figures and themes of Klinger's large-scale paintings, such as *Christ in Olympus* (1897), lent by the Österreichische Galerie of Vienna to the Museum der Bildenden Künste in Leipzig (fig. 5), also recall Puvis de Chavannes. At the same time, however,

2-4. Hans von Marées,
The Hesperides.
Munich, Bayerische
Staatsgemäldesammlungen

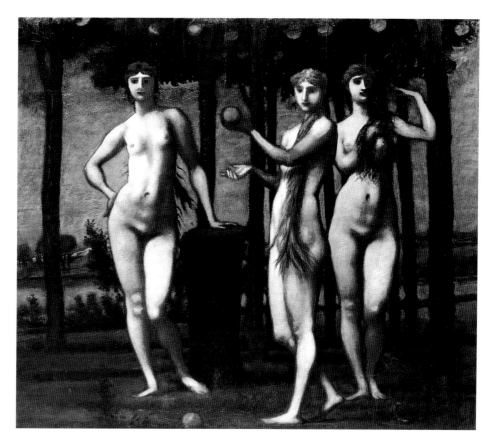

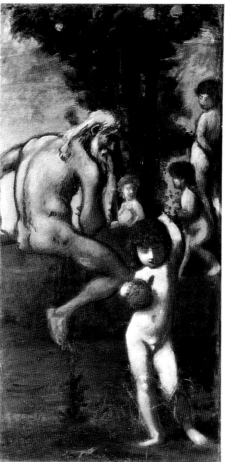

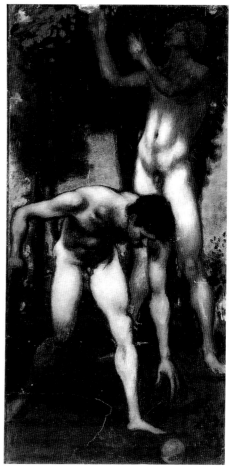

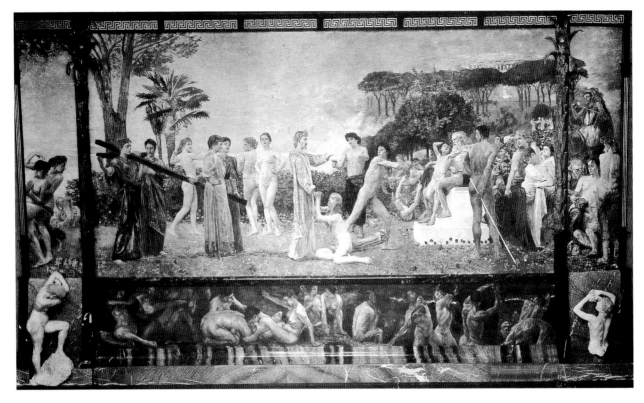

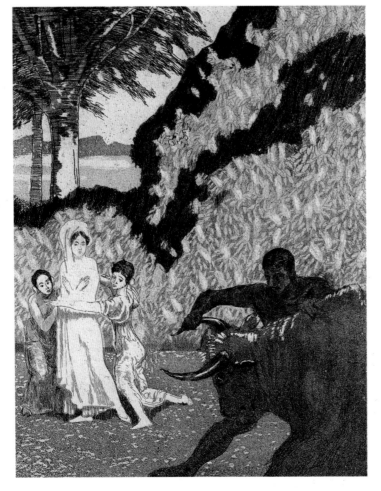

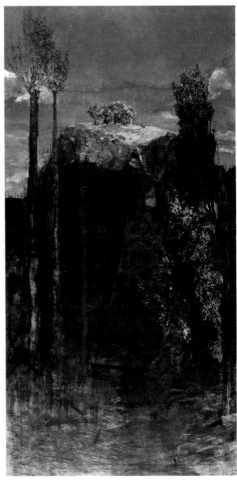

5. Max Klinger,
Christ in Olympus, 1897.
Leipzig, Museum der Bildenden
Künste

6. Max Klinger, *Scene with Bull*.
Darmstadt Landesmuseum

7. Max Klinger, *Nemi*. Halle,
Staatliche Galerie Moritzburg

they are also characteristically different from the French artist's work. In line with his own artistic development, Klinger did not move toward the abstraction of figure and landscape that is so typical of Puvis. Nor did he adopt Puvis's use of color—learned from Quattrocento masters—to create fresco effects in pictures painted on canvas. Rather, he preferred to use the medium of naturalism as a vehicle for symbolist themes, creating a tension which still creates a sense of dichotomy in the viewer, even today. While Puvis sought harmony and balance through theme and idealized form, Klinger placed a Christian or mythological subject in his own present. Puvis's stylized linearity of picture surface and subtle arrangement of chromatic tones contrast with the realistic representation of the body, drawn directly from the model, by which Klinger sought to give his historical painting a sense of both past and present. Puvis de Chavannes was thus completely reinterpreted by the German painter, who shaped the subtle message of his art into a challenge to the viewer to confront the actualization of Christian and mythological truths. In almost brutal fashion, Klinger removed that idealistic component of the classicizing approach to art, inherited from Poussin and Ingres, which Puvis had developed.

In this context, it is not surprising that Klinger's comments on Puvis were unflattering: "What I've seen by him so far was all contemplative in brightness, fraught with world-weariness and trying very hard to be clever. He likes children of nature . . . and quite deliberately leaves them staring ahead, oppressed by the universality of fate. . . . I prefer Impressionism to this kind of thing."[8]

It is revealing that it was exactly this trait of Klinger's paintings which contemporaries defined as "German." In his monograph on the artist, Max Schmid wrote: "We may be proud that we possess an artist who, though he waves no banner with a national motto, is entirely German from the roots of his hair to the soles of his feet; an artist who is unmatched in his own distinctive character by any rival from the other art-producing peoples. For although he long trained abroad, in Brussels, Paris and Rome, although he took in with open eyes the advantages of French painting technique and the greatness of the Old Masters of Italy, Klinger has remained true to himself. . . ."[9] In his efforts to distinguish Klinger from his French sources of inspiration, the author did not even mention the name of Puvis de Chavannes.

Hodler

Although Ferdinand Hodler did study Puvis de Chavannes, did admire his art and was inspired by him in finding his own artistic path, on closer examination the art of the Swiss painter also appears to stand alone. True, Hodler himself felt there was a kinship between his painting and that of Puvis.[10] Their admiration of each other's skills was mutual; as president of the Jury at the Salon du Champ-de-Mars, Puvis advocated the selection of Hodler's masterpiece *Night* (1891). This was an important confirmation of the talent of the Swiss painter, who would have to wait many years before achieving the same kind of recognition at home.

But despite Hodler's regard for Puvis's painting and despite the stimuli which he gained from pictures such as *The Fisherman's Family* and the great decorative paintings, there is no direct route from the delicate idealism of the French artist to the dramatic pathos of Hodler's expressionist art.[11]

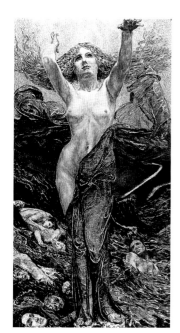

8. Max Klinger, *Beauty*.
Hamburg, Kunsthalle

While Hodler did express a positive judgment of Puvis's work, it remains more significant that his own artistic creativity went in a fundamentally different direction from that of his older French colleague. In contrast to Puvis's religious and mythological themes, Hodler's art is based on his own inner experience. It is an expression of drives, of distress that he had lived through personally, and of concrete fears. While Puvis attempts to shift a traditional figurative heritage to his contemporary context, as an ethical and artistic ideal, Hodler instead breaks with all moral and aesthetic conventions. Alexander Dückers has described Hodler's independence in convincing fashion: "Hodler needed no external impulse to choose his materials; although he had traveled far and wide in art historical terms, he lived in Geneva—far away from the great centers of his day—and it is open to question whether he followed any particular examples in bringing that historical lesson up to the present, say Puvis de Chavannes for *The Dialog* or Courbet for *The Brave Woman*."[12]

It is precisely from this contrast in their respective approaches to art that Hodler's route toward modernism emerges clearly. The artistic world that Puvis dreamed of points to an inner harmony, an Arcadia beyond the reality of metropolitan life, whereas Hodler, starkly driven by existential impulses, needed to destroy just such peace and balance. Puvis's art arose out of a renewal of culture and tradition. His monumental pictorial cycles were made for churches, museums and universities, bound up in an intellectual and spiritualizing context. In contrast, Hodler's paintings are the result of a human being left to his own resources in a secluded natural environment, attempting to free himself from his own drives and impulses through art.

Hodler's flouting of the laws of perspective which seemed brutal to his contemporaries, and his failure to adopt an illusory pictorial space in his works were both elements quite opposed to Puvis's stylized representation of an Arcadian dream.

Hodler's modernity is more conspicuous against the background of the art of Puvis de Chavannes. The French painter can have provided no more than a limited example for the Swiss. Hodler's mental sensibilities needed to break new ground to express themselves fully, shifting from a dream world into existential crises based on real experience. Puvis de Chavannes and Hodler are separated by more than just a generation: they are distinguished by two completely different ways of understanding art. Hodler may have respected and occasionally found inspiration in the Frenchman's work, but it must have come across as fundamentally alien to him, failing as it did to match his own artistic convictions.

On the other hand, Puvis de Chavannes supported Hodler's work and so must have recognized the genius of the younger Swiss painter, despite the fact that he made so few concessions to his own sensibilities.

Ludwig von Hoffman

When Ludwig von Hoffman was studying at the Académie Julian in Paris in 1889–90 he must have admired the work of Puvis de Chavannes.[13] In particular his pictures of the 1890s, with their youthful figures walking through Arcadian landscapes, recall the subject matter of Puvis. His use of color, however, was borrowed from the work of Albert Besnard and the Impressionists. His realistically natural figure drawing is also substantially different from Puvis's manner. Hofmann's paintings do not so much bring up to date the balance and quietude of Puvis's compositions as represent joyously colorful symbols of a new departure in pathos. Marées, Böcklin, Klinger, Ludwig von Hoffman and Hodler are the German-speaking artists whose works allow parallels to be drawn with Puvis. Nonetheless, in the final analysis they all possessed a clearly contrasting artistic attitude. Even in the case of Max Beckmann and Karl Hofer, who acknowledged and later also criticized Puvis's example, it is hard to detect direct results in their paintings.[14]

Puvis's Decorative Style as Seen by German Critics and Art Historians

The wide-ranging, thorough-going response of art critics to Puvis de Chavannes, both during his lifetime and especially in the period immediately after his death, conveys a far more positive judgment overall, attesting to the considerable interest with which Puvis's artistic development was followed in German-speaking countries.[15]

A number of common criteria recur in the articles by visitors to Paris, who regularly reported on the Salons but also looked at the sacred and public buildings with monumental murals by Puvis. Above all, the French master's gift for decorative schemes was noted, principally on the basis of his programmatic work in churches and museums. It is also possible to deduce from their judgments exactly what it was that art historians regarded as "decorative."[16] German visitors saw in Puvis an artist who successfully simplified objects in their form, subordinating them to an overall tone in a composition and thus creating a "style." In his inclination for religious and mythological subjects he was appreciated as a historical painter who attempted to move away from the naturalistic efforts of his contemporaries. He was especially seen as an innovator by those critics who sought to defend the academic tradition and who continued to hold up the model of the ideal of antique art, both that of the Renaissance and that of Poussin.

9. Pierre Puvis de Chavannes,
Summer, 1887–92.
Paris, Hôtel de Ville

One of the first authors to offer an opinion on the art of Puvis de Chavannes was the Swiss Julius Meyer, in his history of French painting. He took the interesting view that the sources for the nineteenth-century revival of monumental painting lay both in the antique and in the Rococo. In this perspective, the works of the young Puvis de Chavannes were judged rather critically as "well-meaning and not untalented attempts to renew the monumental painting of the great masters of the Renaissance. But he fails to bring his groups into an inner relationship, an organic context . . . the drawing lacks definition, especially in the representational modeling of the nude, while the heavy dark outlines . . . are only intended to create a crudely superficial effect. Lastly the colors are too dull and pale, as if extinguished in a misty distance, the flesh tones in particular are chalky, lacking in fiber and tone. The whole execution is quite negligent, blurred and unfinished; it shrugs off the difficult passages, and despite the impressive start the end result is merely a superficially decorative appearance."[17] Already in this early account, it is clear that the "decorative" was to be a point of criticism regarding the painter's work.

Some German art historians were even more negative in their judgments. G. von Guttenberg did not have a good word to say for Puvis de Chavannes in his report on the Salon of 1872: "If I mention a symbolic representation by the Lyon-born artist Puvis de Chavannes, it is only to give an example of just how far a painter can go in giving birth to the ill-formed children of hyper-poetical soppiness." After giving a lengthy description of the painting, Guttenberg supposes that not only must the Allegory of Hope have been buried in one of the cemeteries pictured, but that "the artist's intelligence must have been interred there, too, if he continues to paint such pictures."[18] Such uncomprehending reactions were the exception, however, and the overall response was to alter significantly in subsequent decades.

Puvis as Alternative to Realism, Naturalism and Impressionism
In the 1880s reviews of Puvis's art became more positive. In 1886 it was reported that warlike subjects were all the rage at the Paris Salon. But the works of Puvis de Chavannes must also have attracted attention for their special qualities, since they were noted as having "the

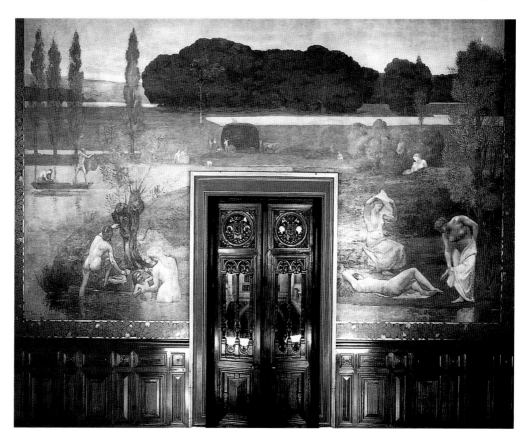

245

10. Arnold Böcklin, *War*, 1896. Dresden, Staatliche Kunstsammlungen, Gemäldegalerie

enrapturing magic of graceful poetry and idyllic restfulness." However, the critic also felt that the "improbability of the drawing and the shortcomings of the figure grouping" lessened his enjoyment.[19]

In a report on the World Exhibition of 1889 in the magazine *Der Kunstwart*, Puvis de Chavannes is cited as an alternative to the Realists and Impressionists.[20] This juxtaposition of his work with the efforts of the Realists, Naturalists and Impressionists continued to be a leitmotiv with German critics.

After the death of Puvis de Chavannes in 1898 numerous articles appeared, paying tribute to his art and work in the historical perspective of his entire œuvre.[21] Walther Hensel summarized his opinion in a monograph study of 1899: "Therein lay his greatness, that in an age which praised formal perfection above all else, whose highest models were Veronese and Correggio, the Bologna school, he created a great, calm, somber and ideal kind of painting that was quite without technical pretensions. While the works of his French contemporaries strike us above all by their virtuoso effects, his paintings breathe the spirit of excellence directly. He responded to the seductive appeal of *L'art pour l'art* with the conviction of *L'art pour l'homme*. . . . In our view his importance is above all ethical. When he started out as a young painter, the last battles between Classics and Romantics were being fought; in his maturity he witnessed the feud of Naturalists and Idealists; in his old age he watched Impressionism and *plein-air*, Pointillism and Luminism, *vérisme* and new idealism tread on each other's heels like the latest Paris fashions: none of them could distract him, however, none could make him swerve from the Ideal he carried in his soul. And thus he showed us that in the end genuine, great art has basically very little to do with all such questions. Thus, too, the deserved, albeit belated recognition that fell to his lot provides an uplifting example of how the true artist need neither pander to the banal tastes of the day, nor have recourse to sensational subject matter and technical artifice, in order to gain his full value."[22]

This is a strikingly typical feature of all criticism of art of the time. The artist, in this case Puvis, is placed in opposition to those trends of his era that have recently passed away. Thus judgment is not so much formed by appreciation of his works, as by his relation to the Impressionist or Realist forms of art that the writer disapproves of. *L'art pour l'art* is juxtaposed with art for man, thus bestowing on the aesthetic judgment an ethical value, implicitly denied to other, criticized forms of nineteenth-century French art. This was also the view taken by Adolf Rosenberg in his widely-read history of modern art, although he added a number of specific critical observations: "His compositions are in the main inadequate and incomplete. The figures, meticulously placed in rows like the tiles in a mosaic, are only superficially connected with each other. Only the uniform style of handling and the overall gray tone link them together." Rosenberg did however acknowledge that his decorative works bore "the seal of majesty and nobility." He went on, "his paintings always seem a little melancholy and old-aged, however merry and sunny the idylls they describe; nonetheless one feels that they are imbued with a spirit that rises above the banal and avoids the vulgar taste of the crowd."[23] In this passage the conservatively minded critic, a staunch supporter of academic painting, alludes to the modern currents of Realism and Impressionism that he disliked, contrasting them with the vastly preferable example of Puvis.

Muther on Puvis de Chavannes

Richard Muther wrote extensively on Puvis. His observation of the works was unusually perceptive and, despite his commitment to proving his own thesis, did contain a serious art historical analysis of Puvis's painting. To Muther, the artist did not seem particularly sophisticated in technique; he was indeed "almost clumsy, for a Frenchman, not at all sure of his craft." In the same context, however—in his review of the Panthéon decorations—Muther judged Puvis to be a groundbreaking figure, one who had shed the deadwood of archaeological pedantry and in his paintings could convey "simple poetry and lyrical magic, a fabulous evocation from the distant past, the atmosphere of legend, casting off the everyday." He saw Puvis as a "modern" artist, since his figures were fashioned "in their every appearance . . . timeless, enrapt in the beyond." He continues, "In Puvis, the whole of the present seems like a day without either beginning or end, paradisiacal, unchanging, eternal. In order to achieve this transcendental effect, he requires no more than modest means: like Millet he general-

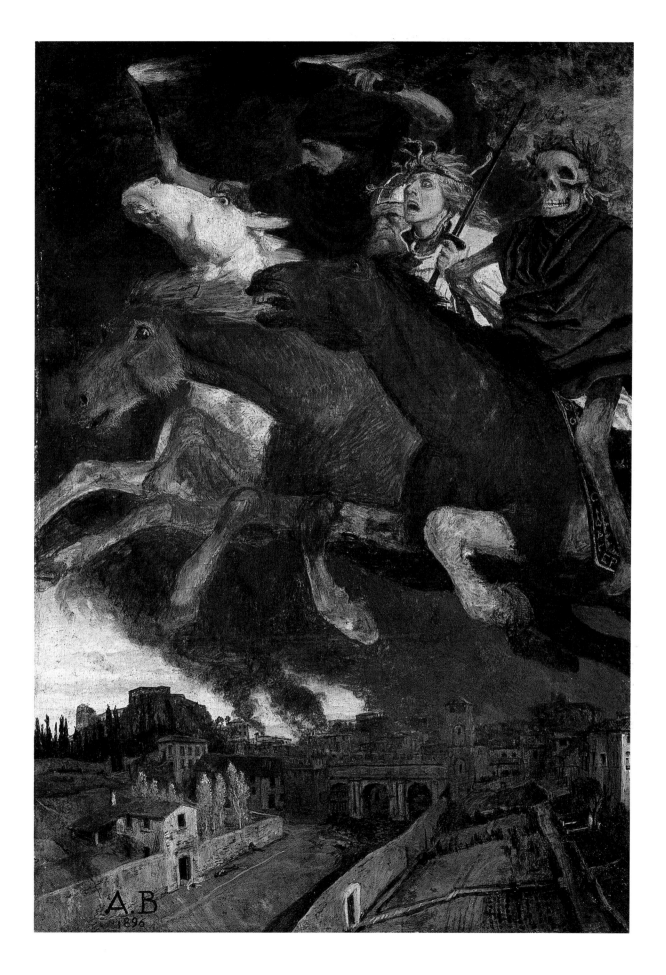

izes the individual, moderating what is given by Nature; antique nudity mixes unforced with modern costume. . . . His paintings have something mistily archaic about them; priestly, if you like, something seraphic, sacred."[24] In the light of this interpretation, Muther's criticism of the artist's craftsmanship appears almost a necessary premise. The "archaic," "priestly" and "seraphic" can only be the expression of a spiritual artistry for which technical execution, the *disegno esterno* of painting, is unimportant.

Only a few years later, Karl Eugen Schmidt was more severe in his criticism of Puvis's painting. He did not fail to note "the striving for quiet greatness and poetical simplicity," which he saw Puvis as trying to obtain "through the gentlest, mattest colors possible, together with quiet lines." At the same time he thought that the paintings were ingenuous to the point where they expressed "so high a degree of simple-minded naiveté" and were "somewhat empty and inadequate" in effect. Schmidt describes the artist's painstaking working method, constantly redrawing his figures in the attempt to achieve the simplicity he intended. But the way that they were then transferred to the painting, made subject to the desired harmonic scheme, left them often looking "as if they had nothing in the least to do with each other." However Schmidt did recognize the "painterly understanding" and "enrapturing poetry" of the works.[25]

Meier-Graefe

Meier-Graefe also saw and praised the poetry that Schmidt discovered in Puvis. In his *History of the Development of Modern Art*, he dedicated a lengthy chapter to Puvis de Chavannes. He saw him as a painter of silence, before whose paintings the habitués of the Salon would stand in quiet contemplation: "It was like being in church."[26] Meier-Graefe goes on to explain that Puvis went beyond everything conventional, superficial narration and ostentatious color, to arrive at a kind of "primitivism" concentrated on the essential. "Stillness seems to be as much of a personal characteristic of his work as, say, movement in Degas or softness in Renoir. He achieves it through an extremely simple form, which could hardly be reduced any further, challenging without depriving." Puvis de Chavannes was thus a kind of outsider who, working outside the hectic mainstream of art, had created "an Arcadia just off the boulevard, a world in which things are beautiful."
With regard to Puvis's use of color, Meier-Graefe took a quite different view from earlier critics, seeking a parallel with the Impressionists: "Puvis was like a filter through which passed all the colors of modernism, emerging in purified form. Thus many diagnosed as pallor and illness what was really healthy restraint of his own mastery." Puvis dealt "wisely" with color, he thought, "using the modernist's colorist only when it could be useful to him." Meier-Graefe concluded enthusiastically: "The German Greeks went no further than the temple porch, while Puvis came near enough to smell the incense of the all-holy, where Aphrodite dwelt."[27] It is unclear whether by "German Greeks" he meant Cornelius, Feuerbach or Böcklin.

For the second edition of his history, entirely revised, Meier-Graefe rewrote his chapter on Puvis de Chavannes. In the meantime he had studied the works of Hans von Marées closely and had written a number of volumes putting forward the work of the German artist, whom he regarded as a groundbreaking modernist painter.[28] Compared with Marées, Puvis de Chavannes's monumental paintings now fell back to the second rank: "Puvis contributed practically nothing to the problem of monumental painting, in which von Marées was a pioneer," ran his revised opinion. In consequence, Meier-Graefe's overall judgment on Puvis, especially when placed alongside the genius of Marées, became rather more reticent: "Basically his was not great art, in particular because his personal, human involvement remained so limited."[29]

German Criticism and French Style

This small selection of critical reactions to his art illustrate how Puvis's work generated an intense response in Germany. However the opinions also show the very different perspectives from which critics judged his painting as attractive or disappointing. In this sense the criticism of his art reflects the debate on contemporary art in Germany around 1900. Several different conceptions of art are clearly visible in the commentaries.

11. Félix Vallotton,
The Jura Mountains, Romanel.
Frankfurt, Städelesches
Kunstinstitut

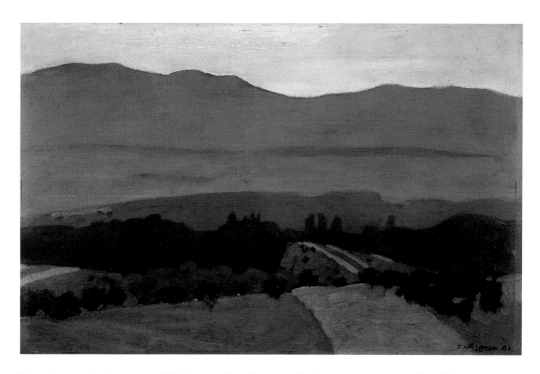

For the academic art establishment, for those in the German Empire who, like Anton von Werner, depicted scenes from German history or from courtly and bourgeois life as a positive, idealized view of reality, Puvis's allegorical subject matter, remote from the everyday and profoundly melancholy, can hardly have seemed an inspiring alternative. On the contrary, it is characteristic of their attitude that Puvis seemed a painter who could be inspiring only for the modernists.

In the modern art camp, a different opinion prevailed. There were still a number of varying reactions, however. Those artists and critics who argued for the renewal of art were unanimous in recognizing the high quality of Puvis's painting. They also agreed that his pictures represented the continuation—or even a renewal—of an academic tradition of religious and mythological monumental painting. It was also clear that Puvis could not be written off just because of his subject matter; rather his simplification of form, concentration on line and delicate chromatic mood entitled him to be viewed as a modern artist.

This, however, was where criticism set in. The German and Swiss artists from the new idealist and Symbolist movements may have admired Puvis's style, but they inevitably found it inappropriate for the time. Even when they chose similar subjects to Puvis, artists such as Marées, Böcklin, Klinger and Hodler preferred to create a more realistic depiction of figures in nature. They could not but find the linearity, unreality and abstraction of Puvis foreign, artificial and aestheticizing. Even Ludwig von Hofmann, whose paintings came closest to Puvis's style in the 1890s, was searching for a combination of realistic and impressionistic painting techniques. For all the above reasons, Puvis de Chavannes found some degree of appreciation, but could not be recognized as an example to be followed by the new idealist and Symbolist currents in German art around 1900.

If the subject matter, compositional sense and magical radiance of Puvis's pictures could win friends among German Symbolists, the artists of the Secession in Berlin and Munich could admire only his sensual depiction of objects. Meier-Graefe's initially very positive judgment derived from his intention to ascertain that Puvis went beyond academic painting in search of a new "purity" of art. A number of critics spoke of a new "style." At the outset Meier-Graefe, too, saw Puvis's refined use of color in the context of the impulse he gave to French Impressionist painters. But the critic toned down his enthusiasm following his studies of Hans von Marées.

The early, favorable opinion of Meier-Graefe does not seem to have made much headway with the German Impressionists. Puvis's art, beyond Realism and Impressionism, failed to gain a positive reception because it did not express an innovative acquisition of reality with which one might strive to overcome academicism. In a period of enormous tension in Franco-German relations, artists such as Liebermann and museum directors such as Pauli and Tschudi among others were attempting to gain recognition in Germany for the French Realists and Impressionists, with the aid of collectors and patrons. It was only with the greatest difficulty that they succeeded in their efforts on behalf of what they saw as the art of the future, in the face of an academic art establishment which enjoyed the strong personal support of the kaiser.

In this context, the German perception of Puvis de Chavannes was easily tainted with prejudice, such that his art was viewed as "typically French" and inextricably bound up with its own, longstanding national tradition. The elegance of his figures, the delicacy of his colors and the classical and mythological subject matter presumably struck German Realists and Impressionists and their collectors as antiquated and old-fashioned, unable to chart the new route away from tradition which they sought. Their indifference must be the chief explanation for the fact that Puvis's art is so little represented in German museums.

[1] On this episode see in particular B. Paul, "Hugo von Tschudi und die moderne französische Kunst im Deutschen Kaiserreich," in *Berliner Schriften zur Kunst*, publ. by the Kunsthistorisches Institut der Freien Universität, vol. 4, Mainz, 1993; *Manet bis Van Gogh, Hugo von Tschudi und der Kampf um die Moderne*, exh. cat., Berlin-Munich, 1996–97; A. Pophanken and F. Billeter, eds., "Die Moderne und ihre Sammler, französische Kunst vom Deutschen Kaiserreich zur Weimarer Republik*," in *Passage/Passages*, Deutsches Forum für Kunstgeschichte, vol. 3, Berlin, 2001.

[2] German museums currently possess: *The Sacred Wood*, Neuss, Clemens-Sels Museum; *Standing Female Nude*, Stuttgart, Staatsgalerie; *The Magdalene in the Desert, Portrait Villiers*, Frankfurt, Städelsches Kunstinstitut; *Allegory of Autumn*, Cologne, Wallraf-Richartz Museum. *The Fisherman's Family*, formerly in Dresden, was destroyed.

[3] Hans von Marées, *Briefe* (Letters), Munich, 1923, p. 32.

[4] Christian Lenz has pointed out that Marées might have seen Puvis's pictures for Marseille at that year's Salon; C. Lenz, "Die Fresken von Marées in Neapel," in *Hans von Marées*, exh. cat., Munich, 1987, p. 62.

[5] Christian Lenz, who has so far given the most extensive consideration to Marées's relations with his contemporaries in France, also left out any comparison with the work of Puvis. See C. Lenz, "Zur Kunst von Marées," in *ibidem*, pp. 19–24.

[6] *Ibidem*, p. 9.

[7] Klinger's paintings for the Hall at Leipzig University were destroyed during World War II. See his sketches in *Max Klinger (1857–1920)*, exh. cat., Städtische Galerie im Städelschen Kunstinstitut, Frankfurt, 1992, cat. 185; *Max Klinger, Bestandskatalog der Bildwerke, Gemälde und Zeichnungen im Museum der bildenden Künste*, Leipzig, 1995, p. 114, no. B 39. D. Gleisberg has pointed out the links between Klinger's *L'Heure bleue* and Puvis de Chavannes's *Young Women by the Sea* (1879, Paris, Musée d'Orsay). *ibidem*, p. 354.

[8] *Max Klinger, Gedanken und Bilder aus der Werkstatt des werdenden Meisters*, ed. H. Heyne, Leipzig, 1925, p. 28.

[9] M. Schmid, *Max Klinger*, Bielefeld and Leipzig 1899, 2nd ed., 1901, p. 132.

[10] See the exhaustive account by R. J. Wattenmaker, *Puvis de Chavannes and the Modern Tradition*, exh. cat., Art Gallery of Ontario, Toronto, 1975, pp. 145–49.

[11] In 1905 Paul Klee visited the Musée du Luxembourg in Paris and observed the relationship between Puvis's *The Fisherman's Family* and Hodler's early pictures. P. Klee, *Tagebücher, 1898–1918*, ed. Felix Klee, Cologne, 1957, p. 191.

[12] A. Dückers, "Der Symbolismus Ferdinand Hodlers," in *Ferdinand Hodler*, exh. cat., Berlin-Paris-Zurich, 1983, p. 236.

[13] See J.A. Schmoll called Eisenwerth, "Zur Marées-Rezeption in der Malerei," in *Hans von Marées*, exh. cat., Munich, 1987, p.151; Seelenreich, *Die Entwicklung des deutschen Symbolismus 1870–1920*, ed. I. Ehrhardt and S. Reynolds, Munich-London-New York, 2000, pp. 62–69.

[14] In 1905 Max Beckmann wrote to Caesar Kunwald: "I can see why you should admire Puvis. Mind you, I hope you will forget him equally quickly, once you're out of Paris again, the same way I forgot him." M. Beckmann, *Briefe* (vol I, 1899–1925), Munich-Zurich, 1993, p. 36. See also Karl Hofer, Munich-Zurich 1993, p.36. See also K. Hofer, *Über das Gesetzliche in der bildenden Kunst*, ed. K. Martin, Akademie der Künste, Berlin 1956, pp. 130ff.

[15] In the database on Franco-German artistic connections compiled by the Deutsches Forum für Kunstgeschichte in Paris, there are a large number of entries for articles by German art historians containing references to the work of Puvis de Chavannes. Only a small selection of these opinions can be cited here.

[16] On the art historical reception of Puvis de Chavannes under the heading "décoration" see: B. von Bismark, *Die Gauguin-Legende, Die Rezeption Paul Gauguins in der französischen Kunstkritik, 1880–1903*, Müster-Hamburg, 1992.

[17] J. Meyer, *Geschichte der modernen französischen Malerei seit 1789 zugleich in ihrem Verhältnis zum politischen Leben, zur Gesittung und Literatur*, Leipzig, 1867, pp. 613–14.

[18] G. von Guttenberg, "Der Salon von 1872," in *Kunstchronik*, vol. 8, 1873, pp. 17ff.

[19] "Aus dem Pariser Salon," in *Die Kunst für Alle*, vol. 1, 1886, p. 258. See also R. Graul, "Die Malerei im Salon von 1886," in *Zeitschrift für bildende Kunst*, vol. 21, 1886, pp. 311–17. In his report from the following year's Salon, Otto Brandes found that Puvis's were not simple and natural enough, too "balletic." *Die Kunst für Alle*, vol. 2, 1887, p. 260.

[20] The author signed his article S.S., "Die deutschen Künstler auf der Pariser Weltausstellung," in *Der Kunstwart*, vol. 3, 1889–90, pp .88–89. See also G. Eller, "Die diesjährigen Pariser Kunstausstellungen," in *Die Gesellschaft, Monatsschrift für Literatur und Kunst*, vol. 8, 1892, p. 945: "Puvis de Chavannes is undoubtedly the most important living painter in France today. No artist of our time has kept his artistic conscience so clean as this master. Every picture that he paints attests to the restless progress of his art. The large canvas exhibited by Puvis de Chavannnes this year, destined for the banqueting hall of the Hôtel de Ville in Paris, is entitled *Winter*. Moving, honest, magnificent!" Hermann Bahr also found modern feeling and a combination of refinement and simplicity in Puvis's art: "Pariser Kunstbriefe, II," in *Der Kunst-*

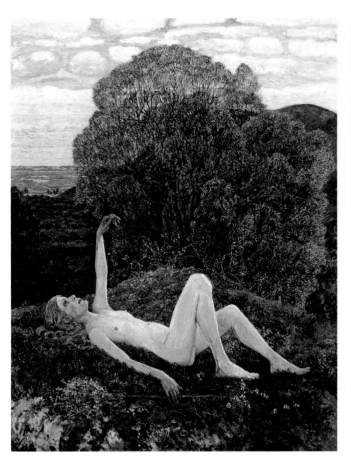

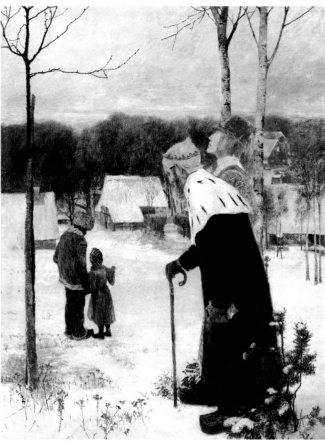

12, 13. Heinrich Vogeler,
Spring, 1909 and *Winter's Tale.
The Magi*, 1897.
Kulturstiftung Landkreis
Osterholz

wart, vol.2, 1888–89, 19, p. 299. A rather more critical view of Puvis de Chavannes is given by E. Zimmermann, "Von den diesjährigen Pariser Salons," in *Bildende Künste, Die Gegenwart, Wochenschrift für Literatur, Kunst und öffentliches Leben*, vol. 43, 1893, p. 71.

[21] See, among others, G. Keyßner, "Puvis de Chavannes," in *Die Kunst für Alle*, vol. 14, 1898–99, pp. 87–92 and Richard Graul, "Pierre Puvis de Chavannes," in *Zeitschrift für bildende Kunst*, 1898–99. pp. 86–92: "Long misunderstood and a late developer in his art, in the evening of his industrious life Puvis de Chavannes has had the rare good fortune not to have become outdated. The ideal that he tentatively explored in the 1850s, and that he sought unflinchingly until his death, first came to life barely twenty years ago. It was precisely in Puvis de Chavannes that the young generation of painters that has taken France by storm saw a worthy leader and counsellor. . . ."

[22] W. Hensel, "Ein Wort über Puvis de Chavannes," in *Die Kunst-Halle*, vol.4, 1899, pp. 113–15.

[23] A. Rosenberg, *Geschichte der modernen Kunst*, 2nd ed., Leipzig, 1894, vol. 1, pp. 174–75.

[24] R. Muther, *Geschichte der Malerei im XIX. Jahrhundert*, Vol.3, Munich, 1894, pp. 574–83.

[25] K.E. Schmidt, *Französische Malerei des 19. Jahrhunderts,* Leipzig, 1905, pp. 76–77.

[26] In 1915, Theodor Däubler was to write of Puvis's paintings in the Panthéon, "How moved, how believing all people are: here, even work becomes religion. . . ." T. Däubler, *Wir wollen nicht verweilen*, Dresden, 1915, p.107.

[27] J. Meier-Graefe, *Entwicklungsgeschichte der modernen Kunst, Vergleichende Betrachtung der bildenden Künste, als Beitrag zu einer neuen Ästhetik*, Stuttgart, 1904, vol.1. pp. 329–35.

[28] See A.-S. Domm, "Die 'Väter' der Marées-Rezeption, Konrad Fiedler und Julius Meier-Graefe," in *Hans von Marées und die Moderne in Deutschland*, exh. cat., Bielefeld-Winterthur, 1988, pp.66–76.

[29] J. Meier-Graefe, *Entwicklungsgeschichte der modernen Kunst*, vol.3, *Die Kunst unserer Tage, von Cézanne bis heute*, 2nd ed., Munich, 1927, pp. 495–96.

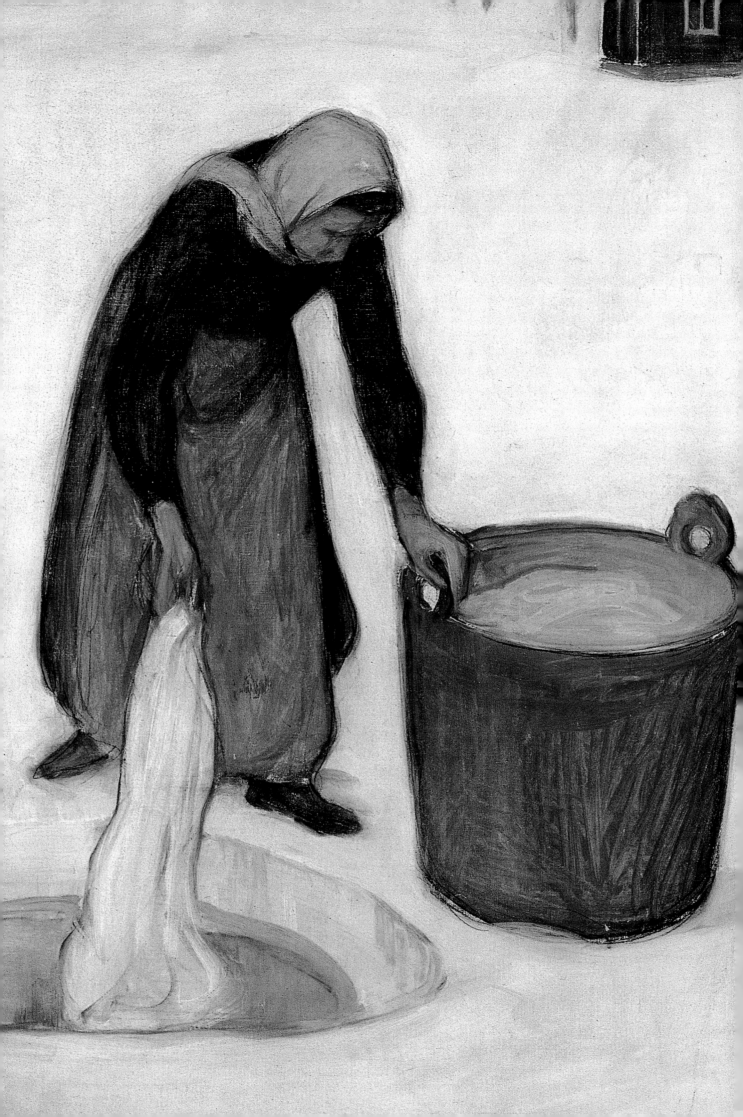

Puvis de Chavannes and the North

For an artist to be admired, celebrated and worshipped by his contemporaries has in many cases foreshadowed impending oblivion, storage and relegation to the periphery of art history. Destiny has treated Puvis de Chavannes with more mercy. After being glorified by his contemporaries towards the end of the nineteenth century, he was, during most of the twentieth century, dismissed and defined as an art historical dinosaur, who belonged to the long condemned Salons of the old world. With the 1970s' rediscovery of Symbolism followed, however, a heightened interest in the movement's more or less pre-Symbolist father figures. Initially this interest rescued Puvis from relative oblivion; later it resulted in a thorough re-evaluation of his work and in a number of retrospective exhibitions, monographs and specialized articles. Without in any way hoping to exhaust the topic, this essay will attempt to reinstate Puvis as the most influential foreign model for Nordic Symbolism.[1] If we consider the modesty of Puvis's current popular impact, not only in the North, the frequency with which he is actually mentioned by his contemporaries may seem surprising. Practically all the Nordic artists, including the most realistic of Naturalists as well as the most esoteric Symbolists, express their respect and their often juvenile enthusiasm for the French master. At an early stage Naturalists such as the Finnish painter Albert Edelfelt and the Danish painter couple Anna and Michael Ancher admired Puvis's insistence on a grand simplicity of composition as well as narration.[2] But even though the Nordic Naturalists and Realists of the 1880s held Puvis's works in great respect, they tended to look to other French artists for direct inspiration: primarily Jules Bastien-Lepage, Jules Breton and Léon Bonnat. The great significance of Puvis de Chavannes as inspiration and model thus belongs primarily to the 1890s.

The Danish Puvists: Vilhelm Hammershøi and Ejnar Nielsen
In Denmark the general public first became acquainted with Puvis de Chavannes's work in 1888. The occasion was an exhibition of French art, organized by Carl Jacobsen at the New Carlsberg Glyptothek in Copenhagen. A few of Puvis's works appeared primarily among French Naturalists and Salon painters, and included a reduced version of the mural decoration for the Panthéon as well as a representation of the *The Beheading of Saint John the Baptist* (which version we do not know). At the 1897 International Art Exhibition, also at the New Carlsberg Glyptothek, Puvis exhibited four pieces: *Pity* (1887; Moscow, Pushkin Museum), *Young Woman at Her Toilette* (1883; London, National Gallery, on loan to Dublin; Paris, Musée d'Orsay), and two untitled pieces. This remarkable degree of representation may indeed be conceived of as a manifestation of the great respect and interest that had surrounded Puvis's works in the previous years. This respect was expressed in clear terms in the following year in an obituary written after Puvis's death on October 24, 1898, by the leading Danish art critic, Emil Hannover, in *Kunstbladet*: "With the death of Puvis de Chavannes the sad decline affecting French painting for a long time now, has become an accomplished fact."

A panoramic view of Danish art of the 1890s reveals many traces of Puvis de Chavannes. The greatest influence is, however, found in the work of two of the period's most significant artists: Vilhelm Hammershøi and Ejnar Nielsen.
That Hammershøi was fascinated by Puvis's ascetic treatment of forms and color is evident from his monumental *Artemis*. Hammershøi visited the World Exhibition in Paris in 1889, and here he must have seen Puvis's *Young Women by the Sea*. Hammershøi generally revealed very little both about his own visits to exhibitions and about his preferences among the works of his fellow contemporary artists; thus he himself has not identified Puvis as a source of inspiration. It seems obvious, however, that he must have gone to see Puvis's works during his visits to Paris, both in the summer of 1889 and a few years later from September 1891 to March 1892.
Puvis was the most admired and discussed artist of the period and he must also have caught Hammershøi's attention; visits to *The Poor Fisherman* at the Musée Luxembourg, to the Panthéon and the Sorbonne, whose walls were decorated with some of Puvis de Chavannes's largest monumental murals, was part of the usual program of Nordic artists visiting Paris.

1. Pekka Halonen,
Washing on the Ice, detail, 1900.
Helsinki, Ateneum, The Museum
of Finnish Art

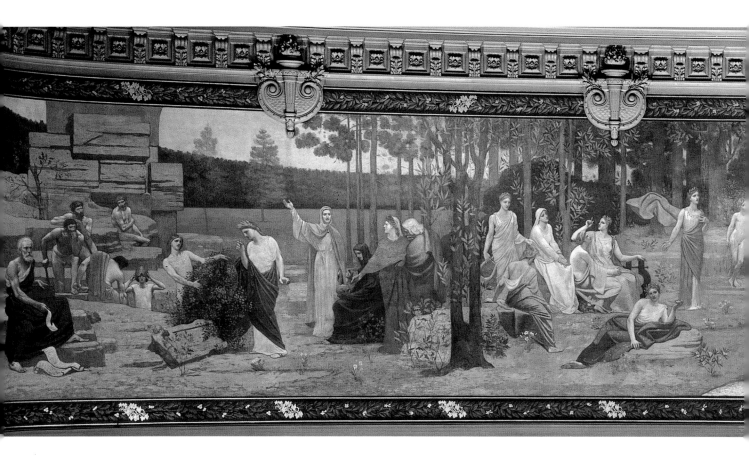

2. Pierre Puvis de Chavannes, *Mural Decoration for the Sorbonne Hemicycle*, 1889.

If asked to identify possible motif correspondences between *Young Women by the Sea* and *Artemis*, one might indicate certain similarities in the two female figures who are viewed from the back. Furthermore, remarkable similarities associate Artemis and the figure who accompanies her with two female figures from Puvis's great decoration for the amphitheater of the Sorbonne (fig. 2), more specifically the two standing Muses representing the Sciences depicted on the right-hand side of the picture.

The decoration was officially inaugurated on August 5, 1889, so that it is unlikely that Hammershøi, who left Paris in July, managed to see it during his first visit to Paris. He did, on the other hand, have ample opportunity to admire the decoration in 1891–92.

If we disregard the similarities of the motifs, Hammershøi's *Artemis* and Puvis's *Young Women by the Sea* both present a coloristic reduction, an accentuation of the flatness of the picture surface, and a mythological mysteriousness which still today fill the spectator with doubt and wonder and with a sense of standing before an unapproachable, secret motif that defies signification. And no matter how peculiar Hammershøi's art, and particularly a work such as *Artemis* may seem, it nevertheless belongs to a European group of works which seem to be associated with Puvis de Chavannes, albeit to greater or lesser degrees. These pictures of monumental figures, which might also include works by Edward Burne-Jones and George Frederic Watts among others, not only veil signification behind inscrutable mythological and pseudo-literary references, but consciously wish to appear "meaningless."[3] Meaningless, however, in the sense that they displace our attention from the narrative to its formal strategies in a modernistic fashion. This is a kind of *existential formalism*, where meaning—for of course there is meaning here too—should be sought both in absence and in presence: mood, beauty, the harmony of colors, rhythm and symmetry. The lack of contact between the figures in *Young Women by the Sea* and *Artemis* alike adds a particular melancholy to the motifs: a feeling of absence and loneliness, as if the modern world has stepped in, rendering the archaic dream present as a painful loss. We also find this melancholy in Hammershøi's interior paintings, where it establishes the pervasive atmosphere.

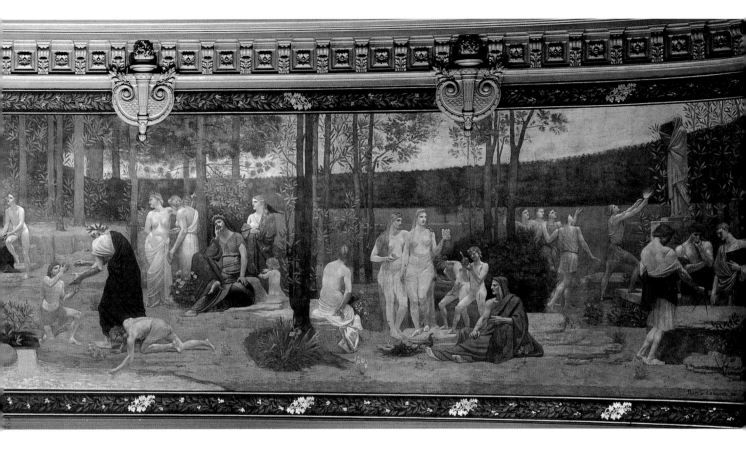

To an even greater extent than Hammershøi, Ejnar Nielsen seems to have been fascinated by Puvis's works, both formally and in terms of interpretation. Nielsen went to Paris relatively late, in connection with the 1900 World Exhibition in Paris. His sojourn there lasted six months, from the autumn of 1900 to the spring of 1901. As documented in all clarity by his principal work from Paris, *The Sculptor Andreas F.V. Hansen and His Wife*, Ejnar Nielsen benefited greatly from the meeting with his avowed model, Puvis de Chavannes: "During my six months in Paris it was probably Puvis de Chavannes who attracted me the most, with his noble and aristocratic use of colors and composition."[4] His enthusiasm and admiration for Puvis are also evident in a letter that Nielsen wrote to his girlfriend, Marie Thaarup. The letter was written in 1899, a year prior to the Paris visit. Here Puvis is spoken of as "the greatest modern painter of France" and as Ejnar Nielsen's "great beloved artist."[5]

In *The Sculptor Andreas F.V. Hansen and His Wife* the spectator's attention is concentrated on the two monumental figures, who are, in psychological as well as symbolical terms, completely separated by the balcony fence from the Parisian life that is taking place in the street beneath their flat. The colors are toned down, and as a consequence the motif remains fixed on the surface, giving to the painting that monumental effect of surface flatness which characterizes many of Puvis's pictures.

It is mainly as a unified enunciation that the picture appears Puvisesque, and it is consequently less important for us to define whether or not the two figures refer to any specific work. Several seated figures, especially in Puvis's visions of antiquity, share their introversive meditative calm. However, the two figures that resemble these the most are found in the already-mentioned decoration in the Sorbonne. We thus recognize "the man" from a figure on the left, seated among a group of Philosophers. He is dressed in a dark suit and holds a skull in his hands. "The woman," on the other hand, is found on the Philosophers' right-hand side, appropriately seated among the Muses of Poetry.

Well before leaving for Paris, Ejnar Nielsen had created a number of his major Symbolist works, including *Death and the Cripple*, executed in Gjern in 1898–99. Here Ejnar Nielsen was not so much interested in Puvis de Chavannes's Arcadian melancholic works, but rather in *The Poor Fisherman*. Ejnar Nielsen was presumably familiar with *The Poor Fisherman* from graphic and photographic reproductions or from illustrations in art journals. Indeed, it seems that the cripple's position owes important features to the poor fisherman, while the composition itself, with its vast landscape and high horizon, has certain similarities as well. On the other hand, *Death and the Cripple* does not possess the religious animism that we find in Puvis. In the work of Ejnar Nielsen, a secularized Protestant, death and human suffering are inserted in a cyclic view of life, the green landscape of spring in the background symbolizing immortality. Man and Nature are united in a symbiosis with no religious connotations, but rather as a simple statement of fact.

A third Danish artist deserves our attention in this connection: the art mediator, craftsman and painter Johan Rohde. Johan Rohde's primary aim as a painter was to turn a landscape into a suggestive contemplative space: an ambition that he successfully realized in a series of landscapes of Holland and Northern Germany in 1892–93, such as *Summer Night at Tönning* of 1893 (fig. 3).[6] These paintings often depict a canal at the evocative hour of twilight as evening turns to night, the perfectly calm surface of the water creating dark decorative reflections of houses and trees, a few ships and bridges. Caspar David Friedrich's romantic moonlight paintings and the Dutch seventeenth-century painter Aert Van der Neers's nocturnal pictures are Rohde's art historical predecessors, while the grand yet simple flat surfaces and decorative stylization, especially of the stagnant water surface, provide a more contemporary allusion to Puvis de Chavannes's *Poor Fisherman*.

Only two months prior to his sojourn in Hoorn, Rohde visited the exhibition at the Champ-de-Mars in Paris. One of the few exhibits that he found of interest was Puvis's *Winter*. In his diary, Rohde wrote: "Puvis de Chavannes reaches greater heights than any other exhibitor with his big decorative picture *Winter*. There is a grandness, a simplicity and a beauty in this great picture that one seeks in vain in all the other big canvases. Especially the landscape with the sea in the background is of great beauty."[7]

Puvis de Chavannes and Finnish Symbolism

In the story of Puvis de Chavannes's influence in the North, the chapter on Finnish art occupies a central position. Not least because a number of the most talented young Finnish artists went to Paris in the early 1890s to see Puvis's works. With these as their point of departure they created a large group of works which combined the great model with Finnish traditions and characteristics in an original fashion.[8] We are primarily thinking here of the artist friends Magnus Enckell, Ellen Thesleff and Beda Stjernschantz, who all went to Paris in 1891, Enckell being the central person of the group and its pioneer. The letters that they wrote home bear witness to the enthusiasm with which they approached Puvis's art. In a letter written in December 1891, Stjernschantz describes the huge impression that Puvis's decorations in the Sorbonne and the Panthéon made on her, and she narrates with wit that the entire group has been affected by an attack of "Puvinism Chavanism."[9]

Stjernschantz only stayed in Paris until 1892. In a series of portraits that she painted during her Paris sojourn, we see how she picked up Puvisesque stylization and coloristic asceticism. It was not, however, until several years later that the influence from Puvis resulted in larger compositions; these, on the other hand, exhibit great originality and energy. In *Everywhere a Voice is Heard* from 1895 she has sought out an old Swedish-Finnish cultural area, the island of Wormsø on the Estonian coast.

Unlike her artist friends, Magnus Enckell and Ellen Thesleff, Stjernschantz did not have and was not to get the financial resources needed for more longer journeys abroad; Wormsø became for her what Brittany had been to Gauguin and to the artists around the Nabis: an unspoiled landscape with a population and a way of life that, in its simplicity and with its religiously based connection to nature, provided a much sought for alternative to the fragmented hectic life of the modern metropolis. With its large monotonous surface, framed at the top by a series of windmills, which seem to be a decorative fret rather than a sign that creates depth, the decorative simplicity of the painting provides convincing references to Puvis de Chavannes.

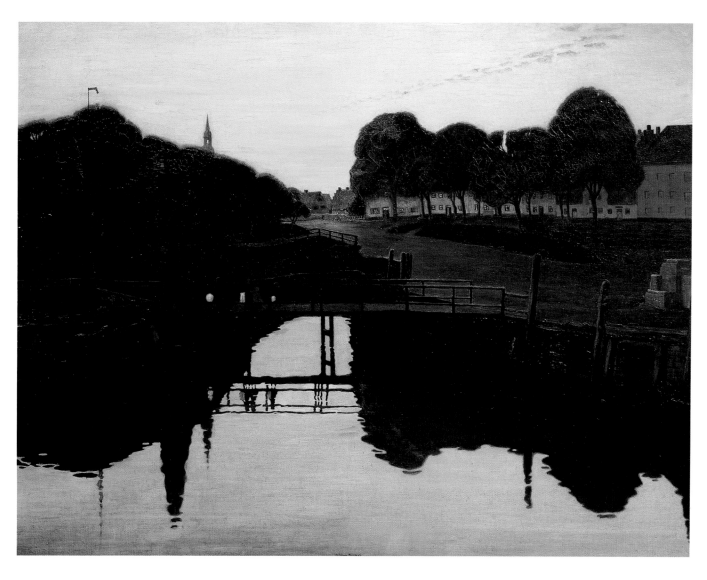

3. Johan Rohde,
Summer Night at Tønning, 1893.
Stockholm, Nationalmuseum

The admiration for Puvis and perhaps particularly for *The Sacred Wood* is also evident in *Pastoral (Spring)* from 1897, an ancient vision of eternal youth and everlasting spring, based on the double myth of Narcissus-Antinous. As in *Young Women by the Sea* and Hammershøi's *Artemis*, Stjernschantz's figures throw no shadow. They thus take on a particular ethereal character, a subtlety and a fragility, which may be detected everywhere in the two pictures, from the largest flat surface to the smallest detail, in the music and the song, and in the transparency of the stylized flowers and leaves. A quiet, almost devout seriousness pervades the figures, who seem to be subjected to the inspiration and motivation of a higher power. By the end of the 1890s Stjernschantz had already cut down on her artistic activities and once the century had turned, she stopped working entirely. Her modest production nevertheless includes several principal works of Nordic Symbolism, and few artists have assimilated and transformed impressions from Puvis de Chavannes with an originality that matches hers.

Magnus Enckell was the intellectual leader among the young Finnish artists and apparently the first to become aware of Puvis de Chavannes. In the autumn of 1891, the Finnish artist, Väinö Blomstedt, described the new development in the following way: "Everything is changing. It is Puvis de Chavannes who has, so to say, first acted as messenger of the new. He is childishly naive, but at the same time so brilliantly grand that it is wonderful; one finds it hard to understand what he has done. At first one wishes to turn one's back to it and laugh out loud, but eventually one is seized by a higher power. God only knows what it is. . . . No one, except Enckell, admires it."[10]
Enckell's assimilation of Puvis's art found its strongest expression in a series of androgynous boyish figures from the years 1892–94. *Waking Up* was produced in Paris in 1894 and represents the culmination of these portraits of boys, all of which seek to create a contemplative space of existential-philosophical consideration with a reduced, almost monochromatic coloring and a simplified composition focused on flat surfaces. Through the removal of all reference to time or space, the existential considerations take on a general validity, pointing to fundamental human conditions. *Waking Up* is painted in oil with thin layers of color that give a particular watercolor texture to the painting. Enckell indeed preferred watercolors because the technique of translucency helps lift the motif from the tangible study of a model to an immaterial and spiritual higher reality.
During a journey in Italy in 1894–95, Enckell moved still further away from a Puvisesque "existential formalism," elaborating and assimilating significant traits, above all from the mythological landscapes of Arnold Böcklin. The color scheme became richer and the motifs more dynamic and illustrative. But at times he returned to his starting point, as we can see in a painting such as *The Golden Age* from 1904. In this study for a decoration of the university library in Helsinki we can recognize both a grand yet simple composition and the tarrying boys, representative of a timeless existence not unlike the one that Enckell had admired in Puvis de Chavannes a decade earlier.

Together with Magnus Enckell and Beda Stjernschantz, Ellen Thesleff went to see Paris and Puvis de Chavannes during the 1890s. Even though she herself would later focus her attention on Eugène Carrière rather than on Puvis, the influence of Puvis on her work seems to have been significant, especially in a series of grayish forest landscapes from the 1890s, including *Aspen* from 1893. As emblematic landscapes, Thesleff's works exhibit a delicate fragility and a spirituality of mellow light, transilluminating the tree trunks and spreading a silver-gray fog over the entire motif. With their silver-gray morning fog the motifs may be archetypally Finnish; the accentuation of the flat surface and the remarkable demarcation and verticality suggest, however, that they are deeply anchored in European Symbolism, primarily in Puvis de Chavannes's works, and especially in his *Winter* (fig. 4), which was exhibited at the 1892 Salon and attracted great attention. Apart from the radiant general blue-purple tone, in *Winter* we find a group of trees with similar slim trunks that divide at the top into a fine complex network of thin boughs. Thesleff was in Paris from the autumn of 1891 to early June 1892, so she must have been familiar with Puvis's composition from the Salon, which had opened in May. The vertical format and the brief demarcation, which underline the composition's simple, decorative attachment to the flat surface, would, on the other hand, seem impossible without a first-hand knowledge of Japanese art, which had been gaining great influence on the European art scene from the middle of the nineteenth century, and especially during the 1880s–'90s. Among the other Finnish artists who went to Paris in the early 1890s and learned from Puvis de Chavannes (albeit to a less noticeable extent), were the already-mentioned Väinö Blomstedt and, especially, Pekka Halonen. Like Enckell, the latter studied at l'Académie Julian; at first he was not influenced by the new Parisian tendencies, but held on to his Realist starting point. Later during the years around 1900, Halonen's art developed a major simplicity and monumentality, culminating in the decoration of the Finnish pavilion for the 1900 World Exhibition. The decoration consisted of six paintings; like *Washing on the Ice* (fig. 5) they all employ a stylization of human beings and landscapes in compositions that are characterized by a Puvisesque grand monumentality and coloristic reduction. The argument that Puvis's *Winter* from the Hôtel de Ville may have been the direct inspiration for this as well as other of the exhibition's winter motifs is certainly not to be dismissed.

As far as Finland's great artist, Akseli Gallen-Kallela, is concerned, the inspiration from Puvis de Chavannes is not immediately conspicuous. During Gallen-Kallela's Parisian sojourn in the middle of the 1880s, the central starting point was Realist open-air painting around Bastien-Lepage. When the young Finnish artists flocked to Paris in order to study Puvis's works closely, Gallen-Kallela was one of the few who expressed certain reservations about the great master, and wished for more "real, lived life."[11] Later in the 1890s, and under the influence of the simplified formal idiom of Symbolism and especially of Synthetism, he developed his own highly stylized pictorial universe, realizing that the Realist formal idiom could not help him visualize his dream of a new monumental art capable of embracing and expressing the particular grand character of Finnish nature and culture. On several occasions his efforts led to works that combine narrative dramas and stories with a pictorial stylization and coloristic reduction. Like Ferdinand Hodler, Gallen-Kallela unites a Germanic tradition with a more French-oriented formalism, which seems indebted to Puvis de Chavannes in several ways.

This observation is exemplified in Gallen-Kallela's *Spring* from 1903. Together with *Autumn*, *Spring* is a definitive sketch for a large fresco decoration executed for the Finnish businessman, F.A. Jusélius, and commissioned for the mausoleum of his daughter Sigrid, who died young. In six large frescoes, Gallen-Kallela describes the themes of "the quiet, winding march of the Finnish people on the edge of life toward the land of the dead, Tuonela." This is how the Finnish national epic *Kalevala* depicts man's journey through life, from the many opportunities of *Spring* and dawn to the last journey of earthly life, crossing the river to the land of the dead. A representation of the victory of death over matter, which is here displayed on the mausoleum's walls. On the stained-glass paintings of the cupola, the two motifs of *Paradise* and *Cosmos* depict the victory of the spirit over death. With its display of the cycle of life, and due to its remarkable use of large color surfaces, a reduced coloring and the stylized meeting between the contours of the landscape and the monotonous surface of the water, the fresco decoration of *Spring* seems to occupy a position that represents a natural continuation of Puvis de Chavannes's efforts.

Puvis and Sweden
Like the Danish, Norwegian and Finnish Naturalists and Realists of the 1880s, the many Swedish artists who visited Paris during the 1880s were full of praise for Puvis de Chavannes's art. This is true of Richard Bergh and Carl Larsson among others; but the writer and painter, August Strindberg, also expressed his admiration for Puvis on several occasions, most remarkably in a letter to Gauguin of February 1, 1895. Gauguin had asked Strindberg to write a text for the catalog of Gauguin's February 18 exhibition in the Hôtel des Ventes. Strindberg answered that he could not take on the job because he did not agree with Gauguin's art. His explanations and observations, which included a definition of Gauguin in relation to Puvis de Chavannes and the latest art developments, were, however, so full of insight that Gauguin chose to print a slightly edited version of Strindberg's rejection in the catalog.

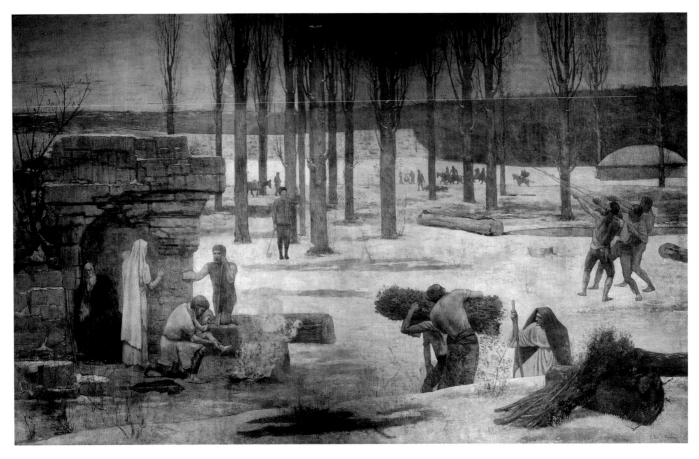

4. Pierre Puvis de Chavannes,
Winter, 1892.
Paris, Hôtel de Ville

5. Pekka Halonen,
Washing on the Ice, 1900.
Helsinki, Ateneum, The Museum
of Finnish Art

To Strindberg, whose own art may seem poles apart from Puvis's, the old master obviously represented the standard by which contemporary art might be measured and which might put its accomplishments into perspective. In order to better understand Gauguin, Strindberg chose to return to Musée Luxembourg to pay another visit to *The Poor Fisherman*: "This morning, I went to visit the Luxembourg Museum in order to look at a Chavannes's work, which kept coming back to my mind. With deep appreciation, I contemplated *The Poor Fisherman*, so attentively awaiting the prey that will bring him the faithful love of both the wife who gathers flowers and his idle child. How beautiful it is!"[12]

The Swedish artist who has provided the most detailed description, not only of his own relation to Puvis de Chavannes but also of that of his contemporaries is Georg Pauli, who concluded in 1892: "All movements need his art—from the old, from the academy fellows, to Impressionist, Symbolists and Synthesists."[13] For several years during the 1870s, Pauli had lived next door to Puvis in Place Pigalle, but had not been aware of the identity of his neighbor at no. 11. In 1905, he nevertheless clearly recollected "the handsome man. Lively and red-cheeked, strengthened through baths and gymnastics, he resembled Henry IV with his brushed-back hair, pointed chin-beard, dominant aquiline nose and alert intelligent eyes."[14] When Pauli, in 1905 and removed from juvenile enthusiasm, also attempts to describe Puvis's art, it is evident to what an extent Puvis was still viewed as having transgressed the many different artistic tendencies of the late nineteenth century, and for that very reason achieved fame among artists for being a pioneer within modern art: "All the schools of the century were assimilated in his art . . . a personal art in which much seems familiar but does not resemble anything else; an art that has found nourishment everywhere

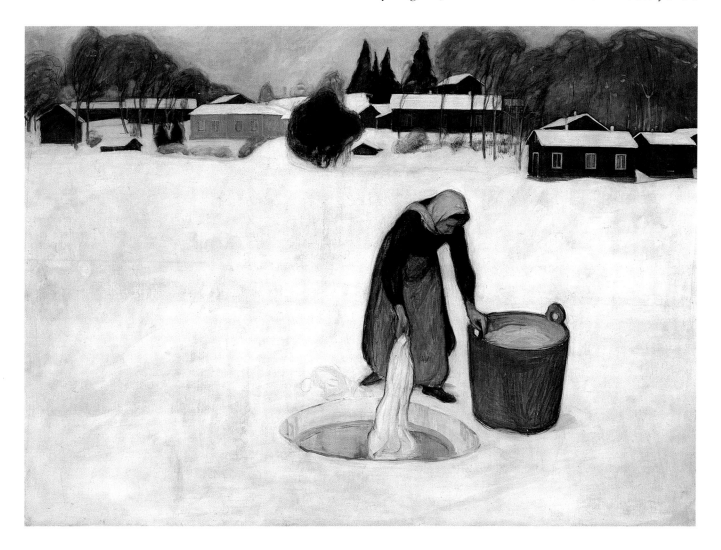

6. Verner Thomé,
Children Playing, 1903.
Helsinki, Ateneum, The Museum
of Finnish Art

7. Magnus Enckell,
Study for "The Golden Age," 1904.
Göteborg, Konstmuseum

and yet, like all great art, has the noble style of sacrifice and finds its greatest strength in *renoncements*."[15]

According to Pauli, it was with his insistence on art and the artistic that Puvis became the primary exponent of a way out of the cul-de-sac of Naturalism, pointing instead toward a "decorative synthetism." In comparison to his influence on contemporary Danish and Finnish art, the direct traces left by Puvis on Swedish art nevertheless remain limited. The many Swedish artists who had turned towards Symbolism in the early 1890s seemed to have oriented themselves directly towards the core Symbolists. This was the case with Ivan Agueli, Helmer Osslund, Karl Nordström and Nils Kreuger, who sought out artists such as Paul Gauguin, Emile Bernard and Maurice Denis. In the case of the latter two Swedes, the list also includes Van Gogh.

Other Swedish "Symbolists," such as Richard Bergh and Prins Eugen, preferred to look to Germanic Symbolism for inspiration, and especially Arnold Böcklin, who together with Max Klinger exercised more influence in Sweden than in the other Nordic countries. Nevertheless it is to Bergh and Prins Eugen that we must turn in order to identify the most direct contacts with Puvis. Prins Eugun had been taught by Puvis during his 1887–89 Paris sojourn. In 1892, he produced several paintings with slim tree trunks as their principal motif, and we should definitely not dismiss the theory that, like Ellen Thesleff's *Aspen*, these depend on Puvis's *Winter*. They do, however, involve a completely different somber melancholy, which might make a German influence more plausible.

To my mind, the most Puvisesque Swedish painting of the 1890s is Richard Bergh's *Nordic Summer Evening* from 1899–1900 (fig. 8). This is a principal work of Swedish national romanticism, but it is also a very international picture which unites impressions from Puvis de Chavannes and the Italian Renaissance with a realist study of Swedish nature. The painting has rightly been compared to a *Sacra conversazione*, in which the two "saints" direct their attention toward the wonderful Nordic nature in the center of the picture rather than the Madonna. Instead of Puvis's visions of antiquity and a concomitant melancholy and desire for times past, Richard Bergh depicts a view of a contemporary Arcadia which admittedly includes sentimental desire, but in comparison with Puvis also a much greater possibility for realization. Contemporary people (the singer Karin Pyk and the painter Prins Eugen) observe Swedish nature; however, the monumentality of the composition and its synthesizing simplicity with the few dominant vertical and horizontal lines and an ascetic coloring that focuses on olive green and white seem impossible without a close familiarity with Puvis's art.

In this essay, I have attempted to identify the most striking contacts between Puvis de Chavannes and the pictorial arts in Denmark, Finland and Sweden. But apart from the obvious similarities in motifs, a number of more general characteristics of late nineteenth-century Nordic art may, to my mind, be related to Puvis de Chavannes. The development of the Nordic landscape, with its preference for the melancholy of the twilight hours, the perfectly still water surfaces, the grand views and an often reduced color, has frequently been considered a particularly Nordic phenomenon. Obviously it is in terms of topography and atmosphere; but when it comes to artistic approach and elaboration, however, I believe to find ubiquitous traces of Puvis de Chavannes: from Eilif Petersson and Kitty Kielland's elegiac Norwegian summer nights to Bruno Liljefors's grand Swedish landscape synthesis, Victor Westerholm's Finnish winter landscapes and Laurits Andersen Ring's Danish landscapes and their accentuation of grand lines and flat surfaces. From *The Sacred Wood* to *The Poor Fisherman*: we can sense Puvis's influence everywhere. Consequently, when in 1905 Georg Pauli "wonders why this pioneer never became a center for disciples and students as well as for a world-wide discussion which his great reputation as an artist would have led one to expect,"[16] Pauli is right, but not entirely. Indeed, Puvis had no disciples; nevertheless his influence, both directly and indirectly, was such that it traveled around the world. Pauli is thus quite right when he writes: "His long opposition to what was academically established, his high ranking as a mature artist, his influence on the developments of modern art, all these justify his being saluted as one of the central personalities of the latter half of the last century."[17]

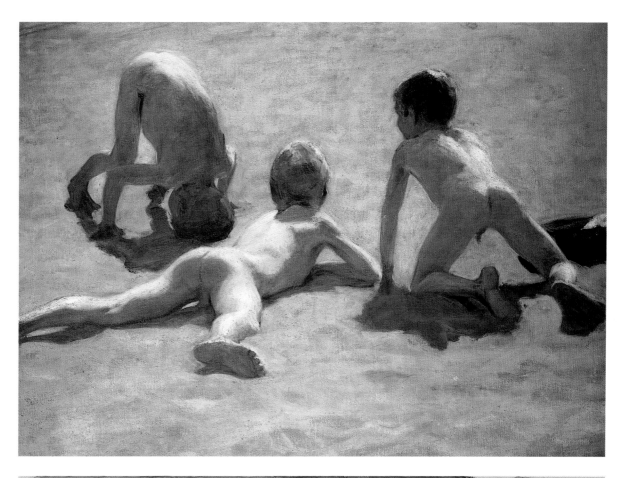

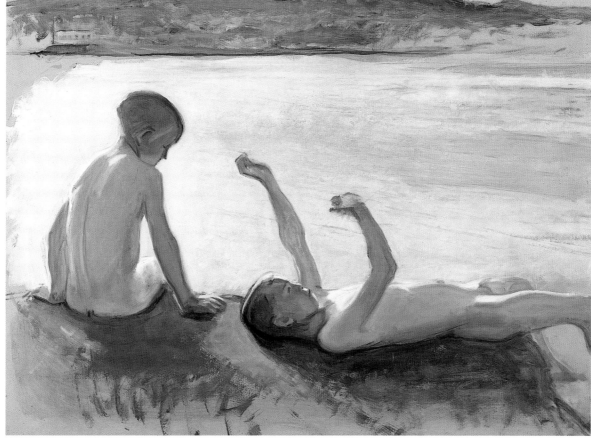

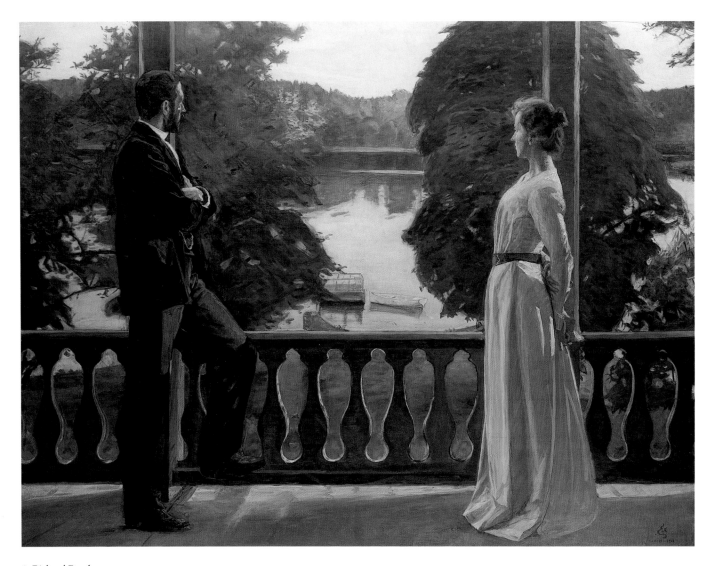

8. Richard Bergh,
Nordic Summer Evening, 1899–1900.
Göteborg, Konstmuseum

[1] With the exhibition *Symbolism in Danish and European Painting 1870–1910*, Statens Museum for Kunst, Copenhagen, 2000, which inserted Danish Symbolist painting in the contemporary European scene, I tried to demonstrate the importance of Puvis for Danish Symbolism. This essay is an elaboration of the findings of that project.

[2] Anna and Michael Ancher visited Puvis in Paris in the spring of 1889. In Anna Ancher's case this led to a couple of months' drawing instruction under the guidance of Puvis.

[3] For related works by Burne-Jones (*Venus Discordia*, 1872–73, Cardiff, Wales, National Museum & Gallery, and *Venus Concordia*, 1872, Plymouth, City Museum and Art Gallery, see *Edward Burne-Jones. Victorian Artist-Dreamer*, Metropolitan Museum of Art, New York et al., 1998, pp. 156ff. For G. F. Watts see *The Three Goddesses*, 1865–72, The Faringdon Collection Trust, England, reproduced in *The Age of Rossetti, Burne-Jones & Watts. Symbolism in Britain 1860–1910*, Tate Gallery, London, et al., 1997–98, p. 115. Individual works by Gustave Moreau may also deserve our attention due to a great similarity with Hammershøi's *Artemis*: first and foremost *Hesiod and the Muses*, which exists in two versions, both the property of Musée Gustave Moreau and reproduced in *Gustave Moreau. 1826–1898*, Grand Palais, Paris, et al., 1898–99, pp. 69ff.

[4] Letter to the Danish art historian Francis Beckett, with the date Paris, November 15, 1907, the Royal Library, Copenhagen. As cited in H. Helge Madsen, *Ejnar Nielsen eller Eventyret om Gjern*, Copenhagen, 1974, p. 41.

[5] *Ibidem*, p. 60.

[6] *Summer Night at Tønning* belongs to a group of paintings that were executed in connection with a major journey in 1892, which put the already well-oriented artist in contact with the most recent tendencies in contemporary European art. The journey has been described in *Journal fra en Rejse i 1892*, published posthumously. In diary form, the book tells of Rohde's many visits to museums and exhibitions and of meetings with a number of leading artists, including Odilon Redon, Maurice Denis and Paul Sérusier.

[7] J. Rohde, *Journal fra en Rejse i 1892*, Copenhagen, 1955, p. 77.

[8] Prior to the early 1890s the influence of Puvis was limited. An exception is Maria Wiik who was taught by Puvis de Chavannes in the spring of 1889, while working in Dagnan-Bouveret's studio. As demonstrated by the painting *Out into the World*, executed in England in 1889 immediately after this study period, she added a greater monumentality and suggestiveness to her realistic representations of ordinary life. This new effect was accomplished by vertical and horizontal lines as well as by a reduced coloring.

[9] As quoted by S. Sarajas-Korte, *Vid symbolismens källor. Den tidiga symbolismen i Finland 1890–1895*, Jakobstad, 1981 (Finnish edition 1966), p. 65.

[10] As quoted in *Lumières du Nord. La peinture scandinave 1885–1905*, Petit Palais, Paris, 1987.

[11] *Ibidem*, p. 76.

[12] One of the books that provide a reduced version of the catalog with Strindberg's French text is G. Söderström, *Strindberg och bildkonsten*, Uddevalla, 1972, pp. 281–82.

[13] G. Pauli, "Bref om konst," *Ord och Bild,* Stockholm, 1892, p. 280.

[14] G. Pauli, *I Paris. Nya konstens källa. Anteckningar ur dagböcker och bref*, Stockholm, 1915, p. 20.

[15] *Ibidem*, p. 19.

[16] *Ibidem*, p. 18.

[17] *Ibidem*, p. 17.

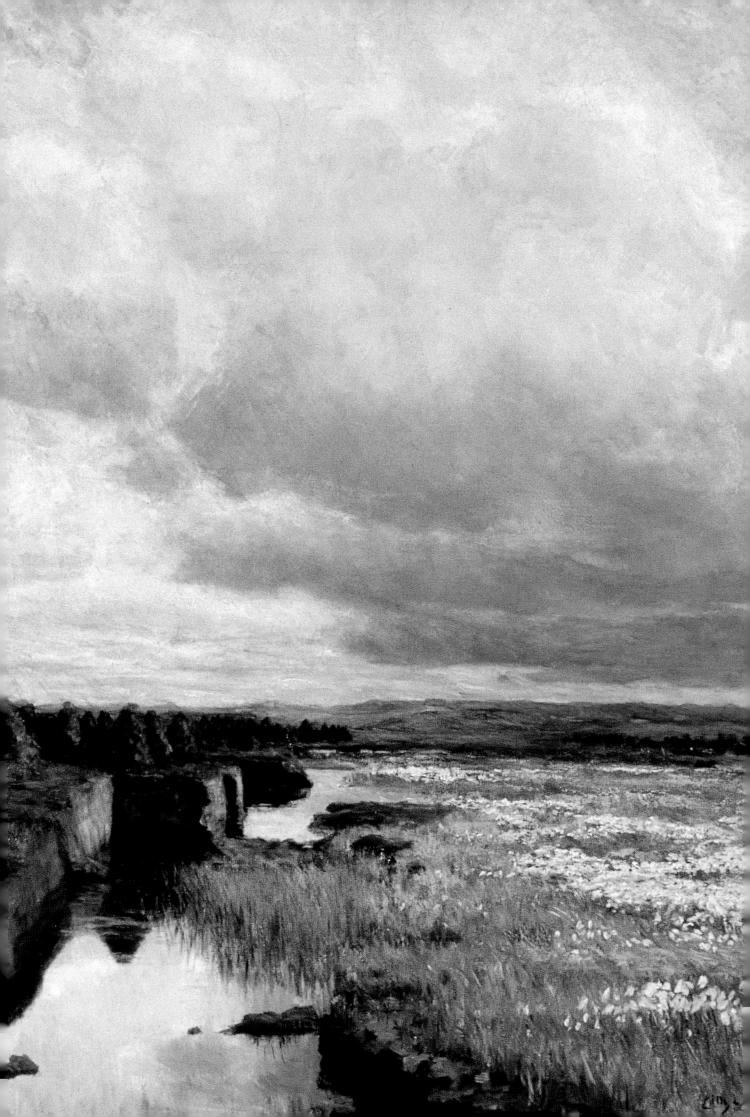

Marit Lange

Between Naturalism and Neo-Romanticism:
Puvis de Chavannes and the Evocative Norwegian Landscape

Norwegian pictorial art, in the modern sense, goes no farther back than to the Romanticism of the very early 1800s. Therefore, Norwegian artists had no classical tradition on which to build. In addition, the country was long without an art academy, an institution that was not established until 1909. Consequently, it is natural that the pictorial art created was founded on actual experiences that concentrated on Norwegian nature and folk life. Similarly, the fact that Norway was such a young nation led to the desire to create a visual expression of national identity.

For those Norwegian artists who had ambitions beyond the amateur status, it was necessary to go abroad and study at the leading art centers in order to acquire an adequate education. Thus, in Norwegian nineteenth-century art history, we are able to follow the development of European painting from the Dresden Romanticism through the late Romanticism in Düsseldorf to a dawning Realism in Karlsruhe, and thence to Berlin and Munich, and finally to Paris of the 1880s. We shall concentrate on Paris in our present context, even though the artists with whom we are particularly concerned carried out the greatest part of their studies in Germany.

Around 1880 the majority of the so-called Naturalist generation were gathered in Paris. Here, we must keep in mind that the Norwegian artists were still basing their work on what might be called a national program, in which the depiction of Norwegian nature and special national characteristics were their most important concern.

The annual Salon exhibitions in the French capital, quite naturally, were of central interest in their minds, and the desire to have a work accepted by the artist jury of this important exhibition was a strong driving force behind the work of these painters. For them, the achievement of international acclaim increased their possibilities of gaining recognition at home, where exhibition possibilities were few and the competition for the scanty resources available to artists was severe.

As a result, the most widely recognized Salon artists were their models while they paid less attention to the radical circles outside the official art milieu. Impressionism was studied, of course, but it had no immediate influence on Norwegian painting during the 1880s. On the other hand, the Salon Realist Jules Bastien-Lepage's poetic combination of figures and landscape clearly left its mark. The same is the case with Puvis de Chavannes's classically oriented landscapes.

In earlier art history, Puvis's painting was usually indicated as a possible forerunner for the decorative and synthesizing tendencies in the Norwegian art of the 1890s. It has been pointed out that a number of Norwegian women painters in Paris chose him as their teacher in the early 1890s; but that this direct contact brought a greater awareness of his art to the Norwegian painters is nevertheless not very likely. Rather, it is a sign that already he was admired both as artist and teacher in the Norwegian art circles.

At first glance, it may seem surprising that Puvis's decorative, classically oriented art had a considerable influence on Norwegian landscape painting as early as the mid-1880s.[1] It is thought-provoking that this takes place at the same time that the ideology of French open-air painting, so to speak, reigns supreme among the most progressive of the younger Norwegian painters. How could the depiction of Norway's rugged nature be compared to Puvis's dreamy, classically oriented landscapes?

At the Window, painted in 1887 by the young Naturalist Karl Jensen-Hjell (1862–88), is an example of the contrasts found in Norwegian painting towards the end of the 1880s. The man at the window portrays his friend, the painter Kalle Løchen (1865–93), in his studio. On the wall to the left, hangs a copy of Puvis's *Sacred Wood*. On the right, we look through a window at a cold winter landscape, a reminder of the demands made on the painter by open-air painting. Here, contrasts in the art of the period are emphasized: Symbolism and fantasy art stand in contrast to the demand for strict naturalism. It is significant that even the rebellious Paul Gauguin could point to Puvis as an important premise for his own radical painting. In his *Still Life with "Hope"* from 1901 we find a reproduction of a Puvis's: *Hope*, now as a conspicuous element on the wall in the background.

Concerning Puvis's influence on the various trends in contemporary art, as early as 1892 the Swedish painter Georg Pauli (1855–1935) made this discerning analysis of the situation:

1. Kitty L. Kielland,
Peat Bog, 1895.
Rogaland, Kunstmuseum

"There is something singular about this Puvis: all trends have a use for his art—from the old, from the academicians to the Impressionists, Symbolists and Synthetists."[2]

By studying Puvis's Salon pictures from the end of the 1870s to the mid-1880s, we are able to follow a slow development in his painting. We see a tendency to reduce the number of figures and, at the same time, allot relatively greater space and importance to the landscape. *The Prodigal Son* (1879), *The Poor Fisherman (1881)* and *The Dream* (1883) show how Puvis expresses the pictorial message and evocative content through the interplay of figure and landscape. The landscape accentuates and amplifies the mood in the image. It was precisely this aspect of Puvis's art that captivated Andreas Aubert (1851–1913), Norway's leading art critic at the time. He uses ample column space on Puvis's paintings in his review of the 1883 Exposition Nationale, where among others *The Prodigal Son* and *The Poor Fisherman* were shown. According to Aubert, the color harmonies were the very heart of Puvis's art. Puvis has attained "harmonies of a wonderful and consummate beauty, which he himself has compared to the long, vibrating quiver of a guitar."[3]

The Sacred Wood Dear to the Arts and Muses is the most important single work in Puvis's production in our context. It drew enormous attention when it was exhibited at the Salon in 1884. Aubert wrote about this painting already after his first impression at the private viewing, and found that the picture "is one of his most brilliant, most distinctive decorative works, wonderfully musical."[4]

Sacred Wood: a quiet evening in the sacred wood. The high horizon with the bluish hills and the edge of the dark forest almost shut out the sky. But we see it fully in the mirror image in the water, glowing in the twilight. The half moon is seen only as a reflection in the calm surface of the water. The dark, forested ridge is profiled in the clear water. For the Muses, this glade, where sky and landscape are reflected in the water is a place for meditation and reflection. Reflection, in its twofold sense, seems to be the fundamental idea itself, the picture's interconnecting idea, such as it was created as a wall decoration for the stairwell in the museum in Lyon. The underlying theme is that nature materializes when reflected in the human mind. It is precisely this process of reflection that is personified by the Muses.

Already at an early stage, it was perceived that the figures—the Muses—were wholly dependent upon the landscape, while the landscape could very well manage without the Muses. In 1898, Robert de la Sizeranne wrote that "Qu'on imagine les figures du *Bois sacré* privée de leur paysage, transportée seules sur un fond uni: on verra, hélas! Ce qu'elles garderont de poésie. . . . Mais on imagine très bien le *Bois sacré* sans ses muses, l'Hiver sans ses bôucherons. Ils resteront des pages magnifiques et leur poésie en sera à peine diminuée. C'est le paysage qui assure aux figures l'harmonie et l'unité."[5]

André Michel, too, laid primary emphasis on the landscape: "Un grand lac . . . y reflète un ciel d'or don't une mince bande paraît seule au-dessus d'une ligne de montagnes, d'un bleu violacé, qui ferme l'horizon. Entre ces deux notes, largement vibrantes, du bleu des montagnes et des eaux dorée du lac, des prairies s'étendent en pentes douces constellées de fleurs rares, narcisses jaunes et blancs, d'arbres aux troncs droits et grêles, pins, chênes et lauriers-roses."[6]

The first Norwegian artist to realize just what painterly possibilities Puvis's masterpiece could have for her own art was Kitty L. Kielland (1843–1914). She belonged to the group of Naturalists who had settled in Paris, and she remained there throughout the entire 1880s. Kielland had been a pupil of the landscape painter Hans Gude (1825–1903) in Karlsruhe, and was solidly imbued with a realistic view of nature. It was the southwestern part of Norway, the district of Jæren with its heather-clad uplands, its endless peat bogs and never-ending sand dunes bordering the open sea that were her chosen subject matter all through her life (fig. 1). However, in the mid-1880s, the influence of Puvis, and especially his *Sacred Wood*, made her turn to other subjects in which a calm water surface reflecting the light of the evening sky was the dominating feature. Given her convincing painterly development of this group of subjects, these pictures had a great impact and are seen today as the introduction to the Neo-Romantic period in Norwegian painting in the 1890s.

Kielland spent the summer of 1885 near Risør, a small city on the southern coast of Norway, and it was here that she found the way to her new circle of subjects. In the subdued light of the evening sky, an old country mansion is mirrored in the calm water. In all simplicity, this

2. Pierre Puvis de Chavannes and his pupils in Paris, 1880–90.

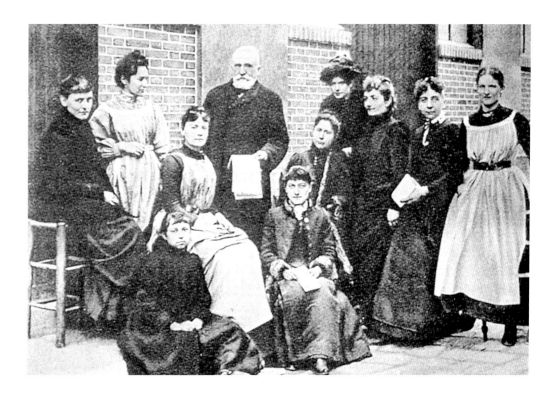

study shows the main characteristics of the composition, the house, the sky and the surface of the water. (fig. 3) The grazing horse and the woman in the rowboat were added later in order to emphasize the peace of the twilight hour and to increase the evocative content. The picture, entitled *After Sunset,* was shown in 1885 at the newly established National Art Exhibition, known as the Autumn Exhibition (fig. 4). Praised by the art critics, this was Kitty Kielland's breakthrough at long last. Aubert reviewed the exhibition and wrote: "The characteristic everyday subject—a white country house with a pointed gable mirrored in a lake—has given her poetry a fixed basis so that it does not melt into the abstract commonplace. It is precisely in this picture's sure *character* that she has reaped the reward for her faithfulness in increasingly linking herself to home. In a French subject she would have had difficulties in plumbing the depths of this feeling, and the intensity of this mood, in the way we see the old country house with its history and its memories standing alone and quiet beneath the summer evening's lingering—slowly fading light."[7]

Inspired by success at home, she repeated the subject for the Paris Salon the following year. She had been represented there each year since 1879, and so was enormously disappointed when the painting was refused. She wrote to friends at home: "It is inconceivable, I daresay, because I had good judges on my side, Dagnan, Courtois and Fantin-Latour; they find it extremely peculiar, but they immediately asked, what in the world can it do to you, your picture was very good." But then we hear that her teacher during her first years in Paris, Léon Pelouse (1838–91), had visited her studio during the winter to see her work, and that he thought "that I had gone badly astray, that I painted like Puvis de Chavannes, and when he saw from my face that I was not displeased at this he said yes, and like Monet and Manet."[8]

At first glance, the similarity between Kitty L. Kielland's evocative summer night images and Puvis's classically oriented landscapes may seem remote. However, the artist herself was pleased by the comparison, and we must keep in mind the goals this generation was striving toward. The artist expressed it very precisely in her article describing the Norwegian stand at the World Exhibition in 1889. Concerning Norwegian dependence on foreign art, she added: "But no, what was learned abroad was well digested, it entered the Norwegian bloodstream and strengthened rather than weakened national feeling." As to the artistic goal, she wrote: "Indeed, those who want to get somewhere, will do it with a new, fresh viewpoint, freed from foreign influence, and they will see our nature and our lives with a Norwegian eye."[9]

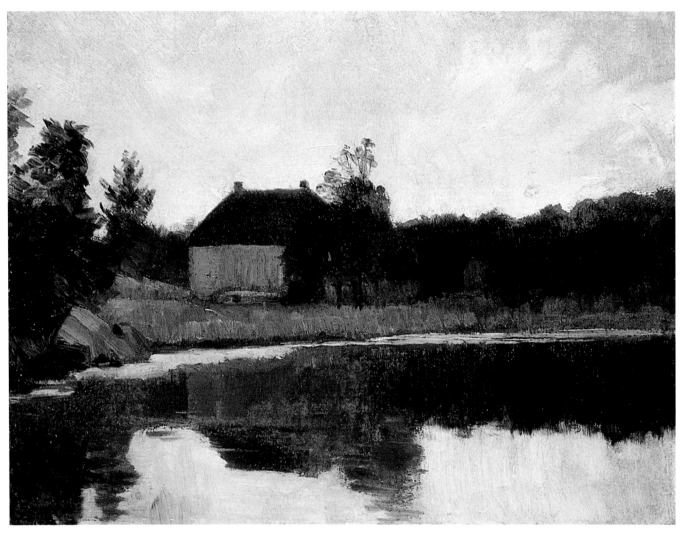

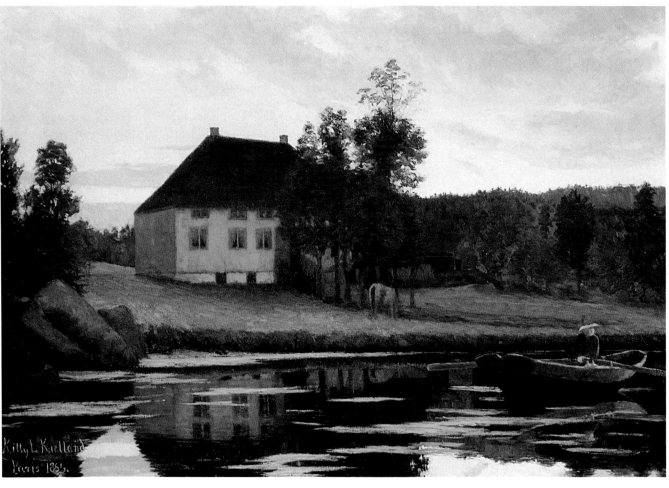

3. Kitty L. Kielland
Study for "After Sunset," 1885.
Oslo, Nasjonalgalleriet

4. Kitty L. Kielland,
After Sunset II, 1886.
Rogaland, Kunstmuseum

In the summer of 1886, a group of painters, friends from Munich and Paris, gathered at Fleskum Farm on the outskirts of Oslo. This so-called Fleskum summer has a special place in Norwegian art history. Here, French inspired open-air painting made its definitive breakthrough. At the same time, we find the seeds of the budding Neo-Romanticism in the pictures from that summer that were to burst forth in full blossom in the 1890s. It is in this dualism between the realistic conception of nature and Neo-Romantic synthesizing tendencies that we find the first signs of influence from Puvis's landscape painting.

Fleskum Farm was idyllically situated beside Lake Dælivannet. This small lake, enclosed by high tree-covered hills, imparted a rare feeling of intimate closeness to nature. The calm mirror of its surface beneath the summer night's fading light became the central subject for Kitty Kielland's and Eilif Peterssen's landscape paintings that summer. Their pictures, both with the title *Summer Night,* were shown at the National Annual Autumn Exhibition the same year. According to Aubert's newspaper review of the exhibition, Peterssen's painting was the exhibition's greatest surprise. If we describe the image, we shall see that it has characteristics in common with Puvis's *Sacred Wood.* Moreover, it is precisely these that Aubert emphasizes. The water mirror, "unfurrowed by the slightest ripple. The pale sickle of the moon and the midnight blue ridge in the west stand firmly but softly down there. . . . We see neither the hills' ridgeline nor the moon's sickle except in the mirrored surface. In the center of the picture the trunk of an alder rises up from the sodden soil, cropped so that we do not see the crown."[10]

With great effect, Peterssen borrowed the idea of the reflected half-moon in the surface of the lake from Puvis de Chavannes's composition. But what is remarkable about this picture is how he managed to transpose the summer night theme from an ideal classical world to an actual and genuine interpretation of Norwegian nature. No matter how strong an experience of reality may be, it is only by means of artistic convention that it attains a satisfactory pictorial expression.

Peterssen's experience of Puvis's pictures in the Paris Salon of 1884 and of 1886 created the basis for his convincing interpretation of this idyllic Norwegian landscape. But his total reinterpretation of Puvis's landscape composition shows how freely and independently he worked with respect to his model.

In addition to these easily demonstrable similarities, the painting also shares something of its fundamental ambience with *Sacred Wood*, namely, a quality called at the time musicality. We have already seen that Aubert drew attention to the musicality in Puvis's art; in particular he found *Sacred Wood* "wondrously musical." *Summer Night,* too, was seen in the same way. It may be of interest to clarify just what this musicality consists of. Aubert writes: "His love of colors is combined with a deep musical sense. . . . Eilif Peterssen wanted to be a Naturalist in full. The picture, however, is not without a faint brownish-violet tone that does not belong to nature. But it is not without musical beauty. . . ." It is evident, in other words, that musicality can stand in contrast to the naturalistic.

It is these musical characteristics found in *Summer Night* that Eilif Peterssen emphasized in his painting, *Nocturne,* the following year. (fig. 6) The title itself reveals the importance he attributed to musical associations. In both title and content we have moved away from the depiction of a summer night that could still be defended from a naturalistic point of view. We are in the same landscape, but this time a dream one. Nature has been abstracted into large bluish expanses, flowers that did not grow wild around the Lake Dælivannet, the previous year have now been added decoratively and meaningfully. We are reminded of André Michel's description of "fleurs rares" in *Sacred Wood.* Here too, it is reasonable to mention Puvis. Wood nymphs such as this had never been seen before in Norwegian nature or in Norwegian art. On the contrary, Peterssen's red-haired woman is an obvious paraphrase of Puvis's nude seen from the rear in his painting *Autumn* (1864), a replica of which was shown in the Paris Salon in 1885.

Summer Night and *Nocturne* show how easily Peterssen had already shifted from a naturalistic to a decorative style by the end of the 1880s. He continued with this for the rest of his life. Some of his finest pictures from this period, however, are based on a combination of the two styles. In his *Salmon Fishermen on Figgen River,* he reinterprets impressions from Puvis's *Poor Fishermen*, but within a naturalistic pictorial imagery.

5. Pierre Puvis de Chavannes,
The Sacred Wood, detail, 1884.
Lyon, Musée des Beaux-Arts

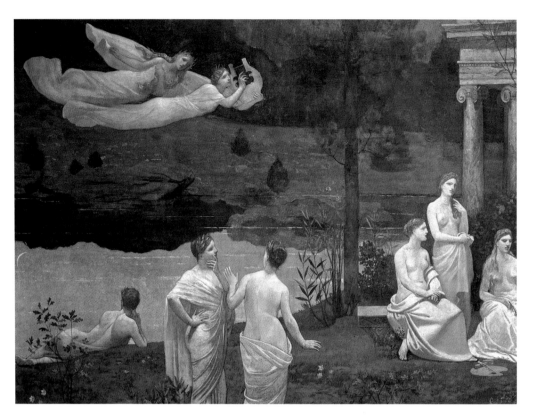

Kitty Kielland, as has been maintained here, was the first to perceive the possibilities Puvis's compositions had for her own landscape art. They did not change her fundamental naturalistic attitude, but encouraged her to find new pictorial formulas for her expressions of nature. If we compare her *Summer Night* (figs. 7–8) with Peterssen's, we find that her perception of nature is far more naturalistic. Nevertheless, Kielland's version of Lake Dælivannet also reflects considerable influence from Puvis's art. As in *After Sunset,* the picture's intimate mood is created through an interplay of the closed composition and the dim evening light. The high, dark crest of the ridge blocks off the view, emphasizing and strengthening the play of the evening light on the calm surface of the water. French art critic Maurice Hamel had seen *After Sunset* at the Nordic Exhibition in Copenhagen in 1888 and noted these characteristics: "En disant les choses plus simplement, Mlle Kielland obtient une impression plus pénétrante [the comparison here is with Peterssen's *Nocturne*]. Quelle pureté diaphane dans son paysage, *Après le coucher du soleil*! Comme la maison blanche au grand toit rouge endort doucement son reflet dans les eaux que le ciel nocturne glace de rose et de vert pâles."[11]

Peterssen's and Kielland's depictions of Dælivannet are marked by a bluish tonality that may be interpreted in various ways. In his reviews of the National Annual Autumn Exhibition Aubert discussed this question. He was aware that this color could be interpreted as a studied effect, but also as faithfulness to the subject matter "based on the blue ridge rising up behind the water." Devotee as he was of open-air painting, he maintained that the Nordic summer night ought to "be a source on which our painters should draw." The summer night with its long twilight allowed, according to Aubert, lengthy studies in the open, in contrast to "Central Europe's short dusk."[12]

An artistic conquest of the summer night was completely in line with the period's naturalistic program, which among other things, meant that art should emphasize the distinctive national character. In addition to being a national innovation, the study of the summer night opened up new possibilities: the light of the twilight hour suggested the idea of simplifying the forms and thereby further increasing the picture's evocative content. It was here Puvis entered the scene and gained his significance in Norwegian art history, at the very time that French-influenced Naturalism finally broke into the Norwegian art milieu.

Among Norwegian art critics of the period there were far greater shades of opinion about the French art situation than we often meet in modern art historic accounts. An excellent

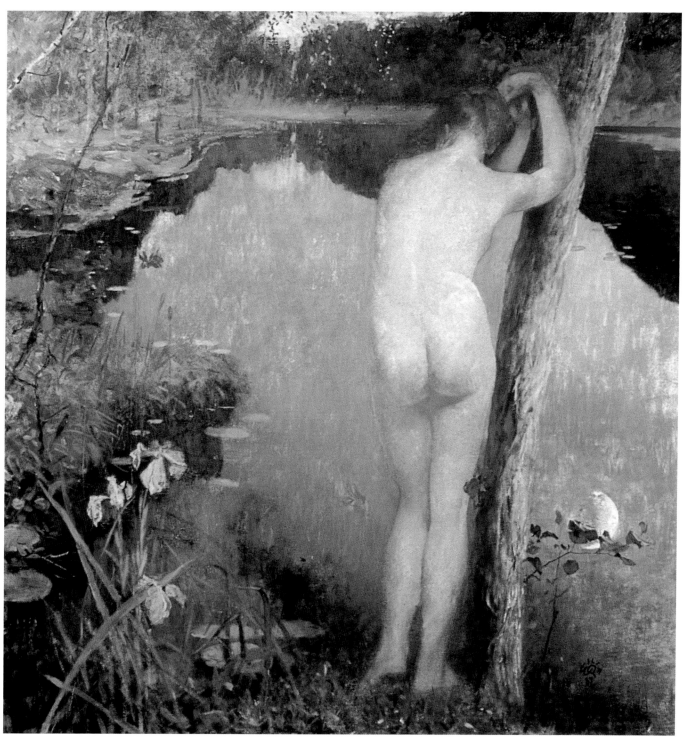

6. Eilif Peterssen, *Nocturne*, 1887.
Oslo, Nasjonalgalleriet

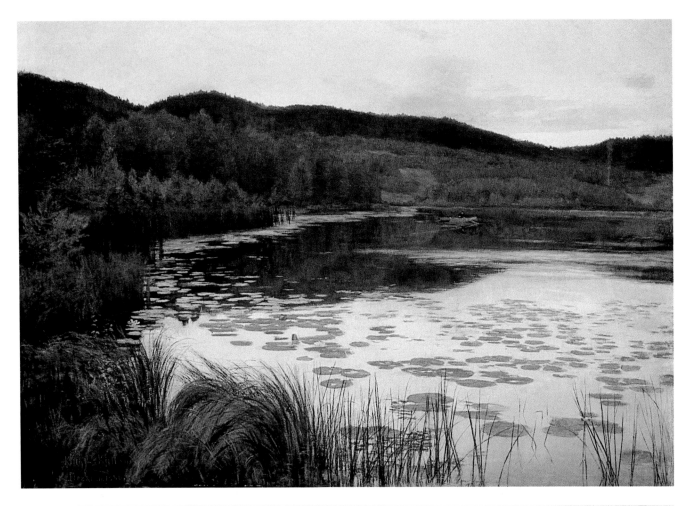

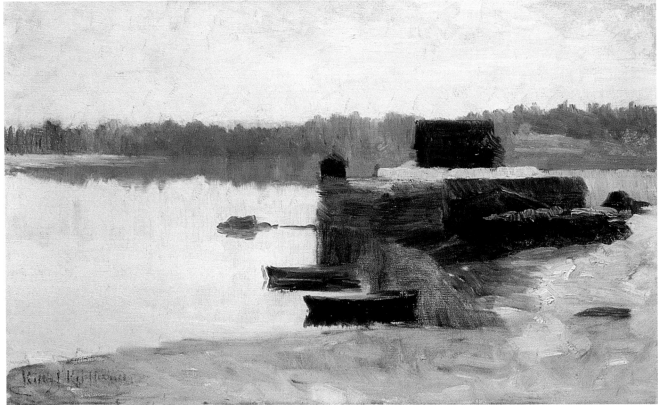

7. Kitty L. Kielland,
Summer Night, 1886.
Oslo, Nasjonalgalleriet

8. Kitty L. Kielland,
Summer Night, 1890.
Private collection

example of this is an article written in 1892 by the painter and art critic Christian Krohg (1852–1925). He reflects upon the relationship between Naturalism and Impressionism on the one hand and Symbolism and Synthetism on the other. Among other things, he says: "In a way, Symbolism has a certain connection with Impressionism, inasmuch as it, too, is not intent upon depicting nature itself, but only the impression it has made upon oneself. But it is always the impression that the small detail of nature that he sees at the moment makes on him. The Symbolist does not confine himself to this. For example, in a single picture he will depict the impression that the entire area he is passing through makes on him, as it appears to him when he thinks about it. Yes, not only that, but also to a great degree what he is thereby led to think about, which with the memory of it creates an entity in his mind, all of which he wants to depict immediately."[13]

Against the background of the above-examined pictures, Krohg contributes to an explanation of how Puvis de Chavannes could be of such decisive importance in an art milieu where faithfulness to nature was still considered binding. In the long drawn-out twilight of the Nordic summer night when all details are blotted out, it was as if the landscape itself had come forth to meet the new synthesizing trends.

[1] This view was first published by M. Lange, "Fra den hellige lund [*Bois sacré*] til Fleskum. Kitty L. Kielland og den nordiske sommernatt," in *Kunst og Kultur,* Oslo 1977, pp. 69–92. See also K. Berg, *Norges kunsthistorie*, vol. 5, Oslo 1981, p. 210ff. Reprinted in *Norges kunsthistorie*, vol. 1, Oslo 1993, p. 451ff.

[2] "Bref om konst," *Ord och Bild,* Stockholm 1892, p. 280.

[3] "Fra det franske nutidsmaleri," II, *Nordisk Tidsskrift,* Stockholm 1884, pp. 451–52.

[4] *Aftenposten,* Kristiania (Oslo), April, 4, 1884.

[5] *Revue des deux mondes,* Paris, 1898, p. 417.

[6] A. Michel and J. Laran, *Puvis de Chavannes,* Paris, n.d., p. 85.

[7] *Nyt Tidsskrift,* Kristiania (Oslo), 1885, p. 526ff.

[8] Letter to the painter Erik Werenskiold, dated Paris, April 15, 1886. Handwriting Collection, National Library, Oslo. This version of *After Sunset* is in the Rogaland Art Museum, Norway, a gift from the artist in 1889.

[9] "Lidt om norsk kunst," in *Samtiden,* Kristiania (Oslo), 1890, p. 223ff.

[10] *Morgenbladet,* Kristiania (Oslo), November, 2, 1886.

[11] "La peinture du Nord," *Gazette des Beaux-Arts,* II, Paris, 1888, p. 402.

[12] *Morgenbladet,* Kristiania (Oslo), November 2 and 4, 1886.

[13] "Willumsen," *Verdens Gang,* Kristiania (Oslo), October 11, 1892. The article was written in connection with the exhibition of the Danish painter J.F. Willumsen (1863–1958) at H. Abel's art shop and gallery in Kristiania.

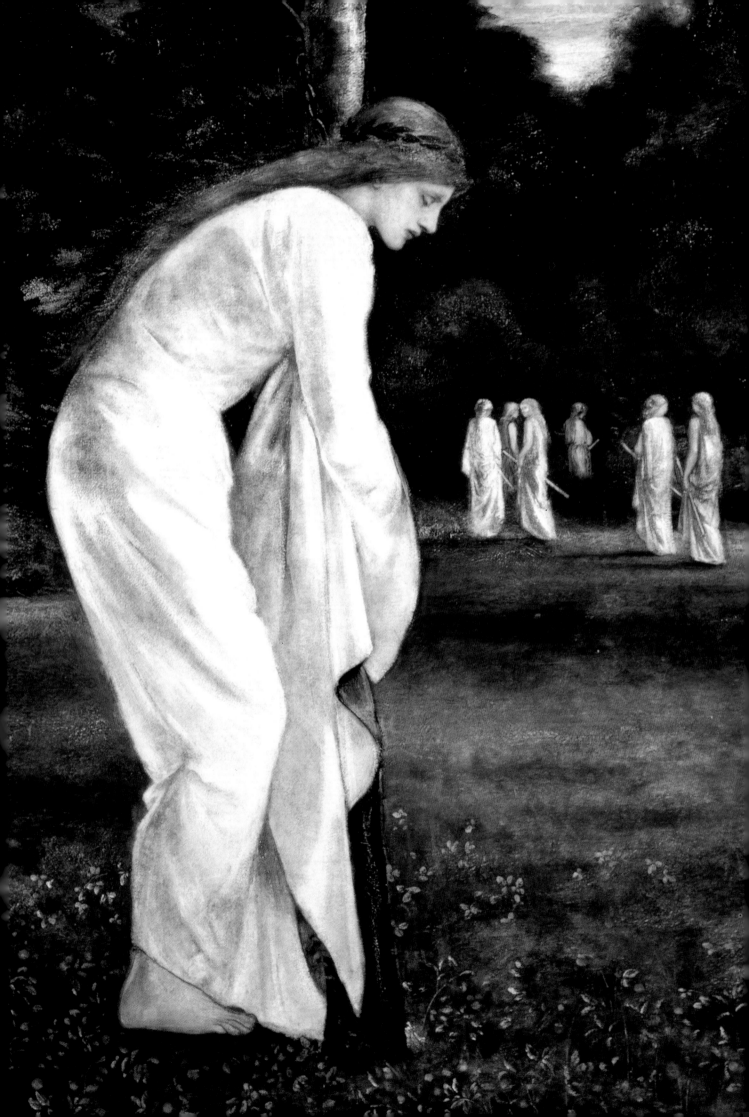

1. Edward Burne-Jones,
The Princess Tied to the Tree, 1866.
New York, The Forbes Collection

Preston is large industrial town in Lancashire, about fifteen miles from the seaside resort of Blackpool in the chilly northwest of England. In the nineteenth century Preston expanded thanks to the cotton trade, and despite fluctuating fortunes its mill owners prospered. As the century entered its final decade Preston sought to signal its achievements by building a public museum and art gallery, as its much larger neighbors Liverpool and Manchester had done in 1873 and 1882 respectively. Paid for from £300 000 the wealthy solicitor Edmund Harris left to benefit his hometown, a museum named after him opened in 1893. It was not simply for the philanthropic edification and enjoyment of the thousands who toiled endlessly in Preston's factories, but would be proof of the town's cultural sophistication and commercial status. The local architect James Hibbert constructed a fine structure in Greek Revival style, an imposing temple to the arts which dominated the main square. Inside, the ambulatories displayed casts of the Parthenon frieze, and around the central square lantern was wall space intended for a mural.

The person the burghers of Preston invited to decorate the lantern was no less a figure than Puvis de Chavannes. This was a surprising choice, not least because in 1893 Puvis was relatively little known in Britain outside of an artistic and aesthetic elite. He was probably recommended by Hibbert, who had travelled widely and is likely to have seen his decorations in Paris. But more than anything else, what made Preston's choice of Puvis so remarkable, or even risky, was that he was French. For much of the nineteenth century French art had been critically derided in Britain, and from the 1880s onwards this denigration reached a fever pitch with the showing of Impressionist pictures, and some young British artists' imitation of them. In the event, Puvis declined the Preston commission because he was busy working on the Boston Public Library. But if it had happened, it would have been the only publicly commissioned decorative cycle in Britain by a French artist, and would have been a considerable coup for Preston.[1]

Nevertheless, for all the aesthetic francophobia in conservative British academic circles, Puvis's high seriousness and epic endeavor fitted exactly with prevailing beliefs about the desirable direction of the national school. George Frederic Watts, for instance, was revered for subject pictures which questioned the timeless uncertainties of human existence. Many considered such pictures as *Love and Death* (c. 1874–77), *Hope* (c. 1885–86) and *The All-Pervading* (1887–c. 93) as the epitome of British artistic achievement, worthy modern successors to history painting and the proper base on which to build the art of the coming new century. Watts's subjects were sometimes slightly more emphatically stated, less ambiguous than Puvis's, but there are close similarities between the two artists in their understanding of the expressive potential of the human figure, and how pose might evoke subtle, indefinable suggestions of mood, atmosphere or states of mind. There are interesting affinities, for instance, between Puvis de Chavannes's *Meditation* (1867) and Watts's *Psyche* (1880; fig. 2), but also with the subjectless pictures of draped female figures made by Albert Moore in the 1860s, with their pale coloring and chalky surface. Puvis's intensity, and melancholy atmosphere, also found comparison and counterpart in the work of Edward Burne-Jones, whom the French painter greatly admired.

In much of his art Burne-Jones was concerned with expressing the possibilities of existential anxiety and disjunction, of the overpowering strength and compulsion of human love, and the inevitability of death and decay. Sometimes these themes were explored through archetypal myth, such as in his series of Perseus or Pygmalion canvases, or those treating Arthurian legend, but other works were altogether more abstract and ideal in origin. In his wide-format pen and ink drawing *Ladies and Death* (1860) a figure of death rings the entrance bell to a garden, where a line of languid girls sit unaware of his proximity. This formed the basis for Burne-Jones's watercolor *Green Summer* (1864; fig. 3) in which a group of maidens sit reading to each other in a verdant, ethereal landscape. Death here is offstage, unseen, but an eerie melancholy pervades the scene and a strange mood of impending doom. Contrasting the careless concerns of youth with the relentless inevitability of death finds interesting expression in Puvis de Chavannes's *Death and the Maidens* (1872), although here death is vanquished. Burne-Jones's placing of figures in the landscape in *Green Summer* echoes and anticipates Puvis, as does his subtly-graded coloring and soft lighting. In the decorative cycle *Saint George and the Dragon*, commis-

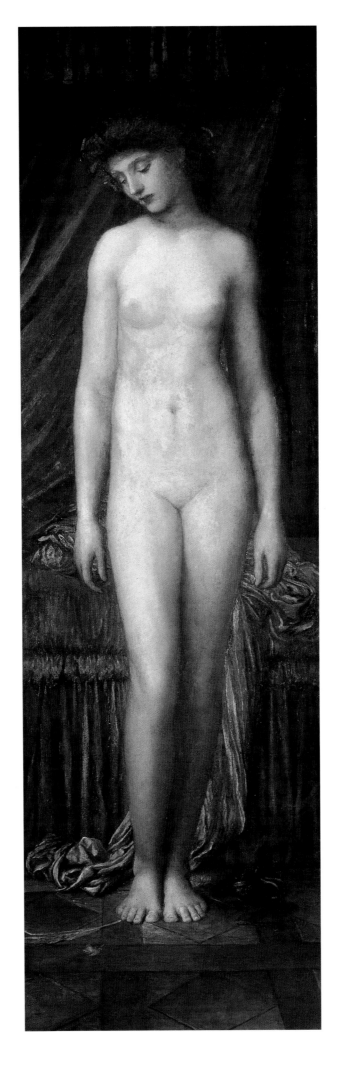

2. George Frederic Watts,
Psyche, 1880.
London, Tate

sioned by Myles Birket Foster, his *Princess Tied to the Tree* (1866; fig. 1) seems particularly close to the disposition of figures found in some of the French painter's designs. There seems little possibility that Puvis de Chavannes ever saw any of these pictures, but their similarities illustrate a shared visual aesthetic and response. Puvis did see Burne-Jones's *King Cophetua* (1884) when it was the triumph of the 1889 Paris Exposition Universelle, and in the early 1890s the two artists entered into correspondence. As president of the Société Nationale des Beaux-Arts, Puvis sought to obtain Burne-Jones's *Wheel of Fortune* (1883) for their annual exhibition. "Most eminent master," Puvis wrote, "The promise of your glorious participation in our exhibition at the Champ-de-Mars is a source of great and sincere personal joy . . . As for drawings, we would consider them also as an expression of the deepest, purest and highest art."[2] In the event, *The Wheel of Fortune* was not shown in Paris, but instead Burne-Jones sent a dozen drawings, including a study for the painting's Goddess of Fortune. "Thank you from the bottom of my painter's heart for your powerful and original symbol of Fortune," Puvis wrote to him, "like everyone I invited to see it, I was deeply impressed by its grandeur."[3] Burne-Jones sent works to the Société the following year, and again in 1895 and 1896. Perhaps as a result of this, or of some personal recommendation, Burne-Jones was invited to contribute to the first Rose+Croix Salon. Sâr Péladan sent him a pamphlet which Burne-Jones described to Watts as "disgracefully silly, but I was in the mood . . . to help in anything that upholds the ideals I care for . . . Do you know Puvis de Chavannes? Who has lifted the same banner."[4] Burne-Jones evidently then wrote to Puvis for advice about the Sâr, and subsequently declined to exhibit.

Contemporary critics noted affinities between the two painters' approach to the subject. In his review of Burne-Jones's retrospective at the New Gallery in London in 1892–93 in the *Gazette des Beaux-Arts*, Paul Leprieur drew attention to "several portraits . . . which he treats in an idealized manner, not unlike Puvis de Chavannes when he works in this genre, synthesizing, simplifying, distilling the essence of the sitter and of life."[5] Puvis's synthesized coloring and concern with unity of facture also finds counterpart in Burne-Jones. His picture surface has a thoroughly modern sensibility in which each area, treated equally, holds an abstract value and emotive potential in itself, divorced from subject or narrative.

If Burne-Jones was well-known to a French audience by the early 1890s, sadly the same could not be said of Puvis de Chavannes in Britain. This was lamented by the critic Claude Phillips in 1885 in one of the earliest articles to examine Puvis in depth. "It may at first appear strange," Phillips wrote, "that an artist who has long been so widely known and so hotly discussed in France . . . should be in England little more than a name."[6] This he attributed to Puvis's principal pictures' large scale preventing their display at sympathetic venues such as the Grosvenor Gallery, and while "The proper place for such works would be the great gallery of the Royal Academy . . . unfortunately the members of that body have not in recent years shown a spirit . . . in the cause of true art that they would grant hospitality."[7]

Phillips hailed Puvis as a great master, but this view was not universal in Britain. The novelist and critic George Moore penned a sneering piece which lambasted Puvis together with Millet, judging "their brushwork is deficient [and] so is their drawing."[8] Moore tapped into visceral language more often reserved by British commentators for Impressionism. In 1887–88 a bitter quarrel had been fought out in the pages of the *Magazine of Art* about French artistic influence. Egged on by Ruskin, the French critic Ernest Chesneau queried the growing fashion for British artists to finish their training in Paris in an article provocatively titled "The English School in Peril." Its rebuttal by George Clausen provoked a blistering tirade from the veteran genre painter and Academician William Powell Frith. Dismissing Pre-Raphaelitism as a "ridiculous movement," aestheticism as "pernicious" and Impressionism and Naturalism as "dangerous," Frith thundered "Born and bred in France what is called Impressionism has tainted the art of this country," and its exponents had minds "in a state of disease."[9] Edward Armitage R.A., who in his youth helped Delaroche with the Ecole des Beaux-Arts decorations, in 1887 blamed Puvis himself for the rise of Impressionism. "There is no doubt," he wrote, "that the great success of M. Puvis de Chavannes (a success totally undeserved) has given an impetus and im-

following pages
3. Edward Burne-Jones,
Green Summer, 1864.
Private collection

279

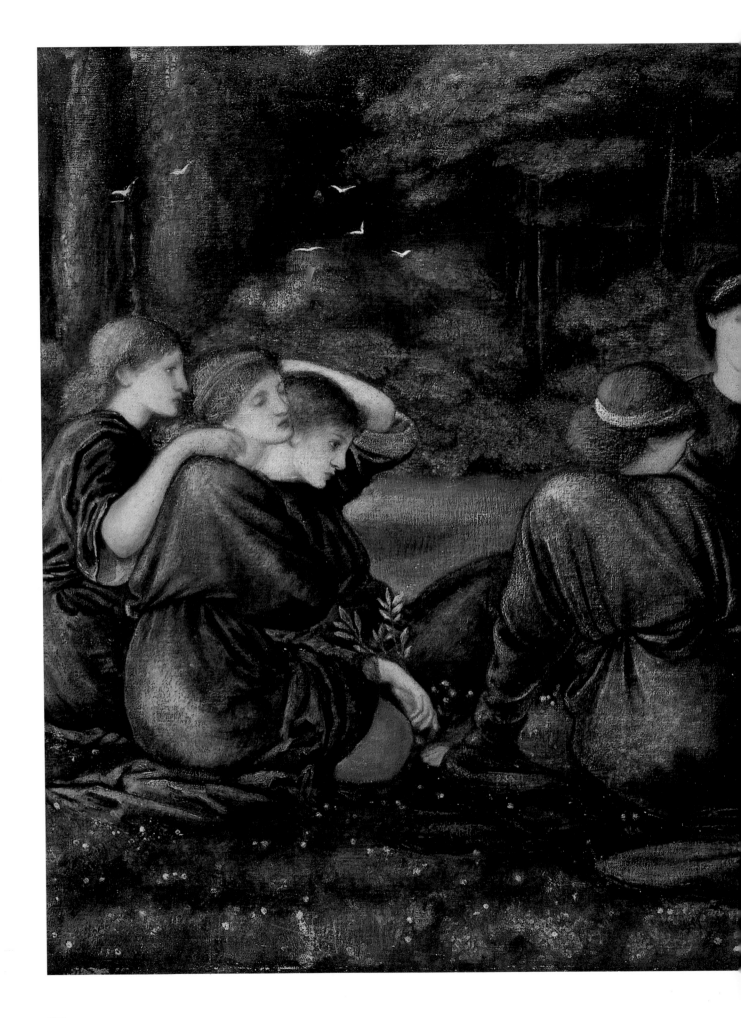

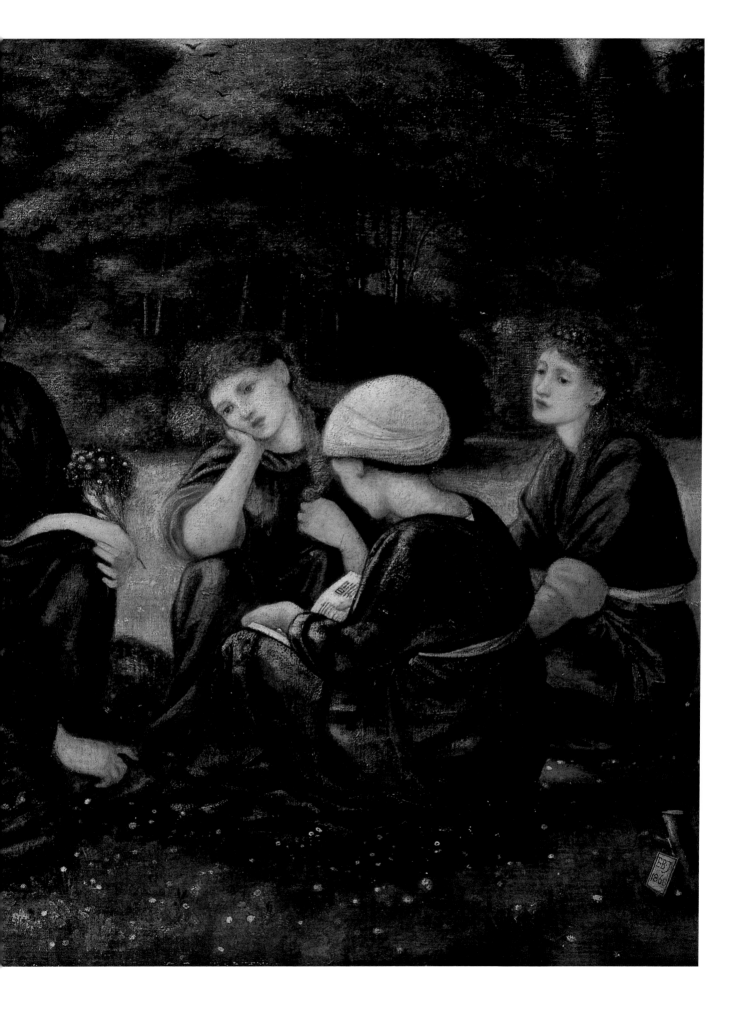

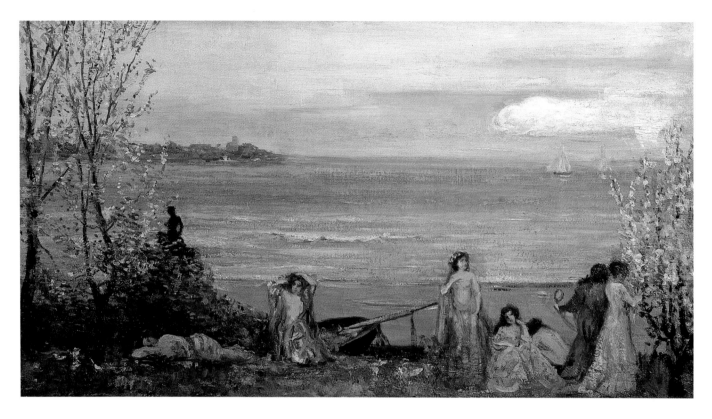

4. Charles Conder,
Spring by the Sea , c. 1905.
London, Tate

portance to this unwholesome phase of French art which otherwise it would not have acquired."[10]

Despite such attitudes, and partly because of them, in the 1880s and 1890s British artists visited Paris in considerable numbers, the advent of the boat train making travel relatively easy. It was increasingly common for students to finish their studies at fashionable ateliers such as the Académie Julian, and to lead the sort of bohemian artistic life celebrated in George du Maurier's novel *Trilby* (1894). Meanwhile in London French art was becoming increasingly visible, with Monet and Rodin sending works to the Grosvenor Gallery, and Durand-Ruel's gallery showing a wide range of painters new to a British audience. But Puvis apparently often slipped from critical attention. Reviewing the 1896 Manet show in Paris, D.S. MacColl recorded how he asked Durand-Ruel why it would not be shown in London, "but M. Durand-Ruel shakes his head, and reminds me how, two years ago, he tried us with a Puvis de Chavannes . . . and vainly essayed to interest, not only our public, but eminent directors of galleries and other leaders of taste."[11]

Nevertheless, for many progressive young British artists in Paris, Puvis was a revelation. Charles Ricketts became a central figure in the emergent aesthetic movement from the late 1880s, and in 1887 he journeyed to Paris especially to meet his idol. "I remember him as the man of his work," Ricketts recalled in 1908, "simple, grave and genial, touched and charmed by our raw and uncultivated admiration for his painting . . . from time to time his speech became admonitory, and he launched forth into disapproval of current tendencies—the photographic drawing of many, 'la perfection bête qui n'a rien à faire avec le vrai dessin, le dessin expressif!' [stupid perfection which has nothing to do with real drawing, expressive drawing] and against 'les pochades d'atelier et de vacance' [rapid sketches of the studio or holiday]."[12] This formed part of a lengthy discussion and defense of Puvis written in 1908, but as early as 1886, Ricketts had published an article about him in the first issue of his limited-edition aesthetic journal *The Dial*.

With his companion Charles Shannon, Ricketts also collected Puvis de Chavannes's work. They had acquired the oil *Fishing* (1866, untraced) by 1904, and Ricketts's diary records his relish in acquiring an Amiens study "for the huge sum of one hundred and thirty pounds. I burst into perspiration at the sight of it, so great was my lust of possession. It had just been refused by the British Museum owing to size and cost . . . a good excuse,

5, 6. Pierre Puvis de Chavannes,
Antique Vision
and *Christian Inspiration*, 1885.
Lyon, Musée des Beaux-Arts

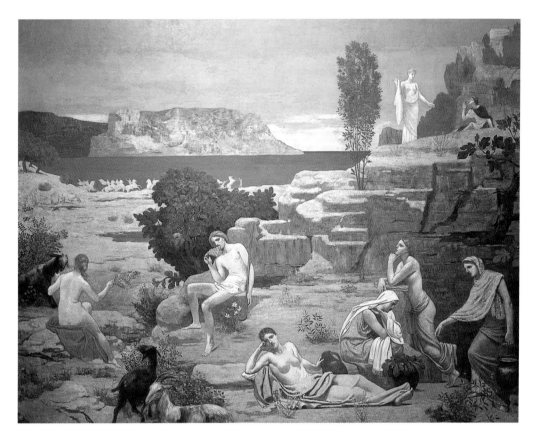

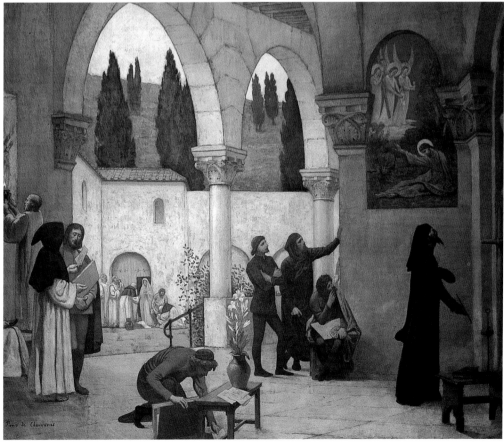

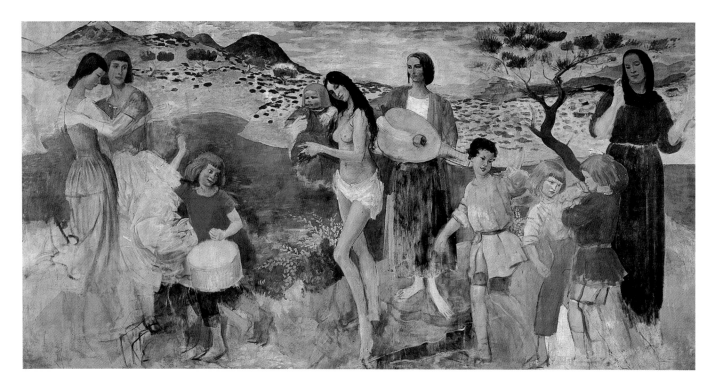

7. Augustus John,
The Lyric Fantasy, 1913–14.
London, Tate

since they do not know how important Puvis is, and how rare is a drawing of this order."[13] William Rothenstein was another young British artist who admired Puvis. Attending the Académie Julian from 1889 to 1893, Rothenstein recalled "Puvis de Chavannes and Monet were the prevalent influences among the more intelligent students."[14] Albert Besnard generously invited Rothenstein and his friend Ludwig von Hoffman to supper to meet their hero, but they appear to have been slightly disappointed: "Could this rubicund, large-nosed old gentleman, encased so correctly in a close-fitting frock coat, looking more like a senator than an artist, be the Olympian Puvis? The only other guest was [Jean-Louis] Forain . . . After dinner we adjourned to the studio . . . we waited breathlessly to hear Puvis's comments, but it was always Forain who played the critic. Puvis was discreetly genial, and said little that was remarkable."[15] In 1892 Aubrey Beardsley visited Puvis, who received him kindly and politely looked through the portfolio he had brought with him. Beardsley presented him with a drawing of children decorating a terminal god, and boasted to a friend of getting "great encouragement from Puvis de Chavannes, who introduced me to a brother painter as 'un jeune artiste anglais qui fait des choses étonnantes.' I was not a little pleased, I can tell you, with my success."[16] Little evidence of imitation seems felt in Beardsley or Rothenstein's pictures, but it is frequently felt in the work of their mutual friend Charles Conder, who was also in Paris in the 1890s, initially a student of the Académie Julian as well. His disposition of figures in Arcadian landscapes in his delicate rococo silk fan designs strongly echo Puvis, and in his oil painting *Spring by the Sea* (c. 1905; fig. 4) the trees, figures and wide compositional plane evoke echoes of *The Sacred Wood*.

Frederick Cayley Robinson also studied at the Académie Julian, from 1891–94 while Rothenstein and Conder were there, and he lived in Paris again from 1902 to 1906. His earliest pictures made in England imitated Newlyn naturalism, but his exposure to Symbolist painting and poetry steered him irrevocably towards the ideal. With its chalky coloring and calm surface, his *Youth* pays open tribute to Puvis. Its expansive, populated landscape punctuated by a gently curving pool drawn with a bounding line is partly inspired by *The Poor Fisherman*, which Cayley Robinson saw on display in the Luxembourg. This evidently had a considerable impact upon him, and he imitated it very closely in his tempera *To Pastures New (Dawn)* (c. 1904)[17] and it still resonates in late works such as *Pastoral* (1923–24).

Cayley Robinson's interest in using tempera, and election to the recently-formed Tempera

Society in 1904, was probably also partly stimulated by Puvis de Chavannes, as his interest in making decorative cycles is likely to have been. The most important of these projects was the series of large-scale murals he made for Middlesex Hospital between 1915 and 1920, which were collectively entitled *Acts of Mercy*, and which are one of the major achievements of British decorative painting. Painted quite dryly in oils, the flat picture space, cool coloring and calm introspection and grouping of the figures immediately recall Puvis de Chavannes's compositions, albeit expressed in a distinctly characteristic and personal idiom.

The end of the old century and the beginning of the new saw a number of such decorative commissions carried out in Britain, testimony to the permeation of belief about the benefits of integrating of art, design and architecture, as well as a flowering of haut bourgeois patronage. Despite being on the eve of modernism and abstraction bursting forth in Britain, to their admirers such cycles embodied belief in the high potential of figuration and the kind of dignified symbolism of expression which embodied the achievements of the Old Masters. With his wild hair and gypsy clothes Augustus John seemed an unlikely advocate of this great tradition, but in 1909 he was commissioned by Hugh Lane to decorate the entrance hall of Lindsey House, his London residence.

Although he was a dealer in Old Master paintings, Lane was a staunch advocate of Impressionist and Post-Impressionist painting, which he collected for himself. Inspired by Puvis's *Poor Fisherman*, John's large *Childhood of Pyramus* had been bought by Lane for the Johannesburg Art Gallery the previous year and he now supported John's development of this new phase in his art. The decorations were to consist of three large canvases, but the commission soon fell into difficulties. Lane objected to the gypsies taken on as models he discovered relaxing in his house, and John himself seems to have been stretched by the large scale of the canvases, and greatly irritated too by Lane's constant admonitions to work faster. Two were finished, and one— *The Lyric Fantasy* (fig. 7)— was left incomplete.[18] None were ever installed, and it appears Lane never paid for the works. When Lane died in the torpedoing of the *Lusitania* in 1915, John abandoned the project once and for all. His inspiration for these large landscapes filled with figures was Puvis de Chavannes. Visiting Paris in autumn 1899 with William Rothenstein, Charles Conder and William Orpen, John was enormously impressed by Puvis's rendering of an idealized humanity, and the harmonious integration of figures and landscape. On his 1906–07 trip to Paris, John's assimilation of Puvis seems to have been completed. He visited Picasso in his studio, and the courtesy was repaid, when they discovered their mutual admiration for the French master. John was rapturous about Puvis, writing "I went to see Puvis's drawings in Paris. He seems to me to be the finest modern . . . full of Greek lightness. Longings devour me to decorate a vast space with nudes and—and trees and waters. I am getting clearer about color tho' still very ignorant, with a little more knowledge I shall at last begin."[19] At this time "almost the only painter, living or dead, who is mentioned in his correspondence is Puvis,"[20] and a response was quickly felt in John's work. His 1907 composition study *Group with a Girl Going to a Boat* is clearly partly influenced by *The Fisherman's Family*, and his decorations for Lane followed this new trend. The many pencil drawings which John made to decide the subjects and compositions for the scheme are potent translations of Puvis.[21] Painted from a full-size pencil cartoon, *The Lyric Fantasy* used members of John's family and circle for its cast of figures in a warm landscape. It stands as an embodiment of the unfettered life John tried unsuccessfully to realize by rejecting social convention, but it is also a lament. His dead wife Ida stands on the right, while his mistress Dorelia, whom he forced Ida to accept in a *ménage à trois*, plays the music of the dance. "It is difficult not to look at this superb painting without sadness," John Rothenstein wrote in 1945, "for it represents something unique in our time, but it remains unfulfilled, not through the painter's fault but through ours."[22]

William Strang was a generation older than John, but he too worked under Puvis's spell well into the twentieth century. He studied at the Slade School of Art from 1876 to 1880, and became a close associate of Ricketts and Shannon. Through them he came to share their enthusiasm for Continental Symbolist artists, particularly Puvis, and also for the Venetian Old Masters and Watts. He became well-known in Europe, mostly in Germany after winning a gold medal at the Dresden International Exhibition in 1897, and here he was exposed to a wide range of Symbolist material. The following year he was one of the small number of British artists invited to contribute to the First Vienna Secession, where he showed five works. Strang's developing Symbolist tendency was most fully expressed in the remarkable cycle of ten paintings he made illustrating the life of Adam and Eve. These were commissioned by the brewer and patron William Hodson to decorate his library at Compton Hall near Wolverhampton (1899–1901). Recognized at the time as landmarks of British imaginative painting of the period, they reflect Strang's growing interest in Puvis. In *By the Sweat of they Brow*, Eve and the babies, and indeed the vegetation, quote from *Rest* in Puvis's Amiens decorations, while Adam appears adapted from a background laborer in *Work*. The cycle was much admired when it was exhibited at the large *Art and Industrial Exhibition* Hodson organized in Wolverhampton in 1902, and again when some of them were shown at the major survey of British art from the last twenty years held at the Whitechapel Art Gallery in 1910.[23] Walter Sickert drew particular attention to them in his review: "These seem to me the works of the greatest importance. They are not for everybody. In these days of incessant lollipops, strong meat does not find a quick or universal favor. Here we have a modern painter setting to work on imaginative subjects in the grand, self-respecting classic manner. A strange, rude fancy of great vitality is served by scholarly ability of a very high order. Every figure, every limb is studied out austerely to the end, for all the significance and beauty that it is worth. The landscapes that form the setting are as full of meaning as the figures. No serious student of art can afford to neglect a careful study of this series . . . it is work like this that year in and year out has a new secret to tell those who live with it. I should like to see Mr. Strang at the head of a great school of art."[24] Strang's admiration of Puvis de Chavannes lasted to the end, and his final major picture *Nymphs and Shepherds* (1921), whose central figure is a nude girl holding out some daisies, partly draws upon *Hope* for inspiration.

The year of the Whitechapel retrospective was something of a watershed in the direction of British art. Puvis had become better known in London, and his work was shown in a solo exhibition at the Friday Club in 1910. He had been included in a number of selections, among which in 1898 the first Salon of the International Society of Sculptors, Painters and Gravers, which made him an honorary member, the survey of French art held at the Guildhall Gallery the same year, and the prestigious 1908 Franco-British Exhibition. But in 1910 Roger Fry staged his Post-Impressionist exhibition, partly perhaps as a riposte to the Whitechapel, and it was followed two years later by a second exhibition of modernist and Cubist pictures which caused considerable shock in some quarters. British art was forced to take stock of recent Continental developments, and before long the rise of modernism was inexorable. But some painters nevertheless continued to try fulfill a modern purpose for figuration. A contemporary of Augustus John, William Orpen was the Slade School's most gifted pupil. In the early years of the twentieth century his paintings were often informed by his profound admiration for the Old Masters, particularly Rembrandt. But in 1914–15 he made a trio of large allegorical canvases in tempera which marked a new stylistic experiment. All three are about the character and renewal of Irish culture, then trying to assert itself from British dominion. The last and greatest of these pictures was *The Holy Well*. Here naked figures of ancient, pagan Ireland are forced to drink from a well which transforms them into God-fearing, clothes-wearing members of the modern world. The process is supervised by a priest, but he looks up at the figure of Orpen's friend Sean Keating, who stares out at us ambiguously. An artist with strong republican sympathies, Keating became an important figure in the new Ireland. Orpen seems partly to criticize the Church, perhaps suggesting that Ireland must free itself from more than one form of dominion, but, as in so many of his works, its full meaning and the target of its irony is reserved. Orpen's responses to the decorations by Puvis he first saw in Paris in 1899 are not recorded. But their echo seems felt in *The Holy Well*, not just in the blond coloring and scale, shallow picture space, and flattened compositional structure, but in its ambition and ambiguous intent.

While Orpen was at work on his trio of pictures about his homeland, a younger Slade-trained painter with a very different personality was creating one of his major visionary

8. Stanley Spencer,
Zacharias and Elizabeth, 1913–14.
London, Tate

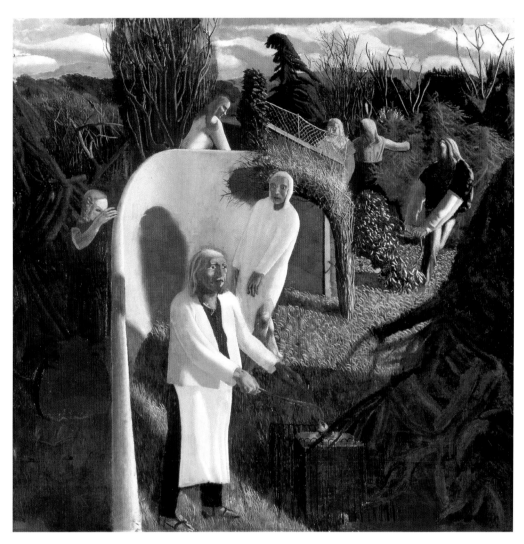

statements. Stanley Spencer was born in the Berkshire village of Cookham, and it became the background setting for his pictures of intense spiritual revelation. The story of Zacharias and Elizabeth begins Luke's Gospel, and is the first miraculous happening in the story of Christ's coming. Spencer imagined the story set like a mystery play in the garden of St John's Lodge behind his Cookham studio (fig. 8). The picture was intended as a summation of his beliefs about Cookham's sanctity: "I wanted to absorb and finally express the atmosphere and meaning the place had for me . . . It was to be a painting characterizing and exactly expressing the life I was . . . living and seeing about me . . . to raise that life round me to what I felt was its true status, meaning and purpose."[25] Spencer shows different moments from the story happening simultaneously. The man on the right was simply a gardener Spencer saw, but his long hair and beard recall images of Christ or John the Baptist. He drags an ivy branch, a traditional emblem of everlasting life and the Resurrection. Behind him Elizabeth's hand touches a yew, a symbol of the same things, and the winter garden itself is symbolically punctuated with evergreens. The sweeping, smoothly sculptural wall seems dramatically modern in this environment, and its pure whiteness, repeated elsewhere in the picture, also strikes a symbolic spiritual note. The picture's force comes from the elusiveness of its narrative, and Spencer's evocation of the spiritual contact between Zacharias and Gabriel. In choosing the story, Spencer was able to treat themes of fertility, spirituality and relationships between men and women which considerably occupied him for much of his life.

Such a picture's relationship with Puvis de Chavannes might at first seem distant, and Spencer, who was interested in a diverse range of artists, never mentioned him in his extensive writings. But his rendering of a spiritualized landscape, and his intention to im-

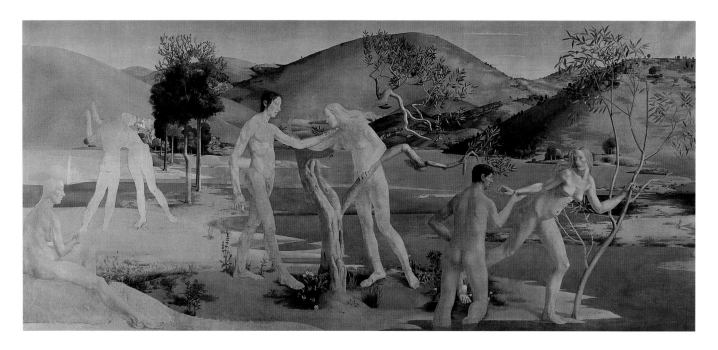

9. Thomas Monnington,
Allegory, c. 1924.
London, Tate

ply that there is much more to express within the poses and attitudes than in the literary interpretation, seems to be a direct descendent of *The Sacred Wood*, inherited perhaps by way of Gauguin and Maurice Denis, painters whose work he had absorbed. In searching for expression, Spencer seems instinctively to have understood the ability of shapes and gestures in certain contexts to communicate indefinable spiritual states. This was far from what was intended by Roger Fry's modernist doctrine of "significant form," but at the same time Spencer seems to express a synthesis of Symbolist, figurative and modernist aesthetics. With the dominance of abstract art, Puvis de Chavannes held little interest or apparent usefulness for the development of British art in the twentieth century. The Rome Scholarship for decorative painting kept the flame alive through the 1920s, and the scheme produced some notable results, such as Thomas Monnington's *Allegory* (fig. 9). An Edenic vision of Monnington's love for his new bride, the painter Winifred Knights, it remains unfinished, a symbolic last whisper of a great tradition which by the next decade was seen as unhealthily conservative and irrelevant. But the revival of interest in figurative painting in the 1980s allowed some partial reassimilation of Puvis's inheritance. The centerpiece of an exhibition put together in Edinburgh by the Scottish artist Ian Hamilton Finlay, famous for the allegorical garden he has constructed at Little Sparta, was a copy of *The Poor Fisherman*.

[1] After Puvis declined the commission, George Frederic Watts was approached, but he too turned it down, on grounds of age—he was seventy-six—and counselled choosing a younger painter. In the event, the commission went to the young and virtually unknown John Somerscales, son of the marine painter.
[2] December 25, 1891; Fondation Custodia, Lugt Collection, Paris; Puvis de Chavannes P.:9308Bb; quoted in *Edward Burne-Jones: Victorian Artist-Dreamer*, exh. cat., Metropolitan Museum of Art, New York, 1998, pp. 30–31.
[3] February 8, 1892; Fondation Custodia, Lugt Collection, Paris; Puvis de Chavannes P.:9308Bc; quoted in *Edward Burne-Jones…, op. cit.*, p. 31.
[4] Quoted in B. Harrison and M. Waters, *Burne-Jones*, London, 1989, p. 177.
[5] P. Leprieur, "Correspondance d'Angleterre," *Gazette des Beaux-Arts*, July 1893, p. 80.
[6] C. Phillips, "Puvis de Chavannes," *Magazine of Art*, 1885, p. 60.
[7] *Ibidem.*
[8] G. Moore, "Chavannes, Millet and Manet," in *Modern Painting*, London, 1893, p. 28.
[9] W. Powell Frith, "Crazes in Art: Pre-Raphaelitism and Impressionism," *Magazine of Art*, 1888, p. 190.
[10] E. Armitage, "The Impressionists," *Athenaeum*, no. 3117, July 23, 1887, pp. 123–24.
[11] D.S. MacColl, "Manet," *Saturday Review*, December 12, 1896, p. 621.
[12] C. Ricketts, "Puvis de Chavannes: A Chapter from "Modern Painters," *Burlington Magazine*, vol. XIII, April 1908, p. 12.
[13] Quoted in J. Darracott, *The World of Charles Ricketts*, London, 1980, p. 102. They also owned a study for *The Prodigal Son* and a drawing of a satyr holding a staff. See *All For Art: The Ricketts and Shannon Collection*, exh. cat., Fitzwilliam Museum, Cambridge, 1979, pp. 66–67.

[14] W. Rothenstein, *Men and Memories: Recollections of William Rothenstein 1872–1900*, London, 1931, p. 43.

[15] *Ibidem*, p. 45.

[16] H. Maas, J.L. Duncan and W.G. Good, eds., *The Letters of Aubrey Beardsley*, London, 1970, pp. 43–44.

[17] Reproduced in M.A. Stevens, "Frederick Cayley Robinson," *The Connoisseur*, September 1977, fig. 6.

[18] The two completed canvases were *The Mumpers* (Detroit Institute of Arts) and *Forza e Amore* which John effectively destroyed by painting white paint over it in 1913.

[19] Letter to William Rothenstein, 1907; quoted in D.F. Jenkins, "Slade School Symbolism," in *The Last Romantics*, exh. cat., Barbican Art Gallery, London, 1989, p. 71.

[20] M. Holroyd, *Augustus John: A Biography*, London, 1987, p. 331.

[21] See *Augustus John: Studies for Compositions*, exh. cat., National Museum of Wales, Cardiff, 1978, nos. 104–11.

[22] J. Rothenstein, *Augustus John*, London, 1945, p. 16.

[23] *Twenty Years of British Art, 1890–1910.*

[24] W. Sickert, "Culture for East-End," *Art News*, May 26, 1910; A. Gruetzner Robins, *Water Sickert: The Complete Writings on Art*, Oxford, 2000, p. 239.

[25] Numbered writings, 1937; Tate Gallery Archives 733.3.1.

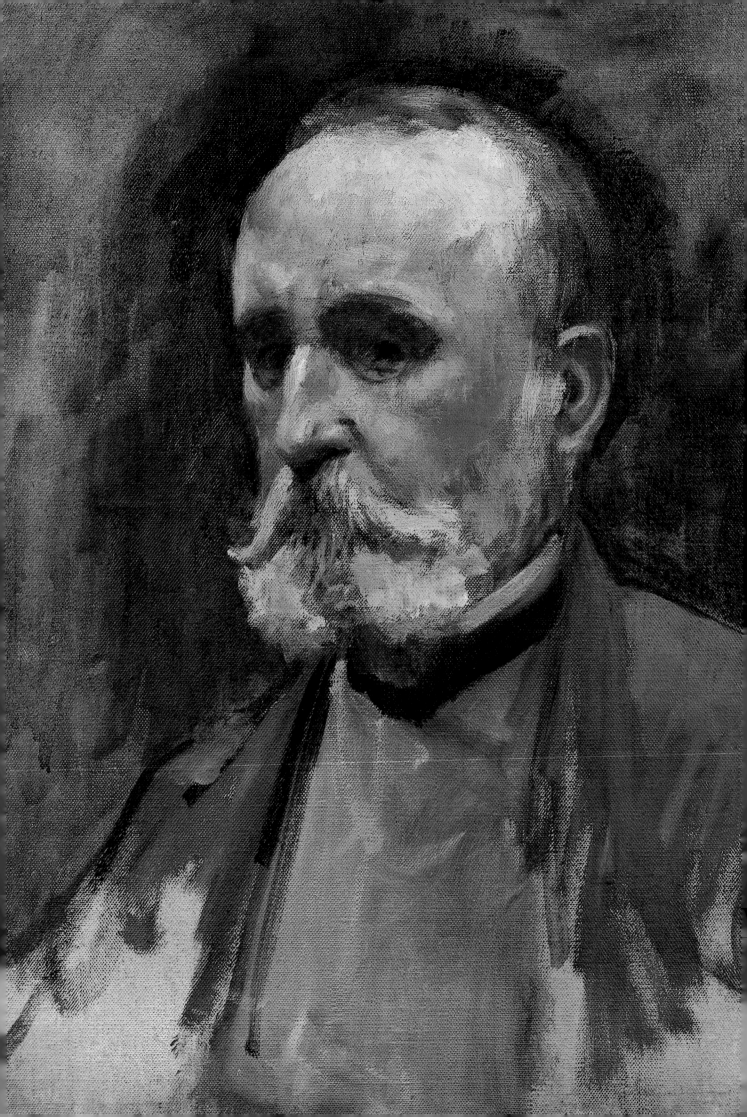

Pierre Puvis de Chavannes played a decisive role in the formation of the modern tradition; his independent and original art led several generations of artists to find in his work a reservoir of intelligently formulated pictorial ideas. His images lent themselves to multiple interpretations, and while they attracted a considerable circle of devotees in his day, it was the moderns who took his forms and adapted them in unsuspected and unimagined new directions. Puvis's plastic ideas were the perfect vehicle for the painters who matured from circa 1880 onward to cushion as well as to modify the vivid broken color and spontaneous naturalism that was the crucial—but limiting—contribution of the Impressionists. His murals were suited to the surroundings for which they were designed, particularly in their majestic, large-scale, dramatic pattern simplifications, relative flatness and rational departures from naturalistic appearances, as well as in their rhythmic ebb and flow of outline and pose. For Puvis, decoration did not imply or entail loss of permanence, complexity, and intellectual substance. Indeed, he was the artist who reinstated its credibility among such artists as Seurat, Signac, Gauguin, Hodler, Denis, Vuillard, and Matisse, among many others.[1] When we see the paintings, embodiments of Puvis's all-embracing economy of means, and note the muffled resonance of their broad areas of color, their subtle patterning textures, their contrapuntal spatial effects, somewhat screenlike, we become aware of the spectrum of plastic ideas that appealed to these dynamic young individualists.

Within little more than a decade after Puvis's death, the quest of simplifying painting had accelerated so rapidly, in many instances toward the total elimination of illustrative matter, that later generations of artists found themselves unable to comprehend the prophetic appeal of Puvis's concepts to the modern masters who were their immediate predecessors and who they considered their true antecedents.[2] Puvis de Chavannes did not possess the qualities found in many whose work was marked by his art. A significant number of those artists emphasized brightness, motion, improvisation, and other characteristics foreign to Puvis's temperament, and they rapidly eclipsed his reputation by their radical innovations. Restoring the historical context helps us to perceive the very personal accomplishments that made Puvis de Chavannes's work so stimulating to those whose ultimate objectives were ostensibly inimical to his own. If the study of the evolution of modern art is to be brought into equilibrium, Puvis de Chavannes must be considered for the catalytic role he played. A practical step in assessing the scope of Puvis's appeal to the great artists of the modern tradition would be to reacquaint ourselves with the independent vision, conviction, and integrity of his art. For to edit Puvis de Chavannes out of the last twenty-five years of the nineteenth century and ignore the network of interconnections between his art and that of the younger artists is to fail to understand those links fully and to overlook a potent force in one of the greatest periods of French art. An exhibition that objectively demonstrated these essential but discrete relationships was the only solution to this impasse.

Already in 1946, Robert Goldwater had published a landmark article entitled "Puvis de Chavannes: Some Reasons for a Reputation,"[3] in which he prefaced his remarks by writing, "A suggestion from Alfred H. Barr, Jr., started me upon the path of this investigation. I wish to thank him for wondering upon what the reputation of Puvis de Chavannes was based. . . . In the course of this study my opinion of his art has risen several points."[4] When I returned in 1970 from a year abroad , I mentioned to Professor Goldwater my enthusiasm for Puvis's work in relation to the moderns. He referred me to his article (which I had not read) and encouraged me to pursue my idea of bringing together work by the moderns with pictures by Puvis, on the grounds that an exhibition based on that premise would be valuable. In 1972, when I departed to take up the position in Toronto as chief curator at the Art Gallery of Ontario (AGO) and told him what I was planning, he wished me well and said perhaps such an exhibition might have more of an effect on how Puvis was perceived by the public than had his 25-year-old article.

Puvis de Chavannes and the Modern Tradition opened at the AGO on October 24, 1975, the seventy-seventh anniversary of the artist's death. Puvis's formative role in the genesis of modern art was at the time largely unfamiliar to most contemporary artists and the museum-going public. The exhibition, which was three years in the making, had been gestating in my mind ever since I had seen throughout France in the late 1960s most of Puvis's public commissions and numerous easel paintings, including studies and reductions of his mural com-

1. Pierre Puvis de Chavannes,
Selfportrait, c. 1887.
Paris, Musée du Louvre

291

positions. The project was conceived to pose as many questions as it sought to answer. It was a show intended to appeal to painters. The core idea was to stimulate visitors to look at paintings they had rarely or never seen, and that the juxtaposition of Puvis's canvases with great paintings of the modern tradition would yield fresh insights, and hence understanding, of Puvis's manifold creative achievements. I proposed to demonstrate a reconstructed model of an epoch we think we all know so well. In other words, the public, including scholars, would confront what the painters of the last quarter of the nineteenth century and first half of the twentieth actually saw in Puvis's art.

The show was not met with enthusiasm on the part of the museum or critical communities, but, rather, with indifference, skepticism, and hostility. More than three weeks into the exhibition, this attitude found a voice in the Canadian biweekly news magazine, *Maclean's*, whose art writer declared that "in the 77 years since [Puvis's] death, he has fallen out of fashion: his works have found their way into museum storage vaults. Today, his cold, monotonous colors and his posturing figures are dated and campy. . . . Nothing serves a curator's career so well as rediscovering a forgotten movement or restoring a lost reputation but Wattenmaker has lost on both counts. By hanging Puvis' work beside that of the men he is supposed to have affected, he simply points out how vital the moderns are and how mannered Puvis is by comparison. . . . The work of the moderns still lives and Pierre Puvis de Chavannes has faded beyond redemption."[5]

Clearer heads prevailed. Hilton Kramer, then chief art critic for the *New York Times*, visited the show and, in a deeply informed article published five days after the piece in *Maclean's*, wrote, "Puvis de Chavannes, though widely admired in his day, is no longer even a name to anyone but a small circle of specialists. He has all but disappeared from recent histories of modern art, and in the museums if his paintings are not completely relegated to the storerooms, they are now unlikely to be found among the acknowledged masterworks of the modern movement."[6] He continued, "Has the later twentieth century lost touch with one of the significant artists of the modern period? . . . [This] exhibition triumphantly restores Puvis to his former place at the center of the modern movement, and does so, not as an act of historical piety but out of a clear perception of his artistic importance."[7] As a direct consequence of Kramer's review, attendance increased dramatically.[8]

A week later, on the last day of the exhibition, Kramer returned to the subject: "Puvis was an exemplary figure—an artist to be emulated as well as admired. For [the artists of the modern tradition], there was no question that he had made a significant and usable contribution to modern painting. . . . We can see the extraordinary refinement and purity of Puvis's style, in which all chromatic contrast is sacrificed to the realization of an exalted decorative ideal. The picture surface, conceived as the pictorial equivalent of a classical frieze, is invested with a gray, even-toned, unearthly light— extremely subtle and without any obvious sensuous appeal—that envelops the eye in a continuous, unbroken plane. The effect of this severe reduction of means is austere, intense, hieratic and spiritually compelling." In his summation Kramer observed, "All at once we are in the presence of something sublime, and we no longer wonder that so many gifted artists responded to its spell."[9]

The range of Puvis's character and impact on his contemporaries was unusually broad. He welcomed young artists to his studio in Paris and was open and encouraging with students in the schools where he taught. It is generally unknown that Puvis de Chavannes's work influenced the decorative arts—glassmakers such as Henri Cross and Emile Gallé—and that he was interested in experimental theater productions. In 1889, along with his friend Degas and many others, including his dealer Paul Durand-Ruel, he contributed to the subscription to buy Manet's *Olympia* for the French state. It will surprise many to learn that in 1894, Puvis donated a work to the benefit auction for Julien [le père] Tanguy's widow along with Monet, Pissarro, Renoir, Rodin, Mary Cassatt, and Berthe Morisot. In 1895, he served on the French Committee of Patronage for the first Venice Biennale and in 1896 exhibited in the first annual exhibition of the Carnegie Institute, Pittsburgh. That year, as president of the Société Nationale des Beaux-Arts, he personally nominated Matisse to be elected a *membre associé*, enabling the young painter to exhibit in the annual shows without submitting his works to a jury. He was the author of numerous caricatures, often made to pass the time during boring jury deliberations, on which councils he was considered a progressive. A collection of these often trenchant drawings, which were cherished by his closest friends, was published in 1906. Another little-known aspect of Puvis's generosity was his donation of two of his most important compositions, *The Balloon* and *The Carrier Pigeon*, of 1870 and 1871 respectively, to a lottery to benefit the victims of the Chicago fire of 1871. These monumental canvases, in frames designed and decorated by the artist, were lost from public view for a hundred years, with the exception of a few weeks in 1915, when they were briefly on exhibit at the Metropolitan Museum of Art in New York. Today they are on permanent display with other major works by the artist at the Musée d'Orsay.

And now, a quarter century later, Professor Serge Lemoine has taken up the baton, reconceived, and greatly broadened the subject of Puvis's importance and pervasive influence in a comprehensive form, *From Puvis de Chavannes to Matisse and Picasso. Toward Modern Art.* This exhibition extends the cycle of historical scholarship that began in 1946 with Robert Goldwater's groundbreaking article. As Puvis de Chavannes was admired and emulated, adapted, and copied, by artists of diverse origins, from Russia to Uruguay, so an international team of scholars has cooperated to render homage and to extend the process of rediscovering and reanimating the reputation of a unique figure in the French tradition.

[1] For example, Puvis de Chavannes's spirit hovered over the galleries of the Metropolitan Museum of Art in which the recent exhibition *Beyond The Easel: Decorative Painting by Bonnard, Vuillard, Denis, and Roussel, 1890–1930* was displayed. In Bonnard's *Le Plaisir: Panneau décoratif*, 1906, 246 x 300 cm (Maeght Collection), the two pale blue figures left and right of the center in the foreground seem to have alighted directly from Puvis's *The Dream* (1883) or *The Inspiring Muses* (1895).

[2] That Monet, Renoir, Gauguin, Signac, and the critics Gustave Geffroy, Roger Marx, and Octave Mirbeau were among the five hundred guests who attended the banquet organized by Rodin in honor of Puvis's seventieth birthday in January 1895 attests to this fact.

[3] *The Art Bulletin*, vol. XXVIII, no. 1, March, 1946, pp. 33–43.

[4] Goldwater, who died in 1973, mentions Puvis frequently in his posthumously published *Symbolism*, New York, Harper & Row, 1979.

[5] S. Littman, "Was all this Puvis de Chavannes really necessary?" *Maclean's*, vol. 88, no. 13, November 17, 1975, p. 83.

[6] "New Light on Puvis de Chavannes," November 22, 1975. Kramer had previously written on the subject, "Rediscovering Puvis de Chavannes," *New York Times*, July 7, 1972.

[7] *Ibidem.*

[8] The Governor General of Canada, Jean Léger, visited the Art Gallery and related to me how much he admired Puvis from his student days before the war listening to lectures and sitting for his doctoral examinations in the amphitheater of the Sorbonne.

[9] "The Revival of a Neglected Modern," *New York Times*, November 30, 1975.

Catalog of Works

1. Pierre Puvis de Chavannes

The Magdalene, 1869
oil on canvas, 53.5 × 37.5 cm
Otterlo, Rijksmuseum Kröller-
Müller

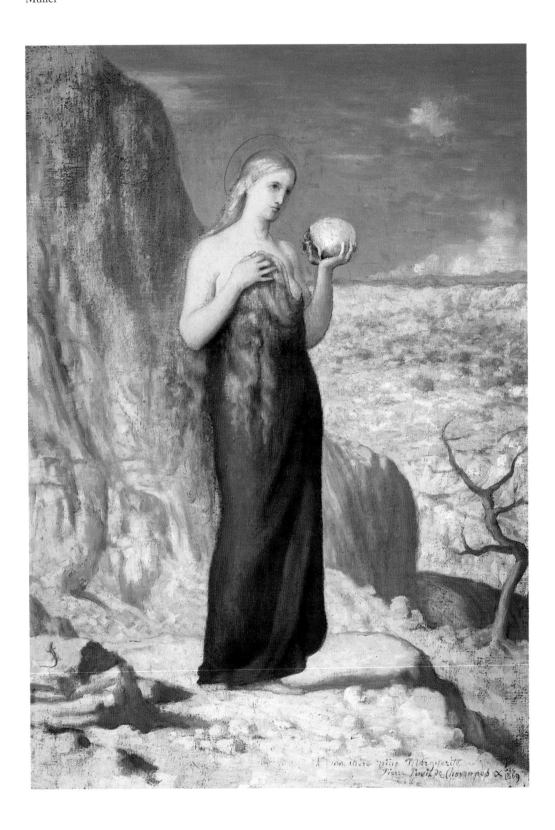

*Greek Colony in Massilia
(The White Rock)*, 1869–72
oil on canvas, 61 × 75 cm
Private collection

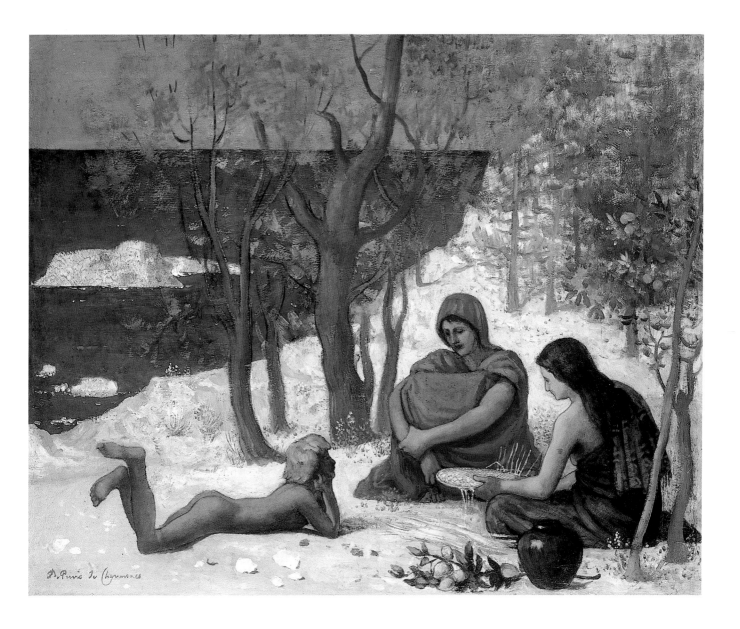

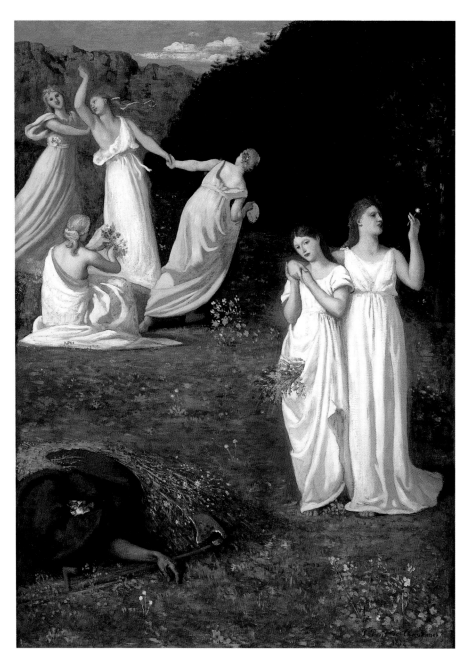

3. Pierre Puvis de Chavannes

Death and the Maidens, 1872
oil on canvas, 146 × 105 cm
Williamstown, Sterling
and Francine Clark Art Institute

4. Pierre Puvis de Chavannes

Hope, 1872
oil on canvas, 102 × 129 cm
Baltimore, Walters Art Museum

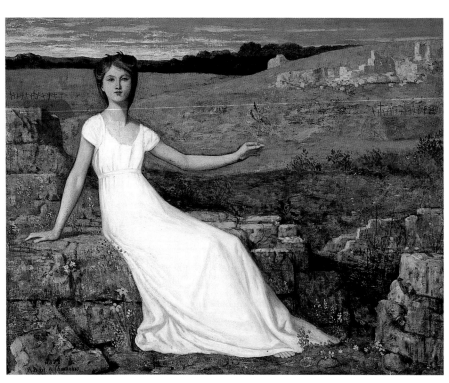

5. Pierre Puvis de Chavannes

*Study for "Saint Genevieve as a
Child in Prayer,"* 1875–76
oil on crepe paper on canvas,
136.3 × 76 cm
Amsterdam, Van Gogh Museum

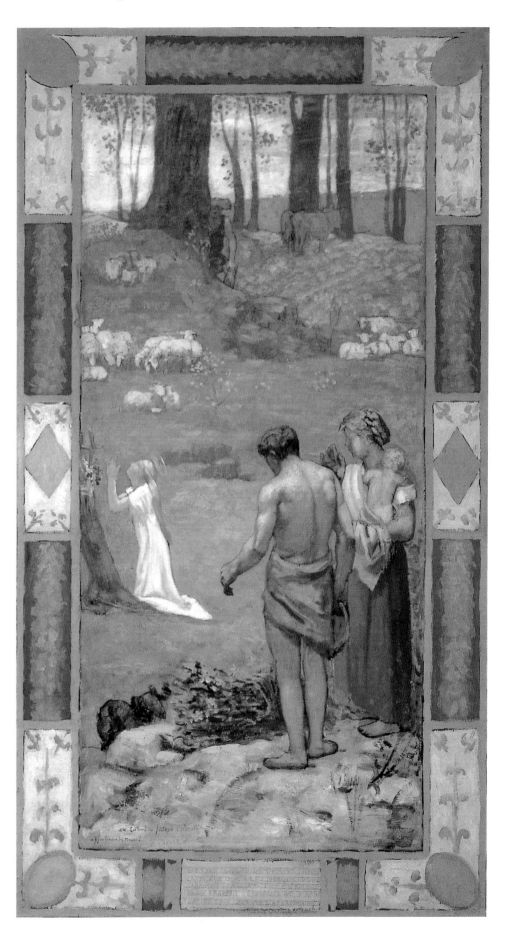

Young Women by the Sea,
1875–80
watercolor, 68 × 52 cm
Paris, private collection

Young Women by the Sea, 1879
oil on canvas, 205 × 154 cm
Paris, Musée d'Orsay

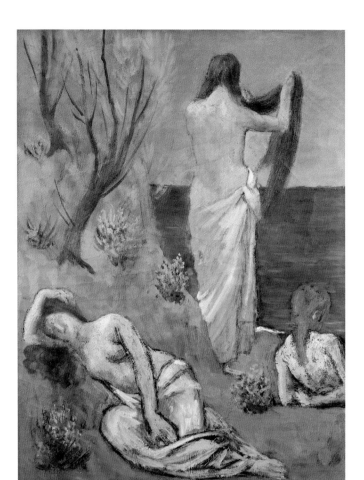

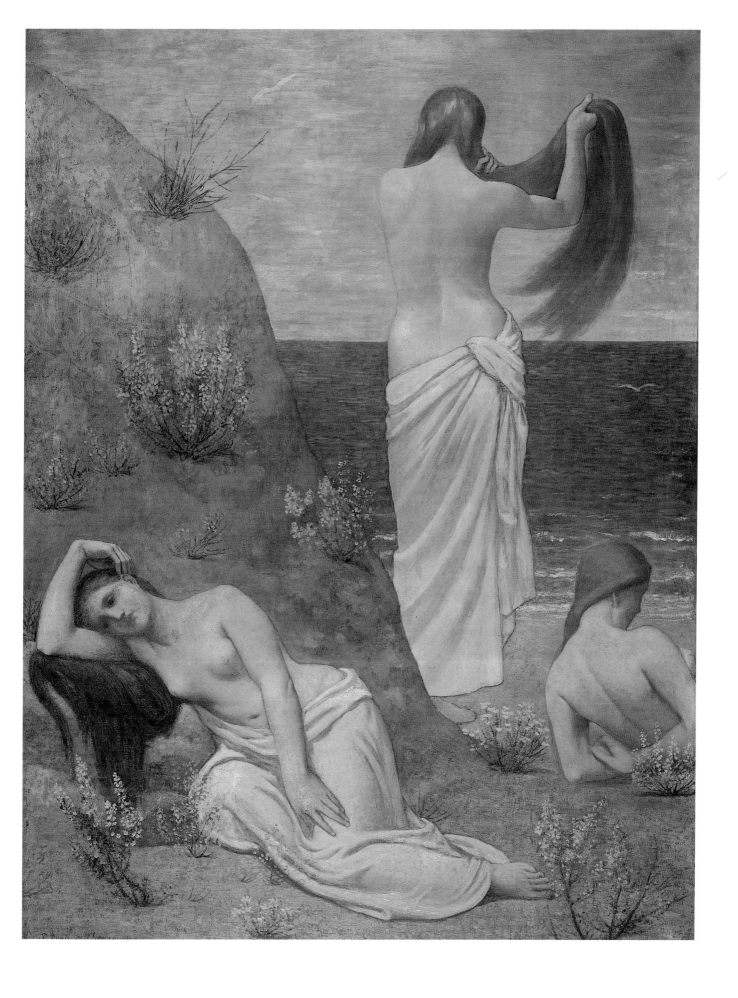

The Prodigal Son, 1879
oil on canvas, 130 × 95.5 cm
Zurich, Stiftung Sammlung
E.G. Bührle

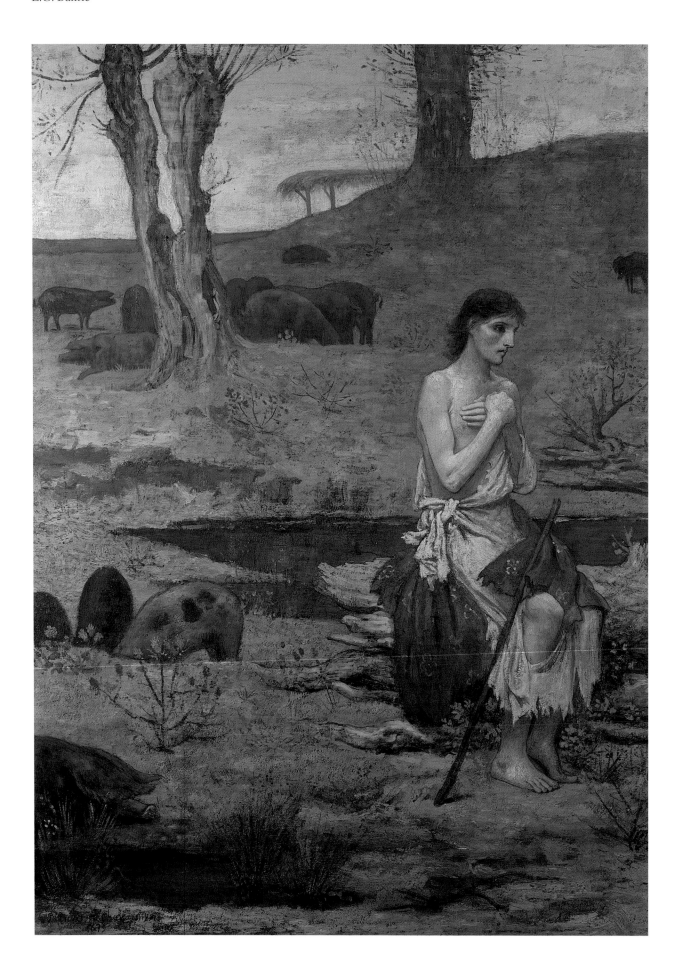

9. Pierre Puvis de Chavannes

The Poor Fisherman, 1879
oil on canvas, 66 × 91 cm
Moscow, Pushkin Museum

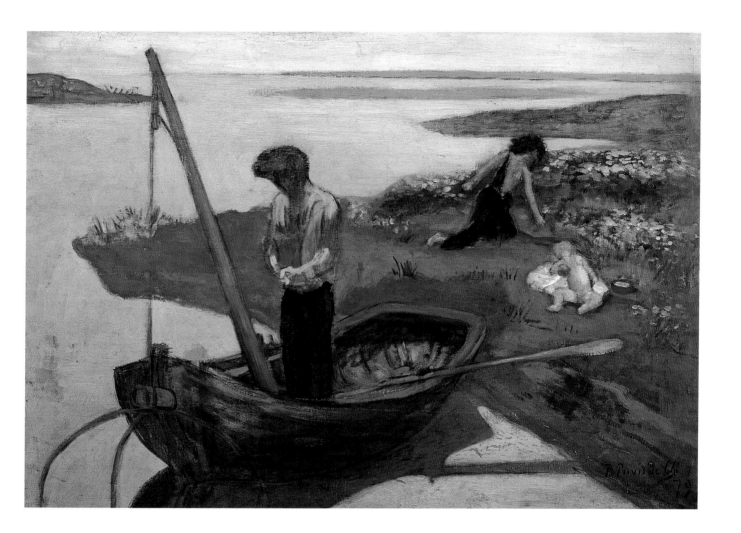

10. Pierre Puvis de Chavannes

Pleasant Land, 1882
oil on canvas, 28.8 × 51 cm
New Heaven,
Yale University Art Gallery

11. Pierre Puvis de Chavannes

Ludus pro Patria, 1882
oil on canvas, 33.4 × 134.6 cm
New York, The Metropolitan
Museum of Art. Gift of
Mrs. Harry Payne Bingham

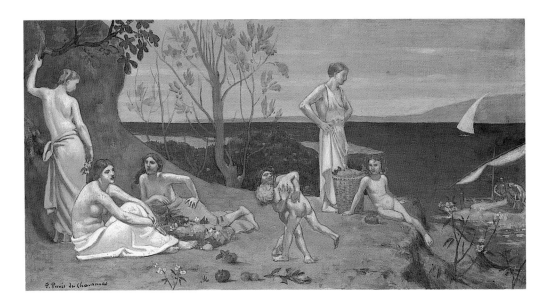

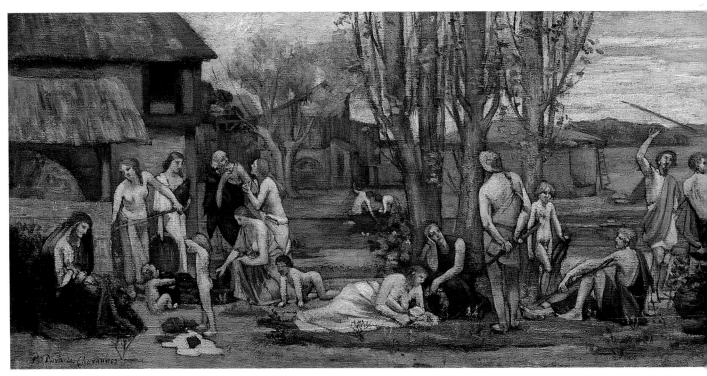

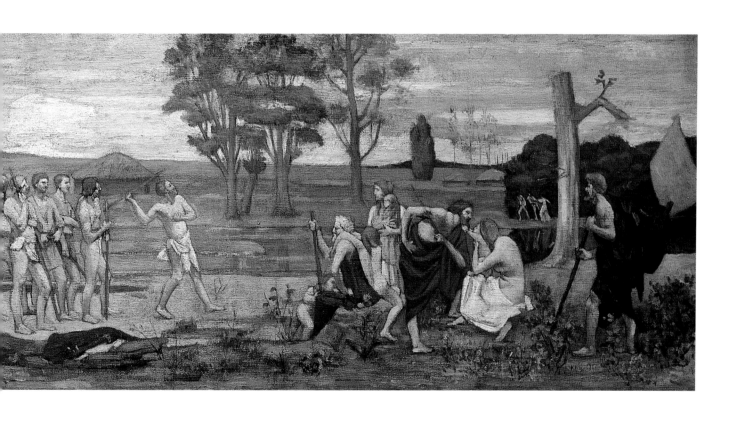

The Toilette, 1878–83
oil on canvas, 32,5 × 24 cm
Dublin, Hugh Lane Gallery
of Modern Art (on loan from
the National Gallery, London)

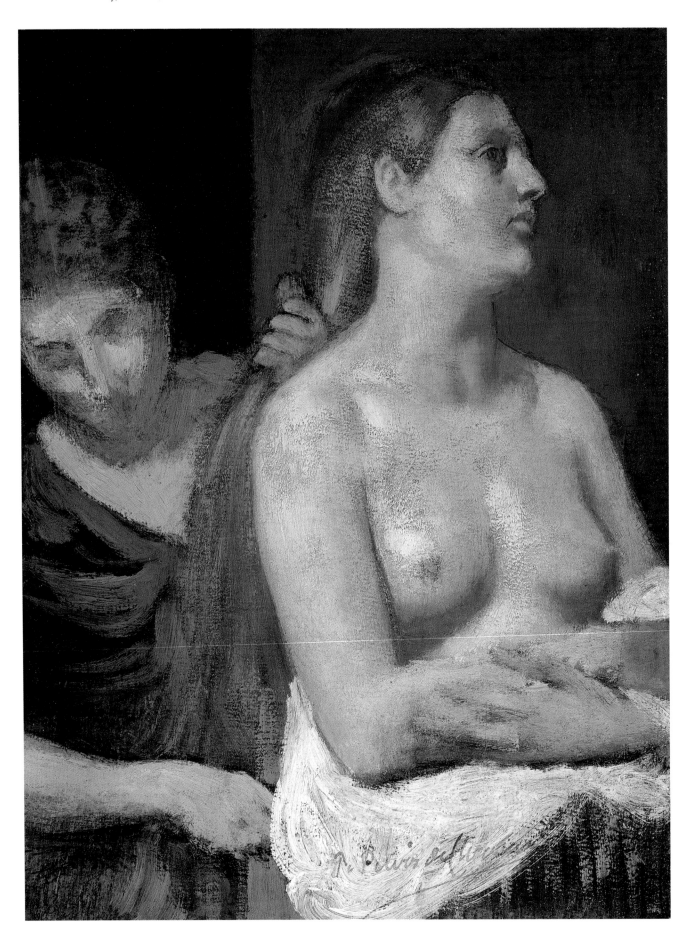

13. Pierre Puvis de Chavannes

Nymph in a Landscape, 1884
olio on cardboard, 50 × 36 cm
Switzerland, private collection

14. Pierre Puvis de Chavannes

*The Sacred Wood, study for
"Pleasant Land,"* c. 1883–84
oil on paper transferred on
canvas, 38.7 × 65.2 cm
Neuss, Clemens-Sels-Museum

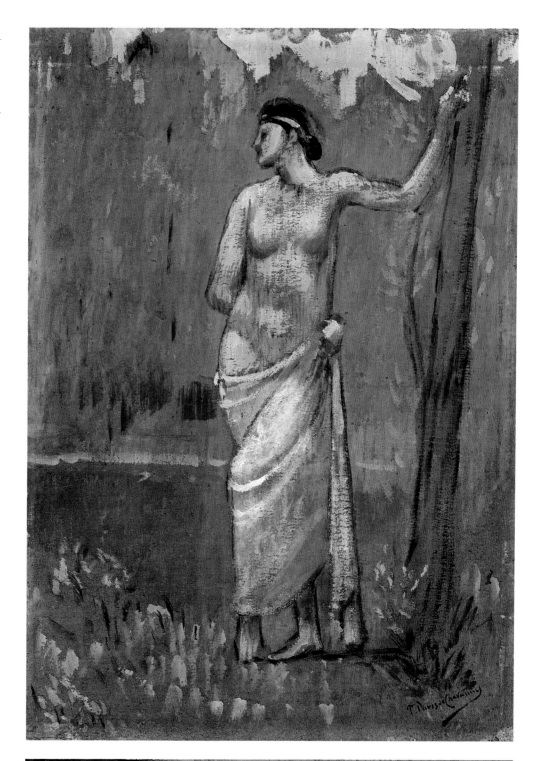

following pages
15. Pierre Puvis de Chavannes

Tamaris, 1885–86
oil on canvas, 25.4 × 30.4 cm
New York, The Metropolitan
Museum of Art, H. O.
Havemeyer Collection.
Gift of Mrs. J. Watson Webb

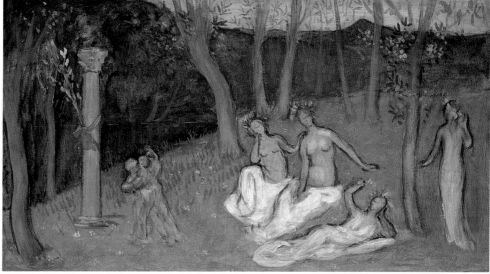

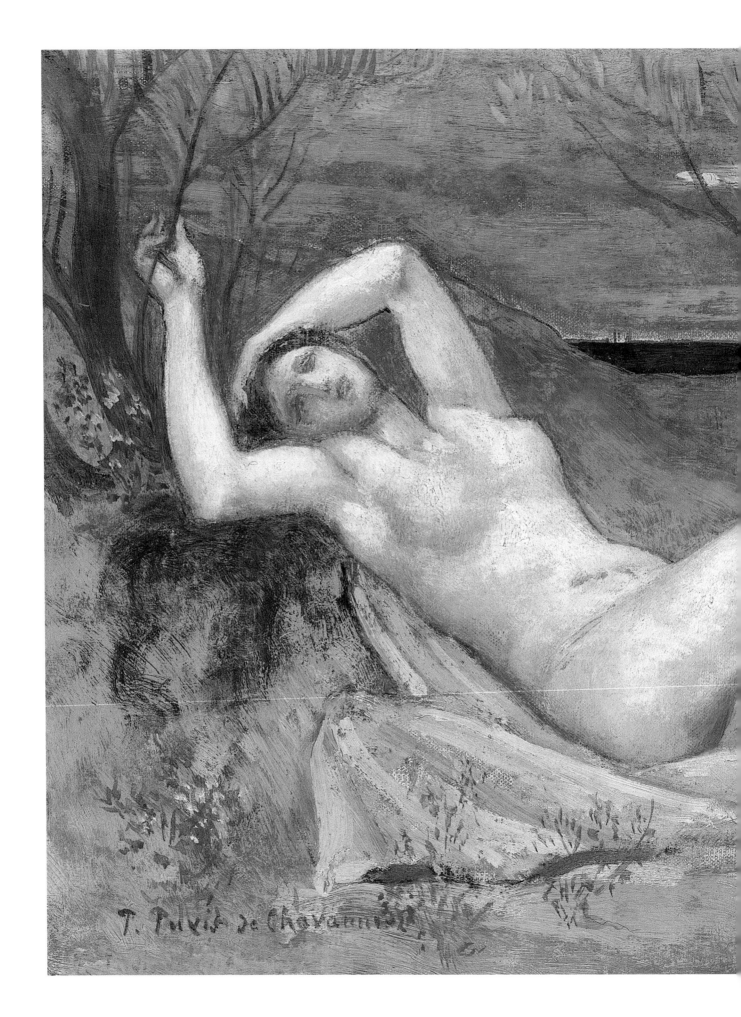

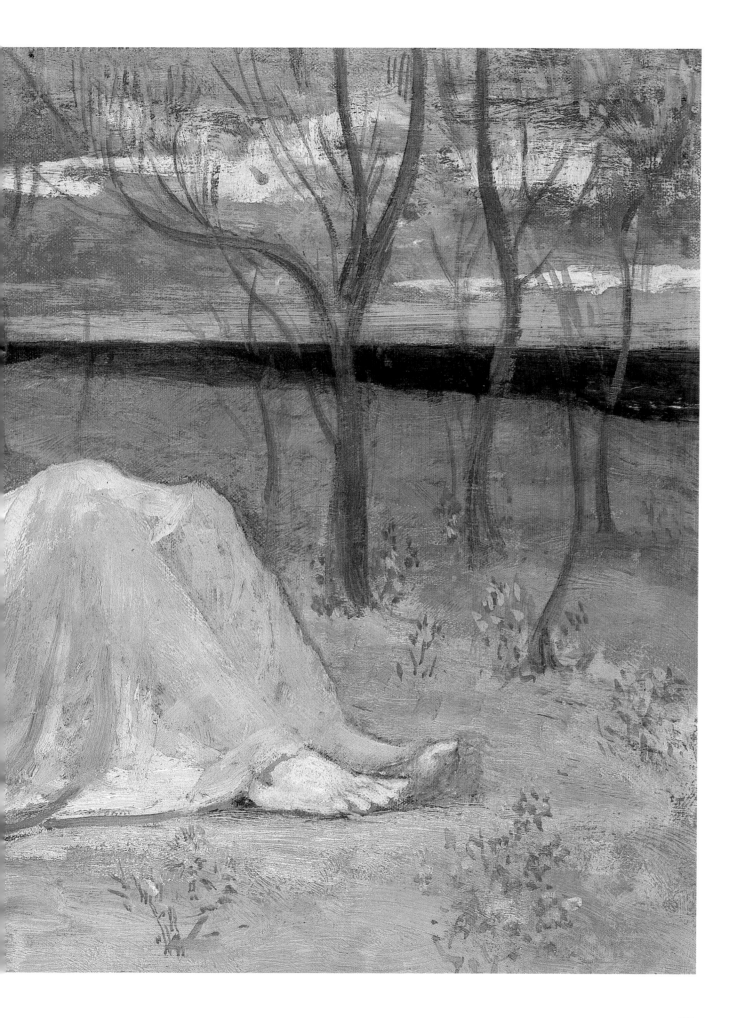

16. Pierre Puvis de Chavannes

Autumn (Children in an Orchard), 1885–89
oil on canvas, 80 × 99 cm
New York, The City College

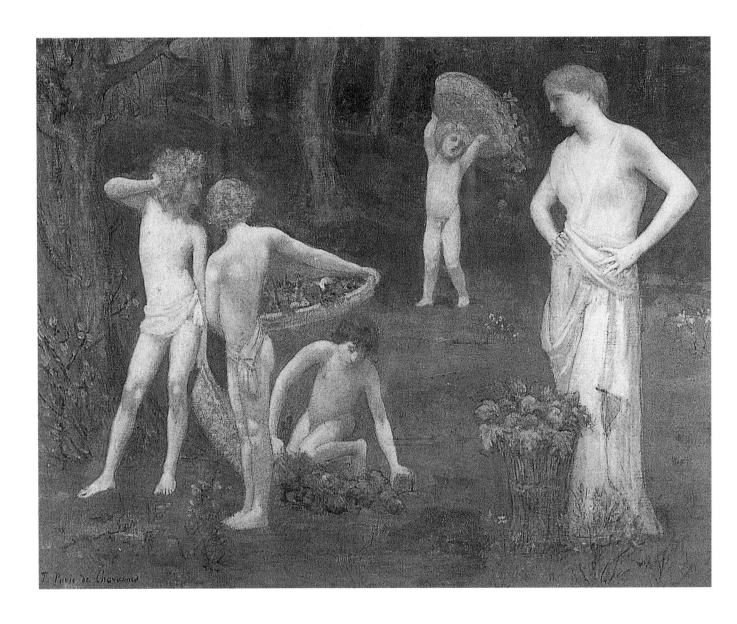

17. Pierre Puvis de Chavannes

Charity, 1887
oil on canvas, 55.5 × 47 cm
Private collection

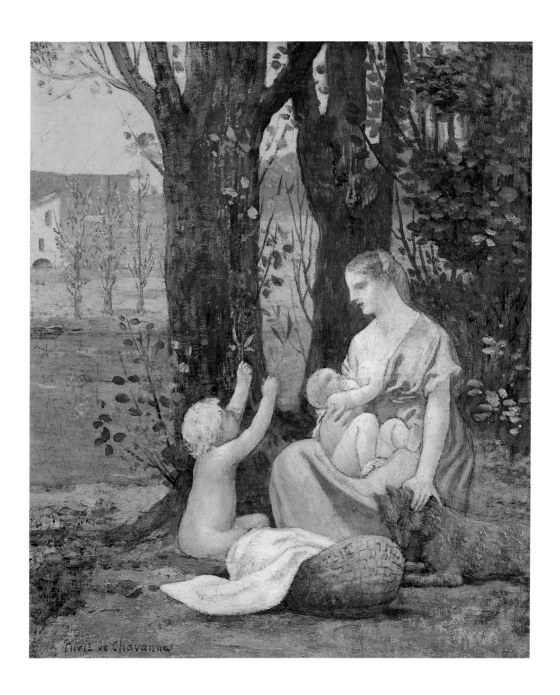

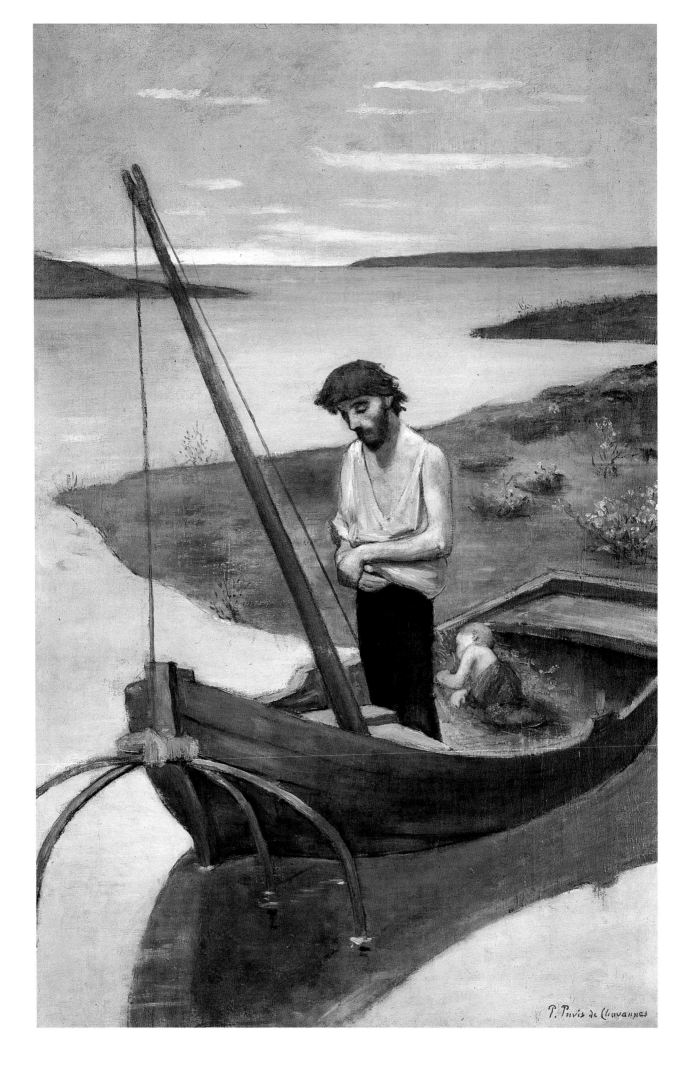

18. Pierre Puvis de Chavannes

The Poor Fisherman, 1887–92,
oil on canvas, 105.8 × 68.6 cm
Tokyo, The National Museum
of Western Art

19. Pierre Puvis de Chavannes

The Bathers, c. 1890
oil on canvas, 55.4 × 35.5 cm
Toronto, Art Gallery of Ontario

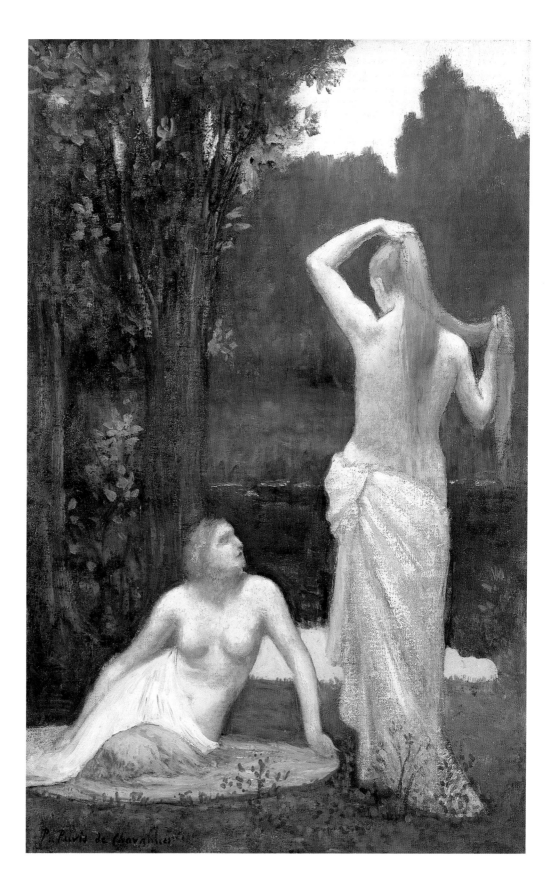

20. Pierre Puvis de Chavannes

Inter Artes et Naturam, 1890–95
oil on canvas, 40.3 × 113.7 cm
New York, The Metropolitan
Museum of Art. Gift of
Mrs. Harry Payne Bingham

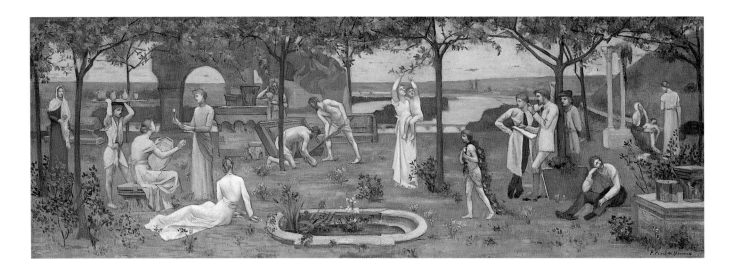

21. Pierre Puvis de Chavannes

The Shepherd's Song, 1891
oil on canvas, 105 × 110 cm
New York, The Metropolitan
Museum of Art, Rogers Fund

following pages
22. Pierre Puvis de Chavannes

Summer, 1891
oil on canvas, 150 × 232 cm
The Cleveland Museum of Art

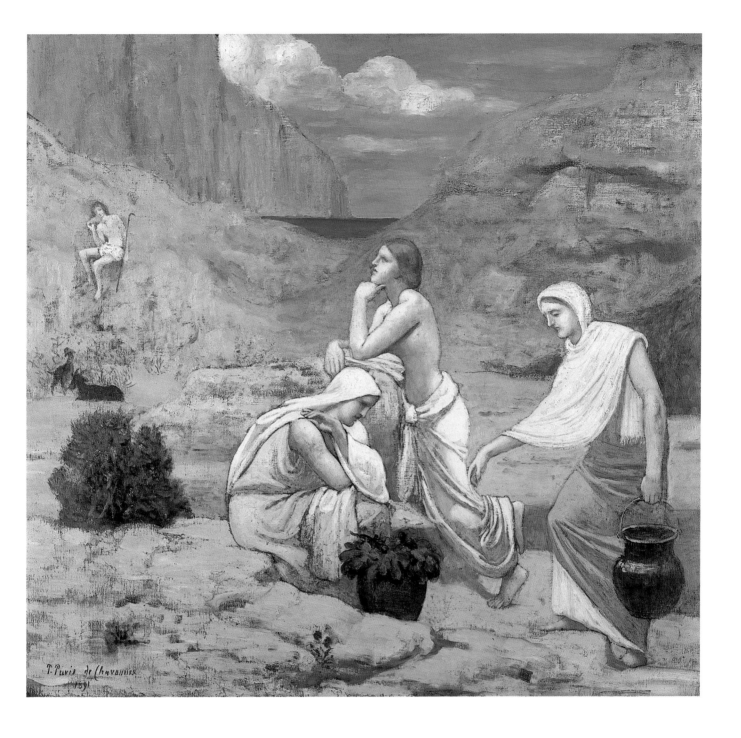

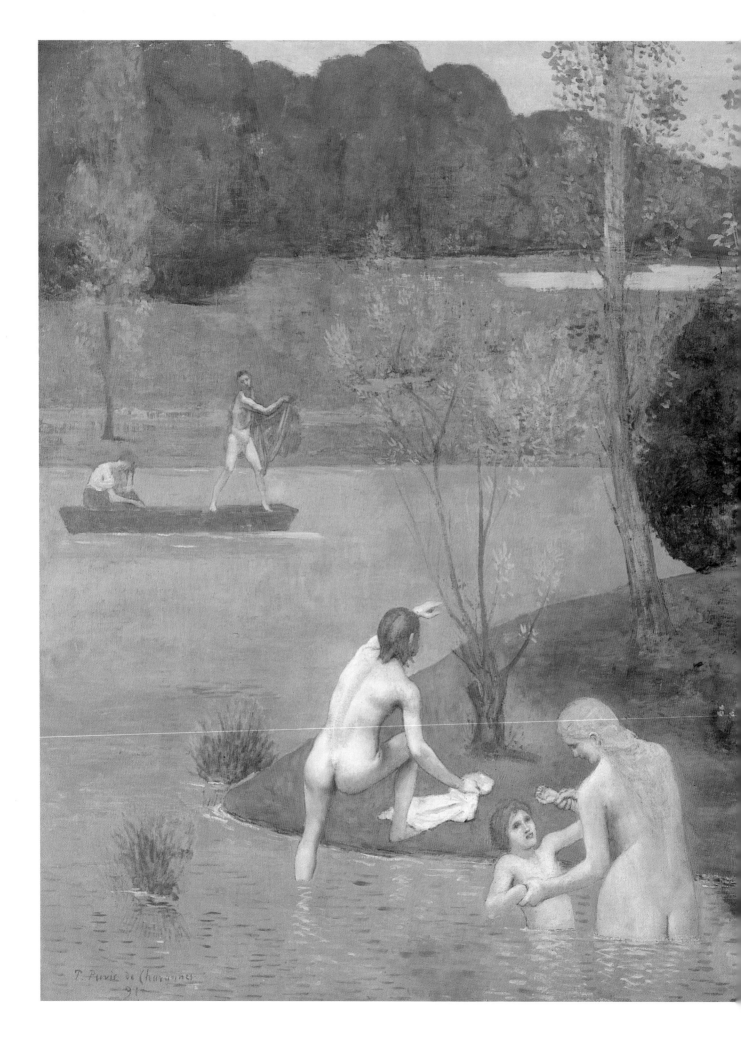

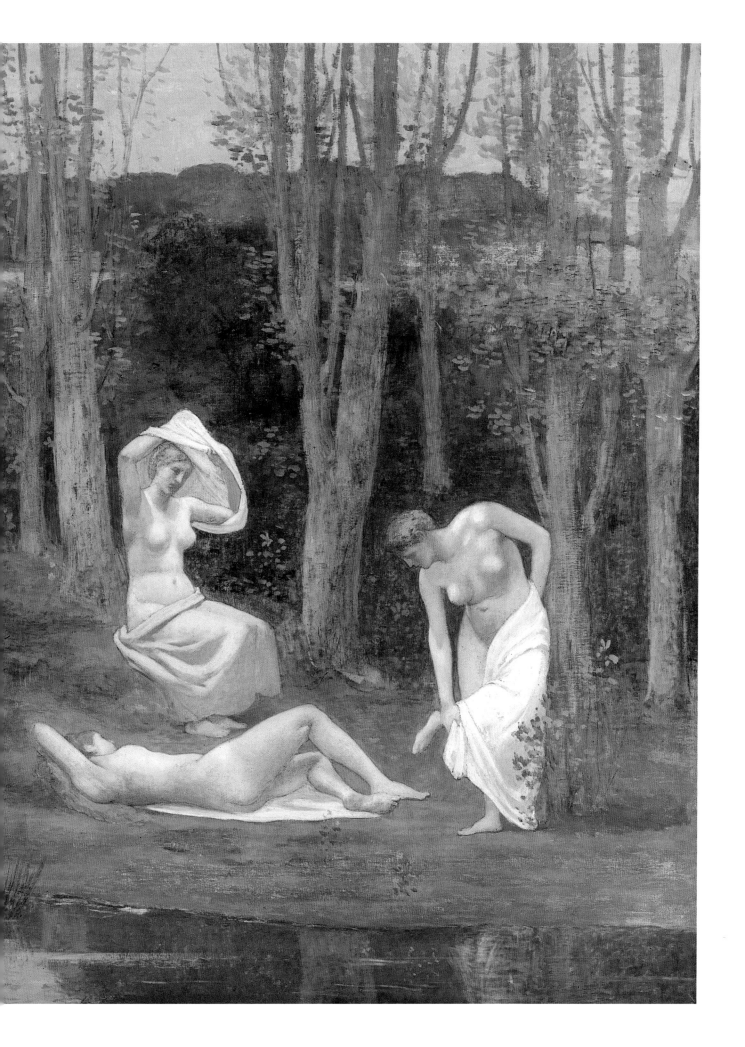

Winter, 1892
oil on canvas, 53.5 × 85.6 cm
Paris, Petit Palais,
Musée de Beaux-Arts de la Ville

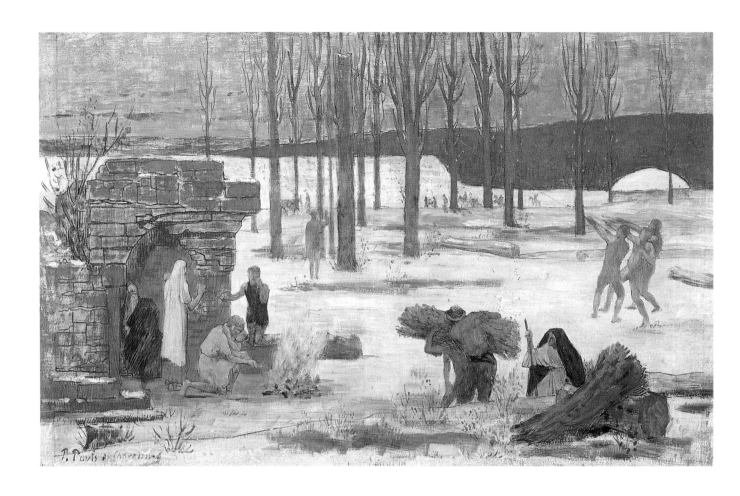

The Goatherd, 1893
oil on canvas, 86.5 × 53 cm
Musée de Mâcon

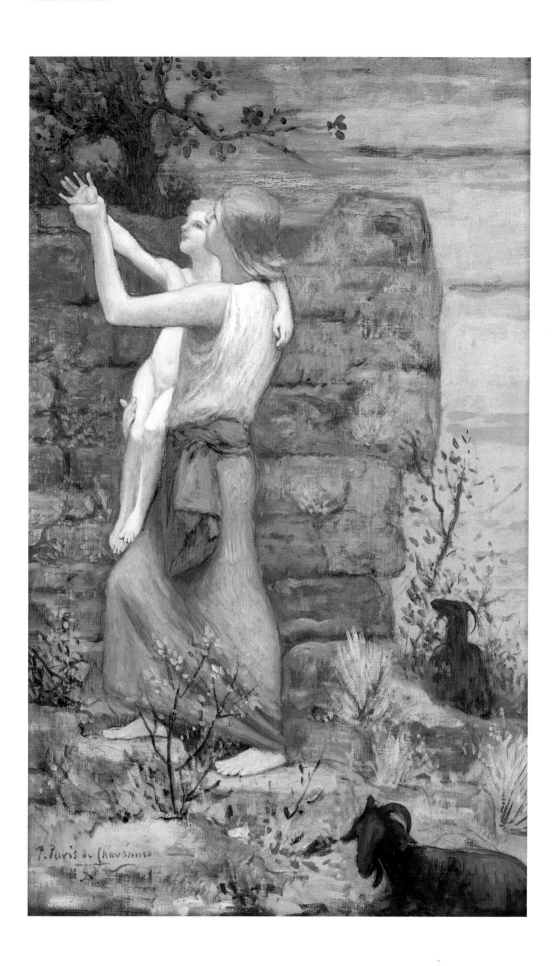

Charity, 1894
oil on canvas, 92.4 × 74 cm
Saint Louis, Washington
University Gallery of Art.
University purchase, Bixby Fund

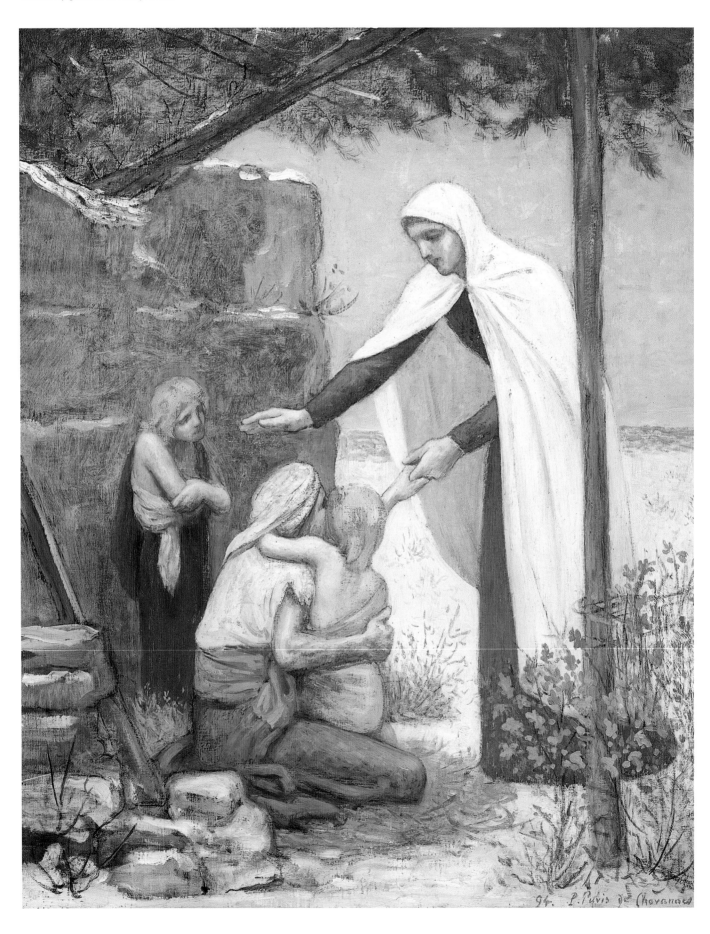

Homer (Epic Poetry), 1896
oil on canvas, 126 × 62 cm
Boston, Museum of Fine Arts

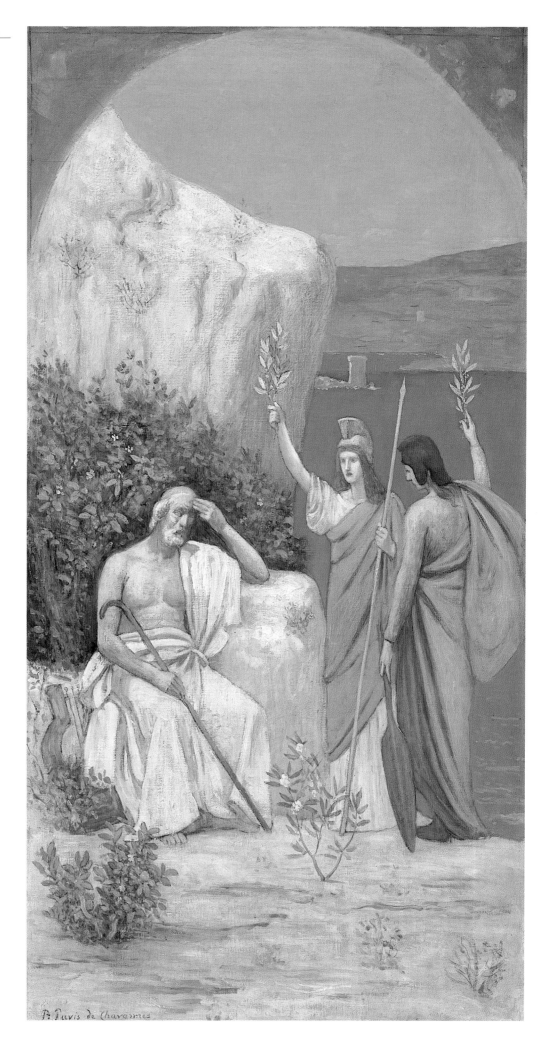

27. Pierre Puvis de Chavannes

Orpheus, 1896
oil on canvas, 67 × 46.5 cm
Oslo, Nasjonalgalleriet

28. Pierre Puvis de Chavannes

The Magdalene, 1897
oil on canvas, 116.5 × 89.5 cm
Budapest, Szépmúvészeti
Múzeum

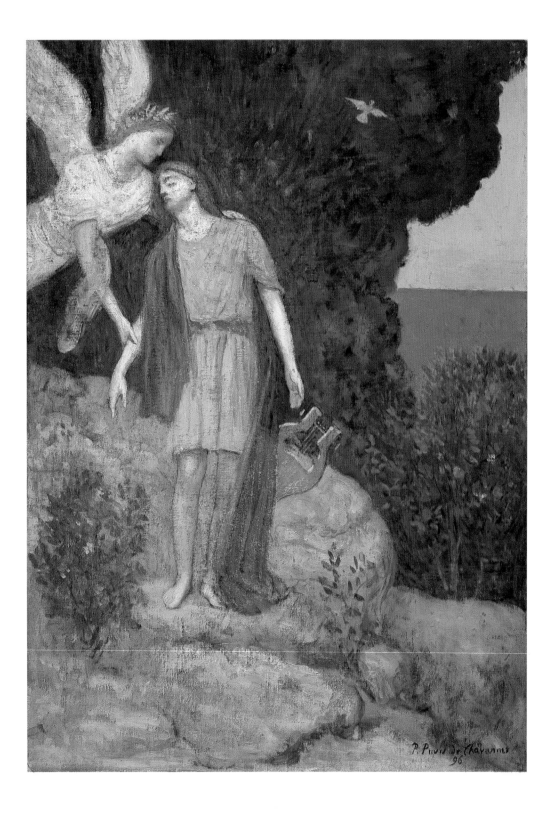

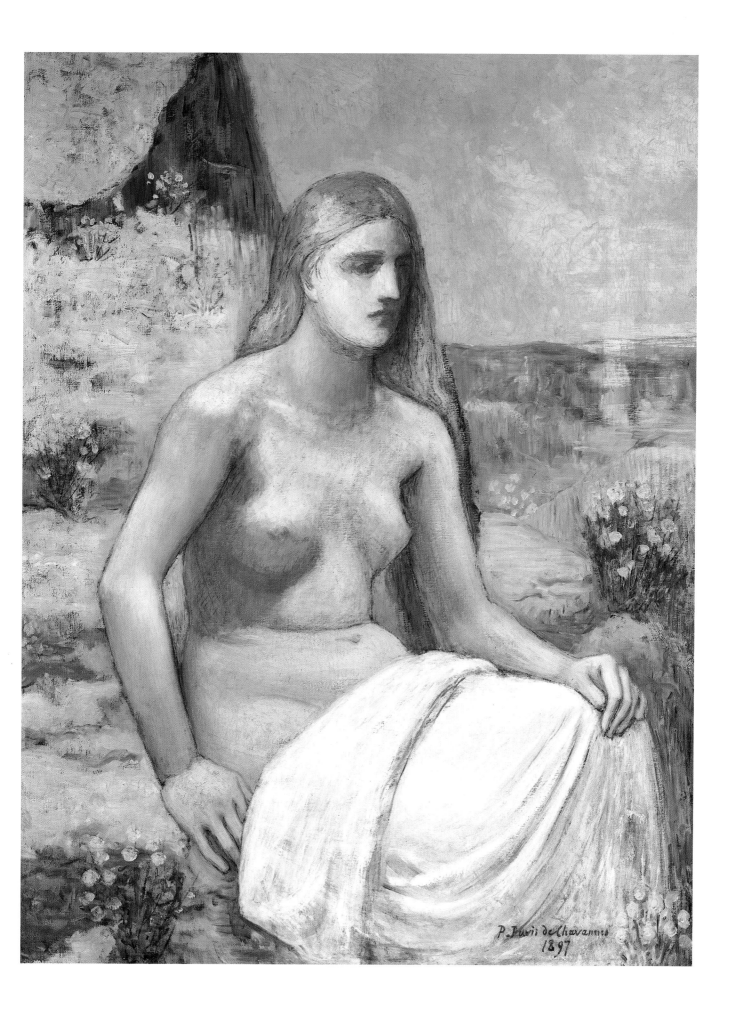

P. Puvis de Chavannes
1897

29. Pierre Puvis de Chavannes

*Sketch of "The Inspiring Muses
Acclaim the Spirit of Light,"* 1895
oil on canvas, 84 × 205 cm
Honk Kong, private collection

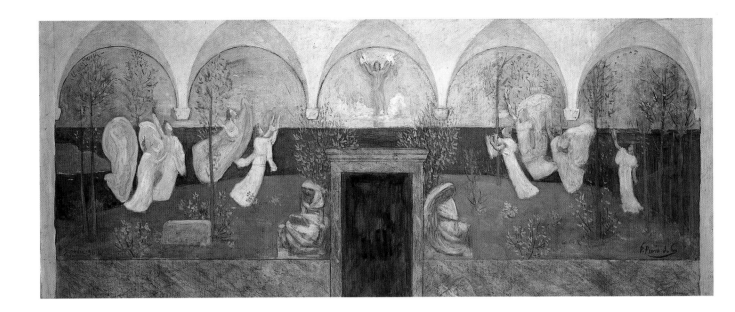

*Study for "Saint Genevieve
Watching over Paris"*
oil on canvas, 92 × 47 cm
Paris, private collection

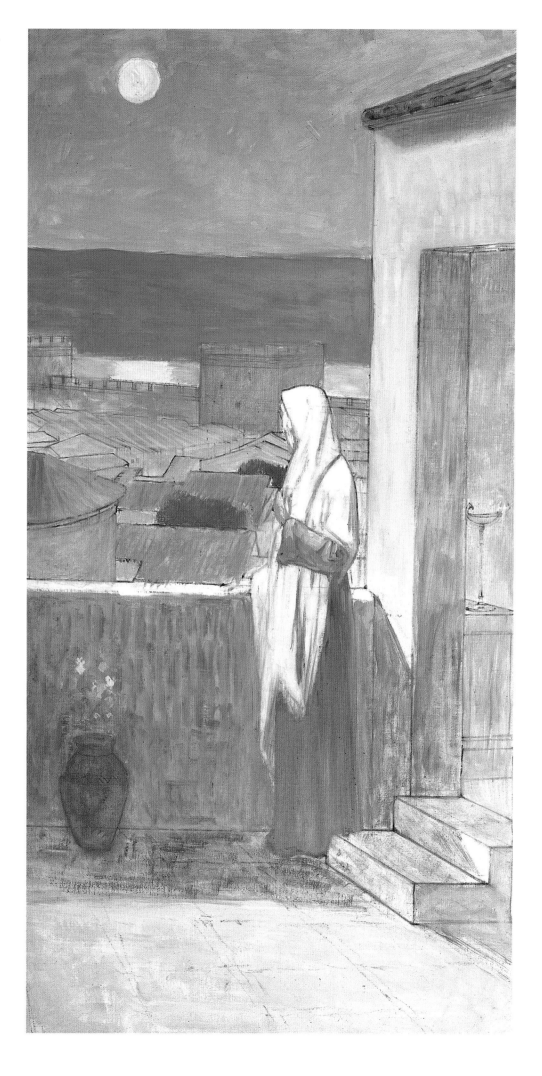

Age of Bronze, 1877
bronze, 174 × 42 × 42 cm
Rome, Galleria Nazionale
d'Arte Moderna

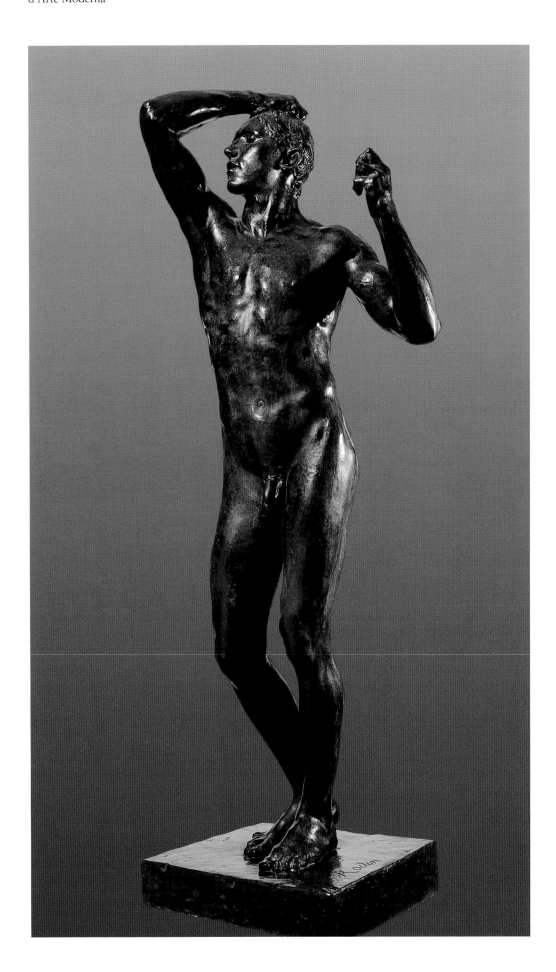

32. Auguste Rodin

Bust of Puvis de Chavannes, 1891
bronze, 51 × 51 × 34 cm
Paris, Musée Rodin

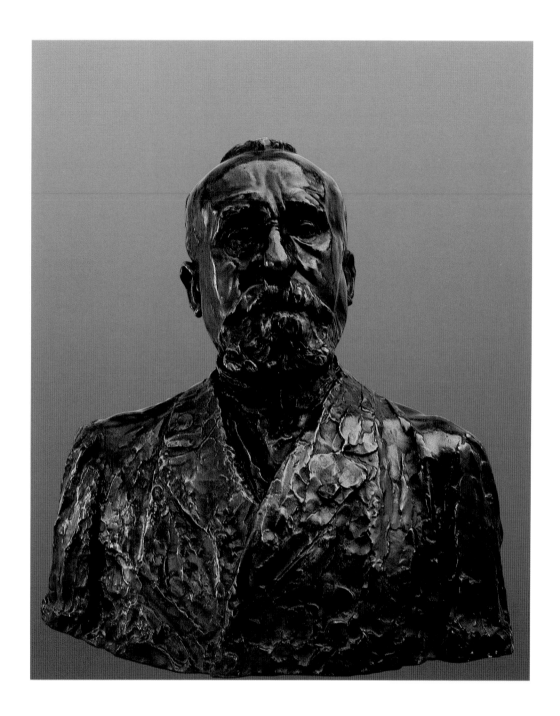

Young Bretons Bathing, 1888
oil on canvas, 92 × 72 cm
Hamburg, Kunsthalle

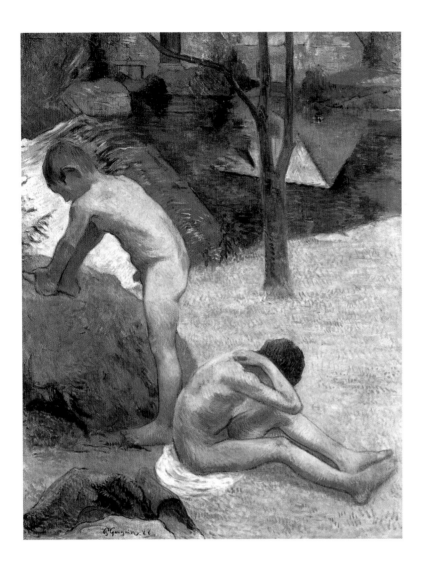

34. Paul Gauguin

Nave nave Mahana, 1896
oil on canvas, 94 × 130 cm
Lyon, Musée des Beaux-Arts

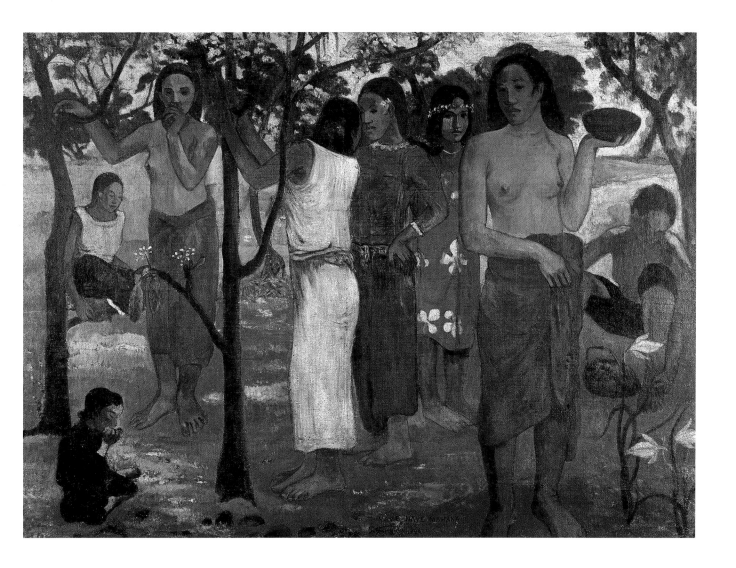

*The Month of Mary (Te avae
no Maria),* 1899
oil on canvas, 96 × 74.5 cm
Saint Petersburg, The
Hermitage Museum

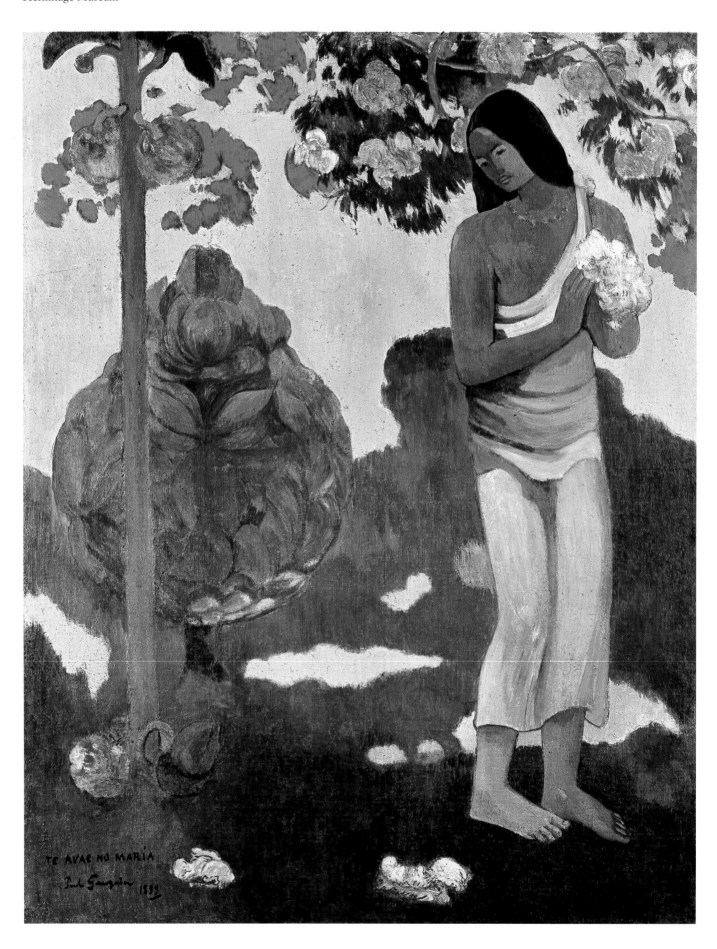

Three Tahitian Women, 1899
oil on canvas, 73 × 93 cm
Edinburgh, National Gallery
of Scotland

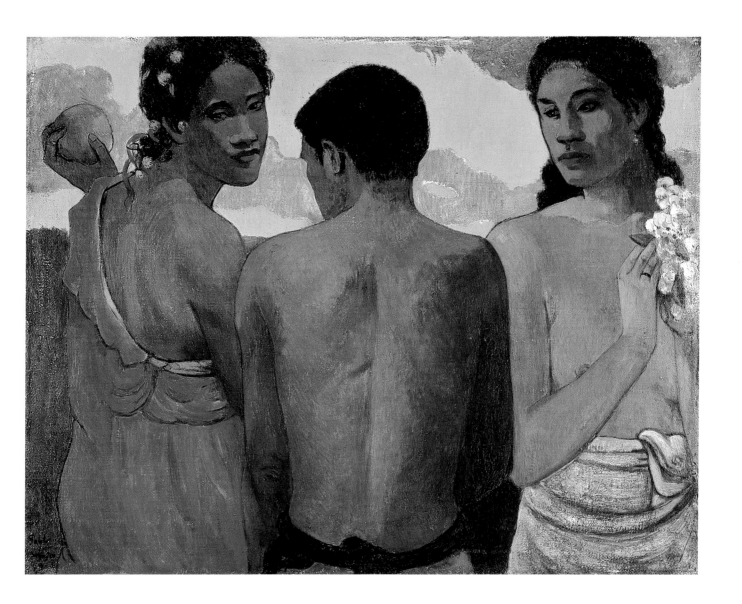

The Large Tree, 1891
oil on canvas, 74 × 92.8 cm
The Cleveland Museum of Art.
Gift of Barbara Ginn Griesinger

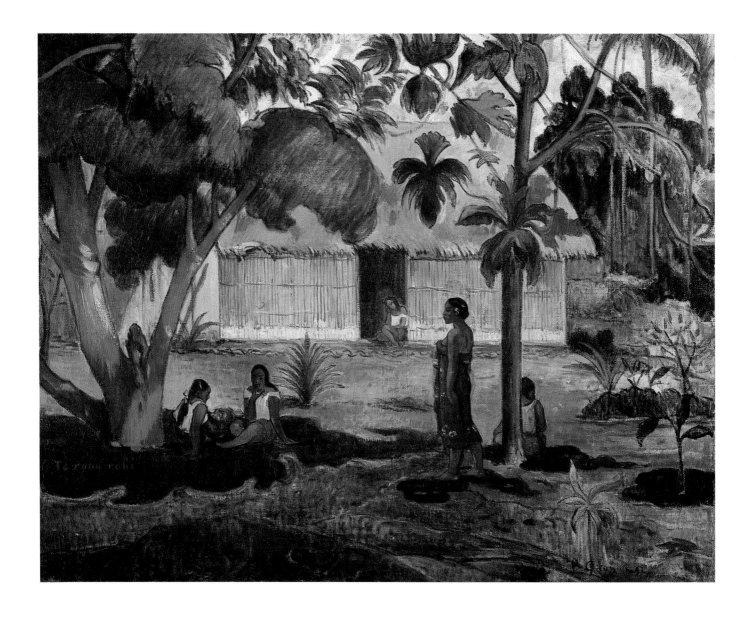

The Poor Fisherman, 1896
oil on canvas, 74 × 66 cm
São Paulo, Museu de Arte

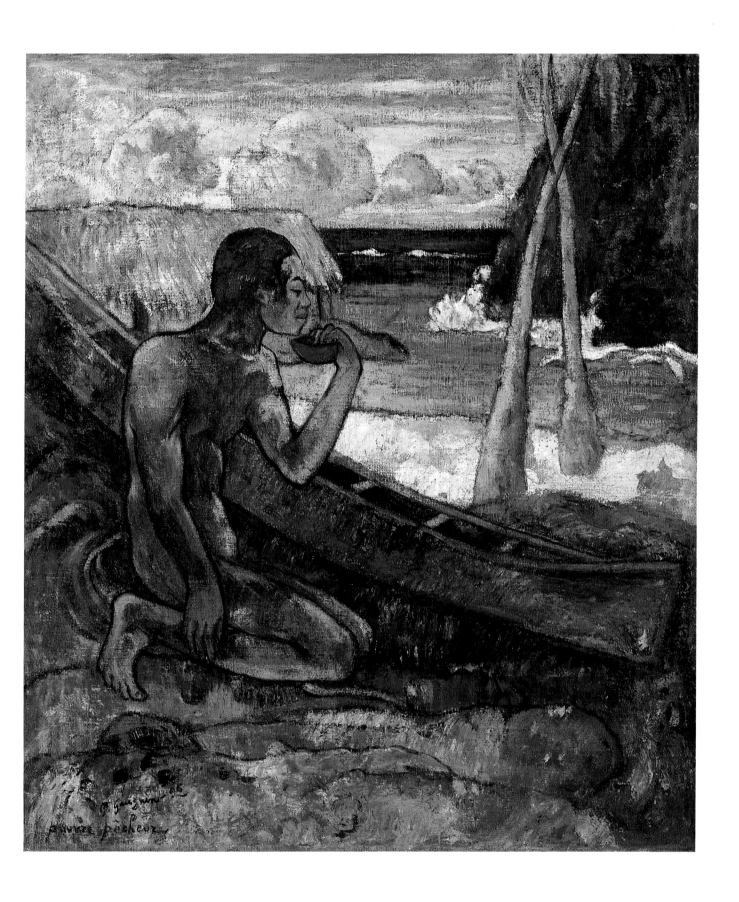

Bathers with Red Cow, 1887
oil on canvas, 92.5 × 72.5 cm
Paris, Musée d'Orsay

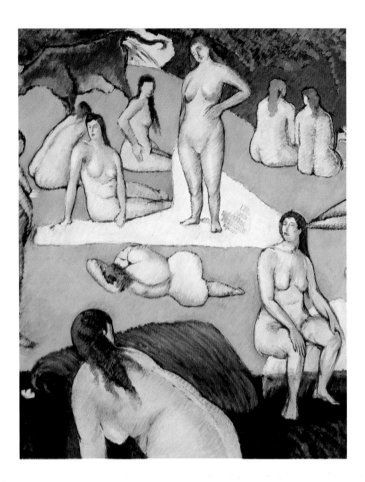

39. Emile Bernard

Madeleine in the Wood of Love,
1888
oil on canvas, 137 × 164 cm
Paris, Musée d'Orsay

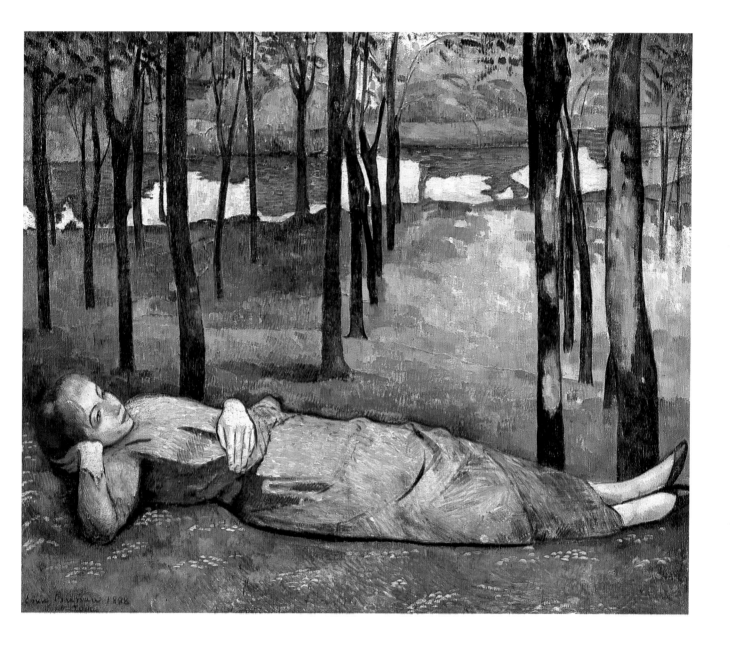

*Tribute to Pierre Puvis
de Chavannes*, 1881
oil on wooden panel,
16.5 × 22.5 cm
Private collection

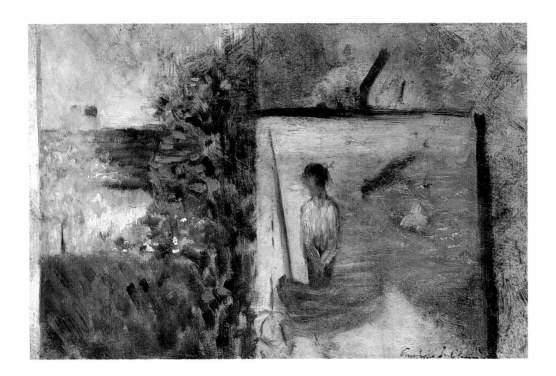

Farm Women at Work, 1882–83
oil on canvas, 38.1 × 46.2 cm
New York, Salomon
R. Guggenheim Museum. Gift,
Solomon R. Guggenheim

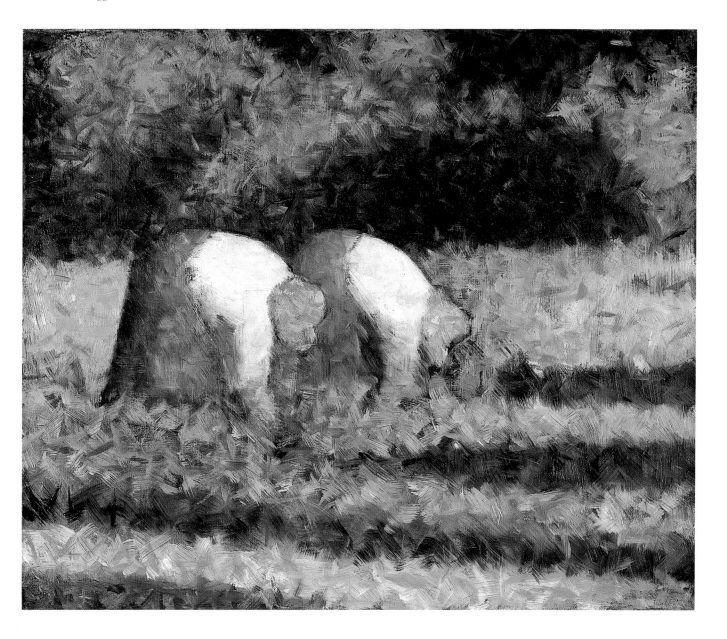

42. Georges Seurat

Study for the "Grande Jatte," 1884
oil on wooden panel,
15.8 × 24.8 cm
Buffalo, Albright Knox
Art Gallery. Gift of
A. Conger Goodyear

43. Georges Seurat

Study for the "Grande Jatte,"
1884–85
oil on wooden panel, 16 × 25 cm
London, The National Gallery

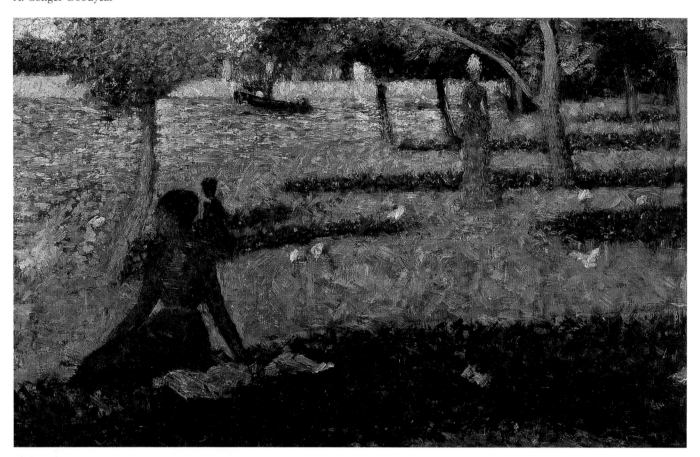

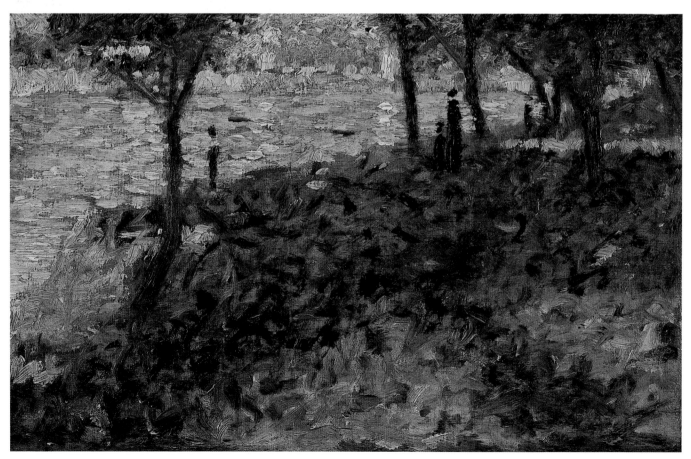

44. Georges Seurat

The Seine at Courbevoie, 1885–86
oil on canvas, 81 × 65 cm
Paris, private collection

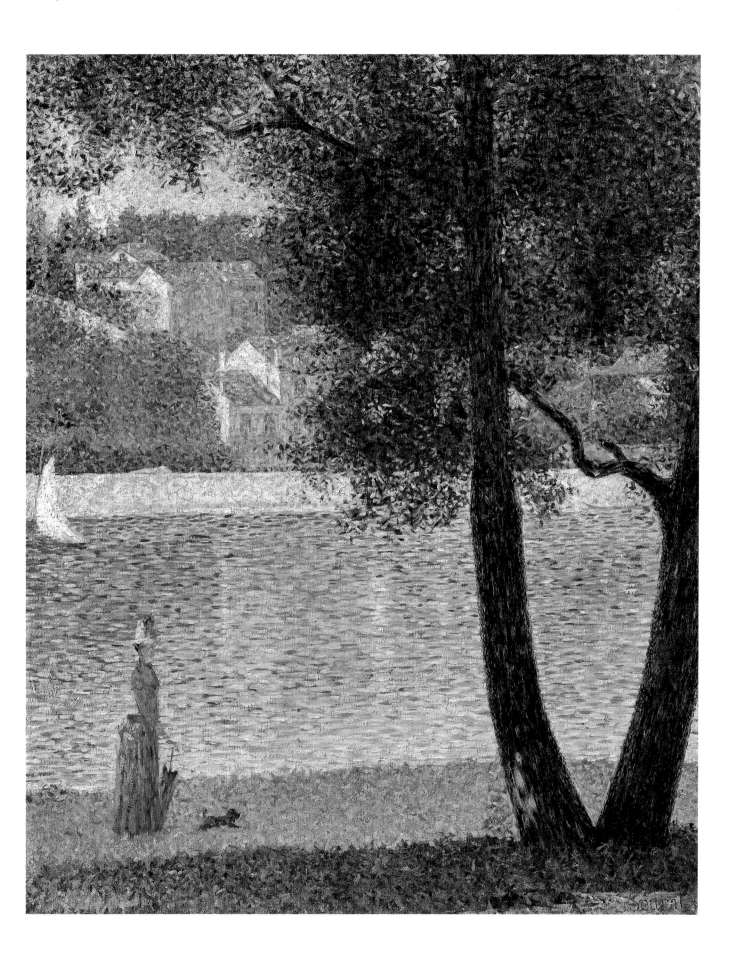

45. Paul Signac

Study for
"In the Time of Harmony"
oil on canvas
Private collection

45bis. Paul Signac

Saint Tropez.
Fontaine des Lices, 1895
oil on canvas, 65 × 81 cm
Freiburg, Diane collection

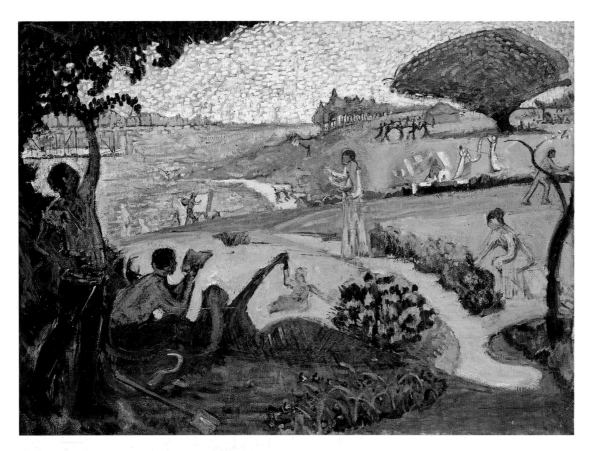

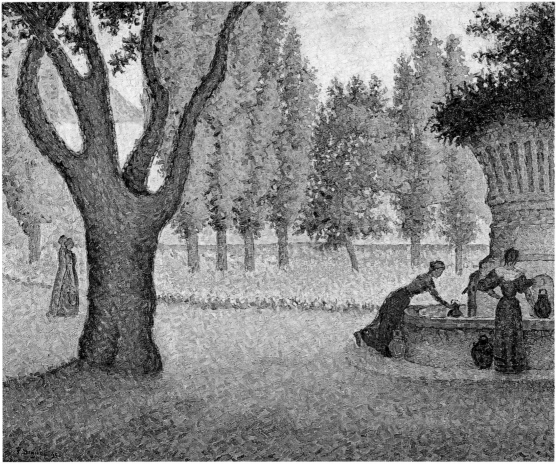

Sails and Pine Trees, 1896
oil on canvas, 81 × 52 cm
Paris, private collection

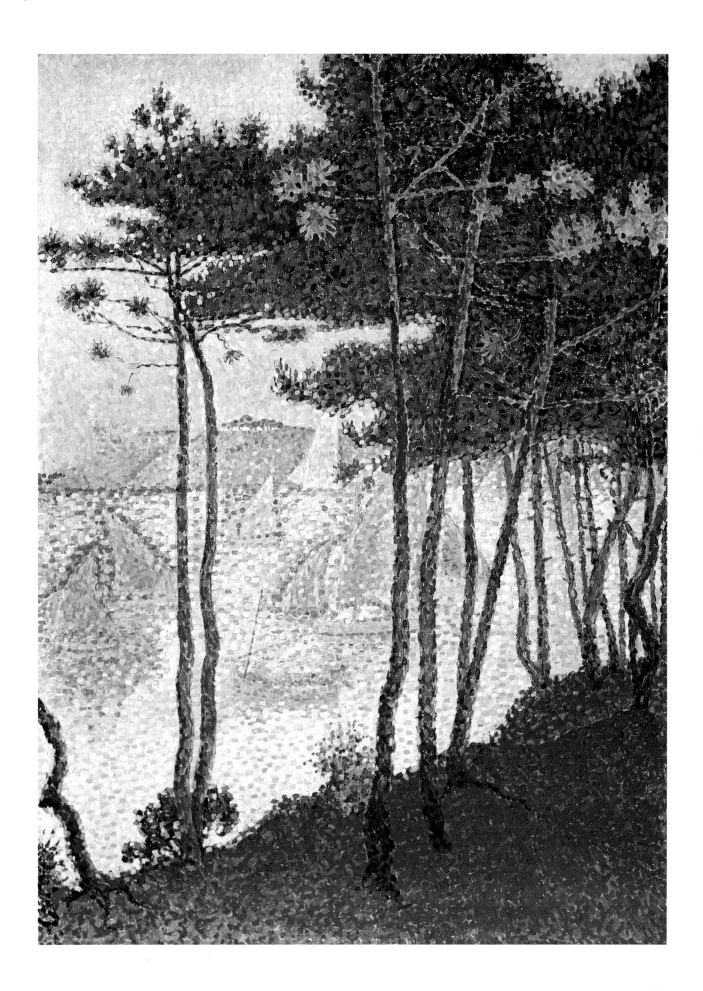

Evening Breeze, 1893.
oil on canvas, 116 × 165 cm
Paris, Musée d'Orsay

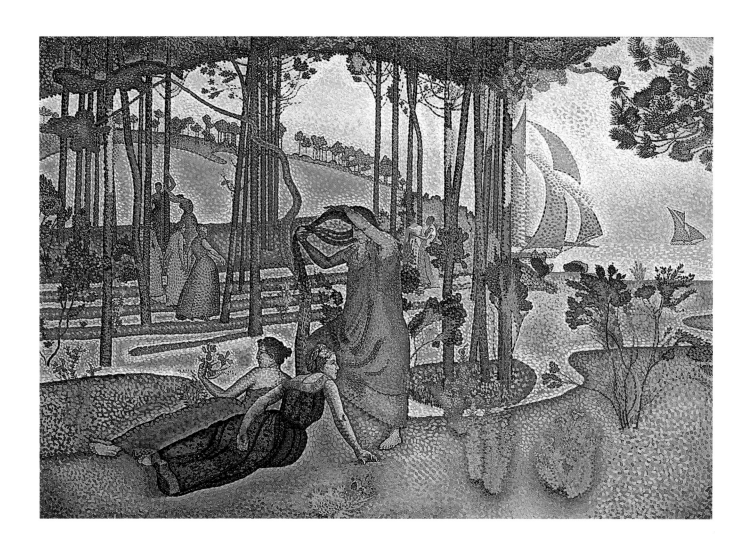

48. Henri Edmond Cross

Mediterranean Shores, 1895
oil on canvas, 65.5 × 93 cm
Walter F. Brown Collection

49. Henri Edmond Cross

Marine Scene with Cypresses,
1896
oil on canvas, 65 × 92 cm
Geneva, Musée du Petit Palais

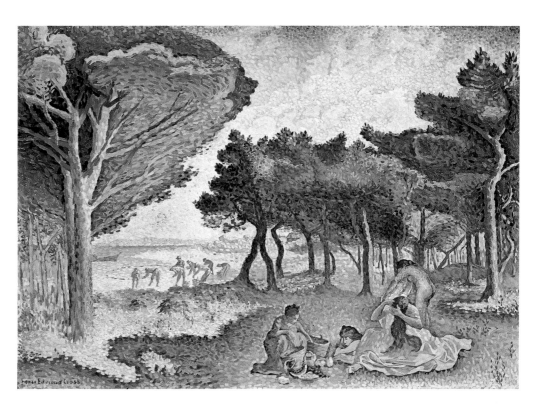

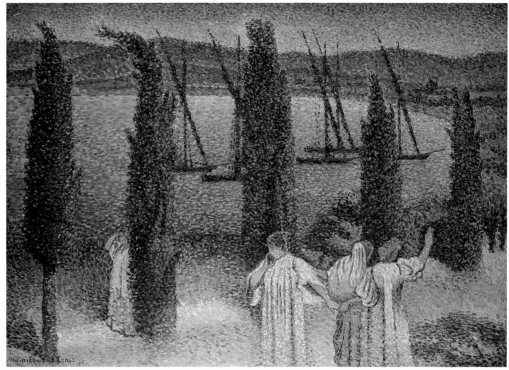

The Pool at Jas de Bouffan, 1878
oil on canvas, 47 × 56.2 cm
Private collection

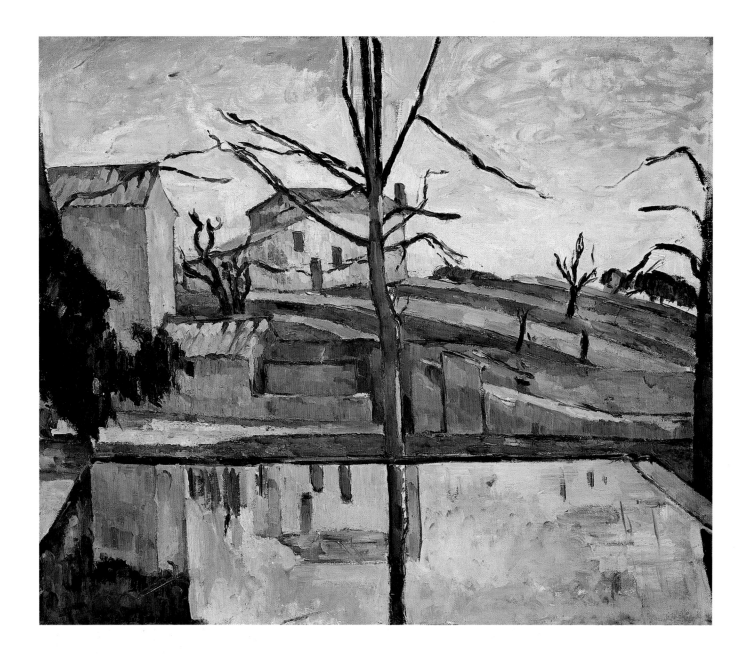

51. Paul Cézanne

Bathers before a Drapery,
1883–85
oil on canvas, 63,5 × 81 cm
Stuttgart, Staatsgalerie

51bis. Paul Cézanne

Bathers, 1895–98
oil on canvas, 29 × 45 cm
Aix-en-Provence,
Musée Granet, in deposit
at the Musée di Orsay

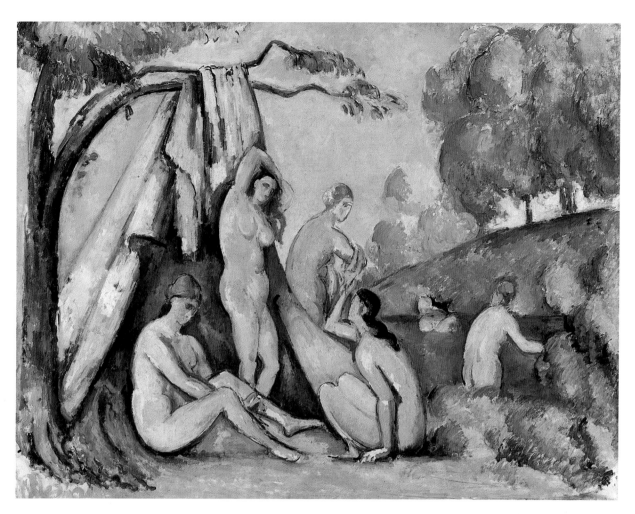

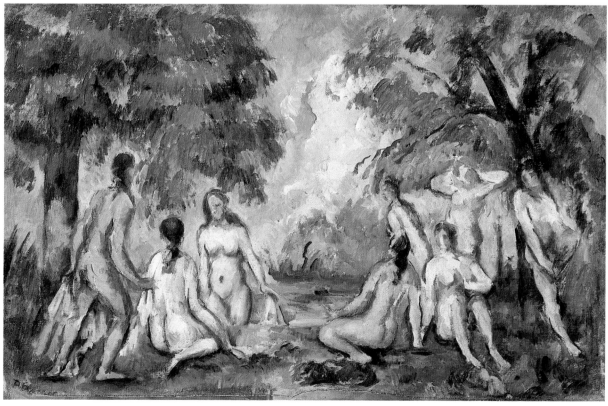

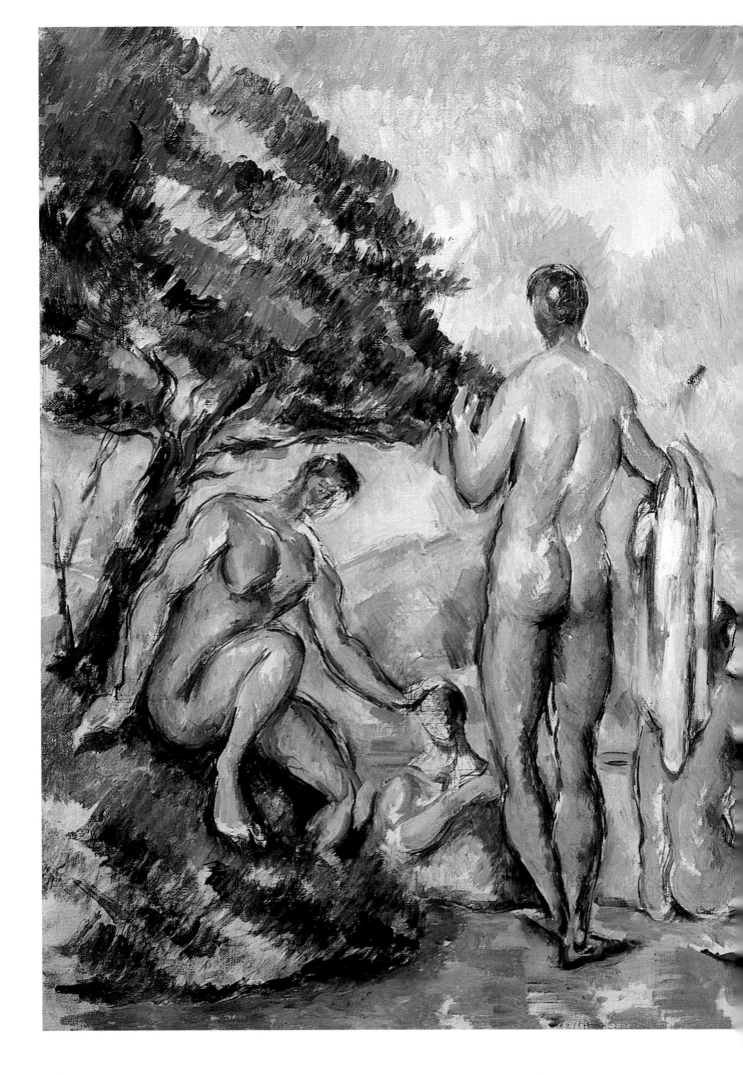

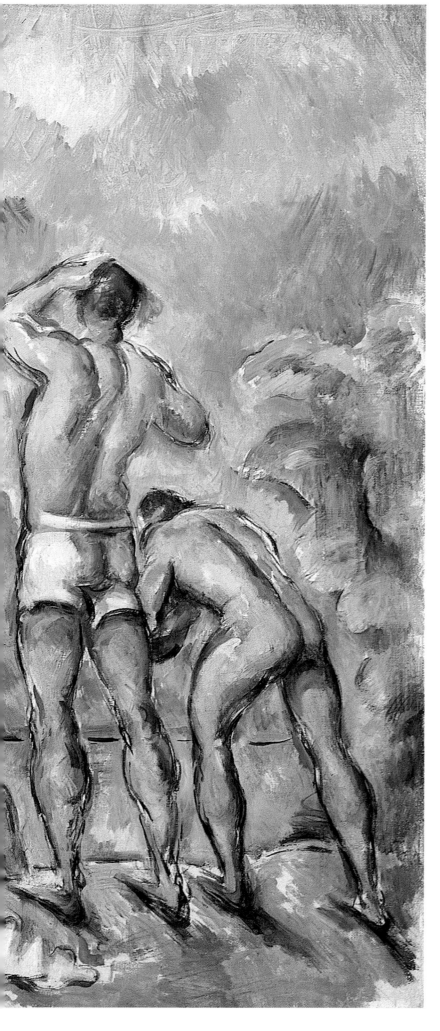

52. Paul Cézanne

Bathers, 1890–92
oil on canvas, 52.7 × 64.2 cm
Saint Louis, The Saint Louis
Art Museum. Funds given
by Mrs. Mark C. Steinberg

*Homer Walking in the
Countryside*, 1889
oil on canvas, 43.5 × 25 cm
Paris, private collection

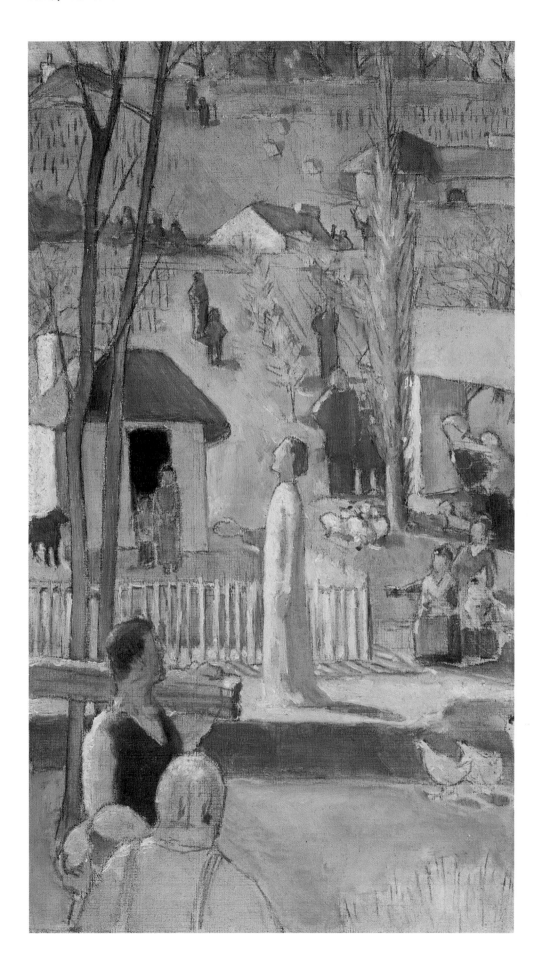

54. Maurice Denis

Portrait of Raphaël Lemeunier,
1889
oil on canvas, 45 × 30 cm
Saint-Germain-en-Laye,
Musée Maurice Denis

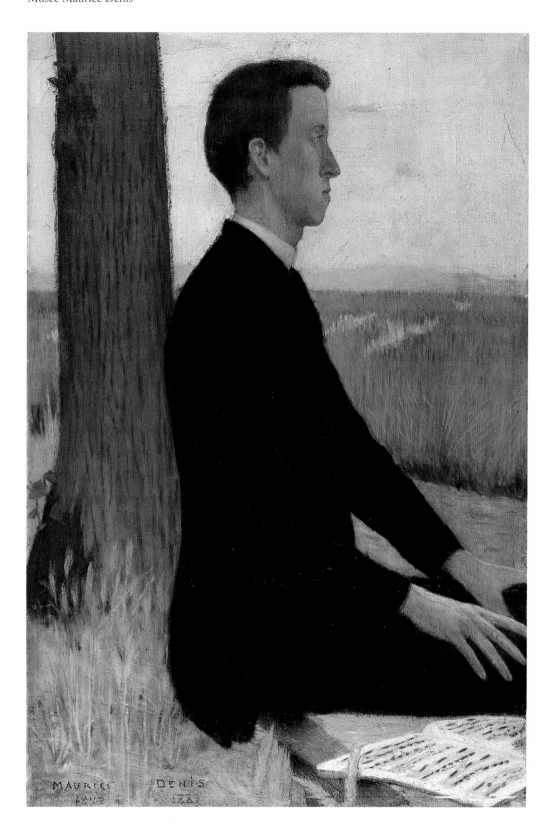

Landscape with Green Trees,
1893
oil on canvas, 46.3 × 42.8 cm
Paris, Musée d'Orsay

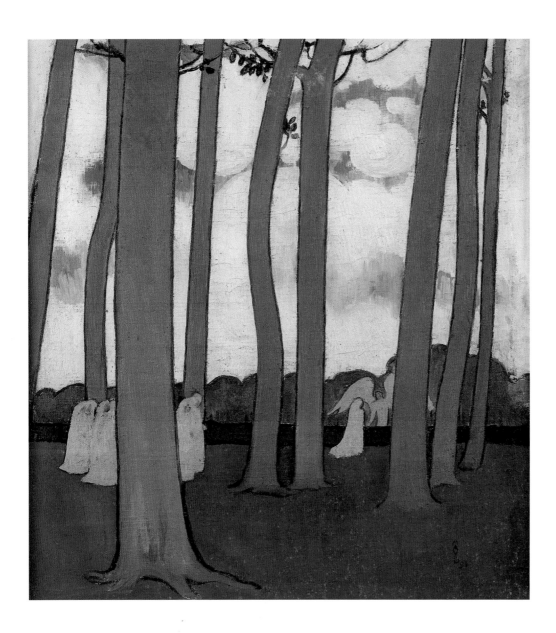

The Orchard of the Wise Virgins, 1893
oil on canvas, 105 × 103 cm
Paris, Daniel Malingue

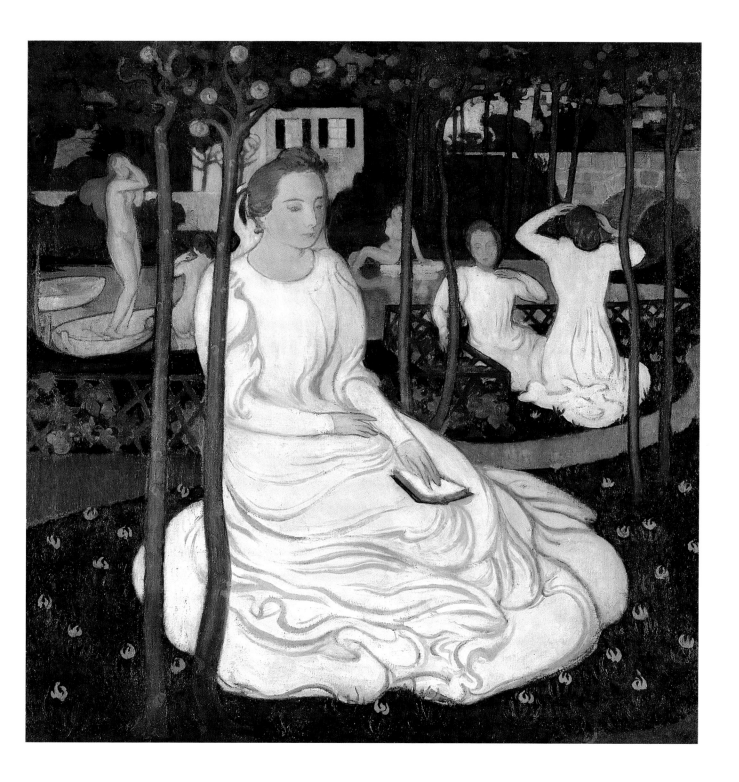

Nude with Bouquet of Violets, 1894
oil on canvas, 54.7 × 74.3 cm
Private collection

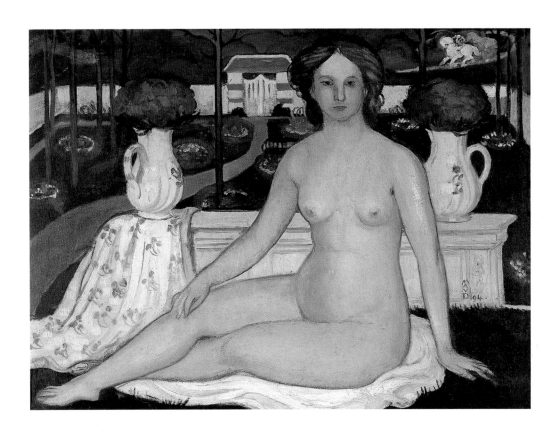

58. Maurice Denis

The Saintly Women at the Tomb, 1893
oil on canvas, 74 × 100 cm
Saint-Germain-en-Laye,
Musée Maurice Denis

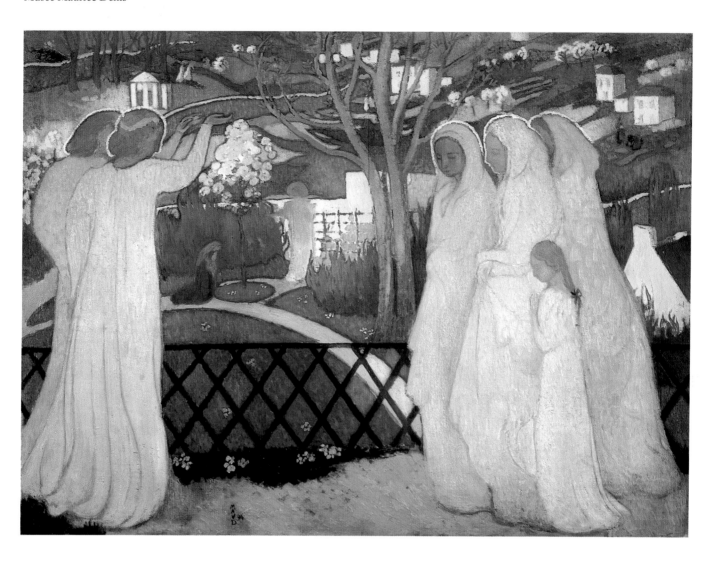

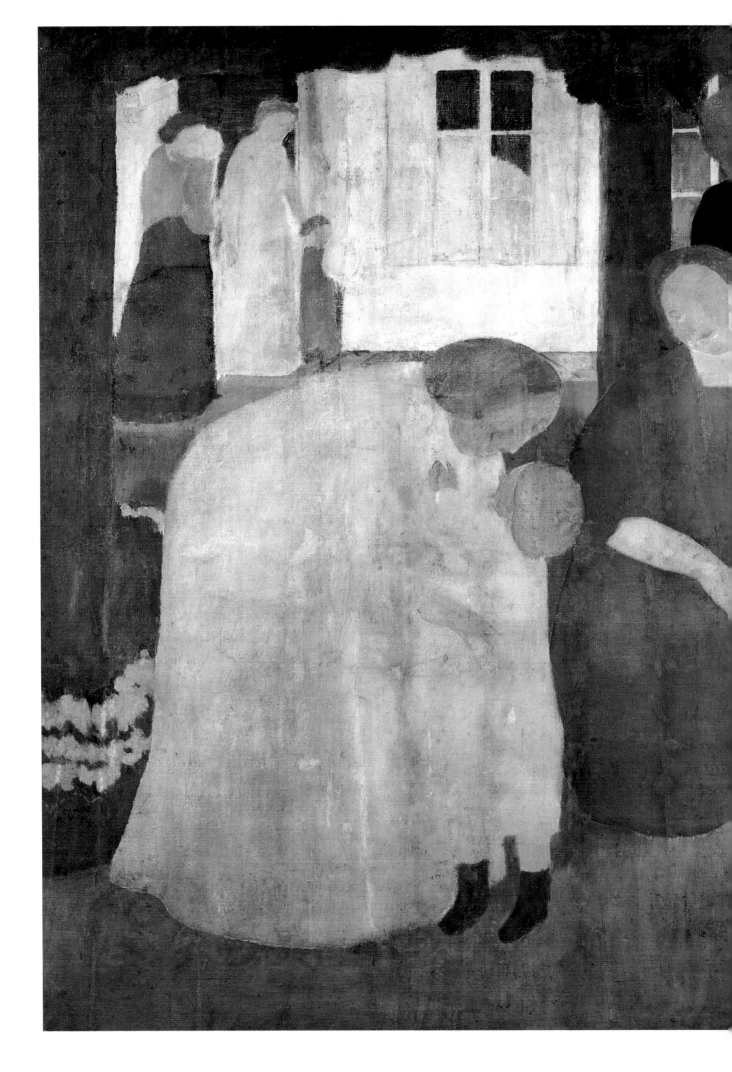

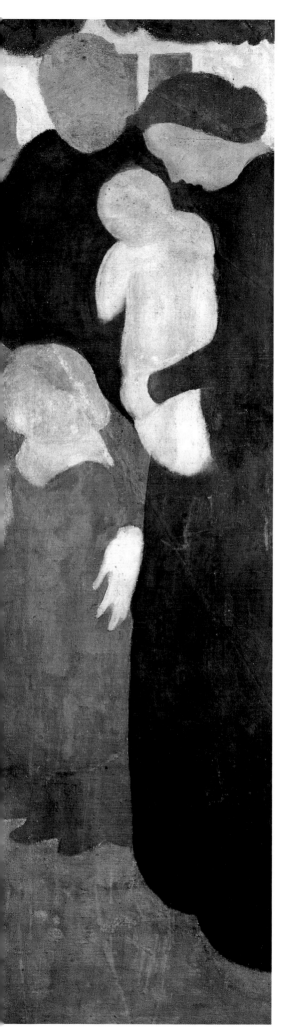

59. Maurice Denis

Let the Children Come to Me, 1899
oil on canvas, 172 × 183 cm
Saint-Germain-en-Laye,
Musée Maurice Denis

Springtime in the Forest, 1907
oil on canvas, 130 × 192 cm
Saint-Germain-en-Laye,
Musée Maurice Denis

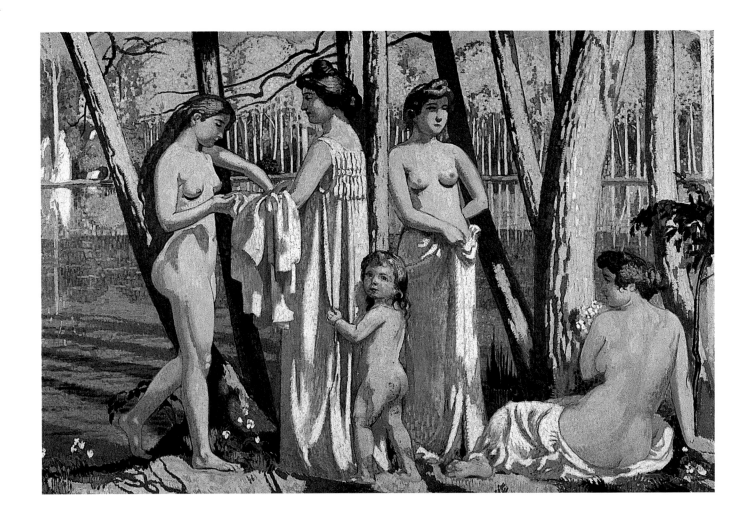

61. Pierre Bonnard

Pleasure, 1906–10
oil on canvas, 230 × 300 cm
Paris, Paul and Adrien
Maeght Collection

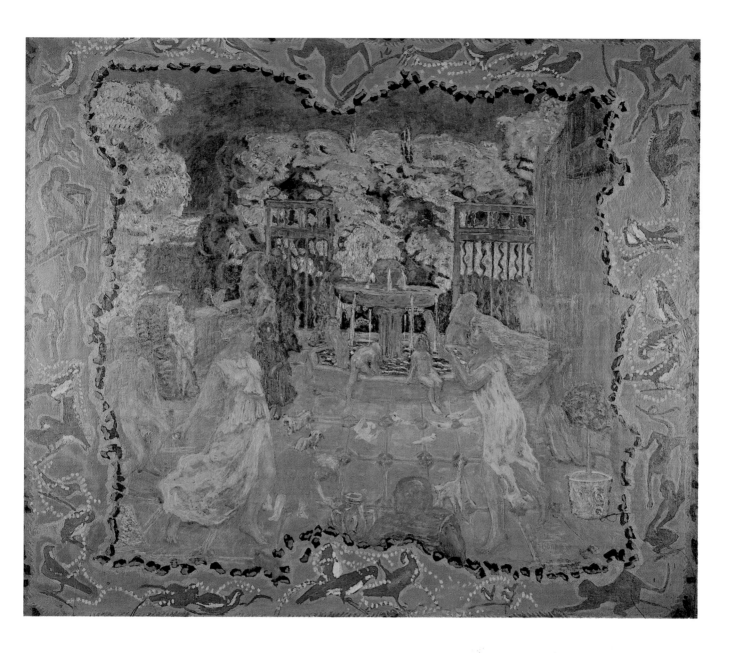

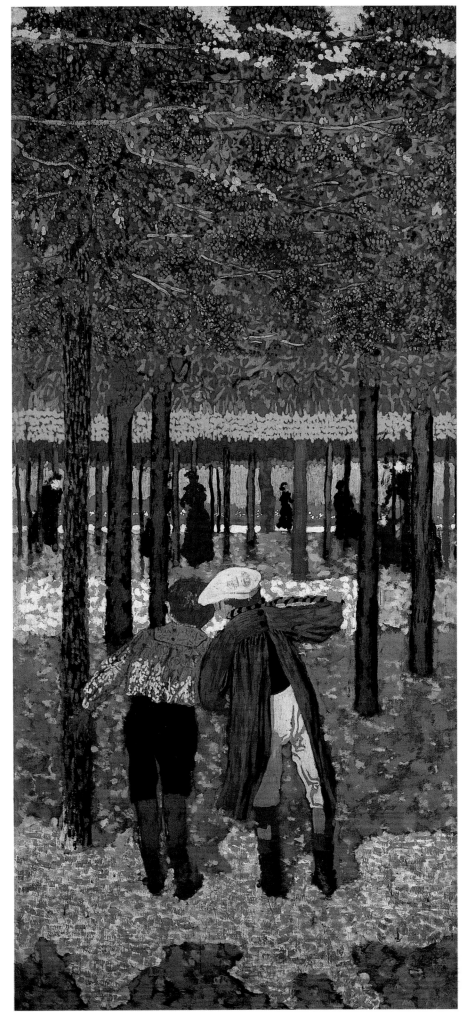

The Two Pupils, 1894
Glue paint on canvas,
214 × 98 cm
Brussels, Musées Royaux
des Beaux-Arts

63. Edouard Vuillard

Misia in Villeneuve-sur-Yonne,
1897–99
oil on panel, 42 × 62 cm
Lyon, Musée des Beaux-Arts

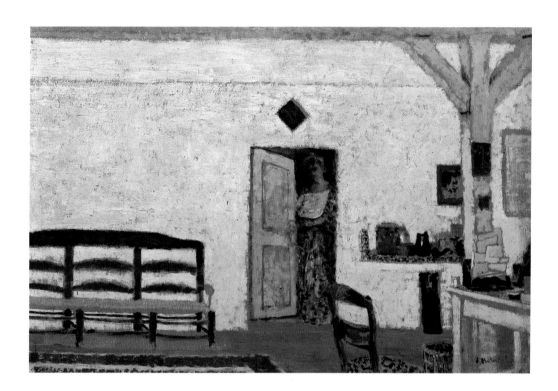

The Spell, 1891
oil on canvas, 98 × 72 cm
Quimper, Musée des Beaux-Arts

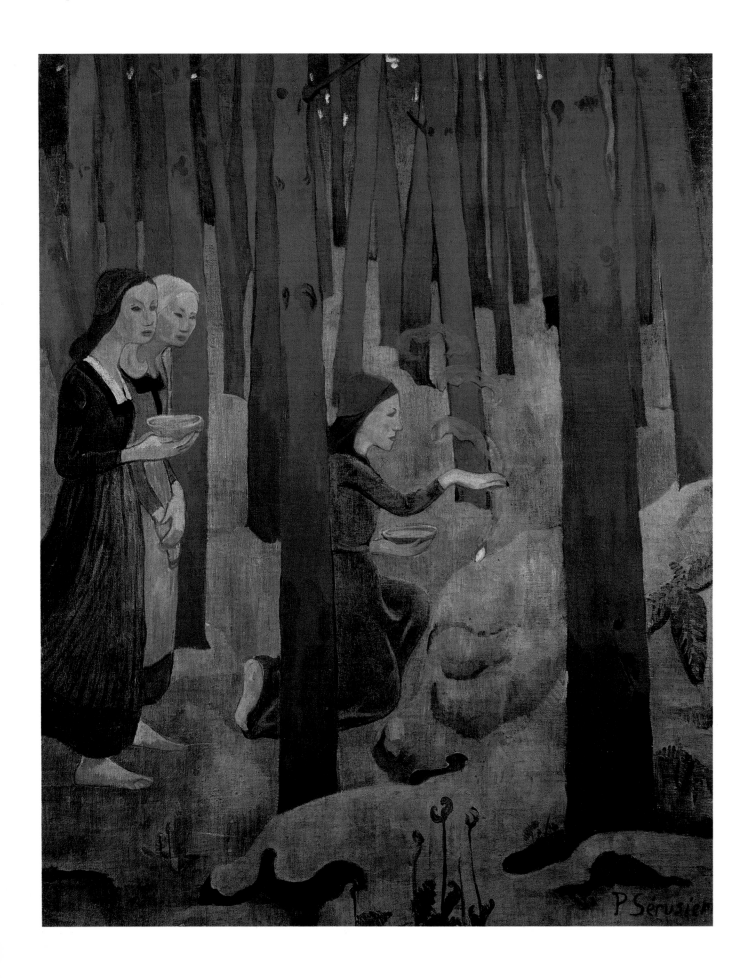

65. Paul Sérusier

The Laundry Bearers, 1895
oil on canvas, 111 × 69 cm
Brest, Musée des Beaux-Arts

66. Paul Sérusier

*Portrait of Jan Verkade in
Beuron*, 1903
oil on canvas, 56 × 46 cm
Saint-Germain-en-Laye,
Musée Maurice Denis

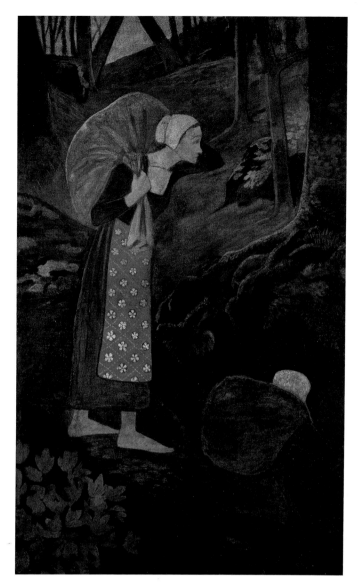

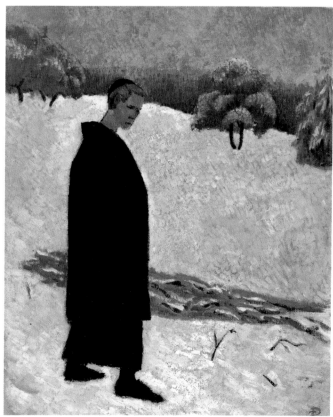

67. Ker-Xavier Roussel

Composition in the Forest, 1890
oil on canvas, 44 × 31 cm
Saint-Germain-en-Laye,
Musée Maurice Denis

68. Ker-Xavier Roussel

Conversation, 1891
oil on canvas, 41 × 32 cm
Toulouse, Musée des Augustins

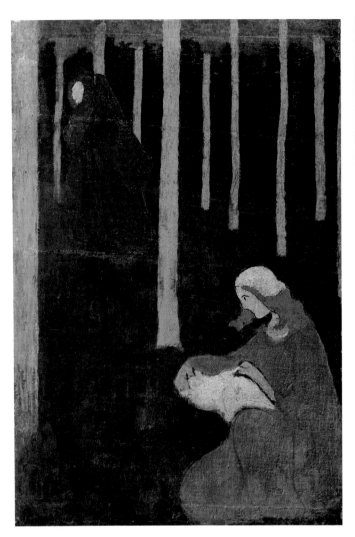

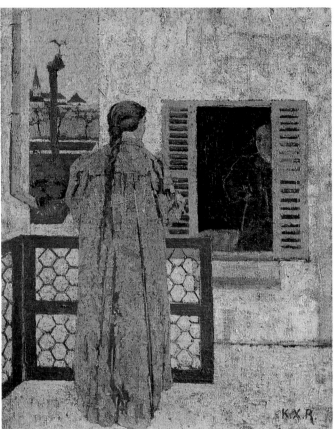

9. Ker-Xavier Roussel

The Season's of Life, 1892
Oil on canvas, 60 × 130 cm
Paris, Musée d'Orsay

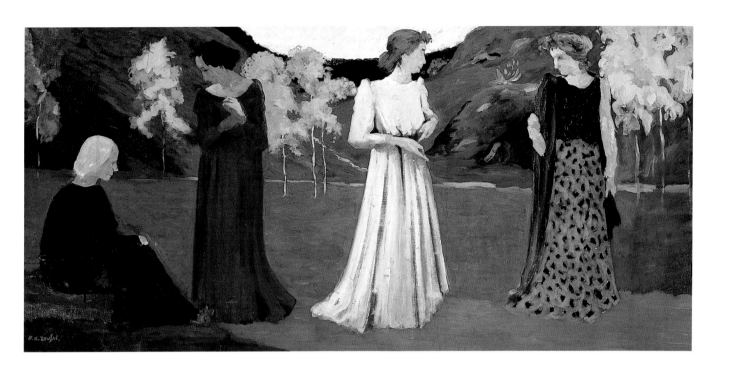

Terrace at the Tuileries,
1892–93
oil on canvas, 36 × 75 cm
Paris, Musée d'Orsay

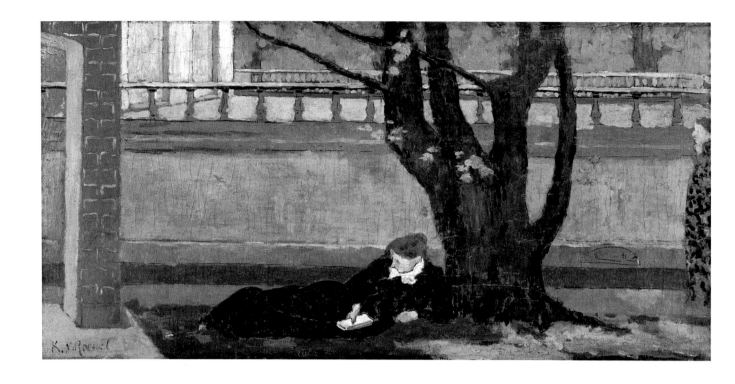

71. Ker-Xavier Roussel

Nymphs, 1899
pastel on cardboard,
57 × 64 cm
Neuss, Clemens-Sels-Museum
(on deposit from a private
collection)

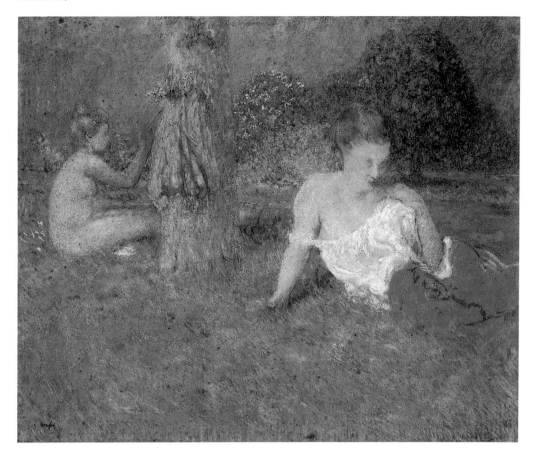

72. Aristide Maillol

Kneeling Young Woman, 1900
bronze, 84 × 40 × 58 cm
Paris, Musée Maillol

73. Aristide Maillol

Cyclist, 1907
bronze, 99 × 30 × 24 cm
Paris, Musée Maillol

74. Aristide Maillol

Nymph, 1930
bronze, 156 × 64 × 43 cm
Saint-Tropez,
Musée de l'Annonciade

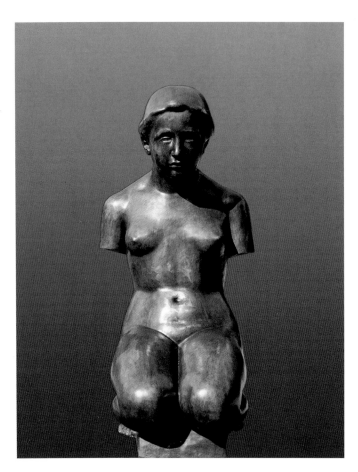

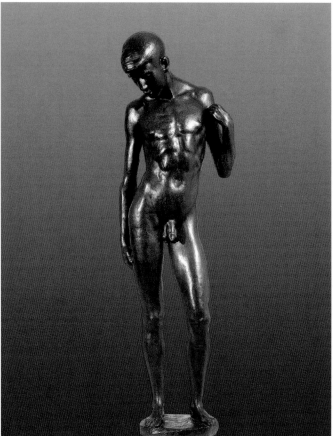

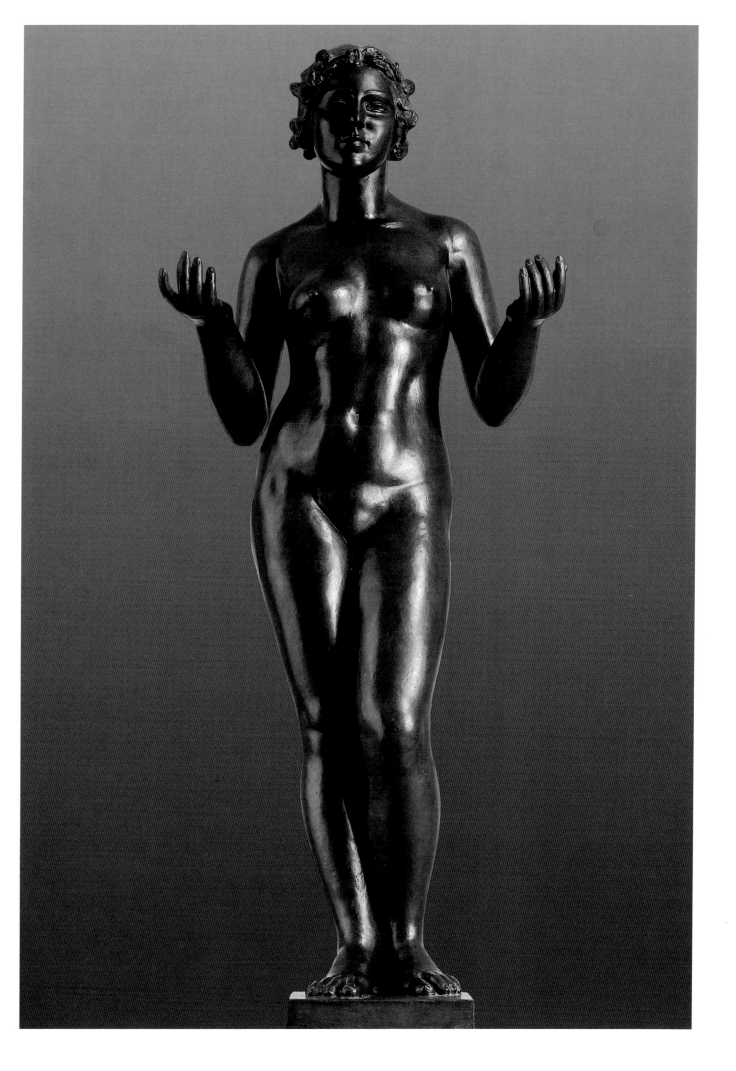

The Poor Fisherman, 1888–89
oil on canvas, 95 × 120 cm
Nancy, Musée des Beaux-Arts
(on deposit from the Musée
d'Orsay)

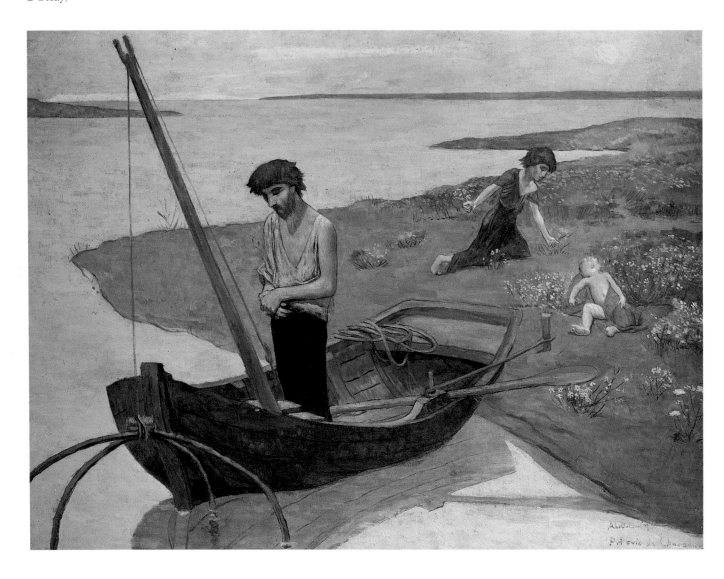

Mediterranean, 1895
oil on canvas 96.5 × 105 cm
Paris, Petit Palais,
Musée des Beaux-Arts
de la Ville

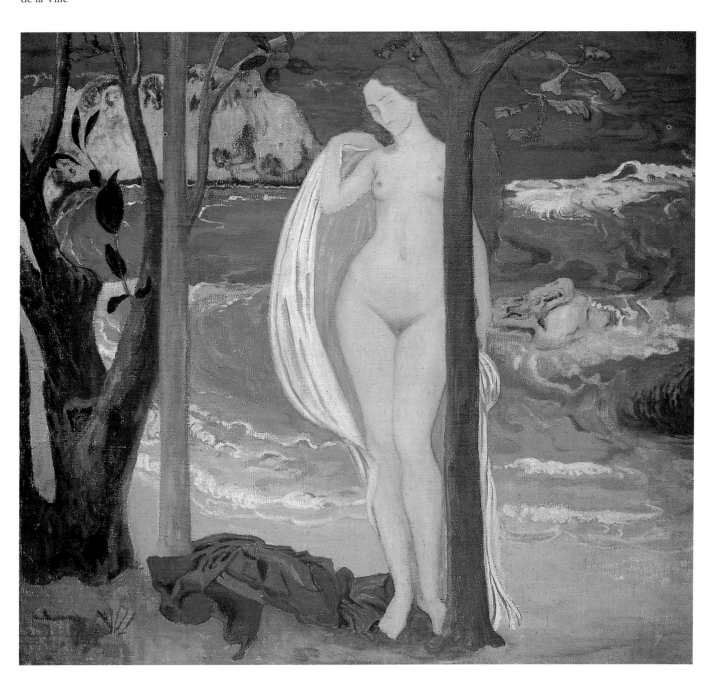

The Prodigal Son, c. 1889
oil on canvas, 88.5 × 108 cm
Private collection

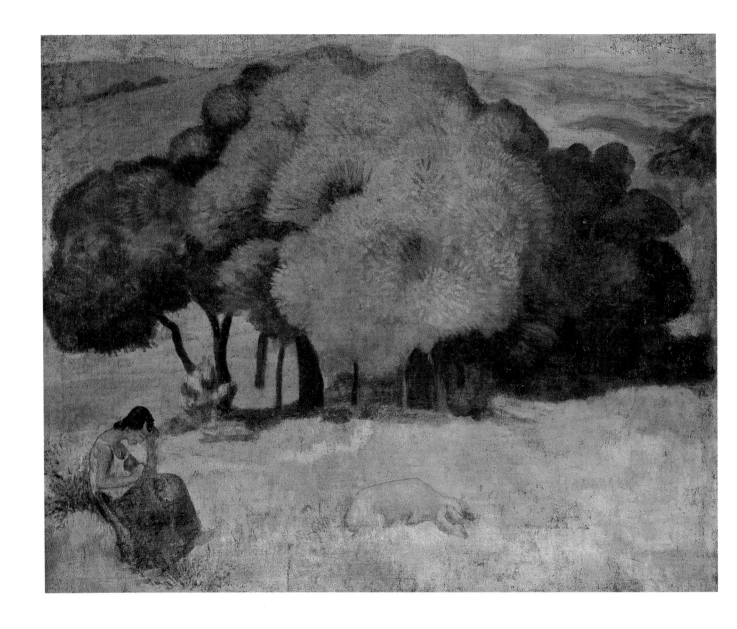

Woman with Parasol, 1895
oil on canvas, 190 × 145 cm
Paris, Musée d'Orsay

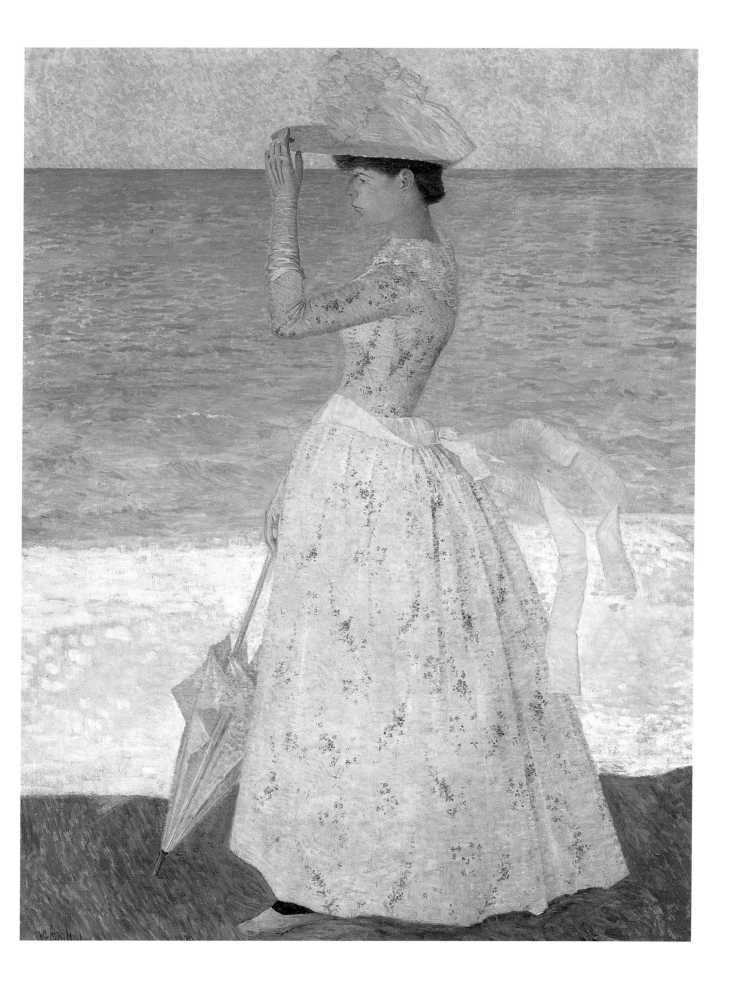

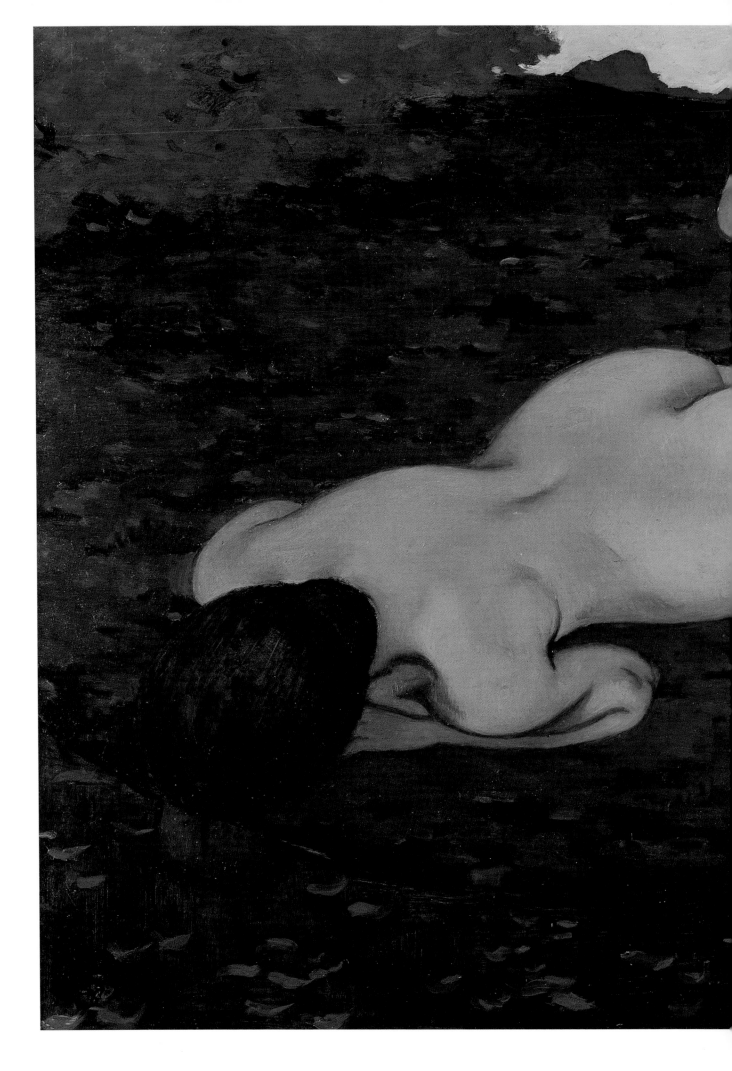

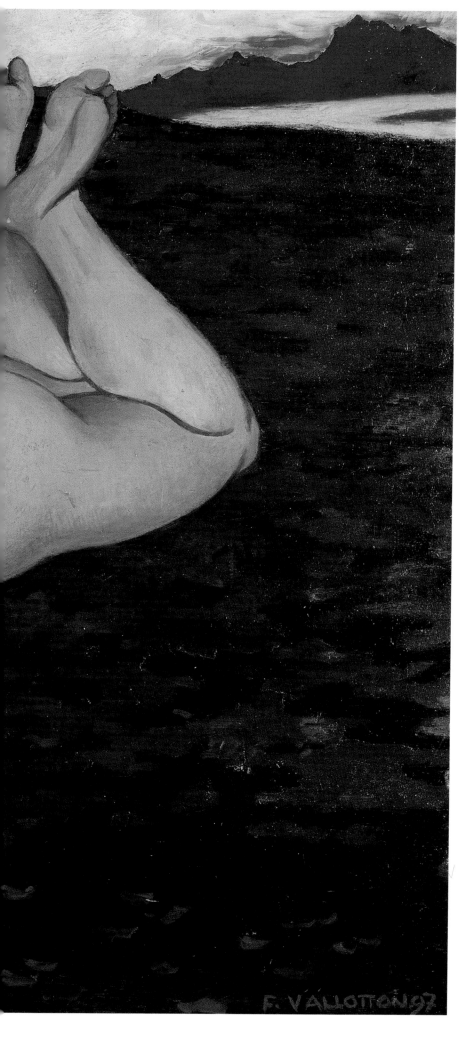

The Spring, 1897
oil on cardboard, 48 × 60 cm
Geneva, Musée du Petit Palais

Houses in Brittany, 1901
oil on cardboard, 67 × 52 cm
Winterthur, Villa Flora,
Hahnloser Collection

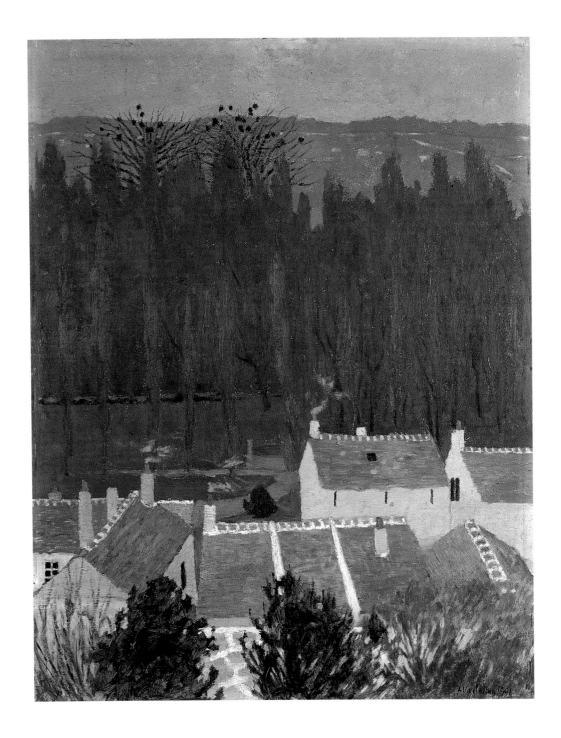

81. Félix Vallotton

Vuillard Drawing in Honfleur,
1902
oil on cardboard, 81 × 60 cm
Private collection

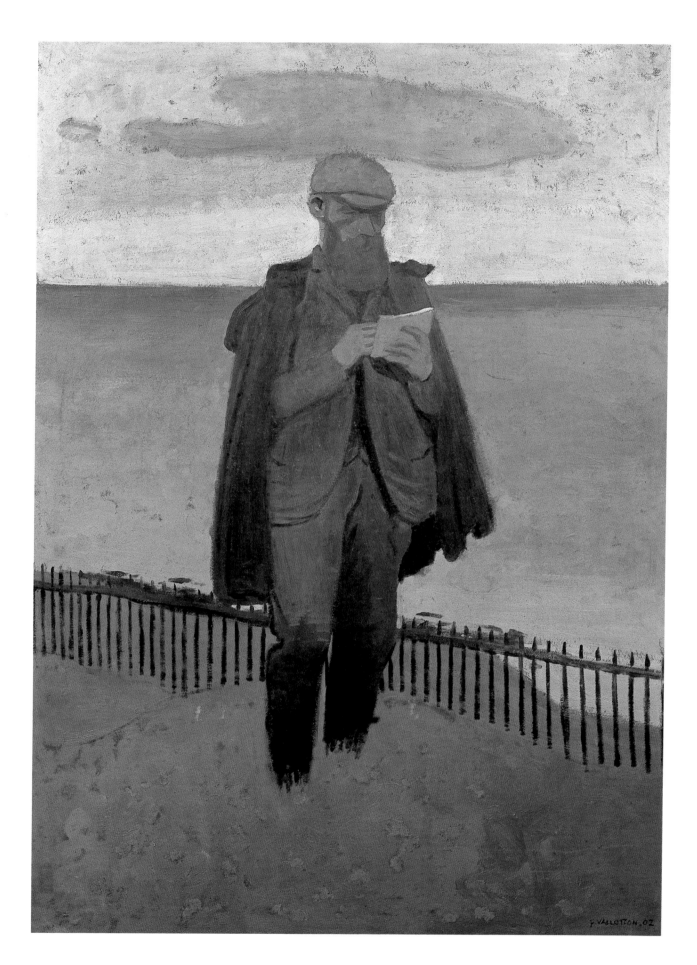

Pentheus, Landscape with
Antique Figures, 1904
oil on canvas, 93 × 142 cm
Private collection

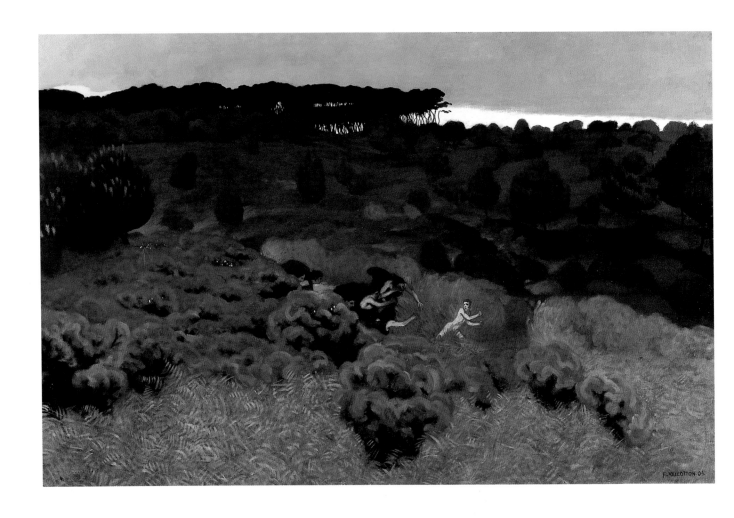

83. Félix Vallotton

*Adolescent Entering in the
Water*, 1907
oil on canvas, 46 × 31 cm
Geneva, Musée du Petit Palais

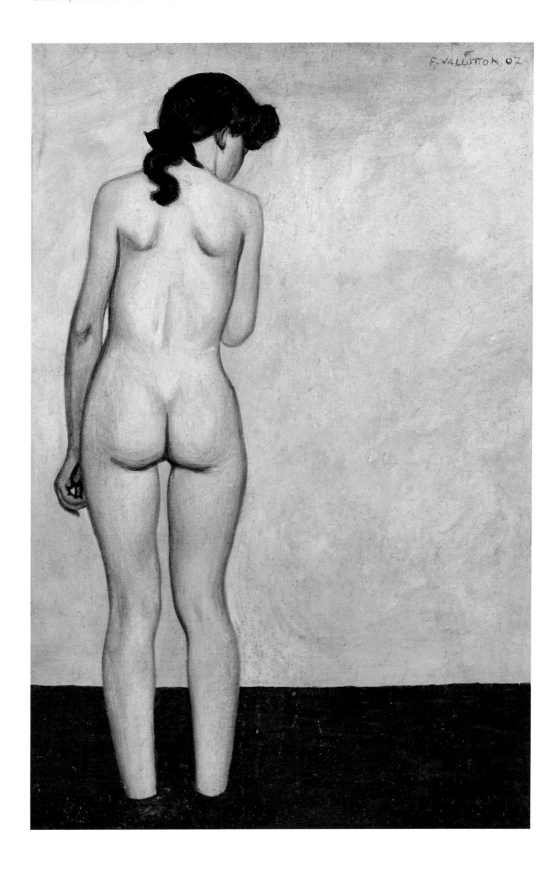

83. Félix Vallotton

*Adolescent Entering in the
Water*, 1907
oil on canvas, 46 × 31 cm
Geneva, Musée du Petit Palais

Forest with Red Soil, 1891
oil on canvas, 71.3 × 50.5 cm
Quimper, Musée des Beaux-Arts

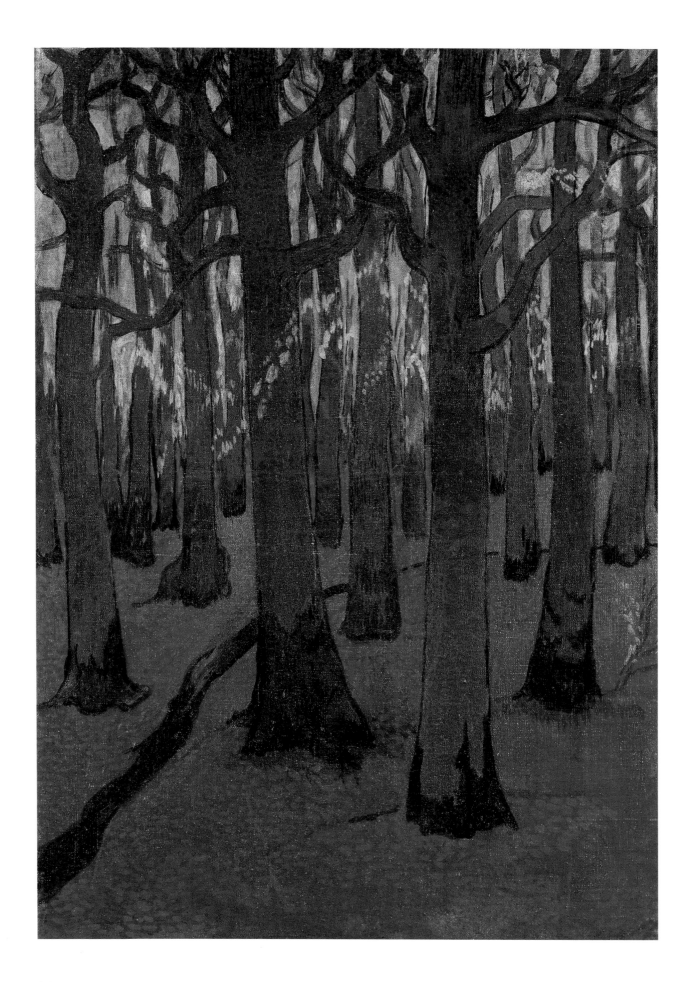

85. Paul Ranson

The Explanation, 1896
pastel on canvas, 58 × 52 cm
Saint-Germain-en-Laye,
Musée Maurice Denis

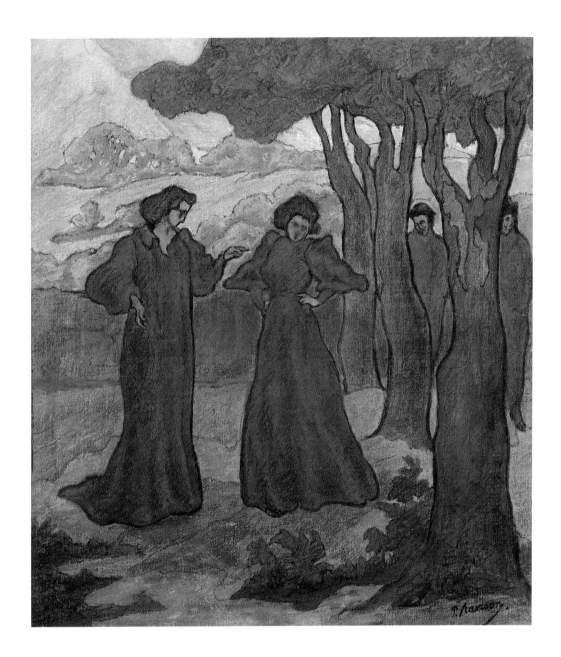

86. Odilon Redon

Closed Eyes, 1890
oil on canvas on cardboard,
44 × 36 cm
Paris, Musée d'Orsay

87. Odilon Redon

Eve, 1904
oil on canvas, 61 × 46 cm
Paris, Musée d'Orsay

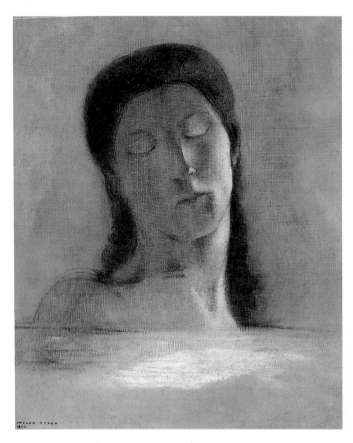

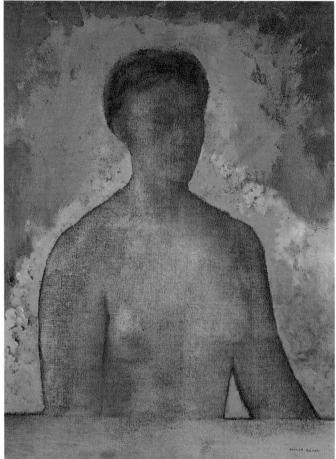

88. Odilon Redon

The Red Tree Not Reddened by the Sun, 1905
oil on canvas, 47.5 × 35.5 cm
Tsu-Shi Mie Kan,
Mie Prefectural Art Museum

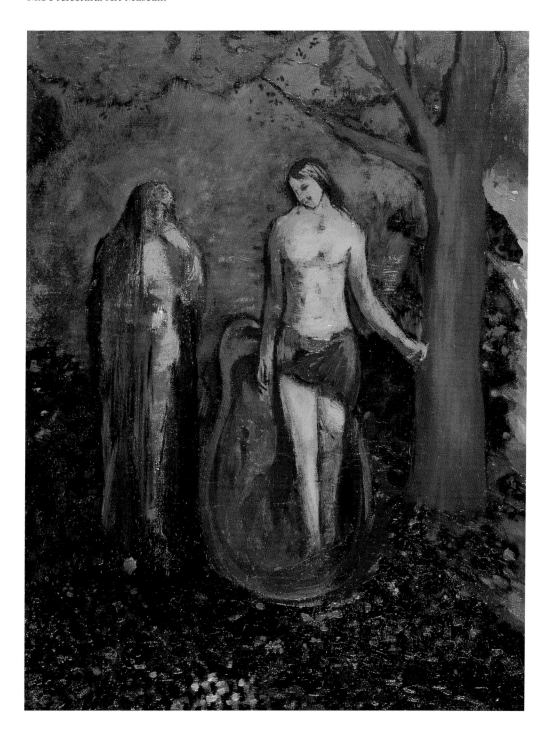

89. Henri Martin

Sketch for "The Elysian Fields,"
1939
oil on canvas, 74.5 × 86.5 cm
Cahors, Musée Henri Martin

90. Henri Martin

The Muse, 1892
pastel on paper, 143 × 90 cm
Private collection

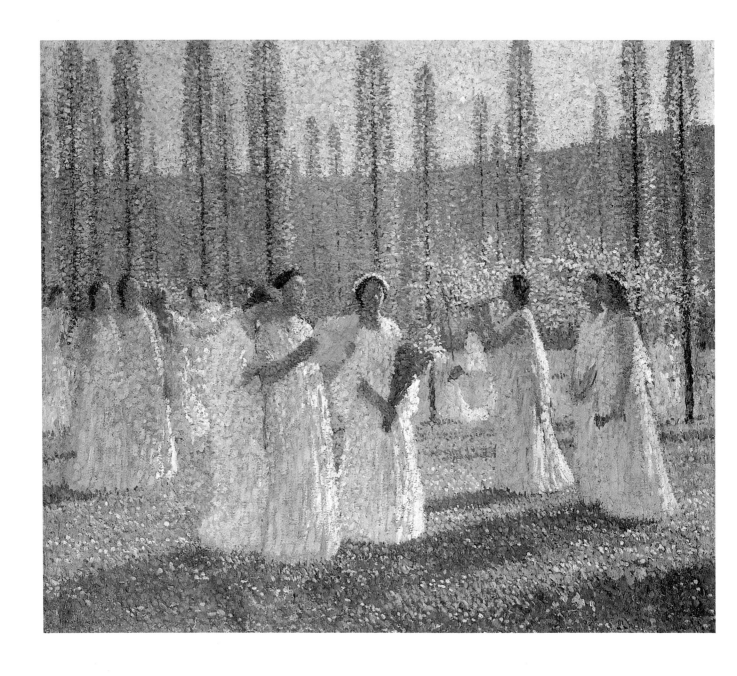

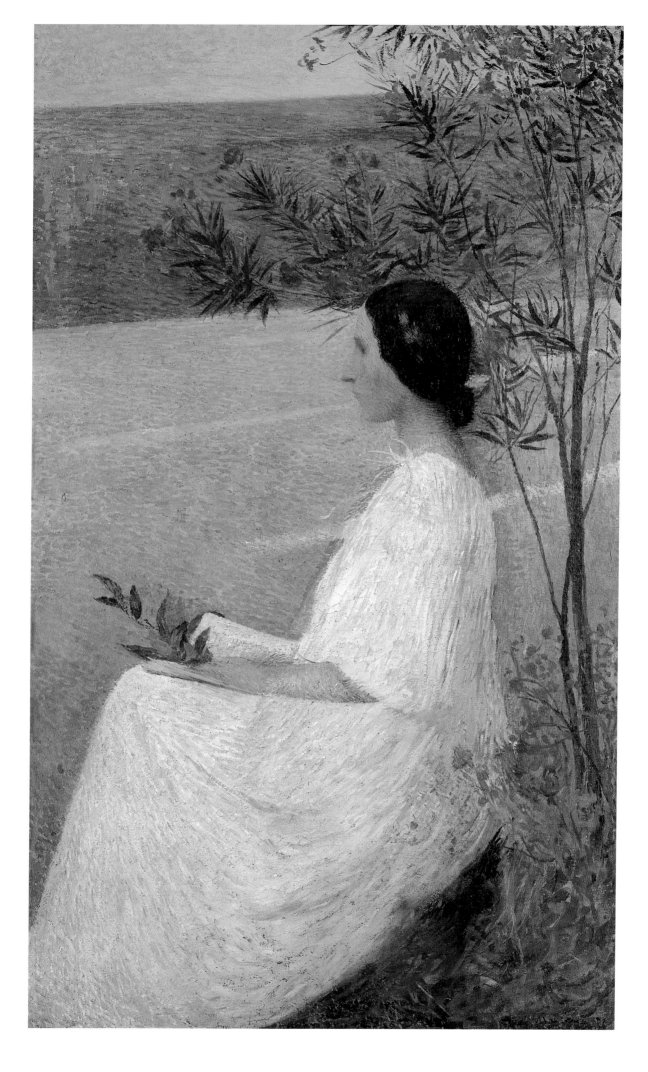

The Lamentation of Orpheus,
1896
oil on canvas, 73 × 116 cm
Paris, Musée d'Orsay

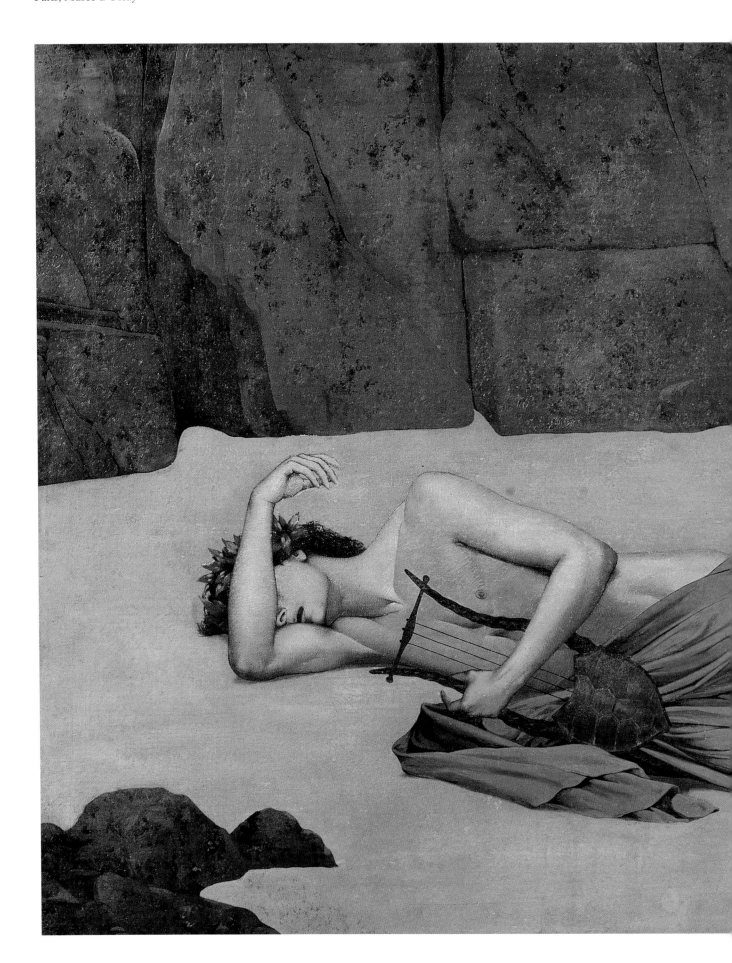

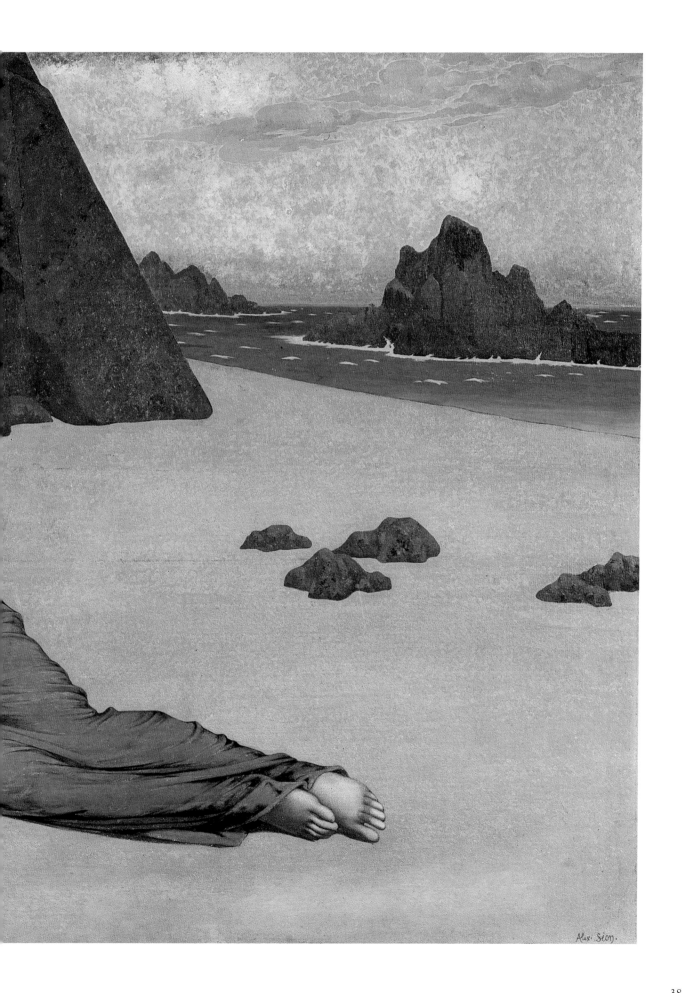

Mystery of the Night, 1897
oil on canvas, 36 × 56 cm
Private collection

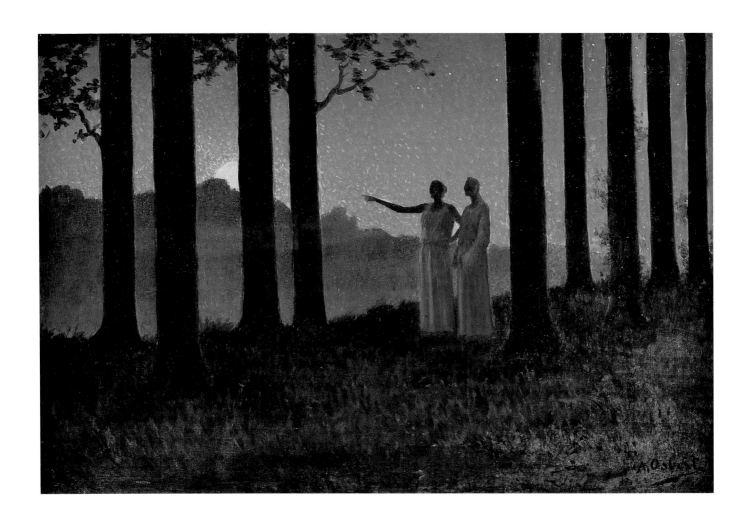

Evening in Antiquity, 1908
oil on canvas, 150.5 × 135.5 cm
Paris, Petit Palais,
Musée des Beaux-Arts de la Ville

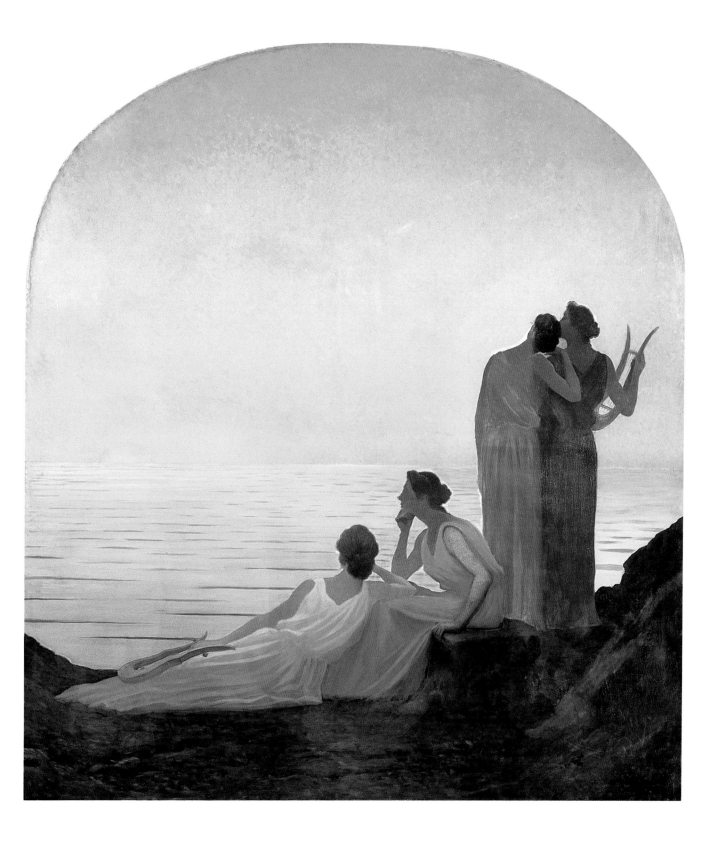

94. Emile-René Ménard

Pastoral, Land of the Ancients,
1919
oil on canvas, 154 × 264 cm
Semblançai, Jean-François
Heim Collection

95. Edmond Aman-Jean

*Verlaine at the Hôpital
Brussais,* 1892
oil on canvas, 125.5 × 70 cm
Metz, Musées de la Cour d'or

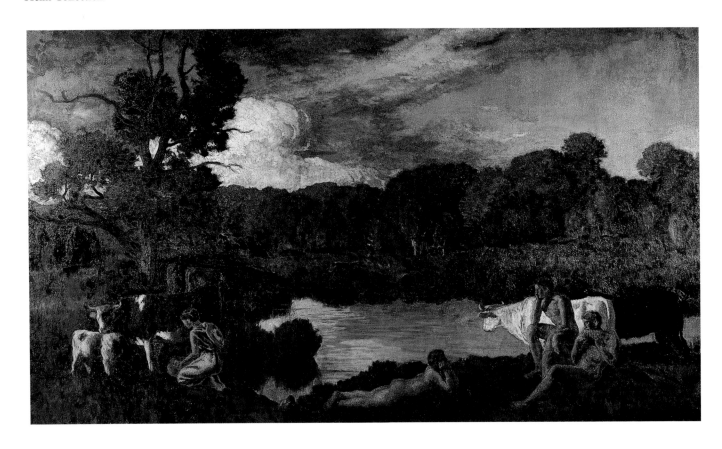

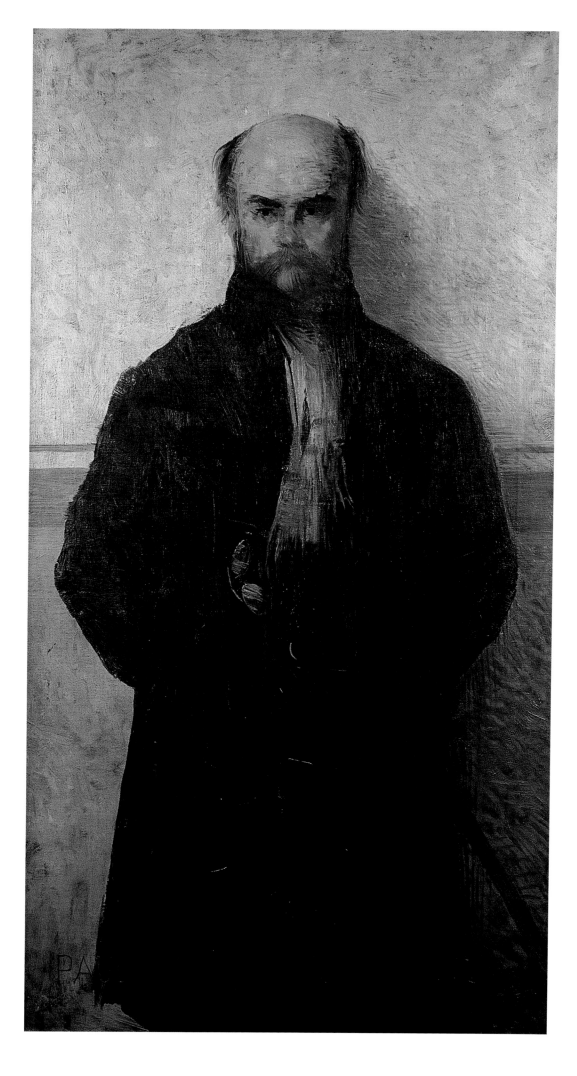

389

The Departure of Tobias, 1894
oil on canvas, 81 × 116 cm
Private collection

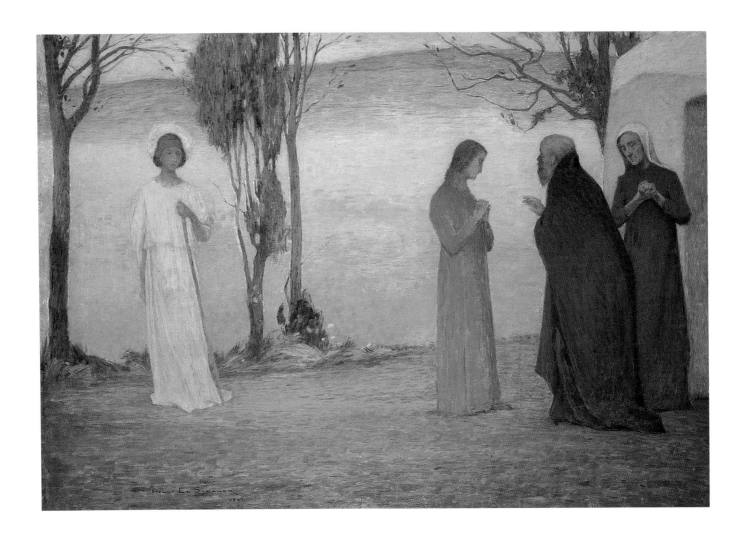

97. Henri Le Sidaner

Morning. Montreuil, Bellay, 1896
oil on canvas, 50 × 78 cm
Dunkerque, Musée
des Beaux-Arts

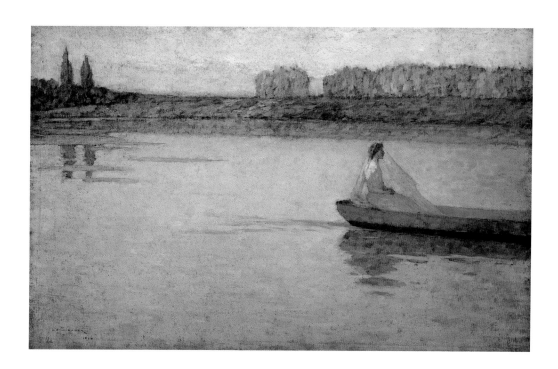

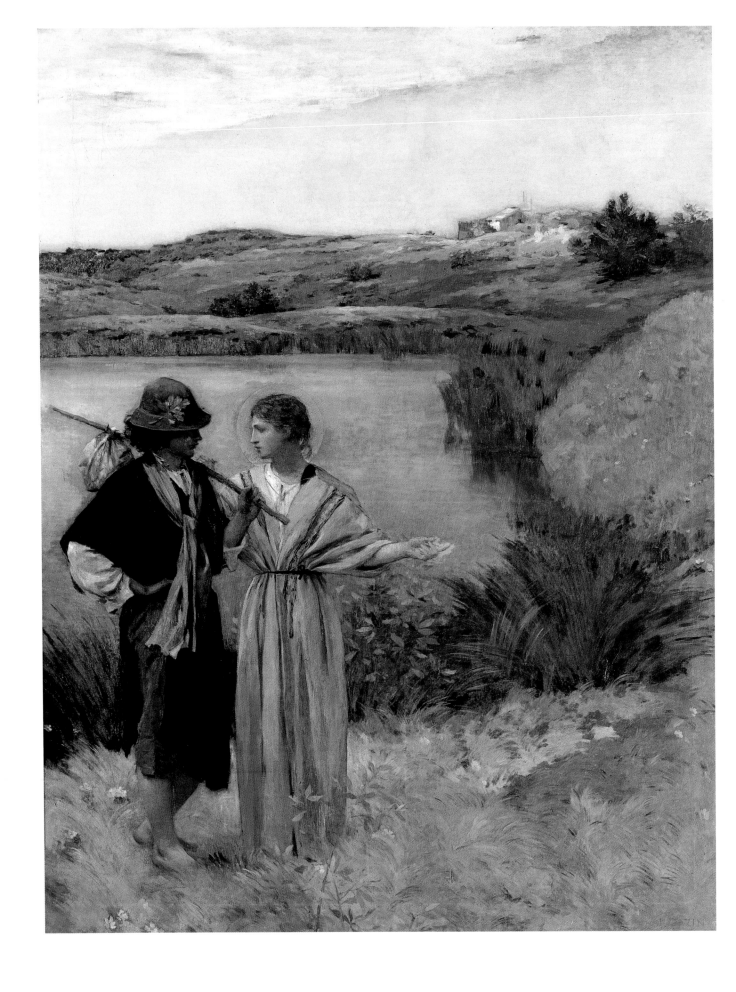

98. Jean-Charles Cazin

Tobias and the Angel, 1880
oil on canvas, 186 × 142 cm
Lille, Palais des Beaux-Arts

99. Louis Welden Hawkins

The Procession of Souls, 1893
oil on canvas, 67.4 × 44 cm
Private collection

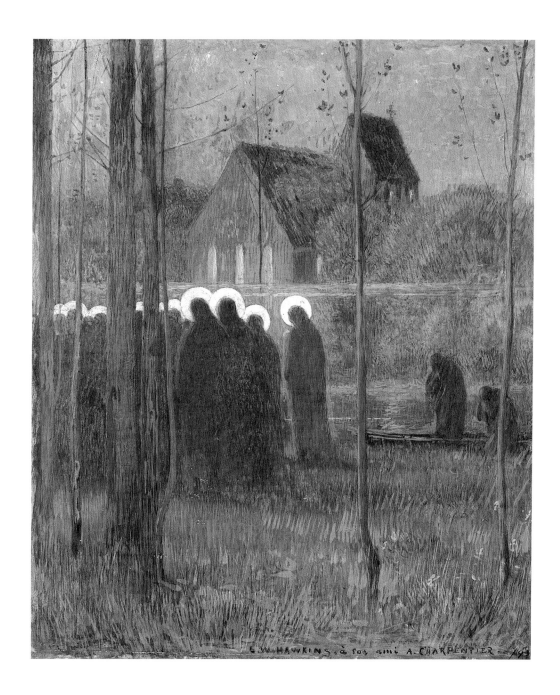

Meditation in the Park
oil on canvas, 38 × 45 cm
Walter F. Brown Collection

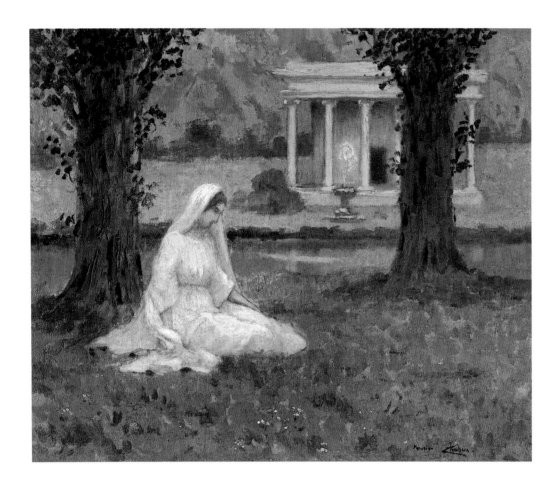

101. Auguste Baud-Bovy

Serenity, 1898
oil on canvas, 90 × 116 cm
Paris, Musée d'Orsay

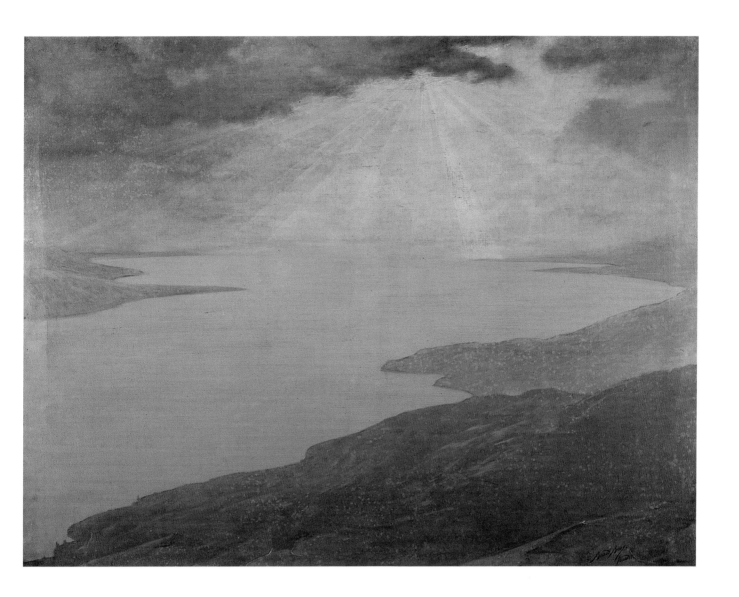

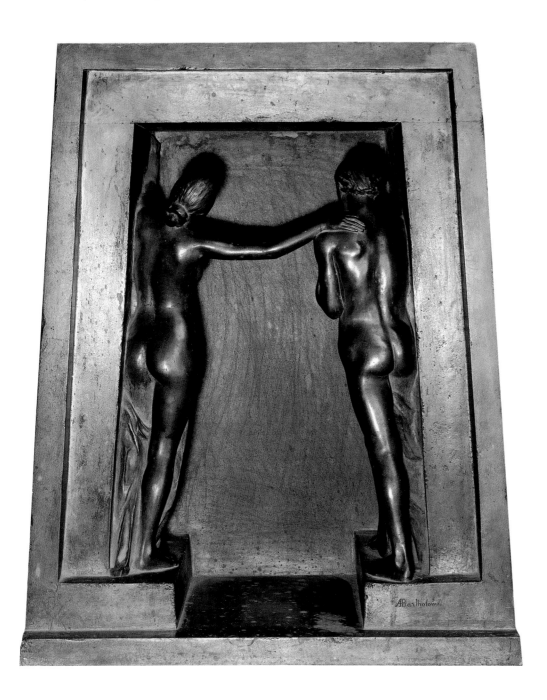

Farewell, 1899
marble, 89 × 53.5 × 10.5 cm
Brussels, Musées Royaux
des Beaux-Arts

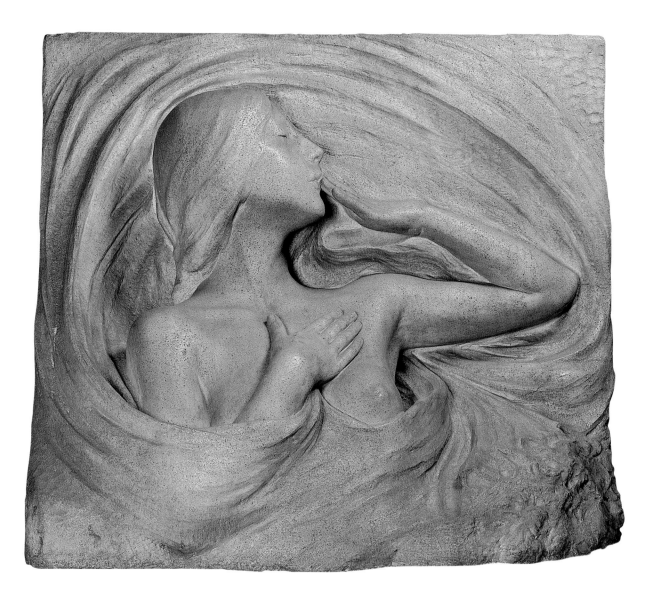

Dance on the Shore, 1904
oil on canvas, 90 × 316 cm
Oslo, Munch Museet

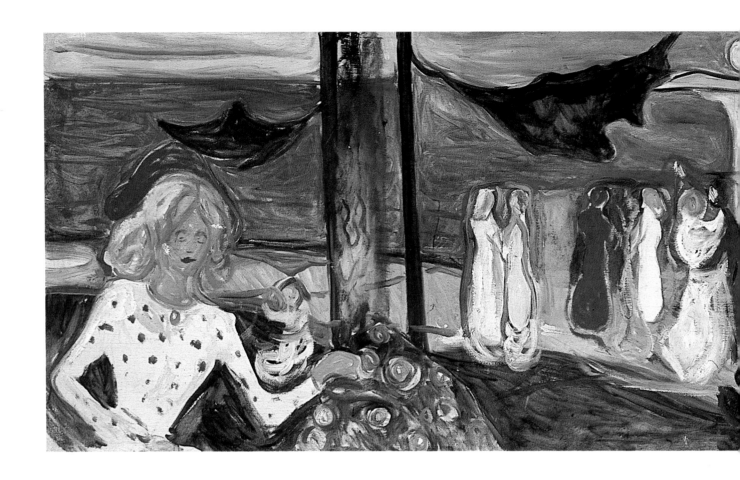

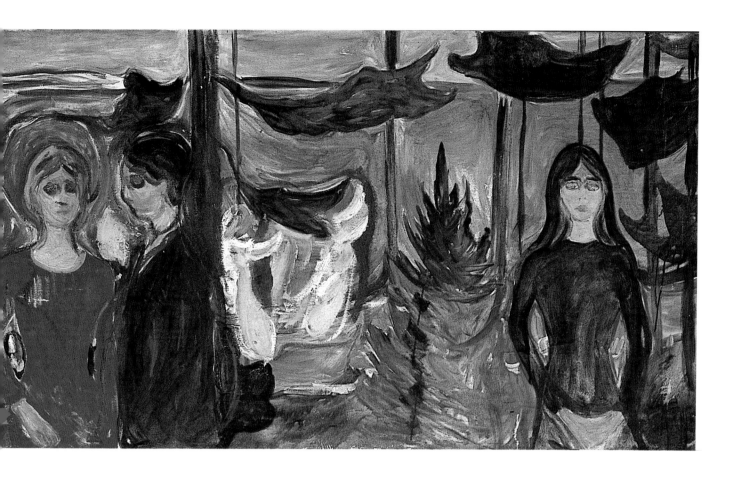

Paris Model, 1896
oil on canvas, 80 × 60 cm
Oslo, Nasjonalgalleriet

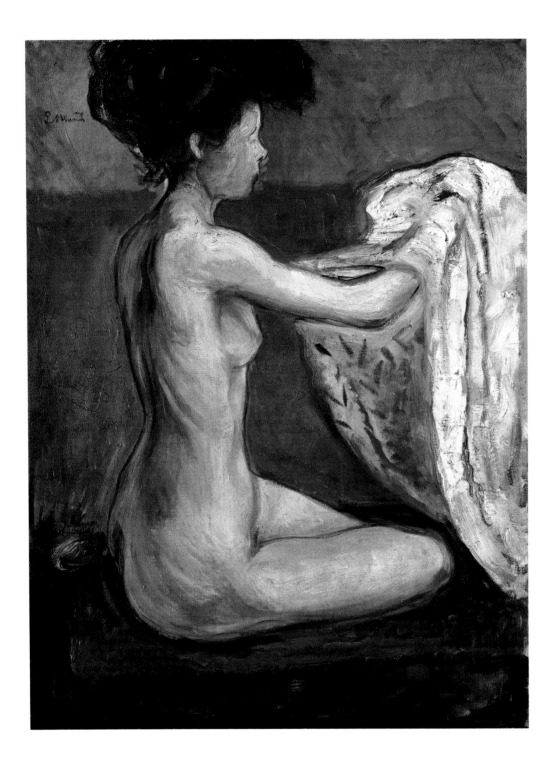

106. Edvard Munch

Bathing Man, 1918
oil on canvas, 160 × 110 cm
Oslo, Nasjonalgalleriet

following pages
107. George Minne

*The Fountain of Kneeling
Youths*, 1905
plaster, 196 × 240 × 79 cm
Gent, Musée des Beaux-Arts

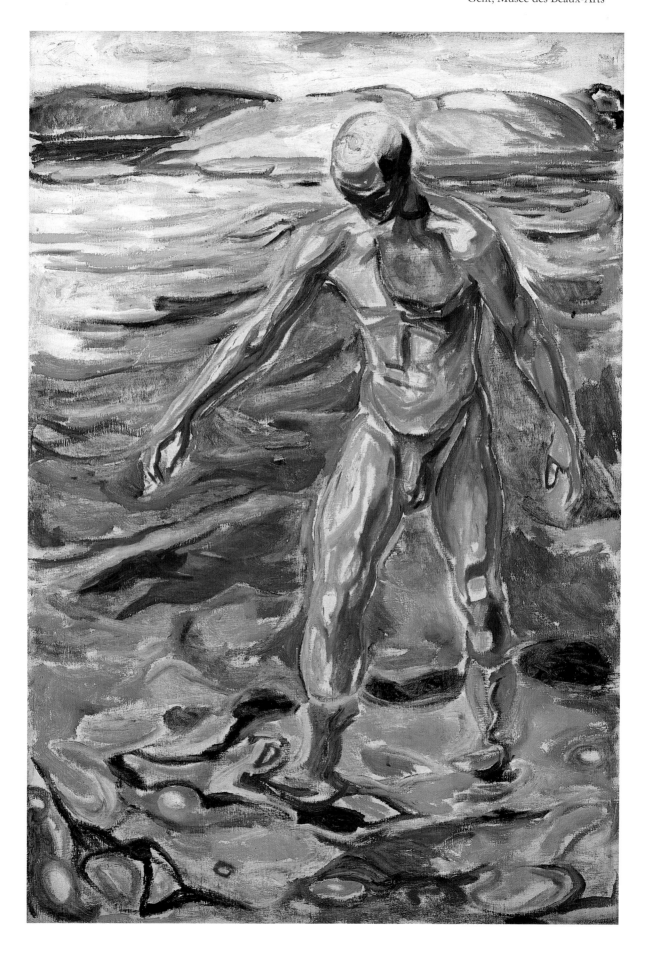

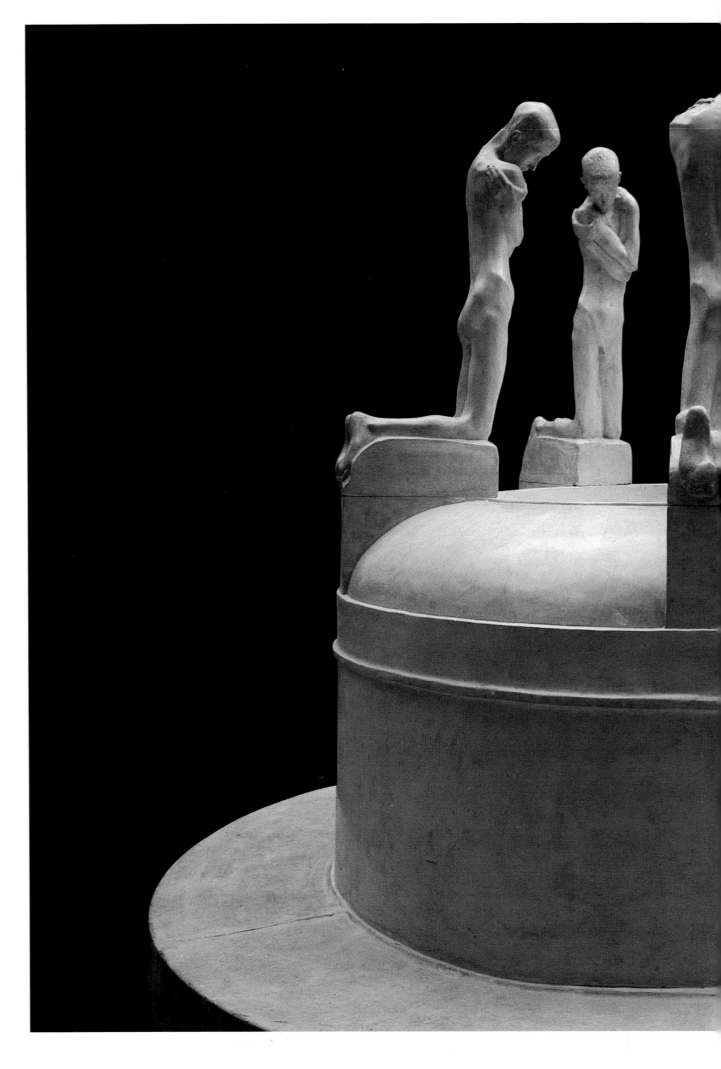

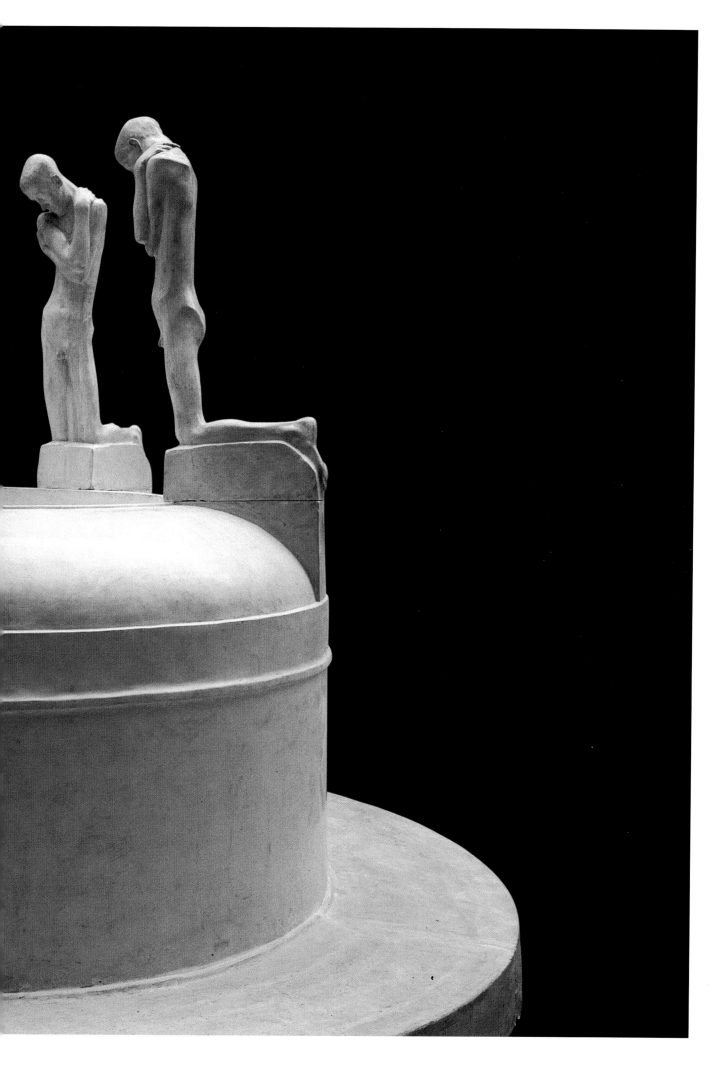

The Ascent into the Cosmos,
1892
oil on canvas, 159 × 97 cm
Basel, Kunstmuseum

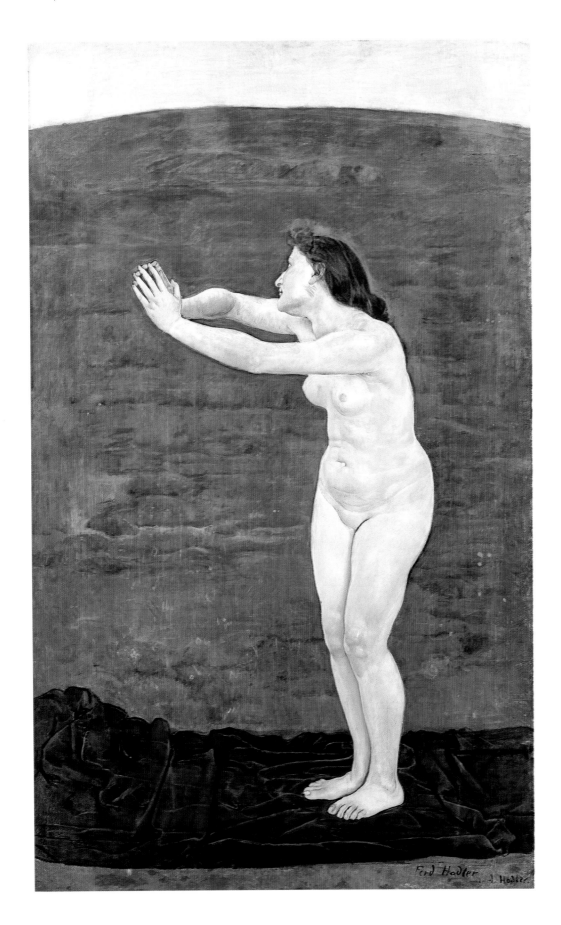

Weary of Life, 1893
oil on canvas, 110.5 × 221 cm
Winterthur, Stiftung für Kunst
Kultur und Geschichte

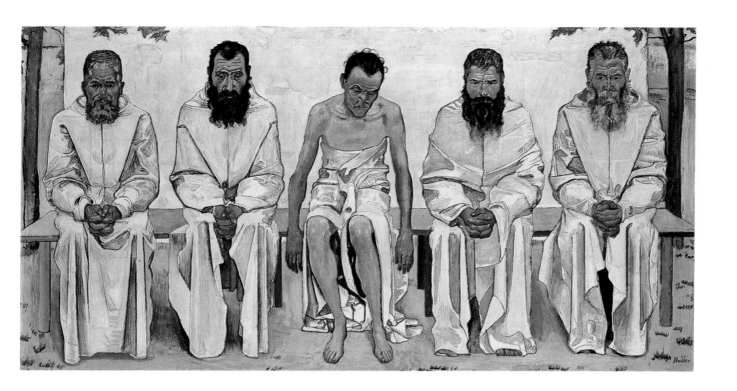

Worship II, 1894
oil on canvas, 81.5 × 101 cm
Lugano, Museo Cantonale
d'Arte (on deposit from the
Kunsthaus, Zurich. Gottfried
Keller Collection)

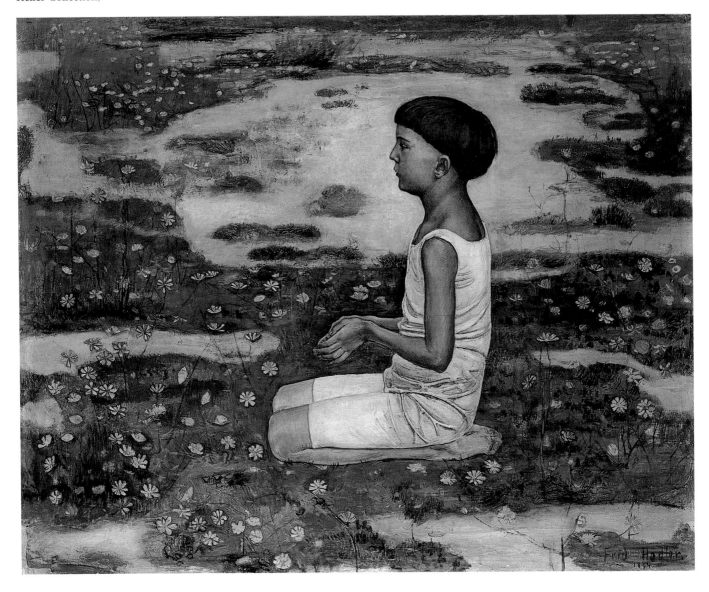

111. Ferdinand Hodler

Portrait of Hélène Weigle, 1896
oil on canvas, 80 × 61 cm
Zurich, Kunsthaus. Gottfried
Keller Collection

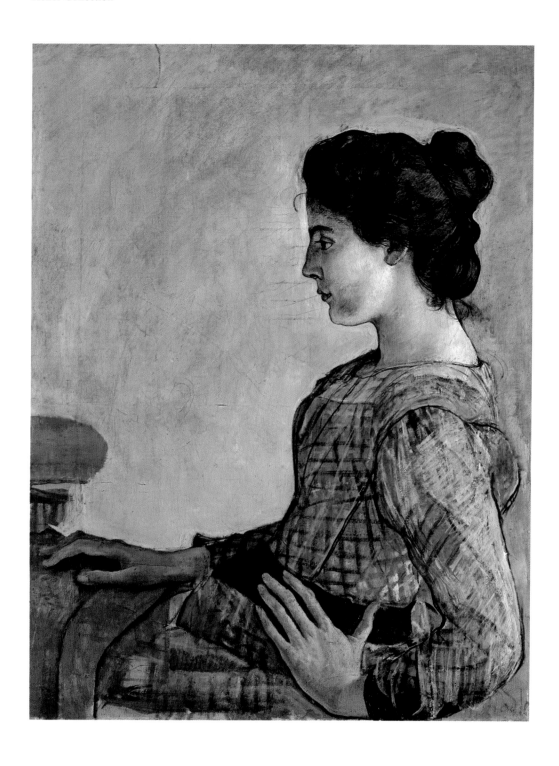

following pages
112. Ferdinand Hodler

Sentiment, 1901–02
oil on canvas, 120 × 172 cm
Thomas Schmidheiny Collection

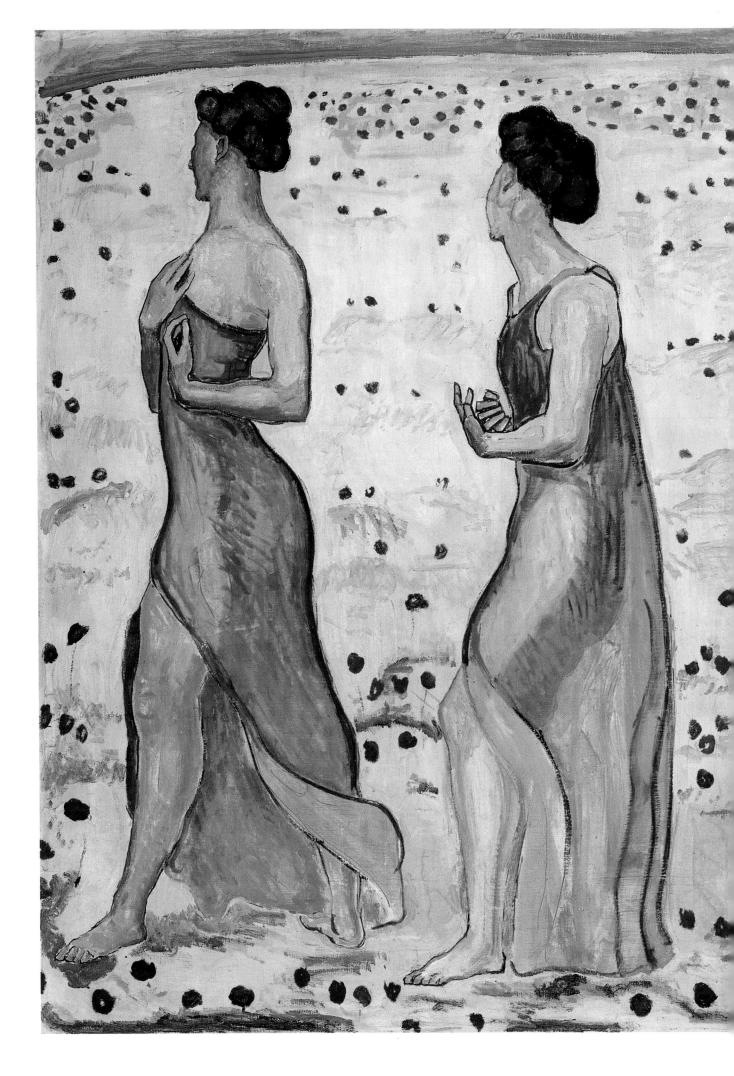

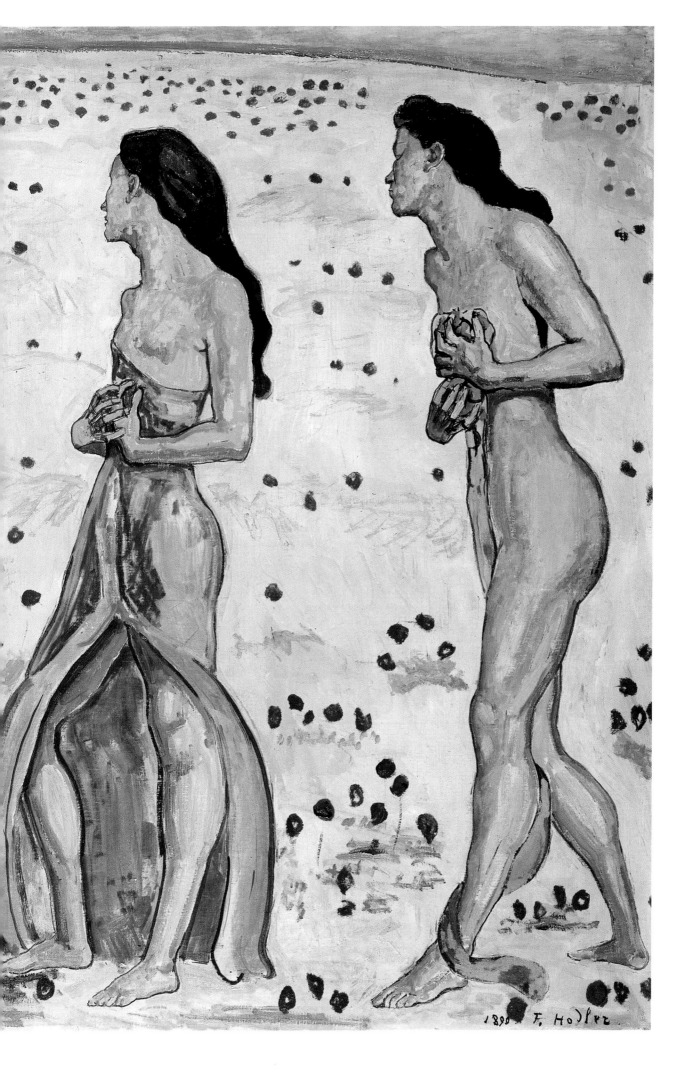

Woman Walking, 1910
oil on canvas, 112.5 × 50.5 cm
Thomas Schmidheiny Collection

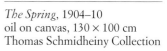

The Spring, 1904–10
oil on canvas, 130 × 100 cm
Thomas Schmidheiny Collection

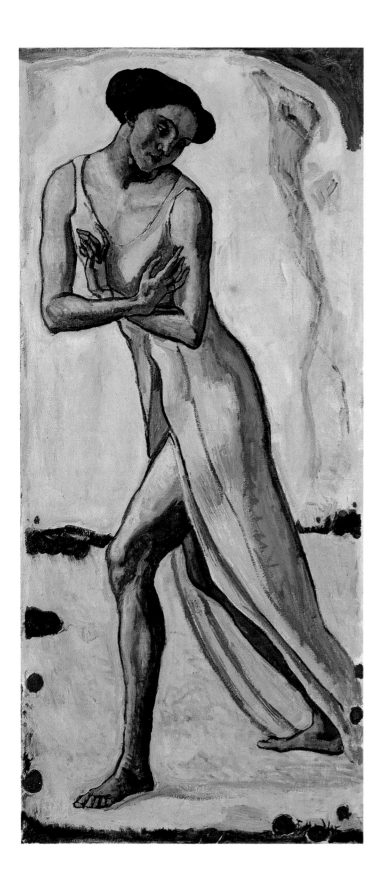

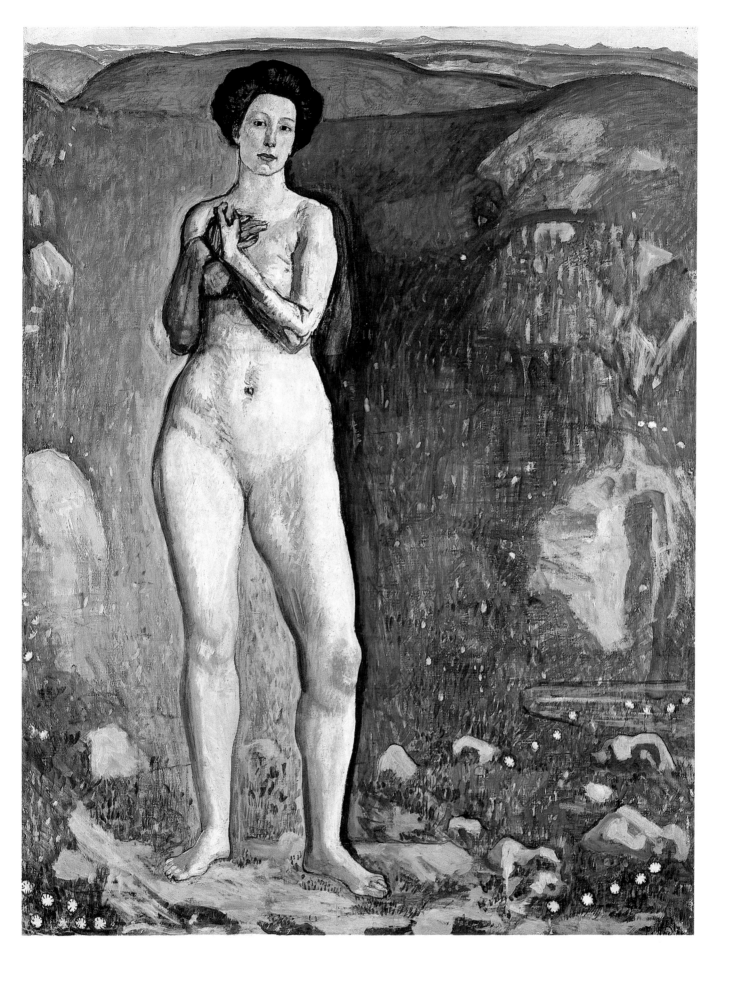

411

*Rider Picking an Orange with a
Female Nude,* 1869–70
oil on canvas, 109 × 77 cm
Halle, Staatliche Galerie
Moritzburg

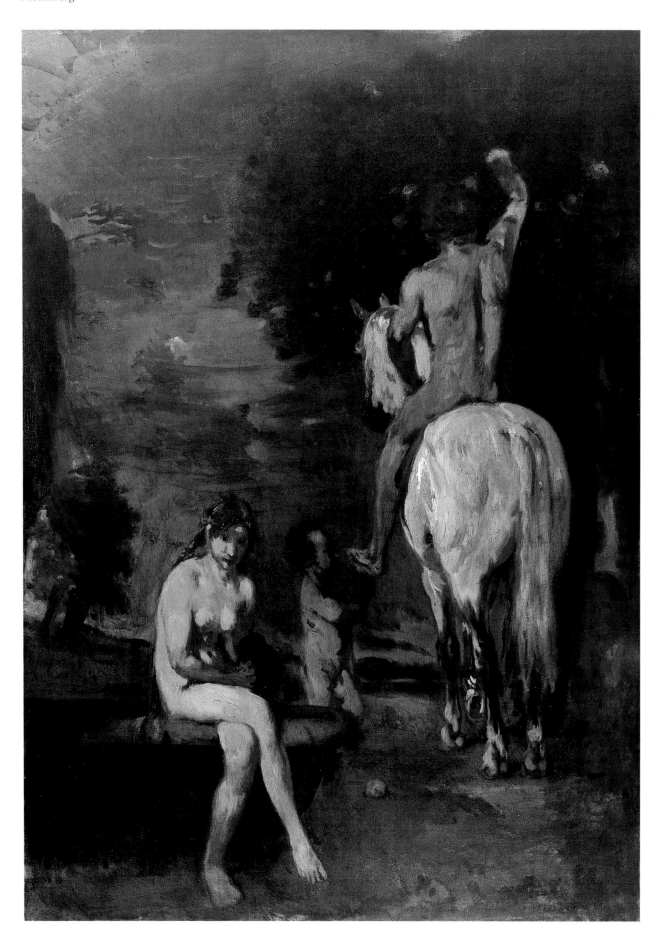

Three Men in a Landscape, 1875
oil on canvas, 80 × 100 cm
Düsseldorf, Museum Kunst
Palast

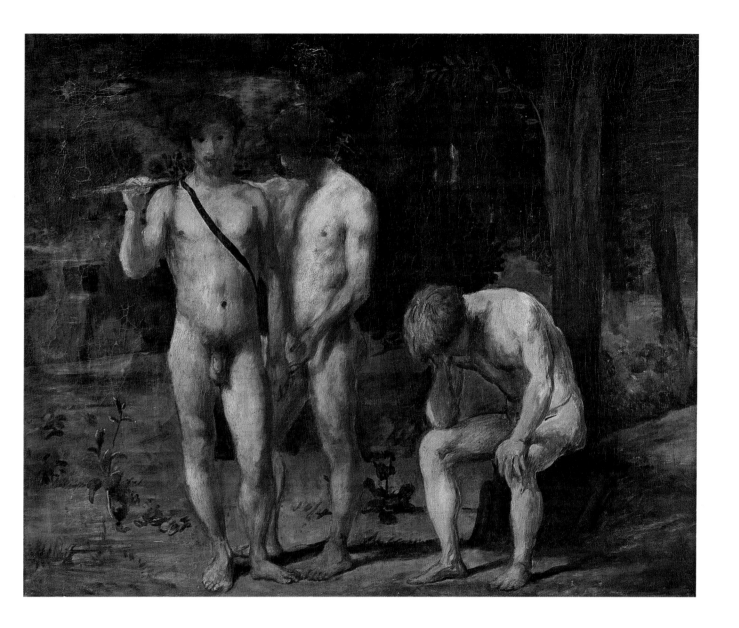

L'Heure Bleue, 1890
oil on canvas, 191.5 × 176 cm
Leipzig, Museum der bildenden
Künste

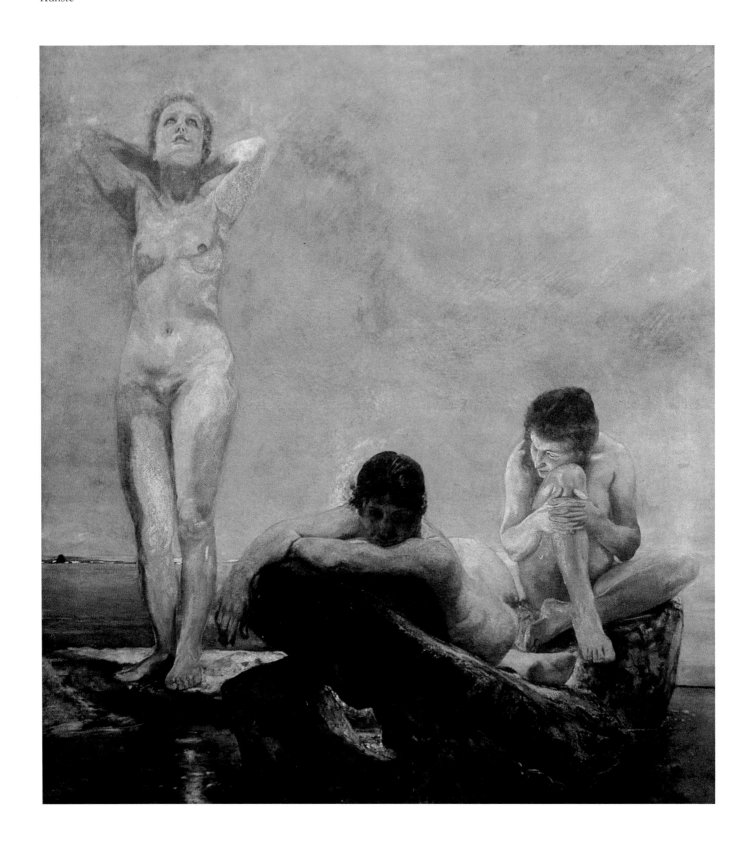

118. Georg Kolbe

The Golden Island, 1898
oil on canvas, 106 × 121 cm
Berlin, Staatliche Museen,
Preußischer Kulturbesitz
Nationalgalerie

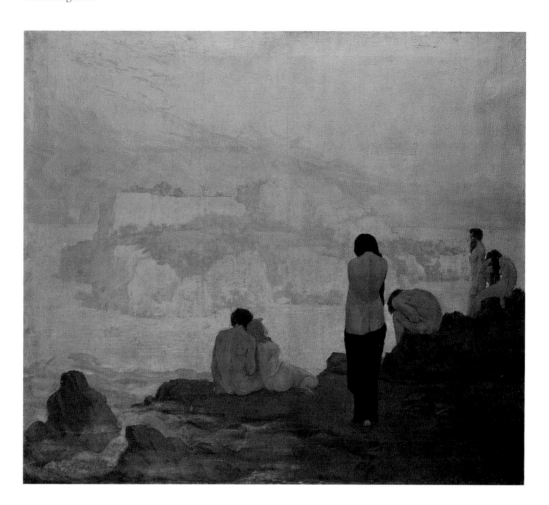

Idolino, 1892
oil on canvas, 190 × 148 cm
Bielefeld, Kunsthalle

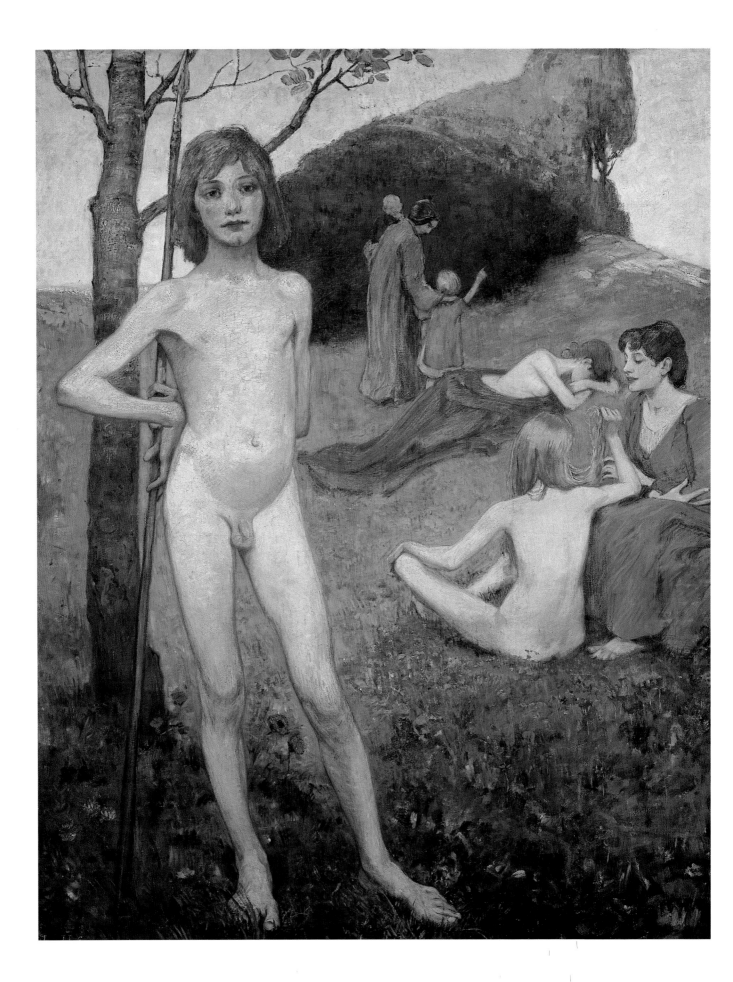

120. Ludwig von Hofmann

Two Youths, 1894
oil on canvas, 60 × 45 cm
Kiel, Kunsthalle

121. Ludwig von Hofmann

Adam and Eve, c. 1895
oil on canvas, 35 × 26.5 cm
Neuss, Clemens-Sels-Museum

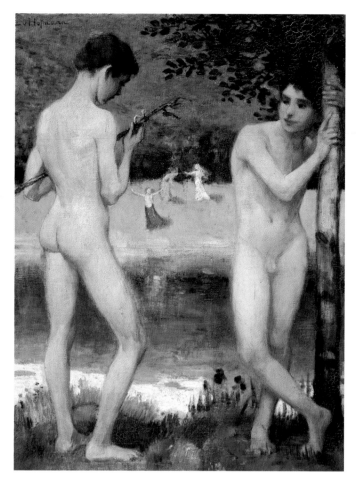

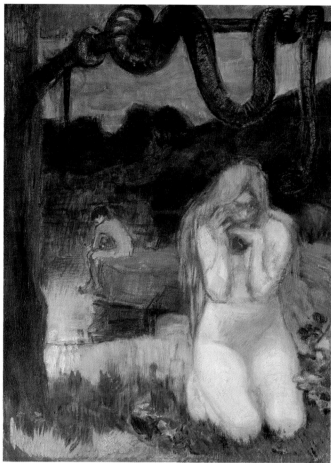

Sunset by the Sea, 1900
oil on canvas, 71 × 73.8 cm
Zurich, Katharina Büttiker Collection,
Galerie Wühre 9 Art deco

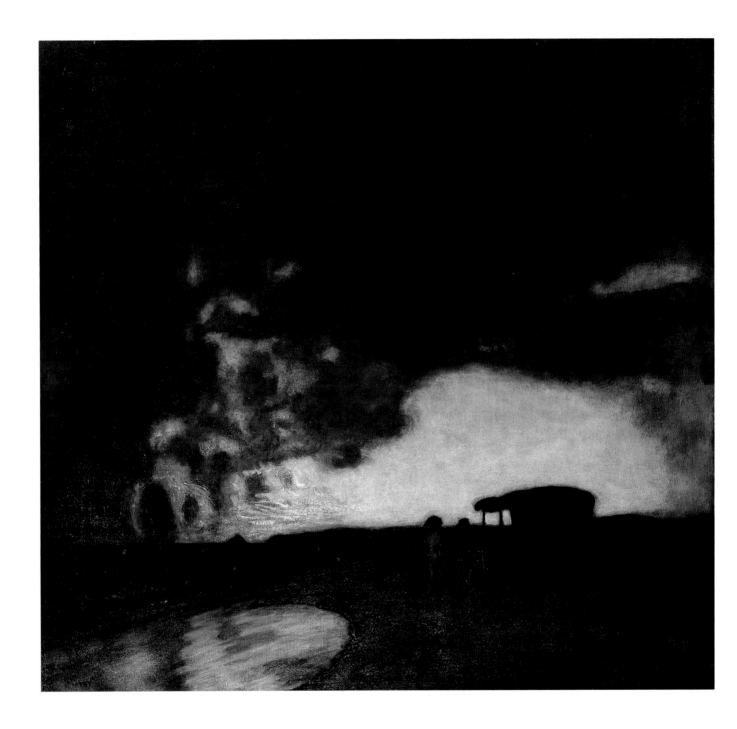

123. Heinrich Vogeler

Melancholy, 1912
oil on canvas, 98,5 × 78,5
Hannover, Niedersächsische
Sparkassestiftung

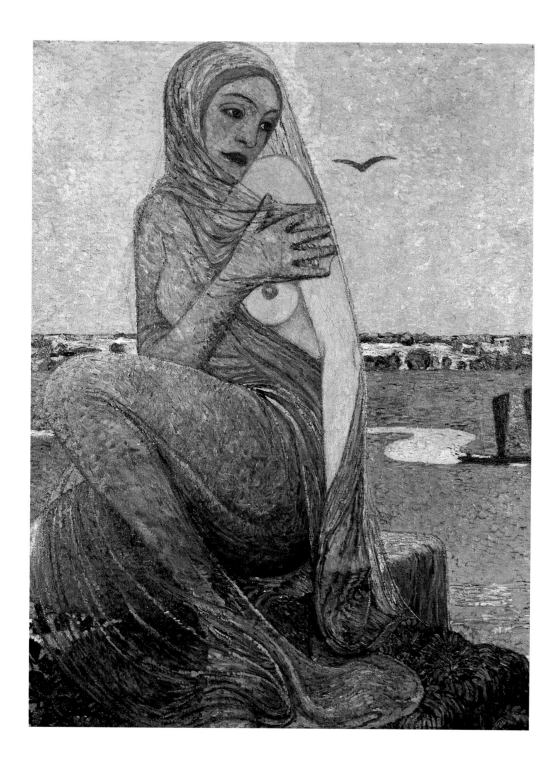

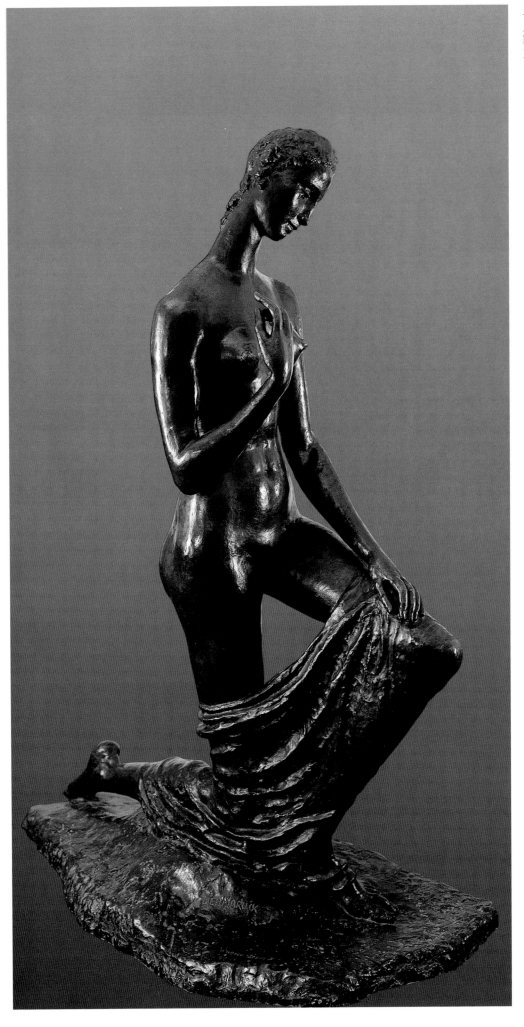

Kneeling Woman, 1911
bronze, 175 × 68.5 × 138.5 cm
Mainz, Landesmuseum

Three Women, 1914
bronze relief, 97.4 × 66.5 × 6.2 cm.
Duisburg, artist's bequest to the
Wilhelm Lehmbruck Museum
Foundation

Standing Youth, 1913
bronze, 221 × 76 × 62 cm
Zurich, Kunsthaus

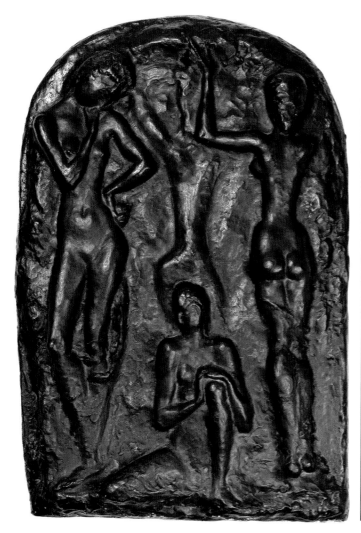

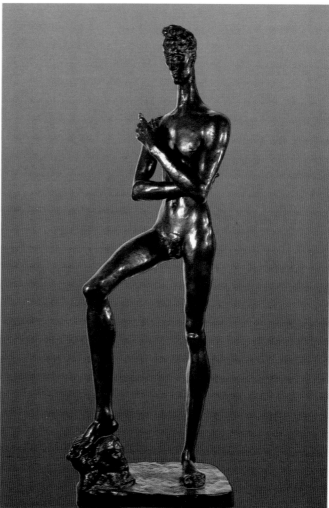

Artemis, 1893–94
oil on canvas, 193 x 251.5 cm
Copenhagen, Statens Museum
for Kunst

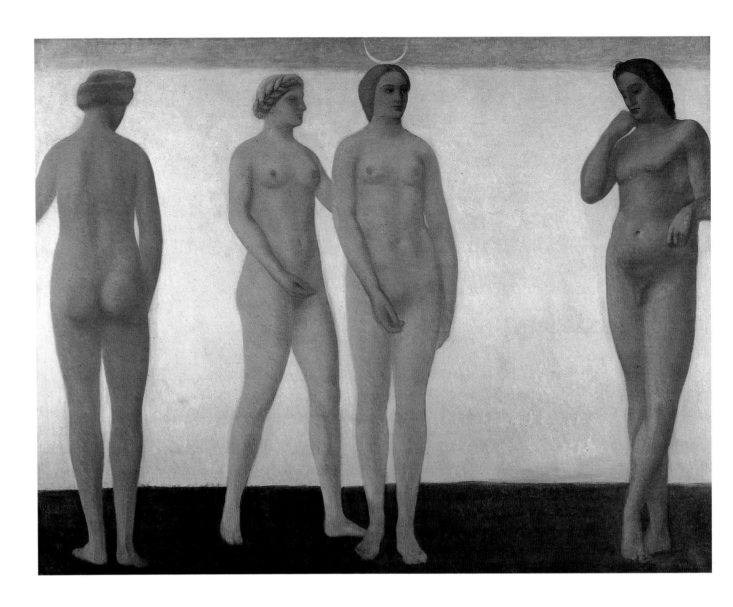

128. Vilhelm Hammershøi

Interior, 1899
oil on canvas, 64.5 × 58.1 cm
London, Tate Gallery, The
National Art Collection Fund,
in memory of Leonard Borwick

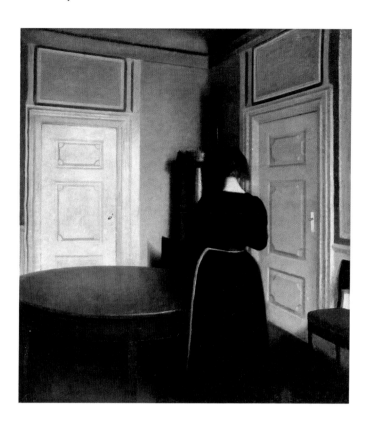

129. Ejnar Nielsen

Death and the Cripple, 1898–99
oil on canvas, 129 × 169 cm
Stockholm, Thielska Galleriet

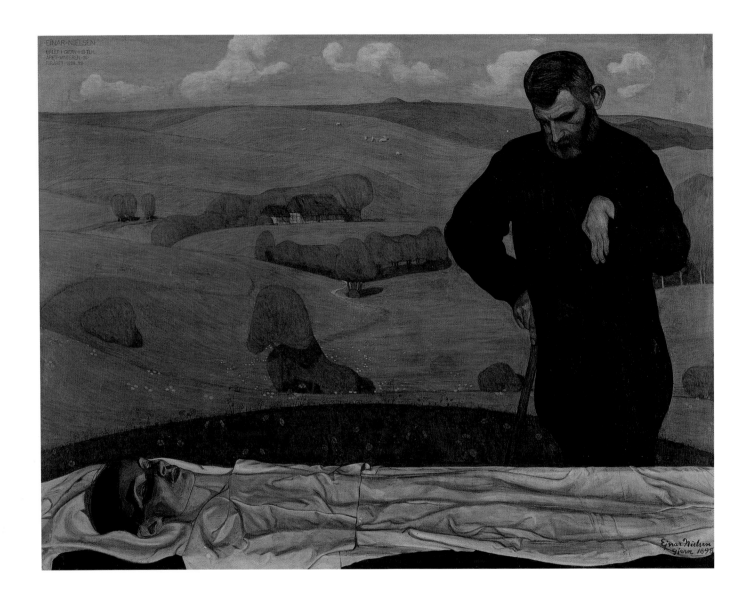

*The Sculptor Andreas F.V.
Hansen and His Wife*, 1900
oil on canvas, 162 × 116 cm
Stockholm, Nationalmuseum

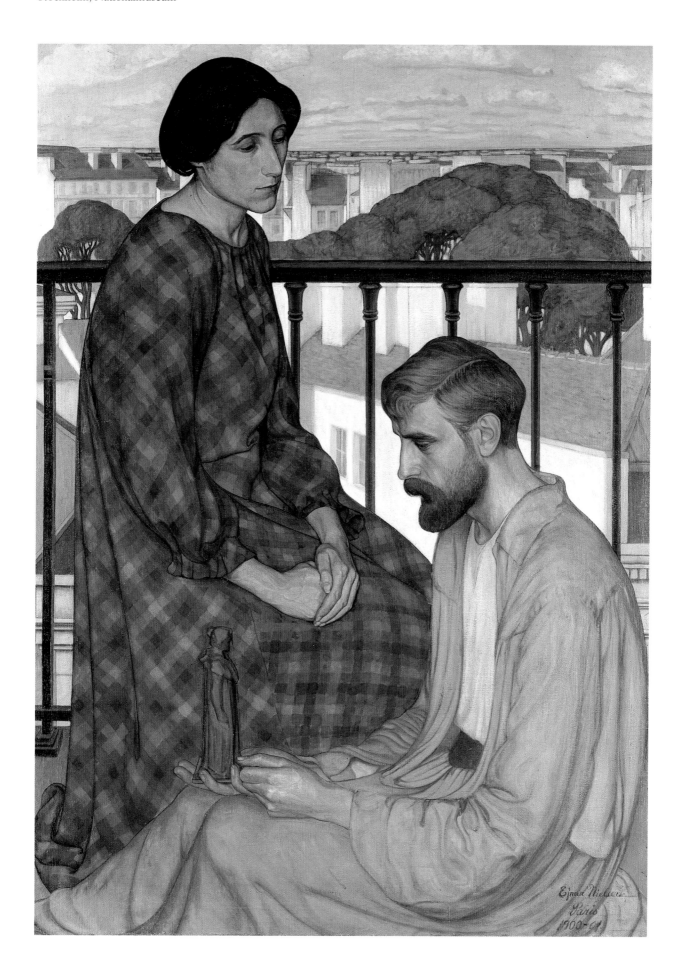

Poplar Trees, 1893
oil on canvas, 54,5 × 28 cm
Helsinki, Ateneum,
Finnish National Gallery

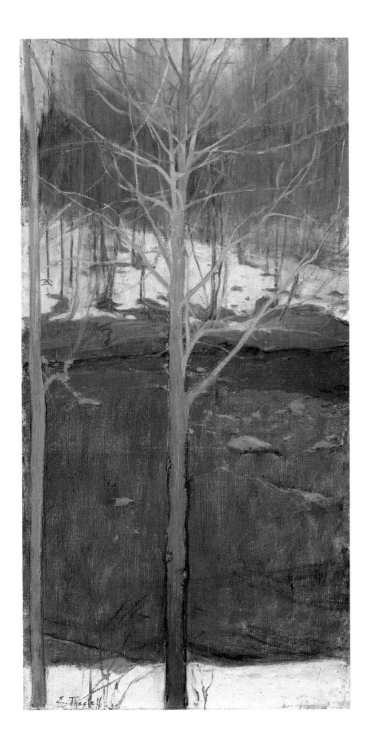

Everywhere a Voice is Heard, 1895
oil on canvas, 85.5 × 129.5 cm
Helsinki, Ateneum,
Finnish National Gallery

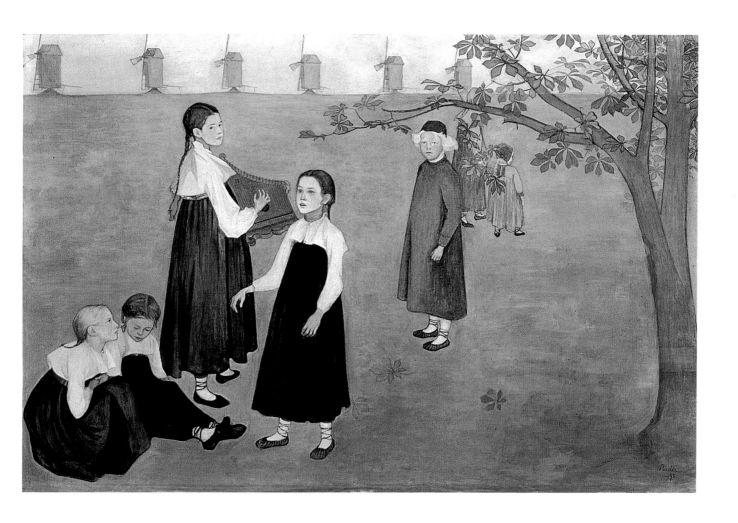

Waking up, 1894
oil on canvas, 113 × 85.5 cm
Helsinki, Ateneum,
Finnish National Gallery.
Antell Collection

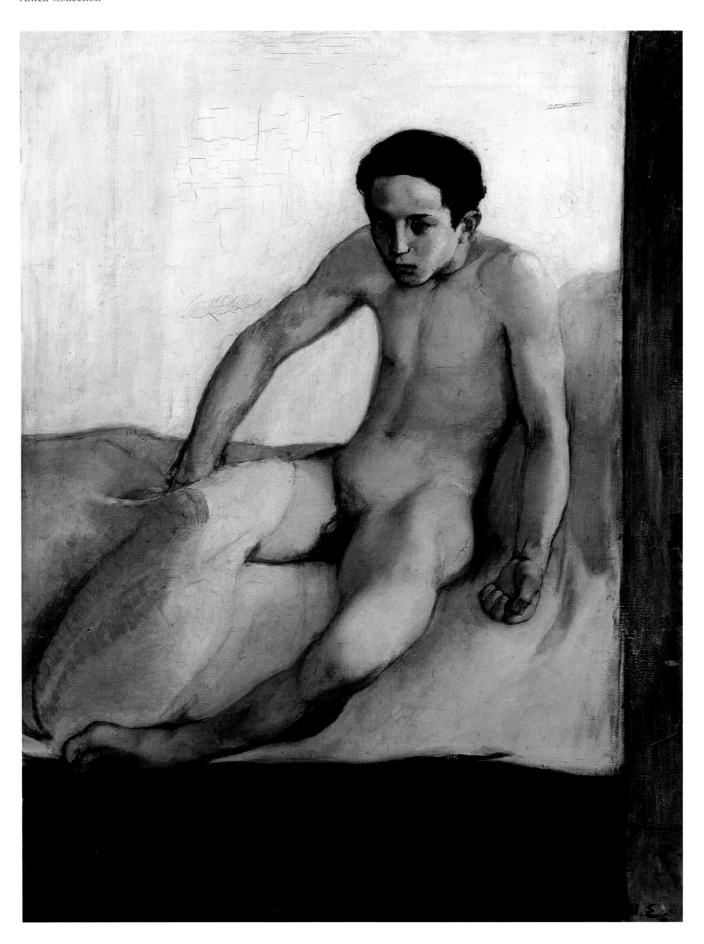

134. Magnus Enckell

Study for "The Golden Age,"
1904
oil on paper, 71.5 × 98.5 cm
Göteborg, Konstmuseum

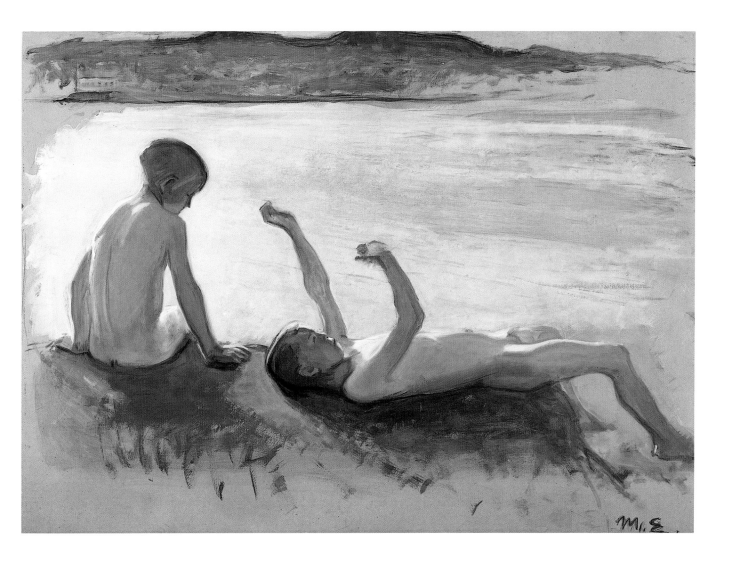

135. Akseli Gallen-Kallela

Autumn, 1902
distemper, 77 × 143 cm
Helsinki, Sigrid Jusélius
Foundation

136. Akseli Gallen-Kallela

*Spring (Study for the Jusélius
Mausoleum frescoes)*, 1903
distemper on canvas,
77 × 145 cm
Helsinki, Ateneum,
Finnish National Gallery

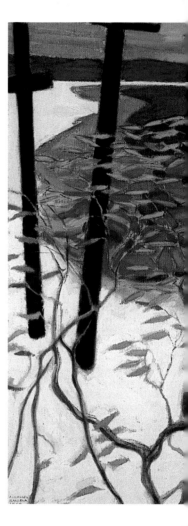

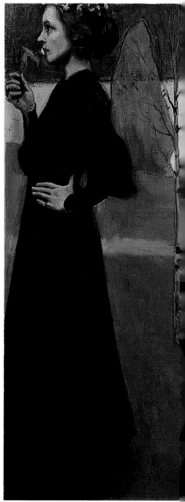

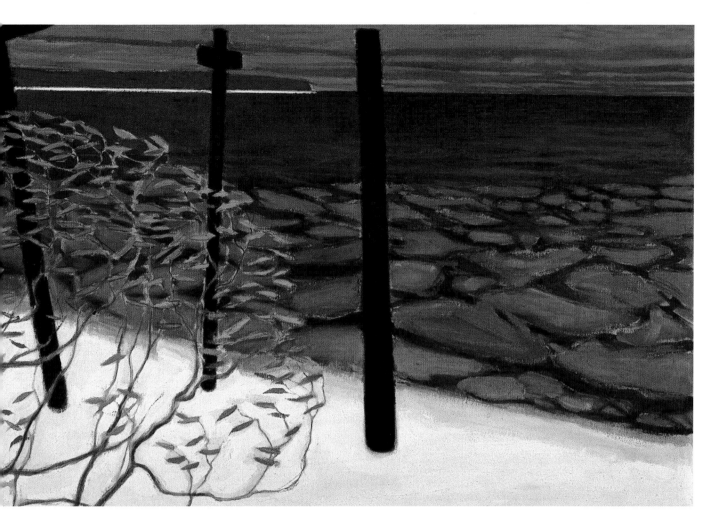

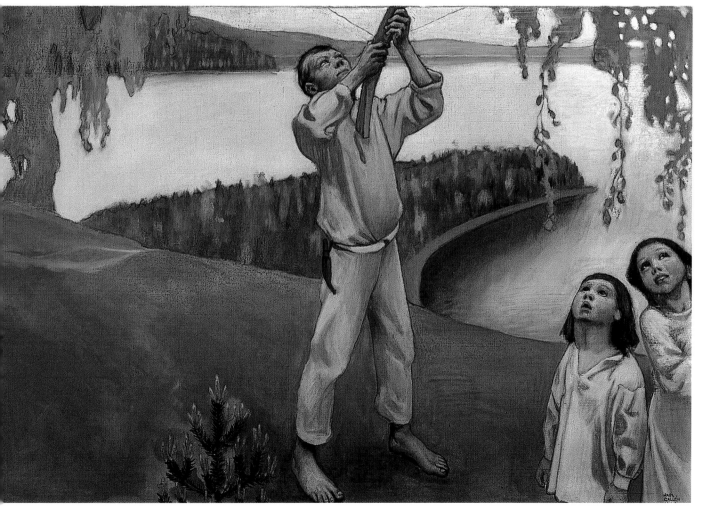

The Wounded Angel, 1903
oil on canvas, 127 × 154 cm
Helsinki, Ateneum,
Finnish National Gallery

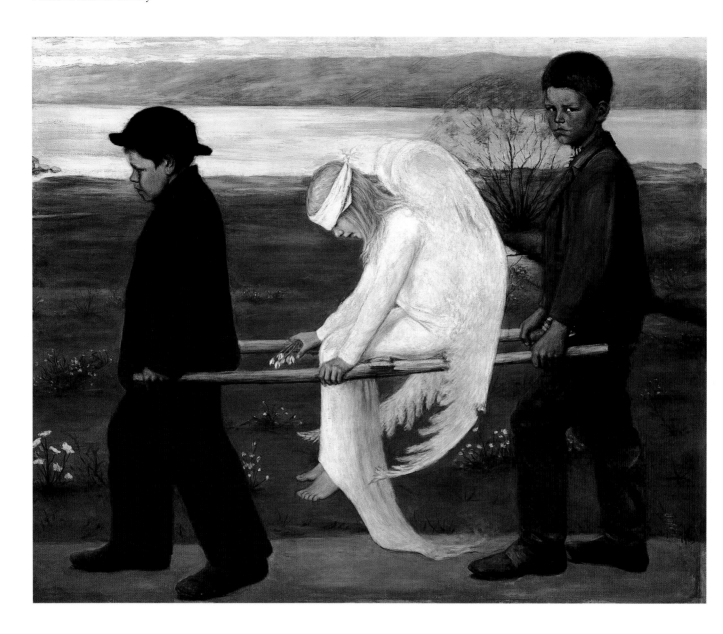

138. Eilif Peterssen

Summer Night, 1886
oil on canvas, 133 × 151 cm
Oslo, Nasjonalgalleriet

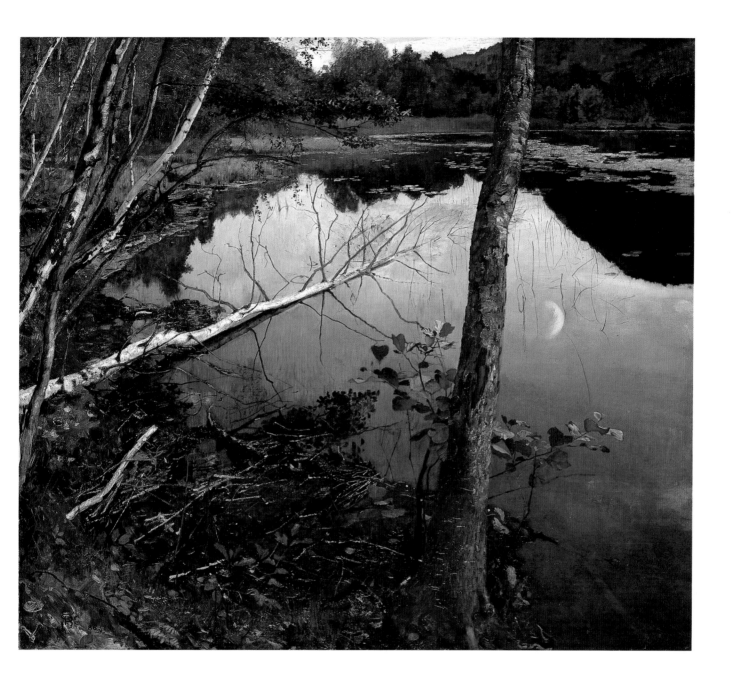

139. Karl Jensen-Hjell

At the Window, Portrait of the Painter Kalle Lochen, 1887
oil on canvas, 73.5 × 99.5 cm
Oslo, Nasjonalgalleriet

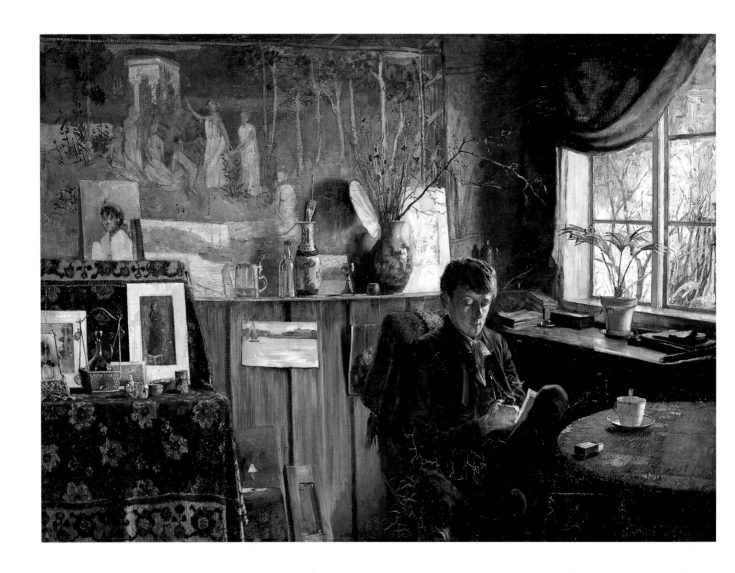

140. Laurits Andersen Ring

June. Girl Blowing a Dandelion, 1899
oil on canvas, 88 × 124 cm
Oslo, Nasjonalgalleriet

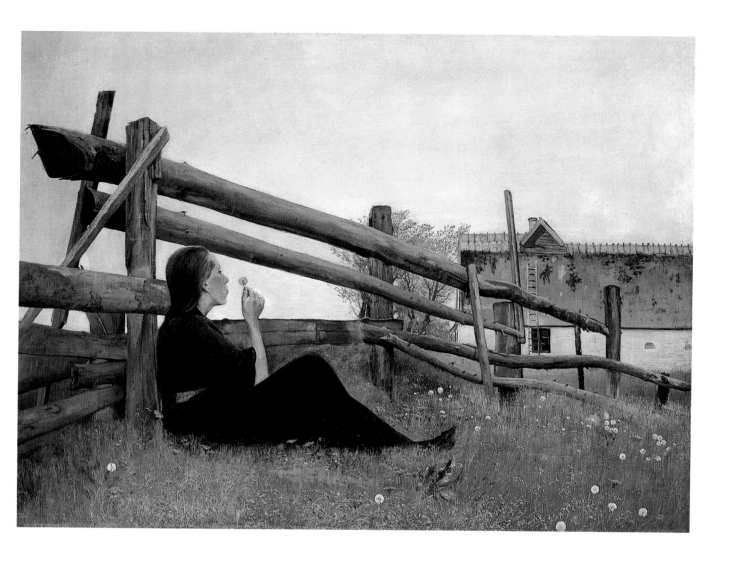

141. Fernand Khnopff

*At Fosset. The Waiting
Gamekeeper*, 1883
oil on canvas, 151 × 176.5 cm
Frankfurt, Städelsches
Kunstinstitut

142. William Degouve
De Nuncques

The Canal, 1894
oil on canvas, 42.4 × 122.5 cm
Otterlo, Rijksmuseum Kröller-
Müller

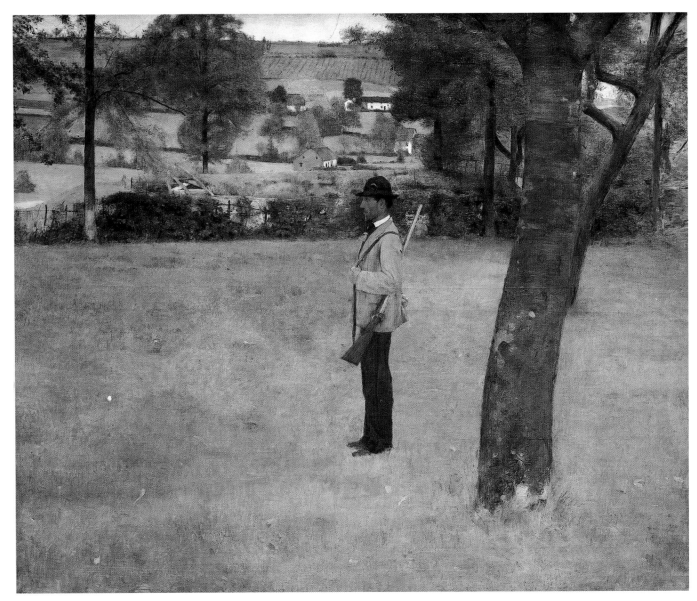

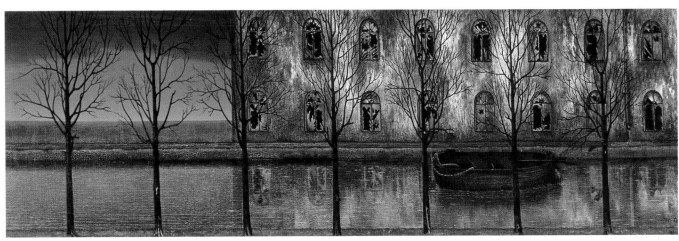

143. Giuseppe Pellizza
da Volpedo

Ring-around-a-rosy. Country
Idyll in the Parish of Volpedo,
c. 1906
oil on canvas, diameter 100 cm
Milan, Civica Galleria d'Arte
Moderna

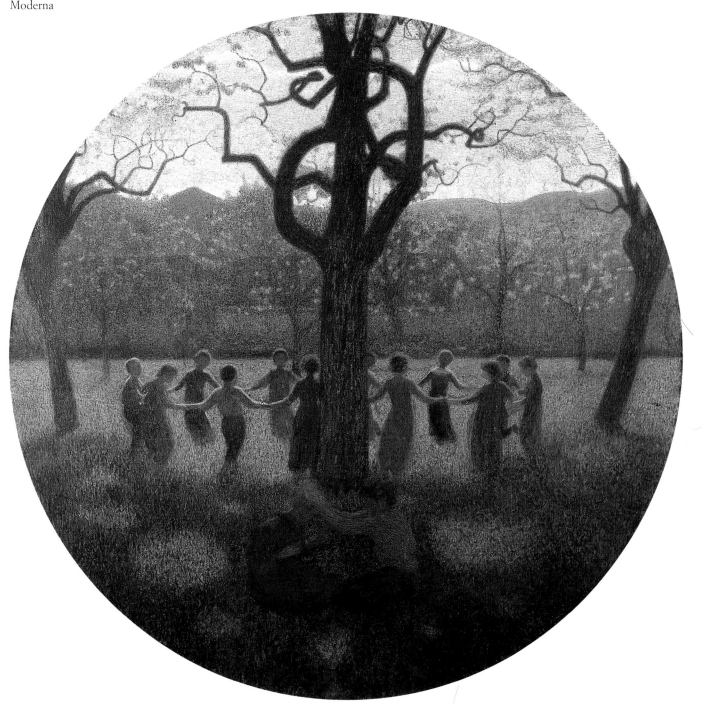

144. Giuseppe Pellizza
da Volpedo

144bis. Giuseppe Pellizza
da Volpedo

Flowering Meadow, 1909
oil on canvas, 88 × 88 cm
Rome, Galleria Nazionale
d'Arte Moderna

April in Volpedo fields, 1904
oil on canvas, 53 × 64,5 cm
Milan, private collection

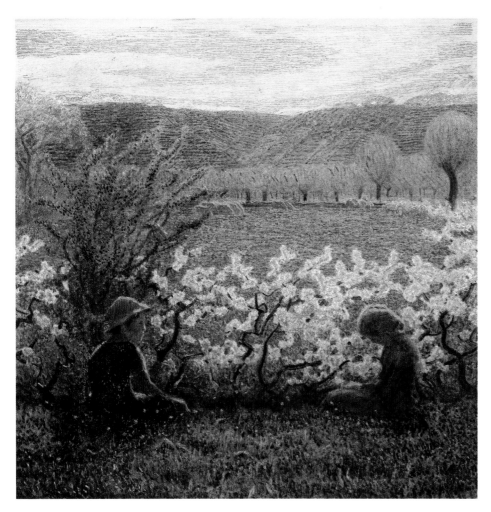

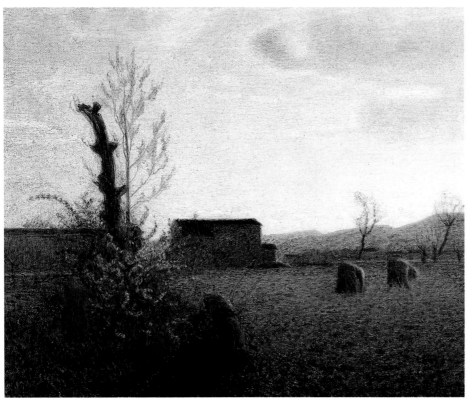

Idyll, 1882
oil on canvas, 56.5 × 84.5 cm
Aberdeen, Art Gallery
and Museums

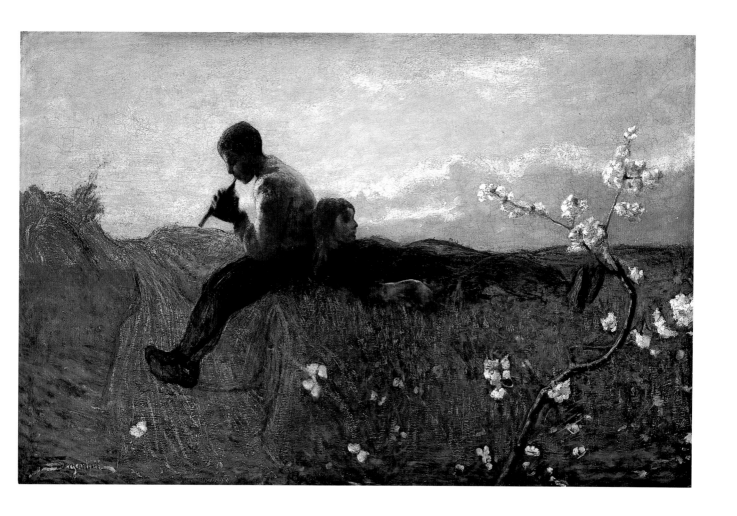

Vanity or The Fountain of Evil,
1897
oil on canvas, 77 × 124 cm
Zurich, Kunsthaus

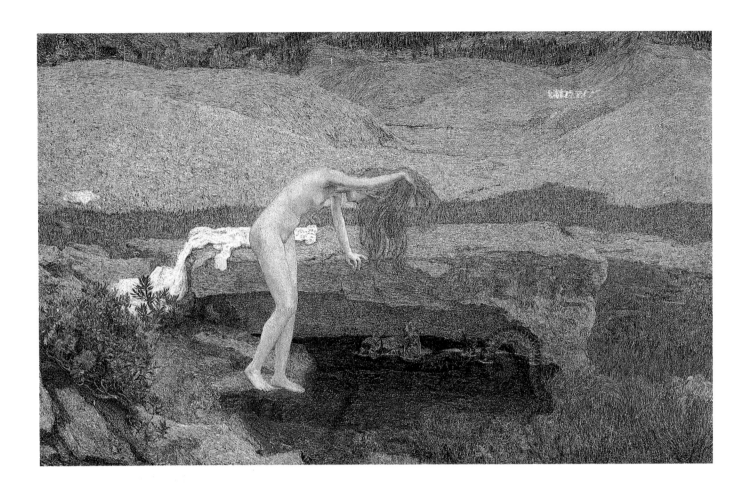

Love at the Fountain of Life,
1896
oil on canvas, 70 × 98 cm
Milan, Civica Galleria d'Arte
Moderna

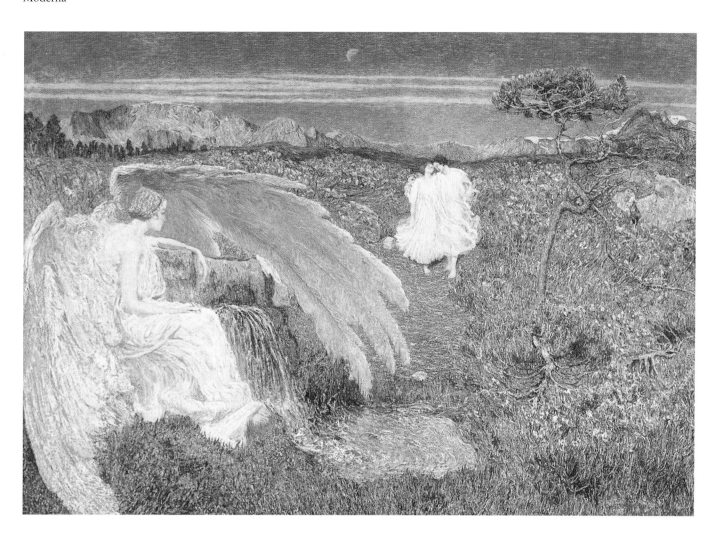

following pages
148. Giovanni Giacometti

Children in the Wood, 1909
oil on canvas, 132 × 200 cm
Neuchâtel, Musée d'Art
et d'Histoire

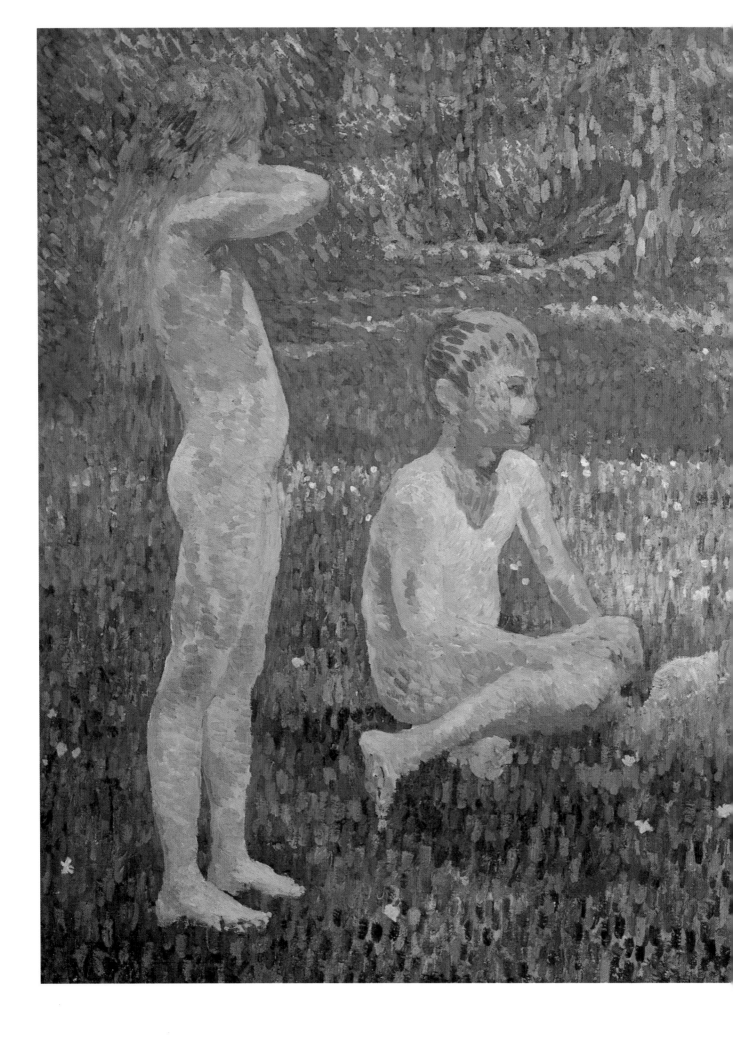

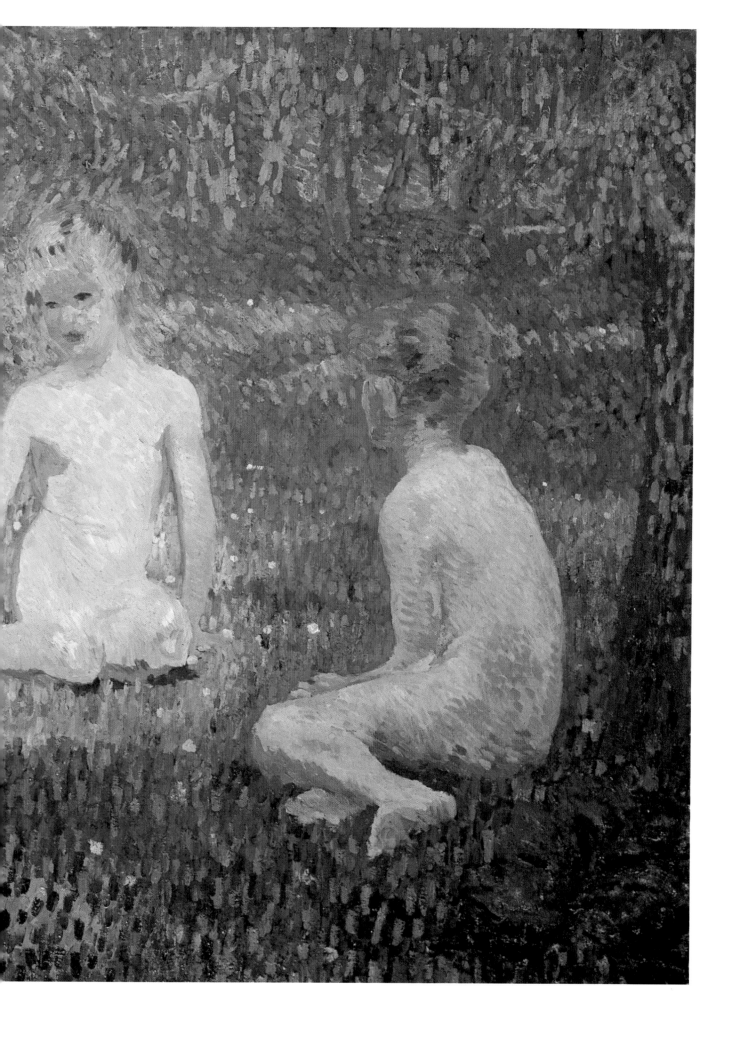

149. Auguste
Niederhäusern-Rodo

The Wave
bronze, 51.5 × 60 × 44 cm
Bulle, Musée Gruérien

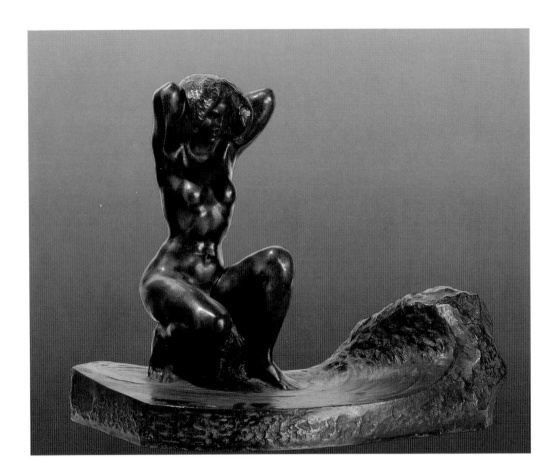

Profound Thoughts, 1900
oil on canvas, 73.5 × 61
Saint Petersburg,
Russian State Museum

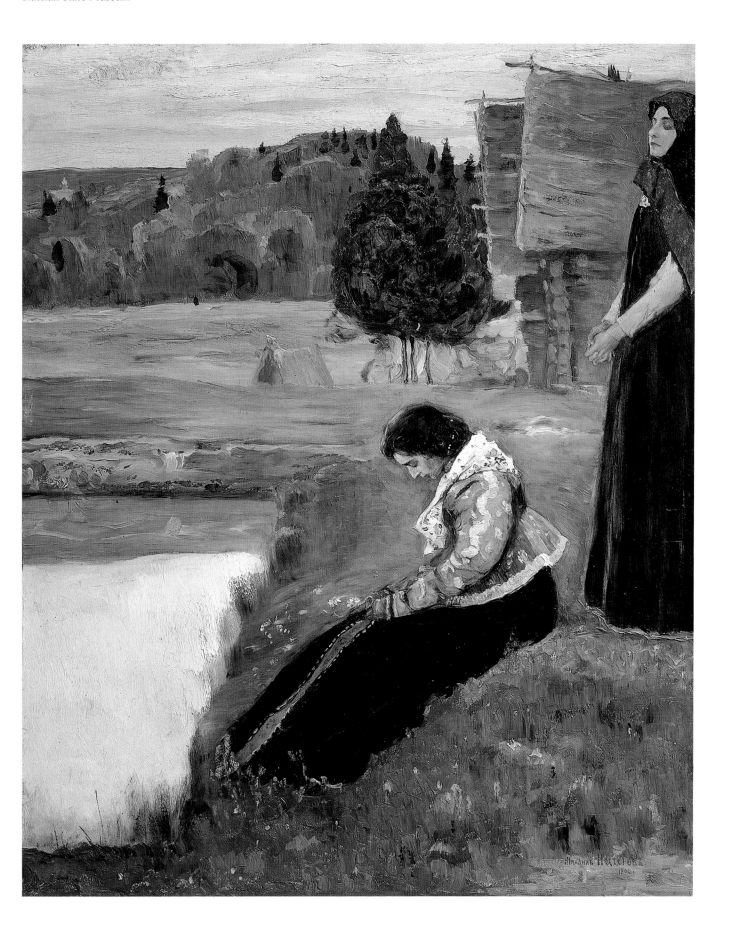

Spring, 1901
oil on canvas, 71 × 98 cm
Saint Petersburg,
Russian State Museum

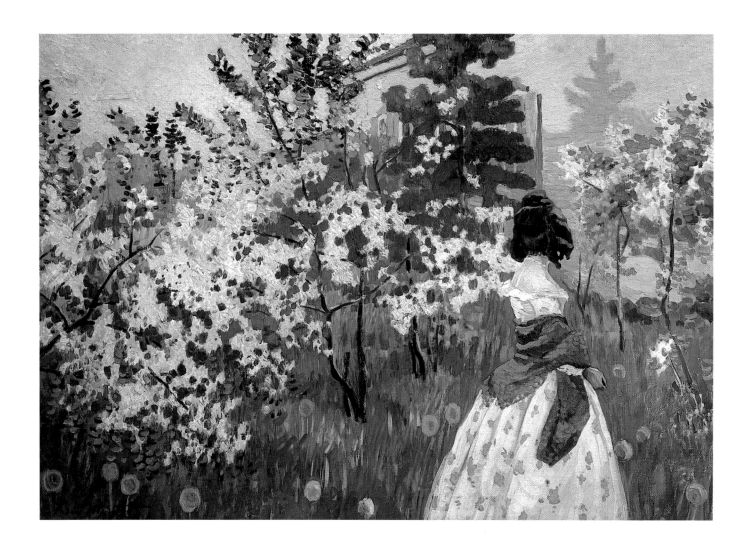

152. Kazimir Malevich

Prayer, 1907
distemper on cardboard,
71 × 107 cm
Saint Petersburg,
Russian State Museum

153. Kazimir Malevich

Sacred Tomb, 1907
distemper on cardboard,
69.3 × 71.5 cm
Saint Petersburg,
Russian State Museum

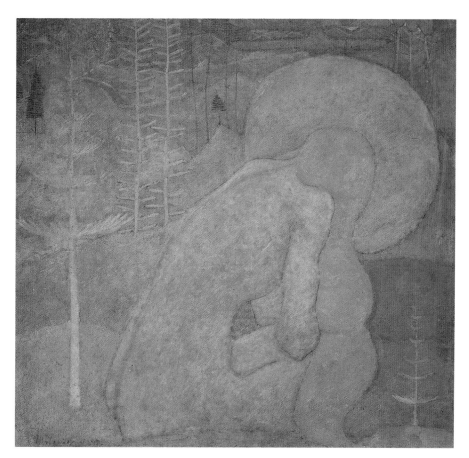

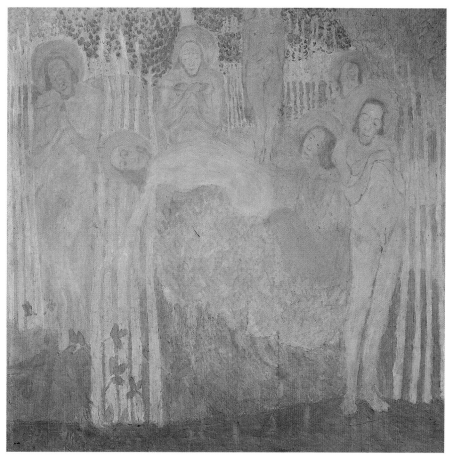

154. Kuz'ma Petrov-Vodkin

Riverbanks, 1908
oil on canvas, 128 × 159 cm
Saint Petersburg,
Russian State Museum

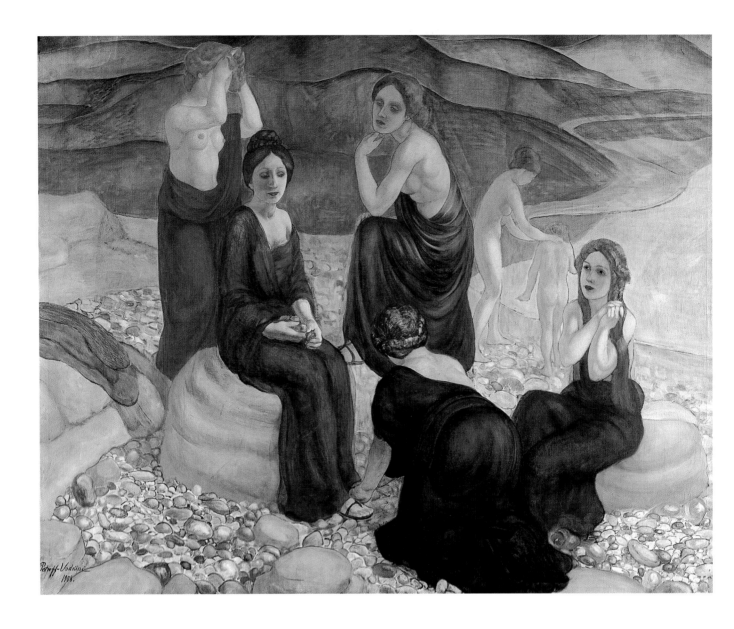

155. Nikolai Roerich

Procopius the Just, 1914
distemper on cardboard,
71 × 107 cm
Saint Petersburg,
Russian State Museum

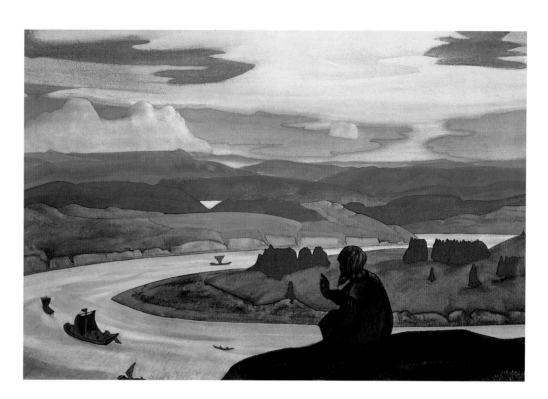

On the Beach, 1918
oil on canvas, 66 × 84.7 cm
The Cleveland Museum of Art

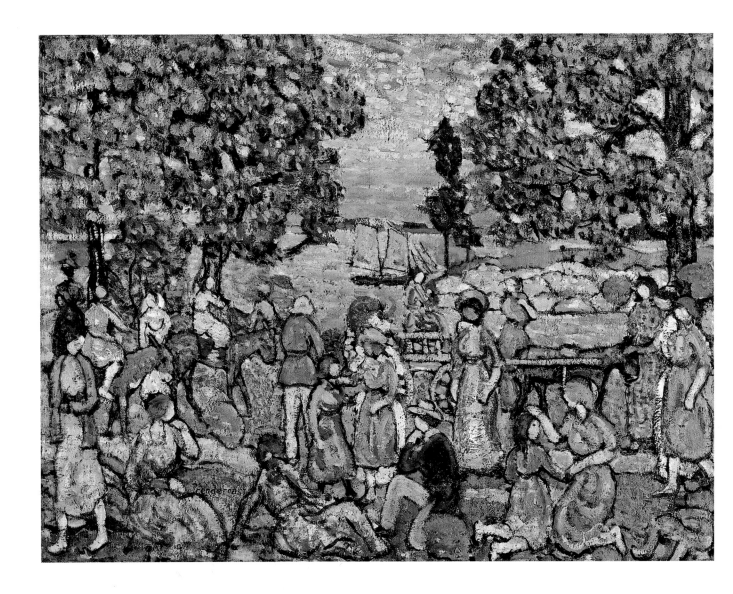

157. Frederick Cayley-Robinson

Youth, 1923
charcoal, watercolor, gouache,
pastel and oil on wood,
46.3 × 62.2 cm
Private collection

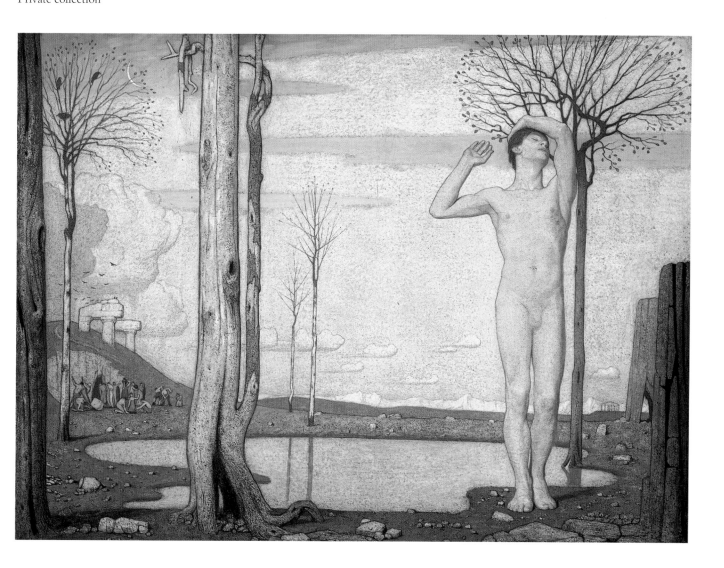

The Water Bearer, 1912
bronze, 175 × 40 × 52 cm
Paris, Musée d'Orsay

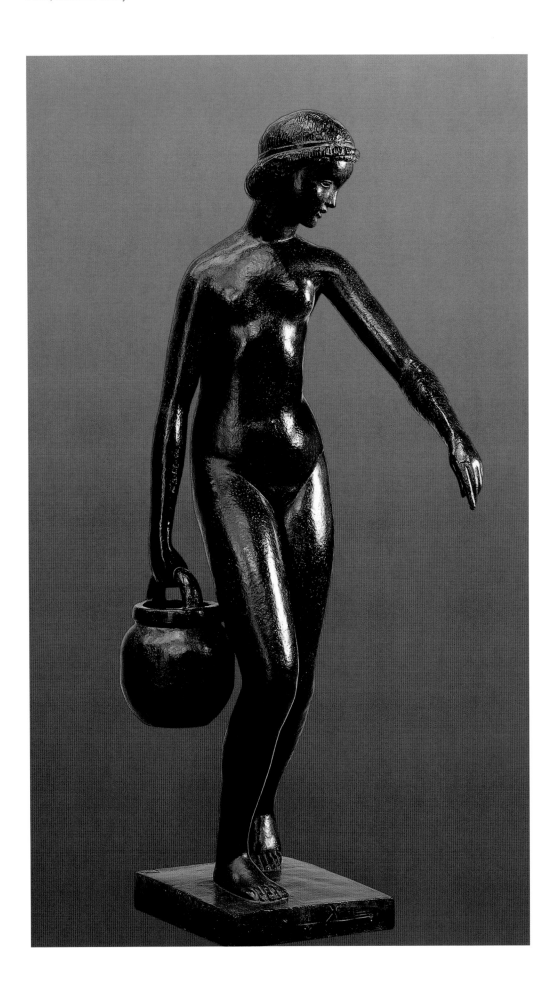

159. Joseph Bernard

Freize of the "Dance,"
left panel, 1913
bronze, 85 × 175 × 8 cm
Saint-Remy-lès-Chevreuse,
Fondation De Coubertin (on
deposit from the Musée d'Orsay)

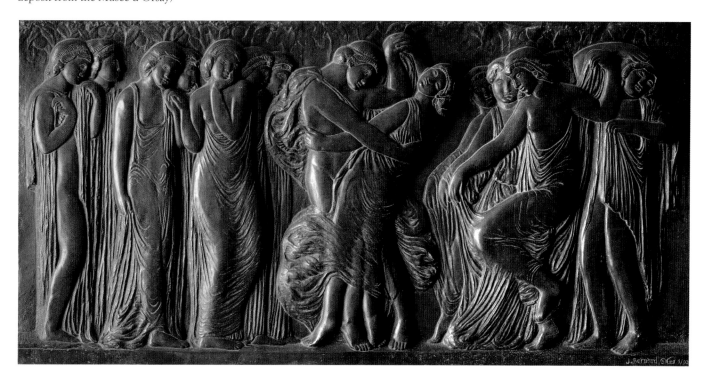

Woman and Child, 1913–25
bronze, 188 × 48 × 76 cm
Private collection

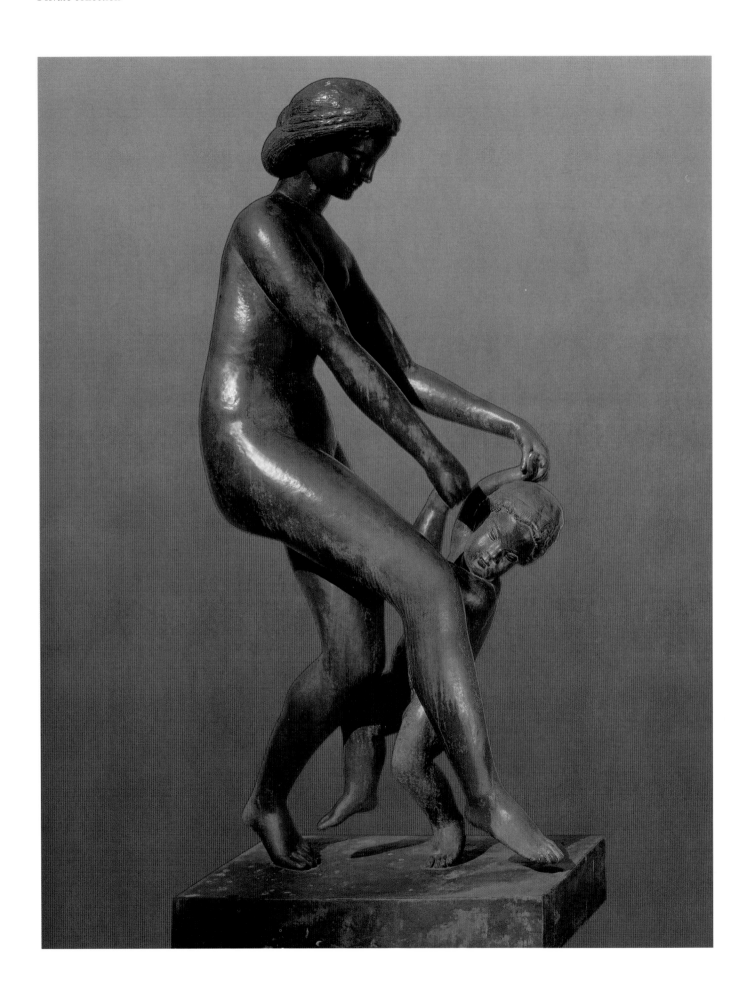

161. Joseph Bernard

Draped Figure of Young Girl,
1926
bronze, height 146 cm
Lyon, Musée des Beaux-Arts

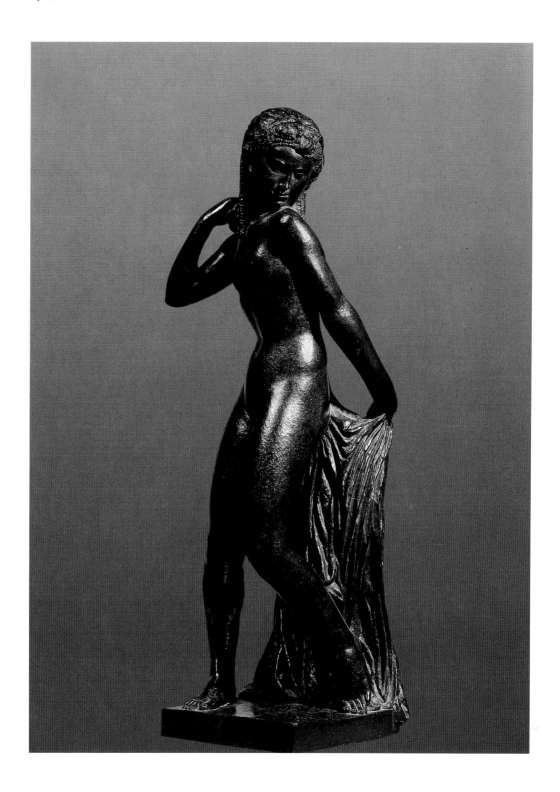

The Offering, 1905
bronze, height 69 cm
Paris, Musée Bourdelle, Rhodia
Dufet-Bourdelle Collection

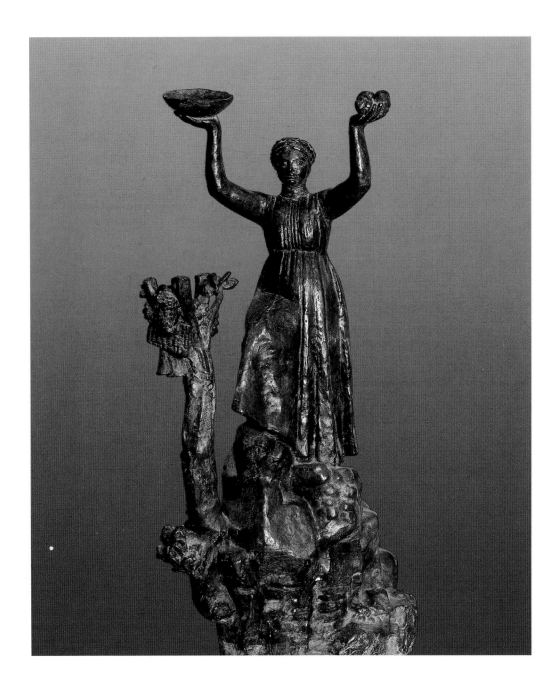

Sappho, 1887–25
bronze, 204 × 90 × 143 cm
Paris, Musée Bourdelle, Rhodia
Dufet-Bourdelle Collection

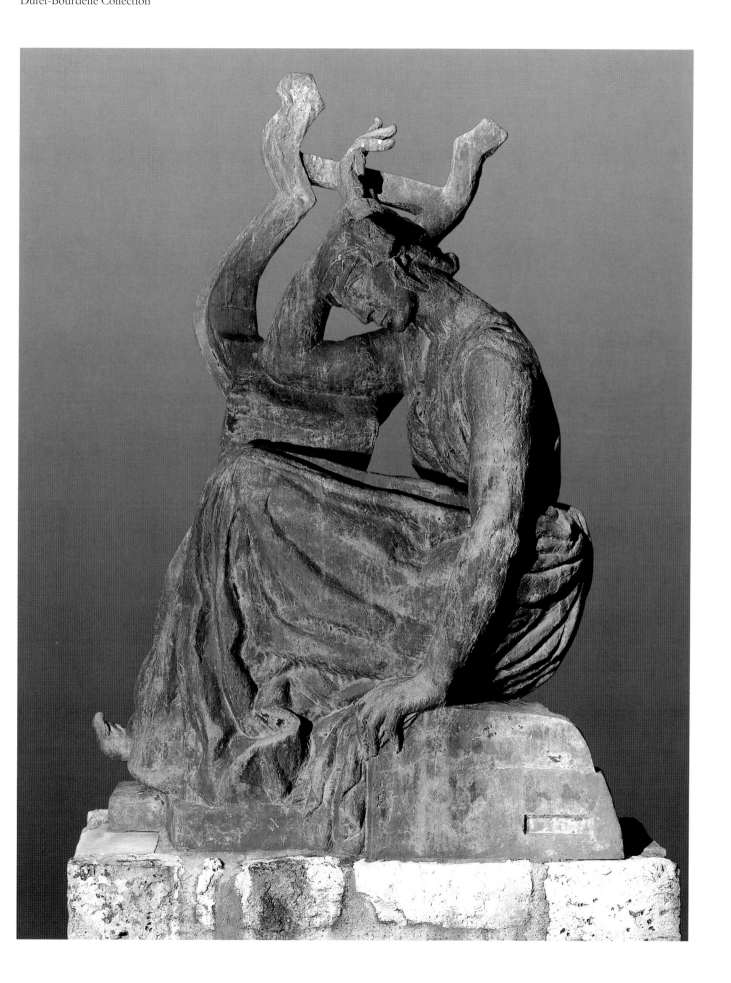

Crouching Bather, 1907
bronze, 102 × 120 × 107 cm
Paris, Musée Bourdelle, Rhodia
Dufet-Bourdelle Collection

Penelope, 1907–26
bronze, 60 × 22 × 175 cm
Paris, Musée d'Orsay

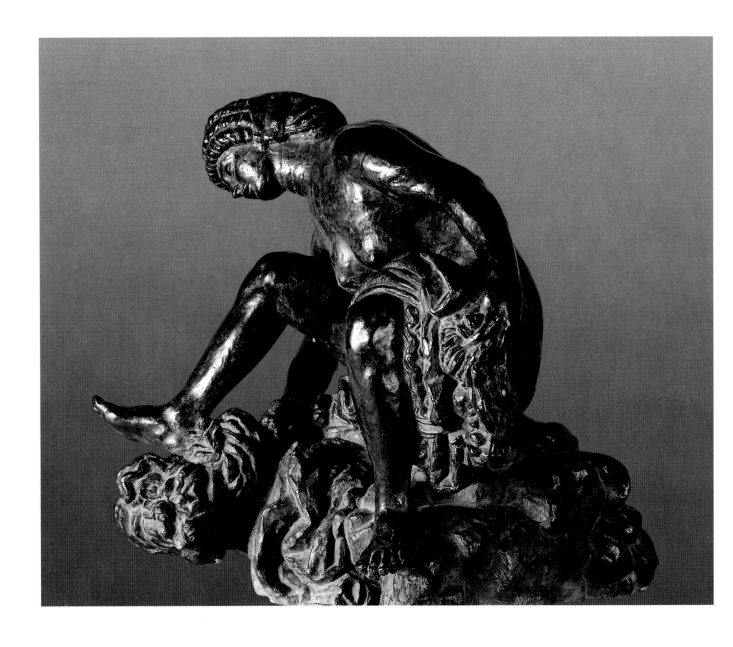

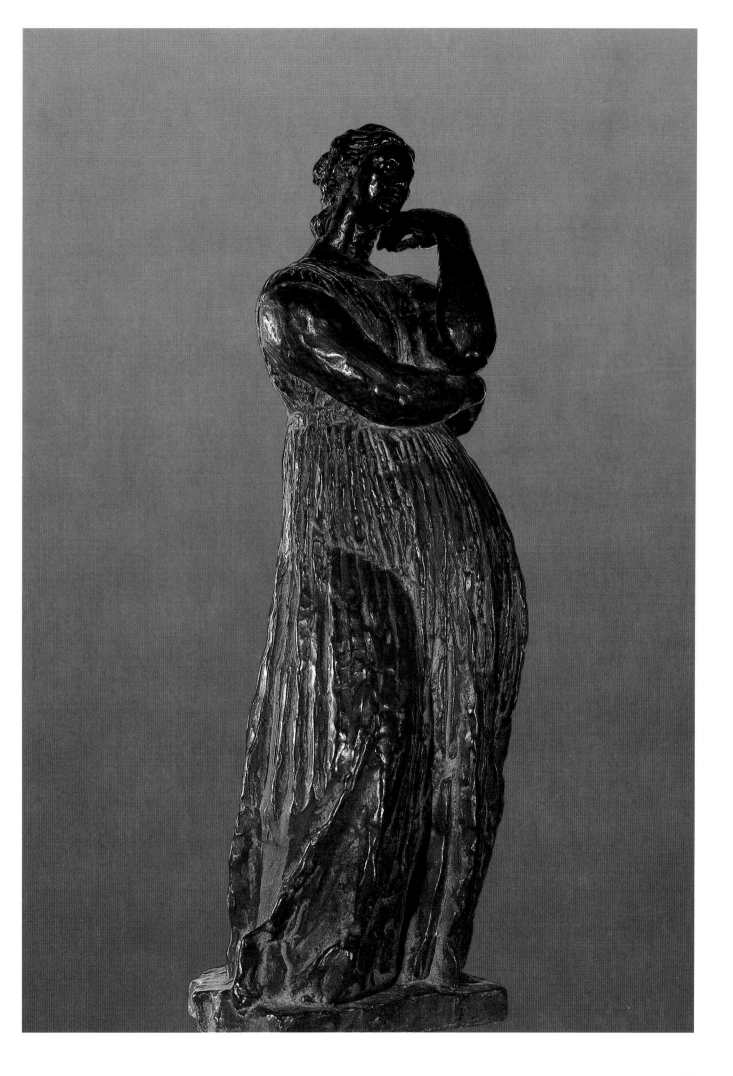

Woman at a Fountain, 1908
bronze, 44 × 32 × 18 cm
Paris, Musée Bourdelle, Rhodia
Dufet-Bourdelle Collection

Fruit, 1909–11
bronze, 226 × 104 × 58.5 cm
Rouen, Musée des Beaux-Arts

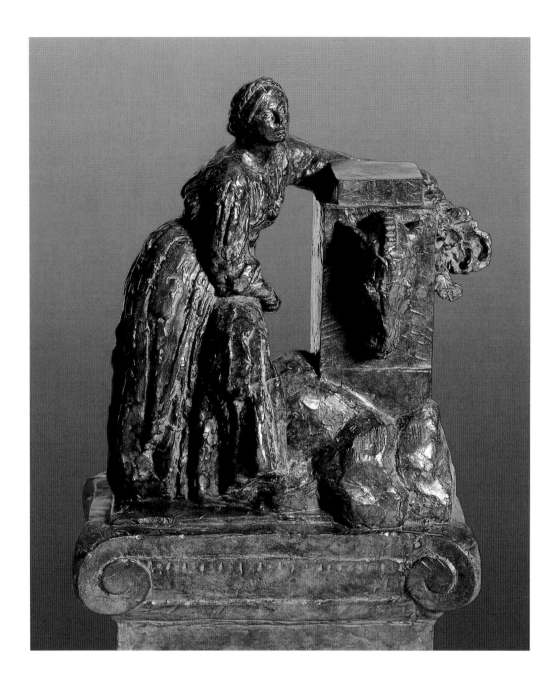

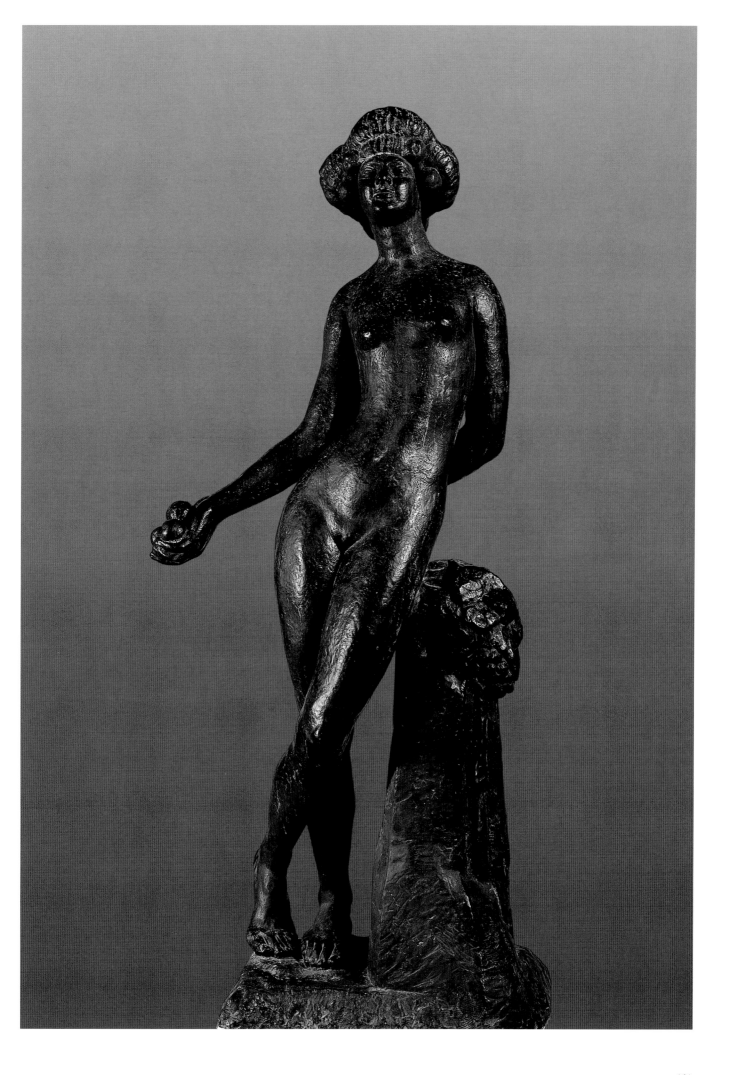

461

168. Emile-Antoine Bourdelle

Orpheus and Eurydice, 1913
watercolor, 200 × 250 cm
Paris, Musée Bourdelle, Rhodia
Dufet-Bourdelle Collection

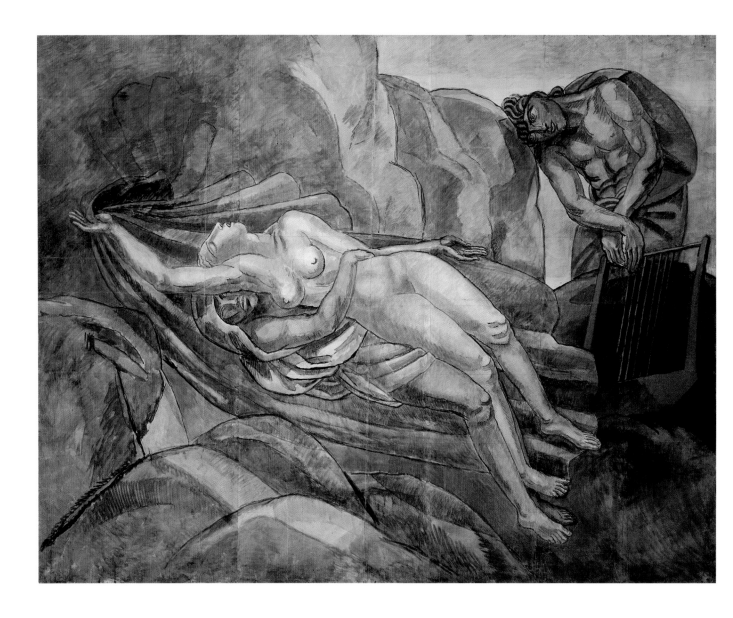

168bis. Pablo Picasso

The Toilette, 1906
oil on canvas, 52 × 31 cm
Saõ Paulo, Museu de Arte

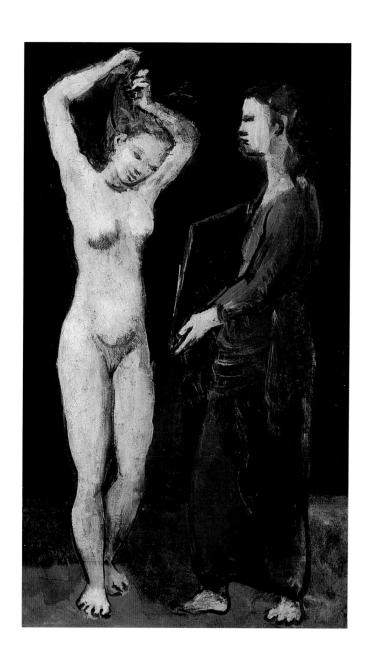

169. Pablo Picasso

Seated Nude (Magdalene), 1905
oil on cardboard, 106 × 76 cm
Paris, Musée National
d'Art Moderne, Centre
Georges-Pompidou

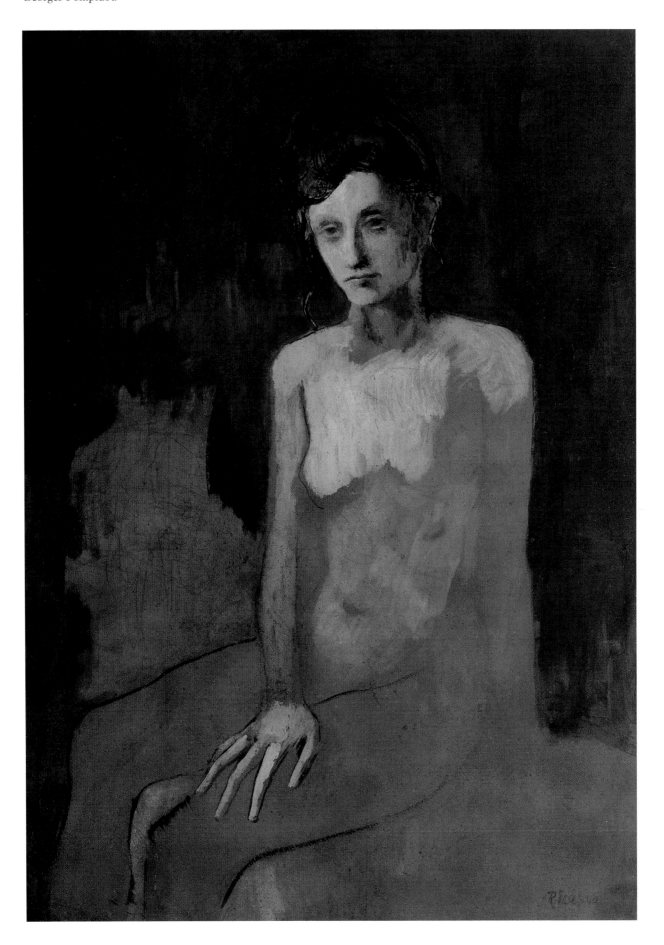

170. Pablo Picasso

Woman with a Fan, 1905
oil on canvas, 99 × 81.3 cm
Washington, D.C.,
National Gallery of Art

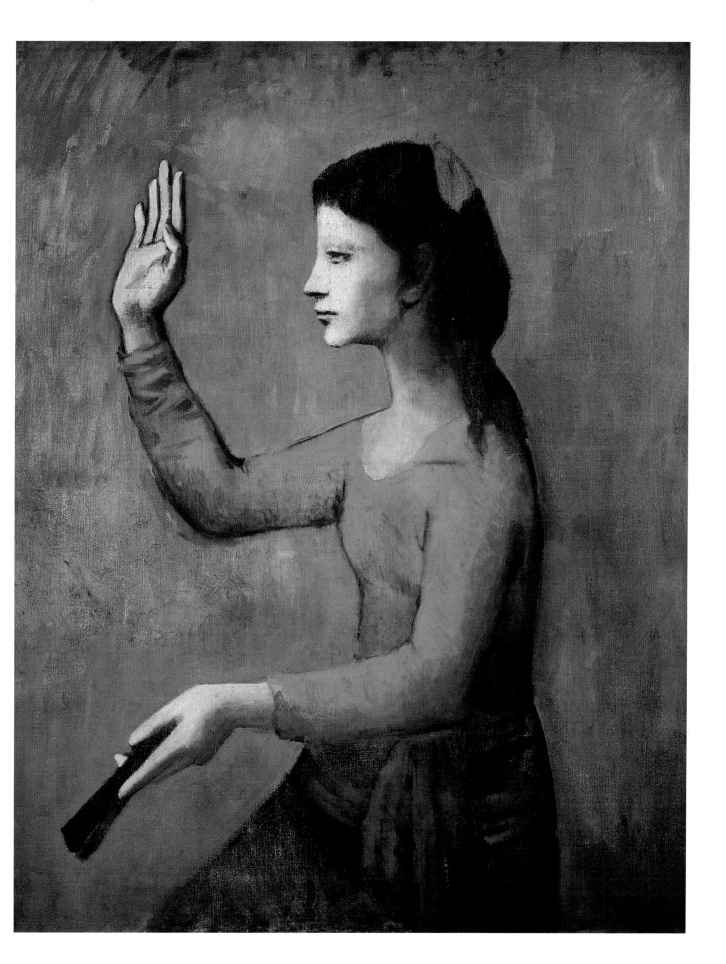

171. Pablo Picasso

Adolescents, 1906
oil on canvas, 157 × 117 cm
Paris, Musée de l'Orangerie

172. Pablo Picasso

The Dryad (Nude in the Forest),
1908
oil on canvas, 185 × 108 cm
Saint Petersburg,
The Hermitage Museum

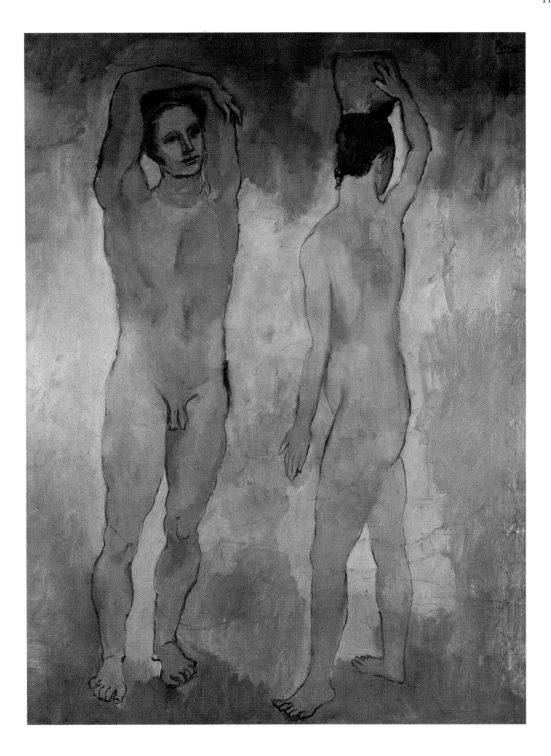

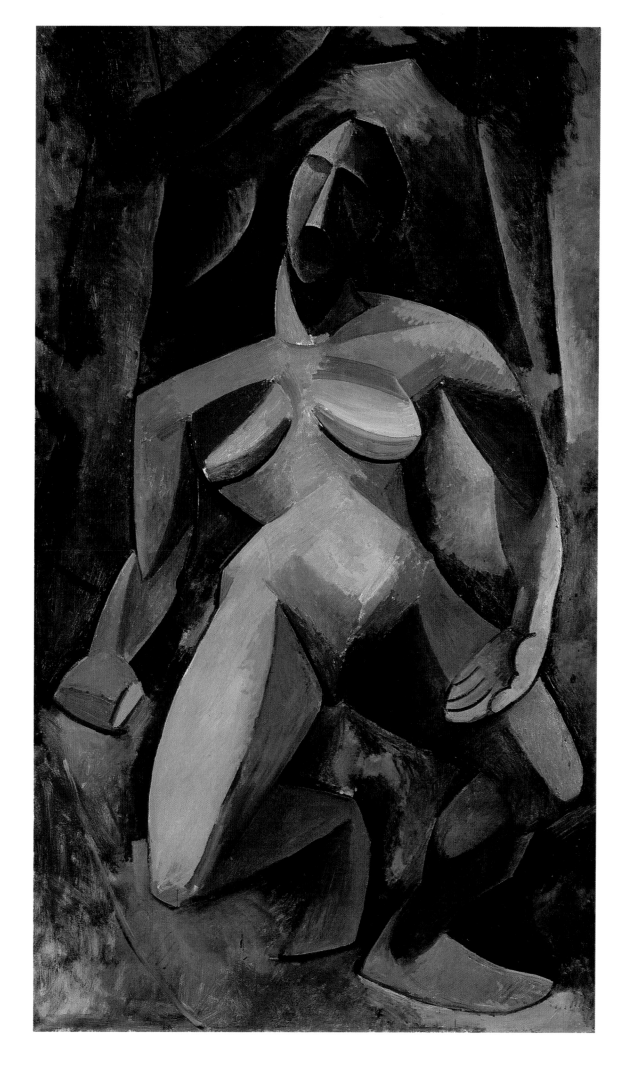

Nude in a Wood, 1906
oil on wooden panel,
40.6 × 32.4 cm
New York, The Brooklyn
Museum of Art. Gift of
George F. Of

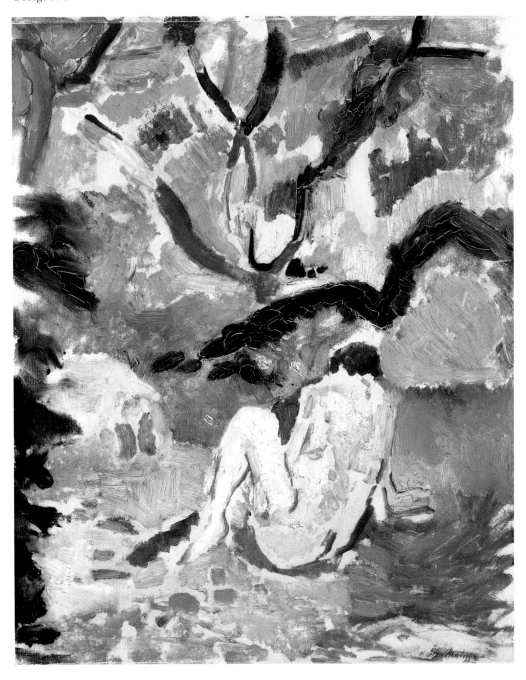

174. Henri Matisse

Study for "Luxe,
calme et volupté," 1904
oil on canvas, 32.8 × 40.6 cm
New York, The Museum
of Modern Art. Bequest of
Mrs. John Hay Whitney

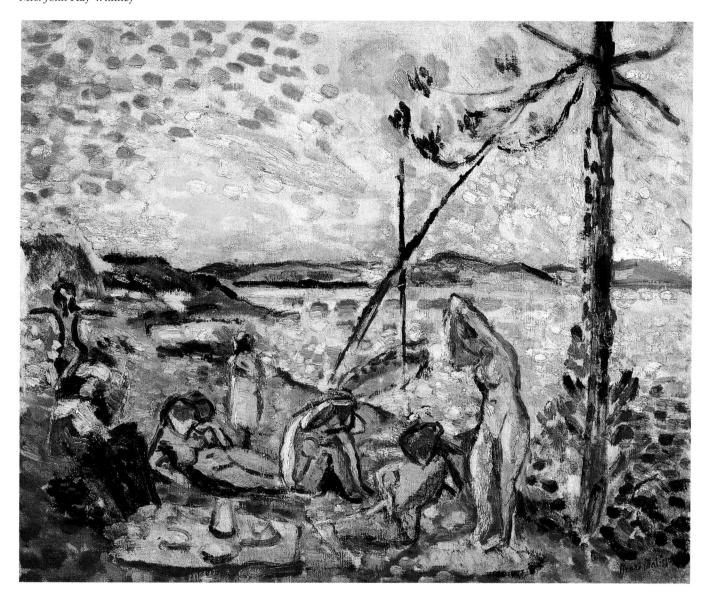

Seated Nude, 1909
oil on canvas, 33 × 40 cm
Musée de Grenoble

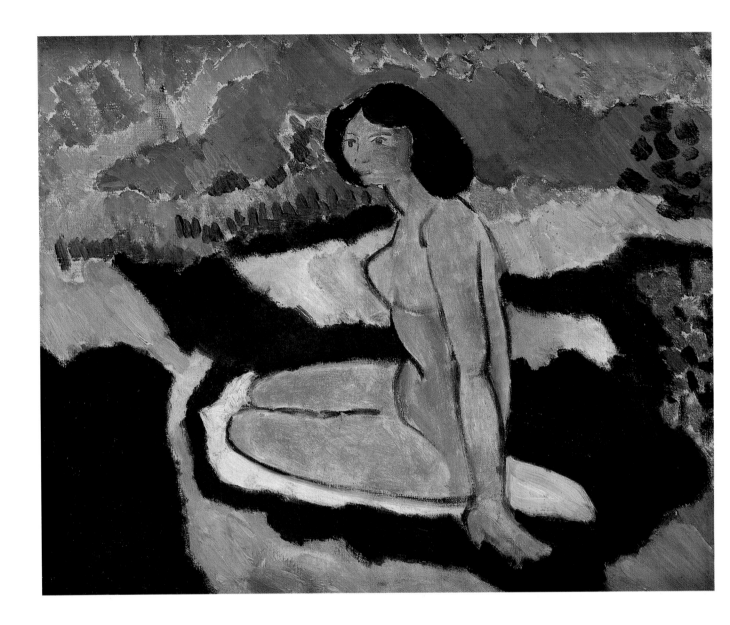

176. Henri Matisse

Sketch for "Music," 1907
oil on canvas, 73.4 × 60.8 cm
New York, The Museum
of Modern Art. Gift of A.
Conger Goodyear in honor
of Alfred H. Barr, Jr.

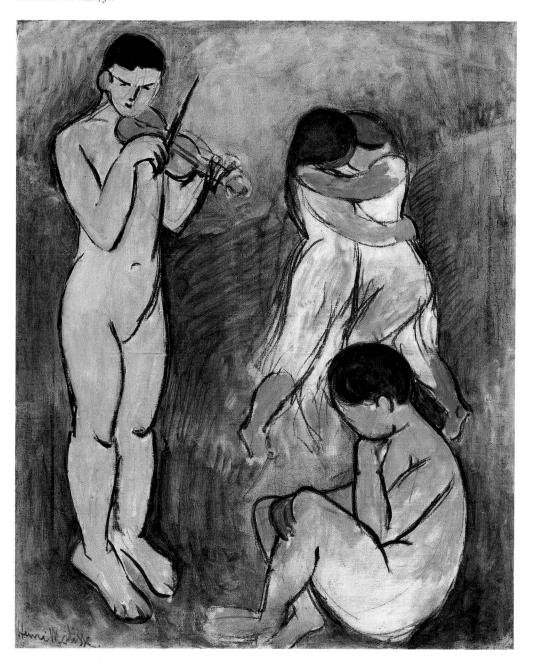

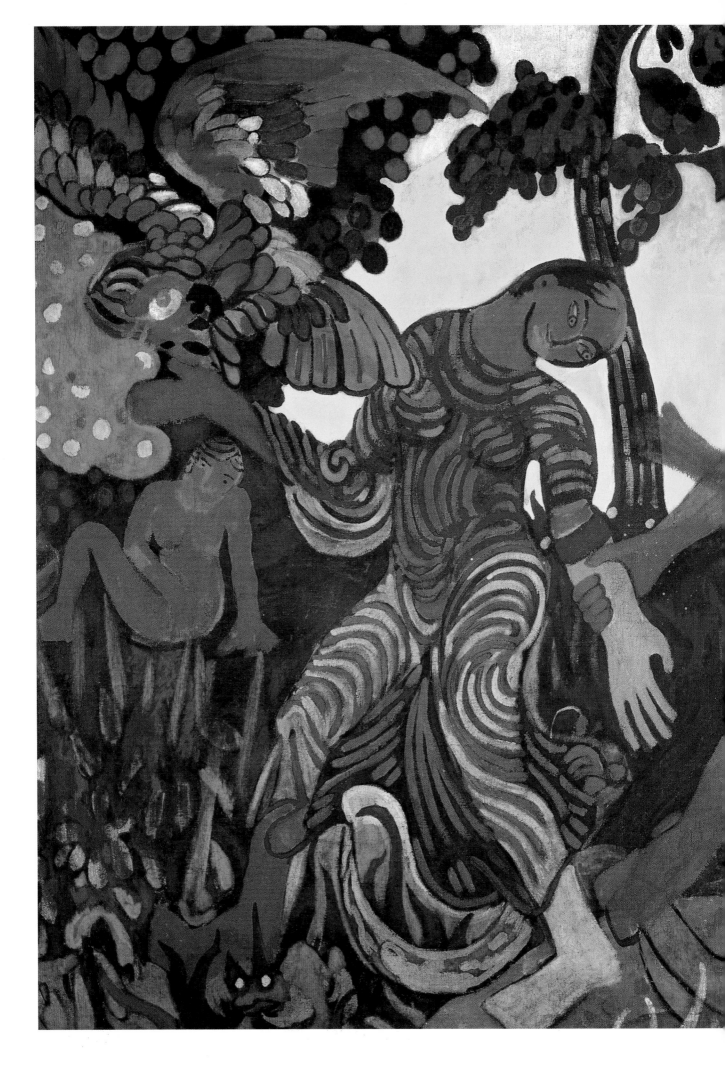

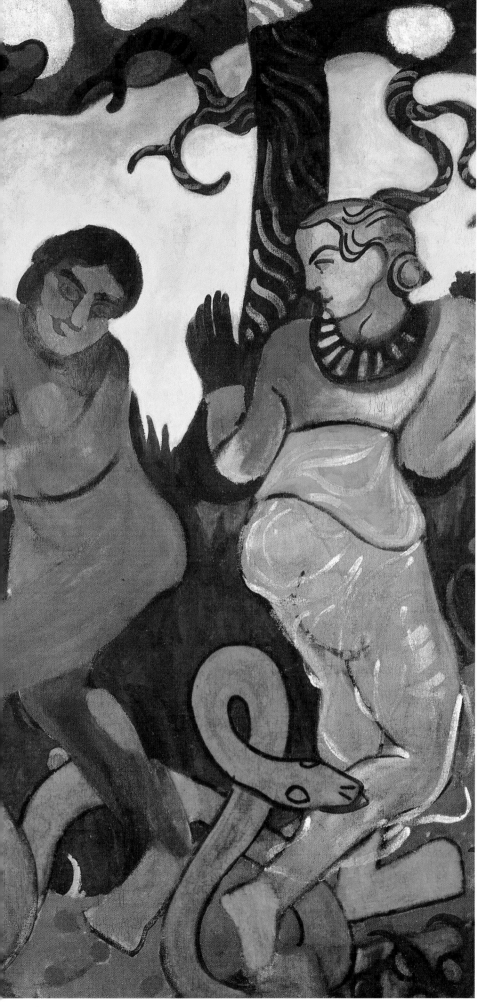

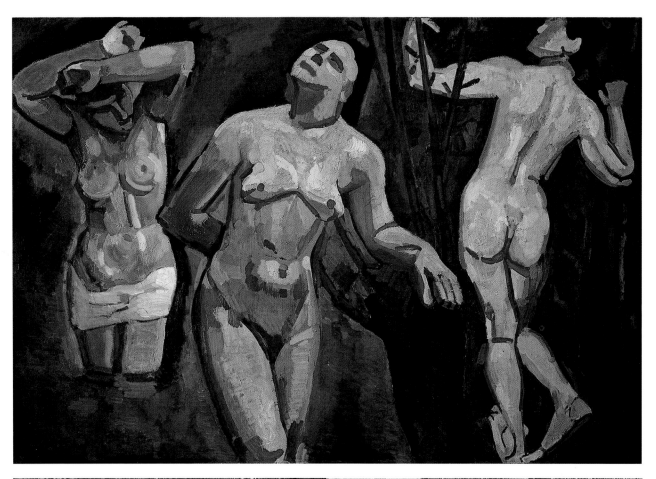

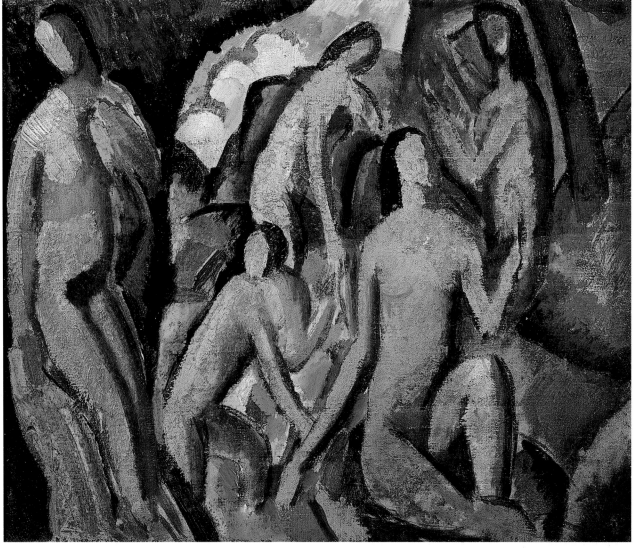

178. André Derain

Bathers, 1907
oil on canvas, 132.1 × 195 cm
New York, The Museum
of Modern Art, William
S. Paley and Abby Aldrich
Rockefeller Funds

179. André Derain

Bathers, 1908
oil on canvas, 38 × 46 cm
Paris, Musée d'Art Moderne
de la Ville

180. Henri Le Fauconnier

The Abundance, 1910
oil on canvas, 191 × 123 cm
The Hague, Gemeentemuseum

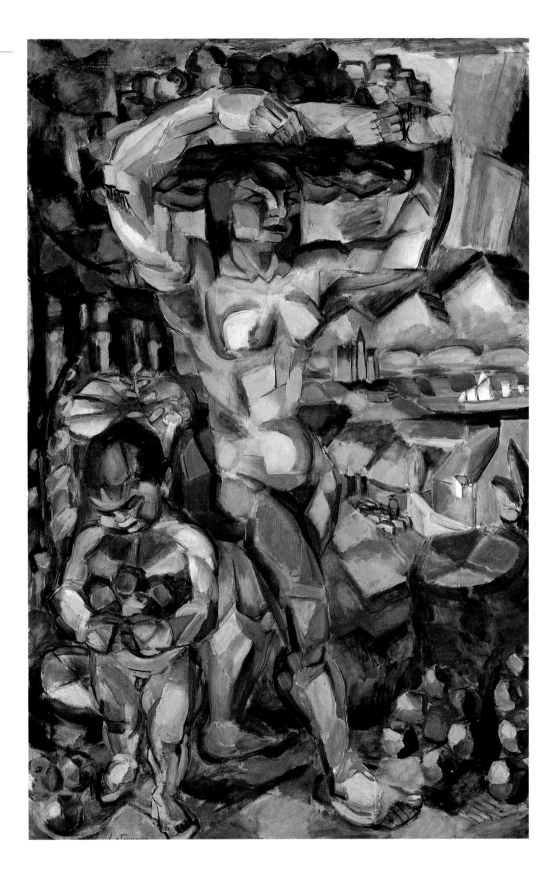

Two Nudes, 1910
oil on canvas, 73 × 92 cm
Paris, Musée National
d'Art Moderne, Centre
Georges-Pompidou

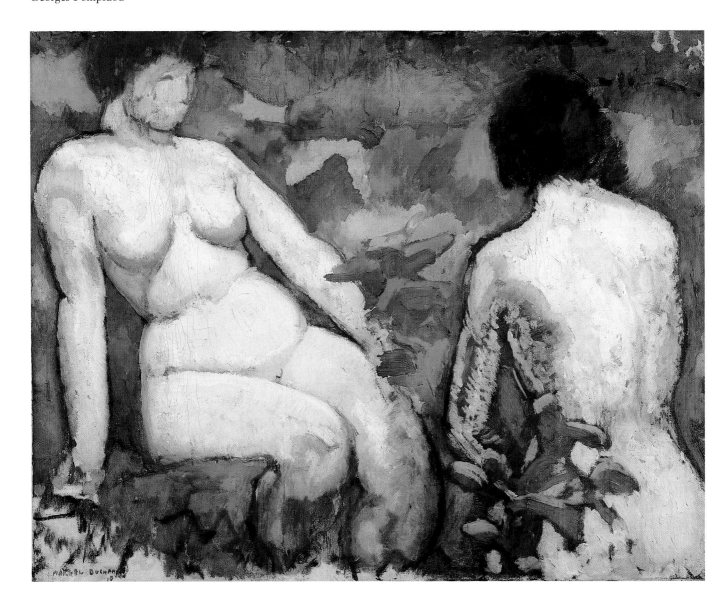

The Bush, 1910–11
oil on canvas, 127 × 92 cm
Philadelphia Museum of Art

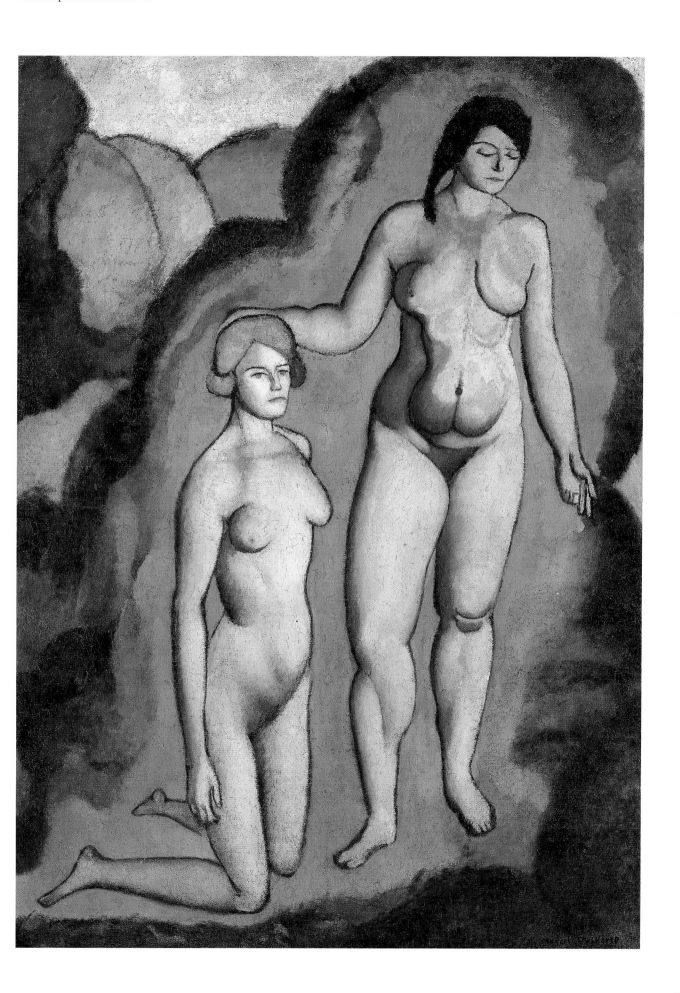

Bathers, 1912
oil on canvas, 105 × 171 cm
Paris, Musée d'Art Moderne
de la Ville

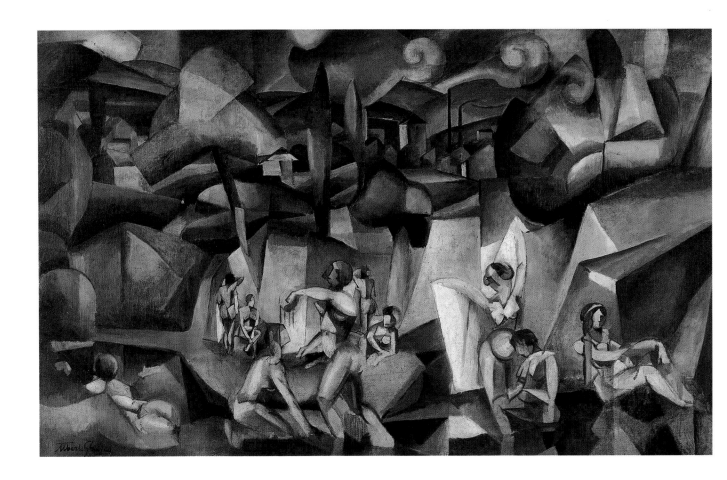

184. Francis Picabia

Adam and Eve, 1911
oil on canvas, 100 × 81 cm
Private collection

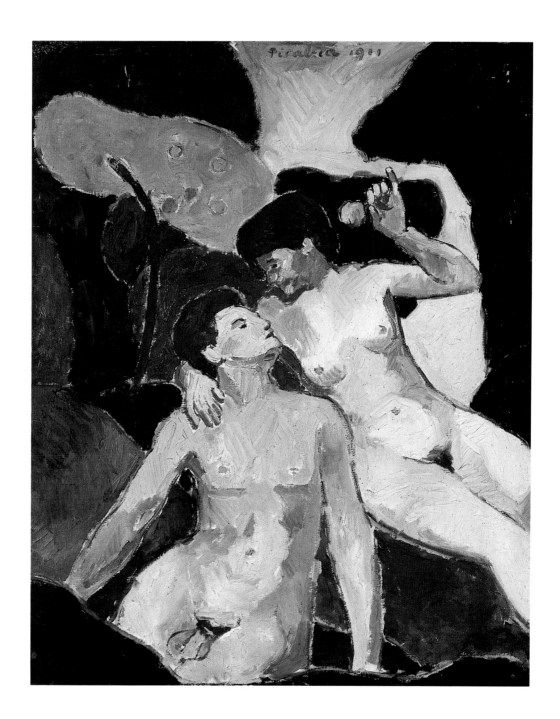

185. Suzanne Valadon

The Casting of the Net, 1914
oil on canvas, 201 × 301 cm
Paris, Musée National
d'Art Moderne, Centre
Georges-Pompidou

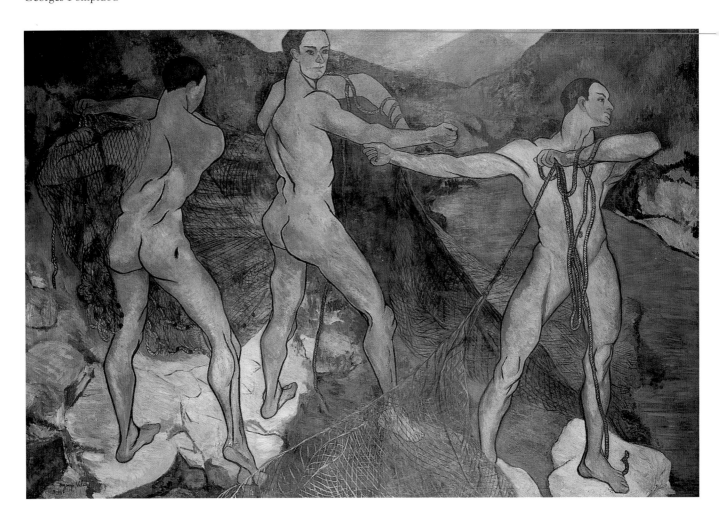

186. Joaquín Torres García

*The Presentation of Philosophy
at Parnassus by Pallas Athena,*
1911
oil on canvas, 113 × 367 cm
Madrid, Centro de Arte
Reina Sofía

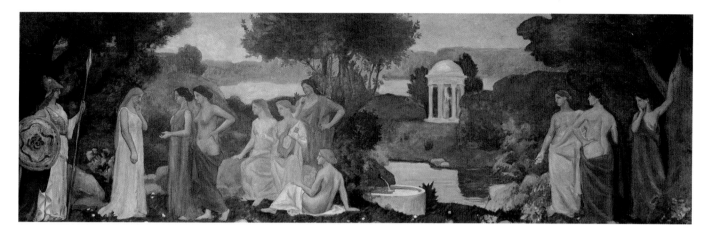

187. Joaquín Torres García

Woman at a Fountain, 1916
oil on canvas, 22.5 × 29.5 cm
Geneva, Alejandra, Aurelio
and Claudio Torres Collection.
Courtesy of Jan Krugier,
Ditesheim et Cie Gallery

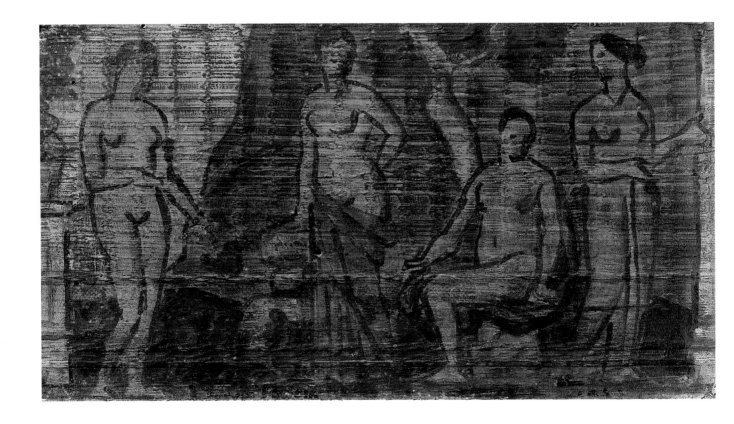

188. Joaquín Torres García

Two Figures Picking Fruit, 1914
distemper on wood, 45 × 33 cm
Geneva, Alejandra, Aurelio and
Claudio Torres Collection.
Courtesy of Jan Krugier,
Ditesheim et Cie Gallery

189. Joaquín Torres García

Classical Figures, 1922
distemper on wood,
34.5 × 49.5 cm
Geneva, Alejandra, Aurelio and
Claudio Torres Collection.
Courtesy of Jan Krugier,
Ditesheim et Cie Gallery

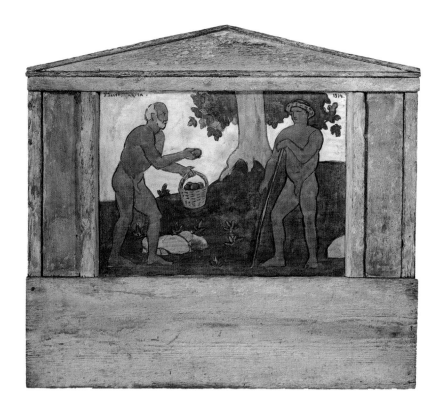

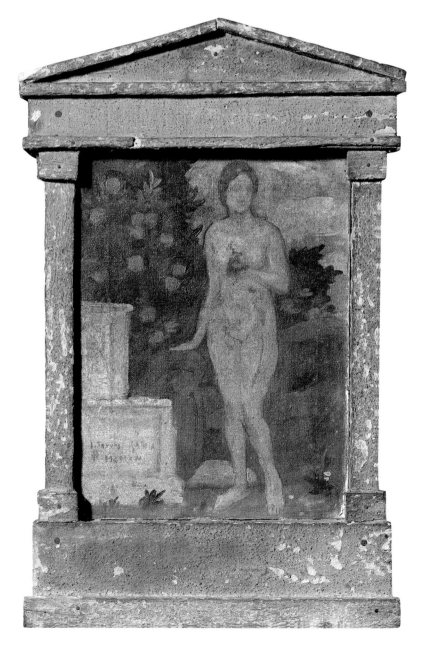

190. Joaquín Torres-García

Pastoral, 1924
oil on canvas, 50 × 73 cm
Geneva, Alejandra, Aurelio
and Claudio Torres Collection.
Courtesy of Jan Krugier,
Ditesheim et Cie Gallery

191. Joaquín Torres-García

Three Classical Figures, 1926
distemper on canvas, 46 × 61 cm
Geneva, Alejandra, Aurelio
and Claudio Torres Collection.
Courtesy of Jan Krugier,
Ditesheim et Cie Gallery

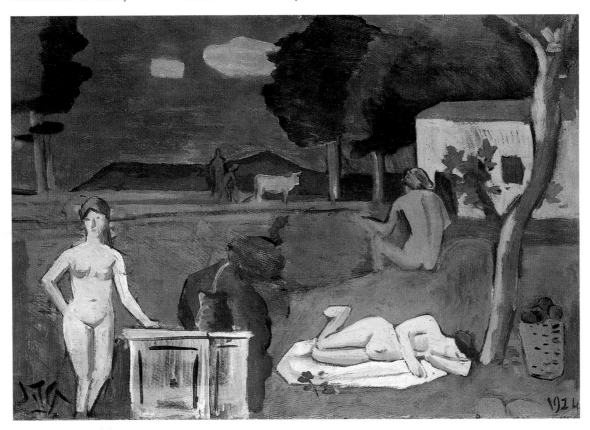

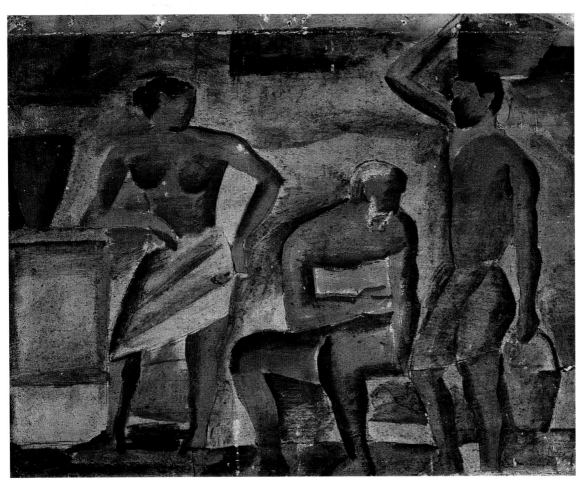

192. Joaquín Torres-García

Four Figures and a Child with a Basket of Fruit, 1943
oil on canvas, 56 × 122 cm
Geneva, Alejandra, Aurelio
and Claudio Torres Collection.
Courtesy of Jan Krugier,
Ditesheim et Cie Gallery

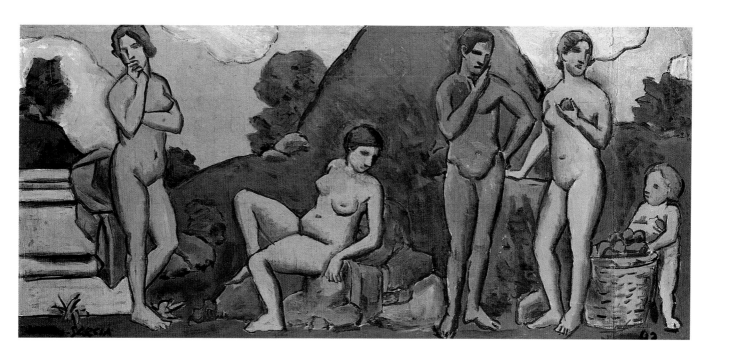

193. Pablo Picasso

Bathers Watching an Airplane,
1920
oil on panel, 73.5 × 92.5 cm
Paris, Musée Picasso

194. Pablo Picasso

Large Bather, 1921
oil on canvas, 182 × 101, cm
Paris, Musée de l'Orangerie

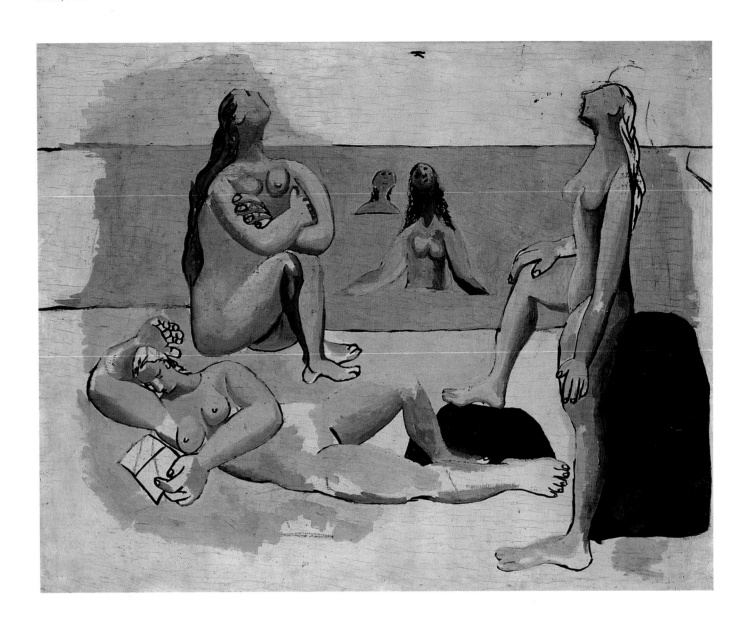

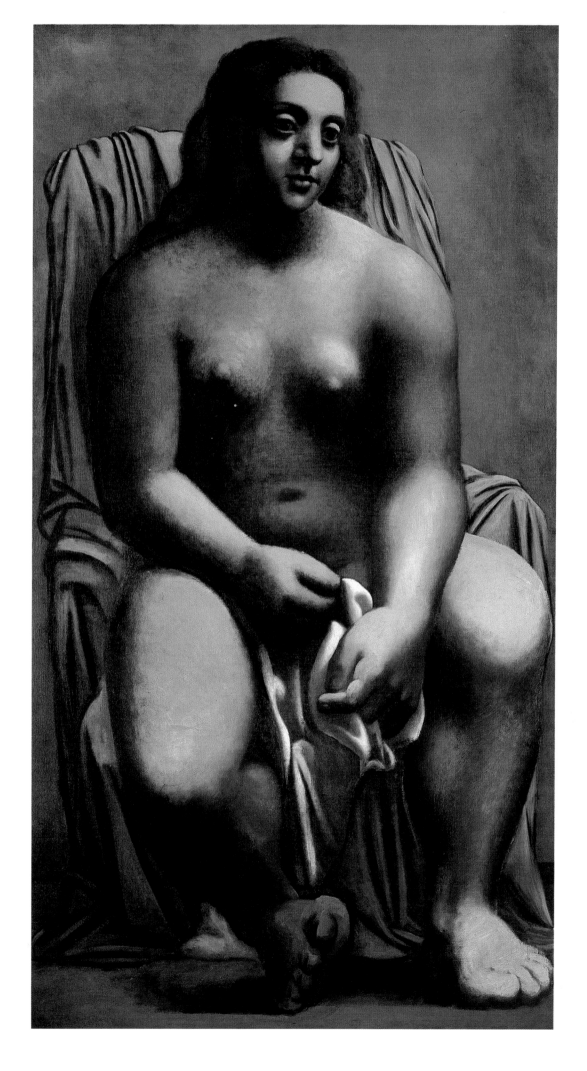

195. Pablo Picasso

The Spring, 1921
grease pencil on canvas,
100 × 200 cm
Paris, Musée Picasso

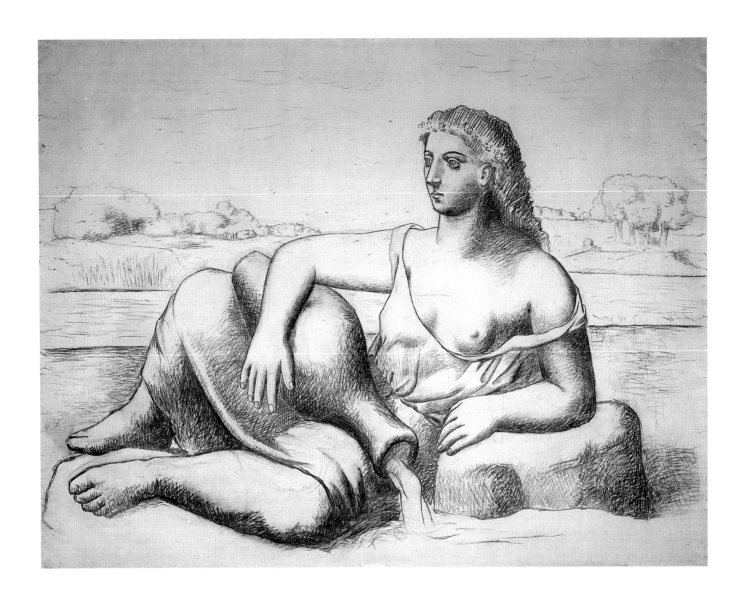

196. Pablo Picasso

Maternity, 1921
oil on canvas, 98.5 × 93 cm
Private collection. Courtesy
of Jan Krugier, Ditesheim et Cie
Gallery

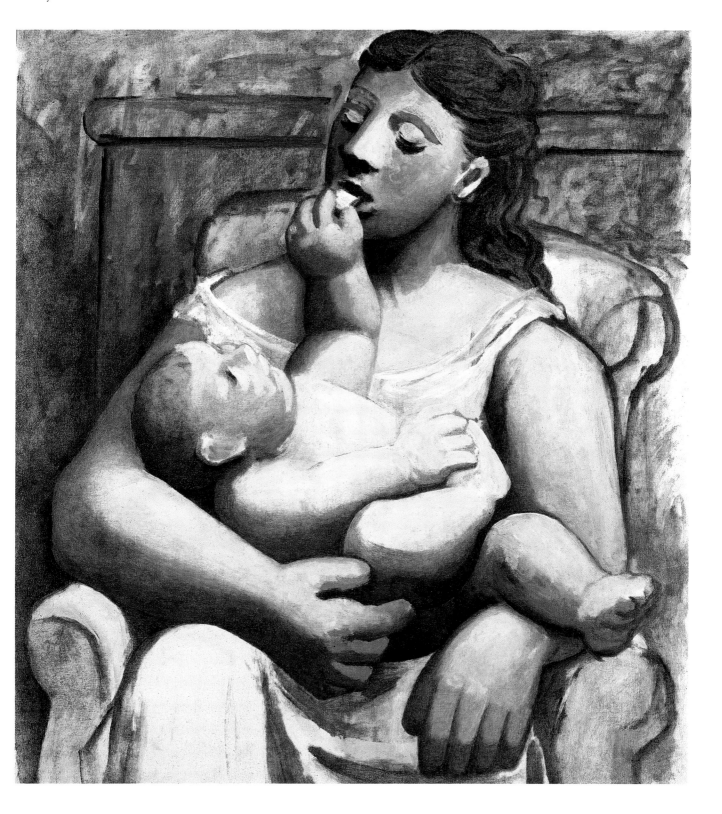

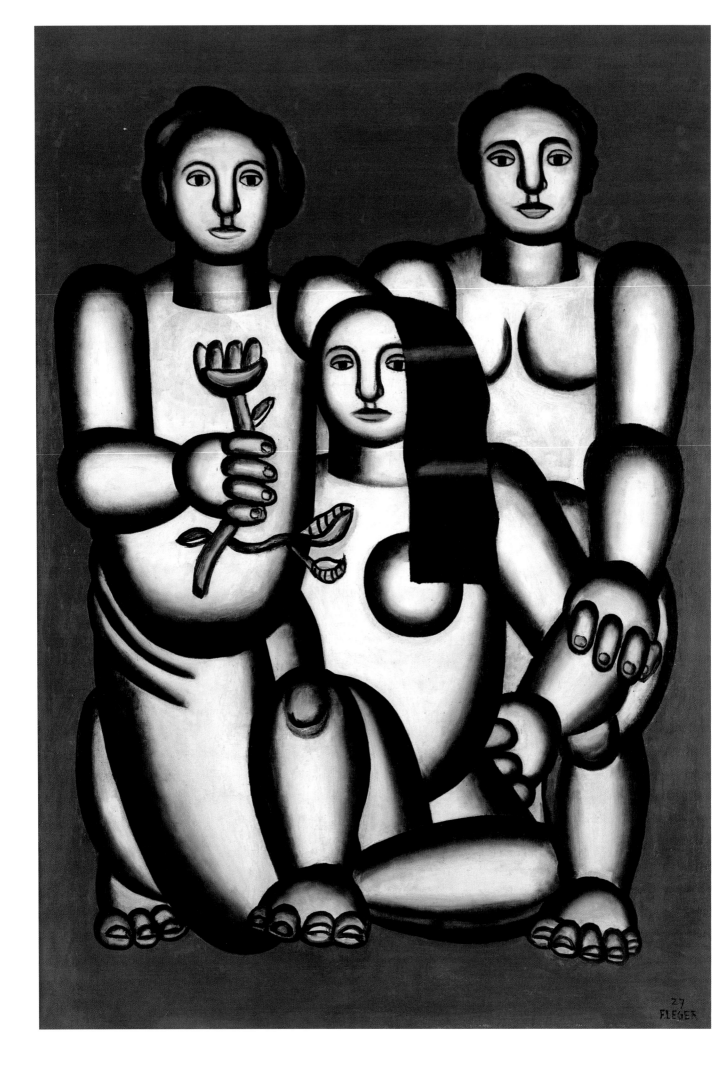

197. Fernand Léger

Three Women against a Red Background, 1927
oil on canvas, 138.5 × 95.5 cm
Saint-Etienne, Musée
d'Art Moderne

198. Fernand Léger

Dance, 1929
oil on canvas, 129 × 90 cm
Fonds National d'Art
Contemporain, Ministère
de la Culture

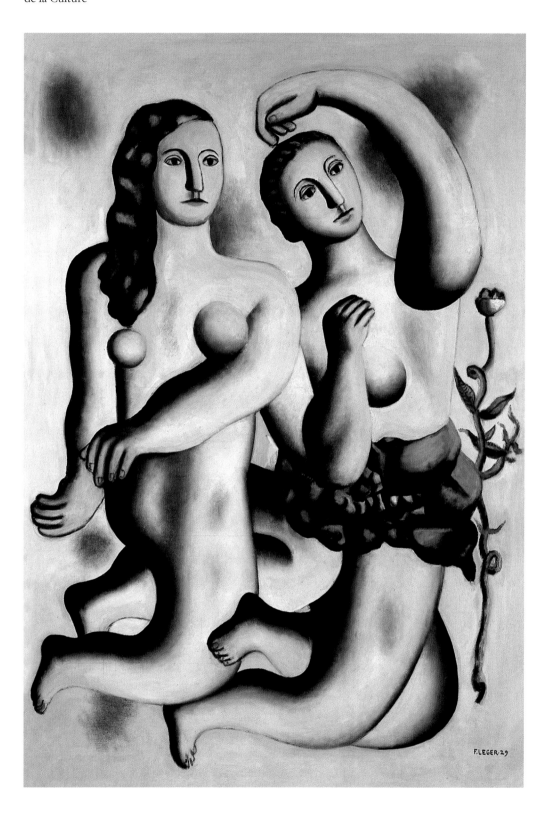

Bathing in the Grotto, 1930–31
oil and mixed technique
on canvas, 73 × 92 cm
Musée de Grenoble

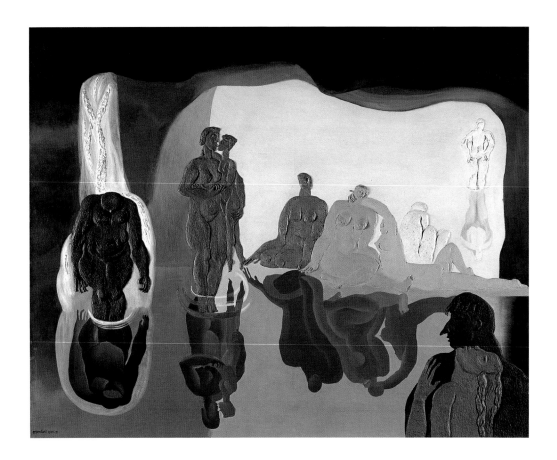

200. Henri Matisse

Dance (Blue Harmony),
1930–31
oil on canvas, 33 × 87 cm
Nice, Musée Matisse

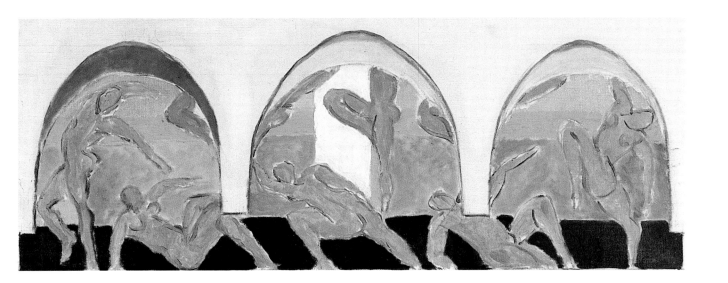

Gipsies, 1928
oil on canvas, 96.5 × 75.5 cm
Museo d'Arte Moderna
e Contemporanea di Trento
e Rovereto. Collezione Giovanardi

Summer, 1930
oil on canvas, 165 × 121 cm
Milan, Civica Galleria d'Arte
Moderna

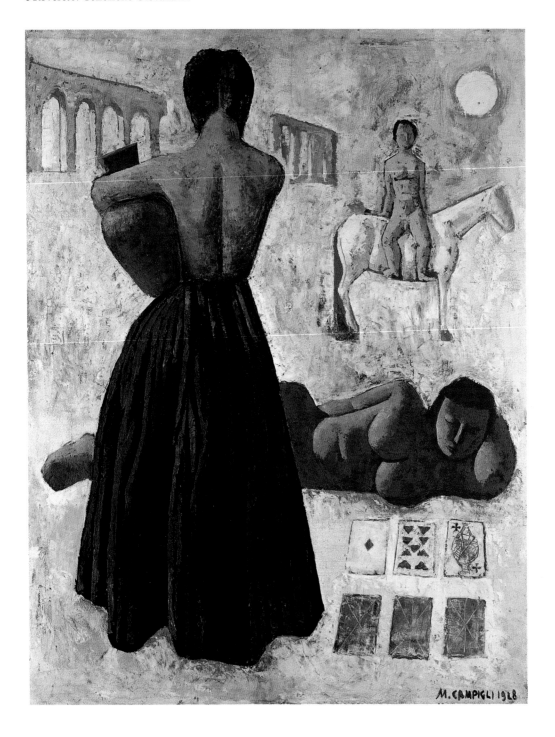

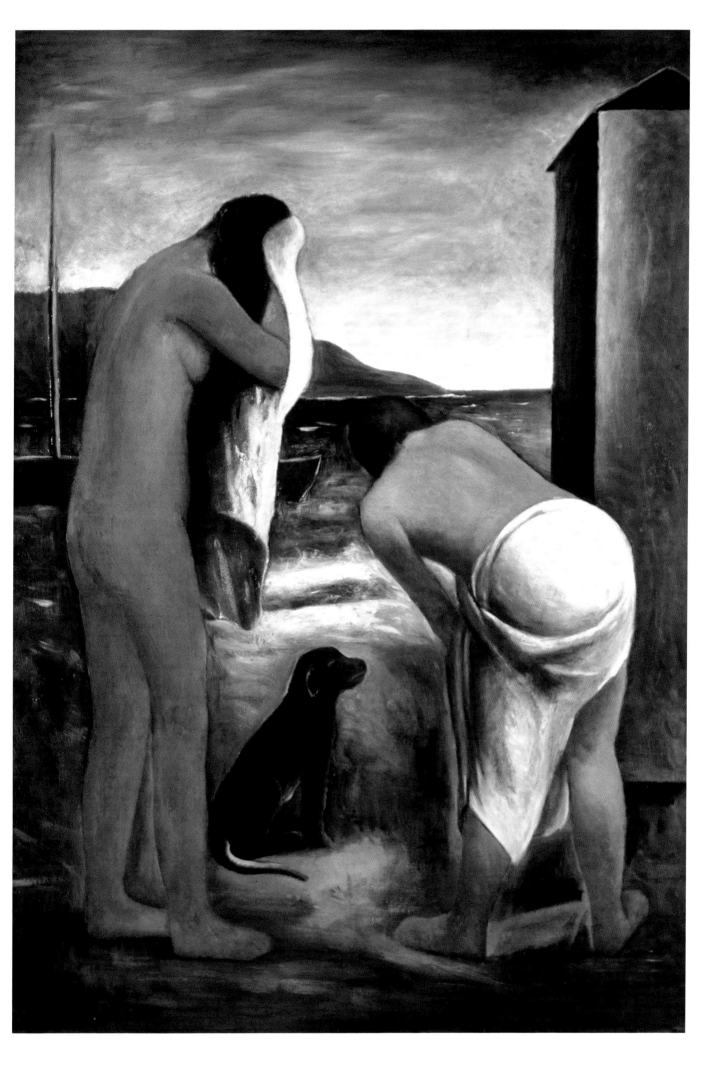

Swimmers, 1932
oil on canvas, 63.5 × 108.5 cm
Museo d'Arte Moderna
e Contemporanea di Trento
e Rovereto

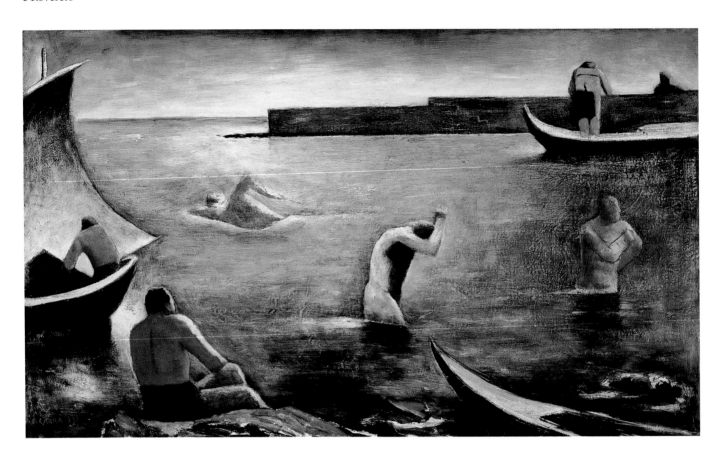

The Family, 1930
oil on canvas, 104 × 83 cm
Rome, Galleria Nazionale
d'Arte Moderna

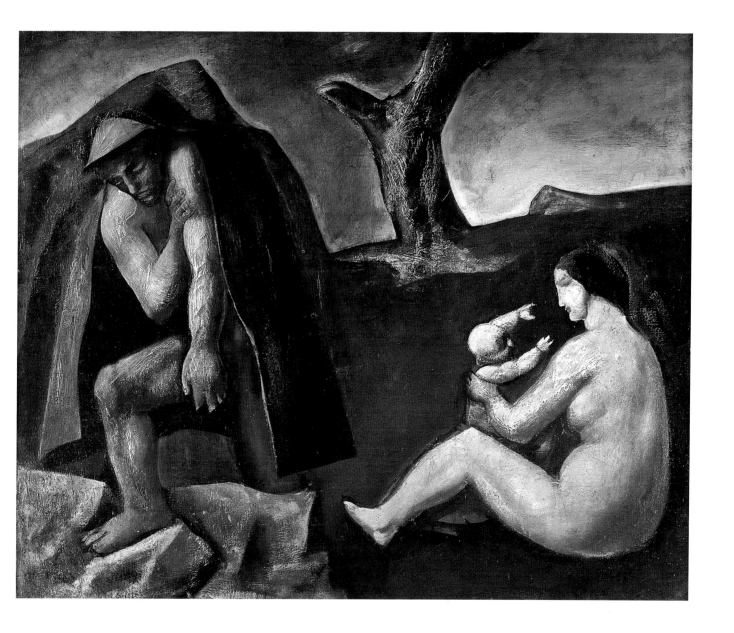

The Fisherman's Wife, 1931
fireclay, 28 × 39 × 18 cm
Milan, private collection.
Courtesy Claudia Gian Ferrari

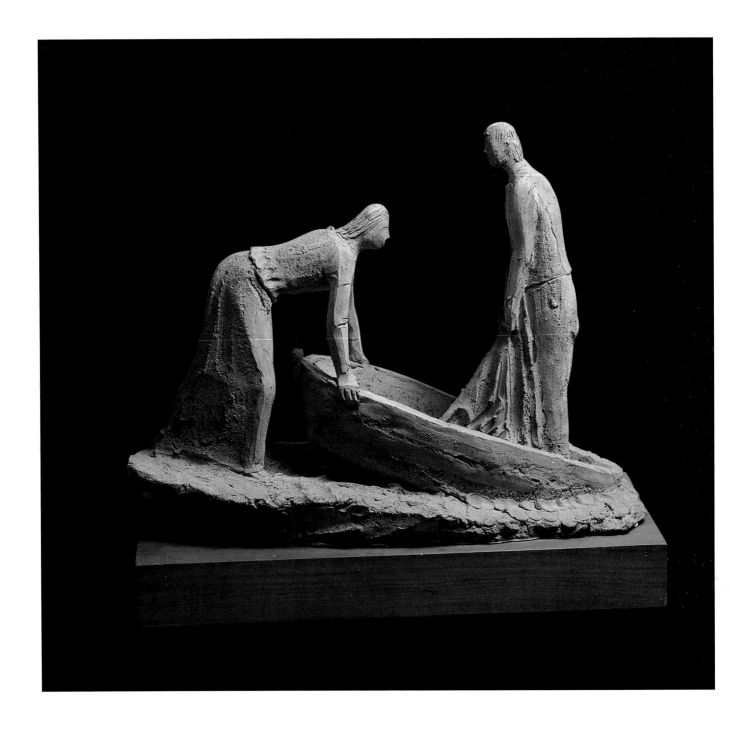

206. Arturo Martini

Hospitality, 1931
fireclay, 33 × 26 × 23,5 cm
Milan, private collection.
Courtesy Claudia Gian Ferrari

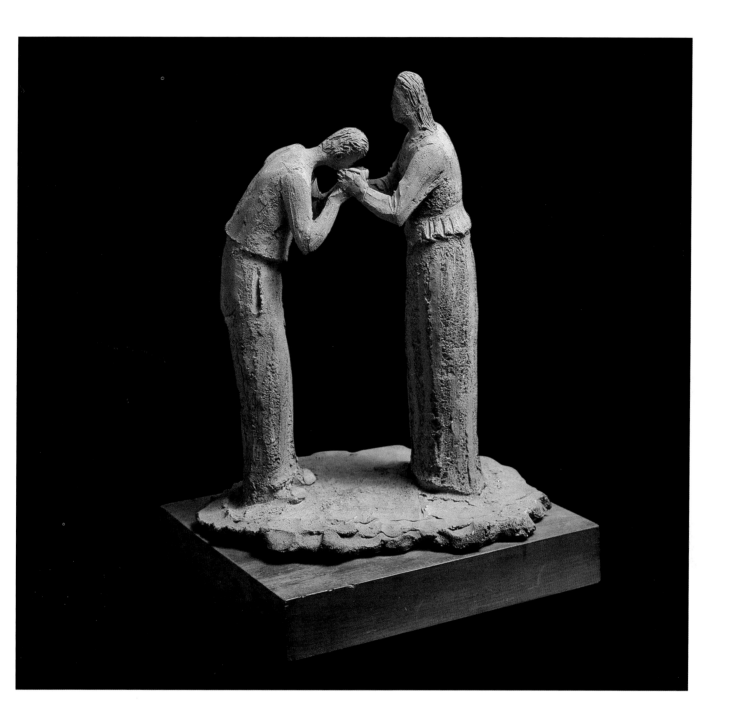

Composition, 1932
oil on plywood, 122.3 × 98.7 cm
Turin, Galleria d'Arte Moderna
e Contemporanea, Fondazione
Guido ed Ettore de Fornaris

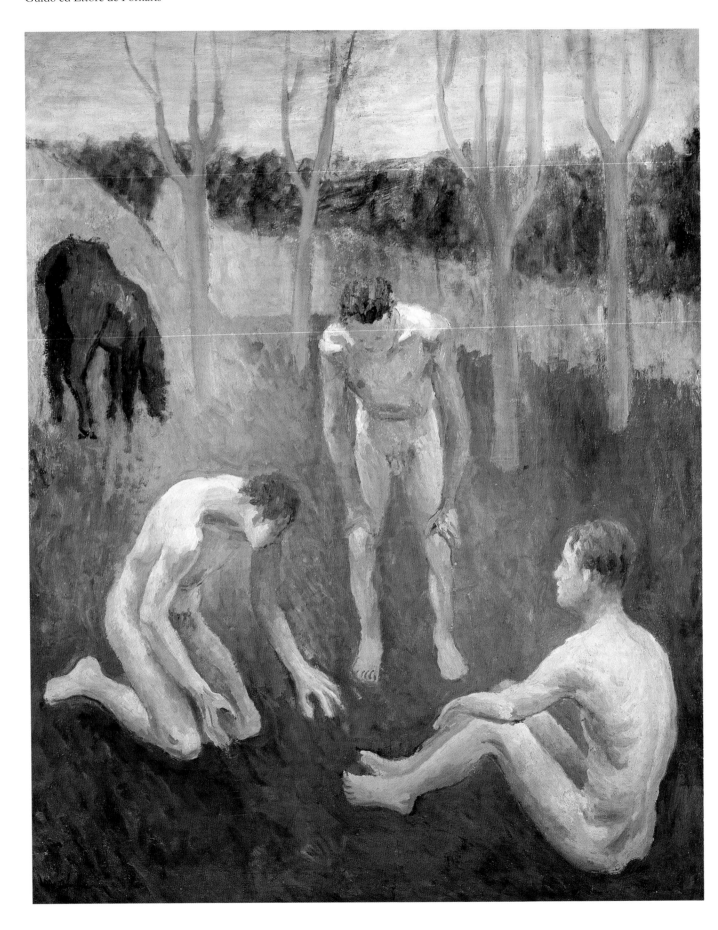

Spring, 1956
oil on canvas, 130 × 195 cm
Paris, Musée National
d'Art Moderne, Centre
Georges-Pompidou

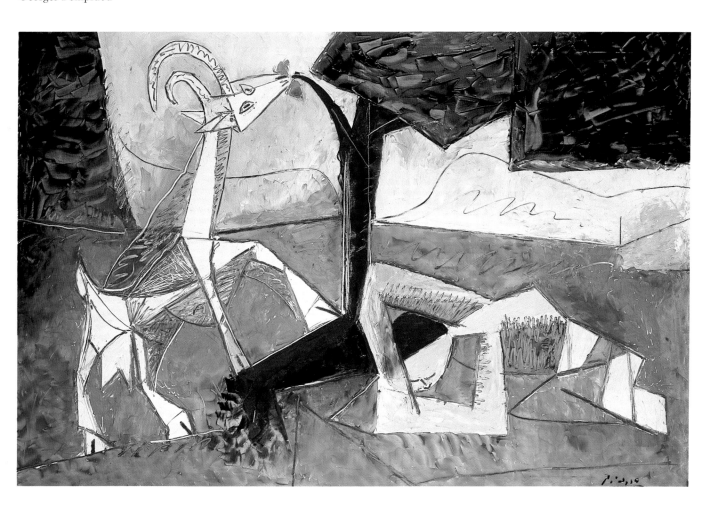

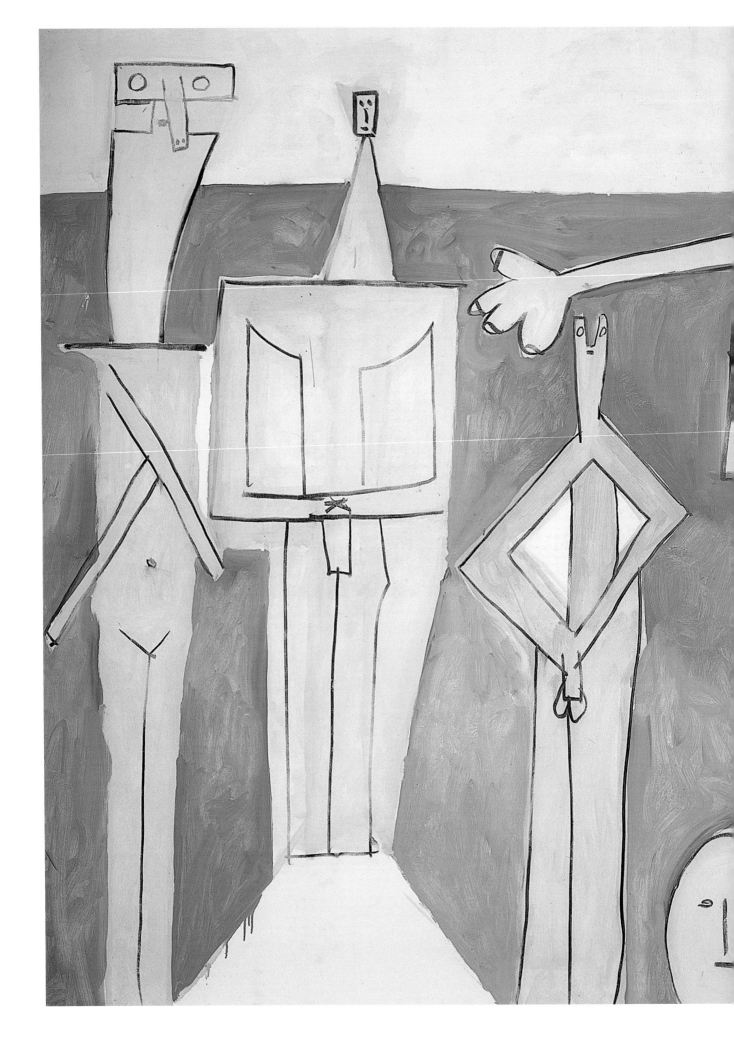

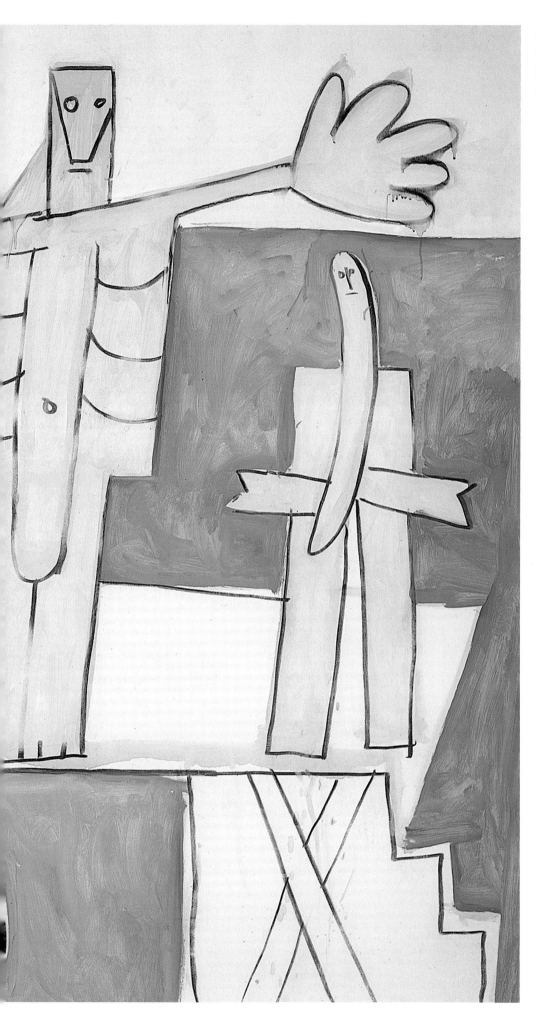

209. Pablo Picasso

Bathers at Garoupe, 1957
oil on canvas, 194.2 × 258.7 cm
Geneva, Musée d'Art
et d'Histoire de la Ville

Appendix

Artists' Biographies

Edmond (François) Jean Amand, known as **Aman-Jean**
(Chevry-Cossigny, 1858—Paris, 1936)

Aman-Jean entered Henri Lehmann's studio in the Paris Ecole des Beaux-Arts in 1878 and there he befriended Alphonse Osbert, Alexandre Séon and Georges Seurat. He also became Puvis de Chavannes's pupil, assisting him in work on *The Sacred Wood*, exhibited at the 1884 Salon. In 1885, during a visit to Italy with Ernest Laurent and Henri Martin, he discovered decorative art, thereafter exhibiting his works at the Salon des Artistes Français and the Société Nationale des Beaux-Arts. In 1890 he published an article on Puvis de Chavannes in *L'Art dans les Deux Mondes*. In 1891 he met Joséphin Péladan and Léonce de Larmandie, who offered him a place as art critic in *La Révolte intellectuelle*, a publication that would have no future. At this point he was frequenting the literary Symbolist circles, having close ties with Verlaine and also participating at the Salons de la Rose+Croix in 1892 and 1893; thereafter, he exhibited regularly at the Galerie Georges Petit. After 1900, he was to be much in demand as a portrait artist, exhibiting at the Salon d'Automne and at the Société des Artistes Décorateurs. Together with Albert Besnard and Antoine Bourdelle, in 1923 he founded the Salon des Tuileries, also producing the murals at the Musée des Arts Décoratifs and the Ecole de Chimie (Chemistry Faculty).
Deeply influenced by the aesthetics of Puvis de Chavannes and his friend Henri Martin, Aman-Jean's works depict pensive female figures which evoke Symbolist themes and concerns; the fairly free style of the artist often finds expression in an arabesque of line which reveals all his mastery of touch.
This portrait of Verlaine bears witness to a friendship that lasted from the first meeting of the two men right up to the poet's death in 1896. The work was painted in the period when Verlaine used to spend parts of the winter at the Hôpital Broussais to receive treatment for his syphilis. Verlaine loved the portrait and dedicated a sonnet to the artist, becoming a regular visit at Aman-Jean's home. The portrait renders without flattery all the force of the poet's powerful personality; the artist has chosen to show him full face in front of the bare wall of the hospital, so that the compact composition emphasizes the sitter's feeble physical condition. The

power of Aman-Jean's portraits comes from this ability to render the sitter's personality, using an Impressionist technique to reveal psychological truth.
M.C.

Albert Bartholomé
(Thiverval, 1848—Paris, 1928)

Bartholomé initially started as a painter, first in Geneva then in Paris, where he became a close friend of Degas. He did not start working in sculpture until 1886, but thereafter would remain faithful to that medium, developing a style that brought together simplicity and restrained emotion, which—as Thérèse Burollet pointed out long ago—are close to "the Attic calm of the figures in Puvis de Chavannes." The parallel was already suggested by Huysmans in a passage in his "Salon de 1885," reprinted in the 1898 *Certains*, which saw a connection between Puvis de Chavannes, Bartholomé and Whistler. For his part, Emile Verhaeren compared the painter's *Inspiring Muses* with Bartholomé's *Monument to the Dead* for their similar sensitivity and gentleness, their simplicity and modesty (*Ecrits sur l'art*, Brussels 1997, pp. 666–67). Later Léonce Bénédite, in a 1899 article on the sculptor, commented on how, unlike his paintings, Bartholomé's sculpture focused on synthesis and a unified harmony—qualities he saw well-illustrated in the *Monument to the Dead* in Père Lachaise and the *Monument to Jean-Jacques Rousseau* ("Art et Décoration," December 1899, pp. 161–74).
Both Bartholomé and Puvis de Chavannes exhibited at La Libre Esthétique, and knew each other—primarily through the Société Nationale des Beaux-Arts, of which Puvis de Chavannes was president from 1891 to the year of his death. Bartholomé exhibited at the Société in 1891, and—together with Saint-Marceaux and Meunier—was part of its examining commission in 1893, 1894 and 1895. He would then be president of the commission in 1905, 1909 and 1910, subsequently becoming vice-president of the Society and ultimately president (in 1914). His correspondence (Document Archives at the Musée d'Orsay) contains many references to Puvis de Chavannes; and the artist often spoke of the painter with Léonce Bénédite, recalling "those pilgrimages made many years ago to Marseille, to Lyon, to Amiens. . . .
In a time when it is scoundrels that

attract the attention of the world, it is good to go with some people to follow in the path of a man who was so great and whose works are so beautiful." (Letter of January 9, 1899, Drouot, April 6, 1981) In 1918, Bartholomé organized an exhibition of Puvis de Chavannes's cartoons in the room dedicated to the great artists (Puvis de Chavannes, Degas and Rodin) who had been presidents of the Société des Beaux-Arts.
C.Ch.

Auguste Baud-Bovy
(Geneva, 1848—Davos, 1899)

Landscape and portrait painter, the Geneva artist Auguste Baud-Bovy was known to the Symbolists of Paris as "the Bard of the Mountains." A pupil of Barthélémy Menn, the young artist frequented the "colony" of the Bovy, who—inspired by the ideals of Fourier—lived in the Chateau de Gruyères as a *phalanstère*. He worked on the mural decoration of the building together with Corot, F. Furet, F.-L. Francais and H. Baron. In 1873 he formed links in Geneva with anarchists and refugees from the suppression of the Paris Commune: Courbet and Rochefort (both of whose portrait he painted), Paul Pia and the Reclus brothers. He lived in Paris from 1882 to 1888, frequenting Symbolist painters and writers, and the critics Roger Marx and Charles Morice. Puvis de Chavannes and Henner visited his studio.
After leaving Paris, he settled at Aeschi, a village in the Oberland mountains near Berne. Like Segantini and other late nineteenth-century artists, he fled from the world of modern civilization, wanting to paint "a vast poem of the mountains." He set up his enormous canvases on the edge of precipices; he painted in the middle of blizzards. In his *The Heroic Deeds of Shepherds* he recorded the epic of a society that had not lost touch with its native soil. And, in 1893, from the height of the Männlichen he prepared his *Panorama of the Bernese Alps*, which was intended for the Universal Exposition of Chicago, but was lost at sea during a storm off the Dublin coast. The final version of that work (112 meters in circumference, 17 meters tall—some 2000 square meters of painted canvas) was completed in Paris, at the Vincennes gasometer. It was there that Puvis de Chavannes, accompanied by Ary Renan, exclaimed: "It is nature itself. It is

perfect!" The esteem was reciprocal. In 1896 at the Musée Rath in Geneva, Bovy organized the exhibition *Puvis de Chavannes, Auguste Rodin and Eugène Carrière* with some four paintings, twenty-nine studies, a poster, twenty photographs and thirty-six drawings by the former artist.
In his later paintings, Baud-Bovy rendered light and clouds in a very transparent palette, with the details of the landscape succumbing to a grandiose spiritual vision of the whole. On the back of the canvases, he wrote that the paintings were not to be varnished, so that they would maintain that matte, fresco-like finish that was so dear to Puvis de Chavannes. He died in Davos, opposite the "Magic Mountain."
V.A.

Emile Bernard
(Lille, 1868—Paris, 1941)

At a young age, Bernard was already painting landscapes and making copies of the works of the Old Masters. In autumn 1884 he entered Cormon's studio, but was expelled for insubordination at the beginning of 1886. He then tried out Impressionist techniques, and explored Seurat's Divisionism, before focusing his interest on a more synthetic style, together with his friend Anquetin. He traveled to Brittany in spring 1888, and then again in autumn, when he visited Gauguin and Laval at Pont-Aven. He painted a portrait of his sister Madeleine there (who had come on a visit with the artist's mother) showing her reclined in a meadow like a recumbent statue. In its decorative approach and muted palette, the work is reminiscent of such Puvis de Chavannes works as *Tamaris*. The same calm reigns in this idyllic landscape, where beyond the screen of "a sacred wood" one can just make out the peaceful course of the river Aven.
That same year Bernard explored the theme of the nude and designed a complex sequence of mural decorations for his new studio. In a Puvisesque sylvan landscape, Bernard aimed to depict a paradisiacal world, where the solidity of forms echoes the work of Cézanne. One can also find this evocation of eternal myths in *Study of a Nude under a Willow*, in which the influence of the elongated figures of the Fontainebleau School is more clearly visible. In this period Bernard also became interested in the Italian Primitives and Byzantine painting. He left Paris for Italy, then continued on to Constantinople and

ultimately settled for a number of years in Cairo, where he painted large-scale mural works and adopted a classicism that distanced him from the avant-garde work of his day.
M.N.

Joseph Bernard
(Vienne, 1866—Boulogne-sur-Seine, 1931)

The son of a modest stone-mason, Joseph Bernard learned to work stone and marble at a very early age. He received a classical training in sculpture at the Lyon Ecole des Beaux-Arts in 1881–86, then moving to the Ecole Nationale des Beaux-Arts in Paris and settling in the city in 1887. He was disappointed by the teaching he received from Cavelier and soon began to neglect his work at the Ecole. The following period (1890–1900) was one of some uncertainty, in which he worked the night shift in a print-works in order to be able to sculpt during the day. While his early works reveal the extent of his admiration for Rodin, he never actually worked for the older sculptor. At the time, he was producing sculptural models in clay—heavily-worked figures that were dramatic in inspiration and clearly influenced by Rodin. This can be seen, for example in the 1891 *Hope Defeated* and the *The Burden of Life. Monument to Peace*—even if these are only known to us through fragments and sketches.

His first public commission was the *Monument to Michel Servet* in his home town. A turning-point in his career, this was a long-term project (from 1906 to 1911) which involved him in the production of a molded model from which he then carved the large-scale figures directly into the stone. In this very fruitful period he carved a number of busts in stone or marble—for example, the 1906 *Effort toward Nature* and the 1908 *Modern Sphinx*—as well as modeling small dancing figures. He held an exhibition of sculpture and numerous drawings at the Galerie Hébrard in 1908, after which he began to work on the figures of young girls, which were to become an important theme in his work. While his *Draped Figure of Young Girl* still seems to be modeled from clay, his *Water Bearer* or *Young Girl with a Pitcher* (1910) and his *Woman and Child* (plaster exhibited on 1914) are modeled directly in plaster, which Bernard then polished to achieve a stone-like finish. The end-results were smooth and highly-stylized statues modeled with a very synthetic hand. Thereafter, Bernard carved one of his masterpieces in marble, the monumental frieze of *The Dance* (1913).

In 1913, he suffered a stroke, and would not resume his work as a sculptor until 1918. The Exposition Internationale des Arts Décoratifs in Paris (1925) highlighted the quality of a number of his works (including an enlarged version of *The Dance* frieze and his bronze sculptures in the Pavillon de Ruhlmann). Since 1921 he had been living in Boulogne-sur-Seine, modeling his very last works and producing a large number of drawings.

Joseph Bernard admired Puvis de Chavannes, as his son, Jean Bernard, wrote in his memoirs. Evidence of this is to be seen in his sculpture and drawings which reflect his return to classicism and his evocation of an idyllic antiquity with synthetic, fluid forms and modeled calm. While exhibiting at the shows of the *Douce France* group, Joseph Bernard remained a solitary figure and did not have any pupils. However, his influence was important not only at a stylistic but also at a technical level (with his rediscovery of the importance of carving directly into the stone).
P.G.G.

Pierre Bonnard
(Fontenay-aux-Roses, 1867—Le Cannet, 1947)

In 1888, one year before he took his degree in law, Bonnard was admitted to the Ecole des Beaux-Arts and also joined the Académie Julian, where he met Sérusier, Ibels, Ranson and Denis—encounters that were at the origins of the Nabi group, with which Bonnard would exhibit from 1891 at Le Barc de Boutteville (the year in which his poster for *France-Champagne* made him renowned). Nicknamed the "Japanese Nabi" because of the similarity between his own works and Japanese prints, Bonnard collaborated with his friends on a number of decorative art projects (glass designs for Bing, furniture, textiles), as well as working on Lugné-Poe's theater designs and (from 1895 onward) producing lithographs for Vollard—for whom he would also illustrate various important books after 1900 (Verlaine's *Parallèlement* in 1900, Longus's *Daphnis et Chloé* in 1902). Parisian life itself was a special theme in both his paintings and his engravings (*Some aspects of Life in Paris*, 1899). His sense of humor and subversive wit (in 1896 he collaborated in the creation of Jarry's *Ubu Roi*, also illustrating other works by the writer) would eventually distance him from Denis, Sérusier and Ranson, whose interest in theoretical questions he did not share. After his first one-man show at Durand-Ruel in 1896, his career—from 1906 onward—flourished thanks to the Galerie Bernheim-Jeune, where he exhibited regularly, and to a number of important private commissions (Misia Edwards in 1906–10; the Muscovite Ivan Morosov in 1910–12, the Bernheim-Jeunes in 1916–20, the Hahnlosers of Winterthur in 1917). Traveling throughout Europe and in North Africa, he eventually acquired a second home in Normandy (1912) and spent various winters in Arcachon. From 1904 onward, he made increasingly frequent trips to the south of France, which ultimately led to his sharing his time between Paris, Deauville and Le Cannet, where he bought the villa "Le Bosquet" in 1926. These new environments contributed to a change in his style, which was now characterized by a flourishing and sumptuously-colored lyricism and a frequent preference for large-scale works. The urban themes that had been predominant earlier in his career now gave way to landscapes, interiors, nudes and an important series of self-portraits.

Bonnard was apparently quite far from Puvis, given the satirical spirit of his painting and his taste for scenes of Parisian life; however, like all his Nabi friends, he, too, came under the sway of the decorative aspect of Puvis's work, and these were the principles he revived in his important decorative works after 1900.
J.P.B.

Viktor (Yel'pidiforovich) Borisov-Musatov
(Saratov, 1870—Tarusa, 1905)

A painter of landscapes, portraits and narrative scenes, Borisov-Musatov was the son of a railway employee. In his early childhood (1873) a chest fell on him, causing a lesion in his spinal column that would lead to a chronic condition of inflammation which eventually left him hunchbacked. This infirmity undoubtedly affected the artist's personality, making him an introverted character who lived in his own fantasy world, a lover of solitude and intense concentrated application to his work. In 1884 Borisov-Musatov started studying painting and drawing under V.V. Konovalov at the Saratov Association of the Lovers of Fine Arts. In 1890–91 and 1893–95 he also studied under V.D. Polenov at the Moscow School of Painting, Sculpture and Architecture. In 1891–93 he frequented P.P. Chistyakov's studio at the Imperial Academy of Fine Arts in Saint Petersburg. In 1895 he went to Paris with the intention of becoming a pupil of Puvis de Chavannes; but the by then aged artist did not accept him. Up to 1898 he worked in the studio of Fernand Cormon (whose real name was Fernand Piestre, 1845–1924). Having returned to Russia, he exhibited his works at the Moscow Society of Painters and the Union of Russian Artists. Borisov-Musatov's art had a significant influence on the "second wave" of Symbolism in painting, though its value was only truly appreciated after the artist's early death. In 1906, at the annual show of the review *Mir Iskusstva* (Russian World of Art) organized in Saint Petersburg by Serge Diaghilev, an entire room was dedicated to his work. In that same year, the paintings in the exhibition of Russian art at the Paris Salon d'Automne aroused great critical interest and received good reviews in newspapers and magazines. A large posthumous exhibition of his work was held in Moscow in 1907, and in Saint Petersburg the following year. The mature phase of Borisov-Musatov's work reveals the undoubted influence of Puvis de Chavannes. Initially, the artist had been drawn to Impressionism, but his encounter with the art of Puvis led him to adopt a more synthetic style of painting, dedicating himself to the production of decorative panels, which reflected the modern style of the period. One can also detect a certain parallel with the work of Puvis de Chavannes in the metaphors he used and in the emotional atmosphere of his paintings, whose idyllic air is tempered with sadness and lucid melancholy.
P.Y.K.

Emile-Antoine Bourdelle
(Montauban, 1861—Le Vésinet, 1929)

This French sculptor soon distinguished himself for his talents as draftsman. At the age of ten he was already modeling from plaster copies of the works of classical antiquity, studying under a photographer-teacher at the local

drawing school; soon after, he was learning the art of wood carving in the cabinet-maker's workshop that he had entered as an apprentice at the age of thirteen. In 1876 he passed the entrance exam to the Toulouse Ecole des Beaux-Arts, and then in 1884 won entrance to the Paris Ecole Nationale des Beaux-Arts; the teaching he followed was academic, but by 1886–88 he was already breaking out in his own direction. His first college works were much influenced by Michelangelo and the Florentine Mannerists, then would come under the influence of Alexandre Falguière's naturalism (Bourdelle frequented his study as well as following courses at the Ecole); by the early 1890s, the sculptor's style had become more synthetic and "idéiste." Frequenting Symbolist poets and writers—such as Moréas and Verlaine—he decided to take for his own Mallarmé's motto: "suggest rather than say." For a time close to the occult movements of the 1890s, he would—together with Khnopff, Minne, Niederhäusern-Rodo and Toorop—take part in the first events of the Ordre de la Rose+Croix in 1892 and 1893. He was also interested in the decorative arts and studied ceramics, following in the footsteps of Gauguin (whose fired stoneware he had seen at Boussod, Valadon & Cie). In 1894 he met Rodin, remaining his assistant until 1907–08. His collaboration with this artist would have a profound effect, and remained dominant until around 1900; thereafter, in an attempt to break out on his own, Bourdelle adopted a sort of proto-Expressionism which led him to break down forms in a style that seems to herald Fauvism (an approach that can be seen both in his sculptural works and in the photography which he had practiced as an independent art form since 1898).
Applying the theories put forward by the Polish critic Mécislas Golberg, whom he frequented regularly at the turn of the century, he would lay the bases for a dissident aesthetics inspired by the work of Cézanne. This comprised an archaic simplification of forms, a tendency to synthesis and a rejection of the classical canons perfectly exemplified by his 1906 *Heracles Archer*, first exhibited in 1910. The teacher of Giacometti and Germaine Richier, Bourdelle would also, in an indirect fashion, be one of the teachers of Matisse, who in the years 1900–01 frequented the sculptor's studio and

absorbed his notions of a purely formal sculpture that eschewed the narrative and the figurative.
C.G.

Massimo Campigli (Max Hilenfeld)
(Berlin, 1895—Saint-Tropez, 1971)

Max Hilenfeld was brought up between Florence and Milan after the family moved to Italy in 1904. In 1914 he was hired by the newspaper *Corriere della Sera* and frequented the Milanese Futurist circles: he became close to Boccioni and Carrà, publishing pieces in *Lacerba* under the pen name Massimo Campigli, and using that name when he volunteered in 1915. After capture and imprisonment, he escaped and returned to Italy where he obtained citizenship (1918). In 1919 he settled in Paris as a correspondent for *Corriere della Sera*. "My life project undoubtedly materialized during my first years of Parisian life," he claimed, "the Ecole de Paris amazed me." In the city of the *Esprit nouveau*, he became interested in painting, spending time with the Italians of the Café du Dôme (de Chirico, De Pisis, Paresce, Savinio, Severini, Tozzi), with whom he formed the *Groupe des Sept*, in connection with *Novecento Italiano* in 1926.
He was a regular museum visitor, "on close, everyday terms with the giants of art" and Egyptian art, discovered Seurat and the timeless immutability of the *Grande Jatte* ("the great love of my life"), to whom he paid a tribute in 1954. In the wake of Cubism he found a response to his own painting's need for order: he was inspired by Léger's geometries and Gris's rigorous Purism. In 1921 he exhibited in the Salon d'Automne and in 1926 in the *Prima Mostra del Novecento Italiano* in Milan.
In 1927 he resigned from the newspaper, and fell in love with Etruscan art in Rome the following year: he gave up his earlier Casorati-style architectural decorations and adopted single-plane backgrounds, where he placed his silent, pre-Hellenic women (De Grada). His one-man show at the Galerie Bucher in Paris was a success, and he was invited to the Venice Biennale.
In 1931 he settled in Milan; he joined Margherita Sarfatti's circle and Giò Ponti, who urged him to apply painting to architecture: he signed the *Manifesto della pittura murale* with Carrà, Funi and Sironi, and executed the frescoes for the Salone delle Cerimonie of the V Triennale in Rome (1933), for the

Hall of Nations in Geneva (1937), for the Law Court of Milan and the Liviano in Padua (1939–40). In these paintings, the classicizing composition acquired further distinction: in works such as *The Sailors' Brides* (1934) the female figures become modules, "permutable cells" (Piceni), rhythmically articulating the perfect balance of the composition.
He returned to Paris in 1946, and the following year an entire room was devoted to him in the Venice Biennale; his graphic production in those years was extensive. In 1955 he took part in the São Paulo of Brazil Biennale, and after 1958 lived in Saint-Tropez. He became interested in tribal sculpture, and in his paintings reduced physiognomies to conventional, archetypal signs. Major retrospectives were devoted to him by the Stedelijk Museum of Amsterdam (1946) and the Palazzo Reale in Milan (1967).
I.P.

Carlo Carrà
(Quargnento, 1881—Milan, 1966)

Carlo Carrà, attracted to drawing since his childhood, moved to Milan in 1895 to work with a decorator and visited museums and galleries, enthralled by Segantini's painting. He went to Paris in 1899 to decorate several of the World Fair pavilions: he discovered Delacroix, Géricault, Manet, Courbet, Millet and Impressionism, that aroused in him a "truly intense emotion." In London in 1900 he mixed with the anarchist political circles, and was carried away by "Phidias's admirable Parcae" in the British Museum, and by Constable and Turner. In Milan he wrote for leftist magazines, attended the Castello Sforzesco Applied Arts school, and as of 1906 the Brera Academy; he met Romani, Russolo, Boccioni, and in 1910 Marinetti. He joined up with Futurism and was one of the signatories of the *Manifesto dei pittori futuristi* (1910): his early Divisionism became a solid pictorial language of balanced masses and volumes, leaning toward the art of Cézanne and the Cubism of Picasso and Braque, whom he had met, as well as Apollinaire, in 1911–12 in Paris, where he successfully participated in the Futurist exhibition at the Galerie Bernheim-Jeune. In 1914 he developed a "formal asceticism," expressed in his collages and his recent interest in the art of Giotto and Paolo Uccello, that induced him to return to concrete forms, immobility, a

blending of art and tradition leading up to the Metaphysics of the years 1916–20.
Drafted in 1917, in Ferrara he met de Chirico, De Pisis and Savinio and, back in Milan, collaborated with *Valori Plastici* in 1919.
A further simplification of the image heralded the period of Magic Realism (Frank Roh) implying a rejection of intellectual notions, in a coherent relationship with nature (1920–30), which in the 1940s would develop into a synthetic spatial articulation: his own aesthetics can be observed from the silent "everyday mythology" (Guzzi) of *Summer* (1930), marked by a formal simplification shared by *Swimmers* (1932), to the frigid stillness of the *Boy on Horse* (1937), permeated with classical undertones.
In 1922 he became friends with Ungaretti and Rosso, and after 1926 spent much of his time at Forte dei Marmi, perfecting his landscape painting. He took part in the Venice Biennales of 1922, 1926 and in 1928 with his first one-man show, and in several Rome Quadriennali (1931); he exhibited at the Galleria Il Milione (1935) and in 1938 executed two frescoes for the Milan Law Court. In 1941 he began teaching at the Brera Academy. Major retrospectives were held in Milan at the Pinacoteca di Brera (1942) and Palazzo Reale (1962).
I.P.

Frederick Cayley Robinson
(Brentford, 1862—London, 1927)

Cayley Robinson was trained at Saint John's Wood School of Art, and then at the Royal Academy Schools. From 1891 to 1894, he studied at the Académie Julian in Paris under Bouguereau and Ferrier. Here he absorbed the other students' admiration of Puvis de Chavannes, and of Gauguin and Japanese art. He was also able to absorb Puvis's decorations and these clearly were a life-long source of inspiration for him. Cayley Robinson rejected his initial adoption of Newlyn naturalism, and from now on devoted himself to mood and symbolic expression. He returned to live in Paris from 1902 to 1906. The years 1898 to 1902 had been passed in Florence, and he studied the work of Giotto, Mantegna and Michelangelo, and developed a great interest in the possibilities of working in tempera. Much of his work after 1901 was in this medium, or more precisely, in different materials with which he experimented to mimic its effects.

Youth is a good example of this wide-ranging technical experimentation, using combinations of charcoal, watercolor, gouache, pastel, oil and pencil on a gesso ground. As well making easel paintings, Cayley Robinson illustrated books, designed the costumes and sets for the first British production of Maurice Maeterlinck's Symbolist play *The Blue Bird*, and was commissioned to make murals for the Dublin Art Gallery and the Middlesex Hospital. Among the major achievements of British decorative painting, these are pervaded with his memories of Puvis's schemes, albeit expressed in a distinctly characteristic and personal idiom.

Cayley Robinson's pictures invariably express a richly Symbolist ethos. But as with Puvis, meaning is usually reserved or implicit, creating an aura of mystery and ambiguity. In *Youth* the principal nude figure represents Youth, stretching as he wakes into life. He serves also as a metaphor for Spring, for tiny leaves have appeared on the trees in this barren landscape. However, the waning moon above suggests the fleeting briefness of youth and, by implication, man's time on earth. The ravens, traditional emblems of death and malefaction, strike a still darker note. Below them figures in the background lever away a boulder from the mouth of a cave, which recalls Christ's tomb, and so the picture seems to be an allegory of the cycle of life and death, and the possibility of ultimate rebirth. Cayley Robinson makes comparisons too with the passing of once great civilizations, represented here by the columns sunk into the hillside, which men with shovels appear to be excavating from below. This was a theme found in a number of his works, and was consciously derived from Claude Lorrain. There are a rich diversity of artistic references in this picture, which is a later version of a work of 1907 now in the South African National Gallery, Cape Town. The figure of Youth partly derives from *The Dying Slave* (c. 1513, Paris, Musée du Louvre) by Michelangelo, whom Cayley Robinson revered. But there are also similarities to Rodin's *Age of Bronze* (1875–77), a cast of which he would have seen in the Victoria and Albert Museum, and to Leighton's influential full-length *The Sluggard* (1885), which was originally entitled *An Athlete Awakening from Sleep*. In modified form, Cayley Robinson reused the central figure in *Youth* for Adam in

his frontispiece to an illustrated edition of Genesis published in 1914, reinforcing the symbolic, multilayered context in which the young male of *Youth* should be viewed. The expansive landscape punctuated by figures and a gently curving pool derives from Puvis. A particular source of inspiration was Puvis's *Poor Fisherman* (1881), which Cayley Robinson saw in the Luxembourg. He imitated it most closely in *To Pastures New (Dawn)* (c. 1904, untraced, repr. Stevens 1977, fig. 6), and to a less pronounced extent in works such as *Pastoral* (1923–24, London, Tate Gallery). As in these other works, the draftsmanship and soft coloring of *Youth* also derives from Puvis.
R.U.

(Stanislas Henri) Jean-Charles Cazin
(Samer, 1841—Le Lavandou, 1901)

Jean-Charles Cazin spent his childhood at Boulogne-sur-Mer, near the Equihen cliffs. In Paris, he first studied at Lecoq de Boisbaudran's Ecole de Dessin, then—from 1863 to 1868—was a teacher of Draftsmanship at the Ecole Spéciale d'Architecture headed by Trélat: in that latter year he was appointed as curator of the Tours museum and also as director of the Ecole de Dessin. After the 1870 war he left for Great Britain and then, in 1874, traveled in Italy. After settling in Paris, he exhibited at the Salon from 1876 to 1883. His first picture on the Tobias theme was his *Voyage of Tobias*, exhibited in 1878 (Art Institute of Chicago); but it was with his *Ishmael*, exhibited in 1880 along with his *Tobias and the Angel*, that he would win the gold medal. He fled from success and honors to return to live in the Pas-de-Calais, exhibiting nothing from 1883 to 1888—a period during which he again traveled in Italy and in Flanders. He learned through free study of the Old Masters and the natural world, as well as coming under the influence of his friend Puvis de Chavannes, who visited him in his Equihen retreat.

Cazin painted landscapes of the area around him, peopled with figures going about their daily lives. His works sold both in Paris and abroad, and by 1891 he was dividing his time between the Var region and the Pas-de-Calais, by now painting only landscapes. At his death, Léonce Bénédite rendered homage to him in these words: "Alongside his great friend Puvis de Chavannes, Cazin will, as a history painter, remain one of the

most refined embodiments of contemporary idealism."

Tobias and the Angel illustrates a scene from the journey of Tobias as recounted in the Apocryphal Gospels, which tell of a young man sent off by his dying blind father to recover property in a distant region. The Angel Raphael accompanies the youth, without however revealing his true identity. The moment depicted here shows the Angel talking to Tobias by the pond in which he will catch a fish that will restore his father's sight. Cazin rewrites the whole tale by setting it in the Pas-de-Calais and offering a realist reading of legend. He had a natural predilection for the more humble incidents in Scriptural History, and his elegant rendition of the simple, atemporal gestures of his characters has something of the art of Puvis de Chavannes. The gentle harmony of color and light reinforces the overall impression of calm, at the same time as suggesting the sacred nature of the incident before one's eyes.
M.C.

Paul Cézanne
(Aix-en-Provence, 1839–1906)

Resisting his father's desire that he become a notary, lawyer or banker, Cézanne decided at the age of twenty-one that he would become a painter, and thus abandoned the study of law. He then trained at the Ecole gratuite de Dessin in Aix and the Académie Suisse in Paris, as well as making copies of the works he admired in museums; but this was not enough to enable him to gain admission to the Ecole des Beaux-Arts in Paris (where he took the entrance exam twice). Shy and emotional, he happily held back from engagement with organized artistic groups or movements, preferring the company of his childhood friends to the discussions at the Café Guerbois that brought together Manet and the future Impressionists (just as at the end of his life, he would prefer the visits paid to his Rue des Lauves studio by such young artists as Emile Bernard and Maurice Denis, to the openings of his exhibitions at the Galerie Vollard). He lived a solitary life within a rather limited geographical area: Provence, Paris (to which Emile Zola introduced him in 1861) and such areas around the capital as Pontoise, Auvers-sur-Oise, Médan and the Fontainebleau region. Only once did he travel abroad, visiting Switzerland in the summer of 1890 on a trip organized by his wife.

His artistic career is generally divided into four periods: romantic (his early years), Impressionist (from 1872), constructivist (from 1878 to 1887) and synthetic (from 1888 to 1906). This eventful development led him from a somber style of thick impasto (much influenced by Courbet) to the experience of open-air painting (under the influence of Pissarro); from Naturalism, he moved to an entirely personal artistic language. Shunned by official art circles, he would only gain recognition late in life; but he was admired by other artists, such has Gauguin, Monet and Renoir. Right up until his death (October 23, 1906), Cézanne worked on a fixed number of chosen motifs: rocks, pine trees, the sea at Estaque, the portrait of Hortense Fiquet (whom he married in 1886), the Jas de Bouffan, card-players, still lifes and the Mont Sainte-Victoire. One subject in particular—the bathers—offered a synthesis of his investigation of both landscape and the human figure. The earliest Cézanne works that show a nude figure in a landscape date from the 1860s and comprise depiction of satyrs and nymphs, of bathers and of animated scenes of passion. The pictures of bathers reveal a wide variety in size and in the combinations of characters and poses, going from the solitary figure of a bather to the sophisticated groups of *Large Bathers*, with a marked predilection for unmixed groups of nudes. The actual meaning of these scenes—which occupy an increasingly important place in his oeuvre from the 1870s onward—remains a mystery. His deliberately distanced view of the bathers—perceived through the filters of classical sculpture and Rubens—even makes it difficult to establish their gender. The painter plays upon ambiguity of outline to remove all narration or anecdote from the scene; he concentrates on the purely plastic problem of the inclusion of a figure within a landscape, without however reducing the latter to a mere background decor, as was required by the rules of academic art. With its heavily-structured surface of oblique brushstrokes, *Three Women Bathers* (1876–77), which once belonged to Matisse (who after bequeathed the painting to the Musée de la Ville de Paris, Petit-Palais), reveals the artist's desire to escape from the graceful and the anecdotal; description of individual figures is eschewed in favor of a treatment that turns each bather into an archetype. Had he at this point seen the monumental forms used in Puvis de Chavannes's *Young Women by the Sea* (Paris, Musée d'Orsay), which was exhibited at the 1879 Salon (in spite of the support of his friend Guillement, Cézanne's own submissions to that exhibition had been rejected)? There is no documentary or anecdotal evidence of any link between the two artists. Given that at least once a year Cézanne traveled from Paris to Marseille necessarily changing trains in Lyon, he probably knew the works that Puvis de Chavannes had created for the Musée des Beaux-Arts (just as he probably knew those in Marseille, a city he visited regularly). In the 1870s–80s he painted his first seascapes, showing coastal bays in which the sea forms a surface of dense and luminous paint.

Cézanne also knew the great mural decorations that Puvis de Chavannes had created in Paris, but he found them too narrative: "He likes oratorical painting, the painting of the people, no more than I do. Yes, there is the Galerie des Batailles at Versailles; but he's not really looking at the painting there. He is reading it as a sort of newspaper, a vast mural newspaper, images of Epinal—just like the Saint Genevieve at the Panthéon." Viewing the works at the Sorbonne, he is said to have exclaimed: "What bad literature!" (J. Gasquet, *Cézanne*, Paris, 1921, quoted in P.M. Doran, *Conversations avec Cézanne*, 1978, p. 129)

However, Cézanne and Puvis de Chavannes shared the same affection for calm and serene light, the same Arcadian vision of bathers seen as monumental figures in a landscape unblemished by traces of civilization. They also agreed on the importance of drawing, even if Cézanne would comment that "it is not a question of fashioning a study—which, all in all, is what Puvis de Chavannes does." (M. Denis, "Cézanne," *L'Occident,* September 1907, quoted in Doran, *op. cit.*, p. 171)

The form of his bathers is not defined by a firm line; it is a line that overlaps, breaks off, gets fatter or thinner, imposing a powerful, animated rhythm on the compositions as a whole. With their vibrant outlines and their schematically-rendered faces, the figures in the Pushkin Museum, *Bathing*, and the Musée Granet *Bathers* (which foreshadow *The Large Bathers* painted toward the end of the artist's life) express a vision unshackled by naturalism in

compositions structured through an animated rhythm of brushstrokes. According to Maurice Denis (*ibidem*, p. 173), the intellectual interpretation of the world championed by Puvis de Chavannes, whose mysterious and idealized antiquity conveyed some sort of symbolic message, may well be linked up with Cézanne's own mystical and idealist primitivism: however, this is open to debate, when one considers the declared aims of the latter painter and his attempts to liberate painting through resort to a lyricism of color. "Painting," Cézanne said, " is the recording of colored sensations." (Cézanne to Emile Bernard, *ibidem*, p. 178) In banishing all literature from his art, all striving for similitude or a revelation of the hidden meaning of forms, Cézanne opened the way to Cubism and abstraction. It was lucky, says Camille Mauclair, that Puvis "never knew Cézanne or, above all, suspected what Cézannism was about! What would he have said, he a man of vast poems and harmonious odes, who in his own day already gave the impression of being a wise man in the midst of neurotics?" (C. Mauclair, *Puvis de Chavannes*, Paris, Librairie Plon, 1928, p. 152)

I.C.

Maurice Chabas
(Nantes, 1862—Versailles, 1947)

Maurice Chabas, brother of the portraitist Paul Chabas, trained under Bouguereau and Robert-Fleury at the Académie Julian. His first exhibition was held at the Salon des Artistes Français in 1885, and he would continue to show work there until 1913. His discovery of the work of Puvis de Chavannes influenced both the style and subject matter of his own paintings. He exhibited frequently, most notably at the Salons of the Amis des Beaux-Arts in Nantes (1890 to 1907) and also in various Salons of Christian-inspired art. A sensitive and mystical artist, he adhered to the ideas of Péladan and took part in all the Salons de la Rose+Croix from 1892 to 1897. Still largely academic in technique, his Symbolist works bore titles evoking the mystic ideal he considered necessary for humanity. His fame spread, and in 1895 he held an exhibition at the Galerie des Arts Réunis in Paris. Divisionism provided him with a less classical style for his dream-like landscapes and ethereal skies.

At the same time, Chabas was also

working on a number of large-scale interior decorations: the town halls of Montrouge (1884) and Vincennes (1898) and the station of Lyon-Perrache (1889). From 1900 onward, though still true to a spiritual ideal of art, he began to simplify his style and by the 1920s was painting in a totally abstract style. Member of the Société Nationale des Beaux-Arts from 1913, he strove for an art that would elevate the spirit. He then became a member of the committee of the Salon des Tuileries and of the Salon d'Automne, as well as of the Société Idéaliste and the Société Moderne. *Meditation in a Park* is a fine example of the peopled landscapes that Chabas produced in the 1890s—works in which one can see the influence of Osbert, whom he had met at the Salons de la Rose+Croix. Bathed in calm and serenity, the work brings together features of the classical landscape (the small temple in the background) and Symbolist themes (the white-draped young girl sitting in the park). The landscapes were inspired by the everyday world around the artist: the Lot, the banks of the Loire, the Ile de France. The world depicted recalls those idealized compositions of Puvis de Chavannes; however, Chabas's young girls are not allegories, but rather serve as figures to aid the spectator to enter an atmosphere of meditation. Woman is the indispensable intermediary who accompanies the spectator toward the Ideal.

M.C.

Henri Edmond Cross
(Douai, 1856—Saint-Clair, 1910)

Henri Edmond Delacroix (the artist's original name) was the son of a local ironmonger and an English mother. A gifted draftsman, he studied briefly with Carolus-Duran in Lille in 1866, before entering the city's Ecoles Académiques de Dessin et d'Architecture in 1878. In 1881 he moved to Paris, where he would exhibit regularly at the Salon, until the foundation of the Société des Artistes Indépendants in 1884. It was then that he first met Signac and Seurat; but he would not adopt the Neo-Impressionist technique until 1891, when he exhibited his *Portrait of Madame Cross* (1891, Paris, Musée d'Orsay). The same year he went to live in Cabasson in the south of France, later having a house built at Saint-Clair, where he would live all year round; it was Cross who encouraged Signac to settle not far away, at Saint-Tropez.

In 1893 he painted his *Evening Breeze* (1893, Paris, Musée d'Orsay), in friendly emulation of Signac, who was then undertaking his *In the Time of Harmony*. As Mediterranean as that work, Cross's "Sacred Wood"—with its draped and immobile Muses, its serene arabesques and muted colors—celebrates an ideal Golden Age without any indications of chronology or geography. There is the same air of an atemporal Arcadia in most of the landscapes that he painted over the years to come. *Mediterranean Shores* (1895, Walter F. Brown Collection) depicts an idyllic repast, just as *Evening Breeze* very clearly heralds Matisse's *Luxe, calme et volupté*. Painted in 1896, *Marine Scene with Cypresses* (Geneva, Musée du Petit-Palais) could well be the nocturnal version of this atemporal Eden. Many of the works painted at this time are redolent of the spirit of Puvis de Chavannes; the correspondence between Cross and Signac reveals their admiration for his murals in Lyon and at the Sorbonne. In 1898, the two friends would also visit Marseille, to see Puvis de Chavannes's paintings there. Introverted, sensitive and frail of health, Cross would then take to painting landscapes peopled with increasingly sensual female nudes which are very different from the calm, meditative Muses painted by the Lyonnais artist. At the turn of the century, Cross developed a sort of vividly-colored lyricism, whose non-realistic palette heralds Fauvism.

M.F.B.

William Degouve de Nuncques
(Monthermé, 1867—Stavelot, 1935)

A scion of the French aristocracy, William Degouve de Nuncques at an early age retreated into a world of reverie and introspection. Aside from a brief period at the Brussels Académie des Beaux-Arts, he was a largely self-taught artist who, from 1892 to 1900, developed a Symbolist oeuvre that mixed together the dream-like and the fantastic, the strange and the surreal. Art, literature, philosophy, science and music are all woven together in this ideal world, which developed outside the real world from which Degouve de Nuncques had totally distanced himself. Having become the brother-in-law of the poet Emile Verhaeren in 1894, the painter found himself introduced to Symbolist circles in Belgium and France. During a trip to Paris in the early 1890s, Degouve

de Nuncques met Rodin, Fritz Thaulow, Maurice Denis and Puvis de Chavannes, whose air of muted melancholy appealed to him. Allegory now became part of his approach to Symbolism, in works characterized by the suspension of time and the theatrical rendition of space as a locus of meditation, by a striving to break free of history and a yearning for poetic fiction. Having both learned from—and been encouraged by—Puvis de Chavannes, Degouve brought together meditation with a subjugation of individuality. For all that he and Puvis de Chavannes had in common, Degouve's work is particular in its—almost total—rejection of the human figure. With its broken windows, damp facades and calm waters (on the surface of which floats an abandoned boat), *The Canal* (1894, Otterlo, Rijksmuseum Kröller-Müller)—painted in 1894 and exhibited that same year at the first Salon of La Libre Esthétique—bears witness to an air of desolation and desertion, which is very different from the calm nobility and serenity seen in the works of Puvis de Chavannes. His numerous travels—from Bruges to Venice, Majorca, Germany and Switzerland—offer us a picture of Degouve de Nuncques as an individual wandering amid a hostile universe, whose "disturbing strangeness" is both revealed and assuaged in images.
M.D.

Maurice Denis
(Granville, 1870—Paris, 1943)

Born in Normandy, Denis lived in Saint-Germain-en-Laye near Paris. At the Lycée Condorcet he met Vuillard and Roussel, and his artistic background was formed by visits to the Louvre, where Fra Angelico revealed to him his vocation as a Christian painter—a revelation further confirmed by the discovery of Puvis de Chavannes in 1887, the meeting with Sérusier at the Académie Julian in 1888 and his first sight of Gauguin's work in 1889. This would be the origin of the Nabi movement, of which Denis's 1890 "Définition du néo-traditionnisme" is a veritable manifesto (it opens with the famous sentence: "It is well to remember that a picture before being a battle horse, a nude woman, or some anecdote, is essentially a flat surface covered with colors assembled in a certain order."). After his marriage to Marthe Meurier in 1893, his honeymoon to Perros-Guirec would

mark the beginning of close relations with the Brittany area (in 1908 he bought the villa "Silencio" there); however, his "second country" was Italy, which he visited a total of ten times (starting in May 1895). A period in Rome in 1898 marked the beginning of a more ambitious, classically-inspired phase in his work, which culminated with the decoration of the cupola at the Théâtre des Champs-Elysées in 1913. He published important theoretical writings, most notably on Maillol (1905) and Cézanne (1907), outlining the principles of a "new classicism" which would then be taken up in his book of 1912, *Théories*, and in his lessons at the Académie Ranson from 1909 to 1919. Numerous sales and commissions in France, Germany and Russia, together with his exhibitions at the Galerie Druet in Paris (from 1904 onward), guaranteed his international success. The peak of his social standing is marked by his purchase of the house "Le Prieuré" in Saint-Germain-en-Laye in 1914 (the building is now the Musée Maurice Denis). The war and the death of Marthe confirmed his commitment to Christian art; in 1919 he and George Desvallières founded the Ateliers d'art sacré, and in 1922 Denis published his *Nouvelles théories*. A large part of his work was dedicated to the adornment of churches, including the Chapel at Le Prieuré (1915–25). His status was further confirmed by his exhibition at the 1922 Venice Biennale, a large retrospective in Paris in 1924 and his election to the Institut in 1932; in the meantime he continued to publish numerous articles and books, including a *Histoire de l'art religieux* (1939). As well as a prolific output as a painter (more than two thousand paintings and around thirty mural decorations), he also worked in the decorative arts (fans and lamp shades, *papiers peints*, furniture, glass, vases) and illustrated various books (Verlaine's *Sagesse* in 1911, André Gide's *Le Voyage d'Urien* in 1893, the *Imitation of Christ* in 1903, *La Vita Nova* in 1907 and *I Fioretti* in 1913).
J.P.B.

André Derain
(Chatou, 1880—Garches, 1954)

Born in Chatou on the outskirts of Paris, André Derain began attending the Académie Camillo in Paris in 1898; there he received comments on his work from Eugène Carrière, a friend of Puvis de

Chavannes, and also met Matisse—an encounter that was to prove decisive for his future as an artist (another equally decisive encounter was that which occurred, on a train in 1900, with Maurice Vlaminck). Self-taught, Derain was a passionate visitor of museums who also fuelled his thoughts upon aesthetics with voracious reading (Zola, Nietzsche, etc.). The key influence of Van Gogh (whose work he discovered in 1901) went together with that of the Neo-Impressionists and, above all, of Cézanne. In 1905 he spent the summer with Matisse at Collioure, confirming his position as one of the important figures in the Fauves group. During two periods in London (1906 and 1907) he was overwhelmed by primitive art, and—in close conjunction with Matisse—continued his investigation of the relation between art-as-decoration and art-as-expression. He was interested in the decorative arts (ceramics, wooden bas-reliefs) and sculpture, producing large panels on the themes of the Golden Age, dance, and female bathers, as well as subjects that echo some of Puvis's great works. From 1908 onward, he drew closer to the art of Picasso, with whom he traveled to Barcelona in 1910. His painting became more somber, and a so-called "Byzantine" period began in 1911, characterized by a sharply reduced palette range and a hieratic simplicity of line. Around this time he began to obtain international recognition, especially in Germany and Russia. In 1915 he was sent to the front, and was not demobilized until 1919. Then he received some commissions for large-scale decorative works (decors and sets for the Ballets Russes and for the Comte de Beaumont, the decoration of Walter Halvorsen's dining room, etc.). During the 1920s his painting contained more and more references to classical French painting. Enjoying increasing success, he moved to Chambourcy, not far from Paris, in 1935. Between 1938 and 1945 he worked on a large composition on the theme of the Golden Age, mixing together a certain primitivism with allusions to the aesthetics of the Italian Renaissance. Overall, the period of World War II was a bleak one for him, and he was criticized for being one of the French artists to visit Germany as part of a trip organized by the occupying forces in 1941. His bouts of depression, which had accompanied him throughout his life, became more sever in older age.

However, after the war he would produce a number of important decorations and sets for theater and opera.
R.L.

Marcel Duchamp
(Blainville, 1887—Neuilly-sur-Seine, 1968)

Marcel Duchamp's first works were those of an artist open to the influence of Impressionist aesthetics. However, from 1910 onward he began to abandon the ideal of visual objectivity which was championed by the main representatives of that movement. Denigrating what he called "retinal" art, he strove to introduce cerebral and intellectual concerns into art—most notably by the choice of subject matter. Hence, without totally abandoning what he had acquired from the Impressionist style, his work, on a chromatic plane in particular, began to embody some of the same esoteric concerns as that of the Symbolists and opened to other influences, such as Puvis for example. This new turn in his art is represented by the two female nudes of the painting *The Bush* (1910–11). To the right of the picture stands a mature woman of rubicund flesh and florid form. With her right hand she indicates, kneeling at her feet, a young woman who is both slimmer and paler of flesh. The title of a painting dating from the same time (the *Baptism* of 1911, Philadelphia Museum of Art) confirms the impression that this is some sort of initiation or rite of passage. But what sort of passage? No doubt the sort that Duchamp's own sister Suzanne went through in 1911, when she married a pharmacist from Rouen. It was to commemorate this wedding that the artist produced the picture *Spring or Young Man and Young Woman in Spring*, which very appropriately shows Adam and Eve tasting the fruit of the Forbidden Tree. His treatment of the subject is not entirely orthodox (for example, the lightly-sketched nude dancers enlivening the background landscape), but the work is clearly linked with another painting of around the same time which is identified as a vision of Eden (*Heaven*, 1910–11, same collection). Knowing the themes that constantly returned in Duchamp's later work, one might see *Bush* and the related pictures as already dealing with the rite of passage from the status of *virgin* to *married woman*. In short, they are concerned with that awakening of sexual desire which

511

would be a leitmotif of Duchamp's work from *The Bride* (1912, same collection) to that masterly summary of the whole theme in his masterpiece *The Bride Stripped Bare by her Bachelors, Even* (1915–23, same collection).
A.P.

Magnus Enckell
(Hamina, 1870—Stockholm, 1925)

Magnus Enckell was the first Finnish artist to break definitively with the naturalistic ideals of the period 1889–91, which he had spent as a student in Helsinki. In 1891 he went to Paris, and it was especially the influence of Puvis de Chavannes that made Enckell move away from Naturalism and closer to the seriousness and intimacy of Symbolism. He showed a keen interest in the spiritual movements of the time, in literature and music, and was to pave the way for and supervise the work of his comrades, the artists Ellen Thesleff and Beda Stjernschantz.
Upon arrival in Paris, Enckell enrolled at the Académie Julian. It was, however, particularly the meeting with the works of Puvis de Chavannes and Sâr Joséphin Péladan's idealist and mystical perception of art that came to influence his development. Enckell joined Péladan in his enthusiasm for the masters of the High Renaissance and introduced Péladan's ideal of beauty—the androgynous youth—as the primary motif of his pictures. This tendency is especially pronounced in a series of pictures of young boys from the years 1892–94, as in the painting *Waking Up* from 1893, in which the young man personifies Enckell's view of the existentialist-philosophical considerations concerning human knowledge and consciousness. Technically he combines a Puvisesque color asceticism with a compositional stringency and a transparency that resembles that of watercolors, in the attempt to attain a spiritual style. After 1900, Enckell began to take an interest in the light and color-saturated paintings of Post-Impressionism. He soon became a central figure among the artists who were striving for a change of style within the trend-setting parts of the Finnish art scene.
The Golden Age from 1904, a lunette painting for the library of the University of Helsinki, is a draft for Enckell's first work within the genre of monumental decorations and was executed in connection with this new orientation. It thus contains both the monumental simplicity and spirituality of the earlier works, but also a major colorist scope, which foreshadows the later brightly colored, almost vitalist, pictures of bathers.
In 1912, together with Verner Thomé and Ellen Thesleff, among others, Enckell founded the exhibition group *Septem* for artists who shared their views on painting.
P.N.L.

Akseli Gallen-Kallela
(Pori, 1865—Stockholm, 1931)

Axel Gallén, who changed his name to Akseli Gallen-Kallela in 1907, began his art studies in Helsinki in 1881. In the autumn of 1884 he went to Paris, where he stayed until 1889 and was taught first at the Académie Julian and then in Fernand Cormon's studio. Gallen-Kallela took his point of departure in Realist open-air painting, on a par with Jules Bastien-Lepage, and he remained faithful to the technical qualities of Realism, even though his Parisian sojourns in the early 1890s brought him into contact with strong Symbolist tendencies. Secluded in Karelia, the eastern border area of Finland, Gallen-Kallela devoted himself to a fascination with Finnish nature and mythology, especially the *Kalevala* epic, and he pioneered the artistic reawakening of the nationalist movement of Karelianism. He was eventually forced to recognize that Realism did not suffice to reproduce the spiritual, Ur-Finnish moods in painting, and consequently in the mid-1890s he approached a decorative style which was more focused on large color surfaces and pictorial stylization. From the mid-1890s Gallen-Kallela expanded his artistic work, now embracing also graphics, monumental mural decorations and applied art: textiles, furniture, metal work and stained-glass painting. He traveled extensively in Europe in order to gather inspiration and technical knowledge and participated in several exhibitions. He established good contacts in Germany after having exhibited in Berlin in 1895 together with Edvard Munch, an exhibition that attracted much attention. In 1907 he was admitted to the artist group Die Brücke. Later, he looked beyond Europe for innovation; in 1909–10 he traveled in East Africa, and in the 1920s he spent several years in the United States.
When the Finnish businessman F.A. Jusélius lost his only child in 1898, an eleven-year-old daughter by the name of Sigrid, he constructed a mausoleum for her in Pori. Gallen-Kallela competed with Väinö Blomstedt and Pekka Halonen for the project and was commissioned to decorate the walls and the ceiling of the central room with frescoes in 1901. The project included six frescoes on the walls, and became Gallen-Kallela's most extensive work: *Spring* and *Autumn* are the final sketches for the cycle of life which was to be realized on the walls in Pori. Having received the commission, Gallen-Kallela took up residence close to the town, near the Bothnian Bay. The coastline in *Autumn*, which is illuminated and full-drawn by the snow, is indebted to this view.
P.N.L.

Paul Gauguin
(Paris, 1848—Atuona, Marquesas Islands, 1903)

A stockbroker, Gauguin started out as an amateur painter with Pissarro and frequented the free courses at the Académie Colarossi. In 1879 he began exhibiting with the Impressionists, whose work he was already collecting. Thereafter, he soon abandoned his job to dedicate himself to his art, gradually distancing himself from his friends—of whom he would later say: "they search around the eye but not at the mysterious center of thought." Gauguin was interested in all forms of artistic expression, and he particularly admired Puvis de Chavannes, who exerted a clear influence on his work (for all that Gauguin may have tried to defend himself against it, given that his aim to rethink nature and search out the essential). At Pont-Aven during the summer of 1888, he painted a series of nudes, including *Young Bretons Bathing*, whose carefully-studied simplification suggests some parallels with *Rest*.
During his first stay in Tahiti, Gauguin painted stories from Tahitian legends as well as scenes of everyday life such as *Tee raau rahi*, a bucolic depiction of native villagers composed to form a sort of frieze. In 1893, ill-health forced Gauguin to return to France, but he still yearned for the calm life of the Tropics. In 1896 he undertook works that were more ambitions, both in theme and size, and in some way measured himself against the large-scale decorations produced by Puvis de Chavannes. *Nave Nave Mahana* is the first of a cycle of majestic works that would end with a somber reflection on life and death *Where Do We Come from?*

What Are We? Where Are We Going? (Boston, Museum of Fine Arts). After a period of crisis and doubt, Gauguin painted *Faa iheihe* (1898, London, Tate Gallery), which marked the start of a new, more peaceful period in his work. This soft-colored pastoral was the first of a cycle of works in which he focused on certain isolated figures from his large paintings—as in the *Teavae no Maria*. During the same period, he painted other works in "close-up"—for example, the *Three Tahitian Women*—revealing a classical vein and refinement that are reminiscent of Puvis de Chavannes. Historians have compared the young girl with the flowers with the figures in the earlier artist's *Young Women by the Sea*, whilst the nude figures seen from the back recall various figures in de Chavannes's mural decorations. In 1901, Gauguin left Tahiti for the Marquesas Islands, settling in Atuona, where he named his tropical studio "La Maison du Jouir."
M.N.

Giovanni Giacometti
(Stampa, canton Grisons, 1868—Glion, canton Vaud, 1933)

Like his colleague and friend Cuno Amiet, Giovanni Giacometti made a lifelong attempt to combine French painting with German Expressionism. His work has both Fauvist and Expressionist traits, but also bears clear signs of Italian influences, especially in the early stage of his artistic development. After studying for a year in Munich, in 1888 the twenty-year-old Giacometti lived for three years in Paris, where he continued his training at the Académie Julian. In 1893 he spent the summer in Rome, where he became acquainted with the *en plein air* works of the Macchiaioli. Shortly after settling permanently in his native land—the Val Bregaglia, between Northern Italy and the upper valley of the Inn in Switzerland—he became friends with Giovanni Segantini, ten years his senior, who had moved to Maloja in 1894. Not only did Segantini open Giacometti's eyes to the beauty of his native mountains, he also introduced him to the principles of Divisionism. After Segantini's sudden death in 1899, Giacometti followed the teachings of Ferdinand Hodler, fifteen years his senior, from whom he learned to use form and color to produce a rigoros, decorative ordering of the surfaces in his canvases.
From 1906 onward, Giacometti

exhibited frequently in both Switzerland and Germany. In 1908 he was invited by the artists of Die Brücke to take part in an Expressionist exhibition in Dresden, but between 1909 and 1912 he also showed his work in Munich, Jena, Düsseldorf and Cologne. After Hodler"s death in 1918 both Giacometti and his friend Amiet began to play an important role in cultural politics in Switzerland.

The large painting shown in this exhibition comes across as an enthusiastic hymn to southern light. Since the children playing in the bright woodland are depicted entirely naked, the scene conveys an almost paradisiacal effect. The children are Giacometti's own offspring; the first from the right is the nine-year-old Alberto, later to reach international fame as a sculptor.
R.K.

Albert Gleizes
(Paris, 1881—Avignon, 1953)

Self-taught, Albert Gleizes began painting around 1901. A landscape artist of the Seine area, he at first appeared as a late adherent of Impressionism. Attracted by literature and theater, he—together with a group of Symbolist writers and friends—would in 1906 found the small literary colony known as L'Abbaye de Créteil. Though this experiment did not last long, it drew the artist toward drawing and book illustration. From 1909–10 onward, Gleizes—largely under the influence of the painter Henri Le Fauconnier—adopted a more synthetic style when rendering the essential forms of his landscapes and his first portraits—a first step toward breaking-down form altogether into multiple facets. In the Paris studio of Le Fauconnier, Gleizes regularly met Jean Metzinger, Robert Delaunay and Fernand Léger. Together with them, he would take part in the scandalous exhibition of Cubist works at the 1911 Salon des Indépendants, showing his *Woman with Phlox* (Houston, The Museum of Fine Art) and a male nude (whereabouts unknown).

The ambitious composition *The Bathers* (1912), which was exhibited at the Salon des Indépendants the following year, confirms an interest in nude and allegory shared by Gleizes and his friends; for example, at that same 1912 Salon, Delaunay exhibited his version of the Three Graces, the large painting entitled *The City of Paris*.

Gleizes shows his bathers in a suburban landscape which has already been affected by the rapid industrialization of the period (see, for example, the number of smoking chimney stacks that appear in the works of the Cubists). Apparently belonging to an age that is now threatened with extinction, the figures clearly draw on the works of Poussin as filtered through Cézanne's *Bathers*. As in the large-scale compositions of Puvis de Chavannes, there is harmonious integration between the figures and the landscape, between the real and the ideal. In the very period in which he was working with Jean Metzinger on *Du Cubisme*, the first theoretical discussion of the movement, Gleizes seems primarily to be striving to reconcile classically-inspired themes and Cubist treatment.
C.B.

Vilhelm Hammershøi
(Copenhagen, 1864–1916)

Vilhelm Hammershøi first presented his work to the public in Copenhagen in 1885. He was interested in the new artistic tendencies of the period, as well as in older art, mainly Dutch seventeenth-century painting, which he went to see on his first journey abroad, a journey that in 1887 took him to Holland and Belgium. In Hammershøi's oeuvre the realist motifs of the Danish Golden Age meet with the classical Greek ideals of form, which he studied at the Louvre and during several trips to Italy. It was primarily during his visits to Paris, the first of which took place in 1889, another in 1891–92, that he familiarized himself with the international trends of the time. On both occasions he had ample opportunity to study the art of Puvis de Chavannes. Hammershøi principally produced interior scenes, as well as architecture and landscape paintings, his motifs including his home, his mother and wife, and the houses and squares in Copenhagen, depicted in stringent formalist compositions.

His favorite motif was the bourgeois interior, often Hammershøi's own rooms, as is the case of *Interior. Strandgade 30* (1906), now at the Tate Gallery. With a characteristic scale of grays Hammershøi created his own particular universe: a world that was at once intimate and domestic, but at the same time disquieting and indefinite, at times even sinister. The picture was originally broader and included the

figure of a woman, standing between the table and the wall to the left. The first owner of the painting, the British pianist Leonard Borwick, reduced the left-hand side by bending the canvas and giving it its present format.

Together with a subsequently darkened representation of *Job*, *Artemis* (1893–94) is Hammershøi's only attempt within the genre of historical paintings. Scholars have been mostly interested in finding Hammershøi's models in past art, paying little attention to contemporary connections, such as a link to Puvis de Chavannes. It has been shown that Hammershøi employed figural elements from Masaccio's and Masolino's frescoes in the Chiesa del Carmine, Florence. Less convincingly, works by Perugino and Signorelli have been mentioned as possible references. Hammershøi found great appreciation abroad. In the 1890s, Théodore Duret advocated him warmly; later he was to count figures such as Serge Diaghilev, Rainer Maria Rilke, Auguste Renoir and Leonard Borwick among his admirers. During his lifetime he exhibited in France, Germany, England, Italy and once in the United States.
P.N.L.

Louis Welden Hawkins
(Esslingen, 1849—Paris, 1910)

Destined for a military career, Hawkins left the United Kingdom in 1873 to enter the Académie Julian in Paris, later entering the Ecole des Beaux-Arts (where his teachers were William Bouguereau, Gustave Boulanger and Jules Lefèbvre). In 1881 he traveled across France to Barbizon in Brittany. He exhibited works of rural inspiration at the Salon des Artistes Français from 1881 to 1891. His first submission *The Orphans* (now in Pouyastruc, Haute-Pyrénées) won a medal. Upon meeting Puvis de Chavannes, he applied to be his pupil; but though he recognized the young man's talent, Puvis refused. From 1892 onward, Hawkins preferred to exhibit in various Salons: the Salon des Indépendants, the Société Nationale des Beaux-Arts, the Salon des Rose+Croix and La Libre Esthétique. He began exhibiting more modern works, which revealed his affinities with the Symbolist movement in literature. His smooth and detailed technique was employed in works whose subject matter was very close to that of the Pre-Raphaelites. In 1899,

given that he was no longer enjoying much success on the British market, he tried in vain to get his pictures bought by the French state. To the end of his life, he lived thanks to commissions for society portraits and his income as a contributor to *L'Oeuvre d'Art International*. He also produced a number of Art Nouveau style masks, reflecting the obsessions of such fin de siècle writers as Jean Lorrain, who would dedicate various short stories to the artist.

His work shows either pensive or mischievous female figures in scenes that provoke introspection. The finish is very classical, but the line betrays the influence of Puvis de Chavannes.

The Procession of Souls bears witness to Hawkins's conversion to Symbolism in the early 1890s. The influence of Puvis de Chavannes is clearly in evidence in the handling of the full, simple figures, the muted pastel palette and the subdued color tone of the whole composition. The subject of the picture remains an enigma: is it a group of religious taking a boat to attend some special ritual; resurrected souls making for the other world; or an arcane gathering of God's elect? The mysterious setting that the artist creates within this picture (and many others) would seem to be the pictorial reflection of the atmosphere in the literary works of Mallarmé, Rodenbach or even Maeterlinck.
M.C.

Ferdinand Hodler
(Berne, 1853—Geneva, 1918)

Hodler ranks as the most important Swiss painter around the turn of the twentieth century. The unique achievement of his art is to have moulded a distinctive Swiss character and Swiss spirituality into so powerful a form that his pictures can stand comparison with those of the greatest artists of his time. He was born in Berne in 1853, the same year as Vincent Van Gogh. After training as a decorative painter, in 1872 he moved to Geneva, where he lived until his death in 1918. His early work was unadventurously in the style of nineteenth-century Swiss Naturalism—Anker, Koller, Calame—but a journey to Spain in 1878 revealed entirely new artistic insights. Hodler began to impose upon the visible a consciously abstract, compositional creative will; his dark tone painting gave way to a bright, almost impressionistically striking chromatism, most often based on a

ground note of light gray.
His painting were first recognized in 1890, however, when he shifted toward Symbolism. The giant figures of *Night* (Berne, Kunstmusem) created a sensation wherever the painting was shown, including at the Salon du Champ-de-Mars in Paris in 1891, where it even drew attention from Puvis de Chavannes. The latter accolade must have pleased the young artist especially, because his admiration for the great French mural painter was as intense as had been his previous enthusiasm for Gustave Courbet. Puvis's work not only encouraged him to attempt a daringly gigantic, mural-like scale; it also taught him how to use form and color as consciously decorative elements in his compositions. Even iconographically, the example of Puvis was decisive. Hodler's liking for paradisiacal images of existence, in which naked or antiquely clad figures engage in a "Dialogue with nature" (to quote the title of one such picture), probably owes much to Puvis, and when in 1892 he decided to take part once again in the Salon du Champ-de-Mars, he did so with *Weary of Life*, an allegory on the autumn of life which pays homage to the great French master in both form and content. The second genre in which Hodler worked intensely during his lifetime was landscape. Here, too, from 1890 onward he stylized his subjects to the point where a lake or a mountain yielded a metaphor of the eternally valid. He achieved success with his bold landscape and figure paintings only after the turn of the century, especially in Germany where he frequently exhibited before World War I, also receiving two commissions for monumental mural paintings.
R.K.

Ludwig von Hofmann
(Darmstadt, 1861—Pillnitz, near Dresden, 1945)

The life-affirming, lyrically decorative pictorial world of the painter and graphic artist Ludwig von Hofmann features rhythmically moving figures—bathing, dancing or riding—in an ideal landscape. After training in Dresden and Karlsruhe, between 1890 and 1903 Hofmann lived mostly in Berlin, where he was a member of the Group of Eleven artists, a founder of the review *Pan* and of the Secession. In 1903 he took up a post as lecturer in the art school at Weimar, where he was a founder member of the league of German

artists. From 1916 to 1931 he was professor of monumental painting in Dresden.
Hofmann traveled to Greece in 1907 and made repeated visits to Italy (1894–99 and after 1906). His desire to set up a studio in Rome was the result of the impact of the work of Hans von Marées, whom he met in 1892. However, despite such a dark, brooding model, Hofmann maintained his cheerful, brightly toned images. In 1889–90 Hofmann stayed in Paris, studying at the Académie Julian. The encounter with Puvis de Chavannes and Albert Besnard was an important influence. While the main work by Puvis he was able to see was the decoration of the Panthéon, the chief model by Besnard was his murals at the Ecole de Pharmacie, which Hofmann copied. He also met Puvis in person at a dinner organized by Besnard.
Two Youths and above all *Idolino*, the ideal of youthful male beauty, are two of the many depictions of nude children and adolescents in Hofmann's work which today seem to verge on paedophilia. Even his Adam in *Adam and Eve* has the body of a young boy. Hofmann's ephebic youths attest to the influence of Marées and of classical models. The figures are represented in Arcadia in a manner that is at once natural and "pure," idealized and transported away from the here-and-now. They enliven compositions that are meditative and timeless, without themselves losing their quietude and moderation. Hofmann's hedonistic work, chiefly decorative in its effect, made him a first-rank interpreter of the "new idealism."
P.K.

Karl-Gustav Jensen-Hjell
(Norwegian, 1862–1888)

The talented Karl Jensen-Hjell died of tuberculosis only twenty-six years old. We know little about his life and we know of only thirteen paintings done by him, all painted between 1884–87. About 1880 he enrolled at the Drawing School in Kristiania (Oslo), already suffering from tuberculosis. In 1882–83, he continued his studies in Munich, probably until 1886. In the summer of 1883, with a group of painters including Edvard Munch, he took part in Frits Thaulow's so-called Open-air Academy at Modum, southwest of Oslo. In 1885 Munch painted a full-length portrait (Oslo, private collection) of his friend as he stands resting arrogantly on his walking stick and with a cigar in his

hand. This work aroused considerable attention when it was exhibited and is one of Munch's most important early portraits. Jensen-Hjell belonged to the younger generation of French-influenced Realists, and his education followed the pattern of the day. He visited Paris in 1884; in 1886, he made a trip to Italy and possibly another visit to Paris. His most important painting is *At the Window* from 1887, which shows his friend, the painter Kalle Løchen in his studio. All the objects in the room are decoratively depicted in strong colors, giving us an idea of Løchen's taste and of the artists he looked to in his art. On the wall in the background hangs a copy of Puvis's *Sacred Wood*, and through the window we see the winter landscape outside. This combination emphasizes the contrasts in the art of that period: Symbolism and decorative discipline in contrast to the demands of open-air Realism.
M.L.

Fernand Khnopff
(Grembergen-Lez-Termonde, 1858—Brussels, 1921)

A major figure among the Belgian Symbolists, Fernand Khnopff spent his childhood in Bruges which left him with a fondness for evoking a past that contrasted with the unchanging rhythm of the natural seasons. An early work, *At Fosset. The Waiting Gamekeeper* (1883, Frankfurt, Städelsches Kunstinstitut) explores this perception of the world using the theme of waiting and expectation—a theme which had figured largely in the monumental compositions of Puvis de Chavannes.
After an education that culminated at the Brussels Académie des Beaux-Arts, Khnopff took an active part in the artistic circles of his day—particularly in the group of *Les Vingt*, who in their first exhibition of 1884 included this picture of a gamekeeper "planted" in the orchard of the Khnopff family property at Fosset, a small hamlet in the Belgian Ardennes. Flattened into the picture plane, the landscape finds there a symbolic meaning similar to that of those unchanging settings so dear to Puvis de Chavannes. And encased within this tapestry, the gamekeeper waits. Khnopff captures him in a hieratic pose; the man is less a part of society than of the cycle of the seasons; his silhouette echoes the outline of the trunk of the apple

tree that encloses the composition. Without resorting to the pretext of antiquity, Khnopff portrays an ideal humankind, separated from the cities and mundanity of modern life. Just as in Puvis de Chavannes, there is a rejection of the notion of progress.
A society portraitist and widely-recognized landscape painter, Khnopff gained an international reputation by the early 1890s. While his works inspired by the writings of Flaubert, Péladan and Mallarmé were attacked by a press hostile to Symbolist innovations, they did mark a milestone in the consolidation of European Symbolism, which following in the wake of Secessionism was becoming established throughout the continent—from London, Berlin and Munich, to Vienna and Saint Petersburg. In Brussels, Khnopff's work became more diversified in the 1900s; he worked on a series of erotic paintings that are still little known and also on the design of productions at the Théâtre Royal de la Monnaie. Yet in all this variety one can see the same imagination at work, combining a feeling for the sensual with musical or literary evocations of myth.
M.D.

Max Klinger
(Leipzig, 1857—Grossjena, 1920)

Of the German artists featured in this exhibition, the painter, graphic artist and sculptor Max Klinger was most closely in contact with French art. Trained in Karlsruhe and Berlin, he lived in Brussels for a time in 1879 and from 1883 spent several lengthy stays in Paris, where he long kept a studio, initially in Montparnasse, in Impasse du Maine and then in the Rue Boulard, later in Châtillon-sous-Bagneux in the outskirts. He read Flaubert, Zola, Goncourt and Maupassant, followed the art shows of the capital and read the reviews, but also lived a very secluded life on occasion. In 1907 he judged that "Paris is the center of art and will be so for a long time to come." Nonetheless he had difficulty adjusting, not only to the French mentality, but also to modernism in France. In Berlin in 1882 he had seen the Bernstein collection of Impressionists and met the critic Jules Laforgue, and he also appreciated Degas and the freshness of Impressionism. Despite this he laid more emphasis on the Louvre, where he was attracted by the works of Leonardo da Vinci, Mantegna and Jan Van Eyck.

Klinger was familiar with the works by Puvis de Chavannes—the closest of his compositions to Puvis, the pen-and-ink drawing *The Start of Spring*, dates from as early as 1874–77—but he was clearly not an admirer of the French artist. He was, however, impressed by Rodin, as by Böcklin and Italian art. From 1888 he lived for a time in Rome, and between 1889 and 1890 he visited Pompeii, Naples, Ferrara, Ravenna, Padua and other art centers.

This was the period of *L'Heure Bleue*. The picture was certainly based on his impressions of the Italian coast (which he preferred to that of Brittany), but can also be seen as a reaction to Puvis, whose representations of the human figure seemed to him to be strained. There is also documentary evidence that his studies of twilight phenomena had led to some early sketches in Paris, which he then developed into the final form in Rome. Klinger himself wrote that his intention was to characterize "three different kinds of peaceful contemplation" at sunset.
P.K.

Georg Kolbe
(Waldheim, 1877—Berlin, 1947)

Georg Kolbe was one of the major German sculptors of the first half of the twentieth century. In his early work, however, he concentrated on two-dimensional media, chiefly painting and drawing. He trained as a decorative painter at the Dresden School of Arts and Crafts and also studied privately in Munich with the Hungarian painter Simon Hollósy, whom he greatly admired. In 1904 Kolbe decided to opt for a career as a sculptor, learning the necessary techniques for full-figure representation from Louis Tuaillon in Rome. The core of his creative work was to be the idealized nude, mostly executed in bronze. His sculptures are detached from any narrative context, attesting to the artist's commitment to representing "pure form." Kolbe took part in the World Exhibitions of 1929 and 1937. His statue *Morning* was shown in the German Pavilion by Mies van der Rohe, while *Proclamation* stood in the entrance area of Albert Speer's pavilion for Nazi Germany. Kolbe's career as an artist promoted by the National Socialist regime was the focus of the exhibition *Taking Positions* (Leeds, Henry Moore Foundation and Berlin, Georg Kolbe Museum 2001–02).
The painting *The Golden Island*

(1898, oil on canvas, Berlin, Staatliche Museen zu Berlin, Nationalgalerie) was completed following a six-month stay in Paris, which Kolbe summed up as follows in a letter of May 1898: "But I must confess that I've got an awful lot out of Paris, and no doubt it's probably the case that, at least for people like myself, there's no city where one can work and get on so much as in Paris." (quoted from Gorka-Reimus in U. Berger, ed., *Georg Kolbe 1877–1947*, exh. cat., Georg Kolbe Museum, Berlin, Gerhard Marcks-Haus, Bremen, Munich and New York 1997, p. 18). The picture's original title was probably *The Land of Longing*, changed only when it was bought by the German National Gallery. In a letter dated June 1898 Kolbe described it as ". . . half lemon-yellow with the foreground dirty green, the nudes are chalky green like newts." There are similarities with Puvis de Chavannes's *Young Women at the Sea* (1879) in the Musée d'Orsay in Paris.
P.K.

Georges Lacombe
(Versailles, 1868—Alençon, 1916)

After a non-academic training from his parents (his father was a cabinet-maker, his mother a painter), Lacombe became part of the Nabi group after his first meeting with Sérusier in 1892; he took part in their exhibitions at Le Barc de Boutteville, later exhibiting at Vollard's (1897) and Durand-Ruel's (1899) and at the other main Salons of Paris. In 1893 he met Gauguin, and the influence of the older artist awoke an interest in (often polychrome) wooden sculpture; he thence became the "Nabi sculptor," producing often esoteric works that revealed his interest in mysticism and his taste for the primitive arts he had discovered thanks to the Exposition Universelle of 1899 (most notably, his *Isis* and the four wooden bed panels of around 1894, Paris, Musée d'Orsay). He also continued to paint, producing heavily-stylized, Japanese-influenced "syntheses" of the Brittany landscape, which he visited (Camaret) every year from 1888 to 1897, when he got married and moved into his house, "L'Ermitage," near Alençon. After 1904—and particularly after his encounter with Théo Van Rysselberghe—the influence of Gauguin and Sérusier gave way to that of Neo-Impressionism, with the production of more descriptive and realistic landscapes. He taught at the

Académie founded by Paul Ranson in 1908. In 1907 he began work on bronze sculpture, though he also continued to use wood right up to the end of his life; he left some strikingly truthful busts (in both wood and bronze) of his Nabi friends (all shown at the 1911 Salon d'Automne): Bonnard (Paris, Musée d'Orsay), Denis (Saint-Germain-en-Laye, Musée Maurice Denis), Roussel, Vuillard and Sérusier—this latter Denis would have placed on Sérusier's tomb at Morlaix.
The fact that he was mainly a sculptor as well as his aversion to the Nabi aesthetic saw to it that Lacombe remained far from Puvis's influence; however, some of his early paintings and an important decorative group show that he too was strongly marked by Puvis's aesthetic.
J.P.B.

Henri Le Fauconnier
(Hesdin, 1881—Paris, 1946)

After studying law in Paris, Henri Le Fauconnier enrolled at the studio of Jean-Paul Laurens before moving on to the Académie Julian. Exhibiting for the first time at the Salon des Indépendants in 1904, Le Fauconnier soon emerged as a straightforward follower of Matisse, with the same daring palette. When he moved to the Ploumanac'h region of Brittany in 1907, the artist began to explore a more personal style: he painted somber interpretations of rocky landscapes in a brown-dominated palette with thick outlines around simplified forms. He also applied this style in nudes and portraits—for example, that of the poet Pierre-Jean Jouve painted in 1909 (Paris, Centre Georges-Pompidou, Musée National d'Art Moderne).
Returning to Paris, Le Fauconnier became part of the literary and artistic circles that gathered around Paul Fort at the Closerie des Lilas. With a certain reputation as an intellectual—Kandinsky would invite him to publish one of his theoretical texts in the catalog of the Neue Künstlervereinigung in Munich in 1910—he was soon throwing open his Rue Visconti studio to those artists who shared his desire to apply the lessons to be learned from the later works of Cézanne. Together with Jean Metzinger, Albert Gleizes, Fernand Léger and Robert Delaunay, he was part of the scandalous group of Cubists who exhibited at the 1911 Salon des Indépendants. His *Abundance* (1910–11), which formed the focus-point of the

famous Room 41, seemed to be an emblematic expression of "le Cubsime des Salons." The picture shows the artist's concern to reconcile the nude with the aesthetics of Cubism—a concern shared with most other members of the group. With its faceted volumes and blue-green monochrome, the work creates a visual continuum that enhances the location within the landscape of the two figures: a woman carrying a basket of fruit and a young boy who is picking fruit. This fidelity to an allegorical vocabulary which is not very different from that of Puvis de Chavannes can be partly explained by Le Fauconnier's resorting to a literary source: *The Abundance* seems to have been inspired by a poem of Alexandre Mercereau on the subject of motherhood, a key link in the transmission of that *élan vital* which was so dear to Bergsonian philosophy.
C.B.

Fernand Léger
(Argentan, 1881—Paris, 1955)

Fernand Léger gave 1909 as the year of his birth as an artist—the year in which he painted the works Louis Vauxcelles described as "tubist," in order to distinguish them from those being produced by the Cubists. As a matter of fact, the artist himself destroyed nearly all the paintings of "Léger before Léger," which revealed the influence of Impressionism and Post-Impressionism. Born in Argentan in 1881, Léger is not known to have painted any early copies of the works of Old Masters (though in 1948–49 he would paint his *Hommage à David*) and was initially more influenced by architectural draftsmanship than by what he learned in Gérôme's studio (from where he passed on to the studio of Gabriel Ferrier and then the Académie Julian). He always declared an admiration for the Symbolist painter Henri Martin and an essential debt to the work of Cézanne, which he first saw at the 1904 Salon d'Automne and then during the show held to commemorate the artist in 1907. Of the Cubists—contemporaries with whom he was often compared—he says: "I was too classical, with that French sense of balance, to adopt the romanticism of Negro art that influenced Braque and Picasso." He did not take up either their subject matter or their "spider's web" style (as he described their dense network of different planes rendered in brown monochromes).

Nudes in the Forest (1909–10, Otterlo, Rijksmuseum Kröller-Müller) might in some way be linked with Picasso's *The Dryad (Nude in the Forest)* (1908, Saint Petersburg, The Hermitage Museum), and yet reveals how the ambitions behind Léger's work were rather different to those behind the work of the Cubists. The picture shows three figures—men at work—in a forest: one, seen in half profile, is standing with his arms raised and his body powerfully arched; another, seen in half profile from behind, is seated; and the third, seen face-on, is standing. The men and the trees are constructed using the same colors and fragmented volumes modeled on tubes; the light is deep green, while the upper central section of the space of the canvas is hollowed out in a lighter section. The vast format—which is horizontally pronounced in two distinct "registers"—the vertical rhythm established by the trees and the two outlines of the standing figures, and the harmony in the unified treatment of figures and objects, reveal not only the lessons learned from Cézanne, but also the influence of the classicism exemplified by the large-scale compositions of Puvis de Chavannes.

The war, during which Léger served from 1914 to 1917, would confirm the direction taken by his art, with compositions based on contrasts, dissonances, a fragmentation of form, a free use of color, a realism of subject matter (drawn from contemporary life), and the construction of a non-imitative reality of convincing plastic and visual coherence.

Up to his death in 1955, he would produce works that were destined to last at the same time as they captured the present "in a useful and social sense."

Hence, the importance given to the rendering of the human figure, the ambitious range of his paintings—which often aimed for the highest genre of history painting—and his attraction to large-scale mural projects.

The figures in *Dance* (1929, Grenoble, Musée de Grenoble) appear to float in space, and remind one of the nymphs in the monumental compositions Puvis de Chavannes created for Lyon and Boston; while *Composition with Three Women (Three Women against a Red Background,* 1927, Saint-Etienne, Musée d'Art Moderne) contains idealized figures that are comparable to those large-scale figures of the "Neoclassical" Picasso. Both works perpetuate that form of the classical tradition into which Pierre Puvis de Chavannes had breathed new life and energy.
M.L.P.

Wilhelm Lehmbruck
(Duisburg, 1881—Berlin, 1919)

From 1895 Wilhelm Lehmbruck attended the School of Arts and Crafts in Düsseldorf with the aid of a scholarship, and between 1901 and 1906 he was a student at the Düsseldorf Academy. In 1905 he found a buyer for his 1902 sculpture *Bathing Woman* and the money from the sale enabled him to travel to Italy for the first time. The interest in Italian art was to stay with him for the rest of his life. In 1907 he produced the first sculptures in the series of the *Mother and Child* theme. In the same year he began traveling regularly to Paris, where he showed his work in exhibitions. In 1908 Lehmbruck was married in Düsseldorf, where the first of the couple's three sons was born in 1909. In 1910 he settled permanently in Paris, where he absorbed the style of Rodin and Maillol; however, with *Nude Woman Standing* (1910) and *The Kneeling Woman* (1911) Lehmbruck found a new formal language of the human body, featuring tectonic composition, volumes and expression interiorized to the point of spiritualisation.

In 1912 the artist made his second trip to Italy. The figures he created show his aesthetic receptiveness to the great masters of the Renaissance and also of antiquity. The relief *Three Women* (1913) is typical of Lehmbruck's formal language during the period. The outsized figures of *Climbing Woman* and *Woman Thinking* take up and extend the form that he had found. At the same time Lehmbruck began to break up his figures, undertaking the series of the *Torso* and *Part-Pieces*. When World War I broke out he moved first to Berlin and later to Zurich (1916–17).

This was the period in which he produced his *Fallen* and *Seated Youth*.

In the anonymity of the deaths they depict, the two figures represent the earliest modern anti-war monuments. Lehmbruck's late work was characterized by many, often unusual portraits. A private crisis in his life drove him to commit suicide in March 1919.
K.L.

Henri (Eugène Augustin) Le Sidaner
(Port-Louis, Mauritius, 1862—Versailles, 1939)

A student from Dunkirk, he won a scholarship which enabled him to move to Paris in 1880. At the Ecole des Beaux-Arts he entered Cabanel's studio in 1884, but soon drew away from such academic teaching. He exhibited at the Salon des Artistes Français from 1887 to 1893, then at the Société Nationale des Beaux-Arts and La Libre Esthétique in Brussels.

From 1882 onward, the artist was a regular visitor to Etaples, where he painted the 1893 *The Cottage at the Edge of the Forest*, in which his art serves to give expression to symbolist dreams; the moment of day depicted is that when natural and artificial light encounter one another; the Impressionist brushwork creates a mysterious, misty atmosphere in a landscape peopled by a sole human figure. A year later he exhibited for the first time at the Société Nationale des Beaux-Arts, where Puvis de Chavannes was then president. In both its composition and subject, his *The Departure of Tobias* reflected Le Sidaner's admiration for the work of Fra Angelico (seen during his 1892 visit to Italy) and Puvis de Chavannes himself. The latter's influence is most evident in the frontal depiction of the figures, and in the flat, rigorous simplicity of spatial composition.

Later, Le Sidaner returned to the more personal style he had developed previously, entering a particularly rich period of his artistic career and establishing links with a number of Symbolist writers and critics. His 1896 *Morning* was the first in a series of landscapes in which the play of light on water serves to create that dream-like atmosphere which his Symbolist friends were striving for in their work. The artist had now found a style and subject matter that were congenial to him, producing often uninhabited landscapes in which the light of different times of day plays on the natural world to create a strange and melancholic atmosphere. After his period in Bruges in 1899, Le Sidaner received widespread recognition; his work was highly appreciated and he signed an exclusive contract with the Galeries Georges Petit. At this point he begin exhibiting throughout the world, and traveled extensively in Europe. After 1910, his art became more decorative, even if remaining faithful to a Symbolist aesthetic; a retrospective of his work was held in Brussels in 1931.

Writing in *La Revue Blanche* in 1901, Gustave Soulier described Le Sidaner as "the Maeterlinck of painting" because of the unfailingly literary inspiration behind his work.
M.C.

Mario Mafai
(Rome, 1902–1965)

Mario Mafai interrupted his studies in 1921 to devote himself to painting.

After his experience at the Industrial Arts night school (1917), he attended the English Academy (1921) and then enrolled in the Accademia di Belle Arti in Rome in 1922. However, his painting did not fit into to the classifications of the avant-garde movements.

A determining event after his military service in 1926 was his friendship with Scipione, M. Mazzacurati, and Antonietta Raphaël, his future wife, with whom he shared an apartment that Longhi called the "Scuola di Via Cavour." Between 1928–30, his painting took on a highly emotional, surreal bent of "orgiastic colorism" (De Grada) that he shared with Scipione. He exhibited at Palazzo Doria and in the Prima Mostra del Sindacato Fascista degli Artisti (1929).

In 1930 he went to Paris where he met de Chirico, Savinio and Chagall who, with Rousseau, was his favorite master, but his enthusiasm was directed more to museums than to culture. Although his painting seemed "diluted in the atmosphere of Paris," it gradually returned to light, realism, and *chiaroscuro*, giving rise to the cycles of the *Dried Flowers*, the *Roman Views* and the *Demolitions*.

Conversely, his *Fantasies* of the war years were visionary and full of anguish.

He had successful exhibitions at the Galleria in Rome and the I Roman Quadriennale (1931), participated in several Venice Biennales (1934–36–38), mounted a one-man show at the II Quadriennale (1935), the Galleria della Cometa (1937), and the Barbaroux in Milan (1940). Between 1948–50 he won international acclaim.

In 1956, he began to teach at the Accademia di Rome. In 1959, his painting took an informal-abstract turn, engaging in a pessimistic controversy with the the artist who in his new role "organizes his instinct and filters it through his clever, calculating intelligence."
I.P.

Aristide Maillol
(Banuyls-sur-Mer, 1861—Perpignan, 1944)

Maillol himself mentions how he had turned to the example of Puvis de Chavannes when producing his first paintings in Banuyls. He repeatedly stressed that artist's influence, not hesitating to say he had provided "the greatest emotions of my youth: those compositions of fine draftsmanship and a charming style filled one with a sense of poetry, thanks to their harmony and the skill they revealed in large-scale decoration. In our inexperience, Puvis de Chavannes provided good counsel. . . . If we had looked at no one but him, we might perhaps have put this counsel to good use; unfortunately, we also looked at the various Laurens and Bonnats, the entire Institut." (J. Cladel, *Aristide Maillol, sa vie, son oeuvre, ses idées*, Paris, Bernard Grasset, 1937, pp. 40–41). Among the sets he painted for the puppet theater of his friend Maurice Bouchor, was "a landscape in a fine silvery light, for *La Dévotion à Saint André*" which received praise and applause from Puvis de Chavannes. Maurice Bouchor, who knew the older artist, introduced him to Maillol; "complimented and invited to visit the famous painter's studio," the young man was, however "too shy, too stupid and never dared to go" (*ibidem*, pp. 42–43). Nevertheless, he always maintained a great admiration for the man: "Puvis de Chavannes has been turned down as a teacher. A man of genius, blackballed at the age of 60! Forain believed that with Puvis at its head, the Ecole would have been saved." (*ibidem*, p. 34).
His sense of form and synthesis, his concision and simplification, would lead to Maillol being accused of *gaucherie*. Maurice Denis brandished that accusation as a banner of pride because it had been leveled for all the great artists in a tradition that he saw running from Ingres through Puvis de Chavannes to Cézanne—a tradition in which he included Maillol: "Reacting against the decline and decadence of the Ingres School, Puvis de Chavannes in his turn rediscovered the ingenuousness of the Giotto School" (M. Denis, *A. Maillol*, Paris, Crés et Cie, 1925, p. 28); the critic would also speak of the "exquisite *gaucherie* of Maillol" (M. Denis, in A. Romain, "Maillol," in *Aristide Maillol*, exh. cat., Musée de Saint-Tropez, 1994, p. 40).
Maillol always denied that his sculpture had been influenced by Gauguin, saying "Gauguin made a mistake when he turned to imitating Negro sculpture. He should have sculpted the way he painted. . . . He had two different approaches, one in painting, one in sculpture; he was, therefore, double as a man and artist." (Cladel, *Aristide Maillol...*, p. 130). Of himself, however, Maillol claimed "I work as if I had learned nothing, as if I was the very first man to carve a sculpture." (Puig, p. 19, in Romain, "Maillol" ..., p. 37)—meaning that he saw no continuity between late nineteenth-century sculpture and his own work, that he was trying to reinvent sculpture by the light of the discoveries he had made in painting, largely thanks to the example of Puvis de Chavannes.
C.Ch.

Kazimir Malevich
(Kiev, 1878—Leningrad, now Saint Petersburg, 1935)

Later in his life Malevich tried to suppress everything about his Symbolist period, which lasted from 1907 to 1910. The first known exhibition of his Symbolist works was at the XIV Exhibition of the Moscow Society of Artists in 1908, and included two tempera works—one of which was *Prayer* (which, in Malevich's own hand, bears on the back the comment: " Sketch for a fresco painting"). The work is characterized by an almost monochromatic use of yellow and a certain spiritual esotericism. It is part of the *Series of Yellows. Saints* that the artist exhibited at the First Moscow Salon in 1911. That series also included the first appearance of *Sketch for a Fresco Painting* (inscribed on the back, in the artist's own hand); though this is the only name for the work that appears in the catalog, due to its subject matter the picture has been arbitrarily named either *Sacred Wood* or *Sacred Tomb*.
These two examples of the *Series of Yellows. Saints* are characteristic of Russian Symbolism, which—in the case of Malevich—draws on the formal qualities of the work of Puvis de Chavannes, Carrière, Whistler, and the Nabis, as well as the example of Vroubel, and Borisov-Mousatov (who owed so much to the Lyon master).
Plant motifs are omnipresent. This is not the natural world of the Impressionists, painted *en plein air*, but an imaginary landscape, a symbolic synthesis of a universal vegetation, of universal growth that is reflected in the rhythm of the picture's color and form. The pantheistic fusion of beings and plants is particularly clear in the "sacred wood" of the *Sketch for a Fresco Painting*. The color yellow, which has powerful Buddhist implications, is also a visual *analogon* of the light of the sun; but this is an inner sunlight that irradiates all space, which flows everywhere without leaving chiaroscuro or shadow. The yellow then blends into bronzes and reds. This is truly an iconic space. Not in the sense of an Orthodox religious icon, but of a picture that offers an essential—rather than imitative—image of the sensorial world; an image that goes to the very heart of things because it draws on the very root of appearances. The tempera shows a lamentation similar to that of Christ's disciples in pictures of "The Entombment." The dead body emerges from among the plants, while its head is hidden among the slim trunks of "symbolic" rather than real trees. One might quote what Marianne Werefkin wrote at the beginning of the 1910s: "The object 'tree' does not exist; it is the word 'tree' that exists, and it is that word that is linked with the concept of a thing that does not exist. . . . There is this tree, and this tree, and this tree; but the tree in itself does not exist. But there is the word 'tree,' and it is the symbol for all that which resembles a tree." Hence, the Verbe—the first abstraction of symbolism which the Greeks considered as constituting the dawn of philosophy. And the pictorial rendition of this verbal Symbolic abstraction to be found in the works of Puvis de Chavannes, Gauguin or Denis consists in the representation of a sign that is a synthesis of all trees rather than the rendition of one particular tree. There are still some characteristics of the physical nature of trees, so one cannot speak here of pictograms or hieroglyphics; however, they are present in embryo.
Even in their evident chastity, the nudes eschew all reference to traditional iconography; though, of course, the mysticism here is more Christian than pagan.
Note that the figures do not look at each other; their gaze is turned inwards in mediation, looking toward a reality that lies beyond the world of the senses—a distinctive feature of Puvis de Chavannes's symbolism which would have profound effects on the painting of the late nineteenth and early twentieth centuries.
Prayer is most heavily influenced by the "Modern Style" (as Art Nouveau was called in Russia). This is particularly clear in the undulation of the hair, which serves as a metonymy for the head lost in mediation. However, it can also be noticed in the inclination toward the monochrome and in the pantheist union of man and Nature (two features which are shared with the other works that make up the *Series of Yellows. Saints*).
Thus for three-four years Malevich was clearly in debt to the purest forms of Symbolism. Just like the Symbolist artists who were his contemporaries, he felt hemmed in, suffocated by a world of objects, by a real world that struck him as vulgar. He took refuge in the soul, in a creative imagination that produced magical worlds that were crammed with memories of other lives. . . . All of this would soon after be totally rejected by Malevich in his struggle against any kind of "illusionism," against "the figurative hotchpotch." That explains his silence on his own Symbolist works, which are of undoubted interest.
J.-C.M.

Hans von Marées
(Elberfeld, 1837—Rome, 1887)

The inspiration for the work of Hans von Marées was his study of antiquity and the Renaissance; with Anselm Feuerbach and Arnold Böcklin he was one of the so-called "Deutsch-Römer" group of German artists based in the Eternal City. Marées first trained as an artist at the Berlin Academy, from 1853 to 1855. In 1857 he moved to Munich, where he received a commission to produce copies of Old Master paintings in Italy. Once there, he met Böcklin in Rome and Feuerbach in Florence. The course of his artistic career was thus already marked out; its high points were the mural decorations for the Zoological Institute in Naples and his pictures of the Hesperides and the Golden Age. Although the impact of Rubens and Italian art was strong—his early enthusiasm was for Venetian Renaissance painting, and from 1875 he settled permanently in Rome—there are also unmistakable signs of the influence of French modernism in his work. The models of Courbet and Manet are especially obvious in his output of the 1860s.
In 1869 Marées traveled to Spain and France. The painting *Rider Picking an Orange with a Female Nude* was completed in 1869–70. While recalling Manet, it also appears close to Puvis de Chavannes's *Autumn*, shown at the

Salon in 1864 and bought by the Musée des Beaux Arts in Lyon. A further parallel between Puvis and Marées can be detected in Puvis's *The Fountain*, 1869. In April 1869 Marées passed through Marseille, where he may have seen Puvis's two-part decoration, completed in 1867–69, for the staircase of the Palais de Longchamp. The work was also shown at the 1869 Salon in Paris when Marées was staying in the city. In the Louvre he admired above all Leonardo and Michelangelo, while he made sketches from Poussin and Bagnacavallo. But he found not one contemporary work in Paris "that could serve for a model." *Three Men in a Landscape* was painted in Florence, inspired by Luca Signorelli's frescos in Orvieto cathedral. The composition does not place the nude figures in a scene; rather it should be understood as a formal variation on the themes of pace, movement, posture and gesture.
P.K.

Henri Martin
(Toulouse, 1860—La Bastide-du-Vert, Lot, 1943)

Around the turn of the century, Henri Martin offered a re-interpretation of Puvis de Chavannes's work in the domain of monumental painting, adopting a style characterized by ellipsis of line, serenity of composition and atemporal white-clad figures that evoked classical antiquity. However, originally from Toulouse—which he left with a city scholarship to study at the Ecole des Beaux-Arts and then at the studio of Jean-Paul Laurens—Martin was not initially predisposed toward the ideals proposed by Puvis. His first works were clearly Realist—and academic—in style, offering no hint of the transformation that would occur after a visit to Italy in 1885 in the company of Aman-Jean and Ernest Laurent. Presented at the 1889 Salon, his *Feast of the Confederacy* celebrates the centenary of the French Revolution in a much lighter palette and with brushwork that reveals the influence of Divisionism (indeed, the painting was attacked both by the champions of a certain type of "academic" painting and by those who supported *les divisionnistes*). History and allegory would remain his chosen subject matter (*Apollo and the Muses*, Hôtel de Ville, 1895), with some works having more than a touch of Symbolism (his Symbolist period would last a

certain time, as Henri Martin first exhibited at the Salon de la Rose+Croix in 1892). It was only with his purchase of his home in Quercy in 1900 and the subsequent discovery of that region's light and landscape during his summer stays there, that the artist adopted a truly luminous palette, rendering shimmering atmospheres with Divisionist brushwork and a draftsmanship that was very reminiscent of Puvis de Chavannes. If *The Muse* is still in theme and treatment a Symbolist work (as well as embodying what was one of the leitmotifs of his entire oeuvre), his *Elysian Fields*, the sketch of which dates from around 1939, reveals the full maturity of the artist. The influence of Puvis de Chavannes can be seen in all aspects of this painting, apart from the treatment of light and Divisionist brushwork. In fact, in 1899, Puvis de Chavannes had recognized Martin as his heir; looking at the painting *Serenity* at the 1899 Salon, he commented: "this man will succeed me." That prediction obviously did not take into account further transformations in the younger artist's work; and yet, nevertheless, Puvis de Chavannes would remain an influence in all Henri Martin's large decorative works. Indeed, this is what makes Martin so original: he combines the Divisionism inherited from Seurat and Signac, with the light of the Impressionists and the geometrical rigor of composition and purity of line that were typical of Puvis de Chavannes. But couldn't one also say that Seurat himself owed Puvis de Chavannes a debt in this area? The large mural works in the Capitole—in particular the Salle Henri Martin (1903–06)—combine all these qualities with a sharp eye for naturalist detail. The same might be said of the works for the Caisse d'Epargne in Marseille, the Palais de Justice in Paris (1914) and the polyptych *The Luxembourg* painted in 1935 for the City Hall of the fifth arrondissement.
E.A.

Arturo Martini
(Treviso, 1889—Milan, 1947)

Of modest birth, Arturo Martini left school in 1901. In 1904, he attended the Night and Sunday Arts and Crafts School in Treviso, and in 1905 he studied with A. Carlini, a local sculptor. Then, in 1907, he enrolled at the Accademia di Belle Arti in Venice where he united his academic studies with a personal bent for realism that was reminiscent of the lessons of

Vincenzo Gemito and Rodin. His first successful show was at the I Mostra d'Arte Trevigiana at which time his first bronze, *Harmony* was cast. During a study-visit to Munich (1909) sponsored by G. Gregorj, he discovered Symbolism, Expressionism and Toorop's linearism, despite a longing for Paris "where I would have found Renoir and the other great artists." He finally did go there in 1912 with Gino Rossi, exhibited at the Salon d'Automne, and associated with Andreotti, de Chirico, Modigliani, Savinio and Rosso, whose luminism impressed him. Receptive to the influences of the avant-garde movements, he executed some "experiments on modernism" that he presented at Ca' Pesaro (1913). An admirer of Carrà, he took part in the Futurist events in Bologna (1914). He was drafted in 1916 and assigned to a bullet foundry where he perfected his technical training. After the war, he published the book of drawings *Contemplazioni* (1918), and exhibited at Ca' Pesaro (1919), at which time he showed an inclination for formal rigor and classicism through his rediscovery of Greek and Roman sculpture. In Milan, he joined Margherita Sarfatti's circle (1920), and his one-man show at the Galleria Buggelli was presented by Carrà. His lecture on sculpture attracted the interest of Mario Broglio, the founder of *Valori Plastici*, which group he joined in 1921. In 1924, he moved to Rome, showed at the III Biennale, and then participated in the first *Novecento Italiano* exhibition (1926) in Milan. Between 1926 and 1930 the combination of classical purity and romantic sentimentality in his work was emphasized, becoming "tactile sensibility" in the terra-cottas (Perocco), while his figurative repertory continued to expand. In works like *Hospitality* and *The Fisherman's Wife* (1930-31), compositional experiments appeared alongside static-dynamic balances of intense emotion. He exhibited at the I Quadriennale of Rome (1931) and the Venice Biennale (1932). His important commissions in the capital include the *Cristo Re* for the church of the same name, and the *Athena* for the University of Rome. He also executed the monument to Livy for the Liviano in Padua, and the high reliefs for the Law Court (1937) and for the Arengario (1942) in Milan. He taught at the Accademia delle Belle Arti in Venice where he was appointed director in 1944.
I.P.

Henri Matisse
(Le Cateau 1869—Nice, 1954)

Born in Le Cateau-Cambrésis (Northern France), Henri Matisse entered the Paris Ecole des Beaux-Arts in 1895, studying in the studio of Gustave Moreau. After an early success at the Salon de la Société Nationale des Beaux-Arts in 1896, where his work had been supported by Puvis de Chavannes, he undertook years of research stimulated by his interest in Neo-Impressionism.
At the 1905 Salon d'Automne he appeared as the leader of the Fauves group.
Thanks to the support of a small number of patrons (the Frenchman Marcel Sembat, the Americans Michael, Sarah, Leo and Gertrude Stein, the Russians Shchukin, Morosov, etc.) he established himself as one of the major figures in European avant-garde painting. Starting with the 1906 *Bonheur de vivre*, his work contains a series of large "decorative" canvases characterized by the influence of non-European art (in particular, Islamic and Byzantine art, which he studied not only in various Paris collections but also on a number of trips abroad—to Algeria in 1906, to Italy in 1907, to Andalusia and Russia in 1911, to Morocco in 1912).
In December 1917 he moved to Nice on the Côte d'Azur, thereafter visiting Paris only for short periods. With the exception of his 1919 decor and sets for the Ballets Russes, his work of the 1920s is characterized by paintings of clearly Oriental inspiration that reveal limited aesthetic ambitions—something which guaranteed him great success but which he ultimately came to see as leading to a dead-end. After his trip to the United States and Polynesia in 1930, he moved beyond this impasse with the large decorative panels on the theme of dance for the Barnes Foundation in Merion, Pennsylvania. This work, characterized by the systematic usage of flat painting, inevitably evokes Puvis and saw the beginning of his use of gouache cut-outs; increasingly present in his investigation of color, this technique would, in his own words, help him to "get to the beginnings of Painting."
Feeling like "a man resurrected" after a 1941 operation for cancer of the intestine, he spent most of the last years before his death working exclusively in drawing and gouache cut-out. These two techniques are

closely associated with his last major work of this period: the decoration of the Chapelle des Dominicaines in Vence near Nice (1947–51).
R.L.

Emile René Ménard
(Paris, 1862–1930)

Raised in the cult of classical antiquity by an uncle who was a philosopher (Louis Ménard) and a father who was the editor of the famous *Gazette des Beaux-Arts*, René Ménard was well-prepared to respond to the idealism in the work of Puvis de Chavannes. Even his home in Paris—in place du Panthéon—and his two-years' apprenticeship with the artist-decorator Victor Galland (1877–78) brought him into direct contact with *The History of Saint Genevieve* and its illustrious creator (Galland at the time was working at the Panthéon, and his work there was clearly inspired by that of Puvis de Chavannes). An apprenticeship spent in the studios of Baudry, Bouguereau and Lehmann—together with a period at the Académie Julian (1880)—did nothing to dilute this essential influence on the young artist. After a series of works inspired by episodes from the Bible or classical antiquity, from 1895 onward René Ménard turned to the production of atemporal works depicting shepherds and dryads who do not seem to be part of historical time, as in *Pastoral, Land of the Ancients* (shown at the 1919 Salon), devoid of a specific subject matter. Just like in the work of Puvis de Chavannes, the study of nature is an exercise in memory, a synthesis of what has been experienced. Extreme simplicity imbues even the most evident things—meadows, water, woodland, twilight—with mystery and opacity. Such a work does not "say" anything apart from itself, which ranks Ménard among the idealists rather than the Symbolists who were his contemporaries. The influence of Puvis de Chavannes can also be seen in the handling of plastic values: there is a taste for the classical nude, for lack of depth in space; a predominance of elliptic draftsmanship and serpentine lines. But Ménard's work also reveals individual characteristics; there is a more tactile quality, which perhaps derives from the artist's admiration for Millet, Corot and Rousseau—whom he had met during childhood holidays in Barbizon. The artist pays particular attention to the depiction of light, rendering those shifts of

chiaroscuro that outline and dissolve contours (the conflict of light and shade has something of the work of Prud'hon or of Ménard's near contemporary, Jean-Jacques Henner). The pictorial values are more definite here than in the work of Puvis de Chavannes, with a darker palette in which blues, browns and pinks predominate. The use of horizontal bands to construct a landscape—together with the presence of atemporal nudes—reveals a classical feel for the natural world; there is also a certain conventionality, which eschews the use of bright, open-air colors, and is obviously far from the dazzling patches of color in Gauguin or the work of the Nabi group. However, Emile René Ménard's work can also be appreciated in the application of his style to monumental paintings—at the Ecole des Hautes Etude (1906), in the Salle des Actes of the Paris Law Faculty (1909, now at the Musée d'Orsay) and the Caisse d'Epargne in Marseille (1918). Alongside the solutions proposed by Maurice Denis or Henri Martin, Ménard offers a more somber, dream-like classicism.
E.A.

George Minne
(Ghent, 1866—Laethem-Saint-Martin, 1941)

It was in Ghent that George Minne first created his drawings and sculptures of grieving and injured figures toward 1886. The emotional power of these works was quickly recognized by Symbolist poets such as Maurice Maeterlinck, Emile Verhaeren and Grégoire Le Roy, whose poetry Minne later illustrated.
Minne was invited to exhibit with the Brussels avant-garde group *Les Vingt* in 1890. He was elected a member the following year, and in 1892 he was one of the Belgian Symbolists who participated in Sâr Péladan's first Salon de la Rose+Croix in Paris. In 1895 he moved to Brussels where he was to produce his most important works, which included the evolution of the figure of a kneeling, introverted youth. In 1899 he returned to Ghent and settled nearby in Laethem-Saint-Martin, which became an artist's colony. Through Henry Van de Velde and the German art critic Julius Meier-Graefe, Minne was introduced to the international centers of Art Nouveau: Paris, various German cities and above all Vienna. He took part in numerous exhibitions,

including the Vienna and Berlin Secessions and the Venice Biennale. His work was noted in Vienna by artists such as Klimt, Schiele and Kokoschka. If Minne's art was thematically and formally limited, its spiritual power was acknowledged by critics and artists alike.
Although he took Auguste Rodin as a major example, he did not wish to compete with his plastic strength; he chose to produce works on a less monumental scale, realized in plaster, and looked to medieval art for his source of inspiration. He developed an expressive formal vocabulary that prefigured the work of the German Expressionist sculptors Ernst Barlach, Käthe Kollwitz and Wilhelm Lehmbruck. It is precisely the rejection of baroque pathos and the search for a surface that holds an inner power, that bring Minne close to Puvis de Chavannes. The relation of the *Prodigal Son* or *The Poor Fisherman* with Minne's introvert and self protecting figures is obvious. However it is less obvious to what degree we have to speak of influence or of mere kinship. Minne seemed to have appeared in Ghent in 1886 almost "out of nothing," with slender primitive sculptures in which his later development was already implied. Maurice Maeterlinck later recalled his astonishment: He was twenty years old, he had seen nothing, he had read nothing. He and his fellow poets were drawn to the young artist and they may well have directed him toward French Symbolism with which they felt akin themselves. Minne is said to have made studies at the Jardin des Plantes already in 1883. In a private collection descending from the artist is a drawing by Minne after a panel from Puvis's *The Childhood of Saint Genevieve* in the Panthéon, done from the original of from a print. The composition shows *Saint Genevieve Marked with the Divine Seal* and comprises kneeling and draped figures of the kind that Minne himself developed. It is almost certain that Minne was further stimulated by Puvis de Chavannes's example when the latter participated with several drawings and photographs after his murals in the Salon d'Art Monumental in Brussels in 1888. This exhibition included the full size cartoon for the Panthéon triptych.
In 1898 Minne created his so-called *Fountain of Kneeling Youths* for which he repeated five identical kneeling figures around a basin.

This work brings the introvert art of Minne to an utmost degree of clarity and simplicity, while at the same time its elegant shape and repetition are linked with Art Nouveau aesthetics. Minne exhibited this fountain for the first time at the Wiener Sezession in 1900. In 1905 he was commissioned a marble version for the entrance hall of the Folkwang Museum in Hagen designed by Henry Van de Velde. The work is now in Essen. The Ghent plaster version is probably the original design of 1905, while the basis is of a slightly later date. Minne in fact used different types of bases. In the 1909 Venice Biennale he even reduced his fountain to only four kneeling youths.
R.H.

Edvard Munch
(Löten, 1863—Ekely, 1944)

Edvard Munch is one of the towering figures in European pictorial art around the turn of the nineteenth century. His painting *The Scream* (Oslo, National Gallery) from 1893 has become an icon of modern man's angst and alienation. Up until the mid-1880s, Munch worked within the framework of Realism. With *The Sick Child* (1885–86, Oslo, National Gallery), he moved away from a realistic presentation, and in the years to follow experimented with various stylistic methods of expression. As early as mid-1880s, the influence of Puvis's *Sacred Wood* made itself felt in Norway, particularly among leading landscape painters. Munch's *Inger on the Shore* (1889, Bergen, Bergen Kunstmuseum) with its dry surface treatment, use of pale colors and its evocative musicality is an example of the widespread interpretation of Puvis's art among Norwegian painters of the period. Munch himself had had the opportunity to study Puvis's painting, both at the World Exhibition in Antwerp in 1885 and at the French Exhibition in Copenhagen in 1888. In 1889–91, Munch was in France where like a sponge he absorbed impressions from current art. While there, he spent a short period as a pupil at Léon Bonnat's studio, where he did not particularly feel at home. During the 1890s, he lived in turn in Norway, Germany and France. Around 1890 his art clearly reveals influence from Synthetism, while at the same time the themes in his images gradually become increasingly symbolistic. During these years, however, he also painted a number of female nudes of quite a different character, depictions taking up problems of form and color rather than the subject's erotic and psychological implications. *Paris Model*, painted about 1896, has a firmly structured simplicity and totally lacks the symbolistic overtones we usually associate with Munch's female depictions from this period. These, however, are not the result of an isolated whim. The picture type has interested the artist, and he has depicted the same model in another painting done at about the same time, now in the Rasmus Meyer Collections, Bergen. This time we see the figure from the back, but the artist's conception of the subject and the painterly idiom are the same. Like a number of artists at that time, Munch had returned to one of western art's chief problems, the representation of the nude human figure. Thus, these pictures also point forward toward the profound change that took place in his painting in the first decade of the 1900s.

In Munch's opinion, his images from the 1890s were connected by a common theme, its origins in modern man's inner life where love, angst and death were the fundamental conceptions. It was this underlying theme that later on, he would call *The Frieze of Life*, and he would return many times to the same themes and rework them in new versions. In *Dance on the Shore* from 1904, he once again takes up the theme in *The Dance of Life,* one of the main subjects in *The Frieze of Life*, first carried out in 1899 (Oslo, National Gallery). This time the picture was milder and paler, understandingly enough as *Dance at the Shore* was intended as part of the decoration for the children's room in the house of Dr. Max Linde, the artist's patron, in Lübeck. Dr. Linde, however, found the erotic content and the free, somewhat nonchalant workmanship unsuitable for the boys room and refused to accept it. Today the Linde Frieze is in the Munch Museum in Oslo. Both the decoration for Max Reinhardt's new chamber theater in Berlin (1906–07) and the Linde Frieze show how Munch now reinterprets what originally was a purely thematic idea into carefully prepared decorations for large indoor spaces, in which the format as well as form and content are joined together in a unified whole.

Despite considerable opposition, Munch finally won the competition for the decoration of the new Assembly Hall (Aula) in Oslo University and fulfilled the task with a series of oil paintings on canvas, carried out between 1913 and 1916. The leitmotif is man in nature, in which the sun plays an important role as the life-giving power. Nevertheless, these images contain clear allusions to the university and its activities. The various fields of science are symbolized by nude women and men who still retain a certain kinship with traditional allegorical depictions. But in one of the largest picture panels, *History* is presented in what is to all appearances a realistic scene that could have been taken straight out of everyday life: an elderly man in patched clothing is recounting tales of bygone days to a small boy who listens with rapt attention to the old man's words. As a counterpart on the opposite wall, the artist has depicted *Alma Mater,* a motherly, fair-haired woman surrounded by small children. Despite the unpretentiousness of both figure and dress, it is as if this woman nourishes and protects the rising generation. Puvis, on the other hand, in his Sorbonne University decoration, allows an idealised central female figure, also surrounded by children, to crown his strictly disciplined composition like a veritable high priestess of the sciences. Unlike the French master, Munch, by means of his direct approach to the task, has held himself surprisingly free from the influence of earlier European monumental painting in the grand style.

It can hardly be doubted that for his pictorial solution, he has looked to both Max Klinger's decorations for the University in Leipzig and Puvis's above mentioned works as his most immediate exemplars. However, Munch's Aula decorations differ substantially from those of Klinger and Puvis. This is, above all, because his new painterly style allowed him to combine a realistic presentation with the symbolic and expressive possibilities in the human figure.

In the period that followed, Munch developed and varied some of the solutions he had devised during the decoration of the University Aula. Nevertheless, he moderates the symbolic content as well as the symbolistic approach in favour of a more direct study of man and nature. In this context, *Bathing Man* from 1918 is an important picture. Here, too, man is seen in interplay with the surrounding nature and life's restless creative powers, while at the same time we realize that only through man does the world take on its meaning. Here are great similarities between Munch's and Puvis's concept of man's place in the universe. Nevertheless, whereas Puvis's heroic figures are timeless and thus classic, those of Munch are physically present in time.

This heroic concept of mankind was something new in Munch's art, although it never became dominant. Many times, however, particularly in the years between 1910 and 1920, it reached the point of being a convincing means of expression. A partial explanation of this development is to be found in the artist's life history and in his personal experiences; but it is also a consequence of new trends in continental art around the turn of the previous century.
M.L.

Mikhail Vasilevich Nesterov
(Ufa, 1862—Moscow, 1942)

A painter of portraits, landscapes, narrative works and large-scale mural decoration, Nesterov was also a book illustrator. Born into a family of the merchant classes, from 1876 to 1880 and again from 1883 to 1885 he studied at the Moscow School of Painting, Sculpture and Architecture under the illustrious Realist painters V.G. Perov, I.M. Pryanishnikov and W.E. Makovsky. In 1881–83 he was in Saint Petersburg, taking drawing lessons and life-classes with P.P. Chistyakov at the Imperial Academy of Fine Arts; he also worked on copies of the works in the Hermitage and enjoyed the advice of I.N. Kramskoy, a portraitist and theoretician of the Company of Wanderers (*Peredvizhniki*). In 1888, Nesterov painted his first famous picture *The Hermit* (Moscow, Tretyakov State Gallery), which was purchased by the famous Russian collector P.M. Tretyakov. With the money he earned, the artist traveled abroad, and in 1889 visited Austria, Italy, France and Germany. In Paris, Nesterov was left spell-bound by the works of J. Bastien-Lepage and Puvis de Chavannes, artists who would have a decisive influence on his subsequent artistic development. Between 1890 and 1905 Nesterov dedicated himself largely to the production of religious works for churches, in which—following the example of Puvis de Chavannes and V.M. Vasnecov—he tried to develop his own personal style of mural art. At the same time, he continued to work on easel paintings, drawing inspiration from the life of Saint Sergei of Radonezh and from the daily life of the "old believer" hermits. The artist exhibited at various shows in Russia—including those organized by the Wanderers (1889–1901), *Mir Iskusstva* (1899–1901) and the 36 Artists group (1901–03)—as well as showing abroad at various Universal Expositions and the International Expositions: Paris (1900), Munich (1898, 1909), Rome (1911) and others. In the first two decades of the twentieth century he worked on large-scale programmatic compositions, whose spirit is similar to that of medieval mystery works, trying to recapture the sense behind the centuries-old history of Russia—for example, in *Holy Rus'* (Saint Petersburg, Russia State Museum), *The Life of Christ* (Moscow, Convent of Martha and Mary), *In Rus' (The Soul of the People)* (Moscow, Tretyakov State Gallery). The artist was very close to certain philosophical circles inspired by questions of religion, and was a close friend of V.V. Rozanov, P.A. Florensky and S.N. Bulgakov. In 1910 he became a full member of the Imperial Academy of Fine Arts. After the 1917 Revolution, he worked mainly as a portraitist, producing fine portraits of leading figures in the Russian intelligentsia. In 1942 he received the Stalin Prize (First Class) for his portrait of I.P. Pavlov, the Nobel-winning physiologist. The fundamental characteristics of Nesterov's art were molded during the last decade of the nineteenth century, and his work reveals a juxtaposition of Symbolism and modern style that is typical of the Moscow school of Realism (which favored *en plein air* painting). The influence of Puvis de Chavannes is to be seen primarily in the choice of subject matter and in certain borrowings of compositional schema—as well as in the emotional power of his works.
P.Y.K.

Auguste de Niederhäusern-Rodo
(Vevey, 1863—Munich, 1913)

After training as a sculptor in Geneva, Rodo entered the Académie Julian and then the Ecole des Beaux-Arts.
However, disappointed with the teaching there, he asked Rodin to take him on as an assistant in 1892; he would work with him until 1898. Since 1886, Rodo had been frequenting the Symbolist circles; a close friend of Verlaine, he enjoyed the esteem of Mallarmé and Charles Morice.
In 1897, Verlaine's friends would commission Rodo to produce

the monument commemorating the dead poet.

Every summer the artist returned to Switzerland, where he met up again with Hodler, Amiet, Giacometti and Trachsel. He also succeeded in obtaining commissions in his own field, although his numerous projects for public monuments were systematically rejected. Before becoming Rodin's assistant, he produced *Avalanche* and *Waterfalls* (1891), followed by *Torrent* (Salon de la Rose+Croix, 1892)—both large groups that were to be part of his *Alpine Poem* which he hoped to carve directly into the stone of the Jungfrau massif. He returned to this dream with *Temple of Melancholy* (1906–09) and *Poem of Fire* (1908–09). These works were left unfinished—indeed, unfinishable—and led to the creation of such individual sculptures as *Offering to Bacchus* (1906), *Andante* (1910), *Psyche* (1910), *Summer* (1910), *Spray of Water* (1911), *Morgenstern* (1911) and *Venus Passing before the Sun* (1913).

After 1904, Rodo abandoned Symbolism and the trend set by Rodin in favor of a sculpture characterized by a striving for "totally personal and plastic form . . . uninfluenced by literature," (*Autobiography*, 1905), a sculpture that reflected his own experience of carving directly into stone. The works of Egypt, Archaic Greece and Khymer Cambodia—together with the example of his friend Maurice Du Plessys and the influence of Moréas—all spurred him toward a return to a strict rhythm of composition, a "return to form." Here, his often reiterated admiration for Puvis de Chavannes, Gauguin, Cézanne and Signac also came into play.

Rarely frequenting sculptors, and gradually breaking away from his old friend Bourdelle, he felt more in tune with Joseph Bernard, Lucian, Gaston Schnegg and Louis Dejean. In 1908, Charles Morice brought together "the new trends in French Art"—represented in the field of sculpture by Bourdelle, Claudel, Halou, Hoetger, Maillol, Marque, Rodin, Niederhäusern-Rodo and Rosso (listed as they appear in the catalog)—in an exhibition directed "against the tyranny of Impressionism," held at the Salon of the Golden Fleece in Moscow. Writing in *L'Intransigeant* (May 6, 1911), Apollinaire included Rodo among the finest of contemporary French sculptors: "Around the sublime Rodin, one finds such great sculptors as Marcel-Jacques,

Bourdelle, Niederhäusern-Rodo—young sculptors who, enlightened by the works of the late lamented Schnegg and the admirable Despiau . . . make straight for a beauty that is both ancient and new. . . . This galaxy of talents is the boast of contemporary sculpture."
C.L.

Ejnar (August) Nielsen
(Copenhagen, 1872—Hellerup, 1956)

Symbolism had its breakthrough in Denmark in 1889–93 when Ejnar Nielsen was a student at the Fine Arts Academy in Copenhagen. Like the artists in the circle around Gauguin, Nielsen looked for an untouched and authentic place to live and work, and eventually settled down in the village of Gjern, close to Silkeborg in central Jutland. Apart from the period 1895–96, Nielsen spent the years between 1894 and 1900 in this isolated village, dominated by a strictly evangelical branch of the Protestant church. Taking his point of departure in the hills of the surrounding moors and the harsh life of the locals, Nielsen created a series of important works, in which the decorative landscape often recedes to the background, forming a symbolic backdrop for solemn reproductions of human destinies in a subdued coloring.

From approximately 1900 Nielsen expanded his horizon to include Southern Europe and European art. His favorite destinations were France and Italy; in 1905–11 he lived in Paris and Rome respectively, but he also went to Spain and Greece. Especially the works by Puvis de Chavannes and the frescoes of the Italian Renaissance left a lasting impression on Nielsen's stringent style. During the 1920s Nielsen taught at the Kunstakademi in Copenhagen. Nielsen went to Paris relatively late. The occasion was presumably the 1900 World Exhibition for which he exhibited two pieces: *The Sick Girl* (1896, Copenhagen, Statens Museum for Kunst) and *Portrait of F. Widow* (1899, Helsinki, Ateneum). He stayed in Paris from the autumn of 1900 to the spring of 1901. As documented by his principal work from this time, *Portrait Group*, Nielsen was successful in his attempt to elaborate the impressions his avowed model, Puvis de Chavannes, made on him. But had Nielsen not provided a date for the painting himself, Paris 1900–01, one would need to know the roofs of Paris in

order to recognize the view. On the back Nielsen wrote that the painting was executed in Rue Vaugirard, where the portrayed couple, the Danish medallist Andreas Hansen and his French wife Celine Delacotte, had a flat. That Ejnar Nielsen incorporated elements from Puvis in his work also prior to his journey to Paris is evident from *Death and the Cripple*, a painting from 1898–99, which in several ways seems to allude to Puvis's *Poor Fisherman*, a work that was much admired among artists. Nielsen presumably owed his familiarity with *The Poor Fisherman* to graphic and photographic reproductions or illustrations in art magazines.
P.N.L.

Alphonse Osbert
(Paris, 1857–1939)

Initially a conventional painter inspired by Léon Bonnat and the Spanish seventeenth-century painting, Osbert quickly developed in the direction of Symbolism; indeed, after his meeting with Puvis de Chavannes, around 1887, this former pupil of Henri Lehmann's broke away from academic painting for good. By 1888 he was declaring himself a follower of Puvis de Chavannes, favoring the theme of a Muse depicted in an idyllic landscape and adopting a decorative style inspired by the older artist's Arcadian visions.

Just like the landscapes painted by the man he took as master, Osbert's reveal a concern for order, simplicity and harmony in their grid-like structure—horizontal bands of natural setting are juxtaposed with the vertical of trees and figures. This division of the surface, taken from the *Sacred Wood* (1884–89), is a main characteristic of Osbert's works of the 1895–1900 period—for example, the *Mystery of the Night* which he exhibited at the Salon de la Rose+Croix in 1897. In this work the artist stresses the verticality of the tree trunks, which almost resemble columns, aligned in a rhythmical sequence that undermines perspective.

The reference to a Golden Age is particularly clear in *Evening in Antiquity*, whose imagery is very close to that of Puvis's *Young Women by the Sea* (1879). The work shows female figures lost in thought on the shore of a blue sea reflecting the last rays of the setting sun. Puvis's influence can be seen in the handling of the landscape, in the pose of the figures and in the simplicity of line. Osbert also owed

him the idea of static figures seen close-to against the background of the sky. Another sign of the older artist's influence is the monumental, atemporal character of the whole picture. *Evening in Antiquity* also echoes *Pleasant Land* (1882) and *Antique Vision* (1885) in its evocation of a better world, in which man lives in perfect harmony with nature.
V.D.

Amédée Ozenfant
(Saint-Quentin, 1886—Cannes, 1996)

A major artist of the modern movement, Ozenfant was far from being part of the avant-garde in his youth. Studying with Charles Cottet and then Jacques Emile Blanche at the Académie La Palette from 1907 to 1913, Ozenfant chose an apprenticeship under the aegis of Romanticism and Symbolism. Reading, traveling and museum-visiting confirmed his taste for a cultured approach to art. He aimed for some sort of continuity between the nineteenth and twentieth centuries, and one of his fixed points of reference in this, along with Cézanne and Seurat, was Puvis de Chavannes, especially the Puvis of *Le Pauvre Pêcheur* in the Musée du Luxembourg. Of the artist, he wrote: "[He] was one of those who formed the Modern School in the fourth part of the nineteenth century—just as much as Delacroix, Ingres and Manet. That is the truth."(1)

In the numerous writings on art he published from 1916 onward, Ozenfant does not mention Puvis de Chavannes; Symbolism no longer enjoyed much standing in the approach to the plastic arts he had adopted after a rereading of Cubism. He envisaged an art of Purism that he applied to the plastic arts with Le Corbusier in *Après le Cubisme. La Peinture moderne*, and in his writings for *L'Esprit Nouveau*. In this key period, Ozenfant worked with Le Corbusier to promote and defend an artistic program that expressed and reflected the developments of a scientific and technological society. Both his abstract-geometrical and figurative painting engaged with the problems of the international avant-garde, even though he himself foresaw a possible continuity between Purism and the traditions of French painting. This continuity sought a constant set of plastic harmonies in its quest for equilibrium and a formal purity of vision (regardless of the subject matter of a painting), which may well explain the very originality of Purism. Dissatisfied with the geometrical abstraction that he had embraced—and soon tiring of the Magic Realism he had dallied with for a while—Ozenfant then headed in another direction, one that more fully developed his concern with the body, matter, and the dream-like. After the excesses of his adherence to a mechanized culture, his *Bathing in the Grotto* (painted in 1930-31) shows him searching for his origins in a sort of lost Golden Age. This painting, which depicts the artist himself in the foreground accompanied by a female figure, paved the way for the first version of his grand composition *Life* (1931-38, Paris, Musée National d'Art Moderne). At this point, Ozenfant returned to those sources of inspiration that reveal the survival within his art of the tradition initiated by Puvis de Chavannes, a source of inspiration that the artist had rediscovered during the course of his development.

F.D.

Giuseppe Pellizza da Volpedo
(Volpedo, 1868–1907)

Giuseppe Pellizza studied at the Accademia di Brera in Milan in 1883–84 and again in 1886–87. In the early months of 1888 he became a pupil of Giovanni Fattori in Florence, while from autumn 1888 to 1890 he frequented Cesare Tallone's School of Painting at the Accademia Carrara in Bergamo. During this time he also visited the most important contemporary art exhibitions: the Esposizione Nazionale in Venice (1887), the Universal Exposition in Paris (1889) and the Brera Triennale (1891); later he was also to visit shows of Italian work in Turin, Milan, Venice, Rome and Florence, as well as returning to Paris for the Exposition Universelle of 1900.
His first works are characterized by realistic themes, which he initially rendered with an impasto of dark and shaded colors before shifting to a brighter, more luminous palette, with refined tonal harmonies created between surface expanses of color (*Memory of a Sorrow*, 1889, Bergamo, Accademia Carrara). Around 1892, his growing taste for painting *en plein air* led him to experiment with the Divisionist technique. The use of little dots and dashes of pure color, aligned to contrast and complement each other, enabled him to achieve faithful renditions of light in works

inspired by social and humanitarian themes as in *In the Hayloft* and *Disappointed Hopes* of 1893–94; *The Fourth Estate* (Milan, Galleria d'Arte Moderna) of 1898–1901 (Pellizza had worked on this painting since 1891) and the almost abstract compositions of *Washing in the Sun* (1894–95) and *The Sun* (1904). From 1895 onward, Pellizza combined his interest in the rendition of the real world with a growing attention to fifteenth and sixteenth-century painting; nature became the source of love and beauty as well as a symbol of the continuity of the cycle of life (*The Mirror of Life*, 1895–98, Turin, Galleria d'Arte Moderna). *Spring Idyll* (whose layout was reused in *Ring-around-a-rosy*, probably completed after Pellizza's death by the young Angelo Barabino) was perhaps the first of these works; the everyday theme of a ring of children is, through a skillful reinvention of an iconographic symbol of the past, turned into an evocative image of life itself, with the couple in the foreground tentatively discovering first love and thus suggesting a more pagan sense of the ritual of coronation and of the symbolism of pain and sorrow in the image of the knotty old tree. It was no coincidence that in 1898 Neera urged Pellizza to take on the role of Symbolist painter as exemplified by Burne-Jones and Puvis de Chavannes.
This symbolic interpretation of nature led the artist to explore the universal themes of life, love and death in a series of paintings, whose variation in composition and palette indicates how the changing light of day reflected the feelings of the children depicted. One such work was *Flowering Meadow*. In *April in the Fields of Volpedo* (1904) the refined rhythm of the landscape suggests the universal value of the cycle of life. It is represented both by the two women gleaners in the field and, in the foreground, by the child in red advancing toward a woman lost in thought in the dense greenery, in which a bare tree stands with newly formed buds on some of its branches. The cosmic whole of immobile figures lost in thought and the natural world that absorbs varieties of color and light can also be seen in such works as *Emigrants*. The celebration of nature as a force that can reabsorb man and society was the dominant theme in the work Pellizza produced between 1902 and 1907, the year in which he committed suicide in his studio in Volpedo.

A.S.

Eilif Peterssen
(Kristiania, now Oslo, 1852—Baerum, 1928)

At the early age of fourteen Eilif Peterssen began his education as an artist at home in Kristiania. He continued his studies at the art schools in Copenhagen and Karlsruhe, then in Munich where he quickly made a name as a promising history painter. Peterssen had a superb mastery of landscape, portrait and figure painting, and about 1880, he was considered the most promising of the younger Norwegian artists. At this time, he had already given up history painting in favor of realistic, contemporary folk-life depictions. Both *Siesta in a Tavern in Sora* (1880, Oslo, National Gallery) and *Piazza Montanara* (1882–83, Oslo, Norske Selskab), are among his major works and are examples of this new trend in his art.
His development during the following ten years was markedly influenced by his encounter with French art of the mid-1880s, and it was particularly the work of Puvis de Chavannes that left a lasting impression. *Summer Night* from 1886 shows how he managed to transfer Puvis's landscape composition of the *Sacred Wood* into a genuine experience of Norwegian nature as seen in the mild, declining light of a summer night. The following year Peterssen painted a large picture entitled *Nocturne* (1887, Stockholm, National Museum): a nude woman, her back turned, placed in the same landscape as his painting from the previous year, arouses immediate associations with Puvis's many female figures in natural settings. The subject can hardly be considered realistic, yet with its perception of nature and rich detail, it has all the characteristics of Naturalism. That same year he painted a smaller version of the subject (1887, Oslo, National Gallery), in which his simplified perception of form and rendering of nature is closer to Puvis's monumental art.

M.L.

Kuz'ma (Sergeyevich) Petrov-Vodkin
(Khvalynsk, 1878—Leningrad, now Saint Petersburg, 1939)

Having trained in Russia, Petrov-Vodkin painted his *The Riverbank* in Paris in 1908, grouping together seven figures within a natural setting. The vertical rhythm of the composition is initiated by the

woman in red who is doing her hair, and is continued by the series of female figures. To the left, an aged woman sits on a rock with her eyes closed in meditation and holding something in her hands—the figure is reminiscent of that in *The Sacred Wood Dear to the Arts and Muses* in the Sorbonne, and is rather different from the old woman in *Ludus pro Patria*. In the center is a half-dressed young woman in pensive mood; with her bent elbow and hand resting delicately under her chin, she reminds one of *Antique Vision*; and the maternal figure seen in profile as she gently dresses a small child echoes *Pleasant Land*. Ultimately, the whole composition is "held in place" by the crouching woman seen from the back in the lower-right of the picture, whose hands are significantly joined in an ardent and silent prayer. The multi-colored ground is constellated, and the winding coastline draws the eye away to the far horizon. Mystery hovers over this coast which is bathed in an atmosphere of harmony; in this place where time seems to have stood still, the static, antique-style figures communicate silently.
The influence of Symbolism is clear here. The painter was clearly rendering homage to Puvis de Chavannes in his treatment of figures and his clear mastery of space. The studies for *Shore* date from 1907, and in 1912 Petrov-Vodkin would paint the work which was a veritable manifesto of his aesthetics—*Red Horse Bathing*—together with *The Death of the Commissar* and a portrait of Pushkin. During his lifetime he was a celebrated master in his native country. His work has been exhibited at the Venice Biennales of 1924, 1928 and 1932.

N.R.F.

Francis Picabia
(Paris, 1879–1953)

Up to around 1908–09 Francis Picabia was a rather unoriginal follower of Impressionism, who nevertheless enjoyed a certain success and reputation thanks to the very brio of his work. However, not settling for the safety of success, he began at that point to produce more de-stylized works in which not only the influence of the Post-Impressionist avant-garde is clear, but also that of some of Puvis's works. One can see this in a painting such as *Adam and Eve* (1911), in which the two embracing nudes, whose pink flesh maintains a

certain verisimilitude, are shown against a background of flat fields of bright and arbitrary colors and rendered with a curving line that considerably simplifies natural forms. Exhibited in May 1911 at the second *Exposition de la Société Normande de la peinture moderne*, this painting showed the artist's tardy adherence to principles close to those behind Fauvism. It should be linked with another outdoor nude exhibited just a few weeks earlier at the Salon des Indépendants, *Spring* or *Women under the Pine Trees* (1911, location unknown), which—because of its "fallacious colors"—the critics of the day linked with the outrages perpetrated by Van Dongen. Before this period, nudes had figured rarely in the work of Picabia, who was primarily a landscape artist. However, the nude was a common subject matter in the Salons of the period—as well as being popular with the avant-garde, who often returned to the theme of the Garden of Eden. Restricting oneself to Picabia's immediate circle, one might mention the *Pastoral* or *Adam and Eve* by Raymond Duchamp-Villon (1910, Paris, Musée National d'Art Moderne) and the *Paradise* (1910–11, Philadelphia Museum of Art) and *Spring or Young Man and Woman at Springtime* (1911, Milan, private collection) by his brother Marcel Duchamp. While there is no certainty that Picabia had met Marcel Duchamp before the autumn of 1911, one cannot help but notice certain stylistic and thematic similarities between their work in this period. They were taking their first steps in an investigation of sexual antagonism which, during in their Dadaist period, would ultimately lead both artists to resort to bio-mechanical images.
A.P.

Pablo Picasso
(Malaga, 1881—Mougins, 1973)

Pablo Ruiz Picasso completed his early artistic studies at the La Corogne School of Fine Arts in Barcelona before moving to Madrid, and thereafter frequenting a circle of avant-garde Catalan artists. In 1900, his painting *Last Moments* was part of the official Spanish exhibition at the Exposition Universelle in Paris—an occasion that first offered Picasso his opportunity to discover the work of Puvis de Chavannes. The influence of this latter is clear in the work of the Blue Period (1901–04) and the Pink Period (1905–06),

with such paintings as *The Interview, The Tragedy, Acrobat on a Ball, The Toilette* and *Boy Leading a Horse*. After frequent journeys between Paris, Madrid and Barcelona in the period 1900–04, Picasso finally settled at the Bateau-Lavoir in Montmartre. He developed close friendships with poets such as Max Jacob, Guillaume Apollinaire and André Salmon, and with such painters as Henri Rousseau, Henri Matisse and Georges Braque. The discovery of Iberian sculpture and of primitive art in general, as well as the influence of the work of Cézanne and Gauguin, played a part in a stylistic development that would ultimately result in *Les Demoiselles d'Avignon* (1907) and the formulation of Cubism over the period 1908–14. The return to figurative art—marked by his 1914 *The Artist and his Model*—opened the way to Picasso's "Classical" period, which began with the "Ingresque" drawings of 1915–17, and the stage curtain for *Parade* (1917) to then continue into the early 1920s. Works inspired by classical antiquity and by the painting of Ingres and Puvis de Chavannes include *Three Women at the Spring* (1921) and *The Pipes of Pan* (1923); and these alternated with paintings that gave a more synthetic reading of Cubism—most notably, *Harlequin and Woman with Necklace* (1917), *Three Musicians* (1923) and *The Dance* (1925). In the period 1925–35—characterized by the emergence of Surrealism and an increasingly-tense international situation—Picasso's work tends to violently distort the human figure and face, as one can see in the series of paintings depicting studios, shipwrecks and individual heads that he produced at Boisgeloup. His *Guernica*, produced for the Spanish Republican Pavilion at the 1937 International Exhibition of Arts and Technology, saw Picasso develop a modern form for monumental political paintings, which would find echoes in such post-war works as *The Charnel House* (1945), *Massacre in Korea* (1951), *War and Peace* (Vallauris, 1952) and *The Fall of Icarus* (1957–58) painted to decorate the UNESCO building. Having settled in the south of France, where he would live for the final decades of his life, Picasso's unfailing creativity found expression in painting (with a predilection for "rereadings" of such Old Masters as Manet, Poussin and Rembrandt), in sculpture (mainly using cut and folded sheets of metal), engraving (especially the

1968 *347 Series* and the 1970–72 *156 Series*) and ceramics (with a sizeable output of Madoura pottery). The 1971 Louvre exhibition, held to celebrate his ninetieth birthday, and the 1973 exhibition of his last works at the Palais des Papes in Avignon were both occasions that underlined the contemporary relevance of his innovative art.
A.B.

Maurice Brazil Prendergast
(Boston, 1858—New York, 1924)

American modernist Maurice Prendergast engaged with the work and ideas of Puvis de Chavannes at several points during his artistic development. While studying in Paris from 1891 to 1894, he formed friendships with many artists who admired the work of Puvis, especially through the Académie Julian where he trained, as well as at Colarossi's. Within this Paris circle were English artists and aesthetes Aubrey Beardsley and Charles Conder, both important promoters of Puvis's work, as well as the Canadian James Wilson Morrice. Through them or on his own, Prendergast may have even met Puvis directly. When he returned to Europe over a decade later, Prendergast approached Puvis's work with greater focus, making sketches after several of his paintings, including *Summer* in the Paris Hôtel de Ville, *Pleasant Land*, and *Young Women by the Sea*. Back in his native Boston in the 1910s, Prendergast again looked to Puvis for ideas and made sketches after three of Puvis's important murals (of 1896) for the Boston Public Library.
All of these sketches as well as *On the Beach, No. 3* (c. 1915, Cleveland Museum of Art, Hinman B. Hurlbut Collection), indicate Prendergast's shift toward broadly classical yet still modernist themes in the years between 1910 and 1918, when he created his crowning series of oils that portray figures at leisure on beaches or in parks. During this period, he actively sought out and often made sketches after major modernist works by Cézanne, Matisse, and Renoir, as well as Puvis. *On the Beach, No. 3* and others like it are distinctly reminiscent of Puvis's work, such as the mural *Inter Artes et Naturam* (1890) for the Musée des Beaux-Arts in Rouen, in which the figures wear modern dress. Virtually everything in *On the Beach, No. 3* has been drawn from Puvis: the frieze-like structure and

composition; the horizontal bands of figures, trees, water, and sky flattening out into the distance; the pastoral theme and its classicizing overtones; the idyllic, Arcadian subject matter; the relationship of the figures; and the distinctively matte, chalky surface. Prendergast employed Puvis's classicism as well as his modernity to create a modern "American" look of his own.
S.E.

Pierre Puvis de Chavannes
(Lyon, 1824—Paris, 1898)

A child of the solid bourgeoisie of Lyon, Puvis de Chavannes received what was then a traditional classical education before dedicating himself to painting. Thereafter he passed through a number of studios—most notably, those of Delacroix, Henri Scheffer and Couture; however, it was Chassériau who perhaps left the greatest mark on him—especially through the large mural paintings he produced for the staircase of the Cour des Comptes [Revenue Courts] in Paris between 1844 and 1848 (works that were destroyed in 1871). The young artist would not truly find his own way until he was thirty years old, when he worked on the decoration of the dining room in his brother's country house (depicting *The Four Seasons* and *The Return of the Prodigal Son*). His debut at the Paris Salon was also a difficult affair (his work was rejected several times; and when he was exhibited, he was heavily criticized). His first success there came in 1861 with his panels of *War* and *Peace*, the former of which was purchased by the state for the Amiens museum. At that point Puvis himself donated the second panel and then worked on two complementary pendants for the 1863 Salon (*Rest* and *Work*), which would be followed in 1865 by *Ave Picardia Nutrix*; the whole ensemble would only be completed fifteen years later, with *Ludus pro Patria*. Thus, produced partly at his own expense, this exceptional project of decorative panels covers a substantial period in his career as an artist. In both theme and style, those works are also representative of his approach to allegory—a genre in which he was to become one of the most eminent practitioners, thanks to a series of large-scale mural projects: the Palais Longchamp in Marseille (1867–69), the Poitiers Hôtel de Ville (1870–75), the Rouen Museum (1888–91), at the Paris Hôtel de Ville (1887–94) and the Boston Public Library (1881–96). Along

with these projects, there were three exceptional ensembles of decoration: the Panthéon in Paris, where he illustrated the life of Saint Genevieve (working over two separate periods, 1874–78 and 1893–98); the Musée des Beaux-Arts in Lyon (where from 1884 to 1886 he decorated the staircase with what, as a matter of fact, forms a thematic manifesto of his art, depicting *The Sacred Wood Dear to the Arts and Muses*, *Antique Vision*, *Christian Inspiration* and allegories of the rivers *The Rhône* and *The Saône*); and the large-scale decor of the Great Amphitheater in the Sorbonne (1886–89), which develops the themes broached in Lyon. For each of these projects there were numerous painted studies and sketches, as well as preparatory cartoons (whose details and color scheme Puvis would follow more or less closely). Together with the copies of the works painted by the artist himself, these would help to enhance the popularity of his art (especially abroad). This exhibition presents a number of such works: a study of *Saint Genevieve as a Child in Prayer* and of *Saint Genevieve Watching over Paris* from the Panthéon, a copy of *Ludus pro Patria*, of *Inter Artes et Naturam* (*The Benefits of Peace*) (painted for the Rouen museum), and of *Summer* and *Winter* (the originals of which were painted for the Zodiac room in the Paris Hôtel de Ville, whose refurbishment after the 1871 fire brought together a remarkable collection of decorative painting, which today affords a very representative collection of official art at the beginning of the Third Republic). The decor produced for the Boston Public Library is here represented by a sketch of the whole (*The Inspiring Muses Acclaim the Spirit of Light*) and an exact copy of one panel: *Homer* or *Epic Poetry*. Similarly, *Charity* is a copy (with some variations) of one of the arches on the main staircase of the Paris Hôtel de Ville, even if it is conceived as an independent painting in its own right.
Other smaller scale works reflect Puvis de Chavannes's main decorative schemes as well: for example, *The Sacred Wood* from the Clemens-Sels Museum is a sketch for *Pleasant Land* painted for the home of the painter Léon Bonnat, who was a friend of Puvis. The artist also took up motifs or groups from the larger compositions using them as independent works: for example, *The White Rock* is taken from *Massilia, Greek Colony* (Palais

Longchamp); *Tamaris*, which is obviously inspired by the famous *Sleeping Ariadne* in the Vatican Museum, also derived from the allegory of *The Saône* in the Lyon Museum; *The Shepherd's Song* is a variation on *Antique Vision*, or again *The Goatherd* which, in part, is taken from *Inter Artes et Naturam* (and has even been incorrectly taken as a study for that earlier work). Puvis was continually returning to motifs and subjects, modifying them in more or less important ways. For example, the 1890 *Apple Harvest* is made up of two motifs taken from the 1873 *Summer* now in the Musée de Chartres. As *Children in an Orchard*, also known as *Autumn*, it draws on the sketch for *Massilia, Greek Colony*, on *Ave Picardia Nutrix* and *Pleasant Land*, generally inverting the figures.
During all this time, Puvis continued to paint small-scale easel works: *Death and the Maidens*, a depiction of the fragility of youth which was distantly inspired by Schubert's "Death and the Maiden"; *Young Woman at Her Toilette* (1883, Paris, Musée d'Orsay)—here represented by another version—can easily be seen in connection with Degas's later paintings of similar subject matter; and the 1883 *Orpheus*, a subject dear to the Symbolists (this painting was bought by the composer Ernest Chausson). The artist was also not averse to painting works with a more run-of-the-mill subject matter (particularly of a religious nature). This was the case, for example, with his 1879 *Prodigal Son* which was so badly received by the critics that same year, probably because of the work's meditative, Symbolist character (something which would, on the contrary, lead to much greater appreciation of the same painting when, in 1887, it was reexhibited with other Puvis pictures at the Galerie Durand-Ruel). Similarly, *The Magdalene*, one of the artist's last paintings, abandons all anecdote to focus on the expression of the figure (in his 1869 treatment of the same subject, the artist had maintained the traditional iconography depicting the female penitent musing upon a human skull in the desert surrounding Sainte Baume in Provence).
Certain works also reflect contemporary events. The Franco-Prussian War of 1870–71 had a deep effect on the artist, and various paintings are a direct response to it (the 1870 *The Balloon*, the 1871 *The Pigeon*, the 1872 *Hope* [known in

two versions, now at the Walters Art Gallery in Baltimore and the Musée d'Orsay, Paris]), while others echo those events more indirectly (*Ludus pro Patria*). However, the paintings which are now most famous are those which maintain the aesthetics of his mural compositions, works which at first glance may be seem easily comprehensible, but as a matter of fact retain an air of mystery. *The Poor Fisherman* is typical of this area of Puvis de Chavannes's output, and sharply divides critics. As for *Young Woman by the Sea*, it further illustrates the artist's habit of returning to themes and motifs already explored (for example, the young girl stretched out in the foreground can be linked with his *Tamaris*). Some twenty years later, in 1890, Puvis de Chavannes would return to the theme in his *Bathers*, which also evokes the work of Ingres (and his *Turkish Bath* in particular). Perhaps this painting by Puvis can be taken as a perfect example of how the artist was at, one and the same time, one of the innovators of his age and also part of a classical tradition—a tradition which he was able to rejuvenate and revitalize and thus hand on to future generations.
B.J.

Paul-Elie Ranson
(Limoges, 1864—Paris, 1909)

After having studied at the School of Industrially-Applied Arts at Limoges, he entered the Académie Julian in 1886, becoming a founder member of the Nabi group (their meetings would, in 1889, be held in his Boulevard du Montparnasse studio). He took part in various of the group's exhibitions at Le Barc de Boutteville from 1891 to 1895, as well as participating at the Salon des Indépendants from 1892 onward and in the Brussels La Libre Esthétique shows from 1894 onward.
In addition, Ranson did work for Lugné-Poe's Théâtre d'Art (later Théâtre de l'Oeuvre) and his own puppet theater (starting in 1894), produced lithographs (particularly for *La Revue Blanche*) and, most importantly, was active in the field of the decorative arts (decorative panels; *papiers peints* in 1893; wallpapers, created for his wife, France, and exhibited at the Société Nationale des Beaux-Arts from 1894 onward; glass panels and fabrics, most notably those used by Van der Velde in 1897). As a decorative artist he worked on the opening of Bing's *L'Art Nouveau* in December 1894, producing

decorative panels to accompany Van der Velde's furniture and Tiffany glass panels.
His interest in theosophy, magic and the occult distinguished him from the other Nabis, even if he shared the same spiritual concerns as Denis and Sérusier (who painted his *Portrait in Nabi costume* in 1890). He produced various esoteric works (*Nabi Landscape*, 1890) which clearly reveal these interests, as well as the strong aesthetic influence of Japanese art (in the complex play of arabesques).
After 1899, as his health gradually declined, his painting moved away from Symbolism. He became close to Georges Lacombe, in 1900 decorating part of his house, "L'Ermitage," near Alençon, and staying with him again in 1901 and 1904.
The last period in his work combines anti-clerical subjects with scenes drawn from mythology, biblical history and sorcery. His last work was the creation of the costumes for Marinetti's satirical work *Le Roi Bombance* in April 1909.
After his death, his wife continued to run the Académie Ranson, which they had opened in October 1908 as a source of income; many of his old Nabi associates—most notably, Sérusier, Denis and Vallotton—taught there.
Although differing in spiritualistic interests, Ranson's particular attention to the decorative arts, notably tapestries and stained glass, often led him to draw closely on the motifs and compositions of Puvis's great decorative panels, including their ornamental frames.
J.P.B.

Odilon Redon
(Bordeaux, 1840—Paris, 1916)

The work of Odilon Redon reveals the full extent of the influence Puvis de Chavannes had on French Symbolism, even if he himself shared none of that movement's interest in the esoteric. This connection has occasionally created some confusion between Symbolist idealism—which was of literary inspiration and much concerned with the mechanisms of dreams and the correspondence of images—and the idealism to be seen in the work of Puvis de Chavannes—which, on the contrary, aimed for the strict simplicity of the universal rather than the tortuous complexities of the individual (it is this difference which accounts for the diversity in his influence, with each artist reappropriating and reinterpreting his work in his own way). Puvis's art speaks a language all can understand, while Redon has a language all his own—a language which is so subjective that some of his works have remained total enigmas. For example, how are we to interpret *Closed Eyes* or *The Red Tree Not Reddened by the Sun*? Various readings have been put forward—most notably, a biblical reading which sees the first as an image of the Resurrection and the second as a metaphor for the Ministry of Christ—but the mystery surrounding the paintings remains intact. What is more, *Closed Eyes* is part of a series of works in which the face appears either crowned with a halo or entirely encircled with flowers—a detail which further complicates the task of interpretation.

The three pictures exhibited here are of particular interest in the context of Redon's work as a whole. The 1890s and the early 1900s marked a period of transition for the artist, with a change in his palette and a gradual move away from the blacks that had previously been dominant in his work. *Eve* is his first female nude from a life study. *Closed Eyes*, painted in 1890 and purchased by the French state in 1904, was considered by the artist to mark an important changing-point in his work. Quite apart from his growing taste for dazzling colors—as can be seen from the glistening red of the tree—Redon was also beginning to pursue the plastic ideal represented by Puvis de Chavannes's work. There was the same elliptic draftsmanship and sculptural rendition of figures, the same flatness of space, the same use of expanses of color to create the composition. All of these qualities give the works an air of atemporal primitivism—something between a biblical Golden Age and a dream-like antiquity.

As we can see from his *Journal*, Redon knew the work of Puvis de Chavannes. He wrote some particularly perceptive comments of the artist he looked upon as one of his masters, jotting down that "Puvis de Chavannes is long-sighted through abstraction." He attributed this sublime simplicity to "a spirit of abnegation which can make the hand work to simplify, to capture basics." Indeed, Redon's definition of his own art could well be applied to that of Puvis de Chavannes: "it also owes a lot to the effects of the abstract line, that agent which arises from a deep well-spring and acts directly upon the spirit."
E.A.

Laurits Andersen Ring
(Ring, 1854—Skt. Jørgensbjerg, near Roskilde, 1933)

Laurits Andersen Ring was born in poverty in the country town of Ring, in South Jutland. In his youth he worked as a house painter in his own neighborhood. His art education lasted a comparatively short time (1874–77), and followed the traditional practice at the Academy in Copenhagen under the direction of the folk-life painter Frederik Vermehren (1823–1910). In 1884–85, he was back at the Academy, this time under another folk-life painter, Johan Julius Exner (1825–1910). Ring's modest country background and his training under the above-mentioned painters were crucial factors in shaping his ideas of what art should express. First, it should tell about the lives of ordinary people, secondly it should transcend the moment and engender a feeling of something eternal, of an underlying reality. His art is therefore naturalistic and symbolistic at the same time. Thanks to the detailed rendering, we have no doubt as to what we see, but we are left with an uneasy feeling of something unseen.
In 1888, a comprehensive exhibition of modern French art was held in Copenhagen. There, Ring was able to study works by, among others, Puvis de Chavannes, Millet, Bastien-Lepage and Raffaëlli, all artists who were to be of importance to him. In 1889, he made his first trip abroad and traveled through Holland and Belgium to Paris. Here he visited the World Exhibition which made an enormous impression on him.
In *June. Girl Blowing a Dandelion* from 1899 brings to mind Puvis's *Hope* (1872, Baltimore, Walters Art Gallery). If that is the case, it is a matter of content and not of painterly execution. Puvis's beautiful young, white-clad girl, a sprig of green in her hand, is seated in a classic pose, in an abstractedly depicted landscape. Ring's black-clad girl, on the other hand, sits in her own daily surroundings, in a meadow beside a worn board fence; with her pointed nose and pronounced cheekbones she is not an ideal beauty, but a figure taken straight out of folk life. She is blowing away a dandelion gone to seed. According to popular belief, if she manages to blow it away in one breath, she can make a wish. A passive and oppressive mood pervades the atmosphere. Ring does not press any interpretations on the onlooker—the paining can just as

easily be a simple country scene as a picture with symbolic overtones. The monumentality of *Hope* is lacking here, but we find the same decorative linear play in the figure's sharply drawn contours.
In his day Ring was often criticized for his uncertainty in figure drawing and for his lack of knowledge of anatomy and perspective. Today, however, it is precisely this break with academic accuracy that marks the strongly personal expression of his art. On this score, we can also point to similarities with Puvis, in whose opinion correct drawing must at times give way to "the style" or, in other words, expressive form. Ring's original composition is carefully thought out and carried out in a consistent manner. As Puvis, he places the figure *in front of* the landscape rather than *in* it, a frequently recurring characteristic in Ring's work. The best-known example of this is *At the Garden Door. The Artist's Wife* (1897, Copenhagen, Statens Museum for Kunst), in which, while emphasizing human presence, the artist draws attention to the mood of the landscape.
M.L.

Nikolai Konstantinovich Roerich
(Saint Petersburg, 1874—Kulu Valley, India, 1947)

A history and landscape painter, as well as mural decorator and stage designer, Roerich was also an archaeologist, philosopher and writer who took a very active stance on social issues. From 1893 to 1898 he studied law at Saint Petersburg University while also being trained in the studio of A.I. Kuindzhi at the Imperial Academy of Fine Arts (1893–97). To complete his artistic training, in 1900 he left for Paris, where he worked in the studio of Fernand Cormon. His attraction to the works of Puvis de Chavannes dates from this period: Roerich found many echoes of his own ideas and aspirations in the life and work of the French master. Having returned from Paris, he exhibited in numerous shows, in Russia and elsewhere, as well as working on various set designs and church interiors, and publishing essays and reviews. From 1906 to 1918, he headed the Society for the Promotion of the Arts, in Saint Petersburg, and in 1910 became the president of the new association *Mir Iskusstva*. In the period 1918–23 he traveled in Finland, England and the United States; then in 1923 he settled in India, where he dedicated his time to painting and to the

promotion of scientific expeditions to investigate not only the mountainous regions of that country but also other areas in Altai, Buratija, Mongolia and China, In 1929 he published the first draft of the so-called "Roerich Pact," a project intended to protect works of art during periods of war. Subsequently, the "Roerich Pact" would serve as the basis for the "International Convention for the Defense of the Cultural Heritage during Armed Conflict" signed at The Hague in 1954. From 1941 to 1944, the artist was honorary president of the America-Russia Cultural Association. Roerich considered Puvis de Chavannes to be one of his own special masters (along with A.I. Kuindzhi and F. Cormon). He was bound to the French master by a deeply-felt agreement on certain fundamental issues: the history of human civilization, the mission of art, the role of work in society, etc.—an agreement which also resulted in close similarities in artistic method. Like Puvis de Chavannes, Roerich set himself to produce cycles of symbolic works. His canvases offer the spectator a monumental panorama of history, drawing on the experience of the great mural painters of the Middle Ages. However, while Puvis de Chavannes had a veritable veneration for the masters of the Italian Renaissance, the Old Masters to whom Roerich was drawn were those of his native Russia; hence his works are less literary and more decorative. Nevertheless, a further affinity between the work of the two can be found in their flowing, musical sense of line, a musical ability that results in their stunning ability to express emotions.
P.Y.K.

Ker-Xavier Roussel
(Lorry-lès-Metz, 1867—L'Etang-la-Ville, 1944)

Roussel's retiring life seems to be overshadowed by his works themselves. The son of a doctor who moved to Paris in 1870 and encouraged his son's artistic vocation, he attended the Lycée Condorcet, where he met Denis, Lugné-Poe and Vuillard (whose sister Marie he married in 1893). After a short period of training at the Ecole des Beaux-Arts (to which he gained admission in 1886), he joined the Académie Julian, where he became a founder member of the Nabi group. He would exhibit with the group at Le Barc de Boutteville, and hold his first one-man show at

La Revue Blanche in 1894; this was followed by exhibitions at Vollard's (for whom he would produce lithographs in the period 1897–98, and again in the 1930s). After 1893, health problems—followed by the emotional trauma caused by the death of his first child (1896)—led to a falling-off in the amount of work he produced. After the birth of a second child in 1898, he left Paris for good in 1899 to settle in L'Etang-la-Ville near Marly-le-Roi, where he would live quietly until his death in 1944; his main contacts during this period were with Denis and Vuillard (with the former he would visit Cézanne in Provence in 1906; while all three of them would work together on the decor of the Théâtre des Champs-Elysées [1913], the Palais des Nations in Geneva [1936] and the Palais de Chaillot in Paris [1937]). Up to 1914 he exhibited regularly at the Bernheim-Jeune gallery, as well as at the Salon des Indépendants from 1901 to 1910; he also received a number of important commissions for the decoration of private interiors (Bernheim and Lugné-Poe in 1909, the Monteux family in 1919–20, Lucien Rosengart in 1925). His work can be divided into two clearly different periods: up to 1899 it is dominated by the aesthetics of the Nabi, being particularly close to that of Vuillard and Denis and revealing a marked interest in Puvis de Chavannes and Seurat (Roussel's own potential as a creator of interior decors would only be fully realized after 1900). After that date, his work—both paintings and engravings—was almost exclusively concerned with the rendition of variations in light and movement within pictures of mythological scenes (most notably inspired by the works of Virgil).
J.P.B.

Giovanni Segantini
(Arco Trentino, 1858—Schafberg, Upper Engadine, 1899)

It is very difficult to describe the exact relation between Giovanni Segantini and Puvis de Chavannes. After an adventurous childhood, the Italian artist trained at the Accademia di Brera (1875–79) made his first, hardly triumphant, public debut with his 1878 *The Choir of Sant'Antonio in Milan* at the Milan National Exhibition in 1879. Despite the modest reception, the work aroused the interest of the critic Vittore Grubicy de Dragon, who would become the young painter's patron. From then on, Segantini would dedicate himself to his art, becoming the leader in Italy of a movement which combined the techniques of Divisionism and the aesthetics of Symbolism. This is how one might first trace a link between him and Puvis de Chavannes: did the 1881 *Poor Fisherman* have some influence on the Italian's first major painting *The Ave Maria on the Boat* (1882, Zurich, private collection; second version of 1886, St Gallen, Otto Fischbacher Giovanni Segantini Stiftung)? For this to be true, Segantini would have had to be very *au fait* with the Parisian art scene. However, thanks to Grubicy—who in return for financing his work had exclusive rights over it—he lived a rather secluded life in Puziano (Brianza), moving to the nearby Carella in 1882 and back to Milan in 1886. In short, he does not seem to have been much interested in European artistic movements, preferring to concentrate on his own work. If one must identify outside references, then they would be the painters made known to him by Grubicy—the Dutch Realists (Israëls, Mesdag, Mauve) and, above all, Jean-François Millet—rather than Puvis de Chavannes.

The years 1888–89 mark a turning-point in Segantini's career, with his works being sent to London and Paris (this is also the period in which the artist broke with Grubicy and turned to his brother Alberto). Moreover, Segantini's international reputation was further consolidated when his work became known in Germany. The artist's paintings became even more Symbolist in tone, even if the subject matter was closely linked with the real world around him in Les Grisons (where he lived from 1886) and the Engadine (where he lived from 1894 to his death). For the 1900 Universal Exposition he painted what must have been his masterpiece—the panoramic triptych of *Nature*—of which only the cartoon (Wintertur, Stiftung für Kunst) and three panels (St Moritz, Segantini Museum) exist. It is here that one can see the closest parallels with Puvis de Chavannes. Already visible in the fine figure of the shepherd shown in profile as he plays the flute in *Idyll* (in which the enclosure of the image within a natural setting is underlined by parallels between the branches of blossom in the foreground and the silhouette of the youth), this link is even clearer in the 1896 *Love at the Fountain of Life* (Milan, Galleria Civica d'Arte Moderna), which takes up the composition of the 1894 *Angel of Life* (same collection) that is equally Puvisesque—a fact underlined by a later drawn version in the form of a fan (1899, same collection). *Vanity, or The Fountain of Evil* marks a further step in this direction: the forms are deliberately simplified, with a figure shown in profile and heavily-scored outline; the realistic landscape is in some sense atemporal; the natural world depicted is calm and unadorned; the more complex meaning of the work is emphasized by the title itself and the presence of the serpent. All these features are reminiscent of Puvis de Chavannes. By this date, Segantini must have undoubtedly been aware of the latter's work; however, there is no proof that he had any great knowledge—or appreciation—of it. He did not speak French; and while he did exhibit with *Les Vingts* as early as 1890 and seems to have subscribed to their journal, *L'Art Moderne*, he could only have read it with the help of those among his friends who did speak the language. In fact, should one not also trace a link here with Seurat, whose *La Grande Jatte*, exhibited in 1886, had an influence that went beyond the strictly technical aspects of Divisionism; or perhaps with Gauguin, whose approach was very similar to—and absolutely contemporary with—Segantini's own? In the absence of any definite answers, it is best to speak of coincidences; not totally fortuitous coincidences, but those brought about by "intermediaries" whose identity is as of yet unknown to us (though it is highly likely they can be identified with figures in the French and Belgian Symbolist circles of the 1890s).
B.J.

Alexandre Séon
(Chazelles-sur-Lyon, 1855—Paris, 1917)

After passing through the Ecole des Beaux-Arts in Lyon, Alexandre Séon entered Henri Lehmann's Paris studio in 1877, there forming a friendship with Seurat. From 1881 he worked with Puvis de Chavannes—first as pupil, then as assistant—also showing his own work at various exhibitions, without much success. In 1886 he exhibited *The Star*, where subject matter, composition and treatment all reveal the influence of his master. The sobriety of the young woman's pose and of her setting highlight the elegant lines in the rendition of the female figure, which is typical of Séon's work: a distant, ideal woman who embodies superior thoughts. As in all of the artist's works, the landscape is a reflection of the inner feelings of the subject.

From 1885–89 he painted the very Puvisesque panels on canvas that were then glued to the walls of the Courbevoie Town Hall. Drawing-master for the schools of the city of Paris from 1881 to 1915, he exhibited at the Salon des Artistes Français from 1880 to 1902, and at the Société Nationale des Beaux-Arts from 1890 to 1906, where he showed *The Lamentation of Orpheus*, which takes up the composition of his 1885 *Orpheus*—except that there the figure is shown standing against a rock, while in the later painting he is lying on the sand in a pose that expresses his sorrow as he weeps over his loss of his wife Eurydice. The inspiration for the landscape—here painted without depth of perspective—was the Ile de Bréhat, which Séon visited frequently. Puvis de Chavannes was the inspiration not only of the composition but also of the theme, having exhibited his own *Orpheus* at the 1883 Salon. In that painting, the poet gives more visible expression to his sorrow, and the flying seagull could be seen as a symbol of the loss of Eurydice. Séon, for his part, chose to rid the landscape of anecdotal detail and depicts the sorrow of the character with great restraint. In fact, only the laurel wreath and the tortoiseshell lyre (the tortoise being a symbol of Eternity) enable us to identify Orpheus at all.

From 1892 onward Séon participated at the Salons de la Rose+Croix and illustrated several literary works. An anti-realist in his theories of art, he worked for a renaissance of idealism—and given his concern with social questions would often be described as an "idéiste" painter by Alphonse Germain.
M.C.

Paul Sérusier
(Paris, 1864—Morlaix, 1927)

After his brilliant studies, in 1885 Paul Sérusier entered the Académie Julian, where he became the *massier* responsible for the collection of communal funds. His meeting with Gauguin at Pont-Aven in summer 1888 resulted in his conversion to the that painter's new aesthetics; in October that same year, his presentation before Denis, Bonnard, Ibels and Ranson of the painting produced under the direction of Gauguin—the work subsequently known as *The Talisman* (Paris, Musée d'Orsay)—contributed to the formation of the Nabi group, of which Sérusier was a founder member. Visiting Gauguin again in 1889 and 1890, he consolidated the link between the artist and his young admirers: "Sérusier's very philosophical mind very quickly transformed Gauguin's word into a scientific doctrine, which had a most decisive effect upon us," Denis would write in 1908. After Gauguin's departure for Tahiti, Sérusier's own painting developed a more hieratic, spare and austere style of muted colors (on which Puvis de Chavannes clearly was one of the influences); the artist was striving for "a grander, more severe and sacred art" (letter to Verkade, 1896). In 1906 he moved to Brittany, taking up residence in a house he had built and decorated for himself at Châteauneuf-du-Faou (a place he had been visiting since 1893, and where he would also decorate the local baptistery in 1912–14). He taught at the Académie Ranson from 1908 to 1912. There are two important phases in his career as a theoretician: first, when he introduced his fellow Nabis to the Neo-Platonism that would become one of the pillars of the group's aesthetics; and then later, when he moved away from that group to further investigation of a mathematical approach to painting—an interest linked with his connections with Jan Verkade (from 1896 onward) and the research into the "Holy Measures" being carried out at the Beuron School in Germany, which Sérusier visited several times from 1898 onward (in 1903 he went there with Denis). Although critical of this change, Denis remained a close friend of his, while Sérusier himself broke away from the theosophy he had been drawn to in the 1890s and returned to the Catholic Church and to a religious concept of art that was close to that of the younger man (they both participated at the 1911 and 1920 exhibitions of Christian Art in Paris). His theoretical writings were published in 1921 under the title *ABC de la Peinture*; Denis would reissue an important new edition plus commentary in 1942.

Sérusier was extremely attentive to Puvis, from whom he literally took certain motifs, but in a form that was faithful primarily to Gauguin, the Nabi to whom he was closest. Around 1890, after his master's departure for Tahiti, it was to Puvis

that Sérusier owed the new orientation of his painting, however, he again moved away from him when he undertook his exploration of numbers.
J.P.B.

Georges Seurat
(Paris, 1859–1891)

Georges Seurat was born into a petit bourgeois family in Second Empire Paris. At sixteen, he left school and enrolled at the municipal art school; there he met Aman-Jean, with whom he would attend the studio of Henri Lehmann at the Ecole des Beaux-Arts in 1878. He very quickly became interested in the work of Puvis de Chavannes—as one can see from an 1881 sketch that shows the latter's *Poor Fisherman* (1881, Paris, Collection Bérès). Seurat completed his artistic education with his study of Charles Blanc's *La Grammaire des arts du dessin* (1867), and developed an interest in the scientific theories regarding color perception. From his first large-scale canvas, *Bathers at Asnières* (1883–84, London, National Gallery), he proved himself worthy of the title of a "modern Puvis." That work, in fact, depicts a scene of contemporary life in the manner of a large, atemporal mural: the stasis, the skillful composition, the synthetically-modeled forms and the muted colors—all recall the work of the painter who was then establishing himself as the master of mural decoration. In 1885 Seurat got to know Camille Pissarro, whom—through Signac—he had first met a year earlier at the meetings that had preceded the creation of the Société des Artistes Indépendants. 1885 would also see him develop a passionate interest in the ideas of Charles Henry, author of *Introduction à une esthétique scientifique*. At this point, Seurat's artistic influences, reading and pronounced dedication to modernity would all come together in the completion of *Sunday Afternoon on the Island of la Grande Jatte* (1884–86, Chicago, The Art Institute); this depiction of a "Sacred Wood" in a contemporary suburban setting is the first concrete expression of his theories concerning the optical blending of colors. Exhibited at the eighth—and final—Impressionist show in 1886, *La Grande Jatte* would immediately become the "manifesto" of Neo-Impressionism. Thereafter, right up until his premature death in 1891, Seurat would produce a series of

masterpieces depicting seascapes and scenes of contemporary life. It was above all in the latter group of works—in particular, *The Models* (1888, Merion, The Barnes Foundation)—that he expressed his unfailing admiration for the man who, in Félix Fénéon's words, "saw painting in terms of large-scale decoration."
M.F.B.

Paul Signac
(Paris, 1863–1935)

Paul Signac was born into the family of a successful Paris shopkeeper. In 1880 he interrupted his studies having discovered the joys of boating at Asnières, and thereafter worked at the Chat-Noir cabaret in Montmartre. In 1882 he rented his first studio, establishing links with members of the literary avant-garde. Most of his works at the time were vivid and brightly-colored marine scenes in an Impressionist style. In 1884 he took part in the creation of the Société des Artistes Indépendants, where he met Georges Seurat, who was exhibiting *Bathers at Asnières*. The two artists became friends, and—along with Camille Pissarro—Signac would be the first painter to adopt the Divisionism technique in 1886. From then onward, he remained faithful to this technique, and in 1899 explained the theory of the entire movement in his treatise *D'Eugène Delacroix au néo-impressionisme*. Throughout his career he always showed great interest in the work of "the great Puvis," sharing Fénéon's and Seurat's admiration for the artist; however, it was above all after the death of Seurat that Signac, who had been living in Saint-Tropez since 1892, gave full expression to this interest. Having realized that, with the premature death of his friend, Neo-Impressionism had lost the one artist capable of producing large-scale decorative works, he decided to tackle more ambitious compositions himself. Enamoured of the Mediterranean landscape, he chose the *doux pays* around him as the subject for significant works. In one of the first of these paintings, *Woman at the Well* (1892, Paris, Musée d'Orsay) the influence of Puvis de Chavannes is clear. Signac would often lament the fact that Puvis's mural decorations in Amiens could not be seen very well—a fault he tried to remedy by using pure, divided colors. His undertaking of large-format paintings continued with *In the Time of Harmony* (1894, Montreuil, Hôtel de Ville), a vast

work that took the artist nearly two years to complete. Here again, in this Mediterranean Arcadia with its calm and ample lines, there are numerous allusions to Puvis. However, his large-scale production was not very well received, and thus the artist returned to what had been his previous subject matter, painting poised and meditative landscapes, whose intensity of color would later attract the attention of the Fauves.
M.F.B.

Hugo Simberg
(Hamina, 1873—Ähtäri, 1917)

Hugo Simberg received his first training in Viipuri and he continued his studies in Helsinki in 1893. Disappointed with the academic Naturalism that dominated the official Finnish art scene, in 1895 Simberg went to Akseli Gallen-Kallela in Rouvesi and became his private student. Gallen-Kallela taught Simberg to work with tempera and introduced him to various graphic techniques, which Simberg was later to employ with great originality. The master's fascination with the mysticism of nature left a lasting impression as well on Simberg, one which recurs in his very personal world of motifs. On a journey to London, Paris and Berlin in 1896–97 Simberg's peculiar pictorial universe reached maturity. Presenting death as our bleak point of destination, Simberg engaged in the great existential questions concerning man's relation to nature, life and death. Stylistically, he chose a consciously primitive technique, which reflected the period's taste for simple and decorative images.
Another important element in Simberg's artistic development was his trip to Italy in 1897–98, where, like many of his contemporaries, he was fascinated by Early Renaissance fresco paintings, which he studied thoroughly. He later benefited from these studies when in 1906–07 he executed a large fresco decoration for the Cathedral of Tampere together with his friend Magnus Enckell. This decoration takes as its departure point the artist's principal work, *The Wounded Angel* of 1903, not only for its subject matter but also for the grandeur of the project. *The Wounded Angel* was produced in the aftermath of a personal crisis involving a serious and life-threatening illness. The work expresses both the awareness of the vicinity of death as well as a recognition of the beauty of life, the latter expressed through a budding landscape that is about to wake up

after a long period of darkness and coldness. The landscape, with its grand and simple lines and gray approach to eternity, recalls Gallen-Kallela's landscapes and ultimately also Puvis de Chavannes's *Poor Fisherman*. Like Puvis, Simberg describes human fragility and the lost paradise; a remarkable familiarity is also evident, however, in the stringent composition and the openness with which the work lends itself to interpretation.
P.N.L.

Mario Sironi
(Sassari, 1885-—Milan, 1961)

Born at Sassari, Sironi studied in Rome but interrupted his engineering studies to devote himself to painting, encouraged by the academician Ximenes. He attended the Accademia di Belle Arti and Balla's studio (1905-10) where he met Severini, Marinetti and Boccioni, with whom he went to Paris in 1906. After recovering from a nervous breakdown, he became interested in Futurism. He visited the *Prima Esposizione di Pittura Futurista* in Rome (1913), moved to Milan, and took part in the *Esposizione Libera Futurista* at the Galleria Sprovieri in Rome (1914).
His Romantic formation, apparent in his copies of Segantini, and his fondness for nineteenth-century Realism and for a Divisionism in the spirit of Cézanne, Pissarro, Seurat and Balla led him to a Pointillism borrowed from Boccioni, expressed in synthetic backgrounds derived from Russian Cubo-Futurism.
In 1915, Sironi enrolled as a volunteer cyclist, joined the circle of Margherita Sarfatti, while in 1916 Boccioni published the article *I Disegni di Sironi*. Sironi then settled in Rome and held his first one-man show at the Galleria Bragaglia (1919), revealing precocious signs of an anxious interpretation of Metaphysical painting. He joined up with Fascism and along with Funi, Dudreville and Russolo signed the Manifesto against any return to the past in painting (1920) in contrast with *Valori Plastici*.
In 1922, he was one of the *Sette pittori di Novecento* and participated in the group show (1923), then the Venice Biennale (1924), the III Roman Biennale (1925) and *Novecento Italiano* exhibitions (1926 and 1929).
The formal solidity of his classicism of the 1920s evolved toward an Expressionist deformation that recalled Rouault and German Expressionism which he had

discovered during his trips to Germany (1908-10), as well as a fondness for emotive subjects, as in the works shown at the First Roman Quadriennale (1931). In *La Famiglia* (1930) the textured chromaticism, rough outlines, unusual forms and thick brushstrokes are hints of a tortured sense of tragedy that gradually became toned down to a muted plasticity.
Sironi designed the poster *La Pittura murale* (1932) for the *Mostra della Rivoluzione Fascista*, published in *Il Popolo d'Italia*, and signed the *Manifesto della Pittura Murale* (1933) with Campigli, Carrà and Funi. He took part in the competition for the Palazzo Littorio, and painted the fresco for the Aula Magna of the University of Rome (1935) and the mosaic for the Law Court in Milan (1936). He participated in the Paris World Fair in 1937.
In 1943, he returned to easel painting, adapting his monumental paintings to the canvas. He also carried out a significant graphic activity in illustration and scenography.
I.P.

Beda Stjernschantz
(Porvoo, 1867—Helsinki, 1910)

Parallel with her studies at the Helsinki Art Association's drawing school in 1889–92, Beda Stjernschantz studied at Gunnar Berndtson's private school together with Magnus Enckell, Ellen Thesleff and Väinö Blomstedt.
In 1891 she left for Paris where she was enrolled at the Académie Colarossi until 1892. Enckell, who had arrived in Paris some months earlier, was already at home in the Symbolist circles and soon the Finnish artists were united not only by their admiration for Puvis de Chavannes but also by a fascination with the simple grandness of Egyptian art.
After having spent the summer of 1893 in Finland, the group of artist-comrades returned to Paris in the autumn; financial problems, however, forced Stjernschantz to stay at home and the feeling of isolation led to desperation and depression. The artist later had the opportunity to go abroad; she visited Italy in 1897 and Paris in 1900, where one of her works appeared at the World Exhibition. Toward the end of the 1890s her production was fairly fragmentary and around the turn of the century she quit her pictorial work altogether. In 1903 she left for the

USA where she worked as a nanny for a while. In the States her depression worsened and in 1910 she committed suicide.
Despite her limited production, she left a series of remarkable Symbolist works, which in an original fashion assimilate and elaborate the impressions from Puvis de Chavannes, her avowed model. Like Ellen Thesleff, Stjernschantz worked toward a simplicity of motif and a harmony of expression, which saw the abstract serenity of music as her goal. Thus *Everywhere a Voice is Heard* represents an attempt to create a picture of music, more specifically an image of the traditional folk music that Stjernschantz encountered on the island of Wormsø on the Estonian coast. In Stjernschantz's reading the simple music and the girls' singing come to symbolize a delicate beauty and an innocent existence. The references to music also include the pantheistic title of the work, *Everywhere a Voice is Heard*: the opening line of Fredrik Pacius's patriotic choral work, which was for many years the national anthem of Finland.
P.N.L.

Franz von Stuck
(Tettenweis, 1863—Munich, 1928)

Franz von Stuck is considered to be one of the "new German painters of ideas," as well as the most important representative of the Jugendstil in Munich, strongly influenced also by Symbolism and idealism. The often erotically charged pictorial world of the painter, graphic artist and sculptor is peopled with amazons, centaurs, fauns and satyrs. Alongside such mythological and allegorical scenes, however, he also worked in the fairytale genre and produced many portraits. *War*, *The Guardian of Paradise* and *Sin* were to become the most celebrated of his works. Stuck first attracted attention for his gifted drawing when still a child. He completed his artistic training in Munich, where he immediately began a successful career as an illustrator for magazines such as *Fliegende Blätter*, *Pan* and *Jugend*.
In 1892 he was one of the founders of the Munich Secession and in 1895 he became professor at the Royal Academy of Fine Arts in the city. Among his students were a number of major artists, including Kandinsky and Klee.
Regarded as one of the last of the "painter princes," in 1897 Stuck had a villa built in Munich which bears witness to his inclination for

the *Gesamtkunstwerk* concept, the all-embracing work of art. He often used photography in preparation for his own art and kept himself fully informed of the work of his contemporaries by means of reproductions. In Munich, which in the years before 1900 was the leading artistic center in Germany, he was also able to view art from both home and abroad at numerous exhibitions. As well as the impact of antiquity and the Renaissance, his work reveals the influence of French and Belgian Symbolism, Whistler and the Pre-Raphaelites in Britain and also of German idealism, though his principal model remained the art of Böcklin. For his landscapes he preferred low horizons, as in *Sunset by the Sea*: Scandinavian in its effect and doubtless inspired by Munch, it is one of the rare pictures by Stuck in which landscape—here in particular with a grandiose and dramatic sky structured by clouds and the red of the sun—is the dominant element.
P.K.

Ellen Thesleff
(Helsinki, 1869–1954)

Like Magnus Enckell and Beda Stjernschantz, Ellen Thesleff attended Gunnar Berndtson's private school in Helsinki from 1890 to 1891; and like her friends she went to Paris to see French Symbolism and the works of her great model, Puvis de Chavannes. At the Académie Colarossi, with which Thesleff was associated during the period 1891–94, she developed a style in which Puvisesque simplicity and harmony were combined with the dark palette of Eugène Carrière. The results were gray-black, almost monochrome portrait and landscape paintings with their very own peculiar melancholy.
In 1894 Thesleff left for Italy, which was to become her favorite country. The study of the Early Renaissance had a lasting effect on her paintings especially in terms of the choice of color, the somber color scheme soon giving way to more lyrical pastels. In her later years Thesleff worked with painting, wood carving and watercolors and created a series of works characterized by a sure sense of color, which attracted international attention.
The majority of Thesleff's relatively few landscape paintings from the 1890s was, like *Aspen* of 1893, painted between winter and spring, in that lapse of time during which the coldness and darkness of winter are about to disappear but have not

left the landscape, while the growth and colors of spring have yet to become dominant. A time of year full of expectation and hope, when Thesleff could best express her feeling for the immateriality of nature. Thesleff chose her subject matter among the elongated aspen trunks of central Finland, in the vicinity of the family's summer residence at Murole.

Aspen is presumably the result of Thesleff's thorough study of Puvis de Chavannes's works and particularly of his *Winter* (1888–92, Paris, Hôtel de Ville), which Thesleff saw at the Salon in 1892. Apart from the similar color schemes, there seems to be a direct reference to several groups of trees in *Winter*—the trees in *Aspen* sharing their slim trunks, dividing themselves at the top into a complex and fine net of thin boughs.

Through the harmony of her colors and a spherical lightness of composition, Thesleff strove to approach the simplicity that she associated with music, the purest form of art. To Thesleff and the Symbolists the correspondence between the various art forms was of major importance, but only few realized the idea more thoroughly than she did. During the 1890s she portrayed her sisters with musical instruments, while several of her later paintings resemble musical interpretations, with titles such as *Chopin's Waltz* and *Elegy*.
P.N.L.

Verner Thomé
(Alajärvi, 1878—Helsinki, 1953)

Verner Thomé studied at the Helsinki Art Association in 1898–99 under the supervision of Helene Schjerfbeck. Later, in 1901–02, he continued his studies at the Fine Arts Academy in Munich under the animal painter H. Zügel and the figure painter Herterich. It seems, however, that the most decisive element in Thomé's artistic development was the inspiring company of Magnus Enckell. Thomé had known Enckell for several years, but from 1903 the acquaintance developed into a close friendship and the two spent the following seven summers together at Suursaari on the southern coast of Finland. With Enckell as his main driving force, it seems that they stimulated one other toward paintings that were increasingly saturated with light and color. This reciprocal exchange may for instance be detected in several of Thomé's paintings of nude boys,

bathing and playing, from 1903–04, as in *Boys at Play*, which is closely related to Enckell's fascination with the same motif, as for instance in his *The Golden Age* from the same year. Travels to Paris, Spain and Morocco (1904), Italy (1906) and the Mediterranean (1908–09) brought even more light and color into Thomé's paintings and in the years around 1910 he became known as the most radical colorist on the Finnish art scene. Not least because he executed a series of Pointillist paintings of above all bathing boys, presumably encouraged by the Belgian-English Neo-Impressionist Alfred William Finch, who was resident in Finland. These pictures are clearly related to Seurat's bathing scenes, but they are also associated with the vitalist tendencies of the period represented by Edvard Munch and Ernst Haeckel.

In 1912 Thomé co-founded the artist group *Septem*, which included Magnus Enckell, A.W. Finch and Ellen Thesleff. The group shared an interest in Neo-Impressionist color theory and the intention to liberate Finnish art from the dominance of a solemn nationalist romanticism and take it instead in the direction of a modernism inspired by French art. Indeed, in the following years *Septem* came to indicate the direction taken by Finnish art toward the dominance of "the pure palette."
P.N.L.

Joaquín Torres-García
(Montevideo, 1874–1949)

The Uruguayan painter Joaquín Torres-García began his career as a book illustrator in Barcelona during the Art Nouveau period. He was close to the great figures of the "Catalan Renaissance," who like him professed great admiration for Hellenistic art. However, soon after the sole source of inspiration for the painter would become the work of Puvis de Chavannes. In a 1907 exhibition he first encountered Puvis's preparatory drawings for the Panthéon frescoes—works which revealed to him how the monumental character of frescoes could be enhanced by the use of a simplified line, a restricted palette of muted colors and the absence of perspective. Unable to apply these insights immediately to a large-scale project of mural decoration, Torres-García used them in his easel painting.

The works shown here—dating from a period that spans more than thirty years—reveal just how

enduring the influence of Puvis de Chavannes was.

When he painted *Elysian Fields*, Torres-García still clearly had a vivid memory of the works by the French artist which he had discovered in Paris a year earlier (in 1910). His rendition of an idealized, calm springtime world is very close to that one finds in Puvis de Chavannes's mythological works such as *Antique Vision* and *Sacred Wood Dear to the Arts and Muses*, which continue a tradition that stretches back to Ingres and Poussin. Later, Torres-García would turn away from mythological subject matter to give a more domestic vision of antiquity in Arcadian landscapes peopled by a simple peasant at harvest time or by graceful female figures gathered around a well. Rendered in a simplified way, these scenes of everyday life—which the artist would return to several times—take on an atemporal, and often allegorical, character. Here again, Torres-García was taking his inspiration from Puvis de Chavannes, who in his simple evocation of family life or work in the fields had depicted his vision of the different ages of man and the cycle of the seasons, using a language that eschewed any symbolist metaphor. The three paintings *Two Figures Picking Fruit* (1914), *Woman at a Fountain* (1916) and *Classical Figures* (1922) show Torres-García paying particular attention to the actual frame of the picture: simple combinations of lengths of wood or else sculpted bas-reliefs, these frames form increasingly summary versions of a Greek temple that contrast with the delicacy of the painted figures; indeed, they are like windows opening onto scenes of the past. This was the artist's first attempt at "constructed " painting—a concern that would, in Paris a few years later (from 1929 onward), culminate in the use of an orthogonal structure in his paintings. *Four Figures and a Child with a Basket of Fruit* (1943) takes its inspiration from those imposing compositions of Puvis which comprise a centrally-placed human figure that, in sequence, is shown full-face, in profile and from behind.

In his first murals, Torres-García had also exploited the same frieze layout, muted palette, frontal organization of composition and use of large solid fields of color. Undoubtedly, he remained closest to the Puvis model in the frescoes painted for the Salon San Jorge in Barcelona between 1913 and 1915.

In 1920 the artist left Spain and went to live first in New York then in Paris. It was logical, therefore, that he should start to explore more contemporary themes and also change his style as a result of the influence of Cubism and Neo-Plasticism—changes evident in such paintings as *Pastoral* and *Three Classical Figures*, which might be seen as related to the works of Matisse or Picasso. Though the Puvis-inspired works of Torres-García were often criticized as naive, childish or primitive, there is no doubt that they ultimately led to that series of "compositions constructives" of the late 1920s which established the artist's "credentials."
C.Ca.

Suzanne Valadon
(Bessines-sur-Gartempe, 1865—Paris, 1938)

Suzanne Valadon began her artistic career in 1883 producing drawings. Her first paintings date from 1892–93. The following year, with the help of Degas, she began to exhibit her work. She became a painter of portraits, nudes and still-lifes, after having been the much-appreciated model of numerous artists, and of Puvis de Chavannes in particular. She started posing for him at the age of fifteen in 1880, and was the model for both the female and male figures in *The Sacred Wood* in the Lyon Musée des Beaux-Arts. For a full seven years she would remain the artist's mistress and model. Suzanne Valadon also posed for Henner, Renoir (to whom she was recommended by Puvis de Chavannes) Steinlen, Toulouse-Lautrec, Forain, Zandomeneghi and numerous others; she also had a close relationship with Erik Satie. Her son was the painter Maurice Utrillo (1883–1955).

Her admiration for Puvis de Chavannes comes out particularly in her drawings, in which she favors outline over modeling of form; the subjects and composition of her work, on the other hand, seems to reveal more the influence of Degas. Nevertheless, the composition and subject matter of her three most important—and most ambitious—paintings do reveal the lessons learned from Puvis de Chavannes: *Adam and Eve* (1909, Paris, Centre Georges-Pompidou, Musée National d'Art Moderne), which shows the two figures facing each other; *Joy of Living* (1912, New York, The Metropolitan Museum of Art), in not only the explicit title

but also the elongated form of the four female figures painted against a flat landscape with a male figure seen in profile; and, above all, *The Casting of the Net* (1914, Paris, Centre Georges-Pompidou, Musée National d'Art Moderne)—her most famous work—which shows the same model of a male nude, in outlined silhouette, depicted from the back, from the side and face-on as his movements unfold in a vertically-aligned composition.
S.L.

Félix Vallotton
(Lausanne, 1865—Paris, 1925)

Vallotton is one of the few Swiss artists who may be regarded as having blazed a trail for modern art, rather than following in the footsteps of others. He made his career in Paris, where he settled as early as 1882, at the age of seventeen. His innovative approach to woodcut technique was so striking as to attract immediate attention when his prints were first shown at the Salon des Indépendants and the Salon de la Rose+Croix in 1891. What was new about his woodcuts was the extreme flatness of the forms and the arabesque sense of line, and also their highly topical range of motifs. Not only did Vallotton use the technique to portray major intellectual heroes of the new age, he also captured the joys and sorrows of modern metropolitan life. Encouraged by the example of friends like Toulouse-Lautrec and Charles Maurin, he subsequently experimented with lithography and zincography, rapidly establishing himself as one of the most sought after illustrators of the fin de siècle. Until the turn of the century he produced relatively few paintings, and much of what he did paint was made up of small-scale pictures that appear to be reworkings of subjects already tried and tested as woodcuts. This is especially true of his 1898–99 series of satirical depictions of bourgeois Salons and their complacent denizens, whose garishly contrasting colors convey an almost painful tension.
After marrying the daughter of a prosperous art dealer in 1899 and acquiring French citizenship the following year, Vallotton turned once again entirely to painting, in an ever more bourgeois manner. From 1903 his output consisted almost entirely of such conventional genres as portraits, nudes, still lifes and landscapes. His starkly artificial structure of color and form gave way to a cool, magically exaggerated naturalism, which seems to anticipate both Metaphysical painting in Italy and the New Objectivity movement in Germany. In this respect Vallotton was one of the first representatives of what Maurice Denis called "néo-traditionnisme". Although he had joined the Nabi group of artists in 1893, he did not feel drawn by Gauguin and Cézanne so much as by Old Masters such as Dürer and Holbein, and the closest to him in spirit among the "early moderns" was not Delacroix, but Ingres. However, he was also a constant admirer of Puvis de Chavannes, whose work he praised in a 1892 newspaper article as "one of the most enduring lessons of our time." He also produced two portraits of the older artist: a lithography in 1893 and a woodcut in 1898.
R.K.

Heinrich Vogeler
(Bremen, 1872—Bud'yonny, near Karaganda [Kazakhstan] 1942)

The painter and graphic artist Heinrich Vogeler is known principally as an illustrator influenced by Jugendstil. As a painter he produced landscapes, portraits, fairytale scenes and figure compositions in a Symbolist vein. In his work he adapted pictorial elements from Böcklin, Hofmann and other German artists, for instance the frescoes by Hans von Marées which he saw in Naples in 1902; on the other hand he was barely influenced by French models. After training at the Düsseldorf Academy, from 1894 he joined the circle of artists who formed the Worpswede colony. He created an "Island of Beauty" in the house which he set up there, Barkenhoff, and its adjoining park, which included a natural theater inspired by Palladio. In Worpswede and district he produced the paintings *Winter Tale*, a modern rendering of the Epiphany, and *Spring*. Vogeler had already dealt with this subject before 1900, but the new painting formed part of a series of nudes depicted against a background of a relationship between nature and the human nude that had altered since the turn of the century. His wife Martha posed for the woman with a blackbird perched on her hand. The figure is clearly derived from Böcklin's *Faun Whistling to a Blackbird*.
He traveled extensively, to Holland and Belgium (1892), Ceylon (1906) and England (1909). In Florence in 1898 he met Rainer Maria Rilke. Heinrich and Martha Vogeler kept in close touch both with the poet and his wife Clara Westhoff, and with Otto Modersohn and Paula Becker, who were familiar with the Paris art scene. Vogeler stayed in Paris in 1894, 1905, 1906 and 1911, but in each case only briefly. Unlike Klinger, he appreciated the attitudes of the French. In the Louvre he was fascinated by the force and charm of Mantegna, Botticelli and Rembrandt, but also by the sheer, quiet beauty of Egyptian and Assyro-Babylonian sculpture. Vogeler also took an interest in Millet and Courbet. Through Rilke and Modersohn-Becker he was introduced to the art of the Paris avant-garde: Van Gogh, Gauguin and Seurat, Rodin and Cézanne—and doubtless also Puvis de Chavannes, whom Rilke admired.
P.K.

Edouard Vuillard
(Cuiseaux, 1868—La Baule, 1940)

It was during his schooldays at the Lycée Condorcet that Vuillard met Denis, Lugné-Poe and Roussel (who would later marry his sister Marie, in 1893). After some time at the Ecole des Beaux-Arts, he enrolled at the Académie Julian (1886–87) and then joined the Nabi group in 1890. In 1891 he exhibited with the group at Le Barc de Boutteville, and also hold a one-man show at La Revue Blanche owned by the Natanson brothers, with whom he was very close. His first interior decoration dates from a year later, and was followed by work for Alexandre Natanson (*Public Gardens*, 1894, Paris, Musée d'Orsay)—which reveals his admiration for Puvis de Chavannes—and other decors for Docteur Vaquez (1896) and Claude Anet (1898). Marking the peak of his work in this period, these—together with his paintings and his colored lithographs for Vollard (starting in 1896, this series of works is best known for the *Landscapes and Interiors* of 1899)—all reveal a new form of intimacy in his approach, which is very different from that found in Denis. Uninterested in theoretical debates, Vuillard did not, in fact, follow the latter when he converted to a more classical style in 1898; true to his initial forms of artistic inspiration, he developed an independent career, exhibiting at Bernheim-Jeune from 1898 to 1914, at the Salon des Indépendants (from 1901) and at the new Salon d'Automne from the year of its foundation in 1903. His close links with the family of the merchant Jos Hessel gained him a number of commissions. Still very close to Denis and Roussel, he took part in the decoration of the Théâtre des Champs-Elysées (1913), the Palais des Nations in Geneva (1936) and the Palais de Chaillot in Paris (1937). The Paris work came in the year of his election at the Institut, and it was followed a year later by a large retrospective exhibition (1938). Although his career unfolded in a regular manner, it embraces two very different styles. The first, which emerged after a brief period of violently-colored works that revealed an interest in synthesis, comprises subtle and refined interiors characterized by a Japanese-inspired flatness of form and rich yet discreet harmonies of composition. The second phase comes after 1900 and reveals a return to a more realistic interest in details, but always rendered with a very personal virtuosity.
J.P.B.

Biographies' authors

A.B.	Anne Baldassari
A.P.	Arnauld Pierre
A.S.	Aurora Scotti
B.J.	Barthélémy Jobert
C.B.	Christian Briend
C.Ca.	Chimène Caputi
C.Ch.	Catherine Chevillot
C.L.	Claude Lapaire
E.A.	Emanuelle Amiot
F.D.	Fraçoise Ducros
I.C.	Isabelle Cahn
I.P.	Isabella Pascucci
J.-C.M.	Jean-Claude Marcadé
J.-P.B.	Jean-Paul Bouillon
K.L.	Katharina Lepper
M.C.	Marie Clarac
M.D.	Michel Draguet
M.F.-B.	Marina Ferretti-Bocquillon
M.L.	Marit Lange
M.L.P.	Marianne Le Pommeré
M.N.	Monique Nonne
N.R.F.	Nadia Richard Filatov
P.G.G.	Pascale Grémont
P.Y.K.	Pavel Y. Klimov
P.K.	Peter Kropmanns
P.N.L.	Peter Nørgaard Larsen
R.H.	Robert Hooze
R.K.	Rudolf Koella
R.L.	Rémi Labrusse
R.U.	Robert Upstone
S.E.	Susan Earle
S.L.	Serge Lemoine
S.M.	Susanne Mersmann
V.A.	Valentina Anker
V.D.	Véronique Dumas
V.G.	Véronique Gautherin

Pierre Puvis de Chavannes's exhibitions
1850-1904

*The following section lists the most important
exhibitions of the years 1850-1904 in which works
by Pierre Puvis de Chavannes were shown.
The data has been transcribed faithfully from
the original catalogs. This reconstruction—which
only takes into account the artist's oil paintings
and omits his vast graphic production—is based
on the often inconsistent documentation conserved
in museums, and therefore has more of an
historical rather than a scientific value.*

1850

Salon de la Société des artistes Français
Paris, Palais National, 30 décembre

2553 – *Christ mort*

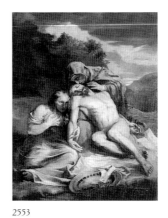

2553

1859

Salon de la Société des artistes Français
Paris, Palais des Champs Elysées, 15 avril

2526 – *Un retour de chasse*
Fragment pour peinture murale

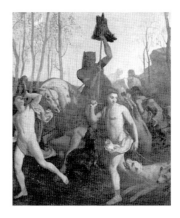

2526

1861

Salon de la Société des artistes Français
Paris, Palais des Champs Elysées, 1ᵉʳ mai

2621 – *Concordia*
2622 – *Bellum*
(Peintures murales)

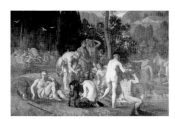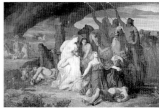

2621   2622

1863

Salon de la Société des artistes Français
Paris, Palais des Champs Elysées, 1ᵉʳ mai

1544 – *Le Travail*
1545 – *Le Repos*
(Complément des peintures décoratives exposées en 1861)

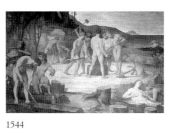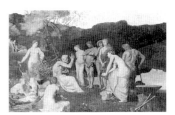

1544   1545

1864

Salon de la Société des artistes Français
Paris, Palais des Champs Elysées, 1er mai

1590 – *L'automne*

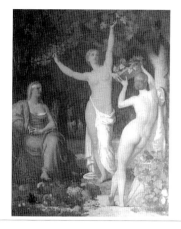

1590

1865

Salon de la Société des artistes Français
Paris, Palais des Champs Elysées, 1er mai

1765 – *Ave Picardia Nutrix*
Peintures décoratives pour le musée d'Amiens
Huit figures monumentales

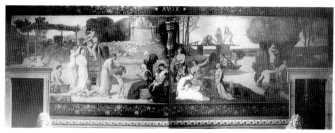

1765

1866

Salon de la Société des artistes Français
Paris, Palais des Champs Elysées, 1er mai

1600 – *La Vigilance*
1601 – *La Fantaisie*
Peinture en camaïeu
Fragment de décoration d'un hôtel

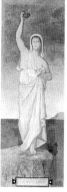

1600

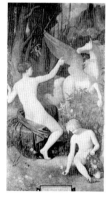

1601

1867

Salon de la Société des artistes Français
Paris, Palais des Champs Elysées, 15 avril

1252 – *Le sommeil*
Tempus erat quo prima quies mortalibus oegris incipit.
(Virgile, Enéide, liv. II)

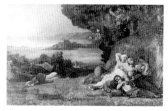

1252

1867

Exposition universelle
Paris, avril 1867

526 – *La Guerre, La Paix, Le Travail, Le Repos*
(réductions de peintures pour
le Musée Napoléon III à Amiens,
et exposées aux Salons de 1861 et 1863)

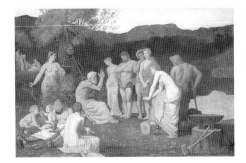
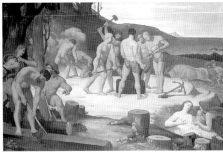
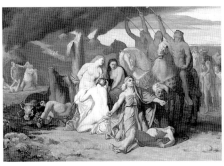
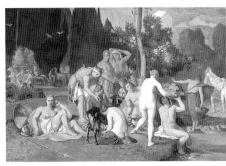

526

1868

Salon de la Société des artistes Français
Paris, Palais des Champs-Elysées, 1er mai

2074 – *Le jeu*
Figure décorative
(Pour le cercle de l'Union artistique)
[détruit]

1869

Salon de la Société des artistes Français
Paris, Palais des Champs-Elysées, 1er mai

1990 – *Massilia ; colonie grecque*
1991 – *Marseille, porte d'orient*
(Peintures décoratives destinées à l'escalier d'honneur
du nouveau Musée de Marseille)

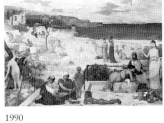

1990

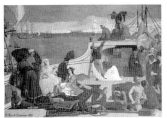

1991

1870

Salon de la Société des artistes Français
Paris, Palais des Champs-Elysées, 1ᵉʳ mai

2346 – *Décollation de Saint Jean-Baptiste*
2347 – *La Madeleine au désert*

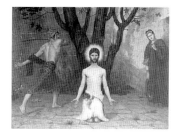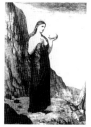

2346　　　　　　　　　　　2347

1872

Salon de la Société des artistes Français
Paris, Palais des Champs-Elysées, 1ᵉʳ mai

1282 – *L'Espérance*

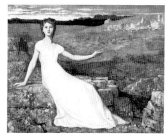

1282

1873

Salon de la Société des artistes Français
Paris, Palais des Champs-Elysées, 5 mai

1229 – *L'Eté*

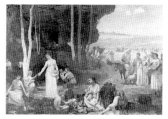

1229

1874

Salon de la Société des artistes Français
Paris, Palais des Champs-Elysées, 1ᵉʳ mai

1526 – *L'an 732, Charles Martel sauve la chrétienté par sa victoire
sur les Sarrasins, près de Poitiers (Pour l'Hôtel de Ville de Poitiers)*

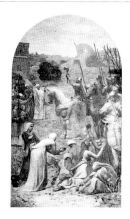

1526

1875

Salon de la Société des artistes Français
Paris, Palais des Champs-Elysées, 1er mai

1688 – *Retirée au couvent de Sainte-Croix, Radegonde donne asile
aux poètes et protège les lettres contre la barbarie du temps –
VIe siècle (Pour l'escalier de l'Hôtel de ville de Poitiers)*
1689 – *Famille de pêcheurs*

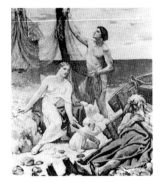

1689

1876

Salon de 1876 Société des artistes Français
Paris, Palais des Champs-Elysées, 1er mai

1694 – *Ste Geneviève.*
*Dès son âge le plus tendre, Ste Geneviève donna les marques d'une
piété ardente. Sans cesse en prière, elle était un sujet de surprise
et d'admiration pour tous ceux qui la voyaient.*
(Pour l'église Ste Geneviève – Panthéon)

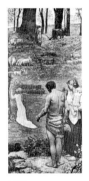

1694

1877

Salon de la Société des artistes Français
Paris, Palais des Champs-Elysées, 1er mai

Église Sainte-Geneviève, à Paris:
Vie pastorale de sainte Geneviève

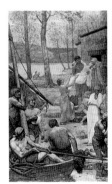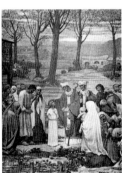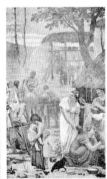

1878

Salon de 1878 Société des artistes Français
Paris, Palais des Champs-Elysées, 25 mai

Église Sainte-Geneviève (Panthéon) :
1.Naissance de Ste Geneviève
*2. Frise : St Paul, St Trophime, St Feréol, St Austremoine, St Julien,
St Lucain, St Crépin, St Crépinien, Ste Madeleine, Ste Colombe,
Ste Marthe, Ste Solange, St Lazare, St Martial, St Gatien, St Lucien,
St Firmin, St Clément, St Paterne*

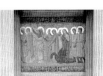

2

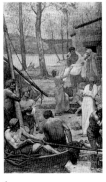

1

1879

Salon de la Société des artistes Français
Paris, Palais des Champs-Elysées, 12 mai

2488 – *L'enfant prodigue*
2489 – *Jeunes filles au bord de la mer*

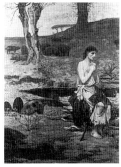 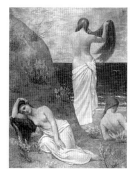

2488   2489

1881

Salon
Paris, Palais des Champs-Elysées, 2 mai

1944 – *Le pauvre Pêcheur*

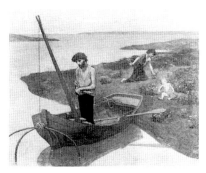

1944

1882

Salon
Paris, Palais des Champs-Elysées, 1er mai

2223 – *Jeunes Picards s'exerçant à la lance* (Pro Patria Ludus)
Peinture murale destinée au Musée d'Amiens
2224 – *Doux pays*
Panneau décoratif destiné à l'hôtel de M.L. Bonnat

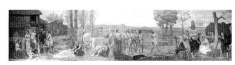

2223

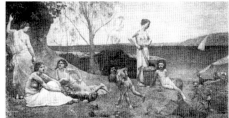

2224

1883

Salon
Paris, Palais des Champs-Elysées, 1er mai

1991 – *Portrait de Mme M. C.*
1992 – *Le Rêve!*
"Il voit dans son sommeil, l'Amour, la Gloire et la Richesse lui apparaître."

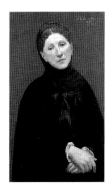 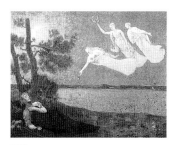

1992

1991

1883

Exposition Nationale
Paris, Palais des Champs-Elysées, 15 septembre

589 – *Femme à sa toilette*
590 – *Jeunes Filles au bord de la mer*
591 – *Le pauvre Pêcheur*
592 – *L'Enfant prodigue*

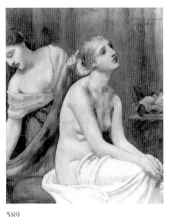

589

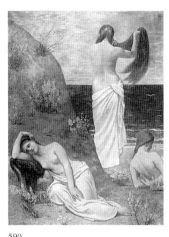

590

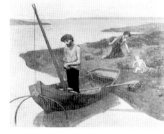

591

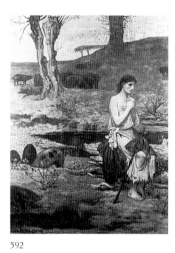

592

1884

Salon
Paris, Palais des Champs-Elysées, 1er mai 1884

1994 – *Le Bois sacré, cher aux Arts et aux Muses*

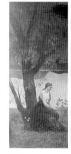
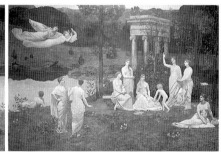
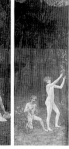

1994

1885

Salon
Paris, Palais des Champs-Elysées, 1er mai

2047 – *L'automne*
Variante du même sujet, appartenant au Musée de Lyon

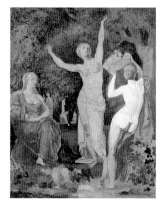

2047

1886

Salon
Paris, Palais des Champs-Elysées, 1ᵉʳ mai

1944 – *Triptyque* :
1 – *Vision antique*
2 – *Inspiration chrétienne*
3 – *Le Rhône et la Saône*
Le Bois sacré cher aux Arts et aux Muses, panneau décoratif exposé en 1884 et placé dans l'escalier du Musée de Lyon, était la composition génératrice de deux autres sujets: Vision antique et Inspiration chrétienne, l'art étant compris entre ces deux termes dont l'un évoque l'idée de la forme, et, l'autre, l'idée du sentiment. – Un quatrième panneau représente le Rhône et la Saône symbolisant la Force et la Grâce.

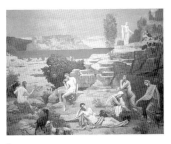 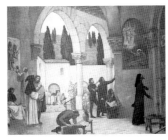 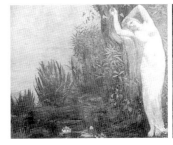 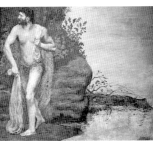

1　　　　　　　　　　　2　　　　　　　　　　　3

1886

Salon
Paris, Palais des Champs-Elysées, 1ᵉʳ mai

1965 – *Carton de la peinture destinée au grand amphithéâtre de la Sorbonne*

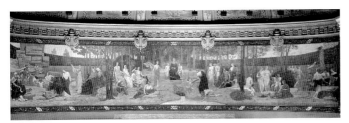

1965

Cette composition, appelée à décorer l'hémicycle du grand amphithéâtre de la Sorbonne, monument élevé aux Lettres, à la Science, à la Philosophie et à l'Histoire, se divise en trois parties.

Au centre, sur un bloc de marbre, est assise l'antique Sorbonne, ayant à ses côtés deux génies portant des couronnes et des palmes, hommage aux vivants et aux morts glorieux. – Debout l'Eloquence célèbre les luttes et les conquêtes de l'esprit humain. – A droite et à gauche sont groupées des figures attentives, symbolisant les diverses poésies. – Du rocher qui les porte s'échappe la source vivifiante; la Jeunesse y boit avidement et la Vieillesse y puise une nouvelle force.

Le compartiment de gauche est réservé à la Philosophie et à l'Histoire, symbolisées, la première par un groupe de figures représentant la lutte du spiritualisme et du matérialisme en face de la mort, l'un s'affirmant par un geste d'ardente aspiration vers l'idéal, tandis que l'autre montre une fleur, expression des joies terrestres et des transformations successives limitées à la matière.

Le second groupe montre l'Histoire interrogeant le passé, figuré par d'antiques débris que l'on vient d'exhumer.

Le compartiment de droite est consacré à la Science. Le premier groupe faisant suite aux Muses se compose de quatre figures, la Botanique, la Mer, la Minéralogie et la Géologie. Des jeunes gens s'émerveillent de ces richesses, tandis que d'autres, groupés devant une statue de la Science, jurent dans un commun élan de se vouer à elle. – Trois jeunes hommes, absorbés par l'étude, ferment la composition.

1887

Paris, Galerie Durand-Ruel, 20 novembre – 20 décembre

1 – *Peintures murales du Panthéon*
Réduction
2 – *La Bresse*
Appartient à M. Duret [détruit]
4 – *Orphée*
Appartient à M. Chausson
5 – *La Jeune mère* [non localisé]
Appartient à l'auteur
6 – *L'Automne*
Réduction avec variantes d'un grand tableau
(Propriété du Musée de Lyon)
7 – *Le Rêve*
8 – *Le pauvre Pêcheur*
9 – *La Toilette*
Appartient à M. Haviland
10 – *L'enfant prodigue*
Appartient à M. Lerolle
14 – *Le Repos*
Réduction des peintures murales du Musée d'Amiens – Appartient à M. H.
15 – *Le Travail*
Réduction des peintures murales du Musée d'Amiens – Appartient à M. H.
16 – *Décollation de Saint Jean-Baptiste*
17 – *Femmes au bord de la mer*
18 – *Portrait de Madame C.*
Appartient à Mme C.

19 – *L'Espérance*
Appartient à M. Paton
20 – *Portrait d'homme*
Appartient à M. Hermann
21 – *La Guerre*
Réduction des peintures murales du Musée d'Amiens. – Appartient à M. H.
22 – *La Paix*
Réduction des peintures murales du Musée d'Amiens. – Appartient à M. H.
23 – *Tamaris*
24 – *Réduction de peinture murale*
Appartient à M. Toulmouche
25 – *Femme debout*
Appartient à M. Chausson
26 – *Le Sommeil*
30 – *Petite Espérance nue*
Appartient à M. Rouart
31 – *Le Rocher blanc*
Appartient à M. Rouart
33 – *Ludus pro Patria*
Réduction avec variantes importantes (d'après le)
34 – *Sainte Madeleine*
35 – *La famille*
Fragment de la réduction de « Ludus Pro Patria »
83 – *Le doux pays*
Appartient à M. Albert Wolff

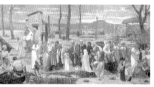

1

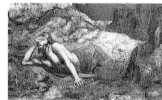

4

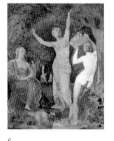

6

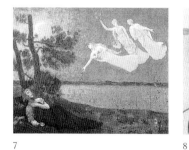

7

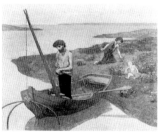

8

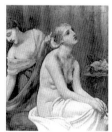

9

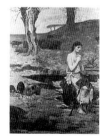

10

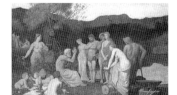

14

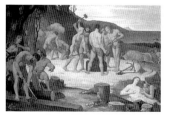

15

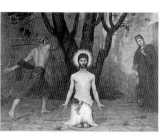

16

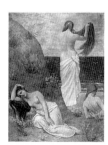

17

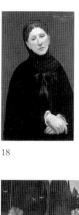
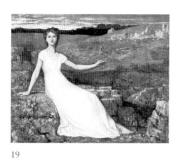
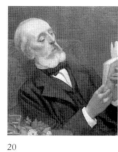
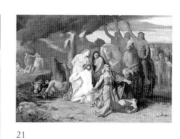

18   19   20   21

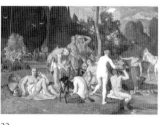
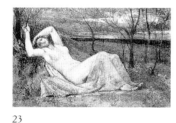
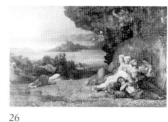
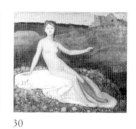

22   23   26   30

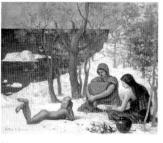
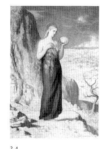
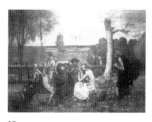
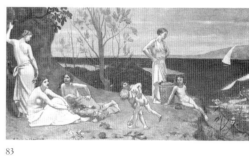

31   34   35   83

1889

Exposition Universelle
Paris, 5 mai - 31 octobre

Groupe 1 Classe 1
1 – *"Pro patriâ ludus"* [sic] *(Musée d'Amiens. – S. 1882)*
2 – *Vision antique*
3 – *Inspiration chrétienne*
4 – *Le Rhône et la Saône*
5 – *Le Bois Sacré (S. 1884)*
(Peintures décoratives pour l'escalier du Palais des Arts, à Lyon)
6 – *Décoration du grand hémicycle de la Sorbonne (S. 1887)*

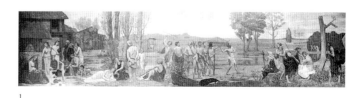

1

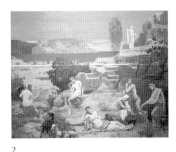
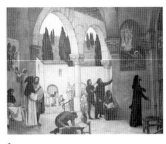
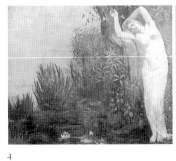
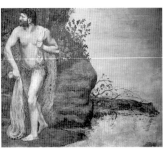

2   3   4

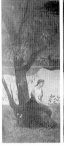
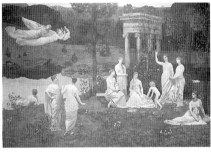
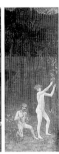
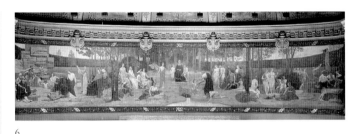

5   6

1889

Exposition Universelle, Exposition Centennale 1789-1889
Paris, Palais du Champ-de-Mars (Galerie des Beaux-Arts),
5 mai - 31 octobre

557 – *L'Automne*
558 – *Décollation de Saint Jean-Baptiste*
559 – *L'Enfant prodigue*
560 – *Jeunes filles au bord de la mer*
561 a – *Vie de Sainte-Geneviève*
561 b – *L'Espérance*
Vision antique
Inspiration chrétienne

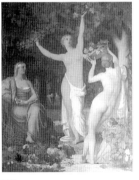
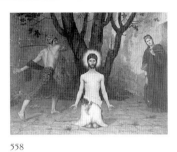

557   558

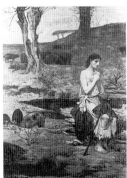
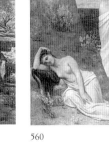
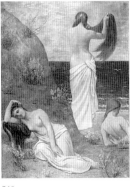
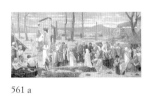
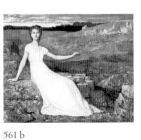
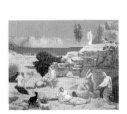
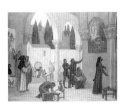

559   560   561 a

561 b

1890

Salon de la Société Nationale des Beaux-Arts
Paris, Champ-de-Mars, 15 mai

718 – *"Inter Artes et Naturam"*
Panneau destiné à l'escalier du musée de Rouen

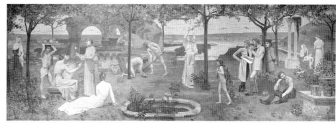

718

1891

Salon de la Société Nationale des Beaux-Arts
Paris, Champ-de-Mars, 15 mai

747 – *L'Eté (panneau décoratif pour l'Hôtel de Ville)*
748 – *La Poterie*
749 – *La Céramique*
Panneaux décoratifs pour l'escalier du Musée Céramique de Rouen

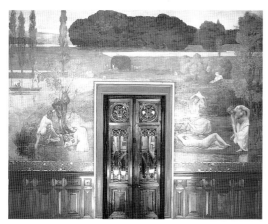 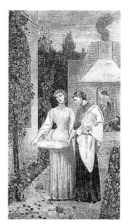 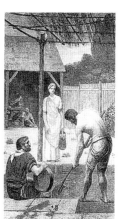

747   748   749

1892

Salon de la Société Nationale des Beaux-Arts de 1892
Paris, Champ-de-Mars, 7 mai 1892

822 – *L'Hiver*
Panneau décoratif pour l'Hôtel de Ville de Paris

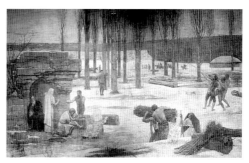

822

1893

Salon de la Société Nationale des Beaux-Arts
Paris, Champ-de-Mars, 10 mai

854 – *Hommage de Victor Hugo à la ville de Paris*
Camaïeu

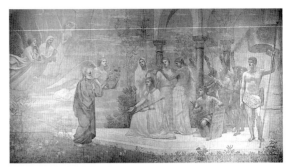

854

1894

Salon de la Société Nationale des Beaux-Arts
Paris, Champ-de-Mars, 25 avril

934 – *Ensemble de la décoration destinée à l'escalier du Préfet,*
à l'Hôtel de Ville
I – *Plafond. Victor Hugo offrant sa lyre à la ville de Paris*
II – *Quatre voussures :*
1. *Patriotisme*
2. *Charité*
3. *Ardeur artistique*
4. *Foyer intellectuel*
III. – *Six tympans :*
1. *Esprit*
2. *Fantaisie*
3. *Beauté*
4. *Intrépidité*
5. *Culte du Souvenir*
6. *Urbanité*

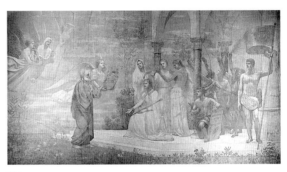

934

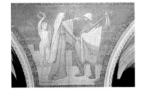

1

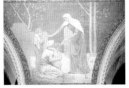

2

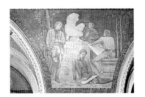

3

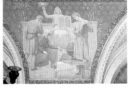

4

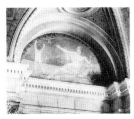

2

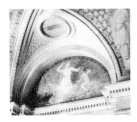

3

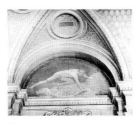

4

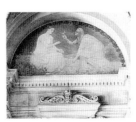

6

1894

Salon de la Libre Esthétique
Bruxelles, 17 février – 15 mars

368 – *L'Enfant prodigue*
(Appartient à M. Henri Lerolle)
369 – *La Mort d'Orphée*
(Appartient à M. Ernest Chausson)

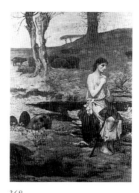

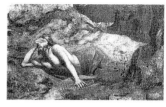

369

368

1894

Paris, Galerie Durand-Ruel, octobre

Le Cidre
La Rivière
La Charité
La Grande sœur

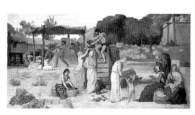

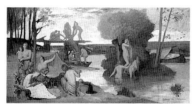

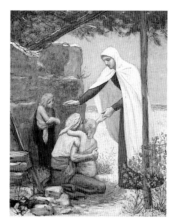

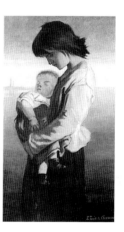

1895

Salon de la Société Nationale des Beaux-Arts
Paris, Champ-de-Mars, 25 avril

1027 – *Panneau destiné à l'escalier de la bibliothèque de Boston :*
les Muses inspiratrices acclament le Génie, messager de lumière

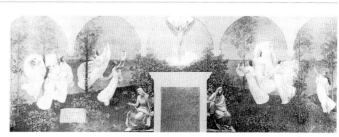

1027

1896

Salon de la Société Nationale des Beaux-Arts
Paris, Champ-de-Mars, 25 avril 1896

1029 – *Virgile (poésie bucolique)*
1030 – *Eschyle (poésie dramatique: Eschyle et les Océanides)*
1031 – *Homère couronné par l'"Iliade" et l'"Odyssée"*
1032 – *L'Histoire (L'Histoire évoque le Passé)*
1033 – *L'Astronomie (les bergers chaldéens observent la marche des Planètes)*
(Cinq panneaux, suite des peintures décoratives pour la bibliothèque de Boston)

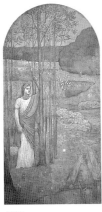 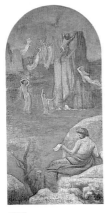 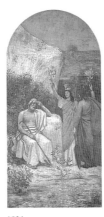 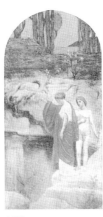 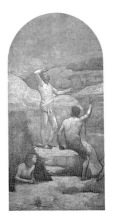

1029   1030   1031   1032   1033

1896

Exposition des trois dernières compositions exécutées par P. Puvis de Chavannes pour l'escalier de la Bibliothèque de Boston
Paris, Galerie Durand-Ruel, 7-19 septembre

Philosophie
Chimie
Physique

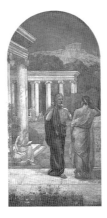 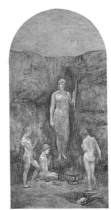 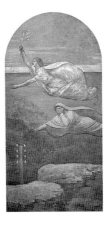

1898

Salon de la Société Nationale des Beaux-Arts
Paris, Champ-de-Mars, 1er mai

1006 – *Panneau destiné au Panthéon*
Geneviève dans sa pieuse sollicitude veille sur la Ville endormie.

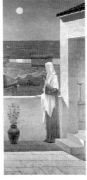

1006

1899

Exposition de tableaux, esquisses et dessins de Puvis de Chavannes
Paris, Galerie Durand-Ruel, juin-juillet

1 – *Portrait de l'Artiste, par lui-même (Appartient à M. Paul Baudouin)*
2 – *Bramante et Savonarole*
4 – *Tête de Femme (Appartient à M. Bracquemond)*
5 – *Pietà*
6 – *L'incendie*
7 – *Julie surprise*
8 – *La Pêche (Appartient à M. M.)*
9 – *La Vigilance*
10 – *Portrait de Jeune Homme. (Appartient à M. Jones)*
11 – *La famille du pêcheur*
12 – *La Décollation de Saint Jean-Baptiste*
 (Appartient à MM. Durand-Ruel)
14 – *Réduction du " Ludus pro Patria ". Seconde partie*
(Appartient à M. Lazare Weiller)
15 – *Femmes au bord de la mer (Appartient à M. Boivin)*
16 – *Le pauvre Pêcheur (Appartient à M. Boivin)*
17 – *Marseille, porte d'Orient*
18 – *Marseille, colonie Grecque*
19 – *L'Espérance (Appartient à M. H. Rouart)*
20 – *Marseille, colonie Grecque (Appartient à M. H. Rouart)*
 – *L'Enfant prodigue (Appartient à M. H. Lerolle)*
23 – *Femmes au bord de la mer*
24 – *La Fileuse (Appartient à MM. Durand-Ruel)*

25 – *La Fantaisie (Appartient à Mme Toulmouche)*
26 – *La Rivière (Appartient à MM. Durand-Ruel)*
27 – *Le Cidre (Appartient à MM. Durand-Ruel)*
28 – *Le Pauvre Pêcheur (Appartient à MM. Durand-Ruel)*
29 – *Ludus pro Patria (Appartient à MM. Durand-Ruel)*
30 – *La Muse des bois (Appartient à Mme Philippe Gille)*
31 – *Tête d'Homme*
32 – *Ave Picardia Nutrix. Fragment (Appartient à M.P. Gallimard)*
33 – *La Famille du pêcheur*
34 – *La Décollation de Saint Jean-Baptiste*
35 – *L'Enfant prodigue*
36 – *Les Saintes Marie*
37 – *Le Rêve (Appartient à M. Moreau-Nélaton)*
38 – *L'Hiver (Appartient à MM. Durand-Ruel)*
39 – *Madeleine (Appartient à MM. Durand-Ruel)*
40 – *Frise pour le Panthéon (En trois parties)*
41 – *Frise pour le Panthéon (Sainte Geneviève)*
42 – *Fronton pour la décoration de l'Hôtel de Ville*
43 – *Fronton pour la décoration de l'Hôtel de Ville*
44 – *Composition pour la décoration de l'Hôtel de Ville*
45 – *Composition pour la décoration de l'Hôtel de Ville*
46 – *Le Patriotisme (Fronton pour la décoration de l'Hôtel de Ville)*
47 – *La Charité (Fronton pour la décoration de l'Hôtel de Ville)*

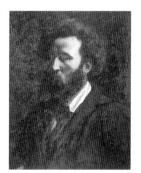
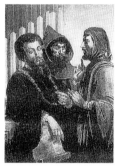
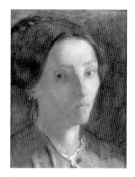
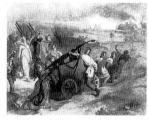

1 2 4 6

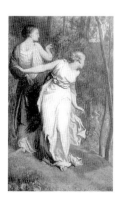
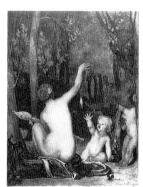
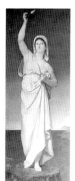
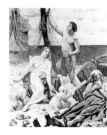
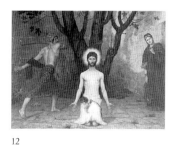

7 8 9 11 12

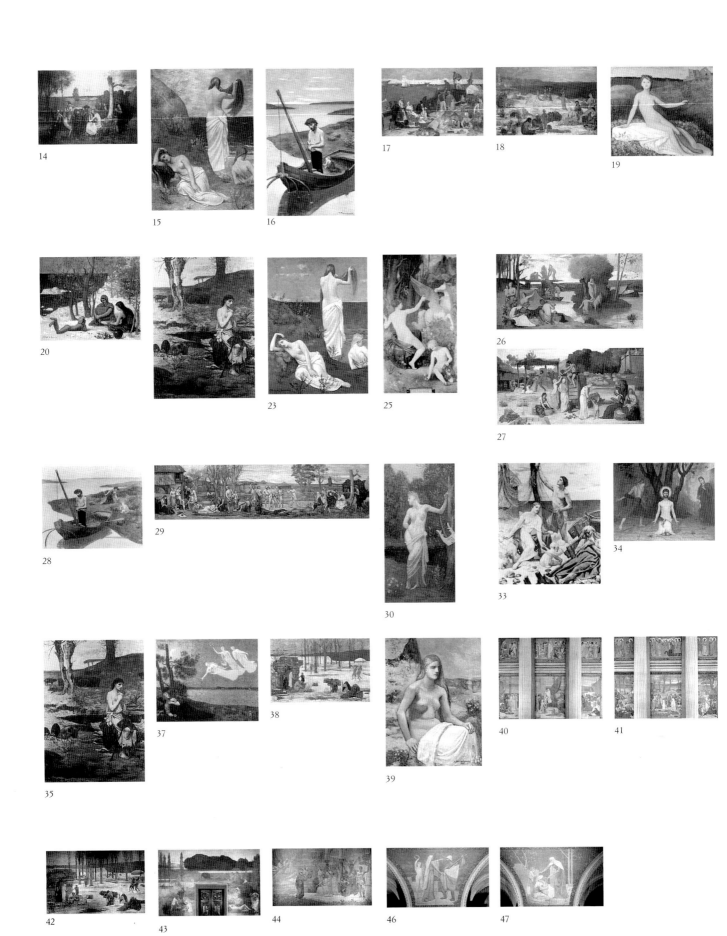

14

15

16

17

18

19

20

23

25

26

27

28

29

30

33

34

35

37

38

39

40

41

42

43

44

46

47

1900

Exposition Universelle – Exposition Centennale
Paris, du 15 avril au 12 novembre

536 – *La Toilette (à M. Haviland)*
537 – *La Famille du pêcheur (à M. P. Durand-Ruel)*
538 – *Jeunes Picards s'exerçant à la lance (Pro patria ludus)*
réduction partielle de la peinture murale du musée d'Amiens
(à M. R. Spaulding)
538 bis – *La Vigilance (à M. P. Durand-Ruel)*

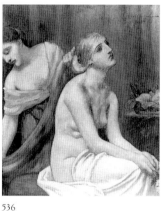
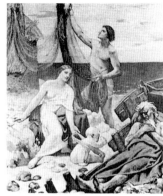
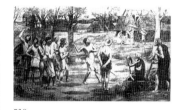
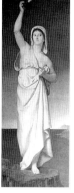

538

536

537

538 bis

1904

Salon d'Automne
Paris, Grand Palais des Champs-Elysées, du 15 octobre au 15 novembre
Salle Puvis de Chavannes

1 – *Famille heureuse*
2 – *Fantaisie*
3 – *" Ludus Pro Patria " (App. à MM. Bernheim)*
4 – *La fileuse*
5 – *Le rêve du poète*
6 – *La fantaisie*
7 – *La pêche*
9 – *La Madeleine*
10 – *La poèsie dramatique*

11 – *La toilette*
12 – *Décollation de Saint Jean-Baptiste*
14 – *L'enfant prodigue*
18 – *Pieta*
19 – *Personnages romains (App. à MM. Durand-Ruel et fils)*
23 – *Espérance*
33 – *La famille du pêcheur*
34 – *L'été*
43 – *Orphée. (App. à Mme Chausson)*

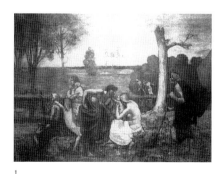
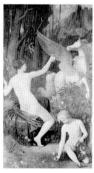
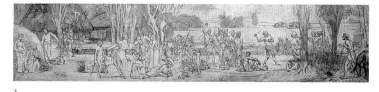

3

1

2

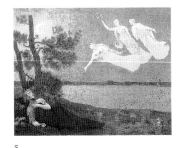

5

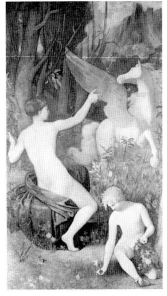

6

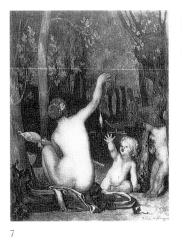

7

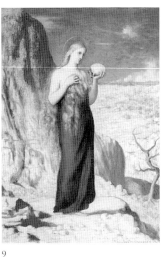

9

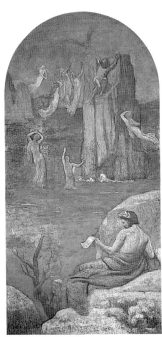

10

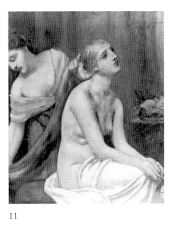

11

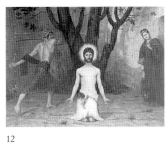

12

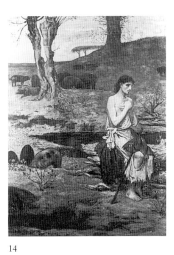

14

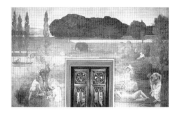

19

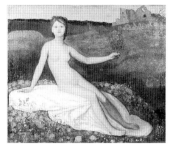

23

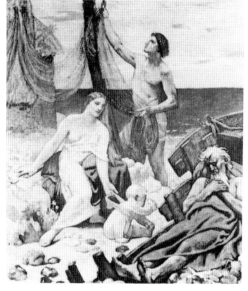

33

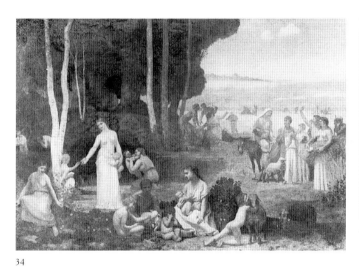

34

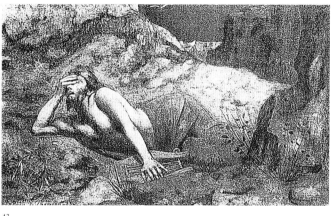

43

Selected Bibliography

The bibliography has been divided into sections referring to different topics; the books appear in chronological order in each section. Catalogs are listed by venue and exhibition date; all other books are listed by author (or editor) and publication date.

• General Reference

BIRD 1987
Alan Bird, *A History of Russian Painting*, London, Phaidon, 1987

BRUSSELS 1988
Le premier groupe de Laethem-Saint-Martin 1899-1914, Van den Abeele, Minne, De Saedeler, Van de Woestijne, Servaes, exhibition catalog, Brussels, Musées Royaux des Beaux-Arts, 1988

CACHIN 1990
Françoise Cachin, ed., *L'art du XIXᵉ siècle 1850–1905*, Paris, Edition Citadelles, 1990

VIENNA 1992
Cornelia Reiter, Jura Bruschweiler, et al., eds., *Ferdinand Hodler und Wien*, exhibition catalog, Vienna, Osterreichische Galerie; Vienna, Oberes Belvedere, 1992

FRANKFURT AM MAIN 1995
Sabine Schulze, ed., *Sehnsucht nach Glueck, Wiens Aufbruch in die Moderne: Klimt, Kokoschka, Schiele*, exhibition catalog, Frankfurt am Main, Schirn Kunsthalle; Hatje Ostfildern, 1995

PARIS 1997
Paris–Bruxelles, Bruxelles–Paris, exhibition catalog, Paris, Grand Palais; Paris, Réunion des Musées Nationaux, 1997

LONDON 2000
Robert Rosenblum, Maryanne Stevens, Ann Dumas, *1900 Art at the Crossroads*, exhibition catalog, London, Royal Academy of Art, 2000

GHENT 2001
Piet Boyens, *Une rare plénitude. Les artistes de Laethem-Saint-Martin, 1900–1930*, exhibition catalog, Ghent, Musée des Beaux-Arts; Ghent, Ludion, 2001

ROME, PARIS 2001
Bianca Alessandra Pinto, Gianna Piantoni, Henri Loyrette, Anne Pingeot, eds., *Italie 1880–1910. Arte alla prova della modernità*, exhibition catalog, Rome, Galleria d'Arte Moderna; Paris, Musée d'Orsay; Paris, Réunion des Musées Nationaux, 2001

CHICAGO 2001
Gloria Groom, ed., *Beyond the Easel: Decorative Painting by Bonnard, Vuillard, Denis and Roussel, 1890–1930*, exhibition catalog, Chicago, The Art Institute; New Haven–London, Yale University Press, 2001

PARIS 2001–02, BARCELONA 2002
Paris–Barcelone, de Gaudi à Miró, exhibition catalog, Paris, Grand Palais, 2001; Barcelona, Museu Picasso, 2002

• Art Movements

Symbolism

LONDON 1972
French Symbolist Painters. Moreau, Puvis de Chavannes, Redon and Their Followers, exhibition catalog, London, Hayward Gallery, 1972

PARIS 1976
Hans Hofstatter, Franco Russoli, Geneviève Lacambre, *Le Symbolisme en Europe*, catalog for the traveling exhibition, Paris, Grand Palais; Paris, Réunion des Musées Nationaux, 1976

DELEVOY 1977
Robert Delevoy, *Journal du Symbolisme*, Geneva, Skira, 1977

MATHIEU 1990
Pierre-Louis Mathieu, *La Génération symboliste*, Geneva, Skira, 1990

MONTREAL 1995
Pierre Theberge, Jean Clair, *Paradis perdus: l'Europe symboliste*, exhibition catalog, Montreal, Musée des Beaux-Arts; Paris, Flammarion, 1995

SAINT PETERSBURG 1996
Symbolism in Russia, Saint Petersburg, Palace Edition, 1996

BRUSSELS 1999
Jean-David Jumeau-Lafond, *Les Peintres de l'âme. Le Symbolisme idéaliste en France*, exhibition catalog, Brussels, Musée d'Ixelles; Ghent–Antwerp, Sdz, 1999

BORDEAUX 2000
Henry-Claude Cousseau, *Le symbolisme russe*, exhibition catalog, Bordeaux, Musée des Beaux-Arts, 2000

COPENHAGEN 2000
Peter Nørgaard Larsen, *Symbolism in Danish and European Painting 1870–1910*, exhibition catalog, Copenhagen, Statens Museum for Kunst, 2000

FRANKFURT AM MAIN 2000
Ingrid Ehrhardt, Simon Reynolds, *Seelen Reich Die Entwicklung des deutschen Symbolismus 1870–1920*, exhibition catalog, Frankfurt am Main, Schirn Kunsthalle; Munich, Prestel, 2000

Neo-Impressionism

NEW YORK 1968
Robert L. Herbert, *Neo-Impressionism*, exhibition catalog, New York, Solomon R. Guggenheim Museum, 1968

SUTTER 1970
Jean Sutter, *Les Néo-impressionnistes*, Paris, La Bibliothèque des Arts, 1970

GRENOBLE 1997
Signac et la libération de la couleur. De Matisse à Mondrian, exhibition catalog, Musée de Grenoble; Paris, Réunion des Musées Nationaux, 1997

Nabis

FRÈCHES-THORY 1990
Claire Frèches-Thory, *Les Nabis*, Paris, Flammarion, 1990

PARIS 1993–94
Claire Frèches-Thory, Ursula Perucchi-Petri, *Nabis 1888–1900*, exhibition catalog, Paris, Grand Palais, 1993–94; Paris, Réunion des Musées Nationaux, 1993

Fauvism

WITTFIELD 1990
Sarah Wittfield, *Fauvism*, London, Thames and Hudson, 1990

ZÜRCHER 1995
Bernard Zürcher, *Les Fauves*, Paris, Hazan, 1995

PARIS 1999–2000
Le Fauvisme ou l'épreuve du feu, exhibition catalog, Paris, Musée d'Art Moderne de la Ville, 1999–2000; Paris, Réunion des Musées Nationaux, 1999

Cubism

LOS ANGELES, NEW YORK 1971
Douglas Cooper, *The Cubist Epoch*, exhibition catalog, Los Angeles, County Museum of Art; New York, The Metropolitan Museum of Art; London, Phaidon, 1971

GREEN 1987
Christopher Green, *Cubism and Its Enemies. Modern. Movements and Reaction in French Art 1916–1928*, New Haven–London, Yale University Press, 1987

NEW YORK 1989–90
William Rubin, *Picasso and Braque: Pioneering Cubism*, exhibition catalog, New York, The Museum of Modern Art, 1989–90

SILVER 1991
Kenneth E. Silver, *Vers le retour à l'ordre*, Paris, Flammarion, 1991

• Individual Artists

Edmond Aman-Jean
PERSIN 1993

Patrick-Gilles Persin, *Aman-Jean: peintre de la femme*, Paris, La Bibliothèque des Arts, 1993

Auguste Baud-Bovy
ANKER 1991
Valentina Anker, *Auguste Baud-Bovy, 1848–1899*, Bern, Benteli, 1991

Emile Bernard
MANNHEIM, AMSTERDAM 1990
Emile Bernard 1868–1941: A Pioneer of Modern Art, exhibition catalog, Mannheim, Städtische Kunstalle; Amsterdam, Van Gogh Museum, 1990

Joseph Bernard
JULLIAN 1989
René Jullian, *Joseph Bernard*, Saint-Rémy-lès-Chevreuse, Fondation de Coubertin, 1989

SAINT-RÉMY-LÈS-CHEVREUSE 1989
Paul-Louis Rinuy, *Pierres et marbres de Joseph Bernard*, exhibition catalog, Saint-Rémy-lès-Chevreuse, Fondation de Coubertin, 1989

Pierre Bonnard
PARIS 1984
Bonnard, exhibition catalog, Paris, Centre Georges-Pompidou, 1984

LONDON, NEW YORK 1998
Sarah Whitfield, *Bonnard*, exhibition catalog, London, Tate Gallery; New York, The Museum of Modern Art; London, Tate Gallery Publishing, 1998

Viktor Borisov-Musatov
OUSAKOVA 1975
A. Ousakova, *Borisov-Musatov*, Leningrad, Aurora, 1975

Emile-Antoine Bourdelle
LAVRILLIER, DUFET 1992
Carol Marc Lavrillier, Michel Dufet, *Bourdelle et la critique de son temps*, Paris, Réunion des Musées Nationaux, 1992

Massimo Campigli
COURTHION 1938
Pierre Courthion, *Massimo Campigli*, Paris, Edit. des Chroniques du Jour, 1938

CHASTEL 1961
André Chastel, *Les Idoles de Campigli*, Paris, Galerie de France, 1961

RUSSOLI 1965
Franco Russoli, *Campigli Pittore*, Milan, Edizioni del Milione, 1965

CORTINA D'AMPEZZO 1981
Massimo Campigli, exhibition catalog, Cortina d'Ampezzo, Galleria d'Arte Moderna Farsetti, 1981

CAMPIGLI 2001
Nicola Campigli et al., eds., *Campigli. Essere altrove, essere altrimenti*, exhibition catalog, Milan, Permanente; Milan, Skira, 2001

Carlo Carrà
CARRÀ 1967–68
Massimo Carrà, *Carrà. Tutta l'opera pittorica*, 3 vols., Milan, Edizioni dell'Annunciata, 1967–68

ROME 1994
Augusta Monferini, *Carlo Carrà 1881–1966*, exhibition catalog, Rome, Galleria Nazionale d'Arte Moderna, 1994; Milan, Electa, 1994

Paul Cézanne
BASEL 1990
Mary Louise Krumrine, *Paul Cézanne–Les Baigneuses*, exhibition catalog, Basel, Kunstmuseum; Paris, Albin Michel, 1990

CAHN 1995
Isabelle Cahn, *Paul Cézanne*, Paris, Editions d'Art Somogy, 1995

PARIS 1995–96
Cézanne, catalog for the traveling exhibition, Paris, Grand Palais, 1995–96; Paris, Réunion des Musées Nationaux, 1995

Henri Edmond Cross
DOUAI 1998–99
Henri-Edmond Cross, 1856–1910, exhibition catalog, Douai, Musée de la Chartreuse, 1998–99; Paris, Somogy, 1998

William Degouve de Nunques
STAVELOT 1990
William Degouve de Nuncques et les intimistes verviétois, exhibition catalog, Stavelot, Musée d'Art Religieux Régional, 1990

Maurice Denis
BOUILLON 1993
Jean-Paul Bouillon, *Maurice Denis*, Geneva, Skira, 1993

LYON 1994
Maurice Denis, 1870–1943, catalog for the traveling exhibition, Lyon, Musée des Beaux-Arts; Paris, Réunion des Musées Nationaux, 1994

André Derain
LEE 1991
Jane Lee, *Derain*, Oxford, Phaidon, Paris, Flammarion, 1991

PARIS 1994–95
André Derain: le peintre du trouble moderne, exhibition catalog, Paris, Musée d'Art Moderne de la Ville, 1994–95; Paris, Réunion des Musées Nationaux, 1994

Marcel Duchamp
VENICE 1993
Pontus Hulten, *Marcel Duchamp*, exhibition catalog, Venice, Palazzo Grassi; Milan, Bompiani, 1993

Magnus Enckell
PUOKKA 1949
Jaakko Puokka, *Magnus Enckell. The Man and the Artist*, Helsinki, 1949

Akseli Gallen-Kallela
HELSINKI 1996
Sinasalo Soili et al., *Akseli Gallen-Kallela*, exhibition catalog, Helsinki, Ateneum, 1996

Paul Gauguin
PARIS 1988
Gauguin, catalog for the traveling exhibition, Paris, Grand Palais; Paris, Réunion des Musées Nationaux, 1988

CACHIN 1988
Françoise Cachin, *Gauguin*, Paris, Flammarion, 1988

Giovanni Giacometti
LAUSANNE 1997
Giovanni Giacometti, 1868–1933, exhibition catalog, Lausanne, Musée Cantonal des Beaux-Arts, 1997

Albert Gleizes
ROBBINS, GEORGEL 1998
Daniel Robbins, Pierre Georgel, *Albert Gleizes: catalogue raisonné*, Paris, Somogy, 1998

BARCELONA, LYON, 2001
Albert Gleizes: el cubisme en majestat, Barcelona, Museu Picasso; Lyon, Musée des Beaux-Arts, 2001

Vilhelm Hammershøi
COPENHAGEN 1997, PARIS 1997–98
L'univers poétique de Vilhelm Hammershøi, 1864–1916, exhibition catalog, Copenhagen, Ordrupgaard, 1997; Paris, Musée d'Orsay, 1997–98; Paris, Réunion des Musées Nationaux, 1997

Louis Welden Hawkins
AMSTERDAM 1993
Louis Welden Hawkins 1849–1910, exhibition catalog, Amsterdam, Van Gogh Museum, 1993

Ferdinand Hodler
PARIS 1983
Ferdinand Hodler, 1853–1918, exhibition catalog, Paris, Petit Palais, Musée des Beaux-Arts de la Ville; Paris, Association Française d'Action Artistique, 1983

BAUMGARTNER 1998
Marcel Baumgartner, *Ferdinand Hodler. Sammlung Thomas Schmidheiny*, Zurich, Schweizerisches In-

stitut fur Kunstwissenschaft (Kataloge Schweizer Museen und Sammlungen 15), 1998

MUNICH 1999
Rudolf Koella, *Ferdinand Hodler*, exhibition catalog, Munich, Kunsthalle der Hypo-Kulturstiftung; Munich, Hirmer, 1999

Ludwig von Hofmann
ALBSTADT 1995
Ludwig von Hofmann, 1861–1945, exhibition catalog, Albstadt, Städtische Galerie, 1995

Fernand Khnopff
PARIS 1979, BRUSSELS 1980
Fernand Khnopff, 1858–1921, exhibition catalog, Paris, Musée des Arts Décoratifs, 1979; Brussels, Musées Royaux des Beaux-Arts, 1980; Paris, Musée des Arts Décoratifs, 1979

DRAGUET 1995
Michel Draguet, *Khnopff ou l'ambigu poétique*, Paris, Flammarion, 1995

Max Klinger
FRANKFURT AM MAIN 1992
Max Klinger, 1857–1920, exhibition catalog, Frankfurt am Main, Städtische Galerie im Städelschen Kunstinstitut; Leipzig, 1992

Georg Kolbe
BERLIN, BREMEN 1997
Georg Kolbe, 1877–1947, exhibition catalog, Berlin, Georg Kolbe Museum; Bremen, Gerhard Marcks-Haus; Munich–New York, Prestel, 1997

Georges Lacombe
PONT-AVEN 1998
Georges Lacombe, 1868–1916, exhibition catalog, Musée de Pont-Aven, 1998

Henri Le Fauconnier
HAARLEM 1993
Henri Le Fauconnier: Cubism and Expressionism in Europe, exhibition catalog, Haarlem, Frans Hals Museum, 1993

Fernand Léger
PARIS 1997
Fernand Léger, exhibition catalog, Paris, Centre Georges-Pompidou, 1997

Wilhelm Lehmbruck
WASHINGTON 1972
Reinhold Heller, ed., *The Art of Wilhelm Lehmbruck*, exhibition catalog, Washington, National Gallery of Art; Washington, D.C., Macmillan, 1972

BERLIN, DUISBURG, MANNHEIM 2000–01
Wilhelm Lehmbruck 1881–1919, exhibition catalog, Berlin, Georg Kolbe Museum; Duisburg, Wil-

helm Lehmbruck Museum; Mannheim, Städtische Kunsthalle, 2000–01

SCHUBERT 2001
Dietrich Schubert, *Wilhelm Lehmbruck: Catalogue Raisonné der Skulpturen 1898–1919*, Worms, Wernersche Verlagsgesellschaft, 2001

Henri Le Sidaner
LIÈGE 1996
Henri Le Sidaner, 1862–1932, exhibition catalog, Liège, Musée d'Art Contemporain, 1996

Mario Mafai
MODENA 1990
Mario Mafai, le fantasie, exhibition catalog, Modena, Palazzo Comunale; Bologna, Nuova Alfa, 1990

Aristide Maillol
BERLIN, LAUSANNE 1996
Aristide Maillol, exhibition catalog, Berlin, Georg Kolbe Museum; Lausanne, Musée Cantonal des Beaux-Arts; Paris, Flammarion, 1996

Kazimir Malevic
AMSTERDAM 1989
Malevic, exhibition catalog, Amsterdam, Stedelijk Museum, 1989

Hans von Marées
GERLACH-LAXNER 1980
Uta Gerlach-Laxner, *Hans von Marées, Katalog seiner Gemaelde*, Munich, Prestel, 1980

MUNICH 1987–88
Hans von Marées, exhibition catalog, Munich, Neue Pinakothek, 1987–88; Munich, Prestel, 1987

Henri Martin
CAHORS, TOULOUSE 1993
Henri Martin, 1860–1943, exhibition catalog, Cahors, Musée Henri Martin, Toulouse, Capitole, 1993

Arturo Martini
PARIS 1991
Arturo Martini, 1889–1947. L'œuvre sculpté, exhibition catalog, Paris, Hôtel de Ville; Milan, Electa, 1991

VIANELLO 1998
Gianni Vianello et al., *Arturo Martini. Catalogo ragionato delle sculture*, Vicenza, Neri Pozza, 1998

Henri Matisse
PARIS 1993
Henri Matisse, 1904–1917, exhibition catalog, Paris, Centre Georges-Pompidou, 1993

SCHNEIDER 1993
Pierre Schneider, *Matisse*, Paris, Flammarion, rev. ed. 1993

René Ménard
DIEPPE 1969
René Ménard, 1862–1930, exhibition catalog, Château-Musée de Dieppe, 1969

George Minne
GHENT 1992
George Minne en de kunst rond 1900, exhibition catalog, Ghent, Museum Voor Schone Kunsten, 1992

Edvard Munch
PARIS 1991–92, OSLO 1992
Munch et la France, exhibition catalog, Paris, Musée d'Orsay, 1991–92; Oslo, Musée Munch, 1992; Paris, Réunion des Musées Nationaux, 1991

Mikhail Nesterov
ROUSSAKOVA 1990
Alla Roussakova, *Mikhail Nesterov*, Leningrad, Aurora, 1990

Auguste de Niederhäusern-Rodo
LAPAIRE 2001
Claude Lapaire, *Auguste de Niederhäusern-Rodo, 1863–1913, catalogue raisonné*, Zurich, Institut Suisse pour l'Etude de l'Art, Bern, Benteli, 2001

Ejnar Nielsen
STATELL 1984
Annette Statell, *Ejnar Nielsen*, Copenhagen, Kunstforeningen, 1984

Alphonse Osbert
HONFLEUR 1977
Alphonse Osbert, peintre symboliste, exhibition catalog, Honfleur, Musée Eugène Boudin, 1977

Amédée Ozenfant
SAINT-QUENTIN 1985
Amédée Ozenfant, catalog for the traveling exhibition, Saint-Quentin, Musée Antoine-Lécuyer, 1985

Giuseppe Pellizza da Volpedo
TURIN, 1999
Aurora Scotti Tosini, ed., *Giuseppe Pellizza da Volpedo*, exhibition catalog, Turin, Galleria d'Arte Moderna e Contemporanea; Turin, Hopefulmonster, 1999

Eilif Peterssen
OSLO 1990
Eilif Peterssen, Summer Exhibition 1990, exhibition catalog, Oslo, Bukowskis, 1990

Kuz'ma Petrov-Vodkin
ROUSSAKOV, BARABANOVA 1986
Yuri Roussakov, Nina Barabanova, *Kuz'ma Petrov-Vodkin, 1878–1939*, Leningrad, Aurora, 1986

Francis Picabia
CAMFIELD 1979

William Camfield, *Francis Picabia. His Art, Life and Times*, Princeton, Princeton University Press, 1979

BORRAS 1985
María Lluisa Borras, *Picabia*, Paris, Albin Michel, 1985

Pablo Picasso
BARCELONA 1992
Picasso: 1905–1906. De l'època rosa als ocres de Gósol, exhibition catalog, Barcelona, Museu Picasso; Barcelona, Electa, 1992

WASHINGTON 1997
Picasso: the Early Years, 1892–1906, exhibition catalog, Washington, National Gallery of Art, 1997

LÉAL, PIOT, BERNADAC 2000
Brigitte Léal, Christine Piot, Marie-Laure Bernadac, *Picasso. La monographie, 1881–1973*, Paris, La Martinière, 2000

Maurice Prendergast
WASHINGTON 1994
Richard J. Wattenmaker, *Maurice Prendergast*, exhibition catalog, Washington, D.C., The National Museum of American Art, Smithsonian Institution; New York, Abrams, 1994

Pierre Puvis de Chavannes
VACHON 1895
Marius Vachon, *Puvis de Chavannes*, Paris, Lahure, 1895

VACHON [1900]
Marius Vachon, *Un maître de ce temps: Puvis de Chavannes*, Paris, Société d'Edition Artistique, n.d. [1900]

MAUCLAIR 1928
Camille Mauclair, *Puvis de Chavannes*, Paris, Plon, 1928

TORONTO 1975
Richard J. Wattenmaker, *Puvis de Chavannes and the Modern Tradition*, exhibition catalog, Toronto, Art Gallery of Ontario, 1975, rev. ed. 1976

PARIS 1976–77, OTTAWA 1977
Louise d'Argencourt, Jacques Foucart, *Puvis de Chavannes, 1824–1898*, exhibition catalog, Paris, Grand Palais, 1976–77; Ottawa, National Gallery of Canada, 1977; Paris, Réunion des Musées Nationaux, 1976

BOUCHER 1979
Marie-Christine Boucher, *Catalogue des dessins et peintures de Puvis de Chavannes au Palais des Beaux-Arts de la Ville de Paris*, Paris, Association Française d'Action Artistique, 1979

MARSEILLE 1985
Puvis de Chavannes et le Musée des Beaux-Arts de Marseille, exhibition catalog, Marseille, Musée des Beaux-Arts, 1985; Le Musée, 1984

AMSTERDAM 1994
Aimée Brown Price, *Pierre de Puvis de Chavannes*, exhibition catalog, Amsterdam, Van Gogh Museum; New York, Rizzoli International, 1994

PETRIE 1997
Brian Petrie, *Puvis de Chavannes*, Aldershot, Vt, Ashgate Publishing, 1997

LYON 1998
Puvis de Chavannes au Musée des beaux-arts de Lyon, exhibition catalog, Lyon, Musée des Beaux-Arts; Paris, Réunion des Musées Nationaux, 1998

Paul-Elie Ranson
SAINT-GERMAIN-EN-LAYE 1997
Paul-Elie Ranson: du symbolisme à l'art nouveau, exhibition catalog, Saint-Germain-en-Laye, Musée Départemental Maurice Denis; Paris, Somogy, 1997

Odilon Redon
LUGANO 1996
Odilon Redon: La natura dell'Invisibile / La Nature de l'Invisible, exhibition catalog, Lugano, Museo Cantonale d'Arte; Milan, Skira, 1996

Laurits Andersen Ring
WIWEL 1997
Henrick Wiwel, *Laurits Andersen Ring*, Copenhagen, Fogtdal, 1997

Auguste Rodin
BUTLER 1998
Ruth Butler, *Rodin. La solitude du génie*, London, Yale University Press, 1993, Paris, Gallimard, 1998

PARIS 2001
Rodin en 1900, exhibition catalog, Paris, Musée du Luxembourg; Paris, Réunion des Musées Nationaux, 2001

Nikolai Roerich
KOROTKINA 1976
Ljudmila Vasielvna Korotkina, *Nikolai Roerich*, Leningrad, Aurora, 1976

Ker-Xavier Roussel
SAINT-TROPEZ 1993
Ker-Xavier Roussel, exhibition catalog, Saint-Tropez, Musée de L'Annonciade, 1993

Giovanni Segantini
QUINSAC 1982
Annie-Paule Quinsac, *Segantini. Catalogo generale*, 2 vols., Milan, Electa, 1982

ZURICH 1990–91
Giovanni Segantini, 1858–1899, exhibition catalog, Zurich, Kunsthaus, 1990–91

STUTZER, WÄSPE 1999
Beat Stutzer, Roland Wäspe, *Giovanni Segantini*, Zurich, NZZ Verlag, 1999

Alexandre Séon
MONTALANT 1992
Delphine Montalant, *Alexandre Séon peintre symboliste*, Paris, A Rebours, 1992

Paul Sérusier
BOYLE-TURNER 1988
Caroline Boyle-Turner, *Paul Sérusier, peintre de la Bretagne*, Lausanne, Edita, 1988

PONT-AVEN 1991
Paul Sérusier et la Bretagne, exhibition catalog, Musée de Pont-Aven, 1991

Georges Seurat
MADELEINE-PERDRILLAT 1990
Alain Madeleine-Perdrillat, *Seurat*, Geneva, Skira, 1990

PARIS 1991
Seurat, exhibition catalog, Paris, Grand Palais; Paris, Réunion des Musées Nationaux, 1991

ZIMMERMANN 1991
Michael Zimmermann, *Les mondes de Seurat, son œuvre et le débat artistique de son temps*, Antwerp, Fonds Mercator, Paris, Albin Michel, 1991

Paul Signac
CACHIN 2000
Françoise Cachin, *Signac, catalogue raisonné de l'œuvre peint*, Paris, Gallimard, 2000

PARIS 2001
Signac, catalog for the traveling exhibition, Paris, Grand Palais; Paris, Réunion des Musées Nationaux, 2001

Hugo Simberg
HELSINKI 1989
Heikki Malme, *Hugo Simberg, grafiikka-Grafik*, exhibition catalog, Helsinki, Ateneum, 1989

Mario Sironi
ROME 1993–94
Mario Sironi 1885–1961, exhibition catalog, Rome, Galleria Nazionale d'Arte Moderna, 1993–94; Milan, Electa, 1993

Beda Stjernschantz
COPENHAGEN, HAMBURG 1983
Salme Sarjas-Korte, *Malerinder fra Finland Sieben finnische Malerinnen Fanny Churberg, Maria Wiik, Helene Schjerfbeck, Ellen Thesleff, Beda Stjernschantz, Ester Helenius, Sigrid Schauman*, exhibition catalog, Copenhagen, Statens Museum for Kunst; Hamburg, Kunsthalle, 1983

Franz von Stuck
MENDGEN 1995
Eva Mendgen, *Franz von Stuck*, Cologne, Taschen, 1995

Ellen Thesleff
HELSINKI 1998
Ellen Thesleff, exhibition catalog, Helsinki, Ateneum, 1998

Joaquín Torres-García
JARDI 1979
Enric Jardi, *Torres-García*, Paris, Cercle d'Art, 1979

MADRID 1991
Torres-García, exhibition catalog, Madrid, Museo Nacional Centro de Arte Reina Sofía; Valencia, Instituto Valenciano de Arte Moderno, 1991

Suzanne Valadon
MARTIGNY 1996
Suzanne Valadon, exhibition catalog, Martigny, Fondation Pierre Gianadda, 1996

Félix Vallotton
LAUSANNE 1992–93
Sasha M. Newman, ed., *Félix Vallotton*, catalog for the traveling exhibition, Lausanne, Musée Cantonal des Beaux-Arts, 1992–93; Paris, Flammarion, 1992

LYON, MARSEILLE 2001
Le très singulier Vallotton, exhibition catalog, Lyon, Musée des Beaux-Arts; Marseille, Musée Cantini; Paris, Réunion des Musées Nationaux, 2001

Heinrich Vogeler
WORPSWEDE 1997
Heinrich Vogeler und der Jugendstil, exhibition catalog, Worpswede, Barkenhoff, Grosse Kunstchau, Haus im Schluh; Cologne, DuMont, 1997

Edouard Vuillard
SAINT-TROPEZ, LAUSANNE 2000–01
Edouard Vuillard, La porte entrebâillée, exhibition catalog, Saint-Tropez, Musée de L'Annonciade; Lausanne, Musée Cantonal des Beaux-Arts, 2000–01; Milan, Skira, 2000

This volume has been published
with the support of Cartiere Burgo
and it is printed on R4 Matt Satin 150 g/m paper
manufactured by Cartiere Burgo.

Grande forEdit – Monza

Printed in January 2002
by Arti Grafiche A. Pizzi
Cinisello Balsamo (Mi)